HANDGUNS 2001

13th Annual Edition

Edited by
Ken Ramage

Published by

krause
publications

700 E. State Street • Iola, WI 54990-0001
Telephone: 715/445-2214
Web: www.krause.com

Please call or write for our free catalog.

Our toll-free number to place an order or obtain a free catalog is 800-258-0929 or please use our regular business telephone 715-445-2214 for editorial comment and further information.

Library of Congress Catalog Number: 88-72115
ISBN: 0-87341-927-8

— HANDGUNS STAFF —

Ken Ramage, Editor
HANDGUNS
Firearms & DBI Books

Ross Bielema,
Associate Editor

Editorial Comments and Suggestions

We're always looking for feedback on our books. Please let us know what you like about this edition. If you have suggestions for articles you'd like to see in future editions, please contact.

Ken Ramage/Handguns
700 East State St.
Iola, WI 54990
email: ramagek@krause.com

About Our Covers...

A new firearms company was born early this year—American Western Arms, of Delray Beach, Florida. A new name, true, but the formerly separate businesses that now comprise the new company are well known.

Classic Old West Styles, perhaps the most prominent purveyor of authentic period clothing, leather goods and accessories to the growing ranks of cowboy action shooters, has acquired the well-known Italian manufacturer of replica firearms, Armi San Marco, SA, which will now be known as American Western Arms Italy. The new entity is marketing an interesting line of cartridge-conversion c&b revolvers, accurate reproductions of the first generation Colt single-action revolver in a variety of models, chamberings and barrel lengths – and a Model 1892 lever-action rifle.

Appearing on the covers of this 13th Edition are two Model 1873 single-action revolver models: the Longhorn, with one-piece walnut grips and the Peacekeeper, which wears authentic Colt-style hard rubber grips. Both models are available in a range of barrel lengths from (3 inches; Peacekeeper only) 3 1/2 inches to 12 inches. A variety of chamberings are also offered for both:

32-20, 38/357 Magnum, 38-40, 44 Special and 45 Colt. This line of firearms is intended for the cowboy action shooter – or

for shooters who enjoy single-action revolvers and lever-action rifles.

Of perhaps greater interest to the former, AWA reports both the Longhorn and the Peacemaker include such authenticity elements as two-line patent dates, correct trigger guard configuration and correctly configured front sights, to mention a few. Both models are available with either the early black-powder frame or the later cross-pin frame, which retains the cylinder pin with a spring-loaded cross-bolt.

Practical shooting touches are not neglected, either. Both the Longhorn and the Peacekeeper are made with accuracy-promoting .452-inch chamber mouths and, especially for cast bullet shooters, a gentle 11-degree barrel forcing cone configuration. Both are advertised to have trigger pulls in the vicinity of 3 1/2 pounds.

The top-of-the-line Peacekeeper features a bone & charcoal color-casehardened frame and a special factory-tuned action. Also unique to the Peacekeeper is the beveled cylinder with first generation enlarged flutes.

For more information, contact American Western Arms, Inc., 1450 S.W. 10th Street, Ste. 3B, Delray Beach FL 33444/877-292-4867. Website: www.awaguns.com

Handguns 2001

Handguns for Sport and Personal Protection

CONTENTS

Page 73

Page 51

Page 7

Page 80

NEW!
Semi Custom
Handgun Catalog

Page 132

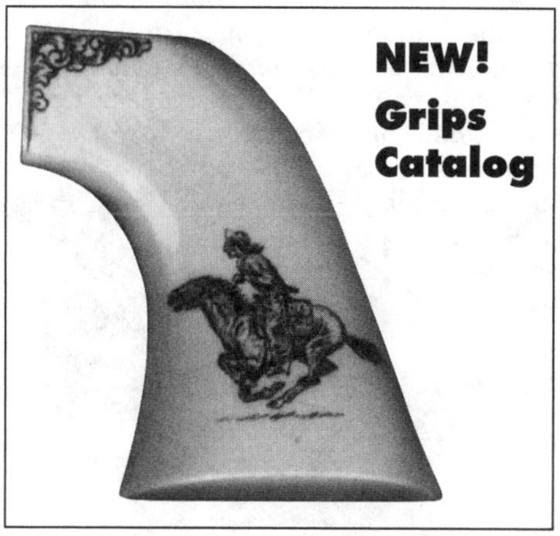

NEW!
Grips
Catalog

Page 218

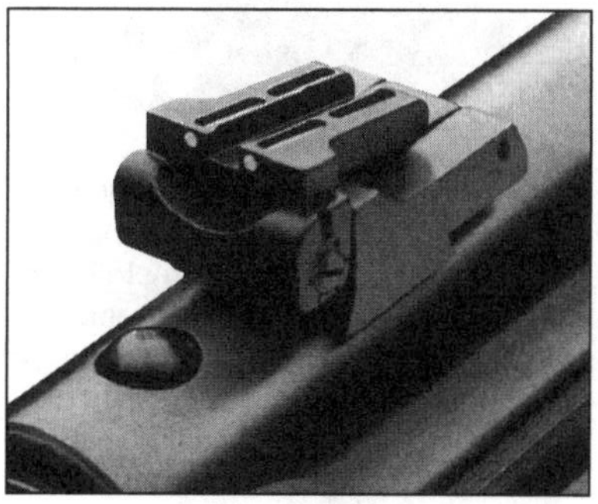

Page 231

HANDGUN ROUNDUP

by Dick Williams

ALCHEMY ARMS: Having made after-market accessories for the Glock pistol, Alchemy decided to manufacture their own unique pistol called the Spectre. One look tells you instantly this is a Glock/1911 hybrid featuring a Glock slide and a 1911 grip frame. It features an internal striker firing mechanism, (*ala* Glock and several other guns,) and an external safety lever courtesy of the 1911. It has the pointing characteristics—or grip ergonomics—of a 1911, but presents the outline of a Glock when looking down the slide. The gun has a 4.5-inch barrel and will come in 9mm, .40 S&W and .45

Cimarron's Wyatt Earp model Buntline with a silver shield in the grip and sporting the movie barrel length of 10 inches instead of the historically correct 12 inches.

AMERICAN ARMS: The unique Mateba revolver is now available in .44 Magnum and can be ordered with compensated and ribbed barrels. AA is working on speed loaders for their revolver and will be offering their own gun case featuring a combination lock. Their Uberti-made line of single-action revolvers intended for cowboy action shooting come in two grades, the Regulator and deluxe Regulator, and are available in .45 Colt only.

AMERICAN DERRINGER: Three options in the new Millennium Series are available this year in the famous little double barrel handgun from the Old West. Built on the Model

ACP. It will be available with either Novak or Ashley sights. It has an internal safety locking device (key-operated) and there will be an optional bore lock available. The sharp grip edges on the prototypes displayed at SHOT will be rounded more like a 1911 before the gun goes into full production.

CIMARRON: Recognizing the stringent demands of cowboy action shooting on the current crop of replica 19th century handguns, Cimarron has introduced the Cowboy Competition Model. Looking exactly like the Peacemaker on the outside, these guns feature major internal changes such as full-size parts, smoother actions and different springs (e.g. coil hand spring). The cowboy competition parts are being integrated into all Cimarron single actions and will be available in all calibers and barrel lengths. Cimarron is also making the Richard Mason conversion model of the 1860 Army with either 5.5- or 8-inch barrels and in either .38 Special or .44 Colt.

BROWNING: While there were no new pistols on display, Browning was showing its slick little Buckmark 22 rifle. Yes, it looks like a Buckmark frame with a pistol-grip stock and long wood forearm. It has "ears" on the rear of the slide to facilitate operation. In fact, all the Buckmark pistols except the Camper Model have the ears to facilitate grasping the slide for cocking. You 22 rimfire handgunners might want to look at the Buckmark rifle to create your own inexpensive "matching set."

1, these will feature special custom grips and roll markings that appropriately reflect the "Gambler", the "Cowboy" and the "Women of Texas" series.

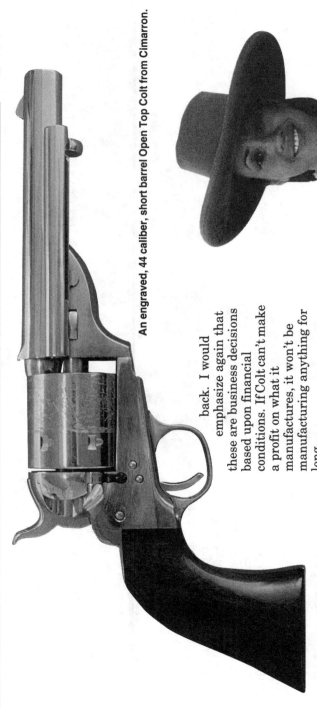

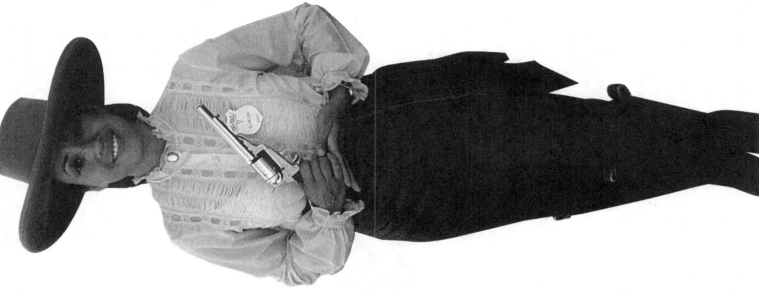

An engraved, 44 caliber, short barrel Open Top Colt from Cimarron.

Most breathtaking was Cimarron's new Wyatt Earp model of the Single Action Army. It is a duplicate of the gun shown in the movie Tombstone featuring a 10-inch (not 12-inch) barrel and a silver shield plate on the right grip. The production versions may come with either 10- or 12-inch barrels as Cimarron is still discussing the requirements with Uberti. Whatever the barrel length, this model will be chambered in 45 Colt only and must be special-ordered since it will not be carried in stock.

COLT: There was some good news and bad news from Colt regarding their decisions on handguns. The overall good news is that Colt will continue in the commercial handgun business with economic realities dictating which models are continued or dropped. From the current production line, the 1991 Mil Spec will continue in both Government and Commander models. The Defender and Gold Cup models will also continue to be available, but the Defender model has been dropped. The Colt Cowboy will continue with a new Royal Blue finish available. Colt is looking at offering the Cowboy in a nickel finish. The Colt Single Action Army will be manufactured by the Custom Shop and sold to the public. The 1911XS series of enhanced models will be produced and will feature Novak-style 3-dot sights with dovetail front blade, aluminum trigger and front slide serrations. The bad news is that all double-action revolvers have been discontinued, and I'm told there is no current planning to bring them

back. I would emphasize again that these are business decisions based upon financial conditions. If Colt can't make a profit on what it manufactures, it won't be manufacturing anything for long.

CZ-USA: Four new models of the famous CZ 75 were introduced at the SHOT Show. The Model PCR Compact features a lightweight alloy frame, decocking lever, front and rear slide serrations and snag-free sights. The DAO is a double-action-only trigger with a clean slide (except for the slide stop), has a bobbed hammer and is chambered in either 9mm or 40 S&W. The SA (single-action-only) is geared for the IDPA competitive shooter and has a straight trigger with adjustment capability for take-up and over-travel. It is initially available in 9mm only. Finally, CZ is building 1000 Silver Anniversary limited editions of their 9mm pistol that feature a nickel finish, walnut grips and the number "25" inlaid into the grips.

DOWNSIZER: No new model versions of this single-shot defensive 45 ACP, but the company is in production mode, and guns are no longer being hand-fitted.

Champion cowboy action shooter "Island Girl" shows off the engraved Cimarron Open Top Colt.

CZ's PCR Compact double-action pistol.

CZ's clean slide double-action-only pistol.

EAA: Displaying its new single-shot pistol, or at least the half that hadn't been stolen, EAA's 1911 frame will carry a single-shot barrel chambered in 45-70. EAA still imports the entire line of Tanfoglio "Witness" self-loaders with a couple of new additions. On the line of steel guns they now offer a decocker model which allows use of your existing conversion kits since the decocking system only modified the gun's frame components. Also new is the polymer frame series of Witness pistols in 22, 9mm, 38 Super, 40 S&W, 10mm and 45 ACP. EAA's revolvers, both their double-action Windicator in 38 Special and 357 Magnum and single-action Bounty Hunters in 357, 44-40, 44 Magnum and 45 Colt are made in Germany and reputed to be quite tough.

ED BROWN: No new handgun developments since starting the new rifle company. Ed continues to manufacture his complete line of 1911 pistols, along with all his custom parts and accessories.

GLOCK: Nothing new reported at the SHOT Show, but considering they just sold Glock #2,000,000, you can see the Austrians have been busy trying to keep up with demand. Interestingly, #2,000,000 was sold at

famous quality control, the gun is also capable of shooting beyond the skills of most of us handgunners. Perhaps not truly a handgun, Freedom is making their large model 454 Casull revolvers with 18-inch barrels in response to some orders from across the Atlantic. Apparently not everyone in *merry olde England* is happy with the new anti-handgun laws and is looking for ways around them. Tally Ho, folks!

With all of Freedom's world-

FREEDOM ARMS: The focus this year is on the down-sized Model 97 revolver from Wyoming, now available in a brand new chambering and with a shorter barrel length option. Rejoice, ye 41 Magnum fans, for Freedom's third offering in the small revolver is this often ignored but excellent hunting round. With a five-shot cylinder and a new barrel length option of 4.75 inches, the Model 97 may be the best-ever trail gun for both serious hunting or mountain meandering. The compact 41 handles all factory ammo (except for Cor-Bon's heavy cast loads which are just a bit too long for the shorter cylinder) and any reasonable handloads.

EMF: The Open Tops are now available in barrel lengths of 5.5 inches and 7.5 inches and in the 44 Colt chambering as well as the 38 Special. Not to worry about ammo for the 44 Colt; it's being manufactured by Black Hills, and if it's even close to Black Hills' 44 Russian in performance, it's a sure winner. If your western preference is for the top-break Schofield, EMF is offering Uberti-made Schofields in barrel lengths from the 3.5-inch Hideout to the 7-inch Cavalry model. And finally, EMF will be offering Buntline single-action revolvers with your choice of the authentic 12-inch Wild West barrel or the Hollywood movie version (and perhaps more useful) 10-inch barrel.

with all his custom parts and accessories.

auction for $9300, a figure which Glock matched in donating $18,600 to the COPS Foundation, an organization that helps the families of police officers killed in the line of duty.

H-S PRECISION: Later this year, shooters will be able to order barreled actions in your favorite caliber from this South Dakota manufacturer. Since their bolt pistol shot half-inch groups at 100 yards in my shaky hands, it's not clear why anyone would think they could produce a finished bolt pistol that's more accurate than one of H-S's production guns. The company reports steady demand for their bolt pistols with the varmint chamberings being particularly popular. Interestingly, there has been a recent surge in demand for 7BR-chambered pistols from South American shooters.

For the IDPA shooter, CZ offers its new single-action pistol with straight, adjustable trigger.

HECKLER & KOCH: H&K's one new handgun this year is their Limited Edition USP in 45 ACP, celebrating their 50th anniversary. The gun is engraved, highly polished, proudly wears H&K's 50th Anniversary logo, and comes in a wood box. Good caliber, pretty gun, but is it really for shooting or just for "oohin' and ahhin'?" That's your call, but if you encounter something that goes bump in the night, you would be well-equipped for dealing with the situation.

ISRAEL ARMS INTERNATIONAL (IAI): Handgun focus of this Houston-based company is on Model 1911s in 45 ACP. U.S.-made variations include full-size military models, full-size stainless steel and two-tones, and a compact with 4.25-inch barrel. All model 1911s feature fixed sights with either rubber or wood grips and GI or combat/ commander-style hammers. Imported models feature the same barrel length and size variations, but magazine capacity is 8 rounds vs. 7, and grips are plastic.

KAHR: Since the only current criticism of the Kahr K-9 pistol is its relatively heavy weight vs. its compact size, (a characteristic not uncommon to guns made entirely of steel,) Kahr is introducing its Polymer frame semi-

In celebration of its 25th anniversary, CZ is offering its Limited Edition Silver Anniversary CZ 75 pistol.

auto to reduce the weight. Not surprisingly, it's called the P-9 instead of the K-9. Initially it will be available only in a full-size pistol and in 9mm caliber. The impact of this on the concealed carry market will be interesting to watch.

KBI/CHARLES DALY: If you need a polymer frame semi-auto in single or double action that holds 10 rounds of 9mm, 40 S&W or 45 ACP, with multiple colors to chose from, check the Charles Daly from KBI. The

TRENDS

KELTEC: Keltec had nothing new to show nor did they report anything new in development. But their incredibly light P-32 is in full production and the company is shipping something like 800 per week trying to catch up with demand. What a wonderful problem!

KIMBER: The "House of 1911" offers five new models in two groups. Group I consists of two off-the-shelf stock guns with night sights in either blue or stainless and ready for shipment. Group II consists of three

offers five new models in two groups. Group I consists of two off-the-shelf stock guns with night sights in either blue or stainless and ready for shipment. Group II consists of three

NAVY ARMS: Navy has added the 1872 Open Top to their product line with either 5.5- or 7.5-inch barrels, but chambered only in 38 Special. Two

gun will have snag-free sights with a grip extension available as an option. They also offer STI polymer frame double-stack 1911s in 45 ACP only. For the would-be cowboy shooter, there are single-action revolvers from Armi San Marco with rebounding hammers finished in brass or other options. Calibers include 357, 44/40 and 45 Colt.

Custom Defense Package (CDP) models with lightweight aluminum frames, tritium night sights, ambidextrous safeties, blended and beveled edges, checkered front straps, premium aluminum triggers and other custom shop features. Defined, chosen and built as Custom Shop guns, the CDP series offer savings of several hundred dollars over guns retrofitted with the same features. Guess what that means in terms of resale value. These guns have either 3- or 4-inch barrels with magazine capacities of 6 or 7 rounds and are definitely ready for concealed street carry. While individual guns have individual preferences for certain types of ammunition, they are not ammo-sensitive with respect to barrel lengths. The minor bit of bad news is that in trying to keep up with demand for 45-caliber pistols, Kimber is no longer offering any guns chambered in 9mm or 38 Super.

EMF's new shorter 5.5-inch barrel Schofield, the Wells Fargo model.

Freedom Arms' new short-barrel, small-frame revolver in 357 Magnum, with fixed sights for the cowboy shooters.

off the line in 45ACP later this year. The SIG PRO 45 is in production in Switzerland and will feature interchangeable 45/400 Cor-Bon barrels, either with or without compensators. The guns at the SHOT Show had really smooth trigger pulls, both single and double action. Production rates have been increased on the BFR revolvers (tested and reported in last year's *HANDGUNS 2000,*) and may be ordered with Hogue wood target grips in either 22 Hornet, 444 Marlin or 45/70.

MAGNUM RESEARCH: The Mark 19 Desert Eagles are in production in Israel and available with fully convertible caliber/barrels. For enhanced concealed carry, the Baby Eagle line has added a polymer-frame model that will vastly reduce weight. Immediately available in 9mm and 40 S&W, polymer-frame Babies will be coming

lightweight aluminum or stainless steel frame, a Comanche-length slide, and comes chambered in 45 ACP.

LES BAER: The hot item from Baer is the new Thunder Ranch Gun, a serious, self-defense Model 1911 in 45 ACP. Conceived by Clint Smith, Director of Thunder Ranch, the gun has all the elements required on a fighting handgun per inputs from one of the premier teachers in the world. The guns use all metal parts made by Les Baer and feature fixed, tritium night sights. Also new this year are the Super-Tac and the Custom Carry models, both geared for serious street purposes. The Super-Tac features special tritium sights (a low-mount LBC adjustable rear and dovetailed front with tritium) and a custom finish for maximum corrosion resistance. It is available in 45 ACP, 40 S&W and 400 Cor-Bon, with the option of two interchangeable barrels in 45 and 400. The Custom Carry has rugged fixed tritium sights, either a

new, and particularly intriguing, black powder models this year are the double-action Starr Model 1858 and the single-action Starr Model 1853. They caught my eye both because I had never seen these particular guns before and because they are extremely unique-looking. Definitely worth a look from the black powder *pistolero*.

NORTH AMERICAN ARMS:

NAA news this year focuses on their Custom Shop's special treatment of their little 32 Auto. The gun can be ordered with a Glock titanium finish, a "meltdown" treatment, stippled front grip strap, and either Trijicon Novak night sights or Ashley sights. The cleanest, least-cluttered profile is still the "guttersnipe" sight where both the rear notch and the

Trijicon front dot are located in the slide rather than the rear sight notch being cut into the frame's top strap. "Slick" is a realistic description of this little pistol with custom shop features.

PARA-ORDNANCE:

Not available at the SHOT Show but

expected later this year is Para-Ordnance's first-ever single-stack handgun. Called the D745, the new gun will be initially offered in a double-action version. Also new this year is Para-Ordnance's compact double-action LDA pistol. The original, full-size double-action LDA has been getting good reviews from the industry, and is the only double-action pistol that incorporates three safeties. Meanwhile, all P12s, P14s and P16s are in production and being shipped to dealers.

REXIO: This Argentinean company has a couple of clever ideas in its new single-shot handgun called the Outfitter. Featuring a cowboy look-alike single-action frame with a release lever in front of the trigger

guard, this comfortable handgun comes with either a 10-inch or 6-inch barrel. Chamberings include 22LR, 22 Magnum and 45 Colt/.410. Changing chokes converts the gun from .410 to 45 Colt. The .410 will shoot either 2.5-inch or 3-inch shells. The guns feature rubber grips, a transfer bar safety, and manual locking safety. Rexio wisely furnishes its own see-through scope mount that attaches to the gun directly in front of the rear sight. The company also manufacturers two economical revolver models, blue and stainless steel, in 22LR, 22 Magnum, 38 Special and 357 Magnum.

ROCK PISTOL MANUFACTURING (RPM): The

extensive list of chamberings available in this semi-production

Freedom Arms' *loooooong-barreled* **454 Casull destined for England.**

Heckler & Koch celebrates its 50th Anniversary with a limited edition USP in 45 ACP.

single-shot handgun remains unchanged, but some of the optional equipment is different. The good news is that RPM will furnish Talley rings and scope bases with the pistol. Number of rings/bases depends on the chambering selected, e.g. a heavy recoiler like the 356 Winchester would get three rings and bases while the milder 223 would get two. On the down-side, the slim octagon barrels are no longer being offered due to the amount of labor involved. Not to appear greedy, but thank goodness I got mine!

ROSSI: Rossi's new single shot is based upon the design of a rifle and looks familiar to those of us who hunt with single-shot handguns. Slightly different is the release latch located at the rear of the receiver on the right side of the gun. The factory-furnished

SMITH & WESSON: Talk about a clever idea for a special edition commemorative! S&W is reviving the Schofield revolver (in its original 45 S&W chambering) on its 125th anniversary. The new Schofield has

The 2 millionth Glock Pistol sold at auction for $9300, with matching funds donated by Glock to the COPS Foundation.

rubber grip and forearm are also a bit different than other manufacturers. Since this is a brand new gun, performance data is not yet available, but offerings initially include 22, 223, 38/357 Magnum and 45 Colt/.410.

RUGER: Although there were no new handguns on display at the SHOT Show, Ruger reports that tests are underway to offer the 22 Hornet in a Ruger revolver. A gun has not yet been selected, but candidates are the Redhawk and Super Blackhawk. No setback problems have been encountered, and one could reasonably expect to see something by next year. Now that the six-shot 454 Super Redhawks are coming off the production line, Ruger reports that some material changes have been incorporated into this gun after proof-testing original steels.

SAVAGE: Their commitment to the bolt-action single-shot pistol continues with Savage's introduction of the 22 Long Rifle-chambered model. The new gun features a scaled-down action, a left-handed bolt and a 10-inch barrel. The gun will have a blue finish and come with Weaver scope bases installed. Available as an "add-on" option, shooters can get B-Square's bipod kit ready for installation.

SIG: Three new models of SIG's 22 rimfire Trailside pistols are available. Reasonably enough, these are the Standard, Target, and Competition models, and the features of each model tend to match the expected application. The guns are in production at Hammerli and being shipped, and all are made entirely of metal. Of greater interest to those who focus on the non-sporting use of handguns, SIG is offering a Model 245 Compact chambered for the most serious of defensive calibers, the 45 ACP.

The three Custom Defense Package pistols offered from Kimber's Custom Shop.

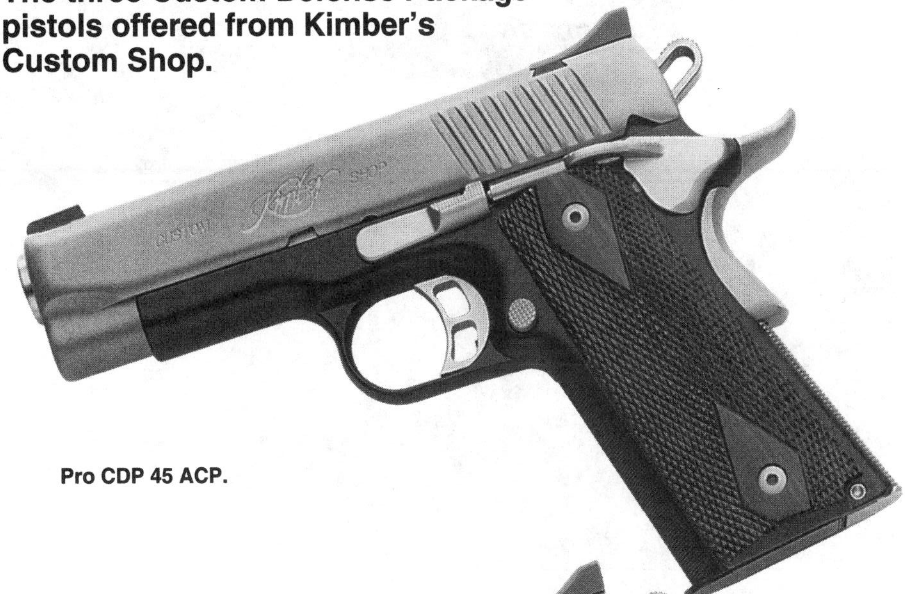

Pro CDP 45 ACP.

Compact CDP 45 ACP.

Ultra CDP 45 ACP.

been reverse-engineered from an original gun with several parts modernized and utilizing a frame-mounted firing pin. The gun will be built by the Performance Center. The first 125 will be the Special Editions and will be sold by credit card bid. The highest bid will receive Serial number 1, the next highest bid will receive Serial number 2, and so on. After the first 125 guns, the Schofield model will be available for general sale, but will still be manufactured by the Performance Center. Slightly less dramatic news is that the Tactical Smith & Wesson (TSW) will replace all Third Generation autos. One of the slick features on the TSW is the "mounting" rail under the slide in front of the trigger guard for little goodies like lasers and flashlights. Additionally, this year's Mountain Gun will be in 45 ACP, an interesting combination of gun and caliber whose performance extends well beyond what its appearance might suggest. And finally, stay in touch with periodic offers from the Performance Center, to wit, a SHOT Show showing of the Model 629 with a custom 12-inch slab-sided barrel and chambered for the inimitable 44 Magnum.

SPRINGFIELD: The Aimpoint mounts are now available, but Springfield admits it has been busy filling its orders with the FBI and making its commercial counterpart, the Professional Model. This used to be called the "Bureau Model" and is still an exact copy of the handgun being sold to the FBI. Their emphasis is on carry guns, IDPA guns and, in general, all kinds of tactical-type guns. Two new things being looked at/ worked on are a revamping of Springfield's custom line of pistols and a safety lock that could be retrofitted on any Model 1911. Perhaps available before year end and on full display at next year's show.

STEYR: The exotic-looking Steyr pistol first reported last year is now available in the small "S" size as well as in the 357 SIG chambering. Chambering offerings are the same, 40 S&W, 9mm and 357 SIG. The downsized version maintains many of its big brother's unique features, like the triangular-shaped sights, dual safeties - inside the trigger guard and in the trigger itself - and a third safety condition that uses a key to disable the

The Desert Eagle with interchangeable barrels is again being made in Israel and is available in 440 Cor-Bon and 44 Magnum.

Between the two 44 chamberings (440 Cor-Bon rounds left, 44 Magnum rounds right), there isn't much the Desert Eagle *pistolero* can't handle.

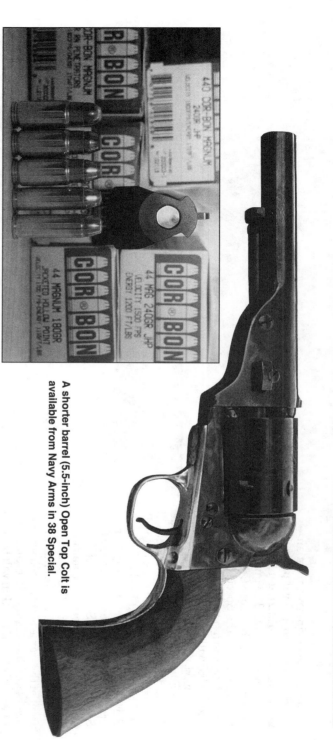

A shorter barrel (5.5-inch) Open Top Colt is available from Navy Arms in 38 Special.

pistol and prevent it from being disassembled. So who needs the government to dictate safety?

TAURUS: The Brazilian company was busy capitalizing on the success of their titanium line with their new semi-autos in both 9mm and 45 ACP. They have also added the 40 S&W to their line of 5-shot snubbie revolvers that will be furnished with polymer full moon clips for truly fast reloads.

The new Tracker Model revolver is being offered in a 5-shot 41 Magnum and 7-shot 357 Magnum with factory porting. And the PT 100 is back, this time in 40 S&W. As one might expect entering a new millennium, Taurus is offering the Millennium Model in two frame sizes. The smaller will handle 380, 9mm, 357 SIG and 40 S&W. A slightly larger frame will chamber the 45 ACP. And finally, check out the various finishes Taurus is offering on several of their models; one might just fulfill a long-time desire.

THOMPSON CENTER: Sitting atop the single-shot handgun world, T/C has turned its attention to the black powder handgun hunter and created the 50-caliber muzzle-loading Encore. With a huge hole running the length of its 15-inch barrel, the new Encore has a great feel and excellent balance. And if you already have an Encore frame, all you need to expand your horizons to black powder

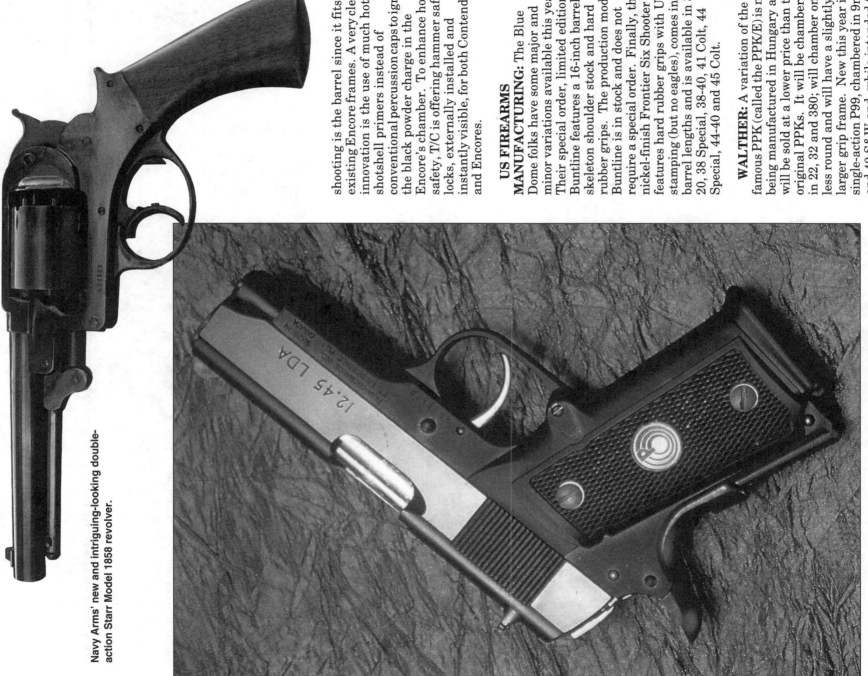

Navy Arms' new and intriguing-looking double-action Starr Model 1858 revolver.

Para-Ordnance's new Compact double-action pistol with double-stack magazine.

shooting is the barrel since it fits on existing Encore frames. A very clever innovation is the use of much hotter shotshell primers instead of conventional percussion caps to ignite the black powder charge in the Encore's chamber. To enhance home safety, T/C is offering hammer safety locks, externally installed and instantly visible, for both Contenders and Encores.

US FIREARMS MANUFACTURING:

The Blue Dome folks have some major and minor variations available this year. Their special order, limited edition Buntline features a 16-inch barrel, a skeleton shoulder stock and hard rubber grips. The production model Buntline is in stock and does not require a special order. Finally, their nickel-finish Frontier Six Shooter features hard rubber grips with U.S. stamping (but no eagles), comes in all barrel lengths and is available in 32-20, 38 Special, 38-40, 41 Colt, 44 Special, 44-40 and 45 Colt.

WALTHER: A variation of the famous PPK (called the PPK/E) is now being manufactured in Hungary and will be sold at a lower price than the original PPKs. It will be chambered in 22, 32 and 380; will chamber one less round and will have a slightly larger grip frame. New this year is a single-action P99, chambered in 9mm and 40 S&W and, while intended for

the law enforcement market, it should work quite nicely for civilian defensive purposes.

DAN WESSON: Several clever new ideas and models from this "never say die" company. Their Hunter Pac revolver comes in an English-style case with two barrels; one with open sights and the other set up with optics. The Pistol Pacs are now furnished with three barrels to go with their magnum revolvers and four barrels on the small frames.

Laser engraving is used to put matching serial numbers on frames and their fitted barrels. Their new model 7460 revolver features a heavy, vented 8-inch barrel and can fire either 45 ACP, the new 45 Roland or 45 Winchester Magnum using the factory-furnished full moon clips. Supermag chamberings include 357, the new 414 (.410), and the 445 (.430). Loaded ammo and brass is available from Starline. As if that were not enough, Dan Wesson has jumped into the 1911 market making full-size guns with Jarvis match barrels and high ribs, plus

The Ruger Super Redhawks in 454 Casull are coming off the production line with the new material changes incorporated.

Scaling down the size (but not the accuracy), Savage offers their smaller-action bolt pistol in 22 Long Rifle with 10-inch barrel.

Smith & Wesson's new Third Generation of autos, the Tactical series, features the accessory mounting rail beneath the barrel for adding flashlights or lasers. This TSW also sports the Tasco Optima 2000 sight.

WILSON: Two new models from Wilson show his range of versatility in Model 1911s. Classically named is his Millennium Protector, a single-stack, economical, "no frills" 1911 in 45 ACP. At the other end of the spectrum is his Model KZ 45, a polymer frame, wide-body self-loader that is even more economically priced than the Millennium Protector and holds 10 rounds of 45 ammo in the capacity-limited new generation of politically correct magazines.

commander-size guns available with either Novak or Bo-Mar sights. Busy year with fun new things for handgunners.

•

HANDGUN ACCESSORIES

by Dick Williams

HANDGUN SALES HAVE been brisk. In those categories and applications where a handgun requires certain accessories to be functional, e.g. cowboy action shooting and concealed carry, associated markets have thrived. When a new handgun needs no assistance, store owners have cleverly promoted some accessories such that new shooters suddenly view an add-on option as a "must have" item. When these items vastly improve a shooter's capabilities or enjoyment of firearms, everyone is well-served. We'll look at handgun optics first.

In talking to different gun store owners and operators around the country, it seems that the various red dot scopes are the leading sellers in handgun optics. It's simple: see better, shoot better. Several brand names have been mentioned as being quality hardware that provide reliable service, like **Leupold, Millett, Simmons, Swift** and **Weaver**. Dot scopes are not the answer for all shooters since they have no place on a nineteenth century single-action replica nor will they comfortably stuff into an inside-the-waistband holster. But for recreational shooters, or those interested in home defense, the scopes definitely enhance performance. And in the dim hours when bad things come stalking, it is very comforting to clearly see your sight on the intended target.

At the SHOT Show, two of the dot scopes caught my attention, not because they're new, but because they've been improved and/or offer advantages. First is the **Tasco** Optima, which is the smallest and lightest optic on the market. Besides the obvious advantages of its size and weight, it stays at the rear of the gun—occupying only slightly more volume than the handgun's original iron sight. This means you can not only carry a compact handgun equipped with an Optima in a properly designed holster, you can carry it concealed. The other huge advantage is that the Optima has no switch to turn it on and off. It is always on, therefore it is always ready. The brightness is based upon demand; the brighter the ambient light, the brighter the dot. When the gun is put aside at the end of the day, a plastic housing slides over the Optima, blocking all light and minimizing the drain on the battery. Even without the cover, when carried in a shoulder or belt holster under a jacket, the relative darkness of that shrouded environment demands minimal battery output. The Optima isn't brand new, but it is now in significant production and available to the shooting public.

The second interesting dot scope is **Bushnell's** new "downsized" Holosight. Though not tiny, the new Holosight is about two-thirds the size and weight of the original, plus the operational controls have been relocated and simplified. Battery change is now extremely quick with no Allen wrench required, and the scope's

Loading a Freedom Arms' downsized 41 Magnum topped with Bushnell's new Holosight leaves a hunter prepared for just about anything.

▲ If you see better, you shoot better, and Bushnell's Holosight has a definite edge over iron sights.

light intensity has been reduced to alleviate the original Holosight's tendency to obscure the target with overpowering brightness. Perhaps best of all, the new Holosight costs $100 less than the old one. Still offering a variety of sight pictures to suit the individual shooter's taste, the Holosight is the "*techie*" darling of the red dot world.

For handgun hunters or long-range shooters, **Simmons** has added a new 3x9 variable power pistol scope to their product line. Can't personally comment on the new kid's performance, but I have had great luck with Simmons' smaller variables on some heavy-recoiling handguns, like 454 Casulls and several single shots chambered for rifle calibers. Hopefully these will be available by the time this annual goes to press.

The demand for suitable holsters to carry handguns concealed is directly proportional to the number of concealed carry permits issued throughout the country. And as more states formally recognize the right of responsible citizens to carry, numbers continue to grow. While I didn't see any new, exotic ways to carry concealed at the SHOT Show, the manufacturers' emphasis was on reducing weight and enhancing

comfort of known techniques. **Bianchi** had a new ankle holster in appropriate shapes and sizes to accommodate small revolvers and semi-autos. Bianchi went with its *AccuMold* technology and built the Triad with three wraparound compression straps and a large, soft pad inside the ankle band to insure a comfortable but snug fit. The two straps that wrap around the front of the leg are secured, the gun is inserted in the holster, and the third strap around the back of the leg is tightened to pull the gun butt close into the leg for maximum concealability. I haven't leaped over any tall buildings wearing this rig, but it has been comfortable for walk-around use, and I would expect the snap retention system to keep a firearm in place for any reasonably-sized buildings you might jump. In the ultra-light weight arena, Bianchi also showed its new *LeatherLite* Shoulder System. It has a thermomolded shell and the Bianchi *porvair plus* finish with an X-style harness for semi-autos or a Y-rig harness for revolvers. The off-side of the X-harness is equipped with a double magazine pouch to maintain the entire rig's balance.

▲ Bianchi's new Triad ankle holster is a comfortable way to conceal smaller handguns like this SIG 230 in 380 Auto.

comfortable.

Galco has their new Cop Ankle Band (CAB) "universal" elastic holster. The word universal is a slight exaggeration in that there are three different size ankle holsters, two semi-auto sizes and one small revolver. Their advantage is their reduced cost compared to some of the beautiful leather gear that Galco offers. New this year is their COP 3-slot belt holster made of molded leather with a magazine/cuff paddle carrier. This is a pancake-style holster where the three slots allow the user to choose either strong-side or cross-draw carry. The beauty of this style holster is that it allows different carry styles to suit different circumstances, and pancakes tend to hug the body well, minimizing those telltale bulges.

Since the holsters are molded, you must choose the right model to fit your gun. However, the holsters are easily removed from the harness and can be replaced by other holsters suitable for different firearms. Once again, no tall buildings, but I have worn the rig enough to verify that it's light and comfortable.

▼ Galco's Ankle Glove.

▲ Larger, more serious handguns are better concealed and carry more comfortably under a jacket in Bianchi's LeatherLite Shoulder System.

▶ While it has been available for years, the Bianchi Askins Avenger belt holster does an excellent job of carrying a new S&W TAC 9 equipped with Tasco's Optima red dot sight.

▼ The new Galco "Cop 3 Slot" Holster and Magazine/Cuff Paddle Carrier system fits popular autoloaders.

A company from Mesquite, Texas, called **Conceal 'N Draw**, had some interesting clothing ideas to handle concealed carry. They make vests and blazers for men and women in denim and leather that feature "universal" inside pockets for your handgun of choice. Starting this year, they will be making sport coats in denim, corduroy, leather or wool with the same internal carry capability. Their ladies' purses feature a center pocket for that "extra little something." Most appealing to me was their 4-inch wide belly band of inexpensive elastic that had two

▼ When "going off duty", the Optima's cover is reinstalled to minimize energy demands on the battery power system.

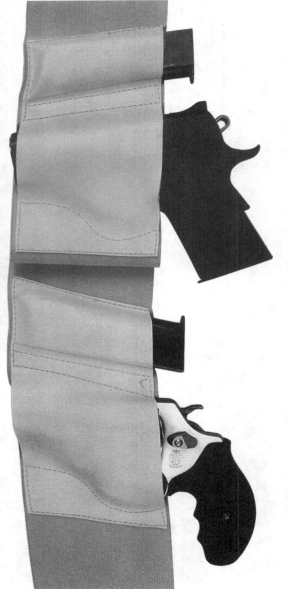

▶ Soft, leather backing on the underside of Conceal 'N Draw's belly band allows comfortable, concealed carry of different model handguns, like this Kimber and S&W Model 60.

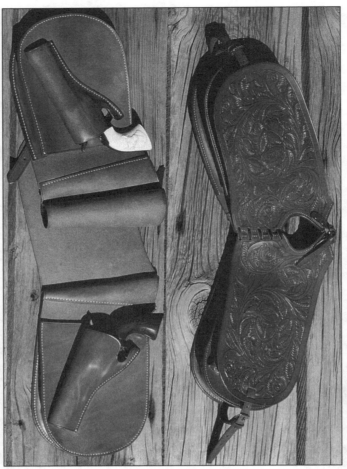

▲ By building the holsters as part of the pommel bags, El Paso Saddlery makes the horse carry the extra weight of one or two handguns.

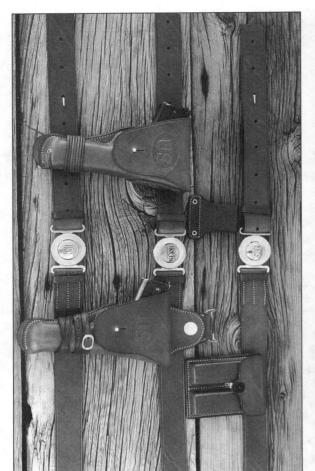

▲ El Paso Saddlery offers two outstanding reproductions of the US military holster in either standard WWII format (left) or cavalry swivel-style (right).

different size leather-backed pockets for either a revolver or semi-auto and two magazines. Simply attach the Velcro and move the band to whatever location puts your handgun where you want it. I wore it around the house for a few nights with a couple of different compact 1911s and was impressed with how well it worked and how comfortable it was.

In the cowboy world of today, there is a greater variety of high quality, authentic leather representative of the frontier period than our ancestors could have imagined. Mixed in with the real stuff, one can see both the influence of television westerns and the artistic touches of the artisans who manufacture today's gear. **El Paso Saddlery** has been making leather goods since 1889, so their research efforts need go no farther than their own files. One of their most unusual offerings are pommel bags, which are saddle bags that fit over the saddle horn and have one or two built-in holsters, that let the horse carry your guns. I understand the big Walker Colts were carried this way in the early days of Texas settlement. El Paso's personal touches are evident in the Wes Hardin holster, a Slim Jim rig with minimal leather for either strong-side or cross-draw use that features six cartridge loops on the outside of the holster. Their Doc Holiday cross-draw

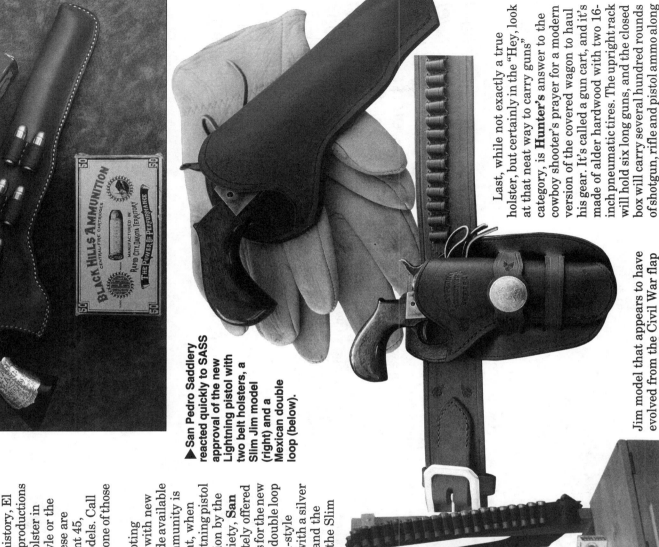

▲ El Paso Saddlery's Wes Hardin holster comes with six cartridge loops sewn on the holster and is available in either cross-draw (shown) or strong-side carry for cowboy guns in all barrel lengths like this Cimarron Wyatt Earp "Buntline".

shoulder holster is a handsome, comfortable-looking rig suitable for wear at the most respectable poker table or cowboy shoot. For those whose interests are in a different period of history, El Paso makes two excellent reproductions of the classic US military holster in either the cavalry swivel style or the standard WWII format. These are available for the Government 45, Beretta, and some other models. Call them if you have other than one of those two semi-autos.

With cowboy action shooting flourishing as a sport, and with new replica handguns being made available every year, the holster community is quick to react. Case in point, when Cimarron's downsized Lightning pistol was approved for competition by the Single Action Shooting Society, **San Pedro Saddlery** immediately offered two authentic-style holsters for the new handgun. One is the classic double loop Mexican-style holster with a silver concho, and the other is the Slim

▲ San Pedro Saddlery reacted quickly to SASS approval of the new Lightning pistol with two belt holsters, a Slim Jim model (right) and a Mexican double loop (below).

Jim model that appears to have evolved from the Civil War flap holsters via the simple expedient of removing the flap. I'm sure other manufacturers will be offering holsters for the Lightning soon, and I suspect San Pedro will be making other models for it.

Last, while not exactly a true holster, but certainly in the "Hey, look at that neat way to carry guns" category, is **Hunter's** answer to the cowboy shooter's prayer for a modern version of the covered wagon to haul his gear. It's called a gun cart, and it's made of alder hardwood with two 16-inch pneumatic tires. The upright rack will hold six long guns, and the closed box will carry several hundred rounds of shotgun, rifle and pistol ammo along with a couple of six-guns. With the lid closed, a tired *vaquero* can sit comfortably on the box waiting for his posse to be called into action. When it's lunch time, the lid opens to a table. It's not what John Wayne dragged across the plains, but I'll bet there were times he wished he had one!

▼ The new gun cart from Hunter Company.

From Downsizer Corporation....

"World's Smallest Pistol"

by Robert M. Hausman

Despite its diminutive size and single shot capability, the World's Smallest Pistol, or "WSP," is a vest pocket-sized pocket-rocket chambered for such no-nonsense rounds as the 45 ACP, making it very suitable for use as a close-range self-defense hideout arm.

A VERY UNIQUE and interesting pistol caught my attention at the S.H.O.T. Show a couple of years ago. It is the product of a new gunmaking firm, Downsizer Corp., of Santee, California and the product is billed as, and in fact named, the "World's Smallest Pistol," or WSP.

Downsizer Corp. was formed with the intention of producing arms of minimum size for the self-defense market. The design of this double-action single-shot arm has indeed been optimized to yield a product of minimum size. The piece makes the most of its single round cartridge capacity by being chambered for the 357 Magnum and 45 ACP. A pistol in the latter chambering was requested from the factory for this report.

Once the sample arrived, the WSP was found to be truly small. Overall length is just 3.25 inches, height is 2-3/8 inches, and its thickness is only fourteen-sixteenths of an inch! Weight (in the author's 45 ACP test sample) was 12 ounces; the barrel length is just over two inches.

This "hammerless" double-action only pistol is constructed entirely of stainless steel and is built without sights. The top of the barrel and receiver top-strap have a smooth, snag-free surface. Early production models were available in 40 S&W, 357 Magnum, 357 SIG, 9mm Parabellum, and 380 ACP. But now only the 45 and 357 Magnum chamberings are available, with the latter providing the capability of firing the milder 38 Special rounds. After the

initial examination of the piece, the urge to fire the gun became irresistible, so it was taken to the range with a box of Remington standard velocity FMJ ammo.

Firing the pistol (particularly with the big heavy slug 45 ACP cartridge) is not something I would recommend to the novice shooter. The muzzle blast was about the loudest of any handgun I have ever fired (use of hearing protection is mandatory). Recoil was considerable as well. In fact, after firing just four rounds, the web of skin between the author's thumb and forefinger rapidly became swollen and sore.

The World's Smallest Pistol is only 3.25 inches long, 2-3/8 inches high and less than one inch thick. At first glance, it could be mistaken for a pistol-shaped cigarette lighter.

Although the pistol has considerable weight for its size, its minimal dimensions, along with the hardness of its steel backstrap and stiff synthetic grip panels, make the recoil sensation even more unpleasant because the design places the chamber/bore line of thrust just above the web of the thumb.

Donning an "Uncle Mike's" padded shooting glove greatly helped dampen the recoil of subsequent rounds. (Note: the manufacturer is considering including a pair of rubberized, cushioned grips with future production, which should greatly aid shooter comfort). While gloves may not always be available during the tactical employment of the pistol, the use of gloves, particularly the padded variety, is recommended while practice firing to enhance shooter comfort. If employing the gun during an emergency to save your life, worrying about getting a swollen hand should be the least of your concerns.

While the recoil is not trivial (as mentioned), the design of the pistol allows the barrel to sit low in the hand and thus the recoil force is essentially straight back, with little muzzle flip. Accuracy was surprisingly good at the 15-foot test range.

There are no sights, making the WSP a true "point-and-shoot" piece for up-close and personal self-defense encounters.

The grip allows no more than a single finger purchase but the gun's fairly considerable weight (due to its steel construction) lends a solid feel in the hand. In addition, the backstrap is intentionally made wide and flat to help distribute the recoil force over the largest possible area of the firer's hand.

Although the author did not test WSP models in other chamberings, the 9mm and particularly the 380 ACP versions should be more suitable for the recoil-shy shooter if an example could be found at a local dealer. The pistol's manual warns against the use of +P or +P+ ammunition. Standard factory ammo generated about all the recoil and blast this author cared to subject himself to. Besides, the use of +P fodder would likely produce no ballistic benefit in the WSP's short barrel.

The WSP cannot be fired, unless the trigger is deliberately pulled, as a passive safety blocks the striker from contacting the primer. In operation, as the trigger is pulled, the striker

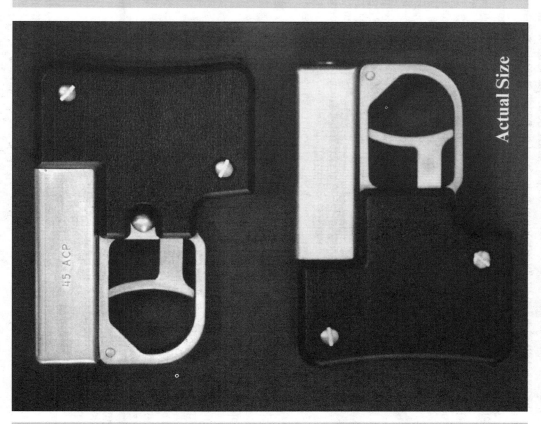

Actual Size

Smaller than a playing card, the WSP's solid construction and craftsmanship make it a pistol fit for a king.

moves rearward and compresses the striker driving spring. Near the endpoint of trigger travel, the passive safety is disengaged and the striker's forward path is no longer blocked.

When the trigger is pulled all the way to the rear, the sear is cammed out of engagement with the striker and the striker is propelled forward by it's driving spring to fire the pistol. After firing, the striker is automatically retracted and again gets blocked by the passive safety when the trigger is allowed to rebound.

In keeping with the nature of the pistol as a unique, top-quality piece for knowledgeable firearms aficionados, the manufacturing process for the WSP is truly top-notch. The WSP is cut from solid barstock. There are no castings or stampings in the pistol.

Quantities of 12-foot long stainless steel bars are received by truck at the factory. These bars are sawed into blanks and then loaded into modern CNC machine tools which are computer programmed to cut each part of the WSP. The entire process is highly automated and produces consistent quality.

Heat-treating is performed in a computer-controlled furnace and deburring is done by automatic machine. Assembly and polishing are accomplished by hand with skill and loving care. Finally, each WSP is proof-tested, function-checked and fully inspected before shipping.

The primary design objective in creating the WSP was to produce the smallest pistol ever made, subject to the constraint that it must fire a respectable cartridge. The small pistols of the past typically fired 25 ACP and 22 rimfire cartridges. Although these guns are often cute and intriguing, their ballistic performance is usually

The WSP is readily concealable within the palm of the hand.

considered less than ideal. The WSP offers the best of both worlds, in that, it is a smaller gun firing a better (more potent) cartridge.

To load, a small button on the WSP's left side is depressed which unlocks the barrel latch. The locking mechanism consists of a spring-loaded pin that engages a latch on the barrel's underside. The latch is not automatically cammed into engagement. The barrel latch button must be manually pushed in to allow closure (and locking) of the barrel. Although this patent-pending opera-

The WSP's barrel is tipped up for loading and unloading by releasing a push-button latch. When closed, it is secured by a solid steel mechanism.

tional aspect makes loading a little less than convenient, this extra step in the process ensures a much stronger barrel lockup, than if just a camming surface were used.

Once the chamber is loaded and the barrel locked into position, the WSP is perfectly safe to carry. As mentioned, a passive safety is utilized which blocks the striker/firing pin until the trigger is deliberately pulled. The passive safety is an

unusual aspect of a firearm in the vest pocket-size gun class, making the WSP a step above most others of its type in the safety area.

The long, heavy trigger pull (about 16 pounds according to my Brownell's trigger pull gauge) virtually ensures this piece will not be subject to unintentional discharge. In fact, some shooters, particularly those with smaller hands/and or minimal hand strength, may have difficulty drawing the WSP's trigger back far enough to fire the piece.

Since it is a single-shot arm not intended for extended firing sessions, there is no extractor. The author found empty shell casings easily dropped out of the chamber when the pistol was turned upside down and shaken slightly. After repeated firing, however, the accumulation of residue in the chamber required the empties to be pushed out with the blunt end of a ball point pen.

In tactical use, the pistol would not be fired more than once so the lack of an extractor would not be a problem. In point of fact, since it is intended to be deployed at very short range, if the first shot missed, the WSP's wielder would likely not have the opportunity to reload (as his adversary would make sure).

Don't let the small size of the WSP fool you. It cannot be compared to the "affordable" pocket pistols of the recent past.

Since it is built and constructed of quality materials, the WSP is not inexpensive, but is not prohibitively costly. At the time of this writing, it's suggested retail price is $429. It is a thoughtfully-engineered and conscientiously-manufactured pistol offering an unprecedented size-to-performance ratio.

The WSP is actually built in its factory, entirely by one person-Dan Chapman, the pistol's designer.

Chapman has had a lifelong interest in firearms, particularly small pistols. After graduating from college, he decided he wanted to work at an established handgun manufacturer. He interviewed with several firms and was treated respectfully by some and quite rudely by others.

"It soon became painfully apparent," Chapman recalls, "that the firearms industry was too small to offer much employment opportunity to an educated and ambitious person.

A reasonable man would have written off the gun industry and taken a good, white collar job elsewhere. However, I decided instead that if the industry couldn't offer me decent employment, I'd start my own gun factory!"

Shortly thereafter, Chapman entered graduate school to study mechanical engi-

The WSP's barrel sits low in the hand so the recoil force tends to push straight back, with little muzzle flip.

neering for the express purpose of learning how to design and manufacture firearms. Downsizer Corp. was formed just before he received his master's degree and he actually studied for his final exams in his factory.

Downsizer Corp. has several designs in various stages of development. They will be introduced to the market as financial, technical, political, and legal constraints allow. While exact details were not available at press time, they all will likely share the distinction of being the smallest pistols of their type ever made.

One hint as to the type of gun Chapman may be planning for the future is his great interest in the Bayard M-1908 pistol. These small pistols were made in 25-, 32- and 380-calibers and were produced by Anciens Établissements Pieper in

Herstal, Belgium. The M-1908 is approximately five inches long and carries a September 8, 1908 patent date. A big-bore derivative of the Bayard M-1908 semi-auto pistol may be in the planning stages, although this bit of information was not confirmed. If true, it would represent Downsizer Corp.'s first repeater.

Though not for the novice, the WSP is worthy of consideration as a second or third backup piece for those treading on dangerous ground. It is of special interest to the undercover police officer. The market for this gun also includes persons licensed for concealed carry, firearms collectors and any qualified person who appreciates a unique, high-quality handgun. Civilians have been known to carry a WSP as their primary arm. Knowledgeable collectors realize the WSP is unlike any other handgun ever made and appreciate the small size, large bore, and high quality of manufacture.

The "World's Smallest Pistol" (or WSP) is produced by Downsizer Corporation, P.O. Box 710316, Santee, California 92072.
Telephone: 619-448-5510.

Dan Chapman, president of Downsizer Corp., designer and builder of the World's Smallest Pistol.

The Liberator
...an earlier small single-shot pistol

While built of much higher quality materials and construction, the WSP is somewhat reminiscent in its concept to the Liberator, a small, sheet-metal stamped arm originally designed in 1942. Chambered for the 45 ACP cartridge, the standard U.S. service pistol round at the time, the Liberator was a single-shot but highly effective (at close range) tool, due to its large caliber. Air-dropped by the Allies behind enemy lines to European patriots, the Liberator was intended for use by citizen soldiers in occupied countries. The gun was also smuggled into the Philippines, as well as China, Burma and India.

Being a single-shot pistol of rather crude construction, it was intended to be used for ambushing Axis soldiers, enabling the patriots to then obtain a more formidable arm, such as a German officer's Luger or P38 pistol, or a soldier's service rifle. The Liberator's smooth bore not only limited its range but also its accuracy.

There was no rifling to stabilize the projectile for its flight and the bullet would often "key-hole," or strike the target sideways. The big 45-caliber bullet's impact contained enough force to cause a disabling wound, at very least, allowing the patriot to rush the enemy and snatch his weapon(s), and thus deliver a coup de grace, if necessary; possibly with the enemy's own gun.

Leaders of the Polish resistance movement originally made the request for a disposable pistol and the U.S. Joint Chiefs of Staff reportedly ordered large quantities (about 1 million) of these low-cost (about $1.72 per pistol), but large-caliber pistols to be produced, mainly by the Guide Lamp division of General Motors, as part of a top secret project.

The barrel was made of seamless tubing and the frame from stamped sheet metal. A vertically sliding breech plate held the cartridge in the chamber while the firing pin was mounted on a die-cast zinc block and the pistol was held together with spot welds and rivets.

Unloaded weight was one pound, length was 5-1/2 inches and thickness just over one inch. The guns were packaged in waxed cardboard cartons containing 10 rounds of ammo, an illustrated pictorial loading and firing instruction sheet without explanatory text to allow comprehension by speakers of a variety of languages, and a wooden ramrod for ejecting spent casings. The pistol's grip contained a hollow cavity to allow storage of extra ammunition.

While a functional arm, the Liberator's main role was for use in psychological warfare. Namely, the demoralization of enemy troops patrolling occupied countries (who never knew which civilian they might encounter could be in possession of a loaded and concealed "Liberator"). Since disarmament of the conquered civilian population is a standard procedure during wartime, the Liberator was intended to give residents of occupied areas the means to resist. The improvement of civilian morale by stimulating the will to resist was an additional benefit.

Smith & Wesson AirWeight and AirLite Revolvers

Pure packing pleasure - then and now!

by Paul S. Scarlata

Photos by James Walters & Sal Scarlata

MOST OF THE important advances in revolver design in the last 130-odd years should be, I believe, attributed to the ongoing competition between two companies that have dominated the American (world?) handgun market since the Civil War – Colt and Smith & Wesson. During the 19th century each company had a lock upon a specific segment of the market with Colt products being adopted by the bulk of those large caliber, holstersized revolvers purchased by civilians. In contrast, S&W's large-caliber topbreak revolvers proved extremely popular with foreign armies while their 32- and 38-caliber guns were the pre-

mier pocket revolvers in an era when a significant percentage of the adult populace went about their daily business and travels armed.

Five decades of S&W compact, light-weight revolvers. Clockwise from the top left: Model 12 Airweight, Model 242 Ti AirLite, Model 37 Airweight and Model 332 Ti AirLite.

U.S. military and accounting for the bulk of those large caliber, holster-

Most of this century saw the two companies competing for the same markets as each attempted to interest military, police and civilian customers in their respective lines of double-action, swing-out cylinder revolvers that - while differing in design - were identical in concept and use. If you wanted a large-caliber wheelgun you could choose between the Colt New Service or the S&W 44 Hand Ejector series; customers seeking a medium-caliber revolver could buy a Colt Police Positive or S&W Military & Police; for concealed carry there was the Colt

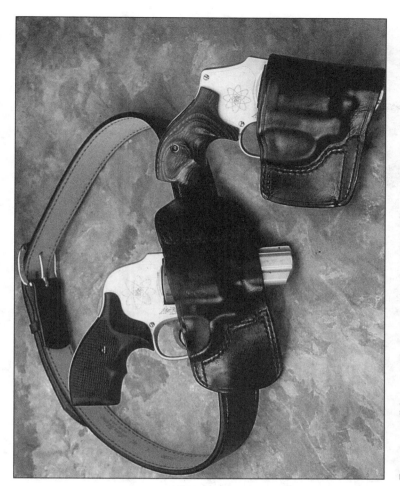

For our test firing exercises, Don Hume Leathergoods supplied us with an H710 holster for the Model 12 and 342, while both the Model 37 and 332 fit nicely in one of their JIT Slide rigs.

38 Special test ammo consisted of Remington standard velocity 110-grain JHP and 158-grain TEMC for the Model 37 and 12 and CCI Blazer 158 grain +P TMJ for the 242 Ti. The little 32 H&R Magnum Model 332 was fired with Federal 85-grain JHPs.

Detective Special or the S&W Chiefs Special. S&W 357s dominated the Magnum market - that is, until Colt brought out their Lawman and Python revolvers. Both firms engaged in a long-running marketing war in a never-ending attempt to gain an edge on the competition and, by 1960, it could be fairly said that these efforts had resulted in the perfection of the modern double-action revolver as we know it.

Around this time, manufacturers began investigating the possibility of producing handgun parts from the new, strong aluminum alloys that had been developed during and after World War II. First off the mark was Colt in 1950 with their 38 Special Cobra. This, the first of the *snake* line, was little more then the popular Detective Special with an alloy frame that reduced its weight by six ounces. In 1951 the U.S. Air Force purchased approximately 1,200 Colt Cobra revolvers fitted with aluminum cylinders that reduced their unloaded weight to only 11 ounces. Known as the Aircrewman Special, they were intended for issue to pilots and other personnel for whom weight was a prime concern.

But S&W's R&D boffins did not take this lying down, and by 1952 they went the Hartford competition one (two?) better by offering the civilian market a pair of revolvers with alloy frames and cylinders - the 38 Chiefs Special Airweight and the 38 Military & Police Airweight. While the five-shot Chiefs Special Airweight used a standard size J-frame, albeit much lighter, the Military & Police utilized an aluminum frame that was identical in height and length to the popular K-frame but, to reduce weight further, was 0.08-inch narrower than steel frame M&Ps while the grips were correspondingly thinner, with rounded edges. Fitted with 2-inch barrels and round butt grips, the Chiefs Special Airweight weighed 11 ounces while the Military & Police tipped the scales at 14.5 ounces, which were respectively - a not inconsiderable - 10 and 11.5 ounces less than their all-steel counterparts!

S&W lost no time in offering their Airweight revolvers to the Air Force, who were impressed enough with the Military & Police version that, in late 1953, they placed an order for a quantity that were officially designated the Revolver, Lightweight, Caliber .38 Special, M13. But within a year the Air Force began experiencing cylinder cracking problems with both their S&W and Colt revolvers. In an attempt to rectify the situation, a low pressure 38 Special load was developed specifically for the Air Force revolvers. But

even this lackluster M41 Ball Cartridge with its 130-grain FMJ bullet moving at (claimed?) 780 fps proved, in some cases, too much for the aluminum cylinder gun. While the Air Force had some of their M13s retrofitted with steel cylinders, the majority were turned in and destroyed in 1959.

But while the military attempted to save the M13 program, in 1954 S&W quickly decided to substitute a steel cylinder for the aluminum one on production guns. Although this increased the weight of both Air-weight revolvers to 12.5 and 18 ounces, they were still extremely con-

TRENDS

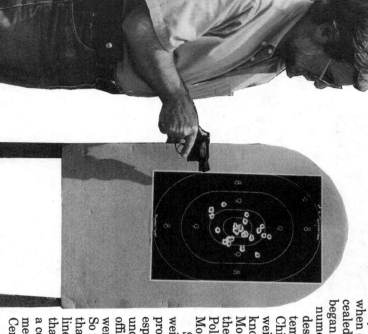

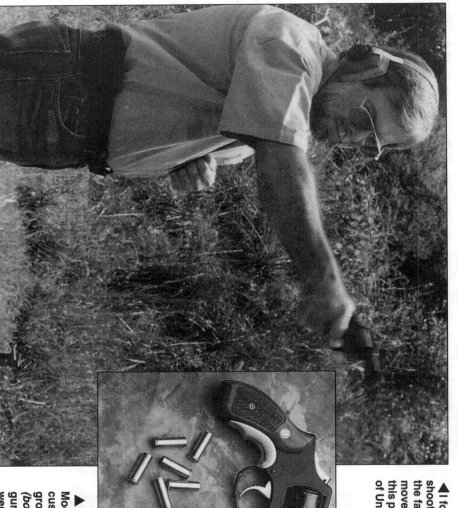

▲ I found the Model 12 Airweight an easy-shooting handgun, although once again the factory wooden grips allowed it to move in my hand under recoil. When I carry this particular revolver, it is fitted with a set of Uncle Mike's Boot grips.

▲ Our two Airweight test 38s included a Model 12 (top) that had been slightly customized by having the hammer spur ground off, and an original Model 37 (bottom). The latter is an early production gun with the flat cylinder release. Both were fitted with Tyler T-grip adapters.

venient handguns to carry - especially when carried concealed. In 1957 S&W began using a numerical model designation system and the Chiefs Special Airweight became known as the Model 37 while the Military & Police became the Model 12.

Smith's Airweight revolvers proved popular - especially with undercover police officers - and sales were encouraging. So much in fact, that the J-frame line was expanded that first year with a concealed hammer version, the Centennial Air-

weight (post-1957 Model 42) and three years later saw the introduction of the shrouded hammer Bodyguard Airweight (post-1957 Model 38).

The Model 12's popularity was sufficient that in 1959 the Massachusetts manufacturer decided to expand the line with the options of 4-, 5- or 6-inch barrels, a choice of round or square butt grips and blue or nickel finishes. While the 4-inch model was an instant success, the longer-barreled models attracted little attention and were dropped from the catalog the following year. The Model 12 maintained a loyal following among police officers - especially, it has been reported, with female officers - and civilians because of its higher capacity cylinder, superior ergonomics and recoil control when compared to the smaller J-frame Airweights.

As were S&W's steel-frame revolvers, the Model 12 line was upgraded with redesigned frames (12-1), more practical sights and grips (12-2) and cylinders (12-3). Beginning in 1984, in an attempt to contain costs by allowing the use of the same machinery, Model

▲ No doubt due to my experience with it, I fired the tightest groups with my Model 12 Airweight.

US in the 1990s, sales of S&W's light-weight J-frame revolvers rebounded from the semiauto slump, leading to the introduction of even more variations including models with stainless steel cylinders, cranes and barrels. S&W's 1999 catalog lists no less then seven alloy J-frame 38 Special revolvers: the Models 37, 38, 442, 637, 638 and 642.

But S&W has never been a company to rest upon its laurels, and it wasn't very long before they broke new ground in the area of lightweight revolvers with their 22 LR Model 317 AirLite. Based upon the ever-popular J-frame, the 317 returned to the original idea of the Model 37 with an alloy frame and cylinder and then went the competition one better by making the barrel out of aluminum, too! S&W had pioneered this new breed of aluminum cylinders a few years earlier with their ten-shot 22 caliber Model 17 and 617-Plus K-frame revolvers. S&W's engineers used parts made from 7075-T6 aluminum, which has a tensile strength of 80,000 P.S.I., similar to many steels. The 317's aluminum barrel features a stainless steel bore liner that is more than capable of standing up to 22 LR operating pressures while several internal parts were made from titanium, reducing weight even further without sacrificing strength.

Wait a minute! What was that strange-sounding metal mentioned in the previous paragraph? Wasn't it...*titanium?* Yeah, that's it. Anyhow, in late 1998 S&W announced two more additions to their extensive line of J-frame revolvers that were the flagships of a new generation of lightweight, concealed handguns - the AirLite Ti Model 337 (exposed hammer) and Model 342

▶ All S&W AirLite revolvers feature a lanyard pin in the groove on the backstrap. This is intended for special retention purposes.

S&W's new line of titanium AirLite revolvers was represented by a Model 242 (*top*), a 38 Special +P L-frame with a 2.5-inch barrel. The 32 H&R Magnum Model 332 (*bottom*) shares similar features: titanium cylinder and internal parts, alloy frame, stainless steel barrel with alloy shroud and a concealed hammer.

Test firing was conducted at seven yards. Here I am firing the S&W 242 AirLiteTi.

12 revolvers (12-4) were produced with frames of the same width as steel K-frame guns. In the mid-1980s - with the burgeoning popularity of semiauto pistols with both police and civilian shooters a fact of life - S&W began to trim their revolver line...and one of the first casualties was the Model 12, when it was dropped from production in 1986. While I have been unable at this time to ascertain total production numbers,

the most common version was the Model 12-2 with a 2-inch barrel and square butt grip. This seems to concur with my own observations, because after three years of collecting Model 12 revolvers, I see more of that version than any other.

But while the Model 12's sales declined, those of the Airweight J-frame remained steady. With the relaxation of concealed carry laws across the

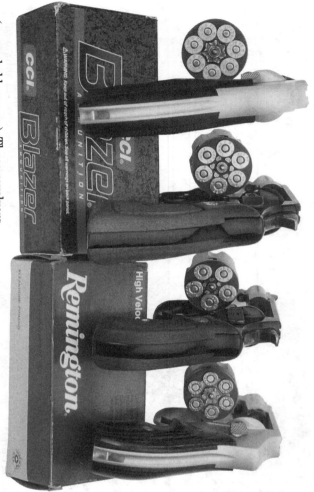

▲Cylinder capacities vary from the Model 12, a traditional "six-shooter", down to five 38s in the Model 37 and back up to the Model 242's seven-round cylinder. While a J-frame, the Model 332 can fit six 32 H&R Magnums in its titanium cylinder.

(concealed hammer.) These revolvers are notable in that they mate cylinders made from titanium with an alloy frame, crane and composite barrel to achieve extreme light weight while still being strong enough to handle 38 Spl.+P ammunition. Titanium - which weighs 40% less than an equal amount of stainless steel - is *extremely* strong and its use, up until now, has generally been restricted to supersonic jet aircraft and space vehicles where weight-to-strength ratio is of critical importance. To help reduce weight even further, the new alloy frames features a number of lightening cuts along the backstrap, trigger guard, trigger, ejector rod housing and barrel rib. Additional strengthening features have been added, including a special, heavy-duty nitrided center pin, a titanium bushing where the center pin passes through the bolster face and four titanium studs that carry the trigger, hammer, rebound and cylinder stop. As did the Model 317, the new AirLite Ti revolvers feature a small lanyard ring inlet into the heel of the grip frame for special retention purposes.

More weight savings are realized by the use a composite barrel assembly that consists of a flat-sided aluminum barrel shroud and a stainless steel barrel tube. The former is held in place by the latter being screwed into the frame (a special tool, only available from S&W, is required to remove or install the assembly.) S&W engineers designed the barrel so the rotational torque of the bullet spinning in the rifling actually tightens the barrel with each shot. The cylinder also features a special surface finish that inhibits wear, corrosion and erosion and in fact, makes extraction of fired cases smoother than from steel cylinders. Because of this, the cylinder or chambers must never be cleaned with any type of abrasive material (sandpaper, Crocus cloth, etc.) since doing so will void the warranty. This combination of titanium and alloy provides enhanced resistance to corrosion from weather or perspiration - an important consideration when carrying a concealed handgun, especially in warmer climates.

One of the first thing one notices about the 337 and 342 is the statement 38 S&W SPL.+P JACKETED laser-engraved on the left side of the barrel

Smith & Wesson has announced that all current production 38 Special Airweight Revolvers are now rated for +P ammunition. This ammunition compatibility update includes (clockwise from left) the Models 642, 638, 38, 442, 637, 642 LadySmith and 37.

Historical Note

The Model 12 family includes one of the rarer S&W K-frame revolvers ever made. In 1966 the Springfield factory produced a small number of Model 12s for French police trials, which were fitted with 3-inch barrels, round butts and a safety catch! The latter device consisted of what appeared to be a second cylinder latch on the right sideplate which, when pushed forward, locked the hammer and trigger. Eventually, the French police decided upon a locally manufactured revolver, and the whole concept of a revolver equipped with a safety (fortunately) ended there! Reportedly, only about a dozen of these remained in the U.S., making them extremely desirable collectors items.

shroud. The explanation for this qualifier is quite simple when one understands that light guns recoil more than heavy guns. Ammunition manufacturers normally use a light crimp to hold soft lead bullets in the case. When such ammunition is fired in a light handgun, with increased recoil momentum, the bullet may be unseated from the casing and move forward. Repeated firings will cause it to eventually move past the front face of the cylinder, preventing rotation and locking up the revolver. For this reason S&W recommends against the use of any +P lead bullet loads in their AirLite Ti revolvers. Literature enclosed with the revolver states that *standard velocity* lead bullet 38 Special loads can be used in the AirLite Ti revolvers.

S&W also offers the AirLite Ti Model 331 and Model 332 titanium revolvers which feature six-shot cylinders chambered for a cartridge that is undergoing a rebirth in popularity - the 32 H&R Magnum. Loaded with 85-grain JHP or 95-grain LSWC bullets this cartridge, the smallest of the handgun magnums, combines the advantages of light recoil and higher cartridge capacity with a cartridge whose ballistics are comparable to the standard velocity 38 Special when loaded with 110- and 125-grain bullets.

But the story doesn't end there! At the 1999 SHOT Show S&W introduced their AirLite Ti Model 242 and Model 296 revolvers. And while the 242 and 296 both display the same construction features as their J-frame brethren, the similarities end there. This is because they are both built on S&W's L-frame, which is slightly larger than the well-known K-frame and was designed to provide a revolver capable of handling Magnum or larger-caliber cartridges without being too bulky. The 296 holds five rounds of 44 Special while the 242 is closer to the concept of the Model 12 with a cylinder that takes seven rounds of 38 Special +P ammunition. Both the 242 and 296 feature Tita-

nium/alloy construction, concealed hammers, 2.5-inch barrels and compact, round butt grips. And while they are indeed larger then their J-frame counterparts, they tend to ape their Model 12 predecessors with a weight of only 18.9 ounces. This combination of light weight, short overall length and round butt grips permit them, with the proper style of holster, to be carried concealed in complete comfort while at the same time their larger size, grips and longer barrels provide enhanced ergonomics, handling and accuracy.

But while the 242 can handle any 38 Special loading, one caveat must be observed when firing the 296. Accordingly, the right side of barrel shroud warns the shooter

.44 S&W SPECIAL CTG. - MAX BULLET 200 GRAIN. The explanation for this warning is identical to that on the 337 and 342: those ammunition manufacturers who produce the 44 Special offer it with lead bullets in the 240-grain range using a light crimp. As was described above, we all know what happens when such cartridges are fired in light-weight revolvers, right? When firing jacketed bullets, with their heavier crimp, this is not a problem.

As it would be downright unethical of me to pass judgment on S&W's Air-weight and AirLite Ti revolvers without actually

▲ Thanks to its excellent ergonomics - and size - the 242 AirLite was a pussycat to shoot and proved quite accurate.

As can be seen here, recoil from the 32 H&R Magnum cartridge in the Model 332 was "quick," but controllable.

The soft-recoiling 332 AirLite proved an excellent performer. With the high performance loads available for the 32 H&R Magnum, it might prove a practical choice for small-stature persons or those who have trouble handling recoil from larger cartridges.

test-firing them, I amassed a fair sampling of the *genre*, both past and present. These included a pair of 1960s vintage 38 caliber Airweights, a Model 37 and Model 12. While the latter has had its hammer spur removed, it is otherwise stock with a 2-inch barrel and round butt grips. My modern AirLite Ti duo consisted of a Model 332 in 32 H&R Magnum and a Model 242 in 38 Special+P. Because +P ammunition is not recommended for older alloy-frame S&W revolvers, the Model 37 and 12 were fired with, respectively, Remington standard velocity 110-grain JHP and 158-grain TEMC Leadless ammunition. Federal's 85-grain JHP loading of the 32 H&R Magnum was used in the little Model 332 while the L-frame 242 was fed a diet of CCI Blazer 158-grain +P TMJ. My test firing coincided with the July 4th weekend and, thanks to the vagaries of Mother Nature, the temperatures were hovering above the 90 degree mark, making the inclusion of a large jug of ice water and a couple of hand towels with my regular shooting

gear all but mandatory! I hope the readers of this fine publication appreciate the hardships I endure to bring you this important information? The life of a gun magazine writer is not an easy one!!!

As I don't believe attempting to shoot little groups from a rest is a valid test of revolvers—intended from the word *go* as close range, defensive weapons—my test firing was limited to off-hand exercises performed at a range of seven yards. Each revolver was run through the following drills:

1. Five/six/seven rounds, slow aimed fire.
2. Drawing the revolver, I fired three sets of rapid fire double taps (yes, the Model 37 had a sixth round loaded!).
3. Drill #2 was repeated, firing the revolvers single-handed.
4. Drawing the revolver, I fired a cylinder-full as fast as I could obtain a flash sight picture.

In the interests of obtaining valid comparisons, my test guns were fired with the factory grips. But as did so

many shooters then - considering the less-than-optimal wooden grips fitted to revolvers of the time - the Model 37 and 12 were fitted with Tyler T alumiinum grip adapters. The Don Hume Leathergoods Company kindly supplied us with appropriate holsters for my test firing while HKS provided a selection of their five-, six- and seven-round speedloaders to help move matters along a bit quicker.

As might be expected of products of the Springfield S&W factory, all my of my test guns proved capable - if I did my part - of keeping their rounds inside in the X, 10 and 9 rings of their respective Birchwood-Casey *Shoot-N-C* targets, although a few of the rounds I sent down-range one-handed wandered out into the 8-ring. In general, handling was admirable and, while the attenuated wooden grips on the Models 37 and 12 permitted them to move around in my (*perspiring*) hands under recoil, the Dymondwood finger groove grips provided excellent control on the

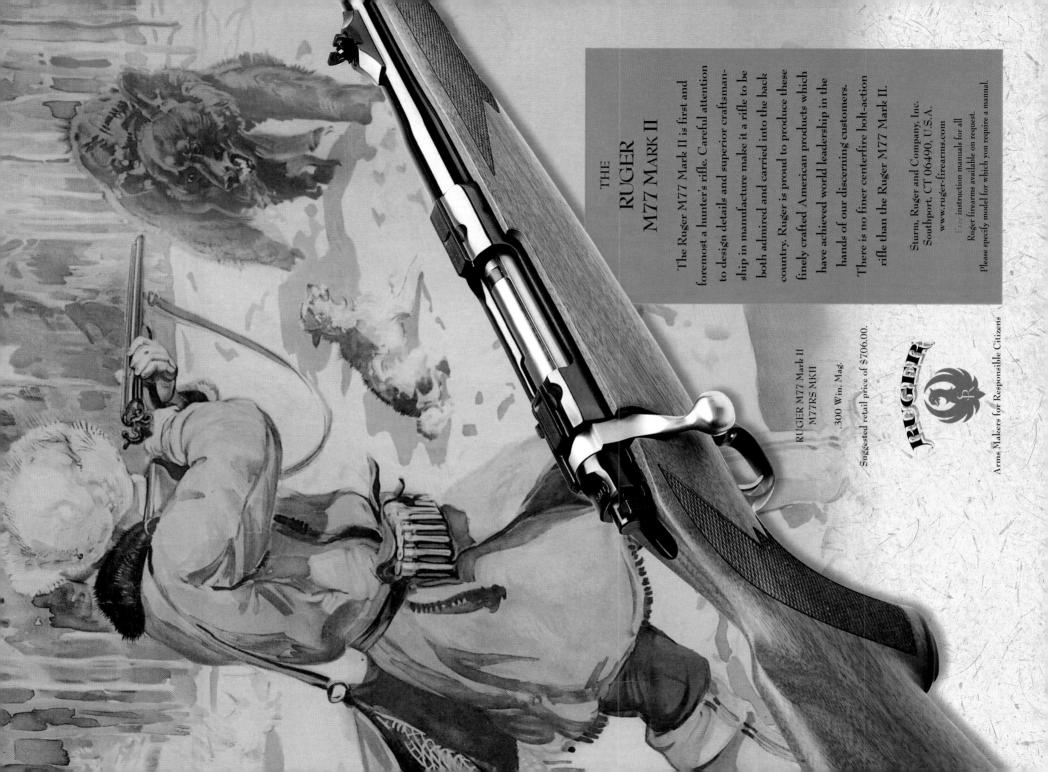

The Guns That Work™

Winchester-guns.com

WINCHESTER

RIFLES AND SHOTGUNS

Licensee

Winchester is a registered trademark licensed from Olin Corporation.

soft-recoiling M332 while the Uncle Mike's Boot Grip-equipped 242 was the handling champion of the day. In general, shootability varied and while the 242 was, even with +P ammo, a regular pussycat to shoot, the little Model 37 proved a trial after the second cylinder full. All in all, I found the Model 12 a practical compromise offering, as it did, less bulk than the 242, superior controllability and an extra round over the Model 37 and a more impressive chambering than the 332. In fact, as can be seen from the photos, thanks to its well-used, and smooth, DA trigger pull I shot the tightest groups with the Model 12. And while I don't want to be accused of trying to tell the marketing types in Springfield their business, I think I would safe in predicting a ready market for a snub-nosed, (eight shot 32 H&R Magnum?) K-frame AirLite Ti.

S&W's Airweight and AirLite revolvers have, for almost a half-century, filled a very important niche. They have provided the police officer and licensed civilian the advantages of light weight, superior shootability and practical chamberings—all in a package that could be carried all day in complete comfort. Or, as one of my friends said after firing our selection of revolvers, *"These were designed to be carried a lot and fired very little! But when you think about it, that is an apt job description for handguns designed for self-defense."* S&W Airweight and AirLite Ti revolvers are a pleasure to carry and will thus be carried more often and, if need be, can be just as practical "shooting guns" as are their heavier brethren. That is one of the reasons why the Model 12 test-fired for this article—one of ten I presently own—has become one of my favorite carry guns. Although now that I've had the opportunity to shoot the 242 extensively I've got to make a big decision - should I send it back to S&W or keep it and retire my faithful old Model 12? This is going to be a very difficult decision!

During its 34-year production run, the Model 12 proved popular enough for S&W to offer it in a variety of barrel lengths, grip shapes and finishes. Reportedly the 2-inch, square butt was the best-selling version.

Specifications:	Model 37	Model 12
Chambering	38 Special	38 Special.
Overall length	6 inches	6 7/8 inches
Barrel length	2 inches	2 inches
Weight (unloaded)	12.5 oz.	18 oz.
Capacity	five	six
Grips	......checkered walnut...........	
Sights front:	..........serrated blade.............	
rear:	..........square notch............	

Specifications:	Model 332 Ti	Model 242 Ti
Chambering	32 H&R Magnum	38 Special +P
Overall length	6 5/16 inches	7 3/8 inches
Barrel length	1 7/8 inches	2 inches
Weight (unloaded)	11.3 oz.	18.9 oz.
Capacity	six	seven
Grips	Dymondwood	Uncle Mike's Boot Grip
Sights front:	..........serrated blade.............	
rear:	..........square notch............	

For further information:

Smith & Wesson -
PO Box 2208,
Springfield, MA 01102.
Tel. 800-331-0852

Don Hume Leathergoods -
PO Box 351, Miami, OK 74355.
Tel. 800-331-2686

HKS Products -
7841 Fountain Dr.,
Florence, KY 41042.
Tel. 606-342-7841.

Alchemy Arms 'Spectre'

A new gun company introduces a new 'hybrid' semi-auto, and this writer was enlisted to help work out the bugs to make it a winner

by Dave Workman

GUN WRITERS ARE usually invited to evaluate a new gun model once it's been fully developed—sometimes tricked out—so that the piece "puts its best foot forward."

Rarely, though, are gun scribes enlisted at "ground level" to take a prototype model, fully evaluate it, then offer criticisms and recommendations while the firearm is still in its pre-production stage.

Offered the opportunity to take the prototype of the brand new "Spectre" semi-auto pistol from Alchemy Arms away from the Auburn, Washington factory — and the watchful eyes of proprietors Brent Mounts and William Smith — to a private range for a demanding test drive, I leaped at the chance.

The Spectre's design intrigued me. It might best be described as a marriage between a Glock slide and barrel assembly, and a somewhat-modified 1911 receiver. Yeah, yeah, that may sound like hell, but the finished product might lay claim to its own little corner of pistol heaven. That's up to shooters to decide.

Chambered in 9mm, 40 S&W or 45 ACP, the Spectre will come in three versions. There's a standard grade — which I tested — built with a 4130 carbon steel slide with black finish, carbon steel barrel and black anodized, one-piece alloy frame. The service grade has a stainless steel slide with either a black anodized or brushed alloy receiver. Still in development at this

GUN TESTS

writing, but promising to be a winner is the Titanium grade, featuring a titanium slide and alloy receiver, with either an all "silver" or "silver/gray" finish.

There are several features that, in my opinion, will combine to earn the Spectre favorable acceptance in the shooting fraternity. Let's take a look at them one at a time:

• Where the ground-breaking Glock design has been criticized by some shooters for lacking an external manual safety, the Spectre has (ready for this?) a thumb safety on the right rear of the receiver — just where you'd find it on a Government Model pistol — and a beavertail grip safety.

• The grip is comfortable, and it's on the same angle as the Model 1911. Checkering is cut on the grip surface.

• Slide-to-barrel lock-up is positive, slide-to-rail fit is tight, and takedown is achieved via the same simple system used on the Glock and S&W Sigma.

• The internal striker firing system works like a champ.

• Last, and certainly not least, is a feature that's going to drive litigation-happy sharks (er, attorneys) and anti-gun hysterics absolutely bonkers. At the base of the mainspring housing is an integral gun locking device.

On my prototype model, this thing operated with a traditional key-lock. On production models, there's an even better version that uses a key-coded cam lock. Simply turn this, a metal tab swivels around that locks into the magazine at the lower rear, and also prevents the grip safety from being depressed. This, in turn, prohibits the trigger from moving.

No other way to say it, this feature is just plain doggone clever. It follows along in the course set by Taurus two years ago, with "key" locking devices on revolver models.

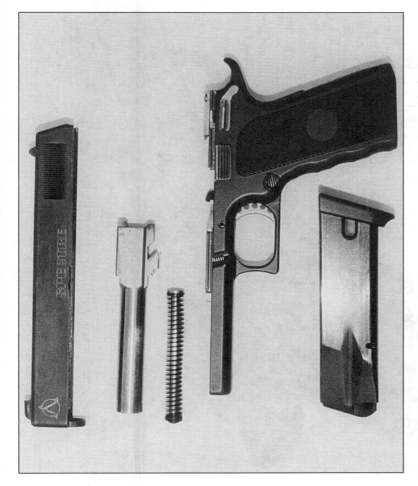

Spectre pistol takes down like Glock, Sigma

A look down inside the receiver of the Spectre shows simple design.

Author Workman tested Alchemy Arms Spectre from a sandbag rest.

Mounts hinted that one of his advertising slogans might well be aimed directly at the gun control zealots who insist on telling industry how to build guns: "Who needs 'smart' when you can have 'safe'?" It has possibilities.

Home on the range

As I said at the beginning, my job was more than a simple test evaluation. Alchemy wanted me to run this pistol through its paces, and "beat up" on it. I certainly did, and I'm delighted to note that every criticism I had of the prototype was put on the priority list, and alterations to production guns will have been made by the time you read this.

Of course, the proverbial "acid test" of any gun is how well it shoots. Despite the bugs in my prototype model, this

Spectre prototype performed well at the 25-yard line. Birchwood Casey Shoot•N•C target tells the tale.

baby delivers downrange.

The 4.5-inch barrel is cut with six lands and grooves, the front sight is from Ashley Outdoors, the rear V-notch sight is an Alchemy production and is dovetailed into the slide.

For my test, Alchemy supplied me with a 45-caliber version of their pistol. I rounded up an assortment of ammunition including Remington Golden Sabre (230-grain JHP), CCI/Blazer (200-grain Gold Dot JHP), Federal Hydra Shok (230-grain), Winchester Silver Tip (185-grain), Federal Classic Hi Shok (185-grain JHP), Black Hills (230-grain Gold Dot) and Federal (230-grain ball).

What happened next surprised me, for a prototype gun.

Shooting over my Chrony Delta chronograph, placed at ten yards from the muzzle, the best velocity came out of the Remington Golden Sabre with an average of 972.5 fps, followed by the Winchester Silvertip at 952.6 fps. That's what I expected.

At 15 yards, that Silvertip ammo amazed me, putting three bullets through the same hole in a 2.5-inch overall group, shot on a Birchwood Casey Shoot•N•C target. That got my attention!

I moved the range out to 25 yards, and again found this prototype pistol, despite its pre-production flaws, capable of shooting into very small groups....as in one-hole groups.

Thanks to the ample ejection port, spent brass clears the Spectre without a hitch. I experienced some jamming and failures to feed, which I blamed directly on pre-production magazines from a large-volume commercial vendor. After talking with Alchemy, I learned that they have decided to produce their own pistol magazines — having experienced the same problem in their function firing tests before placing the prototype in my abusive little hands. Alchemy engineers have also re-aligned the magazine well ever so slightly, and production guns are slick.

William seemed amused. "Hey, you wanted the gun. You were in a hurry." Okay, okay, I deserved that.

While the standard and service grade Spectre pistols are certainly not to be dismissed, I'm really eager to see the titanium model, which was not available at test time. Having seen titanium used on Taurus and S&W handguns, it's a cinch this full-size pistol is going to be surprisingly light and strong.

Cartridges come up in line with feed ramp and barrel breech.

GUN TESTS

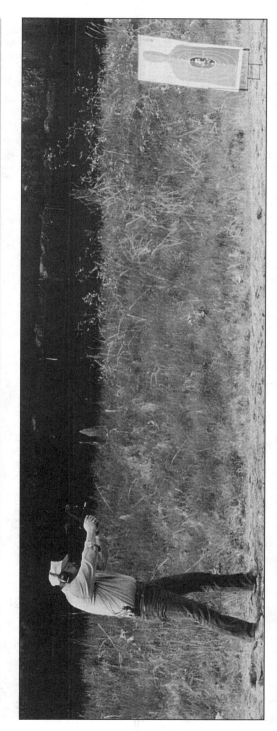

Workman runs Spectre through its paces at ten yards. Look at the tight, rapid-fire groups on that Shoot•N•C.

▶ Rear wide V-notch sight is dovetailed into slide...

▲ ...While front Ashley Express tritium sight is a post model.

▲ Thumb safety shown in "on" (up) position...

▲ ...and in the "off" (down) position ready for action.

If the titanium gun's engineering is faithful to that of the present crop, it's going to delight anybody who carries a pistol for extended periods.

Another thing important to the armed citizen is the Spectre's grip frame. It is contoured along the front strap to accommodate the fingers, and there are vertical grooves in each one of these finger contours for a no-slip hold.

The frame also features a squared trigger guard, almost identical to a Glock's, so this gun easily fits just about any holster built for a standard polymer pistol.

I can't imagine the Spectre not being right at home in any good leather from folks like maestro Mitch Rosen, Greg Kramer, Milt Sparks or several other popular makers.

The Spectre's aluminum alloy frame is tough. Due to the double-column magazine, it may feel a bit wide at the grip, but it is less

Alchemy Arms Spectre Specifications

Action:	'Safe Action' semi-automatic
Caliber:	Available in 9mm, 40 S&W and 45 ACP
Finish:	Available in matte blue/black (slide) and anodized alloy frame, brushed frame and stainless slide or titanium slide and brushed frame.
Barrel:	4.5 inches
Capacity:	Ten rounds, all calibers
Sights:	Ashley front tritium, V-notch rear fixed
Weight:	Aprox. 30 ounces
Height:	5.72 inches
Length:	8 3/8 inches
Price:	Basic - $685
	Service Grade - $850
	Titanium - $1,190

Alchemy Arms Spectre...on the range @10yds

Brand & Bullet	Velocity	Group
Federal / 230 gr. FMJ (ball)	822.5	3.5"
Winchester /185 gr. Silvertip	952.6	2.5"*
CCI Blazer / 200 gr. Speer Gold Dot	919.2	2.5"
Federal /185 gr. Hi- Shok	946.8	4.5"
Black Hills / 230 gr. Gold Dot	824.3	3.35"

* Includes one hole with three bullets through it.

bulky than some other wide-grip frames I've held. For a normal-sized hand, getting a good hold on the Spectre will be a snap.

There are no sharp edges on the slide or frame. Barrel-to-grip axis is low, so it's a natural shooter. The barrel projects about 3/8-inch beyond the slide, and is well-crowned.

The slide release is located comfortably within reach of the thumb for right handers. Likewise, the ample magazine release is right where it ought to be. Each Spectre pistol is supplied with two double-column ten-round magazines.

As for value, this pistol has a recommended price tag right in the ballpark for handguns of its genré.

One thing that may give it the edge as time goes by is that integral locking system. While other handgun makers may be adding dollars to their price tags to pay for re-tooling or adding security locks of some sort, this one is already ahead of the curve.

I'm guessing the Spectre pistol will be well-received by folks who find this handgun's lines and safety features irresistible. Because of the external manual safeties, I can see the Spectre earning high marks in corners where semi-auto pistols of the traditional "safe-action" design may not be completely acceptable.

It was a challenge to test, and it changed some of my notions about all the things involved in engineering a handgun.

Best of all, when it goes "bang!", you know there's going to be a hole in whatever you're shooting at. In the first and last analysis, that's the only thing that counts.

•

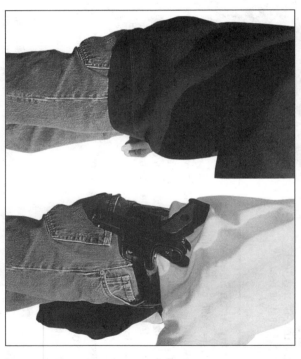

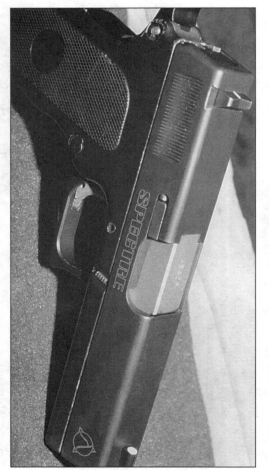

Now, does that slide profile look somewhat familiar? Spectre is a combination of a Glock-type slide assembly and a receiver with features found on a Government Model pistol.

Is Spectre conceal-able? Author's friend Tammy Kynett tried gun in her belt slide holster, and it van-ished under her sweat-shirt...

...Only to appear when the sweatshirt came off. Unpleasant sur-prise for bad guys!

Spectre with just some of the ammunition Workman put down the tube.

GUN TESTS

GUN TESTS

The Smith & Wesson Model 27:

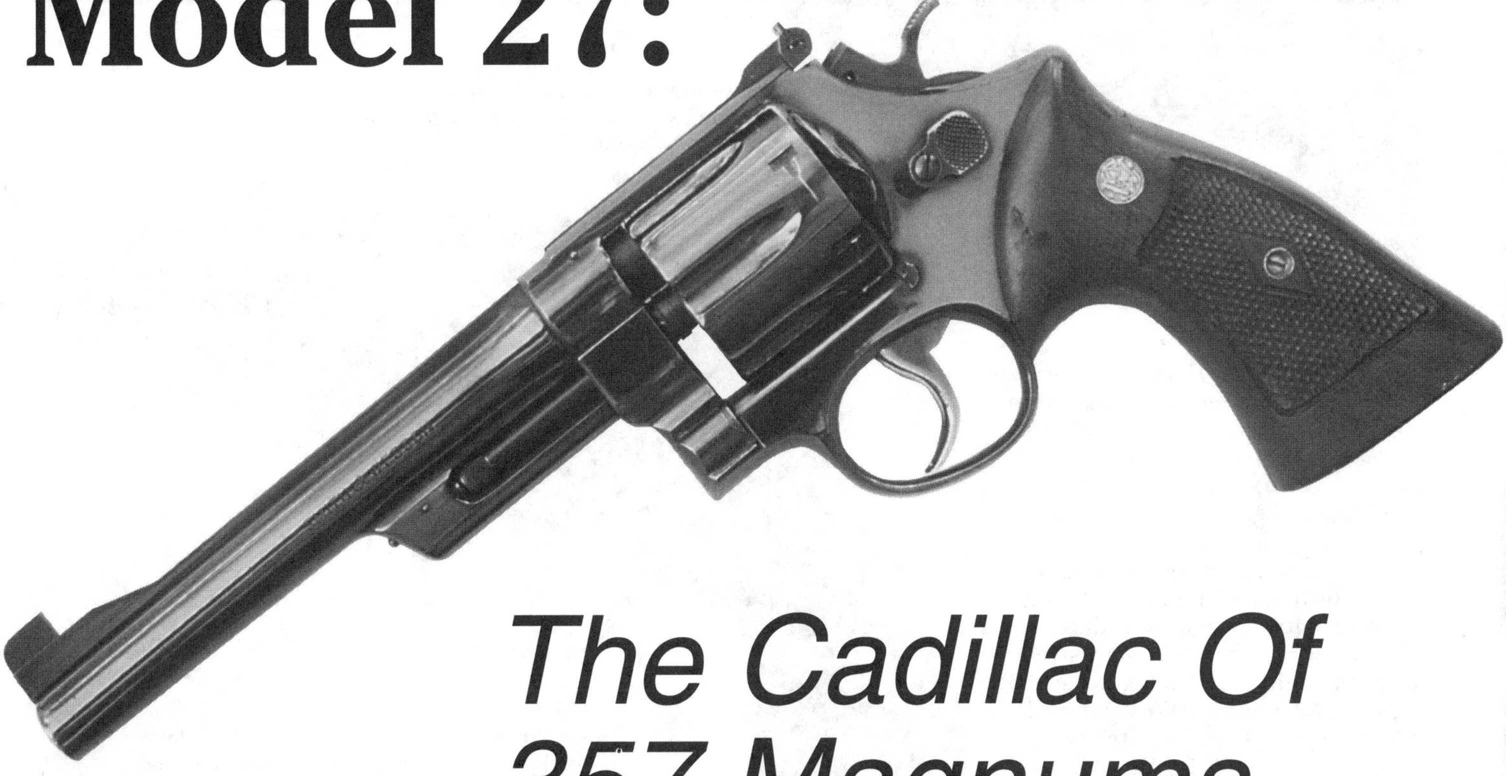

The Cadillac Of 357 Magnums

by Chuck Taylor

Left side view of one of author's vintage M27s, this one with a 6-1/2-inch barrel. Developed from the famous M23 38-44 Outdoorsman, it represented a quantum leap in handgun technology and enjoyed a long production life. Although unfortunately discontinued in the early 1990s, it remains a favorite of many handgunners and is still a sought-after revolver.

SINCE 1935 WHEN the 357 Magnum cartridge first appeared, thus launching us into the magnum era, there have been myriad handguns chambered for it. But of all the guns sporting the ".357 Magnum" stamping, one in particular has distinguished itself as being the Cadillac of the breed – Smith & Wesson's Model 27.

The result of the Keith/Sharpe/Wesson project to upgrade the performance of the 38 Special, the slightly longer 357 subsequently evolved, thus eliminating the potential problem of someone unknowingly chambering the super-

hot, but outwardly identical, 38-44 in a light-framed 38 Special.

Pressures with the new cartridge were high—up to 35,000 psi—with velocities to match. And, perhaps not surprisingly, the recoil, flash and concussion levels it produced were sufficient to send the unprepared scurrying away with a grimace and their hands pressed tightly over their ears!

Original velocities in the 1500 fps range from a long barrel, and excellent penetration, gave rise to the claim that the 357 was the "World's Most Powerful Handgun," an honor it held until the appearance in 1956 of the mighty 44 Magnum. Naturally, the 357's special performance demanded

that Smith & Wesson build a special handgun for it and on April 8, 1935, the first "Three-Fifty-Seven" was presented to FBI founder and then-Director, J. Edgar Hoover.

Based upon S&W's highly successful S-frame series, the new behemoth was finely checkered on both its top strap and barrel rib, offered with seven different combinations of front/rear sights and shipped from the factory with barrel lengths from 3.5 to a full 8 3/4 inches (later reduced to 8 3/8 inches to accommodate NRA competition rules). Sales of the new revolver were brisk and outstripped S&W's 120 gun-permonth capacity to build them, a condition that persisted until the onset of World War II when, along with many of their other handguns, it was temporarily discontinued to allow S&W's full attention to wartime military contracts. Total prewar production of the "Three-Fifty-Seven" was 6,642 guns and when manufacture again commenced in 1948, the 3.5, 5, 6 1/2 and 8 3/8-inch barrel lengths became standard.

Sales continued to be very strong, with an additional 6,322 guns sold by June, 1952, and in 1957 when S&W assigned model numbers to their guns, the "Three-Fifty-Seven" became the Model 27, the designator it retains to this day. In fact, buyer-interest was so strong that it overshadowed the popularity of the two guns that spawned it—the 38-44 Model 23 Outdoorsman and M-20 Heavy Duty, causing their production to cease permanently in 1964.

Throughout the next two decades, S&W made continuous improvements on the M-27 and, by September, 1975, it was offered with a target hammer, target trigger, checkered Goncalo Alves target stocks and a mahogany presentation case. In the early 1990s, the 3.5, 5 and 6.5-inch barrel lengths were dropped, and 4, 6 and 8 3/8-inch barrels became standard. Then, a few years later, the unthinkable happened—along with a number of its other best offerings, S&W discontinued the M27 in all its configurations! However, in view of the fact that its career spanned over five decades, there are still plenty of them around if one just looks a bit.

Accuracy with my two M27s, both vintage 3 1/2- and 6 1/2-inch versions,

The term ".357 Magnum" was made famous by the M27 and quickly became synonymous with it.

Right side view of the 3 1/2-inch version. Intended primarily for law enforcement use, it achieved considerable long-term popularity among police personnel of all types for nearly fifty years.

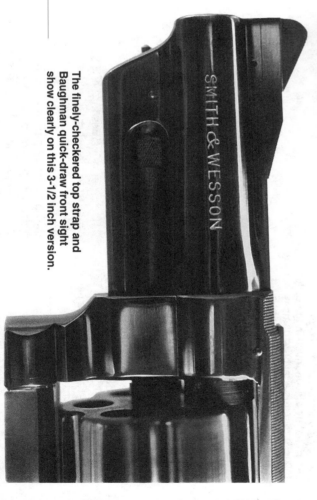

The finely-checkered top strap and Baughman quick-draw front sight show clearly on this 3-1/2 inch version.

▲ Initial versions of the M27 featured a grooved, narrow trigger; on later versions a wide, target-type trigger was also offered.

▲▼ Another popular feature of the M27 was its white-outlined rear notch and gracefully-angled serrated front blade. Later, both were included on nearly all S&W revolvers that utilized adjustable sights.

▼ Wide target hammer, adjustable sights were also hallmarks of the M27 and remained popular with the majority of its aficionados.

is excellent, with 50-meter Ransom Rest groups of around 2 inches being the norm. Generally speaking, the M27 is a forgiving handgun, meaning that it shoots well with pretty much

anything one cares to stuff into it. Nonetheless, best accuracy in my guns is consistently achieved with a healthy handload

S&W M27 357 Magnum Performance Specifications

Test Gun: S&W M27 with 6 1/2-inch barrel.

BRAND	TYPE	WT (grs.)	VEL (fps)	KE (Ft. lbs.)
Glaser Blue Safety Slug	prefrag	80	1563	434
Winchester-Western	JHP	110	1146	321
Super Vel	JSP	110	1466	525
Super Vel	JHP	110	1478	534
Cor-Bon	JHP	115	1344	461
Winchester-Western	JHP	125	1411	553
Federal	JHP	125	1421	561
Remington-Peters	JHP	125	1414	555
Cor-Bon	JHP	125	1423	562
Super Vel	JSP	137	1433	622
Speer	JHP	140	1321	543
Handload 17.0 grs. #2400*				
	XTP-JHP	140	1549	746
Winchester-Western	SWCL	158	1267	563
Federal	JHP	158	1158	471
Remington-Peters	JHP	158	1134	451
Federal +	JSP	158	1310	602
Handload 15.5 grs. #2400* +				
	SWC	160	1387	684
Handload15.0 grs. #2400* +				
	SWC	173	1334	684

* = intended for heavy-framed gun only (S&W "S" or "N" or Colt "I"). Not recommended for use with S&W "K" or "J" frame.

Author firing one of his 5-inch M27s with his favorite handload – Keith 170-grain SWC and 15.0 grains of 2400. Perhaps the most powerful load in the 357 category, it duplicates the original 1935 load and exhibits superb accuracy, penetration and general performance on game.

Nearly any of the factory loads listed will serve well for hunting purposes, too. The 110-grain JHP, for example, is great for small game, while the 158-grain JHPs serve well on larger game such as whitetail or mule deer–and even elk, with proper shot placement. For the best penetration on big game, the Keith 170-grain SWC, loaded over 15.0-grains of 2400 is the way to go. I've shot dozens of deer with this load and always had complete penetration of the target from all angles, as well as nearly universal one shot kills.

The Keith bullet load is a stiff one, approximating the original 357 Magnum factory load of 1935, and is intended only for use in the heavy-framed M27 or its bread & butter counterpart, the no-frills M28. However, since both are based on S&W big S and, later, N-frames, there is little concern about the gun being shaken to bits in only a few hundred rounds. Use of loads like this in lighter-framed guns, however, is NOT recommended.

So, in summary, the Smith & Wesson Model 27 is without a doubt the Cadillac of 357 Magnum revolvers and produces excellent results with

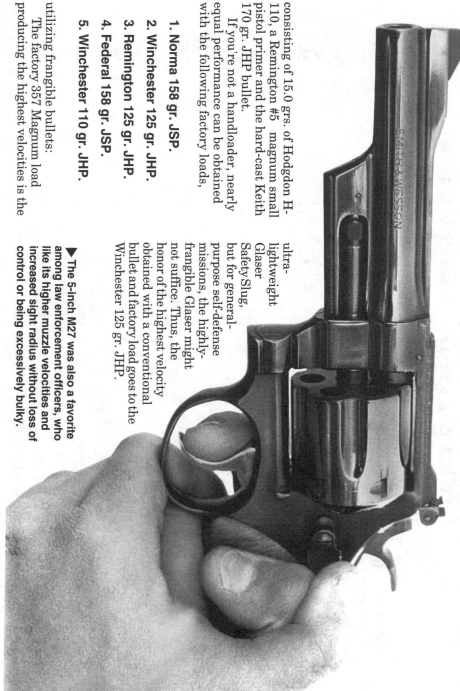

▶ The 5-inch M27 was also a favorite among law enforcement officers, who like its higher muzzle velocities and increased sight radius without loss of control or being excessively bulky.

consisting of 15.0 grs. of Hodgdon H-110, a Remington #5 magnum small pistol primer and the hard-cast Keith 170 gr. JHP bullet.

If you're not a handloader, nearly equal performance can be obtained with the following factory loads,

1. **Norma 158 gr. JSP.**
2. **Winchester 125 gr. JHP.**
3. **Remington 125 gr. JHP.**
4. **Federal 158 gr. JSP.**
5. **Winchester 110 gr. JHP.**

ultra-lightweight Glaser Safety Slug, but for general-purpose self-defense missions, the highly-frangible Glaser might not suffice. Thus, the honor of the highest velocity obtained with a conventional bullet and factory load goes to the Winchester 125 gr. JHP.

utilizing frangible bullets: The factory 357 Magnum load producing the highest velocities is the

Highly accurate, reliable and easy to shoot well under stress, the longer-barreled M27 has always been a popular hunting handgun.

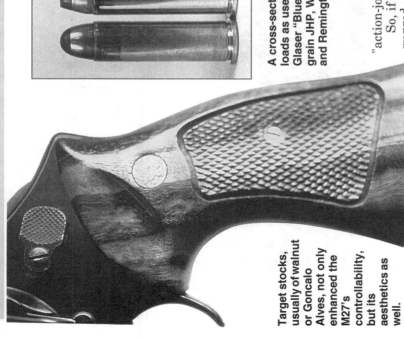

Target stocks, usually of walnut or Goncalo Alves, not only enhanced the M27's controllability, but its aesthetics as well.

A cross-section of popular 357 factory loads as used in the M27, left to right: Glaser "Blue" Safety Slug, Federal 110-grain JHP, Winchester 125-grain JHP and Remington 158-grain JHP.

virtually any kind of ammunition. It is rugged, strong, aesthetically pleasing, functionally reliable, very accurate and thus well worth its price. In addition, its internal works are amenable to the ministrations of any good gunsmith, allowing superb

"action-jobs" to be performed on it.

So, if you have need for a rugged, good-looking, high-performance 357 for either self-defense or hunting purposes, check out the Model 27. Although a bit on the large side—the price one must pay for a long service life when high-pressure cartridges are involved—it offers by far the best value obtainable in a 357 today. Even though it's now a discontinued item,

it can still be found without too much trouble and is well worth the search.

It was for nearly five decades the preferred revolver of not only the FBI, but literally hundreds of police departments across the country as well. Officers swore by their M27s and cherished their many attributes. Try one and I think you'll agree – it's a great handgun and one which belongs in the armory of any serious handgunner.

The potent Federal 125-grain JHP in full muzzle rise. Due to its heavy frame, M27's recoil with standard 357 loads is the lowest found in any type of handgun, making it relatively easy to control.

GUN TESTS

THE KEL-TEC P-32

Weighing only 6.6 ounces, the Kel-Tec P-32 is one of the lightest centerfire self-defense pistols available today.

by Frank W. James

MANY YEARS AGO—and long before my time—32-caliber handguns were not only common, but extremely popular. Yet, the experiences carried by many returning combat veterans from World War II became a catalyst in changing this preference and point of view as more and more authorities viewed the caliber and corresponding pistols with some disgust. I was born soon after the war and grew up in the Fifties. I can remember a few of my father's friends who kept or sometimes carried .32s, but those who had been involved in some sort of fighting in the Pacific or Europe—if they owned a pistol at all—had a 45-caliber 1911

pistol and few of them had anything good to say about the lowly .32.

Of course, this emphasis on heavy calibers became the stuff of legends for writers like Elmer Keith, Bill Jordan and Charley Askins. They were not only proponents of powerful and quick defensive pistols, they absolutely demanded them.

There is nothing wrong with any of this except that powerful big-bore defensive pistols tend to run large in size and heavy in recoil. These physical aspects sometimes make it difficult to have a gun with you all the time. If we all lived in a cold northern climate twelve months out of the year,

concealing any of these items beneath various layers of outer clothing would be far easier and more practical than when you live near a warm, temperate seashore community.

Naturally enough, the need for concealment is driven by the self-defense logic that you don't bring a knife to a gunfight, so you always want to have a gun—with you or on you–at all times…even if it's a little one.

When I was a kid growing up in the Midwest, the local town marshal carried a double-action, swing-out cylinder 32-caliber revolver in a full-flap holster hung on a Sam Browne belt, complete with an over-the-

The Kel-Tec P-32 fieldstrips down to these basic components: the slide, a chin piece that dovetails in the front of the slide for positioning the recoil spring assembly, the recoil spring assembly, the barrel, the take-down pin, the grip and subframe assembly and the magazine.

shoulder strap. I know he shot it frequently at the town dump because he would join us when we were using our 22 rifles to shoot rats from the refuse. Once, I watched him show it to a businessman in our small town. It was a Smith&Wesson and, although it showed evidence of much holster wear, it was well-oiled and reliable.

The father of a childhood friend also had a 32-caliber pistol, only his was a Colt Automatic. Specifically, it was a Model 1903 Pocket 32. He kept it in a soft suede shoulder holster and he would show it to us kids about twice a year if we bugged him long enough. (Unlike children today, we knew better than to examine any gun without permission from the adult responsible. Adults when I was a kid *believed* in corporal punishment and they had no idea that, years later, someone would interpret actions similar to theirs as child abuse. Those days were more clearly defined in many ways for everyone!)

The Colt Model 1903 in 32 ACP was issued by the U.S. Army to a number of general officers during World War II as a means of providing them with some degree of self-protection. The idea was not to give them a gun that would guarantee long-range accuracy or provide the ultimate in stopping power. The Army had more powerful small-arms to accomplish that, but they were unhandy and, therefore, not likely to be used—or even carried—by an all-important general. The military wanted its generals to have a gun they would have with them if they actually needed a gun for self-defense.

The situation hasn't really changed all that much today.

The 32-caliber handgun is not much of a defensive handgun in terms of stopping power, but the main point is, packaged properly, you are more likely to have it with you when you need it

than something larger, heavier and more effective ballistically. This brings us to the subject at hand; the Kel-Tec P-32.

I first saw the Kel-Tec P-32 at the 1999 SHOT Show and I couldn't get over how thin and light this little pistol was. I realize the 32 ACP cartridge is often the subject of scorn from many commentators and small-arms experts, but I have yet to meet the guy who, after being shot in some part of his anatomy with one, said, "Yeah, but he only shot me with a 32!" I think the idea of being shot with anything, regardless of how small the caliber, is abhorrent to any member of the human race intelligent enough to imagine the pain, suffering and damage to their internal organs that accompanies a gunshot wound.

To illustrate the P-32's dropping barrel design, all one has to do is retract the slide slightly and the underbarrel cam will start to disengage the barrel from the slide.

The Kel-Tec P-32 is a double-action-only semi-automatic pistol chambered in 32 ACP. Because of its light weight and flat, thin design it fits perfectly the mission statement for a self-defense pistol.

The Kel-Tec P-32 is shipped in a small blue nylon zippered pouch.

The Kel-Tec P-32 fits the mission statement of any defensive pistol primarily because it is lightweight. The silly thing only weighs 6.6 ounces.

The alloy sub-frame is what carries the slide; the concept was pioneered on Kel-Tec's P-11 pistol, a compact 9x19mm caliber handgun which has won raves for its durability, good balance and low cost. The rectangular-shaped sub-frame is machined from a solid piece of 7075 T-6 aluminum. The steel slide reveals the first evidence of something really different about the P-32. The slide is manufactured from 4140 steel as is the barrel, but the barrel is heat-treated to 48 HRC. That's not so unusual, but its method of operation is.

Normally, today's 32 ACP semi-automatic pistols are blowback operated. In a blowback-operated firearm, like most 22 rimfire pistols, the barrel is fixed solidly to the frame in some manner. A big benefit is increased accuracy because—essentially—the frame, grip and barrel are one unit.

In a blowback-operated firearm when the cartridge fires the pressure within the chamber and barrel builds to the point where the inertia presented by the slide mass is overcome and the breech

That means it is not a burden to carry at all times. How is this possible?

The basic construction of the Kel-Tec P-32 consists of a polymer grip assembly, a sub-frame and a carbon steel slide and barrel. The polymer grip assembly is available in a variety of different colors, but my pistol came in basic black.

However, if you want, the gun can be had in pink(!), blue, gray and other hues of the rainbow. The polymer employed in this venture is a high-impact DuPont ST-8018 synthetic. The grip assembly has a fine checkering pattern on either side of the flat grip and the front of the grip is left smooth while the front corners are grooved with seven closely-spaced lines for a better purchase on the grip by the shooter.

GUN TESTS

Specifications:
Kel-Tec P-32

MANUFACTURER:	Kel-Tec CNC Industries Inc. P.O. Box 3427 Cocoa, Florida 32924-3427 407-631-0068
MODEL:	P-32
MECHANISM TYPE:	double-action-only, Browning-style dropping barrel, recoil-operated action
SAFETY:	No external safeties
CALIBER:	32 ACP
OVERALL LENGTH:	5.07 inches
WIDTH:	.75 inches
HEIGHT:	3.5 inches
BARREL LENGTH:	2.6 inches
WEIGHT, empty	6.5 ounces
MAGAZINE CAPACITY:	7+1 rounds

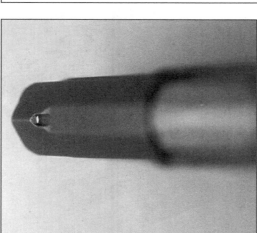

The rear sight on the P-32 consists of nothing more than this rectangular pattern of white paint in a milled u-shaped channel at the rear of the slide.

The front sight is a corresponding white-painted dot located behind the raised portion of the front of the slide.

opens. Generally speaking, the 380 ACP cartridge represents the upper limit on blowback-operated handguns because the slide mass required by more powerful cartridges becomes prohibitive.

The Kel-Tec P-32, however, is not a blowback-operated handgun. It is a locked-breech design utilizing a conventional Browning-style dropping barrel mechanism. This is truly new and different in a gun so light and small as this one. Obviously, the designer of the P-32, George Kellgren, had concerns over slide weight and the easiest means to keep the slide weight low was by utilizing a locked breech design in the P-32.

I know some may take issue, but it is my belief the locked-breech P-32 is actually stronger than any other blowback 32 Auto pistol on the market. I have worked with

different submachine guns using blowback actions and, because of inadvertent case failures, I am convinced the average locked-breech handgun is far stronger than any blowback submachine gun in the same chambering. Many feel this is wrong simply because the average sub-gun usually weighs so much more but, in working with high-pressure handloads, I have found pistols using a dropping barrel design will regularly digest handloads that will sometimes deliver bulge cases as well as deliver occasional case failures when fired in a blowback-operated submachine gun. It is for this reason I feel the Kel-Tec

P-32 with its locked breech design is a far stronger gun, even though much lighter than any other contemporary 32 ACP blowback-operated handgun.

The Kel-Tec P-32 is a double-action-only pistol and has no external levers or mechanisms, other than the DAO trigger. There isn't even a slide release. The slide does lock open after the last round has been fired, but the magazine must be lowered, changed or

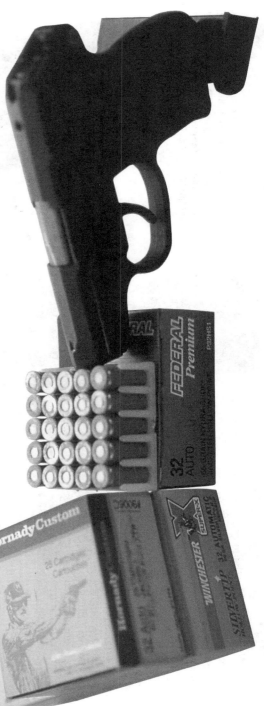

The author fired a wide variety of 32 ACP and 32 Auto ammunition through his P-32 and found it to be a reliable and dependable self-defense pistol. Shown here are three of the better self-defense hollow-point loads available from different manufacturers and a plastic training round that was produced in Germany by Dynamit Nobel.

released in order for the slide to move to the *forward* position. To release the slide—once it has locked open—all you have to do is pull slightly to the rear and the slide will return to battery.

The magazine on the P-32 is manufactured by Mec-Gar in Italy and holds seven rounds of 32 ACP ammunition in a single vertical column. Unlike many of the increasingly popular "mini-pistols" in 32 ACP, the Kel-Tec P-32 shot all kinds of 32 Auto ammunition during testing without a bobble or problem. Some of the new mini-pistols in 32-caliber will handle only the Winchester SilverTip round, but the Kel-Tec P-32—in our testing—worked perfectly with everything, including the handload.

Because of the renewed interest in small diminutive self-defense pistols, research was begun a few years back on improving the performance of this cartridge formerly compared to the 22 Long Rifle round in terms of effectiveness.

Winchester was the first with the 60-grain hollow-point SilverTip load. It quickly became the standard by which others were judged simply because it was the first hollow-point load from a major ammunition manufacturer for the 32 ACP round. Seven rounds of Winchester SilverTip averaged 803 feet-per-second from my

The magazine for the P-32, manufactured in Italy by Mec-Gar, is a single-column design that holds seven rounds of 32 ACP ammunition.

The magazine release, a push-button design, is located at the familiar junction of the trigger guard and frame.

The Colt Model 1903 Pocket pistol (above) was a popular 32 ACP pistol prior to World War II, but the Kel-Tec P-32 is both smaller, lighter, thinner and more reliable than this legendary Colt product.

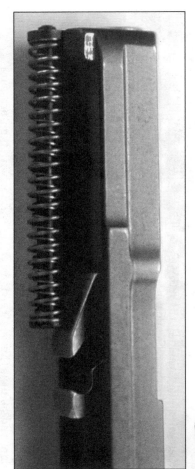

Even though the P-32 is chambered in a cartridge, the 32 Auto, scorned by many for its lack of power, the recoil spring assembly still features dual springs for reliable performance.

Kel-Tec P-32, the group measured just over four inches at seven yards, but an explanation-following is necessary about the "sights" on the P-32.

Cor-Bon's Bee-Safe ammunition achieved the highest velocity reading over the chronograph with an average of 1,096 fps. The Cor-Bon Bee-Safe employs a 52-grain pre-fragmented projectile that demonstrates an admittedly limited penetration in the little testing I've done in a Fackler Water Box.

Hornady also offers a 60-grain hollow-point loading that averaged 825 fps, but the best overall performance, in my opinion, was that found with the Federal Hydra-Shok 65-grain load that averaged 813 fps for seven rounds and clustered in a group measuring two and a half inches across at a distance of seven yards.

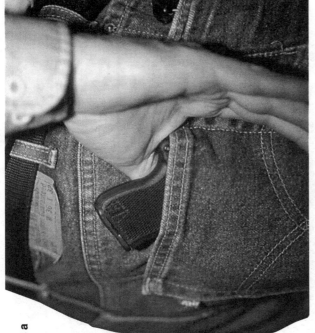

The author, who holds a valid concealed carry permit for his home state, found the best way to carry the little P-32 was to simply slip it in a rear pocket of his jeans. It conceals easily and is unobtrusive.

About the only feature the author didn't appreciate on the Kel-Tec P-32 was the knife-like side clip. He had a difficult time finding a practical use and eventually removed it from the pistol.

All of the test rounds were fired at a distance of twenty-one feet. Some may question this short distance, but the accuracy of the gun is limited by its "sights." The front and rear sights consist of two white-painted rectangles at the front and rear of the slide. The rear white paint mark can be found at the front of a u-shaped milled channel located at the rear of the slide while the front sight is a small, round white paint mark behind a raised angle at the front of the slide. Both are beyond rudimentary and can only be described as primitive—at best. However, this should not be judged too harshly. These sights were not—nor was the pistol—intended for formal target work. This is a pistol that will be carried long and often—because it is so convenient and, most importantly—reliable.

The average groups for seven shots at seven yards ranged from the smallest with the Federal Hydra-Shok to four and a half inches for the Winchester SilverTip, the USA White Box FMJ load, and the one handload I tried in testing the P-32.

The handload consisted of a CCI #500 small pistol primer, 2.5 grains of Winchester 231 powder and a cast 80-grain lead round-nose bullet. Velocity averaged 847 fps for seven rounds and grouped no worse than the Winchester SilverTip or White Box factory FMJ load. I had cast the bullets, using Lyman's #2 formula, from a Lyman round-nose bullet mould and sized the resulting projectiles to .311-inch. To some this may seem ridiculous, casting bullets for the lowly 32 ACP cartridge, but with the present anti-gun legislative trends one never knows what future political restrictions await. I want to be able to keep my guns working with reliable ammo regardless of their caliber...and casting my own projectiles is one sure way of guaranteeing my ammunition supply. This load functioned well in the Kel-Tec P-32, as I shot over fifty rounds without a malfunction.

The trigger pull was smooth and registered a consistent 5.5 pounds on my RCBS trigger-pull scale. The trigger movement is lengthy, in relation to the pistol's small size, but the pull is smooth and certainly not difficult. For a double-action-only trigger mechanism I found the pull better than expected—or even encountered among pistols of this size and classification.

I've fired over 250 rounds of assorted ammunition through the P-32 and have yet to experience a malfunction. It is one of the most reliable pistols I have experienced in this caliber. About the only thing I didn't like about the P-32 was it came with a side-mounted spring clip—like those seen on some folding knives—and I had a terrible time finding a practical use for this device. Eventually, I came to the conclusion this feature didn't fit my needs and I removed it. The gun conceals much easier for me, now.

The Kel-Tec P-32 is light enough it can be carried in a shirt pocket without a betraying bulge or unsightly sag. I find I can just slip it into the right hip pocket of my jeans—and pull my handkerchief around it to prevent it from being seen—as the most convenient mode of concealed carry. I think enough of it that, during a law enforcement training class with a local

sheriff's department, I passed it around among the assembled personnel for their review as a possible back-up weapon.

No, the Kel-Tec P-32 is not a magnum giant-killer and the 32 ACP won't meet the minimum in terms of penetration and projectile expansion, but the fact remains—IT'S A GUN. And it is *a lot better* to have a gun and not need one—than to need a gun and not have one.

Since my childhood days I've had a love affair with the old Colt Model 1903 in 32 ACP. Maybe the affection shown by the men of my childhood memories was contagious, but now I've found a 32 ACP pistol that, to me, is far more practical—and certainly more reliable—than the old Colt pistol.

I can give no higher recommendation for the Kel-Tec P-32 than to say you should look at this gun if you seek a small, extremely light, easy-to-conceal self-defense pistol. •

The U.S. M9 Service pistol.

All photos by Lawrence Ventura. Property of the Wisconsin Department of Justice, Crime Laboratory-Milwaukee

The Beretta 92FS, Just how durable is the U.S. M9?

The M9/92FS is put through a 20,500 round endurance test.

by Christopher R. Bartocci

THE BERETTA M9/92FS hs served the U.S. military for fifteen years now, but not without its critics. On January 14, 1985 the M9/92FS was adopted as the official sidearm of the U.S. military. It was seriously challenged only by the SIG Sauer P226; none of the other competitors' handguns survived the grueling test. After the most exhausting testing a military pistol has ever gone through–followed by competitive

bidding–the contract was awarded to Beretta U.S.A. Much controversy surrounds the entire M9 project– everything from the so-called inferior 9mm Parabellum cartridge to lack of durability has haunted the M9/92FS. The competitors took great exception with the fact a foreign-made weapon would equip the U.S. military and claimed that Beretta used specially-made pistols for the testing phase which did not represent

their standard production. After the announcement that Beretta was the winner, the manufacturers of the rejected pistols asked the U.S. Congress for a retrial–and got it.

The trial results were the same and the contract award held. Today, there are more than 540,000 pistols in U.S. arsenals, according to Beretta U.S.A. The M1911A1 was the issue military pistol from 1911 to 1985. After that

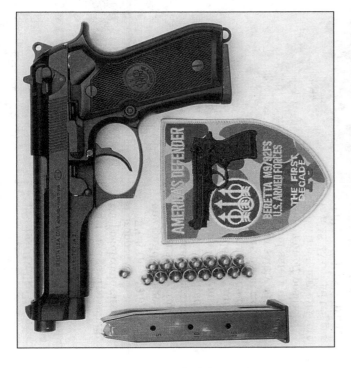

The Beretta M9/ 92FS pistol. Note the 16-round capacity. 15 in the magazine, 1 in the chamber.

The M1911A1 service pistol (top) with 7 rounds of 45ACP ammunition and the M9/ 92FS service pistol (bottom) with 15 + 1 rounds of 9mm NATO ammunition.

many years of reliable service the pistol was bound to have serious supporters. The reasons for the M9 project arose from many different considerations.

The last shipment of M1911A1 pistols to the Department of Defense was back in 1945. The pistols in inventory were well-used, to say the least, and needed to be replaced.

Further, the U.S. military is the only military in the world using a 45-caliber sidearm. NATO standardized on the 9x19mm (9mmNATO/9mm Luger/9mm Parabellum) many years ago. Ammunition compatibility is a very important issue considering the wide array of military units that deploy the H&K MP5, Colt SMG, UZI–and all the various other 9mm subguns in service today. The interchangeability of ammunition only makes logistical sense...the 9x19mm cartridge is on every battlefield in the world regardless of which side you are on.

One cannot dispute the fact the 9mm Parabellum cartridge does not have the stopping power of the 45ACP; however, there are two schools of thought on this issue.

The first is *the bigger the bullet, the better.* The other school is *better shot placement with a lighter bullet with less recoil.* The author belongs to the *lighter bullet* school. You are more likely to hit your target with a well-placed 9mm round than with a larger caliber that is harder to shoot accurately due to greater recoil.

My first experience with the M9/ 92FS was at Fort Benning, Georgia. When we fired for qualification, there was only a handful of troops that did not qualify on the first try. In fact, around 25% of the people qualified as *Expert.* The military needed a pistol that all the troops–male and female–would be able to fire accurately and efficiently. With its lighter recoil and reduced muzzle blast the M9/92FS has proven to be popular with the troops.

The military also wanted a pistol that could be safely carried loaded, with the hammer down. To carry the M1911A1 loaded, one would normally carry the pistol "cocked and locked," meaning a round in the chamber with the hammer cocked and the safety engaged. This condition is not considered safe by many gun experts. Another unsafe carry method for the M1911A1 was to load a round into the chamber and manually de-cock the hammer. This is an extremely unsafe

Group fired at 15 yards with the M9/92FS using issue M882 Ball ammunition.

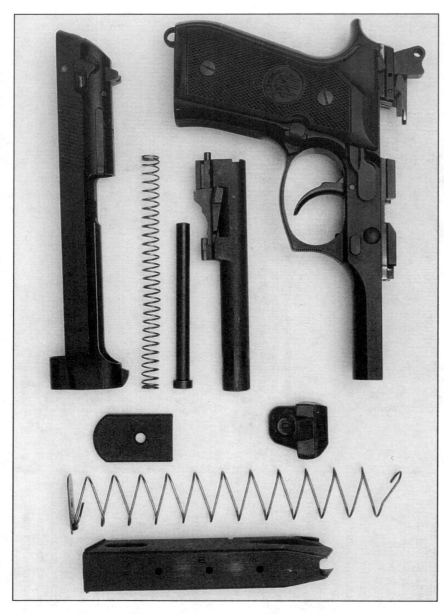

The M9/92FS field-stripped. The ease of disassembly has proven a major selling point to the military as well as law enforcement.

practice. Unlike the new Series 80 Colt pistols, the Government-issue M1911A1s did not have a firing pin block safety. There is a good possibility the pistol could discharge if dropped.

With the M9/92FS one could engage the manual safety, insert the loaded magazine, cycle the slide and safely load the firearm. While the slide locks up, the hammer will de-cock. Now the pistol can be carried safely with the manual safety in either the *on* or *off* position. With the safety off there is a 16.25 pound trigger pull as well as a firing pin safety block deactivated only when the trigger is pulled all the way to the rear. When the pistol is carried with the safety *on*, the firing pin plunger is disconnected from the firing pin and the firing

pin is locked in place by the firing pin safety. The trigger bar is then disengaged from the hammer; in turn, disengaging the trigger.

Magazine capacity was also an important issue: the M1911A1 magazine carried 7 rounds of 45ACP while the M9/92FS carried 15 rounds of 9mmNATO. One could provide cover fire with 15 rounds! The typical soldier would carry 21 rounds (3 magazines) of ammunition for his M1911A1 and the troop with the M9/92FS would carry 45 rounds (3 magazines).

Both the M9 and the M1911A1 are comparable in empty weight. The M1911A1 weighs in at 38 ounces; the M9 at 34.4 ounces. Both guns are comparable in size: the M9/92FS has a 4.9-inch barrel and the M1911A1 has a 5-inch barrel.

One complaint against the M9/92FS is that people with small hands have a hard time holding onto the pistol and that the trigger is hard for them to reach in the double-action mode. However, by cocking the hammer the trigger is well within reach for those with the smallest hands. The reason for the easy access of the M1911A1 trigger is that the pistol is single action only. The M9/92FS has an excellent Bruniton finish on the slide cracking problem was ammunition-related, the replacement of slides and barrels was halted, deemed unnecessary. However, concern about the +P+ ammunition used by U.S. troops and special operation groups sharing ammunition with submachine guns caused the D.O.D. to ask Beretta U.S.A. to develop a slide over-travel stop so the user would not be in danger. Thus, from the model 92F the model 92FS was born— the *S* stands for *safety*. What was done was to

The live cartridge indicator, which is the extractor, showing a raised portion with red paint on it. The red paint offers visual confirmation of a loaded chamber. As well, the raised area can be felt with the trigger finger in low light conditions.

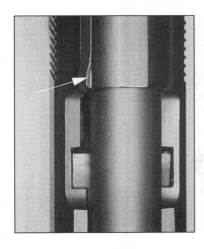

▶ The area of the slide that failed was the area where the locking block locked the slide into battery.

to protect the steel from the harsh environment. This finish is much superior to the Parkerizing of the M1911A1 pistol. The plastic grip panels on the M9/92FS are extremely durable. The checkering on the grips, as well as the grooves on the front and backstrap of the grip, make the M9 easier to hold securely with sweaty or muddy hands than the M1911A1 grip design allows. Both pistols incorporate chrome-lined barrels but I am sure you will still find non-chrome barrels for the M1911A1 in the government inventory.

Chrome-lining of the barrels does a few things for the pistol. First, when the barrel heats up, chrome has a self-lubricating property which reduces the likelihood of a failure to extract. Secondly, chrome plating makes the inside of the barrel corrosion-resistant. Lastly, chrome-lining a barrel (now standard in all U.S. military small arms) can increase barrel life two to three times over that of a standard steel barrel.

Another unique feature of the M9/92FS is the open slide design that leaves the barrel exposed. This acts as a cooling mechanism as well as enhancing reliability. With an open ejection port there is no obstruction for a spent cartridge case; a "stove pipe" malfunction is very rare.

The M9/92FS also has a live cartridge indicator. The extractor protrudes enough from the slide that with one

swipe from your trigger finger you are able to tell if the pistol is loaded. A visual check would note the red paint on the protruding extractor.

The issue of durability was one of the biggest controversies about the M9 after one of the SEAL units broke seven slides. The area of the slide where the locking block locks the pistol into battery cracked and that rear portion of the slide hit a SEAL in the face. To my knowledge he was not injured seriously and the other six incidents produced no serious injuries, either. Since these pistols had anywhere from 5,000 to 20,000+ rounds through them. D.O.D. and Beretta USA went to investigate these incidents. The results showed it was not a problem with the pistol; rather, it was ammunition-related. (When has the U.S. military messed up a firearm with improper ammunition before? Does "M16" sound familiar?) The ammunition being used was +P+ submachine gun ammunition...basically proof loads. The M9 was driven 'way past its operating parameters and eventually failed. This ammunition also cracked frame rails of SIG P226s. During the investigation into the slide failures, round counts were kept on slides and they were replaced regularly, as were the barrels. After the investigation concluded the frame-

enlarge the head of the hammer pin and cut a notch in the bottom of the left wing of the slide. In case of over-travel the slide would thus catch on the hammer pin, preventing the slide from flying off the rear of the pistol. Beretta U.S.A. claimed they did not feel this was necessary on their pistol and, if the military wished for it to be added onto the M9, it would cost them. So D.O.D. paid for the research & development and tooling for the slide overdrive mechanism. Because this was an isolated incident, Beretta U.S.A. never offered this as an upgrade to civilian or law enforcement handguns. According to Beretta U.S.A., this condition has never been duplicated on a civilian or law enforcement pistol under normal conditions. When slides have broken, it was due to a careless handloader. However, all M92/96-series handguns come with this new feature—to standardize parts, according to Beretta U.S.A.

The other part under criticism was the locking block itself. The life of a locking block was approximately 8,000 to 10,000 rounds. Constant use of high-power ammunition decreased the life of the part. Subsequently, Beretta U.S.A. developed a new-style locking block that will increase round counts up to 17,000 to 22,000 rounds.

At the 1995 SHOT Show, Beretta U.S.A. introduced a new member of the 92/96 family, the Brigadier. The

The ambidextrous safety also works as a decocker.

Original 92F   M9/92FS

The slide over-travel stop, note hammer pin of the original 92F (left). The hammer pin/slide over-travel stop (right). Notice the large hammer pin head and notch cut in the bottom of the left rail.

The Brigadier (top), note the more "beefed-up" reinforced slide, high profile rear sight and removable front sight. The standard M9/92FS (bottom).

Brigadier weighs in at 35.3 ounces, over an ounce heavier than the M9/92FS. This pistol was designed with abuse in mind. It is functionally the same as the M9/92FS but is built wider and stronger. There is significantly more metal in the slide. The locking block recess in the slide has been reinforced and a more aggressive rear sight fitted. The new rear sight has a higher profile, permitting the slide to be cycled with a boot heel in an emergency. The pistol is set up with a three-dot sight system. The long-awaited removable front sight has also been added. This pistol was designed for military training units that fire thousands of rounds per week and for units that use steady diets of high-pressure ammunition. The Brigadier is one of the rarest Beretta handguns. The U.S. Department of Immigration and Naturalization has adopted the model 96 Double Action Only Brigadier as their duty weapon so Beretta U.S.A is manufacturing the Brigadier for the first time in the United States. That order consisted of 16,400 96D Brigadier 40-caliber pistols.

Field-stripping the M9/92FS is very simple and straightforward. As with all firearms you want to be sure the weapon is clear. With your finger off the trigger, release the magazine, engage the manual safety and pull the slide to the rear, while simultaneously pushing upward on the slide stop. Visually inspect the chamber to verify the weapon is not loaded and, after you are satisfied the weapon is in a safe condition, release the slide. Grasp the pistol in your right hand and with your left forefinger depress the disassembling latch release button; with your left thumb rotate the disassembling latch until it stops. Push the slide assembly off the frame. Depress the spring guide and lift up and remove the spring guide and recoil spring. Depress the locking block plunger and lift the barrel out of the slide. To assemble reverse the process.

With the gun's major criticisms in mind, I wanted to see how the M9/92FS would stand up to a 20,500 round torture test using mostly +P and +P+ ammunition. I purchased a stock 92FS from a local gun distributor and made some calls for some high-power ammunition. The ammunition used in this test is as follows: 9x19mm (NATO, Parabellum/Luger) manufactured by Winchester/Olin Corporation.

Beretta U.S.A. claims their pistol is serviceable to 35,000 rounds and that it

The new improved-style locking block removed the square corners to prevent any chance of cracking (*left*). The original locking block (*right*).

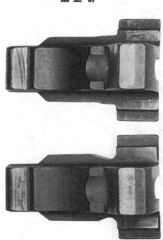

▶ Close-up of the differences in the slides of the M9/92FS and the Brigadier. The Brigadier slide (top) has more metal around the locking block recess as well as a new high-profile rear sight and the long-awaited removable front sight. The Standard M9/92FS slide(below).

will function under the most adverse conditions. Beretta U.S.A. claims "the average reliability of all M9s tested at Beretta U.S.A. is 17,500 rounds without stoppage." The ammunition I chose was the hottest ammunition available and I would not recommend anyone put high round counts of +P+ ammunition through any alloy-frame pistol regardless of the manufacturer.

The first thing I did was fire for out-of-the-box accuracy. I used the 115-grain +P+ ammunition and at 15 yards the 15-shot group measured 1.5 inches. I had nine magazines loaded up and someone loading magazines as I emptied them and, within 20 minutes, I fired 500 rounds with no malfunctions of any type. I guess it is safe to say the pistol has been broken in! I came to appreciate the crisp break of the pistol's single-action trigger pull, at an even 5.25 pounds. Rapid fire was quick and accurate.

The next day I began firing 2,000 rounds of the 127-grain +P+SXT, by far the hottest 9mm ammunition I have ever fired. There were no malfunctions of any type using this ammunition. Over the next 3 days I fired 8,000 rounds of 9mm NATO, the standard M882 Ball ammunition issued to U.S. military personnel. The

M882 ball cartridge is rated as a +P cartridge by SAAMI specifications.

The barrel was cleaned every 2,000 to 3,000 rounds. It would take us 45 to 50 minutes to fire 1,000 rounds and, at times, the pistol would become too hot to handle. I fired 1,000 rounds of Winchester USA 115-grain 9mm ball with no problems and the pistol, after 11,500 rounds, was still delivering groups in the 1.5-inch range.

At this point, the pistol was totally disassembled and cleaned. Then I fired an additional 6,000 rounds of the 115-grain FMJ with only one malfunction. There was one *failure to extract* due to an under-powered cartridge, not the pistol.

After about 15,000 rounds I began to notice some pitting on the right wing of the locking block. I recommend changing this part when pitting is noted, but this was a torture test and we wanted to see how long the gun will last. As of now 17,500 rounds have been fired and I headed back to the range

to fire the remaining 3,000 rounds. Finally at round count 19,498, I had a locking block failure. The left wing of the locking block broke and the pistol's slide locked up. By pushing down on the broken wing with a drift punch, the action was freed and the pistol subsequently disassembled, revealing some minimal frame damage—but nothing that would affect the operation of the pistol. I changed the locking block and within 10 minutes I was back in action and concluded the test with no other malfunctions. The last 15 rounds were fired for accuracy; the group measured about 1.75 inches at 15 yards. The accuracy had hardly changed at all.

The locking block survived 19,498 rounds, which included 2,500 rounds of +P+, 8,000 rounds of +P and 10,000 rounds of *standard* 9mm ball. One friend of mine put it best: "You fired $4,000 dollars worth of ammunition out of a $450 handgun and broke a $60 part after 19,498 rounds were fired, what more could you ask?"

I feel very few pistols will ever see this round count—except for a military pistol. For many years I have heard people claim the Beretta M9/92FS was a fragile gun because of those early, isolated incidents. Following this torture test, I *know* this gun is far from fragile! There is no question in my mind the pistol is serviceable to 35,000 rounds; I would not be surprised to see it last 50,000 rounds. The Beretta M9/92FS is, in my opinion, one of the most reliable firearms ever produced–and this test proved it.

Ammunition	Muzzle Velocity	Muzzle Energy
127-grain +P+ SXT	1250 fps	440 ft/lbs
115-grain +P+ JHP	1305 fps	437 ft/lbs
124-grain FMJ NATO	1185 fps	387 ft/lbs
115-grain FMJ	1160 fps	345 ft/lbs

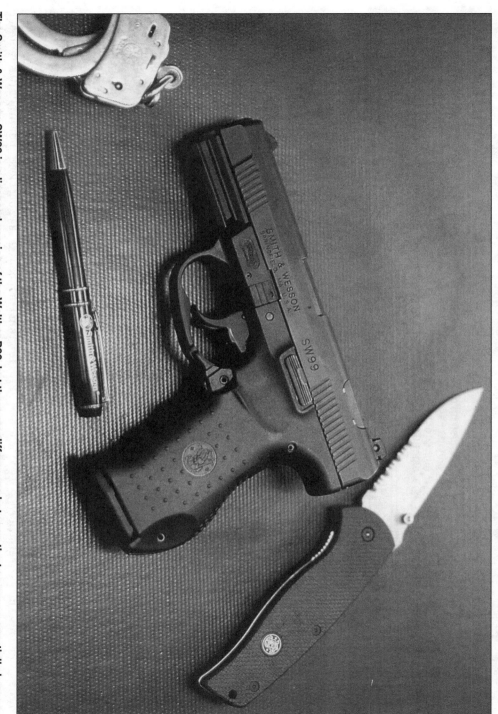

The Smith & Wesson SW99 is a licensed version of the Walther P99, but there are differences between the two guns essentially because some of the SW99's major components for the SW99 are made in the United States, not Germany.

THE SMITH & WESSON SW99

by Frank W. James

It DOESN'T HAPPEN often in the realm of smallarms but when Smith & Wesson arranged to license, produce and market a copy of the Walther P99 semi-automatic pistol the agreement between these two giants of the handgun world came not as the result of the coercion which results when one of the coercion which results when one conglomerate takes over a smaller firm. Nor was it the result of capricious and arbitrary governmental threat or lawsuit. Instead, it was a merger of two historic names in the firearms business; one from the United States and the other from Germany, and it was done solely for the mutual benefit of each firm.

These two competitors examined the world situation and each concluded they were going to have to find a willing partner to co-exist with them, while at the same time forming a temporary alliance that could prove beneficial to each, either on a short-term basis or—possibly—on a long-term basis.

Umarex, the parent company that owns Walther, initiated the business arrangement by seeking a license from Smith & Wesson to build a gas-powered copy of the Smith & Wesson revolver for the domestic European market. They also inquired if Smith & Wesson would be interested, or available, as a subcontractor on

various internal parts for the Walther P99. Smith & Wesson declined the invitation because of their own work at the time on the Sigma project, but after some investigation by S&W's executives, an agreement was reached for the gas gun license and, most importantly, a dialog between the two firms was established.

Walther has been marketed in the United States by Interarms for over fifty years. Interarms was founded by Sam Cummings, a man who became a living legend in the world of international arms trafficking during the fifties and sixties. Sadly, the living legend is no longer alive and neither is the firm he founded.

GUN TESTS

The Smith & Wesson Model SW99 pistol is made from parts produced in both Germany and the United States. In fact, all of the parts—save the slide and barrel—are manufactured in Germany. The slide and barrel, of course, are manufactured at the Smith & Wesson plant in Springfield, Massachusetts. The two guns, the Walther P99 and the Smith & Wesson SW99, however, are not the same pistols. There are differences which came about because of the differences in specific market preferences.

The 9x19mm cartridge, best known as the 9mm Luger round in America, has always been controversial to American shooters. Many shooters disparage this round because of a preference for big-bore calibers and big-bore handgun performance. Controversy also enters the picture when the subject of hollow-point ammunition effectiveness in law enforcement applications enters the discussion. Even though such ammunition is illegal in Germany, hollow-point ammunition is essential to selling 9x19mm handguns to both American law enforcement and civilian self-defense consumers—the biggest handgun market in the world.

Americans have a demonstrated love affair with big-bore pistols; many feel the introduction of the 40 S&W cartridge established the bare minimum in terms of lethal force effectiveness with any handgun chambering. This belief has made the 40 S&W

The author, shown here at the Smith & Wesson Academy, testing the SW99 in 40 S&W when it was first introduced.

To sell handguns to police departments in America today takes much more than a well-designed pistol. It takes support on a level only a Napoleon or Caesar could envision. Today, of course, the issue is clouded further by the controversy over Smith & Wesson's agreement with H.U.D. and the participating cities. Some cities are supposed to give preference to Smith & Wesson handguns for law enforcement purchases. It is also important to mention a number of cities *did not agree* to the government pact and that a large distributor of S&W handguns dropped Smith & Wesson completely from its distribution operation…so the issue is a complicated one, to say the least.

Regardless, in 1997, Smith & Wesson approached Walther to see if they could come to an mutually beneficial agreement, not on an contract concerning gas guns, but in a cooperative effort on a real gun.

There was interest and general agreement on both sides, but now Smith & Wesson had to get U.S. State Department approval

before they could even start discussing the technical details of this joint endeavor--or begin sharing design specifications. The delay in securing U.S. State Department approval set the project behind, by one estimate, between four to six months. Until S&W received approval they couldn't even discuss specifics over the telephone. However, once that approval was received the project moved rapidly.

The SW99 is a well-made and extremely well-designed service pistol. Whether it proves a sales success will most likely depend upon factors totally outside the parameters of the gun's design, but the author is one who endorses the SW99 pistol and design.

cartridge the most popular chambering in U.S. domestic law enforcement handgun purchases today.

Unfortunately, it is a cartridge not widely distributed in Europe. The end result was that, while the Walther P99 9x19mm pistol, there were some performance problems with the 40-caliber version. These were traced directly to the German manufacturer's lack of experience designing for a wide range of ammunition from multiple manufacturers.

Added into this mix was the fact that Smith & Wesson made the decision—early—that their version of the P99 would be offered first in 40 S&W. It is then easy to understand why a close scrutiny of the Walther P99 began and some re-engineering was subsequently found necessary by Smith & Wesson.

Upon comparing the two pistols you will notice many differences in the polymer frame, or receiver. These will be listed briefly and then we will examine the more important ones in greater detail.

The SW99 has a rounded trigger guard instead of the squared-off trigger guard of the Walther pistol. The SW99 has the same style of checkering on the front and back strap as found on the Sigma. There is slightly more palm swell on the sides of the SW99 grip and there is an obvious difference in the side panels of the SW99—as opposed to the P99. The recurve at the rear of the polymer Walther P99 receiver has been eliminated and made straight on the

The SW99, like the Walther P99, features a very large flat wire recoil spring for increased durability and reliability.

S&W version. There is a continuous 'fence' around the slide release tab and there has been a change in the slide profile to make the SW99 blend in more naturally with other members of the Smith & Wesson centerfire auto-pistol product line. At the front and bottom of the grip there is a flat area to facilitate grabbing a magazine that might hang up for some reason and, at the very front of the polymer frame near the dust cover, there is a Picatinny-style rail for the installation of a tactical lamp.

The similarity between the SW99 (below) and the original Walther P99 (above) is easy to see, but there are differences. The majority of the differences are there to establish a Smith & Wesson appearance/identity for the SW99.

obvious; such as the addition of a S&W-marked floorplate and a different color follower: in this case, orange. The floorplate has also been radiused to avoid pinching the palm on big hands, when inserting a fresh magazine.

A great improvement is the Picatinny-style rail forward of the trigger guard. Essentially, it is an upside-down Weaver-style scope mount rail. One could even use a Weaver-type scope ring and base to easily and inexpensively mount a tactical flashlight at the front of this pistol.

Because the 40-caliber chambering was heavily emphasized, the removal of the rear receiver 'hook' was a needed modification. In testing 40-caliber P99s at the S&W factory this feature proved painful on the test shooters with medium to large hands.

Of course, one of the best features of the P99 has been retained: the changeable grip inserts that allow personalization of the grip size for the individual hand. 'One size fits all' is a fallacy. It doesn't work with overshoes, panty-hose or women's bras. In fact, the grip inserts will interchange perfectly between the SW99 and the P99, to the point that each looks like it was made for the other. Like the Walther P99, the SW99 comes with three different size inserts; small, medium and large.

Some of the changes were made mainly for cosmetic purposes or to

Changes to the magazine include the

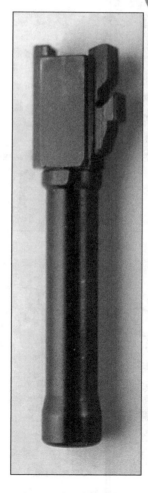

Because the SW99 was originally designed for the 40 S&W cartridge, those SW99S chambered for the 9x19mm round feature barrels with a 'barbell' appearance because the muzzle has the same outside diameter as the 40-caliber barrel.

The front surfaces of the trigger on the SW99 are wide and flat and the most distinctive part of the SW99 trigger system is its lengthy, but smooth, pull.

Specifications: The Smith & Wesson

SW99 MANUFACTURER:	Smith & Wesson
	2100 Roosevelt Ave.
	P.O. Box 2208
	Springfield, MA 01102-2208
	tel: 413-781-8300
MODEL:	SW99
MECHANISM TYPE:	Short recoil operated, Browning-style dropping barrel, semi-automatic pistol
SAFETY:	Four; Striker Safety, Trigger Safety, Decocking Safety and Drop Safety
CALIBER:	9x19mm and 40 S&W
OVERALL LENGTH:	7.08 inches
WIDTH:	1.14 inches (1.26 inches with large grip insert)
BARREL LENGTH:	4 inches
WEIGHT, empty	23 ounces (without magazine)
MAGAZINE CAPACITY:	10 rounds (USA civilian capacity)
	16 rounds for 9x19mm Law Enforcement
	12 rounds for 40 S&W Law Enforcement
SIGHTS:	White dot front sight with two white dot windage-adjustable rear sight.
ACCESSORIES:	Plastic carrying case, trigger lock, spare ten round magazine, a total of three different size grip inserts and four front sight blades plus the installation tool.

establish a Smith & Wesson identity for the new pistol. These modifications include the slide profile, the trigger guard shape and the changes to the grip proper.

A problem area for some shooters with the Walther P99 is the location and position of the slide release tab. World champion shooters like Rob Leatham and Jerry Barnhart have proven the advantages of gripping a pistol with two hands and having both thumbs pointed forward, one on top of the other. Sometimes referred to as the 'high thumb' position when applied to the 1911 pistol, shooters who use this technique with the Walther P99 may find their right thumb rides the rear of the P99 slide release tab. This often results in the slide closing on an empty chamber after the ammo supply has been exhausted.

Smith & Wesson has built a raised polymer 'fence,' for lack of a better term, around the perimeter of this tab. Smith & Wesson test personnel suffered this malfunction with the 40-caliber gun, but they felt it was due to a weak slide stop spring and a subsequent redesign mandated a heavier slide stop spring…which then necessitated a heavier magazine follower spring in order to properly engage and operate the slide stop when the magazine was emptied. For this reason the magazines of the Walther P99 and the Smith & Wesson SW99 in 40 S&W should not be interchanged. The Walther magazines will have a spring that may be too weak to engage the slide stop in the SW99.

Smith & Wesson has said previously they have no intention of discontinuing the Sigma, but the SW99 was designed to use a Sigma 416 stainless steel slide forging as the starting point for the SW99 slide. Walther machines the P99 slide from a carbon steel extrusion. Does that mean the Smith & Wesson SW99 slide is stronger because it's made from a forging? Nobody knows and, in truth, nobody cares. They both work.

There is slightly more mass in the SW99 slide in 40 S&W than there is in the comparable Walther slide, but S&W personnel report Walther has increased their slide mass to the S&W specification.

The SW99 slide also features forward serrations that are noticeably absent on the Walther slide. This was a feature developed from action competition shooting. The serrations make it easy to grasp the slide from under the pistol and behind the muzzle, while pointed downrange, and slightly retract the slide to check if the chamber is loaded. Yes, there is the same loaded chamber indicator on the SW99 at the rear of the extractor as found on the P99, but many shooters want the reassurance they get from a visual, physical verification.

The barrels are different between the SW99 and P99. Mainly because Smith & Wesson started with the 40-caliber version first, the 9x19mm SW99 has a barrel with the same outside diameter at the muzzle as the 40-caliber pistol but it narrows soon after the muzzle, which gives it a kind of barbell appearance.

It is important to mention that all SW99 barrels are made from 410 stainless steel with a *melonite* coating. *Melonite* is not equivalent to the *tennifer* process used by their competitors, but it does have some similar properties. The SW99 stainless steel slides are also treated with the *melonite* process.

I have shot the SW99 in numerous IDPA competitions and find the gun to be exceedingly accurate and reliable, but there are shortcomings. The biggest problem

The SW99 features the same decocking button as found on the Walther P99. Depressing this button decocks the striker fired mechanism.

It is easy to tell if the striker-fired mechanism of the SW99 is in the 'cocked' position, because if it is, the firing pin will protrude (as shown here) and expose it's red-painted tip.

has to do with the slide release tab—and my unknowing engagement of the tab as I fire the last round in the magazine. This causes the slide to go forward over an empty magazine onto an empty chamber, rewarding me with a loud "click" as the firing pin strikes—nothing.

In an effort to correct this condition, I cut the slide release tab away from my personally-owned SW99 in 40 S&W and realized an improvement; even so, I still sometimes engage the stub because of the increased recoil of the 40-caliber pistol over its milder 9mm brethren.

The SW99 and the Walther P99 share a common heritage and design. Many who are used to other polymer-framed pistols are disappointed after shooting the SW99 because of its long double-action trigger pull, very different from any other double-action-only pistol.

Probably the best way to describe the SW99 trigger pull is to compare it to the traditional double-action revolver, like a Smith & Wesson K-38. If you are an old DA revolver shooter it will feel natural to you; if you are not and have been raised on single-action automatics, then more likely you will be uncomfortable with the action and feel of the SW99.

Smith & Wesson uses the same front and rear sight Horst Wesp, the Walther P99 designer, created for the P99. Smith & Wesson's comment was, "It works, why change it?" Like the

James, who worked extensively with the SW99, feels it is an accurate pistol. It offers some of the advantages found in the traditional DA revolver: the interchangeable grip inserts and smooth double-action trigger pull.

Every SW99 will be shipped with what is seen here; a trigger lock, three different-sized grip inserts, a tool to drive out the pin holding the grip insert in place and three extra—but different height—front sight inserts as well as the tool necessary for their installation.

The magazine release on the SW99 is like that found on the P99 and similar in operation to that seen on the HK USP and USP Compact. The lever must be pulled down to release the magazine, but it is an ambidextrous design.

now also the Walther importer the marketing and sales situation is clouded by the consumer boycott in reaction to S&W's pact with H.U.D. and the participating cities.

Each SW99 will come to the S&W factory in a 'pistol assembly kit' consisting of six different groups which will then be assembled with the American-produced slides and barrels. The S&W engineers have gone over every change with the engineers at Walther and in some cases, such as the slide mass of the 40-caliber P99, Walther adopted those changes for their own production.

Smith & Wesson now has a product that compares most favorably with any other polymer frame pistol in the world. The question now, of course, is who will distribute them and—*more importantly*—who will buy them?

●

The idea that one size fits all is a fallacy and one of the most difficult challenges in auto-pistol design. The SW99 comes with three different-sized grip inserts to adjust the grip circumference to the individual shooter's hand. This, in the author's opinion, is a big step forward.

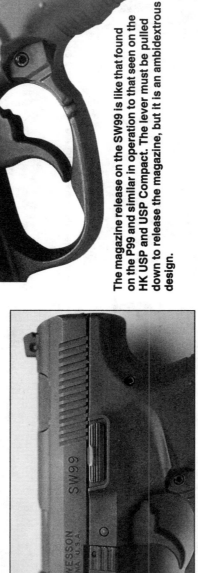

The SW99 has a small 'fence' surrounding the slide release tab. This is in marked contrast to the Walther P99 which has only a raised ridge under the slide release tab.

Walther P99, the SW99 will come with three extra front sight inserts, as well as a spare ten-round magazine for the domestic American market.

The magazines, interestingly enough, are being sourced in the States direct from the importer, Mec-Gar, not from Walther. That way the management at Smith & Wesson doesn't have to deal with the import paperwork concerning ammunition feeding devices.

Smith & Wesson's goal for the acquisition of the SW99 was the addition of a high-end polymer pistol to their product line. It retails in the States for less than the original Walther, but since Smith & Wesson is

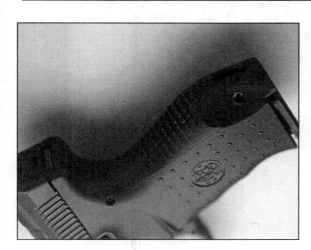

James cut the tab portion of the release off his pistol in an effort to avoid unintentional engagement of the slide release after the last round from the magazine has been fired.

Rats in the barn? Shotshells like these in a Super Blackhawk can help.

Shotshells for Revolvers

How to make and load shotshells that offer good payloads, good patterns, no leading, reloadability and low cost compared to commercial shotshells for the 38 Special/357 Magnum; 44 Special/Magnum; 38-40 and 44-40 WCF, 44 American, 44 Russian, 45 Schofield, 45 Colt and 454 Casull, etc. The shotshells are also adaptable to rifle use in the 44 Magnum, 444 Marlin, 45-70, etc.

by Kirk Paradise

WHEELING AS I caught sight of the fleeting brown form, I leveled the Super Blackhawk, firing instinctively. The rat was transfixed, instantly passing from a blur into a heap; from life to death. "A clean kill," I thought. Indeed it was, for the target, a brown rat, had just

emerged over the top of a mound and had run directly toward me as I fired from a range of six feet. I was not using the buck-and-bellow 44 Magnum round the revolver was chambered for; rather, I was using a handloaded shot cartridge more suited for the game at hand.

That night, my companions and I were scouring the local city dump for vermin. A 38, 357 or a 44 handloaded with shot was a popular tactic for such adventure but, except for a few clean kills like this one, mostly ineffective. Incredulously, I watched first one and ultimately many rats walk through a

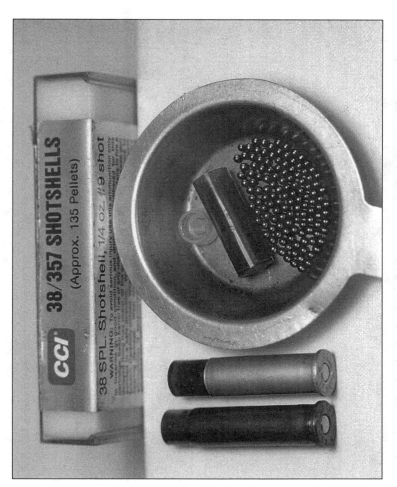

CCI 38/357 shotshell 1/4-ounce/135 pellet loads beside a 357 Maximum shotshell.

CCI 44 Magnum shotshell 1/3-ounce/210 pellet loads beside a 44 Magnum shotshell.

pattern of shot with little effect. I vowed to find a more effective handgun shotshell than what we had.

My search first concentrated on the 44 Magnum and then, as the techniques were learned, I applied the lessons to other revolver cartridges as well. I found shotshells can easily be fashioned for the 357 Magnum, 44 Special and Magnum and the 45 Colt. And, although I haven't done so, there isn't any reason why 38-40, 44-40, 44 American, 44 Russian, 45 Schofield or 454 Casull shotshells cannot be fashioned as well. Commercial shotshells are readily available for the 38 Special, 357 and 44 Magnums—but not for the others. The shotshells described here may be the only ones available for them.

To start with, the ideal revolver shotshell would obviously have to be much better than what my companions and I had first tried. My goal was to make a shotshell capable of cleanly killing small animals out to 15 feet, about the maximum effective range of shot fired in a rifled barrel. The shotshell would be useful not only for shooting vermin but also for survival and, where legal, hunting small game. It should have the virtues of being easily and inexpensively reloadable as well.

My starting point, the load we'd used for rat shooting, was a 44 Magnum case loaded with 6 grains of Unique, a gas check as an over-powder wad, an average load of 117 grains of shot and a second gas check crimped on top. Patterns consistently formed "doughnuts"; some hits in the middle and then alternating, concentric rings of voids where no shot hit and shot holes. This explained why many rats survived; too few hits (and firing from too far!). These doughnuts occurred only when gas checks were used and not with any other technique described below.

In comparison, the commercial 44 Magnum CCI shotshell patterns well and comes with a cartridge-length capsule carrying an average load of 127 grains of #9 shot, 8.5% more. The CCI package advertises "1/3-ounce of shot" (145 grains) and "Approx. 210 Pellets" but, when dissected, the shot weighed 127 grains, the combined weight of the capsule and the shot weighed only 141.5 grains and pellet count averaged 167. Perhaps the shot in this particular lot was a bit larger than #9 shot; that could account for the reduced weight and pellet count. The CCI 38/357 load advertised "1/4-ounce shot" (110 grains) #9 shot and "Approx. 135 pellets" but had only 96 grains of shot; 105 grains combined

with the capsule. Pellet count was right on at 135 pellets. This again showed an inconsistency, but it's a minor problem since we are dealing with very small quantities of a not-

very-uniform product. My own loads, which used #9 shot from different lots, showed similar inconsistencies. The fact the loads were a bit shy of the advertised weights is minor; what is

HANDLOADING

more important is they are not reloadable, offer only #9 shot and, at the prices I paid, $4.30 per box of ten 38/357s or $5.75 for the 44 Magnums, expensive. They offer convenience but not optimum performance. Because of this, they were not the solution I wanted. The answer occurred to me one day as I examined the Super Blackhawk's cylinder. I looked first at the cylinder and then at an empty case. The cylinder is 1.75 inches long; the case 1.29 inches. The solution: find a case long enough to fill the cylinder all the way to the chamber mouth!

The first idea on how to use all that chamber volume came from the rolled-paper shotgun shell. A length of typing paper was rolled into a cylinder and glued into an empty, primed case. This had the advantage of adapting standard cases with readily available material. However easy it appeared to be, this route proved so unpromising it was abandoned without test-firing a single round. It wasn't that making the inserts was difficult; I concluded that, first, it was impractical and second, but more important, it was unsafe. The problems were reduced volume and uniformity. When rolled thick enough to be sturdy (and hence *reloadable*) the coiled paper reduced case volume significantly. For safety, the paper insert had to be seated to the bottom of the case. Only if seated as deep as possible would there be enough area for the glue to make a durable bond to the case. The interior taper of the case prevented this and the paper insert stopped about .15-inch short of the web, forming a lip. I envisioned the powder gasses pushing on the lip, dislodging the insert and shooting it out of the barrel or, worse, halfway out. Even epoxy may not survive repeated firings.

The idea of a one-piece all-brass case presented itself. Such a case must have proper rim and base dimensions–plus extend all the way to the chamber mouth. Such a case must be a rifle case since the 44 Magnum was the longest handgun case in existence at that time. Did such a case exist? Studying Frank C. Barnes *Car-*

tridges of the World revealed three cases had suitable rim and base dimensions: the 30-40 Krag; 303 British and 444 Marlin. Nominal dimensions of the candidates are:

The 30-40 and the 303 have correct base dimensions but are too large across the rim. The 444 has the correct rim but is too fat across the base. All three have rims thicker than the 44's. Samples of all four cases were measured and found to agree closely with the nominal dimensions.

The significance of the case dimensions depends on the characteristics of the revolver for which you are loading. Initially, an old model Super Blackhawk with countersunk chambers was used. Current new model Super Blackhawk, Redhawk and model Super Blackhawk, Redhawk and S&W Model 29-3 and later revolvers do not have countersunk chambers. Shotshells made with unaltered rims fit into sample Redhawk and S&W 29-3 revolvers without problems but, interestingly, shotshells for new model Super Blackhawks without countersunk chambers require shotshells trimmed the same as for old models with countersunk chambers. If you try making a shotshell, try one for fit; if the shotshells easily drop into the chambers and the cylinder turns freely, without binding, the shotshell should work well. The directions for reducing the diameter of the rims, given below, are important only to those who have revolvers with

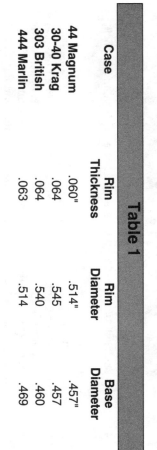

357 Maximum case shown with a 357 Maximum shotshell, a 223 Remington case annealed and trimmed prior to fire-forming and a fire-formed 357/223 shotshell. The 357/223 shotshell holds insignificantly more shot, is much more difficult to make but its 223 Remington parent is much easier to find than 357 Maximum cases.

357 Magnum case compared to a sized 357 Maximum case and another, neck-sized in a 32 S&W die, ready to load as a shotshell.

Basic 44 Magnum shot load; gas checks as over-powder and over-shot wads.

Table 1

Case	Rim Thickness	Rim Diameter	Base Diameter
44 Magnum	.060"	.514"	.457"
30-40 Krag	.064	.545	.457
303 British	.064	.540	.460
444 Marlin	.063	.514	.469

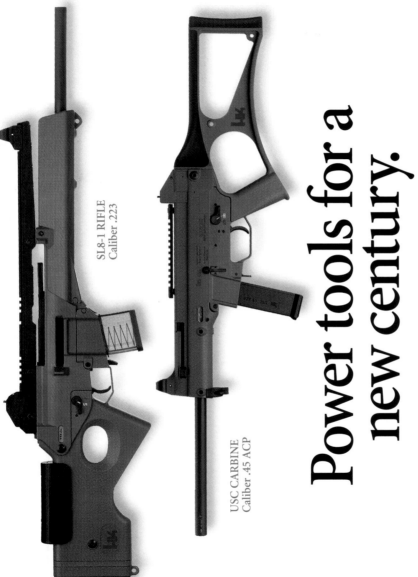
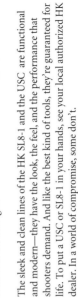

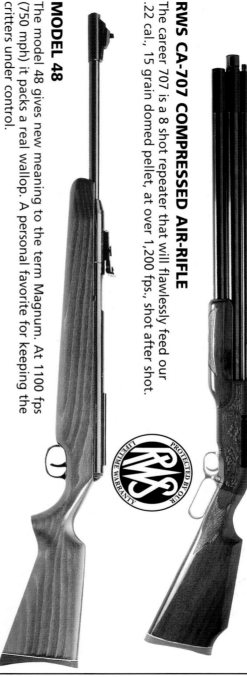

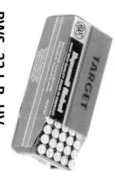

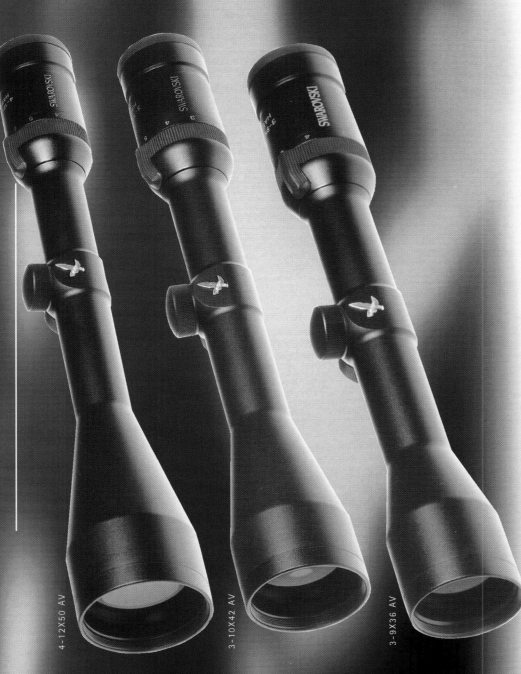

consequently it took considerable time to produce one case. It proved so unsatisfactory a method that only two cases were produced this way. Each was then chucked in a case trimmer and shortened with a fine-toothed hacksaw. The case trimmer was then used in a normal manner to bring the finished case to a length of 1.70-inches. Even though shotshells can be successfully made this way, the excessive time it takes makes it unattractive. I turned my attention to the 30-40 and 303 cases in search of a better way.

A technique was developed to keep the case head stable while filing the rim by keeping the primer pocket centered on a ball bearing. This kept the primer pocket from being marred in the least degree. The primer pocket is a critical area and the smallest gouge or other deformation destroys the case. A handloader with a 3/8-inch electric drill, a bench vise, a 3/8-inch nut, a ball bearing about .30-inch in diameter, a mill file and a triangular file has all the tools needed to produce shotshells.

Here's how it works: first, chuck the neck of a 30-40 or 303 case in the drill. (If you have only a 1/4-inch drill, the necks may be sized down in a 257 Roberts or 250 Savage sizing die). Second, secure the nut in the vise and place the bearing on the hole. Then, center the primer pocket on the ball bearing and start the drill. No part of the primer pocket's interior is touched and the smooth surface of the bearing does not harm the primer pocket lip, even when turned at high speed. No lubricant was necessary. Holding the drill and case in one hand and the mill file in the other, guide the file against the rim until it is small enough to easily slip into all chambers in the cylinder or to clear cases in adjacent chambers without any binding. The triangular file is used to thin the inside of the rim. This reduces the rim thickness so there is sufficient clearance between the cylinder and the breach to allow the cylinder to freely rotate. Only the inside of the rim should be thinned; thinning the headstamp side reduces the depth of the primer pocket. No measurements or special gauges are required since each case can be individually tried for fit in the chambers in which it will be used. Deburr the rim with coarse steel wool and then compare the fit with a regular case. The shotshell should protrude no more than the regular case; if it does, it may bind the gun when the cylinder rotates. Be sure to thin enough because, after the bottleneck

countersunk chambers or have binding problems. Try the technique with your revolver and see how it works. Revolvers chambered for the 44 Special, such as the Charter Arms Bulldog, have relatively small diameter cylinders which position the cases so close together the cartridge rims nearly touch one another; shotshells for these revolvers will need the rim diameter reduced. In the case of the Bulldog, the chambers are not countersunk *per se*, but the extractor on a sample gun is cut with a slight lip which acts like a countersink. Try the cases in your revolver; if they won't fit, trim as needed.

Once suitable cases close to the desired dimensions were identified, the next step was to develop a practical method for someone like me–who didn't have access to a lathe, drill press or the like–to use in working the cases into final form.

My first efforts were with the 444 case. It appeared it would be the easiest to convert since its dimensions were correct except for the base. However, I could find no way of removing the excess brass other than turning it off with a lathe, which I did not have. I improvised with an electric drill, using a mill file to remove brass. The case neck was held securely enough in the chuck but the base end was unsupported. The case was turned at medium speed with the file pressed against the base. Even slight pressure on the unsupported case caused it to wobble;

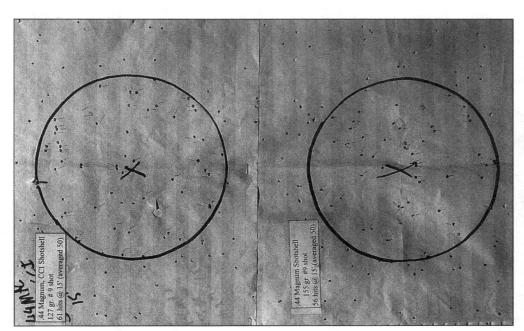

Comparison patterns fired at 15 feet with CCI and handloaded shotshells for a 44 Magnum.

44 Magnum, CCI Shotshell
127 gr. # 9 shot
61 hits @ 15' (averaged 50)

44 Magnum Shotshell
155 gr. #9 shot
56 hits @ 15' (averaged 50)

44 Magnum shotshell, CCI 44 Magnum & 38/357 and 357 Maximum shotshells.

is cut off, the case will not fit the 3/8-inch drill any longer. For Super Black-hawks, thinning is essential; however, on sample Redhawk and S&W 29-3 revolvers, unthinned, untrimmed rims had adequate clearance and cases had only to be trimmed to proper length.

One can readily gain a feel for how much brass should be removed. With a little practice, one can produce a shotshell in one or two minutes. Once the rim is finished, the case is ready to be trimmed. With 30-40 or 303 cases, a 30-caliber pilot is needed, initially. With the case in position, use a fine-toothed hack saw to cut the cases to about 1.8 inches. Then, switching to a .40-inch or 10mm pilot, trim the case to about .01-inch shorter than cylinder length. The .40-inch pilot is needed because the taper of a 30-40 or 303 case will not admit a larger one; the new case mouth is very nearly .40-inch. Once cases are thinned and shortened, they should be annealed before being loaded. This may be done in the conventional manner for annealing and fire-forming cases.

Stand cases in a pan of water 1 inch deep. Heat the necks with a propane torch. When the necks begin to turn red, tip them over to quench. Once the cases are thoroughly dry, they are ready to be fire-formed. When fire-forming, the over-powder wad needs to be flexible enough to fit through the .40-inch mouth but expand to about .42-inch over the powder and to provide a good seal when fired. Gasket cork 1/16-inch thick - or similar material - will work. A 44 case with a sharpened mouth easily cuts wads from a sheet of cork.

▲ 45 Colt and 44 Magnum shotshells shown, respectively, with their parent cartridges: the 444 Marlin, 303 British and 30-40 Krag.

Two such wads provide a good gas seal. To fireform the cases in a 44 Magnum, standard CCI large pistol primers were seated in the shotshell case followed by 6.0 grains of Unique and two wads. The wads were inserted individually and seated with a dowel. The case was filled with #7 shot and another wad seated on top and sealed with GE Silicon Windshield Glass Seal.

After firing, none of the cases split and each was now a bottlenecked copy of the 44 Magnum chamber. The cases had shrunk to about 1.725 inches, .025-inch shorter than cylinder length. The resulting shotshell is able to use the full capacity of revolvers chambered for the 44 Magnum. It carries more shot than competitive shotshells, can be made with common tools almost every handloader has and is easy and inexpensive to reload.

Equally important, the shotshells pattern well. The first loads produced a nice, even pattern 12 inches in diameter at 10 feet-with no *doughnuts*. Maximum effective range is about 15 feet where the pattern opens to 18 feet. At that range, the pattern thins and holes appear. Handguns, with their rifled barrels, spin the shot column; the centrifugal force so distorts the pattern they are effective at just a few

yards. Barrel lengths seem to be a minor factor. Effective patterns, all at 10 feet, averaged 12 inches in diameter from a 3-inch-barreled Bulldog, 12 inches from a 5-inch Model 629, 15 inches from a 7 1/2-inch Super Black-hawk, 12 inches from a 20-inch-barreled Marlin 1894 and 10 inches from a 4 5/8-inch 45 Colt. The rifling is an inherent limitation. The only way to overcome it would be to have a smooth-bore (which is not only illegal but makes the gun useless with regular ammunition) or to have a device like that used by Thompson/Center. Thompson/Center uses a removable, patented choke tube which counteracts the effect of rifling, stabilizes the shot and, in the 45 Colt/.410 shotshell version, has an advertised effective range of some 30 yards. The removable choke has also been advertised in a 44 Magnum version but it requires a specially-loaded cartridge.

▲ 45 Colt, 44 Magnum and 44 Special shotshells shown before and after fire-forming. Note the rims of the two previously fired 44s are bright after having been thinned and trimmed. Their rims had to be altered before they would chamber in a Ruger Super Blackhawk and a Charter Arms Bulldog, respectively. The two unfired 44s are destined to be fired in a S&W Model 629-3 and require no alteration. The 45 Colt shotshell also fit without alteration.

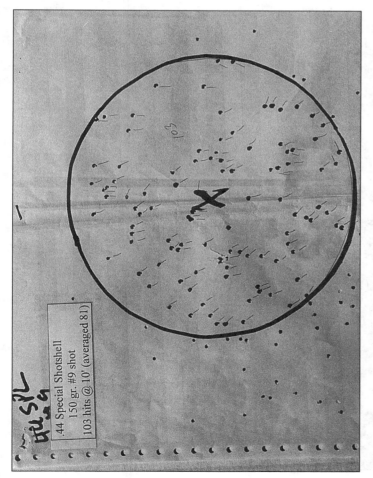

.44 Special Shotshell
150 gr. #9 shot
103 hits @ 10' (averaged 81)

A pattern from a 44 Special shotshell; it is nearly as effective as one from a 44 Magnum. Make this shotshell a little shorter and it could fit a 44 American or 44 Russian.

Neither version can be fired with ball ammunition with a choke tube attached. T/C also marketed their shot cartridges in 357 Magnum. These shotshells use regular cases but have a long plastic shot capsule. They can be used only in the Thompson/Center Contenders since the cartridges are too long to fit a revolver cylinder.

After fire-forming, a standard load was developed. Since case volume was now greatly increased, the powder charge was stepped up to 8 grains of Unique. Initially, the two cork over-powder wads were used, followed by an average load of 210 grains of #7 shot and then the Silicone Seal. After the Silicone Seal cures, it provides a tough, waterproof seal which withstands the repeated firing of a 44 Magnum in an adjacent chamber.

After the first firing, the shotshells need to be resized before they will re-chamber. Their bottleneck form does not match any existing case. However, by using a 30-40 Krag or 303 British sizing die, you can size the neck down slightly so cases easily re-chamber. The completed rounds were tested on aluminum and steel cans, plus plastic drink bottles—completely penetrating both sides, even on the tough plastic. They should give excellent results out to 10 or 15 feet on any target. Once the design was perfected, I gave some to friends to shoot and then sat back to wait for their praise.

Their comments were more like *"Sure they work fine, BUT ... look in the barrel after you fire one."* Their comments were directed to the dark, dirty gray deposits, or rather the dark, dirty gray *hard-to-remove* deposits left in the barrel. It was true. One drawback of shooting soft shot in a rifled barrel is that it rubs and smears off, leaving a mess behind. If only one or two shotshells are used and then the barrel cleaned promptly, lead build-up is not a serious problem. However, if more than a few are used, leading becomes difficult to remove and can impair the accuracy of ball cartridges—or even preclude their use. Another fortunate coincidence eliminated the leading.

The use of plastic wads in shotgun shells is almost universal. The wad rides down the bore, prevents contact between the shot and the barrel, eliminates leading and greatly reduces shot deformation. Plastic wads for .410-bore shotshells are close enough in size to be useful in 44- and 45-caliber revolver shotshells. Both Remington and Winchester make .410 wads but the Remington Power Piston has a base which uses up too much of the valuable shot space. The Winchester AA wad has a plain base which allows more shot to be carried. Shot capacity is greatly reduced compared to the basic shotshell, but with the 44 Mag-

num/8 grains Unique load, 155 grains of shot still fits inside, 22% more than the commercial CCI shotshell. With 6 grains of Unique, the load grows to 166 grains, some 30% more. After some experimenting, the 6 grains Unique/166 grains shot seems the better of the two. Best yet, with either load, leading is completely eliminated. The cylinder-length shotshell and .410 AA wad combination offers a good payload, good patterns, no leading, reloadability and low cost.

To use the AA wad, first prime the case with standard large pistol primers, charge the case with 6 grains of Unique, insert the wad and seat it firmly on the powder by pushing it with a dowel. The wad will protrude about .3-inch; use a sharp blade to trim the wad flush with the case mouth. Pull the wad out of the case mouth about 1/2-inch, put a thin coat of Silicone Seal on the outside of the wad and re-seat the wad. Charge the wad with shot, leaving the last 1/8-inch or so empty. Place a large drop of Silicone Seal in the mouth and add enough shot to fill the case. The idea is to coat several layers of shot inside the wad to fully seal the shotshell and prevent the wad from shifting forward. Make sure the petals are evenly arranged and do not overlap. Set the completed shotshell aside to cure for 24-hours. No separate over-powder wad is needed with the AA wad.

Once the basic design of the shotshell was developed, it was easy to transfer the principle to other cartridges. The 44 Special is a natural since it involves only shortening the case a little more and using a little less shot and powder. A sample 44 Bulldog had a cylinder 1.58 inches long but, since it does not have chambers that are truly countersunk, cases were cut to 1.64 inches. They measured 1.637 inches after fire-forming and resizing. The load selected was 6.0 grains of Unique and 150 grains of shot. This Bulldog patterned well, as shown in **Table 2**, in comparison to other shotshells. Perhaps the 3-inch barrel did not impart as much spin as longer barrels. A 44 shotshell made for the S&W Models 24 or 696, Colt New Service, Single Action Army or clone, Rossi 720 or Taurus 431/441, etc., could be left longer and the payload increased. Cylinder length is the controlling factor. Shotshells for the cowboy action shooter who has a pistol in 44 American or 44 Russian should also be easy to make by adapting this method.

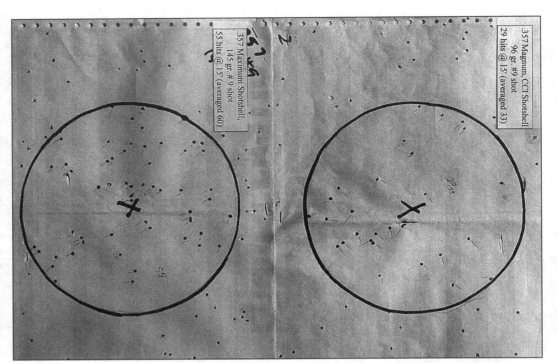

357 Magnum, CCI Shotshell
96 gr. #9 shot
29 hits @ 15' (averaged 33)

357 Maximum Shotshell,
145 gr. # 9 shot
55 hits @ 15' (averaged 60)

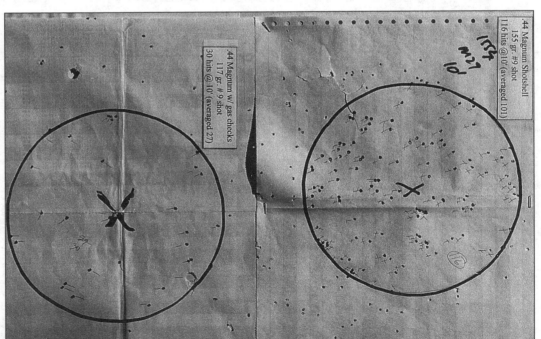

44 Magnum Shotshell
155 gr. #9 shot
116 hits @ 10' (averaged 101)

44 Magnum w/ gas checks
117 gr. #9 shot
30 hits @ 10' (averaged 27)

Sample patterns fired at 15 feet with CCI and handloaded shotshells for a 357 Magnum. In this, and the other tests described below, different combinations were fired at the aim point "X" from 5', 10', 15' and 20'. To count the number of hits, a 8-inch diameter template was centered on the X and the circumference drawn. The total pattern diameter and density varied considerably from one gun/barrel length to another but all combinations were judged only on how many hits went into the 8-inch diameter circle around the X. That is, after all, where the target will be. Sometimes the wadding would strike within the 8-inch circle, but more often it did not. Results are summarized in Table 2.

Patterns fired from 10 feet from two different 44 Magnum shotshells. The upper pattern is from a shotshell loaded with 155 grains of shot, held by a Winchester .410 AA wad. The lower pattern is from a plain 44 Magnum case holding 117 grains of shot between two gas checks.

Do you have a Winchester, Marlin, Browning, Rossi or Uberti carbine or rifle? A little work produced a usable shotshell for a Marlin 1894 44 Magnum. The shotshell had to be trimmed shorter than for a Super Blackhawk, to 1.675 inches, before it loaded and extracted through the Marlin's action; this length may need to be adjusted for other makes. The shotshell works through the magazine and ejects normally but does not chamber readily; the case mouth hits the chamber mouth. Cases need to be loaded singly, directly into the chamber.

hawk. It maintains an effective pattern, 14 inches in diameter, out to 15 feet. Apparently, the ride down the 20-inch barrel doesn't affect the pattern until it passes 15 feet, so that it is just as capable as a handgun. Once the pattern passes 15 feet, it seems to open more rapidly than one from a handgun, ending up about 20 inches at 20 feet. I should add that effectiveness of the shotshells was not judged by how wide a pattern they throw but rather by how many shot hit an 8-inch circle, which is about the space a rat would occupy, at any given range.

ber. The shotshell holds a few grains less shot than one for a Super Black-

It should be noted the Marlin has micro-groove rifling and conventional rifling may give different results. Results in the Marlin are found in **Table 2.** Modify the shotshells described below for use in lever actions in 38-40, 44-40 and 45 Colt. Cases for a 444 Marlin or 45-70 should not have to be modified in any way; just loaded with powder, wad and shot.

Now for the 45 Colt and other cartridges with similar base dimensions. Remember the 444 Marlin case? While the base of the 444 is too fat for a 44 Magnum chamber, it is exactly right for a 45 Colt. Rim thickness is also satisfactory. This is the simplest shotshell to make (well, almost; the absolute simplest is just stuffing

powder, a wad and shot into a 444 Marlin or 45-70 case for use in a rifle). Just trim the 444 case to cylinder length and it is ready to load. Annealing is not even necessary. With 6 grains of Unique, the AA .410 wad seated, trimmed and sealed as for the 44–and 178 grains of shot–you are in business. Shotshells made from 444s for a 38-40, 44-40, 45 Schofield or 454 Casull should also require no more than trimming to appropriate cylinder length. Even the 38-40 may be able to use the AA .410 wad if the shotshell mouth is belled like a "regular" case mouth is before seating a bullet. Assuming a chamber throat is .400-inch, the shotshell neck would probably have to be sized to .398-inch outside diameter to fit. This means the inside diameter would be about .370-inch (.398 - .028 for the thickness of the brass.) The AA wads are flexible and may be able to be pushed, undamaged, through the neck if the mouth is belled first. Just make sure any pistol you use is in good condition and the loads are appropriate to it.

Finally, an effective 357 shotshell is possible, but it cannot use the plastic wad. The only rimmed cartridge case able to be trimmed to cylinder length is the 222 Rimmed from Australia. Huntington Die Specialties may import Bertram 222R cases but I have not tried them. The 222 Remington family of cartridges has the proper base diameter but they are rimless. The regular 222 or 223 may be used if, after they are trimmed, annealed and loaded, a small piece of flexible tape is wrapped around the case head before the round is chambered. The tape will be pushed into the extractor groove as the round is chambered and act as a rim. It will have enough strength to hold the case in place when the round is fired and the neck fireforms in the chamber throat to form a bottleneck. After firing, the tape is removed; it is not needed again. The case will then headspace on the bottleneck like any rimless case. Since this is a rimless case, it will not extract from double-action revolvers but a dowel may be used to push the case out of the chamber. In a single-action revolver, it makes no difference. I once tried 351 Winchester Self-Loading cases. While they are rimmed, they are but 1.38-inches long and do not hold as large a shot load. If you can find any Remington 357 Maximum cases, use them because they are the best compromise. They are 1.60-inches long and, while not as long as the cylin-

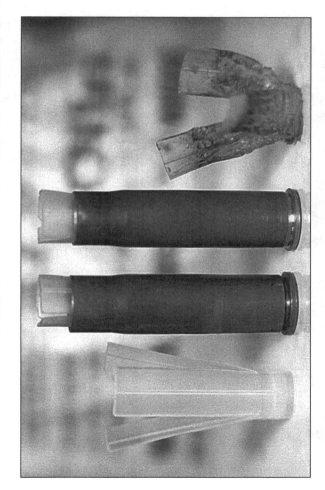

45 Colt and 44 Magnum shotshells showing the Winchester AA .410-bore wads which eliminate leading in rifled bores. The wads are seated on 6 grains of Alliant Unique. The wads are ready to be trimmed to case length. Afterwards, they will be glued to the case side with GE Silicon Seal, filled with shot and then topped with Silicon Seal. A new, and fired, wad are shown for comparison.

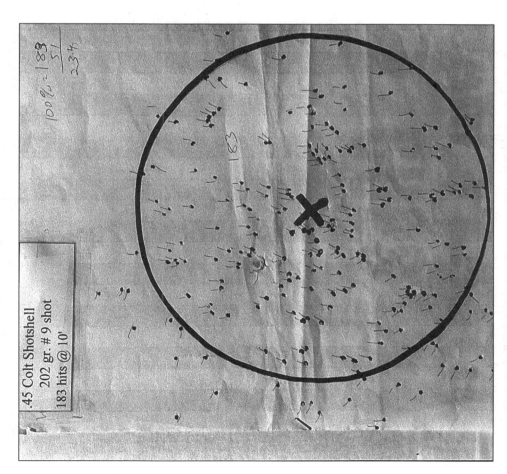

.45 Colt Shotshell
202 gr. # 9 shot
183 hits @ 10'

A pattern from a 45 Colt shotshell shows how dense and effective these can be. No commercial version is available and this shotshell can be adapted to the 38-40 and 44-40 or 45 Schofield as well.

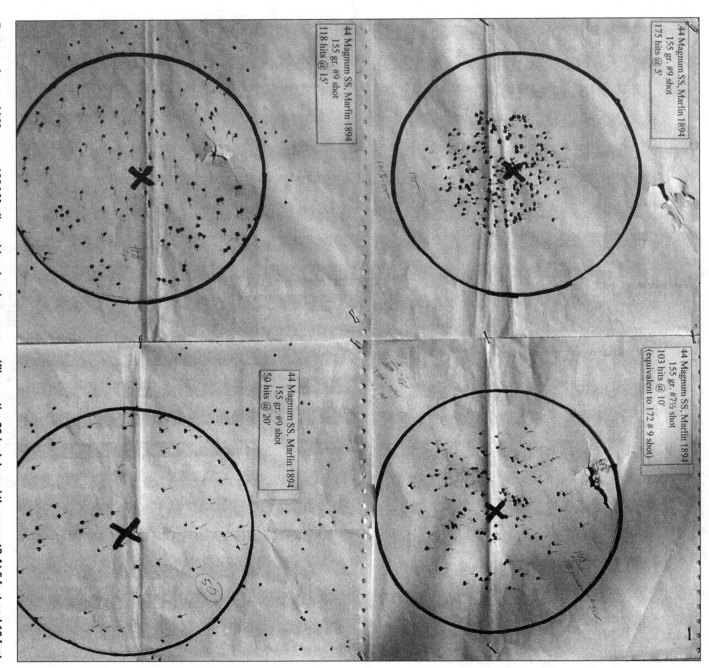

44 Magnum SS, Marlin 1894
155 gr. #9 shot
175 hits @ 5'

44 Magnum SS, Marlin 1894
155 gr. #9 shot
118 hits @ 15'

44 Magnum SS, Marlin 1894
155 gr. #7½ shot
103 hits @ 10'
(equivalent to 172 # 9 shot)

44 Magnum SS, Marlin 1894
155 gr. #9 shot
50 hits @ 20'

Patterns from a 44 Magnum 1894 Marlin carbine. Is micro-groove rifling or the 20-inch barrel the secret? At 5 feet and 10 feet, 100% of the pattern remains inside the 8-inch circle. At 15 feet, it is nearly so but at 20 feet, the pattern thins out. Revolvers with conventional rifling could not pattern as close as this. Perhaps Marlin should offer a special "Guide" version with choke tubes!

ders of many 357s (they are close to cylinder length for some small-frame 38s), the rims make them much more convenient to use. Unlike the tapered 222/223 case that will readily chamber before fire-forming, a 357 Maximum case must have the neck diameter reduced to be able to enter the chamber throat before they can be chambered. After sizing in a regu-

lar 38/357 full-length sizer, sizing the last .4-inch or so with a 30 Carbine or 32 S&W sizer forms the bottleneck. For subsequent firings, after full-length resizing, run the cases into a 38/357 Magnum crimping die until the shotshell mouth just touches the crimp ring. This should taper the mouth enough for the shotshell to easily rechamber. A charge of 5.0

grains of Bullseye, an over-powder wad and 145 grains of #9 shot will fit into the case. Regrettably, no AA wad or substitute is available. Over-powder wads are cut from a wax-coated paper milk carton with a sharpened 38 Special case. Since there is no plastic wad to take up space, this load comes near the 44 Magnum load and exceeds the payloads of both the

Table 2: Shotshell Comparisons

Case/Shotshell	*Powder,* Grains	*Shot wt.,* Grains	Load Index	# Shot in ctg.	*Average # Shot in 8" circle at:* 5 Feet	10 Feet	15 Feet	20 Feet.
38/357 CCI Shotshell	factory	96	1.00	135	101	54	33	21
357 Maximum Shotshell	5.0 Bullseye	145	1.51	143	143	113	60	25
44 Magnum CCI Shotshell	factory	127	1.00	167	152	87	50	20
44 Special Shotshell, AA wad	6.0 Unique	150	1.18	194	168	81	88	67
44 Magnum, gas check	6.0 Unique	117	0.92	85	68	27	-	-
44 Magnum Shotshell, AA wad	8.0 Unique	155	1.22	181	162	101	50	18
44 Magnum Shotshell, AA wad	6.0 Unique	166	1.31	199	198	111	53	23
44 Mag SS, AA wad in Marlin	6.0 Unique	155	1.22	175	175	172	118	50
45 Colt Shotshell, AA wad	6.0 Unique	178	1.40	202	202	183	89	36

CCI 38/357 and 44 Magnum loads. Just be ready to scrub your barrel as these loads *WILL* lead the bore. These shotshells may also be adapted for other obsolete calibers such as the 38 Short or Long Colt if the powder charge/shot load is adjusted to keep pressures at a safe level in the pistol used.

How well do these shotshells work? They can't be directly compared to a .410-bore or any other shotgun but they provide effective patterns to at least 15 feet–and 20 feet in some instances. A 2 3/4-inch .410 shell with its 1/2-ounce (219 grains) load holds much more shot than any shotshell described here and is effective to 25 or 30 yards, about 6 times the effective range of these shotshells. However, these revolver shotshells offer convenience, versatility and solid performance up close where it counts. Shotshells of each type described here were assembled and patterned at 5, 10, 15 and 20 feet. Comparisons of various shotshells with different combinations of powder and shot are in **Table 2**. The ***Load Index*** column shows the comparative payloads of the various combinations with both the CCI 38/357 and 44 Magnum shotshells rated as "1.00" in their respective categories. **Table 2** also shows the average weight and number of shot taken from sample shotshells as they were loaded–plus the number of #9 shot striking within 8-inch diameter circles–for each combination at each distance. **Table 2** contains some apparent inconsistencies, but I did weigh one load at 150 grains and count 194 pellets and count fewer, 181 pellets, in a load weighing 155 grains. I lay this to variations in the average size/weight of the pellets in the different lots of shot.

I planned to chronograph these loads and had the foresight to use two layers of transparent plastic to armor the LCD readout of my Shooting Chrony chronograph. Velocity averaged 881 fps at 5 feet and 871 fps at 10 feet for the 44 Magnum/6 grains Unique/166 grains shot load. However at 15 feet, the second shot in the string registered 1572 fps, enough of a change to make me examine the instrument. Despite my efforts to aim the shot string high up in the guide rods, a few shot had zinged the LCD readout, case and rear Skyscreen. The armor protected the LCD readout but the case was dented and Skyscreen pocked! Subsequent tests with ball ammunition of known velocity showed the Shooting Chrony still works properly but that ended all velocity tests on the shotshells! Let's just say the shotshells have enough velocity to get the job done.

Costs? Each CCI 357 Magnum shotshell cost 43¢ and the 44 Magnum 57¢; prices may vary depending where you buy them. For around 2-3¢ for each component, primer, powder, wad and shot–and even including the cost of the GE Silicone Seal, you can load shotshells for about a dime each. In addition to the low cost, there is also the added flexibility of using shot sizes other than #9. In addition to #9 shot, I experimented only with #7 shot but others may wish to try #8, #9 or #12 shot–or even larger sizes, *like #6 shot for those hard-to-kill super rats.*

Shotshells for revolvers are very useful in some situations and have no substitute in others. There is no alternative to making your own for the newly-popular Cowboy Action cartridges. When shooting vermin, they offer the advantages of less report and recoil than a ball cartridge while providing greater assurance of hitting and killing the animal. They are more effective and much less expensive than commercial shotshells. Handloaders may easily tailor them to their needs with different powders and by using smaller or larger shot. Try these simple techniques to produce your own revolver shotshells. •

Warning:
Neither the author or the publisher assume any liability for accidents using the information contained in this article. The loads listed in the article are safe only in the guns in which they were developed and tested. Readers assume all liability and proceed at their own risk. Consult reloading manuals and references and be thoroughly familiar with handloading techniques before attempting any work described in this article. Death or injury may result from misuse of tools, improperly loaded ammunition or with unsuitable firearms. The information contained in the article was checked for accuracy but neither the author or the publisher take responsibility for misprints or other errors.

ENGRAVED GUNS

Handgun Engraving -
Better Than Ever!

by Tom Turpin

A really unusual engraving job. It is from the shop of Alaskan Don Scarberry and, if engraving was categorized in the same way as oil painting, I suppose Don's work would be called either Impressionistic or perhaps Art Deco. *Photo by Mark Ross, courtesy of Guns Magazine.*

MAN HAS BEEN decorating his personal stuff for a long time. In the old days, he would bowl over an eagle or grizzly bear and use the feathers and/or claws to adorn something that was special to him—usually his means of survival. That meant his spear, bow–or whatever weapon was in vogue at the time. Of course, those ancestors of ours learned quickly that some of the decorations came pretty dear as Old Griz didn't give up his claws, or anything else for that matter, without a fracas. Often primitive man learned it was considerably safer and less painful to find a more tranquil source of adornment.

At some point in our past, a particularly gifted fellow, at least I assume it was a fellow, successfully tried cutting designs into metal and the art of engraving was born. Presumably, the art form came along before the invention of firearms as the museums in Europe are full of swords, spears, maces (or is it *maci*?)–as well as suits of armor and other neat stuff–that were decorated by engraving.

When firearms were invented they quickly replaced bows, arrows, spears and the like as the weapons of choice. It didn't take our progenitors long to learn the firearm was infinitely more

ENGRAVED GUNS

▲ This magnificent Colt Dragoon was embellished by Texan Ron Smith. Reminiscent of some of Sam Colt's presentation pieces, this piece would certainly make Gustave Young proud. *Photo by Alan Richmond.*

▼ This Ruger Black Powder Single Action was decorated by the Teutonic Master, Claus Willig. The Ruger is one of several handguns being theme-engraved by Herr Willig for a collector client. *Photo courtesy of Claus Willig.*

▲ Robert Strosin engraved this Colt Gold Cup National Match Model 45 Auto. Strosin's work on this handgun is impeccably executed. *Photo by Alan Richmond*

engraving has been reserved for smaller sporting arms - shotguns, rifles–and the subject of this piece, handguns.

While many firearms were engraved long before Sam Colt came onto the scene, he did much to popularize having one's handgun beautified. He offered factory engraving on most, if not all, of his models. He made a practice of presenting highly-chiseled and ornate handguns to VIPs of the day as a means of advertising his products on the world market. Not only did Mr. Colt do a lot of presenting on behalf of his company, he also convinced heads of state, both here and abroad, to use highly decorated Colt handguns as presentation pieces. Abe Lincoln took advantage of the Colt factory on at least two occasions, having presentation sets made for King Charles XV of Sweden & Norway and King Frederick VII of Denmark. He probably had others made as well.

Many ornately-embellished Colts ended up in Russia, thanks to the Czars. In those pre-Lenin days, the rulers of the country were great Colt

efficient at warding off one's adversaries than were the previous armaments. The engravers of the day saw the handwriting on the wall and moved from blades to guns. They have been doing so ever since...although knives run a close second to guns in engraving popularity, even today.

One finds engraving on all types of firearms. I don't think I've yet come across an engraved 105mm howitzer, but just about everything smaller than that has been, on occasion, adorned by engraving. Mostly though,

▶ Washington State engraver Ken Warren adorned this Colt Single Action with deeply-cut Germanic Scroll. Warren did a similar single-action revolver for the late singing cowboy, Gene Autry. *Photo courtesy of Ken Warren.*

fans. Decorated eggs weren't the only things they collected!

Colt employed many engravers over the years. The names of Kornbrath, Nimschke, Helfricht, Young, Ulrich and others are well known to Colt *aficionados.* Now I'm the first to admit the lesser grades of engraving found on old Colts are usually pretty poorly done. However, the same can be accurately said of factory-engraved Winchesters, Parkers, Foxes—and the rest.

It is exceedingly obvious that the engravers doing the work were not paid very much for each of the lower-grade jobs, so they didn't take a lot of pains with the work. Doing so would have taken much too much time to be profitable. On the higher grades, though, the work was ordinarily very good and often exquisite - particularly on the presentation pieces.

One need not be exceptionally observant to note that none of the early Colt engravers had common American names. Only Young is close—and even that name is a misnomer as it is an Americanization of the German name "Jung." Instead, all were Germanic in origin and training. That situation remained basically the same in this country up until just a few short years ago.

These days, though, magnificently-executed engraving is coming from guys (and a few gals) with names like Churchill, Smith, Evans, Wallace, Rabeno, Welch, Swartley, Gold, George, Tomlin and many, many others. A few of our current crop of American engravers received some of their training from German engravers, but most are essentially self-taught.

The Germans have long had a formal apprenticeship program for skill training in just about every trade, including engraving. We Americans have not. Current American engravers that learned at least a part of their skills from German Masters were Bob Swartley and Winston Churchill who worked under Josef Fugger; Terry

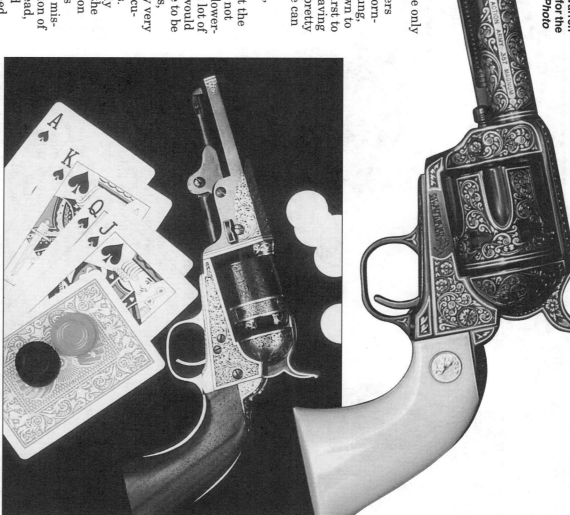

A Colt Black Powder Model from the shop of Sam Welch. Engraved in the style of some of the older Colt presentation pieces, it is exquisite. *Photo courtesy of Sam Welch*

Theis studied under Erich Boessler; Ray Viramontez labored under the tutelage of Werner Schuck. There are probably others as well.

Naturally, most engravers spend the preponderance of their bench time working on firearms although a few specialize in embellishing custom-made knives and adorn almost nothing else. The majority, however, will perform their artistry on practically any "canvas", but most work primarily on guns. There are also two or three engravers I can quickly think of that seem to do far more handguns than other types of firearms, but again, the vast majority decorate all types.

As far as I know, there has been no poll taken among our engravers to determine which type of firearms, if any, receives the most attention. Judging from what I see at various exhibitions, including the combined American Custom Gunmakers Guild - Firearms Engravers Guild of America annual exhibition, I can't tell that any particular type receives significantly more consideration than any other. One sees engraved rifles, shotguns and handguns in almost equal numbers. At least, that appears to me to be the situation.

Clearly, though, the handgun receives plenty of the engraver's attention. One of the most beauti-

ENGRAVED GUNS

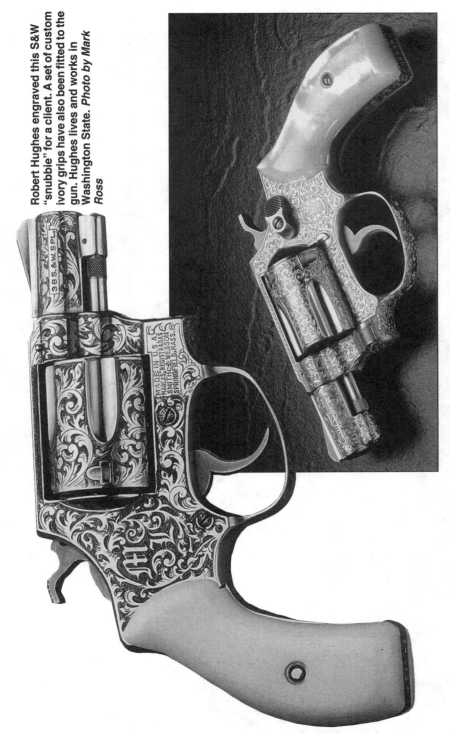

Robert Hughes engraved this S&W "snubbie" for a client. A set of custom ivory grips have also been fitted to the gun. Hughes lives and works in Washington State. *Photo by Mark Ross*

The Georgia shop of Ralph Ingle turned out this beautiful Smith & Wesson "Chief" model, pearl grips and all. Ralph does a lot of handgun engraving for his clients. *Photo courtesy of Ralph Ingle*

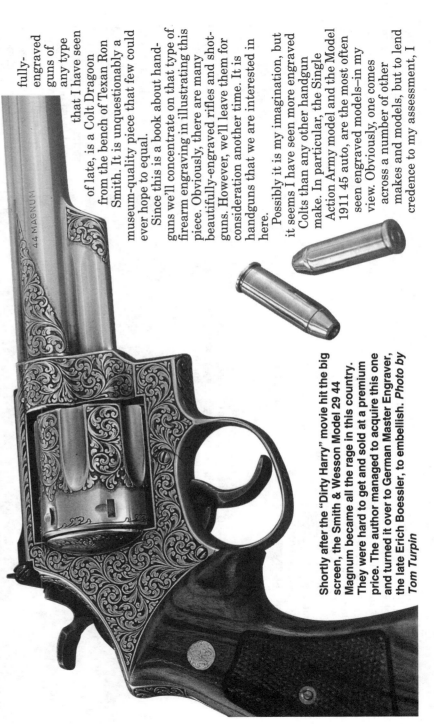

Shortly after the "Dirty Harry" movie hit the big screen, the Smith & Wesson Model 29 44 Magnum became all the rage in this country. They were hard to get and sold at a premium price. The author managed to acquire this one and turned it over to German Master Engraver, the late Erich Boessler, to embellish. *Photo by Tom Turpin*

fully-engraved guns of any type that I have seen of late, is a Colt Dragoon from the bench of Texan Ron Smith. It is unquestionably a museum-quality piece that few could ever hope to equal.

Since this is a book about hand-guns we'll concentrate on that type of firearm engraving in illustrating this piece. Obviously, there are many beautifully-engraved rifles and shot-guns. However, we'll leave them for consideration another time. It is handguns that we are interested in here.

Possibly it is my imagination, but it seems I have seen more engraved Colts than any other handgun make. In particular, the Single Action Army model and the Model 1911 45 auto, are the most often seen engraved models—in my view. Obviously, one comes across a number of other makes and models, but to lend credence to my assessment, I

ENGRAVED GUNS

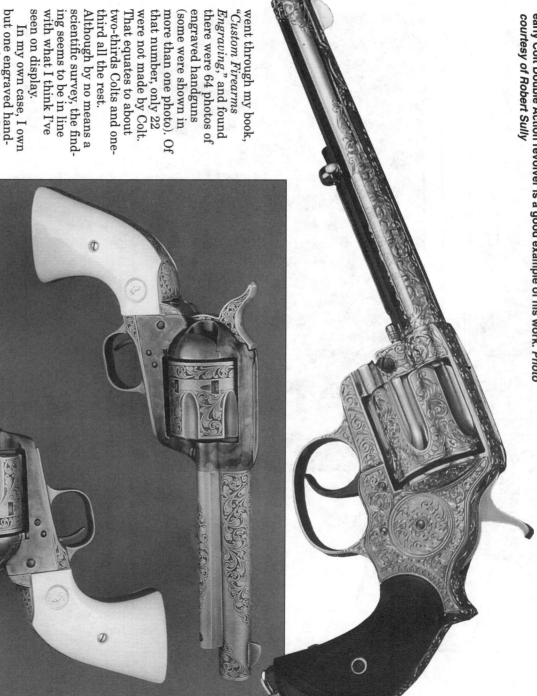

Robert Sully prefers to execute period-style engraving patterns on Western-style firearms from his Albuquerque, New Mexico shop. This early Colt Double Action revolver is a good example of his work. *Photo courtesy of Robert Sully*

went through my book, *"Custom Firearms Engraving,"* and found there were 64 photos of engraved handguns (some were shown in more than one photo). Of that number, only 22 were not made by Colt. That equates to about two-thirds Colts and one-third all the rest. Although by no means a scientific survey, the finding seems to be in line with what I think I've seen on display.

In my own case, I own but one engraved handgun and it is not a Colt. Rather, it is a Smith & Wesson Model 39 that my late engraver friend Erich Boessler engraved for me many years ago. It features full coverage engraving in an oak leaf pattern, but is not a test of the artistic abilities of the late *Herr Boessler*. I couldn't afford that degree of engraving as my budget simply wouldn't permit it. Nevertheless, it is a very nice handgun.

I have only owned one other engraved handgun - also a Smith & Wesson. It was a Model 29 .44 Magnum and was likewise worked on by *Herr Boessler's* hammer and graver. Since I've never been much of a pistolero—concentrating much more on rifles and shotguns—those two 'Smiths were my only embellished

handguns. The big .44 I traded to a close friend years ago.

Getting back to the question of what type of firearm is most often engraved, I have given my opinion. Having said that, however, it would seem the handgun should be the most commonly-decorated arms type, and for two reasons. First, I believe there are more handguns in circulation than there are rifles and shotguns.

While serving a tour of duty with the US Air Force in Germany, Ray Viramontez arranged to study engraving under the guidance of Master Engraver, Werner Schuck. He engraved part-time until his retirement from the service and has been at it full-time since. This pair of Colt Single-Action revolvers was done in his shop. *Photo courtesy of Ray Viramontez.*

For that reason alone, if the presumption is true, one would think there would be more handguns sent off for adornment.

In addition, although there are many that have love affairs with their shotguns and rifles, I believe a handgun is, for most, a more personal gun. It is, after all, the most common type of firearm relied upon for personal defense. To trust one's life to a

The oak leaf engraving pattern, as well as the scrimshaw artistry on the custom grips, were both executed by the late German Master, Erich Boessler. *Photo by Tom Turpin*

Three examples of the handgun engraving of Georgian Ralph Ingle. I'm not sure that Ralph specializes in handgun engraving but most of his work that I've seen was executed on them. *Photos courtesy of Ralph Ingle*

▶ This S&W Model 66 features an unusual relief-sculpted oak leaf and acorn pattern. This work is very Germanic in both design and execution. A beautiful piece of work, it come from the Georgia shop of Ralph Ingle. *Photo courtesy of Ralph Ingle*

▲ A custom single-action handgun and the engraving are both the work of Daniel Love. His firearms design work leaves him a very limited amount of time to devote to his very fine engraving, therefore he accepts only a limited number of engraving projects each year. *Photo by Alan Richmond*

▲ John Barraclough was once a jockey, highly skilled interior designer–and still is an avocado farmer–in addition to his wonderful engraving talents. Not only does John execute exquisite engraving, he also teaches engraving in several programs around the country. This beautifully engraved and gold-inlaid Colt Government Model is a wonderful example of his artistry. *Photo by Alan Richmond*

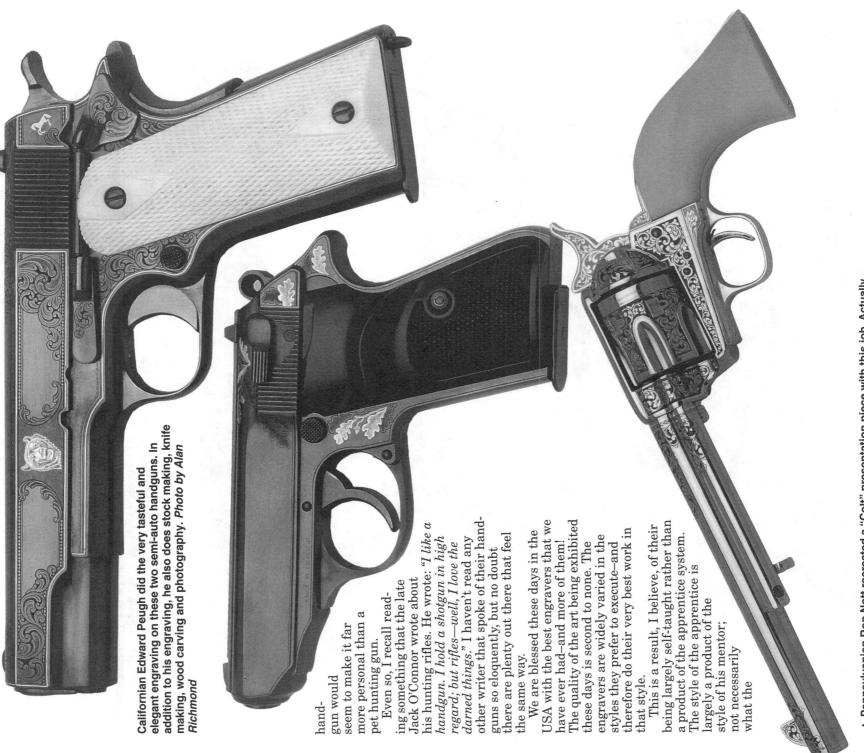

Californian Edward Peugh did the very tasteful and elegant engraving on these two semi-auto handguns. In addition to his engraving, he also does stock making, knife making, wood carving and photography. *Photo by Alan Richmond*

hand-gun would seem to make it far more personal than a pet hunting gun.

Even so, I recall reading something that the late Jack O'Connor wrote about his hunting rifles. He wrote: *"I like a handgun. I hold a shotgun in high regard; but rifles—well, I love the darned things."* I haven't read any other writer that spoke of their handguns so eloquently, but no doubt there are plenty out there that feel the same way.

We are blessed these days in the USA with the best engravers that we have ever had—and more of them! The quality of the art being exhibited these days is second to none. The engravers are widely varied in the styles they prefer to execute—and therefore do their very best work in that style.

This is a result, I believe, of their being largely self-taught rather than a product of the apprentice system. The style of the apprentice is largely a product of the style of his mentor; not necessarily what the

▲ Pennsylvanian Ron Nott recreated a "Colt" presentation piece with this job. Actually, the single-action revolver is an Italian-made reproduction of the original Colt model. The custom ivory grips and gold-plated hammer, grip straps and ejector components completed the job. *Photo by Alan Richmond*

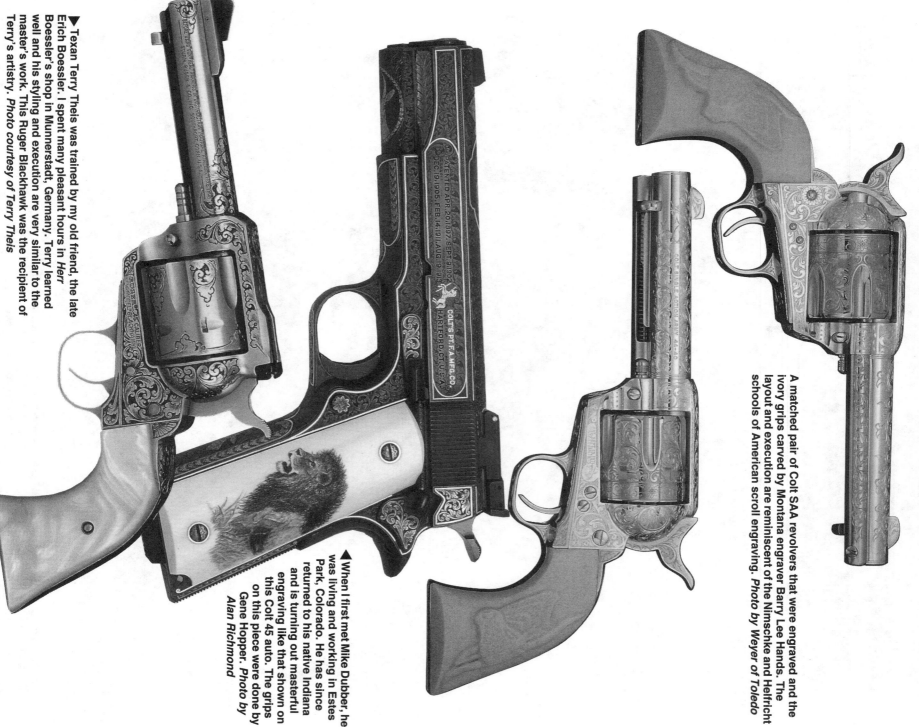

▶ Texan Terry Theis was trained by my old friend, the late Erich Boessler. I spent many pleasant hours in *Herr* Boessler's shop in Munnerstadt, Germany. Terry learned well and his styling and execution are very similar to the master's work. This Ruger Blackhawk was the recipient of Terry's artistry. *Photo courtesy of Terry Theis*

▶ When I first met Mike Dubber, he was living and working in Estes Park, Colorado. He has since returned to his native Indiana and is turning out masterful engraving like that shown on this Colt 45 auto. The grips on this piece were done by Gene Hopper. *Photo by Alan Richmond*

A matched pair of Colt SAA revolvers that were engraved and the ivory grips carved by Montana engraver Barry Lee Hands. The layout and execution are reminiscent of the Nimschke and Helfricht schools of American scroll engraving. *Photo by Weyer of Toledo*

Richard Boucher has done engraving work for five presidents, Eisenhower, Kennedy, Johnson, Regan and Bush. His adornment of this Chris Dahl custom knife and Colt SAA are good examples of his superlative work. *Photo by Mustafa Bilal*

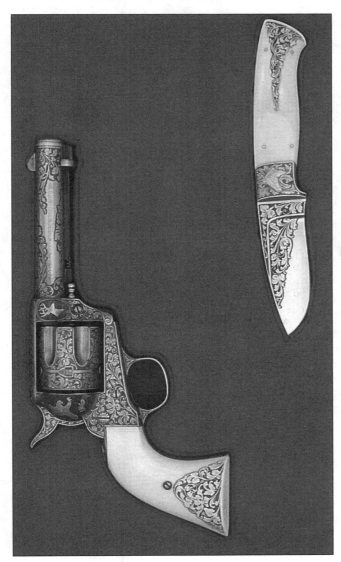

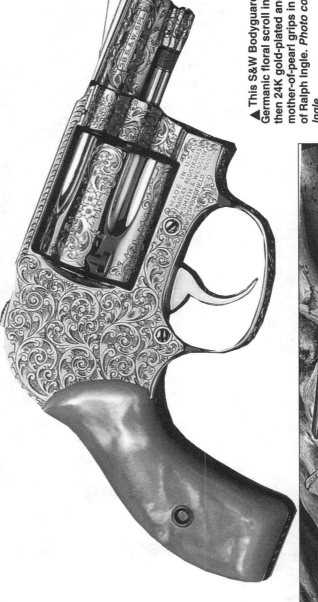

▲ This S&W Bodyguard was engraved in Germanic floral scroll in high-relief and then 24K gold-plated and fitted with mother-of-pearl grips in the Georgia shop of Ralph Ingle. *Photo courtesy of Ralph Ingle*

apprentice prefers. That is not all bad but it does sometimes stifle creativity.

Because we have many fine engravers in this country these days, it is not difficult to find one whose styling preference matches the client's taste. That is the best of both worlds.

If you have a yen for some decoration on your favorite handgun, or any other gun for that matter, I suggest the best place to start researching engravers is the Firearms Engravers Guild of America. Not all of America's fine engravers are members–but most are. It is a good starting point.

•

Hoosier engraver Mike Dubber did the wonderful engraving on this Colt SAA and the grips were executed by Gene Hopper. The combination of the two make this one beautiful handgun. *Photo by Milt Borchert.*

CUSTOM GUNS

There's more to this game than simply calling a gunsmith and ordering a 'No. 3 Deluxe'. You could get onions and fries...or just a lemon.

So, you want a custom pistol, eh?

by Dave Workman

PERSONAL HANDGUNS ARE like tailor-made suits. One size does not fit all, and what appeals to one shooter may cause the next guy nothing but heartburn. Whether your tastes run to single- or double-action revolvers, black plastic guns or cold blue steel, sooner or later the desire to own a personalized piece is going to grow like a hunger for the perfect steak.

When that urge becomes so strong that you stop dreaming and start shopping, there are several considerations to ponder beyond the price tag. Indeed, price may be your least concern.

Not long ago, I decided to add a custom-built pistol to my arsenal. My criteria were straightforward: It would be a semi-auto "working gun" as opposed to a glass-case collector's piece, yet appealing to the eye. It must be chambered in a serious caliber, built on a full-sized frame, yet be con-

cealable, and fit my hand comfortably. Above all, it needed to be reliable.

Sound like a spruced-up Model 1911 in 45 ACP to you? Me, too.

There are lots of great M1911s on the market, from some of the top names in the business. As I started shopping and imagining what this gun would be in its final form, I read reviews, and quietly searched out pistols such as those from Les Baer, Nowlin, Clark Custom, Wilson Combat and the Springfield Custom Shop.

An incredibly fortunate coincidence in timing led me, however, just down the road from my home to the workbench of Richard Niemer, one-time guru at Detonics and now residing at Olympic Arms and its subsidiary, Schuetzen Pistol Works. Olympic has been producing handguns on a modified 1911 design for some time, and I had only the year before tested that firm's Carrier

model—also a Niemer production—for the *Handguns 2000* annual.

So, I knew this outfit, and this gunsmith, were capable of turning out an exceptionally accurate pistol. What I did not know, but would soon learn, is that Niemer is a maestro of the 1911, and that my request would have an uncanny resemblance to a gun that he had been considering for production for several years, and help set the stage for creation of Olympic's custom shop.

What began, then, as a simple e-mail to Olympic asking for a price estimate on a pistol would be the catalyst for Olympic proprietor Bob Schuetz to "turn Niemer loose" on his pet project, the "Street Deuce" full-frame model, and its Commander-sized little brother, the "Journeyman." Indeed, fallout from this single project helped solidify startup of the Schuetzen Pistol Works Specialty Shop, with Niemer in command.

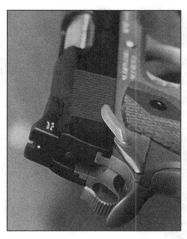

Workman's Street Deuce shown with bull barrel installed; match barrel, bushing and recoil spring assembly.

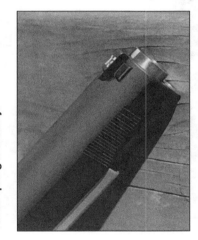

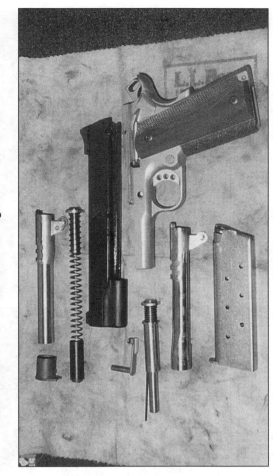

Deuce wears front and rear Heinie dovetailed sights with tritium inserts.

Stripped for cleaning, the custom Street Deuce takes down like any typical 1911. Author was impressed with fit, finish and functionality.

Purchasing a custom-built gun is like buying a car, with your favorite options. To his credit, when interviewed for this article, Niemer strongly recommended that gun buyers sit down, list the features they want on their personalized handguns, and call for bids from several gunsmiths and custom shops.

Most of these outfits have one or more "stock/custom" guns, such as Baer's Thunder Ranch Special or Springfield's "Professional" model based on that company's pistol for the FBI SWAT teams. But custom gun builders can modify their "basic" models to suit individual clients. Quite frankly, all it takes is money.

Niemer's "basic" Street Deuce is a two-tone (stainless frame, black Parkerized slide) pistol with a Videki trigger, raised front strap, flat or arched Smith & Alexander mainspring housing with 20 *lpi* checkering (mine is flat), high-ride grip safety, checkered magazine release button, lowered and flared ejection port, extended thumb safety, GI slide stop and double-diamond checkered grips. The buyer has a choice of either an LPA adjustable rear sight with white dot front, or Heinie Slant Pro fixed sight.

What will likely become known as the "Workman package" substitutes Heinie Slant Pro Straight 8 tritium sights, dovetailed front and rear, and includes front slide serrations, ambidextrous thumb safety and two barrel assemblies (all of these are extras to the basic model). My package includes a match-grade stainless steel barrel with fitted bushing and plunger-type recoil spring setup, plus a bushingless bull barrel and full-length recoil spring guide rod, both with 18.5-pound recoil springs.

My pistol was supplied with three seven-round Metalform magazines. These are Niemer's favorites, though I happen to prefer Chip McCormick Shooting Star eight-rounders. I've got a good supply of those, and they function just fine in the Street Deuce.

Looks good, functions great

A lot of people can make good-looking handguns on the 1911 design. It happens to be the most customized pistol model on the planet. But just because a handgun looks snazzy, doesn't mean it will work reliably.

The acid test for any sidearm upon which lives may one day depend is that it functions on demand, even though 99 percent of such "street guns" will never be fired in life-or-death situations.

I've had the occasion to sample a few 1911 pistols over the years, including a

Business end of Street Deuce shown with match barrel and standard bushing installed.

Street Deuce from Olympic Arms' Schuetzen Pistol Works custom shop digests every type of personal defense ammo author selected for test.

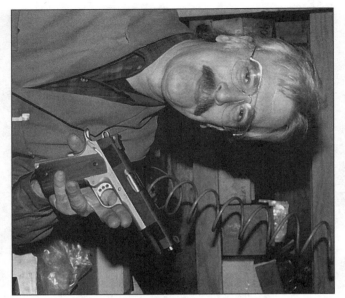

Custom gunsmith Richard Niemer and finished Street Deuce. "It's my gun," he told Workman. "I'm just letting you use it."

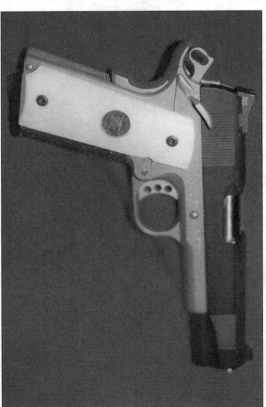

Workman, an NRA-certified instructor, had Mike Prater at Prater & Co. of Flintstone, Ga. mold a set of ivory polymer grips with an NRA instructor's pin inset in right grip.

couple of so-called "custom" numbers. Some were sloppy, rattled horribly and didn't shoot worth a darn. One or two were built with such a tight rail-to-rail fit that they required a rather stout pull to get the slide to cycle—and in my humble opinion, that's too tight. A grain of sand might lock the thing up and, in an emergency, no self-defense pistol should make its user struggle to cycle the action.

Niemer's Street Deuce does not sacrifice accuracy for ease of function. To the contrary, it cycles smoothly, yet consistently shoots to point of aim at 25 yards. To my delight, during a couple of extended range sessions, the "Deuce/Workman" digested every type of .45 ammunition I fed it, from 230-grain ball to 185-grain Speer Gold Dot with its wide hollowpoint mouth.

My selection of test ammunition included Winchester SXTs and Silvertips, Remington Golden Sabres, Black Hills with Gold Dot bullets, Federal Hydra Shoks and Hi Shoks, and Normas, with bullet weights in all three common offerings: 230, 200 and 185 grain. I even ran through a few magazines stoked with my pet handloads that press a 185-grain Speer Gold Dot over 7.2 grains of Hodgdon HP-38, and the 185-grain Nosler JHP over 5.5 grains of Hodgdon Titegroup.

I'm still waiting for the pistol to jam. So far, it has functioned without flaw. And it has fired some incredibly tight groups from a sandbag rest, as evidenced by the accompanying photos.

Once you've selected a gunsmith, discuss the project with him at length. Hey, it's your nickel. Lots of 'em, in fact! You'll find that a good 'smith wants his clients to be absolutely satisfied, and may offer suggestions—not to make his job easier—but to make sure the customer is happy with the finished project.

For example, when I first spoke with Niemer about the slide finish, I requested one of the slick new coatings that have been publicized of late

CUSTOM GUNS

Specifications:

Olympic Arms
Street Deuce

Action:	Single-action semi-automatic
Caliber:	45 ACP
Finish:	Black Parkerized slide, bead-blasted stainless frame
Barrel:	5 inches
Capacity:	7 + 1
Sights:	Heinie fixed, with tritium inserts
Weight:	40 ounces
Height:	5.5 inches
Length:	9 inches
Price:	P.O.R.

Street Deuce...on the range

Ammo Brand	Bullet type & wt.	Distance: 10yds Velocity (fps)	Group (in.)
Remington	185 gr. Golden Sabre	1,021	2.75"
Federal	230 gr. FMJ (ball)	839.7	3.75"
Winchester	185 gr. Silvertip	964.5	3.75"
CCI Blazer	200 gr. Speer Gold Dot	919.8	5.0"
Federal	185 gr. Hi- Shok	935.2	4.0"
Black Hills	230 gr. Gold Dot	815.7	1.5"

From 25 yards, two-hand hold, Street Deuce delivered these groups with alternate barrels installed. Somebody asked Workman how well this pistol performed. He was kidding, right? (Check the serial number 'DPW 0001'...author's personalized number. There's a 0002 waiting for you.)

Workman knocked together this D&D Gunleather IWB holster for his new Street Deuce.

Author Workman function-fired his Street Deuce from a sandbag rest....

performed. Now the sear releases crisply at exactly 4.5 pounds.

When you order a pistol from the 'smith of your choice, be sure to specify how light or heavy your trigger should be. I didn't, and the result was a trek back to the gunsmith that would not have been necessary, had I spoken sooner.

So, uh, just what should someone expect to spend on a custom-built sidearm like the Street Deuce? You will part with something in the neighborhood of $1,300 to $1,600 for the "basic level" gun from any good gunsmith operation, and that's reasonable. You are, after all, paying for some very talented work, and a good gunsmith is worth every penny. Want options? Reach for your wallet.

You can purchase a "stock" Nowlin, Les Baer, Wilson, Clark–or Schuetzen's Street Deuce–and you will own a very fine pistol. But when you go custom, you go for something special, something personal, something you believe could save your life. You decide what that's worth.

•

in the gun press. To my eventual satisfaction, the gunsmith talked me out of that, noting that it adds to the cost of the gun, and arguing at the same time that the Parkerized finish wears longer. True enough. I've run this gun in and out of a brand new IWB holster I whipped up, and I have yet to notice any holster wear. And against the bead-blasted stainless steel finish on the frame, that slide looks sharp.

I had initially specified a different brand of night sight, one that gets lots of ink, because of its three-dot

configuration. Niemer counseled me to try the two-dot Heinie, with tritium inserts made by Trijicon. It takes a bit of getting used to, but my final analysis of this suggestion is that Richard was right for what I intend to do with this gun.

My early testing found the Deuce's trigger to be a very light 3-pounds, with a crisp let-off. As it happens, I don't like that light a trigger for a street gun, so back went the pistol to Niemer's bench, where some stoning and spring adjustment was quickly

SELF DEFENSE/CONCEALED CARRY

A Combat Magnum with Ajax stag grips; it doesn't get any better than this!

The Revolver's Last Hurrah?

I Don't Think So!

by Bob Campbell

A LOOK AROUND the gun club shows interest in the revolver at an all-time low. Autos are the "*in*" gun. Revolvers are perceived as old-fashioned, inefficient and slow to reload. They also lack "*firepower*."

Personally, I associate the term "*firepower*" with the capabilities of an infantry squad, but this is not the majority interpretation.

The police establishment's move to autoloaders has diminished interest in shooting revolvers. Those new to shooting look at the cop's holster, see a black gun and wish to purchase a reasonable facsimile for their own use. In doing so, they miss the charm and character that is the essence of a revolver.

Technically, many criticisms of the revolver are true. A good autopistol is

a fine handgun, truly superior for most of what we term combat. But everyone should be familiar with the revolver and its mode of operation. For many shooters the revolver is the best choice, as a bit of familiarization will show. The revolver is not just for a novice. A number of very experienced individuals favor the revolver for good reason. A well-schooled individual is

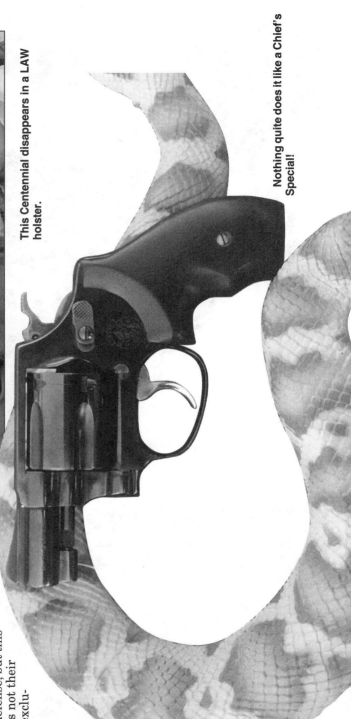

▲ An expanded 38-caliber FBI load.

This Centennial disappears in a LAW holster.

Nothing quite does it like a Chief's Special!

capable of defending himself against most threats—short of a gang attack or riot—with a revolver. One wonders if any handgun is adequate defense against such threats!

Shooting the revolver well is one thing, adroitly handling it, another. The most glaring shortcoming of the revolver is reloading time. At least one trainer has suggested swing-out cylinder double-action revolvers are "*practically disassembled*" as they are reloaded. The swing-out cylinder revolver is, in fact, easily manipulated and shows us immediately whether the revolver is loaded.

We are venturing into a realm where "*technical*" and "*tactical*" clash. Perhaps "*practical*" should be included as well. Ammunition capacity, as it relates to reloading, must be kept in perspective. Most actions are decided in the first three rounds fired. If you haven't stopped your adversary or found cover during these first few rounds, your battle is probably over. If it can't be done with six rounds, how could it be done with ten—or fourteen? At this point it might be useful to list both the strong and weak points of the revolver and the autopistol.

The revolver might be a second choice in some situations but it is a formidable fighting tool just the same. The autopistol has advantages—but so does the revolver. Some advantages are more "*technical*" than "*tactical*." The use the gun will be put to is most important. Handguns were designed for defense, but this is not their exclu-

SELF-DEFENSE/CONCEALED CARRY

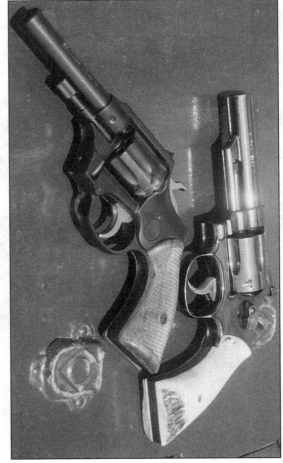

Two favorites, the Combat Magnum and the High Standard Sentinel.

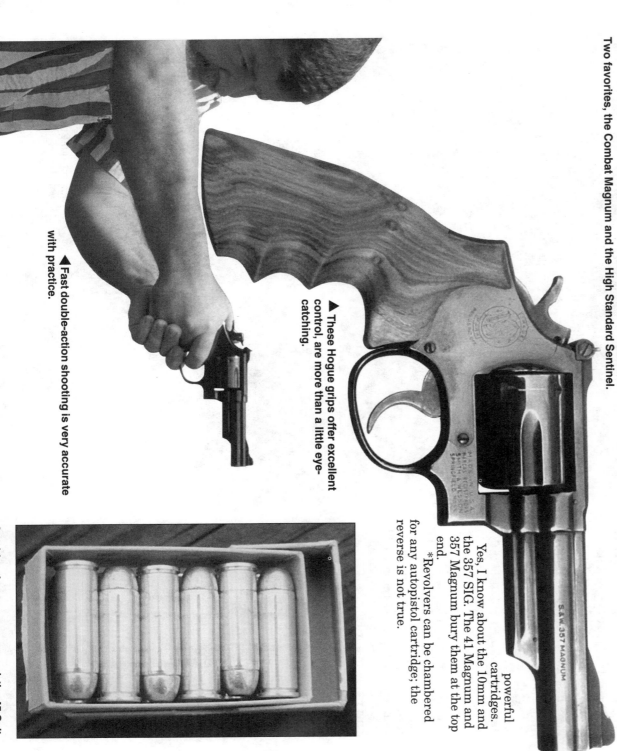

▲ These Hogue grips offer excellent control, are more than a little eye-catching.

▲ Fast double-action shooting is very accurate with practice.

An old and very proven round, the 45 Colt.

sive province. Revolvers are well-suited to short-range hunting and pest control. The revolver is superior, for the most part, for field use.

*Revolvers can be left at ready, fully loaded, in a dry condition (*unlubricated*) for an infinite period of time–and come up shooting!

*The revolver is simple to manipulate.

*Revolvers are not as sensitive to ammunition quality as autopistols. I don't like substandard ammunition of any type, but the revolver is more forgiving of bad crimps, long or short bullet seating.

*Revolvers may use a wider range of ammunition, from wax bullets and shotshells to very heavy, blunt bullet loads.

*Revolvers chamber more powerful cartridges.

Yes, I know about the 10mm and the 357 SIG. The 41 Magnum and 357 Magnum bury them at the top end.

*Revolvers can be chambered for any autopistol cartridge; the reverse is not true.

*Revolvers are usually more accurate than comparable autopistols.

The following two advantages are considered critical by those who prefer the revolver as a defensive handgun:

*The revolver offers more than a second-strike capability. The revolver does not strike the same cartridge twice, but moves a new round into position. My research indicates very few dud rounds will fire when stuck a second time; finding two duds in a row is extremely rare.

*At contact range, a revolver can be placed against an adversary's body and fired repeatedly. This is not true of *any* autopistol. Many who carry the autopistol as a service gun carry a revolver backup, for this reason.

The auto has it's advantages as well, which include:

  * A larger ammunition reserve.
  * Faster reloading time.
  * A low bore axis, which results in less muzzle *flip*.

*Autos are flatter, easier to conceal than a revolver.

* The autopistol uses relatively smaller charges of fast-burning powder to deliver

▼ **Smith and Wesson's proven and desirable Centennial.**

about the same power as comparable revolvers, while producing less recoil.

Combined with the auto's reciprocating action and the ability of some pistol frames to absorb recoil, the autopistol always kicks less with loads of comparable power—even if the auto is somewhat lighter than the revolver it is being compared to.

Some folks naturally fire one type of handgun better. But a number of authorities note the autopistol delivers a *higher hit probability* under stress than does a revolver. I agreed—until I read the Police

▼ **Smith and Wesson's geometrically-designed, hidden-hammer Centennial.**

▲ **Smith and Wesson's old Long Action–very smooth with a bit of practice.**

Making a good thing better—

▲ A very hi-tech DAO Ruger Magnum with Hogue grips, stainless construction and 'keeper' recoil-reducer system.

handgunners pack a autopistol all day—but rely upon a revolver to defend their *castle*. I am one of these. Any number of trainers have combated *spray and pray* tactics with compelling students to download their autopistol to only six rounds. What occurs afterwards is interesting. Concentrating upon reality-based scenarios with a finite amount of ammunition, the shoot-

ers bear down on their target and concentrate upon marksmanship. Problems are solved with a few rounds. I realize a reserve of ammunition is desirable, and that many adversaries require multiple hits before they are stopped by handgun calibers. But marksmanship and a solid first shot hit count for the most.

▼ A modified cylinder latch that will not bust the thumb in recoil, courtesy of the Action Works.

▲ Night sight insert, by the Action Works.

It isn't just autopistols when it comes to appropriate subjects for custom work. Custom gunsmiths can carefully smooth the trigger action of a revolver to the point where the gun is much easier for a trained hand to use well. Unlike single-action autopistols, the revolver's *pull* will never be so light as to invite clutching. I am told 9.75 pounds *pull* is the lower limit at which reliable ignition can be maintained. A ten-pound revolver action is very nice.

Other touches include *breaking* sharp and offending edges by chamfering the cylinder, including the

chambers themselves, for easy loading. This makes the gun easier to use in everyday shooting. A very nice addition to any revolver is hand-filling, well-designed stocks. Factory grips are just OK for the most part; some are all wrong. Hogue, Blu Magnum and Eagle grips will change handle geometry to something more usable.

Another modification, performed by the Action Works, is drilling the front sight and inserting a small tritium night sight. This makes the wheelgun a 24-hour protection handgun. Revolvers high tech? You bet.

Marksman's Association Study. When switching to the auto, a number of agencies experienced a drop in *hit probability* or *hits per shots fired*. According to the PMA, the 38 Special revolver and the harder-kicking 357 Magnum revolver had higher percentages of hits per rounds fired than any autopistol. It is not easy to isolate such results but the revolver seems to have a *first shot hit probability* at least equal to that of the autopistol. As a rule, 9mm-armed cops expended four times as many rounds per hit as revolver-armed

shooters. So much for the hard-kicking revolver!

The conclusion drawn from the PMA study is that skill and training are better predictors of survival than is the weapon type.

What does this mean to the armed civilian? It means the revolver is not an also-ran, but a viable defense handgun. There are many shooters who perform well with a revolver. For home defense, the revolver makes a lot of sense. More than a few savvy

SELF-DEFENSE/CONCEALED CARRY

With proper indoctrination, the long, but smooth double-action trigger of a revolver can reduce the incidence of *pulled* or *jerked* shots. It forces shooters to concentrate upon marksmanship, but does not overly challenge them. *Pulled* or *clutched* shots are less likely.

For this reason, the revolver has been most successful in certain forms of competition. Bowling pin

Ruger duty gun in flawless Wm. Davis duty holster.

shoots are one of these forms. The long, rolling trigger action of a revolver seems well-suited to the task of knocking five or six bowling pins off the table within a finite time period.

My handguns are not specialized self-defense tools, but all-around shooting and working implements. They serve for small game hunting, back-up hunting rifles, keep predators off the farm and serve as recreational shooters. The revolver is often my best bet. A four-inch Combat Magnum is a great all-around handgun. It will take small to medium game at appropriate ranges, with proper load selection. There is no more proven combination for municipal police or self-defense use; no better handgun, ounce-for-ounce.

For a slightly heavier handgun, the model 1917 45 Auto Rim revolver is an unbeatable package. This revolver combines a top-rated defense cartridge with the most efficient revolver reloading system of all time...full-moon ammunition clips. Full-moon reloading clips beat any speedloader. The gun may be reloaded from any angle, and there is no danger of *a case rim under the ejector star*-malfunction. This goes a long way to combat one drawback of the revolver–that being it does not unload itself. Manually-operated bolt

Combat Magnum in Don Hume 'Inside the Pants' holster, a good choice for deep concealment.

and is more controllable in rapid fire. At longer ranges the revolver comes into its own, however.

I am not preaching a return to the revolver, but pointing out the revolver is far from a dead shooting system. It is a viable–sometimes even the best–choice for novice and experienced shooter alike. For an outdoorsman it is the best choice.

Take a hard look at the wheel gun. You can't go wrong.

and pump-action long guns unload themselves, requiring only that they be reloaded after firing each round. The manually-operated revolver requires less manipulation...but must be unloaded before reloading, a drawback unique to the revolver, single-shot and double-barrel sporting long guns.

Automatic ejectors have been tried on break-top revolvers, but the 1917's system is more efficient. I like the 1917 and it's 'moon clips very much. When confronting the choice between a revolver or autopistol, it is good to refine the choice by taking a hard look at the use the gun will be put to. The revolver often comes out ahead.

If the use will be self-defense, a short-range firing program on the local range will answer many questions. You will find the revolver is accurate and easy to use quickly, as are most autos. However, the autopistol offers an instant following shot

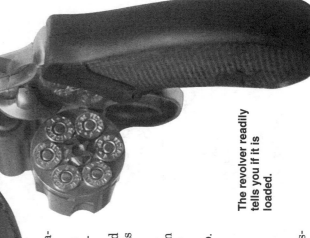

The revolver readily tells you if it is loaded.

THE GLOCK LONGSLIDES:
High Performance "Sleepers!"

by Chuck Taylor

I'T'S CERTAINLY NO secret to anyone that over the last twelve years, Glock pistols have taken the shooting world by storm. With the 9mm Model 17 appearing in the mid-1980s, and the compact Model 19 9mm shortly thereafter, it quickly became plain the Glock had arrived.

Then, only a few years later, Glock stunned the firearms community by producing and successfully marketing the Models 22 and compact M23, both chambered for the then-new 40 S&W cartridge. In fact, both guns appeared nearly a year before Smith & Wesson could produce and market

their own 40-caliber offerings, a true coup in every sense of the word. Clearly, Glocks were here to stay.

Then came the 10mm M20 and 45 ACP M21, both featuring a larger frame than their early counterparts and, in the summer of 1995, the sub-compact M26 9mm and 40 Auto M27. These captured both the heart and mind of the combat shooter because they reflected a cognizance by Glock of their needs. And, needless to say, they've been red-hot sellers ever since.

As if this weren't enough, Glock did it again in March, 1997, by introducing the long-awaited compact Model

With their enhanced balance, long sight radius, higher muzzle velocities and excellent accuracy, the Glock M17L and M24 are a great choice for both SpecOps use and hunting.

SELF-DEFENSE/CONCEALED CARRY

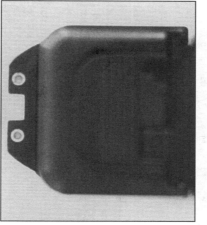

Both M17L 9mm and M24 40 Auto come from the box with low-profile plastic sights adjustable for both windage and elevation. Rear sight (shown) features a white-outlined rear notch, while the front sight utilizes a white dot. Taylor feels they're a bit fragile for serious tactical or hunting use and so, for best performance, should be replaced with steel Trijicon sights with tritium 3-dot horizontal pattern.

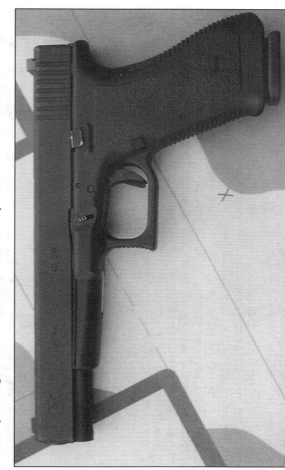

Left side view of Glock M24 40 Auto. This weapon and its 9mm counterpart, the M17L, are seeing increased use by SWAT and other SpecOps units throughout the world.

29 10mm and M30 in 45 ACP. Writers nearly fought to get a glimpse and perhaps actually get their hands on the Model 30 in particular, for it represented a pocket-pistol in a potent caliber that could truly be called a counterpart to Colt's highly successful Officer's Model.

Throughout all of the period 1987-97, Glock continuously stayed ahead of the competition by configuring their pistols in such a way as to answer the various tactical needs of the self-defense shooter, whether he be a police officer, civilian or military man. And, as well, the compact and sub-compact Glocks in both 9mm and 40 Auto quickly found much favor with the ladies, too, with many of them finding their way into fanny packs and purses carried on a daily basis.

But while all this was going on, Glock also introduced two other pistols—the Model 17L (for longslide) in 9mm and M24 40 Auto. The M17L appeared within just a few months of the original Model 17/19 9mms, but saw only cursory attention. Too, when the now-famous 40 Auto Models 22 and 23 appeared, so did the Model 24, a longslide version in that caliber.

Strangely, the shooting public considered both of these guns to be "target" pistols, a label that I, too, placed on them until a few years ago when I realized that there was hardly a need to a target pistol chambered in 40 auto. The 9mm, perhaps; but in 40 auto? No way!

Then it occurred to me that both longslides are nearly ideal special operations and hunting handguns. As they come from the box, both have:

1. A 3.5 lb. connector, providing an excellent trigger pull.

2. A 1.53-inch longer barrel than the standard M17 or M22, thus producing higher muzzle velocities and enhancing the potential for frangible bullet expansion.

3. A 1.58-inch longer slide, thus moving the point of balance forward, assisting in muzzle flip control during fast shooting sequences.

4. An optional vented muzzle-brake, to further enhance control, even though muzzle flash patterns were altered and channeled upwards, rather than expanding outward from the muzzle during firing. For hunting

and other recreational uses, the muzzle brake was therefore a useful addition, but for tactical shooting it could, depending upon the ammunition used, be a liability due to the loss of low-light vision.

Since all Glocks are also virtually sharp edge-free as they come from the box, I realized that the longslides possessed nearly every attribute required of a superior special operations pistol and began to pay closer attention to them in my training endeavors around the world.

I didn't have to wait long, for almost immediately I encountered the 9mm M17L in use by one of Europe's most famous—and efficient—law-enforcement special teams. Known as RAID, the French National Police special team captured the hearts of the American public only a few years ago by successfully neutralizing a dynamite-wrapped madman who was holding nearly two-dozen Paris elementary school children hostage.

Even though he was literally clad in explosives and had planted additional charges strategically around the room and hooked them all into a central detonator which he held in his hand, a M17L-armed RAID entry team was able to execute a dynamic entry into the room and neutralize him with three 147-gr. Federal Hydra-Shoks to the head before he could trigger the explosives.

I'm proud to say that less than two months earlier, "the shooter" and most of the members of that team had been students of mine in a special training session here in the USA. And strangely enough, we had used a similar scenario during that training visit. I must also say that I have never met more professional and courageous men than they.

After that, I encountered more and more M17Ls in Europe and, within the following year, a number of M24 40 Auto longslides were in use by several teams here in the U.S. In fact, I began to see enough of them that I procured both a M17L and M24 for my own use and began to evaluate them in comparison with standard-sized Glocks and a few other so-called "special ops" pistols.

During the course of the evaluation, I decided to carry the M24, loaded with 155-gr. Hornady XTP JHPs, on a hunting trip during which I was able to drop a mule deer buck at 75 meters with a single shot. This attests to the accuracy capabilities of the M24 and, thinking back, I can recall how handy its 8.03-inch sight radius was as I went kneeling and took the shot. As the buck hit the ground, my companion,

Author's preferred hunting 40 Auto load – Hornady's factory 155-grain XTP JHP. Accurate, dependable and exhibiting good expansion, he's used to efficiently take all manner of small and medium game.

The largest of the Glock series, the Longslide (upper right) represents the apotheosis of the tactical or hunting self-loader, producing superb accuracy and good recoil control, even with heavier loads.

who was armed with a rifle as my backup, was perhaps more surprised than I and remarked, "Wow, that thing really puts 'em where you aim 'em!" Yeah...it sure does!

The extra length and weight of the longslide causes it to be a bit slower from a holster, but it should be remembered that special ops guns aren't presented in the traditional manner. Instead, they're brought to and deployed (presented) from a Ready Position, thus negating any slowness from a holster in the traditional sense. Presented in this manner, the fact that their point of balance is somewhat forward of center and their longer sight radius make them superior in fast controlled pairs (2 shots) on single adversaries or in high-speed multiple target (1 shot on each) encounters.

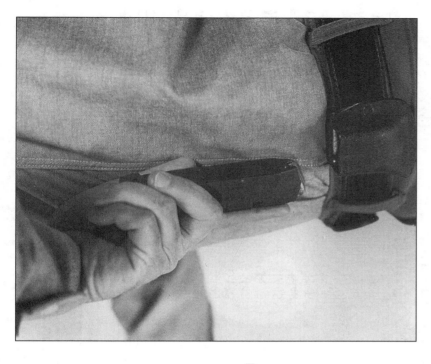

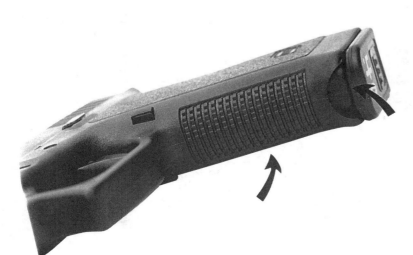

▲ For fast reloading, both the 10-rd. and original high-capacity magazines are well shaped and contoured.

▲ Excellent grip index is maintained in cold or wet weather with factory checkering found on all Glocks. Cutaway front strap also allows quick removal of magazine in the field for reloading or stoppage clearing.

Accuracy from both the M17L and M24 is excellent, even superb, with nearly everything I tried in them producing 25-meter 3-shot Ransom Rest groups of from as small as .69- to 1.89-inches. The most accurate 9mm load tested was my own handload, consisting of the Hornady 90-grain XTP JHP, loaded with 6.0-grains of Unique, which grouped into a phenomenal .44 inches. The Federal Hydra-Shok 124-grain JHP was second, printing a .69-inch group, followed closely by the Winchester Black Talon 147-grain JHP, whose groups measured .86 inches.

My M24 40 Auto shot Ransom Rest groups of from 1.01 to 1.42 inches, the most accurate being a 1.01-inch group by the Winchester 180-grain FMJ and a 1.06-incher with the Remington 155-grain JHP. Even lead-bullet handloads were impressive, the two that I tested printing 1.13 and 1.42 inches respectively.

Functional reliability is always a critical issue with combat weapons and in this category, the longslides have performed quite admirably. Since I began using them nearly three and a half years ago, I've run over 18,000 rounds through both of them and, to date, haven't experienced a single stoppage. Many of you will recall that, for the last ten years, I've been trying to wear out an early Model 17 9mm, but have so far (135,000 rds.) been unable to do so. It appears that both the Model 17L and M24 will continue this trend.

I've run them through what I call 'The American Small Arms Academy Pistol Evaluation Test', consisting of four stages. Stage One - Close Range Emergency Techniques, deals with when the fight erupts at arm's length. Two drills are involve—the Stepback, in which the shooter must gain stand-off distance from his adversary while bringing his own weapon into action.

The shooter takes a long step rearward with his shooting-side foot, keeping his weight forward on his supporting foot, as he begins to present his weapon. Then he takes a short step rearward with his support-side foot as the presentation takes place, bringing him into a firing stance that is outside of arm's reach of the target. He fires two shots, then, as he brings the weapon back down to 'Ready', he executes the Stepback procedure once again to gain additional standoff in the event of a Failure To Stop. This is a perfect simulator for building searches, etc., where a suspect comes from an unexpected place, such as a closet, et al.

Next, to test the weapon's abilities when there is no distance available behind the shooter in which to gain

The prize! Moments after photo was taken by hunting companion, Taylor dropped this beautiful whitetail buck with a single shot behind the shoulder from Glock M24 40 Auto from 30 meters. Hornady 155-grain XTP JHP expanded well and was found on ground beside downed buck. This is that elusive textbook performance we all look for in a gun/load combination.

Test Gun: Glock M17L with 6-inch barrel.

Chronograph: Oehler M35P with Skyscreens.

9mm Parabellum Performance Specifications

Bullet	Vel	K/E	HRSP* (1)	(2)	TRSP+ (1)	(2)
Glaser Safety Slug 79 gr.	1455	202	31.6	25.3	11.4	14.2
Hirtenberger 100 gr. JSP	1381	307	24.3	30.4	17.1	13.7
CCI 100 gr. JSP	1254	279	34.5	27.6	15.5	12.4
W-W 115 gr. FMJ	1069	302	24.3	----	10.9	----
Chicom 115 gr. Ball	1143	336	26.0	----	11.7	----
R-P 115 gr.	1176	366	37.2	29.7	16.7	13.4
Federal 115 gr. JHP	1142	335	36.1	28.9	16.3	13.0
W-W S/T 115 gr. JHP	1175	345	37.1	29.7	16.7	13.4
115 gr. JHP "P+" (M)	1443	424	45.6	36.5	20.5	16.4
Federal 123 gr. FMJ	1048	352	25.5	----	11.5	----
124 gr. NATO	1146	391	28.1	----	12.7	----
Federal H/S 124 gr. JHP	1109	379	37.8	30.2	17.0	13.6
Federal H/S 147 gr. JH	1000	480	40.4	32.3	18.2	14.6
W-W (LEO) 147 gr. JHP	979	470	39.6	31.6	17.8	14.2
W-W B/T 147 gr. JHP	988	474	39.9	31.9	18.0	14.4

Test Gun: Glock M24 with 6-inch barrel.

Chronograph: Oehler M35P with Skyscreens.

40 S&W Performance Specifications

AMMO/BRAND	TYPE	WT (gr.)	VEL (fps)	KE (ft/lb.)
Handload: Hornady XTP 6.5 grs. Unique	JHP	155	1150	405
Cor-Bon	JHP	150	1327	587
Remington-Peters	JHP	155	1012	353
Hornady Custom	JHP	155	1018	364
CCI-Speer	JHP	155	1023	360
Cor-Bon	JHP	180	1034	365
Winchester-Western	JHP	180	956	365
CCI-Speer GD	JHP	180	941	354
Federal Hydra-Shok	JHP	180	930	346
Winchester Blk Tin	JHP	180	933	348
Winchester SXT	JHP	180	936	350
Remington-Peters	JHP	180	932	347

Legend:

(1) denotes "score" if bullet expands.
(2) denotes "score" if bullet DOES NOT expand.
* denotes Hatcher Relative Stopping Power. Generally, a minimum "score" of 60 is considered "passing."
+ denotes Taylor Relative Stopping Power. Generally, a minimum "score" of 20 is considered "passing."
S/T = Silver Tip H/S = Hydra-Shock LEO = Law Enf Only
JHP = Jacketed Hollow Point JSP = Jacketed Soft Point BALL = FMJ FMJ = Full Metal Jacket
W-W = Winchester-Western B/T = Black Talon
"+P+" = Loaded to higher than industry specifications.
(M) = Loaded by Mullins Custom Ammunition. Not recommended for sustained use, as it will considerably shorten weapon service-life. FPS = feet per second. KE = Kinetic Energy, expressed in foot-pounds (ft. lbs./fpe) VEL = Muzzle velocity, expressed in feet per second (fps)

Slim is in!

With the new "Slimline" GLOCK 36

6+1 rounds of potent .45 Auto... in a package that fits the hand of almost any shooter.

Renowned for its safety, accuracy, reliability, durability, and ease of use, GLOCK's proven "Safe Action" technology has now been applied to the grip-slimming single-stack magazine concept. The result should come as no surprise: The GLOCK system makes shooting the high-performance .45 Auto a pleasure, while the reduced width of the finger-grooved grip frame, ambidextrous thumb rests and extended magazine floor plate make handling the G36 a breeze!

GLOCK has slimmed the width of the G36 to an incredible 1.13 inches, making it the slimmest GLOCK yet.

Rule #1: Handle all firearms as if they were loaded.

Nominated as
Shooting Industry's Academy of Excellence
Handgun of the Year 2000

GLOCK®

PERFECTION

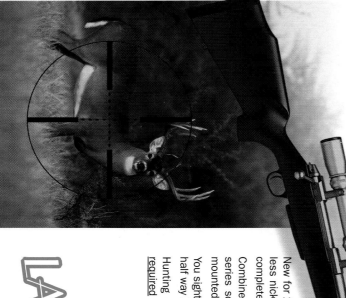

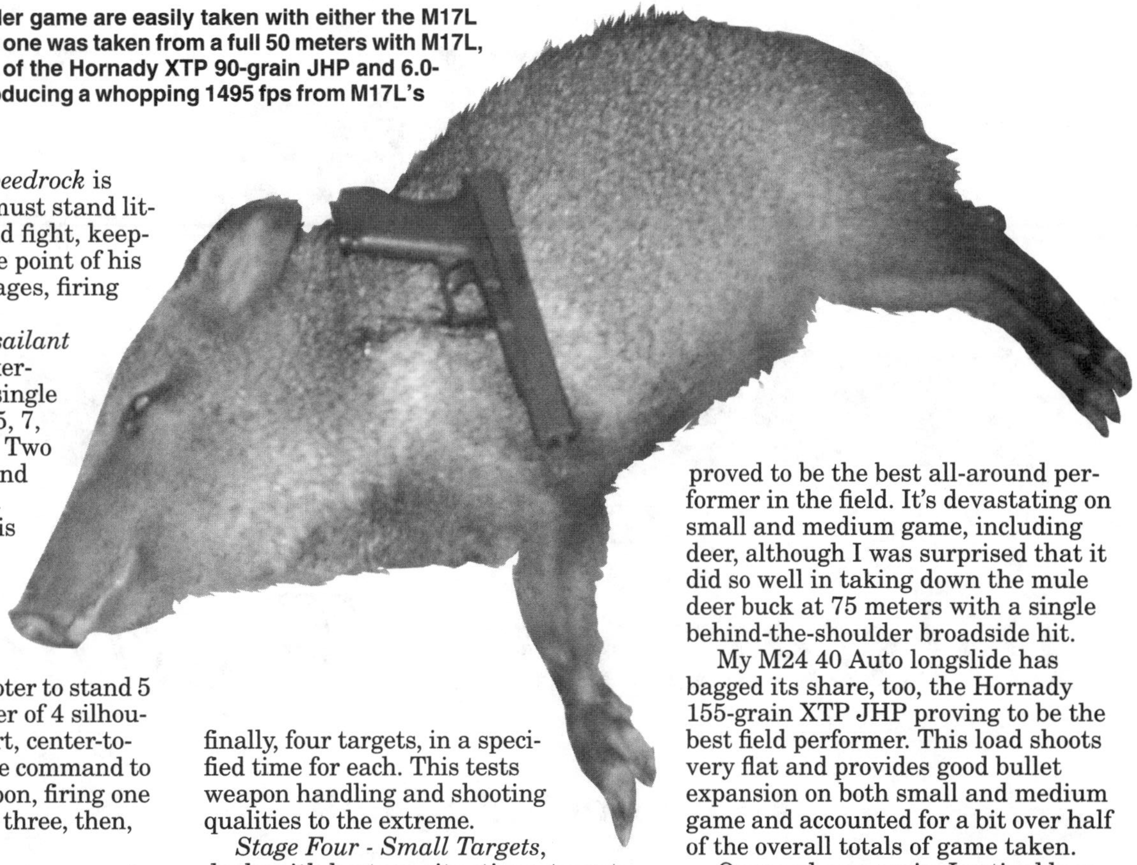

▶ Javelina and other smaller game are easily taken with either the M17L 9mm or M24 40 Auto. This one was taken from a full 50 meters with M17L, using handload consisting of the Hornady XTP 90-grain JHP and 6.0-grains of Unique, safely producing a whopping 1495 fps from M17L's 6-inch barrel.

standoff distance, the *Speedrock* is used. Here, the shooter must stand literally at arm's length and fight, keeping the weapon above the point of his firing-side hip as he engages, firing two quick shots.

Stage Two - Single Assailant Encounters (Standard Exercises) deals with typical single attacker situations at 3, 5, 7, 10, 15, 25 and 50 meters. Two shots are fired on command from each range within a specified time at each. This tests the handling and shooting qualities of the weapon in typical situations.

Stage Three - Multiple Targets, requires the shooter to stand 5 meters in front of a cluster of 4 silhouettes placed 1 meter apart, center-to-center. Upon receiving the command to fire, he presents his weapon, firing one shot on each of two, then three, then,

▶ Contemporary laws governing magazine capacity allow only 10 rounds. However, this is no drawback in the hunting field.

finally, four targets, in a specified time for each. This tests weapon handling and shooting qualities to the extreme.

Stage Four - Small Targets, deals with hostage situations, targets only partly visible, etc. In this drill, the shooter must stand 5 meters from a single silhouette, weapon at the Ready. Upon command, he must present the gun and fire a single shot at the head only. Then, the process is repeated four times, for a total of five shots. Here, the sight radius and weight of the gun exerts significant influence upon performance.

A total of 160 points is possible on the test, but both the Model 17L and M24 sailed right through with perfect scores (160 points)! This more than amply demonstrates their excellent handling and shooting qualities under stress and explains why an ever-growing number of special ops teams prefer them.

In the last three years, I've also used them both as hunting handguns on numerous occasions, bagging no less than a dozen Javelina, a couple of hundred jack and cottontail rabbits, five coyotes, a mule deer buck and a half-dozen whitetails. All were one-shot kills, even though the ranges on some of the shots approached 75 meters

In my M17L, the 90-grain Hornady XTP JHP load mentioned earlier

proved to be the best all-around performer in the field. It's devastating on small and medium game, including deer, although I was surprised that it did so well in taking down the mule deer buck at 75 meters with a single behind-the-shoulder broadside hit.

My M24 40 Auto longslide has bagged its share, too, the Hornady 155-grain XTP JHP proving to be the best field performer. This load shoots very flat and provides good bullet expansion on both small and medium game and accounted for a bit over half of the overall totals of game taken.

Over and over again, I noticed how well both pistols handled in the field. They balance well, point well and their long sight radius makes them most forgiving of sighting errors. In fact, they handle so well, that I can only think of one improvement on them—the addition of Trijicon tritium sights with horizontal 3-dot pattern, for improved low light performance. The "dot & outlined notch" front and rear sights featured from the factory are not only plastic and therefore somewhat fragile for either SpecOps or hunting use, but don't offer as good a combination as does the horizontal 3-dot tritium pattern.

In summary, I find the Glock Model 17L 9mm and Model 24 40 S&W longslides to be excellent handguns. They're tough, accurate, handle well under stress and offer a wide variety of tactical abilities. Their increased weight and forward balance makes them easier to control at high shooting speeds, and their longer sight radius makes super-quick sight alignment and sight picture a relatively easy task.

With such attributes, it's no wonder many of the elite SpecOps teams, like RAID, prefer them. As tactical weapons and hunting handguns, they're definite winners and offer a great package for a price that is more than fair. So, if you're in the market for such a piece, I highly recommend that you give them a try. ●

▼ For SpecOps or other tactical use, original Glock high-capacity magazines are favored. M24 mag shown here is the same as used in the M22 and holds 15 rds. "Plus-two" floorplate (shown) increases capacity by an additional two rounds, for a total of 17.

The Crossdraw....

Holsters and Technique

by Bob Campbell

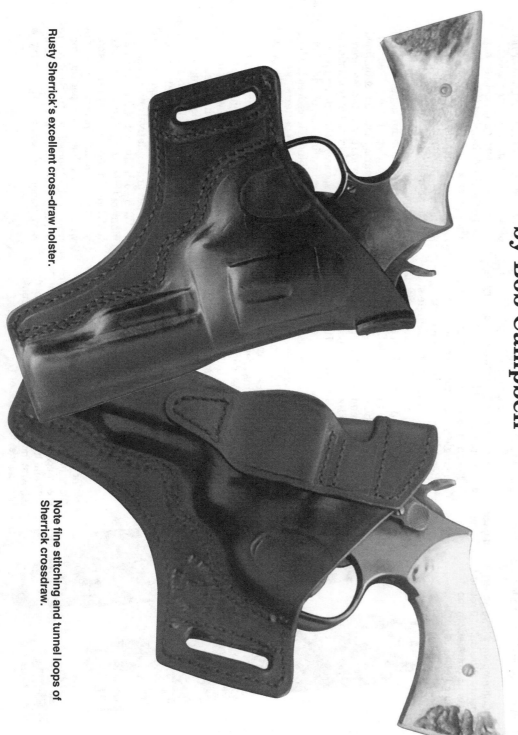

Rusty Sherrick's excellent cross-draw holster.

Note fine stitching and tunnel loops of Sherrick crossdraw.

The crossdraw is a good option when backing up a long gun.

THE CROSS-DRAW HOLSTER has been criticized, ignored and even condemned by most modern trainers. Yet, there is a hard core of users who appreciate the crossdraw, although few of them rely exclusively upon it. This situation has been different in the past. At one time the crossdraw was popular, seen on the belts of municipal officers. It was also popular with outdoorsmen. More than one cowboy adopted the crossdraw because it kept his handgun out of the way of the roping activity; a demanding three-part evolution while on horseback.

The crossdraw fell into disfavor for several reasons. The most often stated criticism is that the weapon is openly presented to a gun-grabber. Some holsters do thrust the gun butt forward in a rakish fashion that seems to shout 'grab me'.

FBI statistics warn us of such perils. One in five officers assaulted with handguns are shot with their own weapon. However, a case may be made that holster selection has little to do with these attacks. Many handguns are snatched from the user's hands. The most common attack planned in prison seems to be a grab from the rear, with the left arm going around the officer's neck, slightly lifting him off the ground. The crossdraw would be only slightly more difficult, with the felon using his right arm to cross the neck and drawing with his left hand 'cavalry-style.'

I wore a crossdraw holster with a Colt 38 early in my career, until I was told to trash this holster during one of my first firearms training classes. The criticism leveled at the crossdraw in this class related to the draw (This same argument was well-presented by Bill Jordan in his treatise on gunfighting, *No Second Place Winner*). Crossdraw is slower than strong-side draw, even with quality holsters. The motion requires we reach to the weak side with our draw, arrest this motion, then draw and pivot the gun. Just as important, when drawing from a strong-side holster we will draw *through* a target. The gun's muzzle will be on the target somewhere from the ankles to the head during a strong-side draw. We have a good chance of connecting somewhere. The cross-draw arc is across an assailant's body-at least that is conventional wisdom.

There are a few defenders of the crossdraw. One of these is Chief R. E. Cogdell. Gene has had dealings with many miscreants who preferred the crossdraw. He told me the Hell's

Angels preferred cross-draw holsters for easy access when on their bikes. Many of these men, knowledgeable about firearms and tactics, carried cocked and locked Colt 45 autos. More than a few made their own ammunition in the days before reliable factory jacketed hollow-point ammunition. A favorite rig of the local branch was the classic Wm. E. Davis crossdraw.

Gene notes the crossdraw might be easier to defend than some types of holsters. With modern retention techniques, we are taught to clamp our strong hand on the weapon and attempt to strike a blow with our weak hand. With the crossdraw, it is the weak hand that clamps down while the strong hand strikes a more telling blow. He also feels an attack from the front is easier to defend against than an assault from the rear.

The crossdraw may not be for peace officers *but just may be the best choice* for many civilian gun carriers. This design has real utility in certain needs. A well-made cross-draw holster is much more versatile than any specialized driving holster. You don't have to leave a crossdraw behind in the car, simply wear it out of the vehicle. When seated, behind the wheel or behind a desk, the crossdraw allows the user to easily have his or her hand on the gun butt and ready. This is the very pinnacle of martial arts - being ready without giving away this prudence in the face of a threat. Indeed, brushing back a covering garment and placing your hand on a strong-side holstered pistol is a move sure to escalate any situation.

The movie "Walking Tall" featured the capable Joe Don Baker as legendary lawman, Buford Pusser. Pusser was portrayed as wearing his Magnum in a cross-draw holster. Hollywood is very appearance-conscious and the crossdraw looks rakish. I have been able to ascertain Pusser used both 357 and 41 Magnums in his career, but the holsters used could not be positively identified.

Any lawman who spends a lot of time in a vehicle would have adopted the crossdraw. A cross-draw holstered pistol would be out of the way. Pusser was once a successful professional wrestler and certainly understood more than a little about handgun retention.

A well-know lawman and adventurer who adopted a form of crossdraw to his profit was James Butler Hickok.

A popular form of carry in the late 1860s was the *cavalry carry*. However, since Hickok was known to have executed the draw from a seated position, he must have used a more conventional crossdraw at times. A gaming

SELF-DEFENSE/CONCEALED CARRY

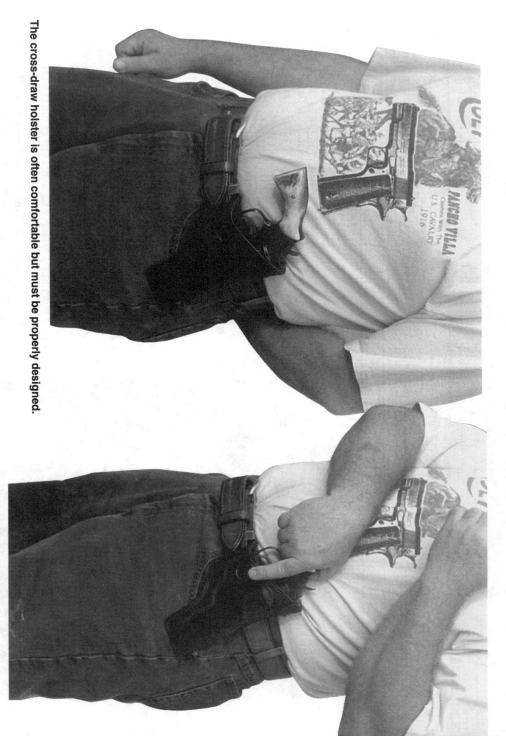

The cross-draw holster is often comfortable but must be properly designed.

Beginning the draw.

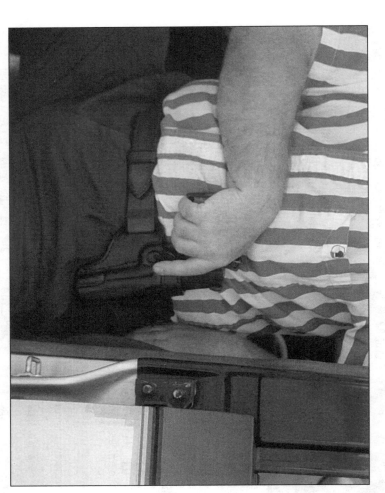

Crossdraws are especially handy when seated (Del Fatti holster, Colt 45).

man, Hickok appreciated the speed a practiced man could demonstrate when seated with a cross-draw holster. When dealing, or at play, his hands were practically upon his gun butts. It should be noted that when Wild Bill was killed, he was shot from behind.

A *cavalry draw* required more manipulation than most. The butt-forward handle was grasped with the hand on the same side as the gun. The gun barrel was twisted forward; during most of its travel the muzzle pointed toward soft body parts, although it seems self-wounding was not a common thing. Firearms were respected and, when not in a life-or-death fight, folks took their time drawing and cocking their weapon. Only a handful, Hickok included, practiced their craft. I would be loathe to attempt the draw with modern weapons, but this is exactly the weak-hand draw executed with a modern crossdraw. If the strong hand is injured this draw just might be a lifesaver.

After a fair amount of historical research, I find the crossdraw had its

Self-Defense/Concealed Carry

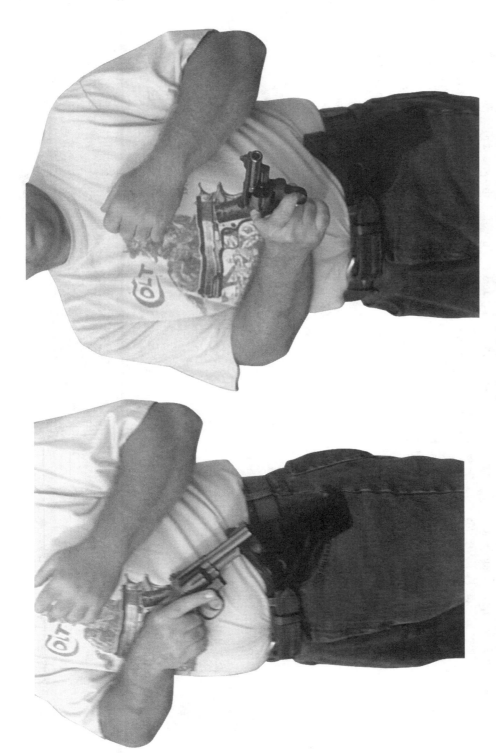

On target at close range.

Pivoting under the arm.

adherents in the cop and gunfighter school...but seems better suited to civilian use. When hunting, casually shooting or carrying a heavy handgun concealed, the crossdraw is among the best choices. A shopkeeper who stands behind a counter or desk most of the day, a courier who drives a great deal, or even a tow truck driver who is called often at night–would benefit from a good cross-draw holster.

Selecting a well-designed holster, rugged and well-executed, is a beginning. A poorly-made cross-draw holster is more of a nuisance than bad holsters of other types. A top flight example should be chosen. The holster must ride high to clear obstacles and must ride close to the body.

I have done a number of range tests with most popular types. I have earned a grasp of the capabilities of each. Sometimes, I really needed a good holster and other times I was simply curious.

I have determined that, quite aside from its other attributes, the cross-draw is the best carry when relying on a long gun as a primary firearm. A lot of hunters like to carry a Magnum revolver as backup, and should choose

Crossdraws cannot equal the speed of a well-designed strong-side holster such as the Sherrick NTT version–under most conditions–but if you are seated, even this hi-ride holster might not equal the crossdraw.

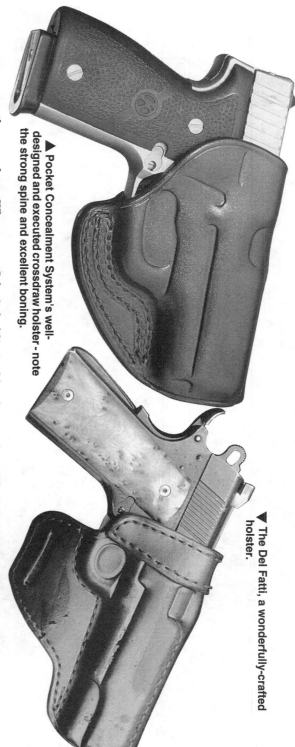

▲ Pocket Concealment System's well-designed and executed crossdraw holster - note the strong spine and excellent boning.

▼ The Del Fatti, a wonderfully-crafted holster.

kneeling or sitting, no other holster is as out-of-the-way of the long gun-or as accessible.

The few cross-draw holsters in my collection are the finest available. My most frequently-carried handgun on the *back forty* is the able Combat Magnum, but I also have on hand examples for my semi-auto pistols.

The Magnum and the 45 Auto are very versatile, doing anything I need to do. Pests, snakes and wayward larger animals are readily dispatched or dissuaded with either of these capable handguns. They have taken larger game animals when the opportunity has presented itself.

As for self-defense-if such a need arises in my rural area, it would probably be at longer range and the Magnum would be the bet. In self defense,

the crossdraw. When kneeling or sitting, no other holster is as out-of-the-way of the long gun-or as accessible.

I don't feel limited by the revolver. If you don't hit your adversary or find cover within the first three seconds after the fight begins, your personal battle is over. The revolver will serve well.

I am not interested in carrying more weight than is needed, and the light, strong horsehide holster by Rusty Sherrick is among the best options. It holds its form well and is brilliantly fast when needed. There are those who feel horsehide is not worth the slight premium, but I am slowly becoming a believer.

I suppose if I were to attempt to sell anyone on the crossdraw, the Sherrick holster would be the best holster example to reference.

The late, great Ed McGivern is considered a trick shooter but made more than a few tactical observations worth quoting during his many experiments in the handgun

field. One of his favorite carry rigs was a three-inch barrel Smith and Wesson Military and Police 38 Special carried in a cross-draw holster. Sometimes, McGivern used suspender holsters.

McGivern held with conventional wisdom concerning the crossdraw. But he noted that when confronting an adversary attacking from the weak side, the crossdraw offered excellent reaction time. As detailed in his seminal work, *Fast and Fancy Revolver Shooting*, McGivern understood the crossdraw was slower against an opponent 'squared' to the defender. But against a weak-side attack, the crossdraw proved quite fast.

These drills point out the wisdom of hard work with our survival gear. Quality equipment is not inexpensive, while proficiency at arms is purchased with a different coin. *Practice hard...or don't bother!*

I have used Matt Del Fatti's crossdraw with

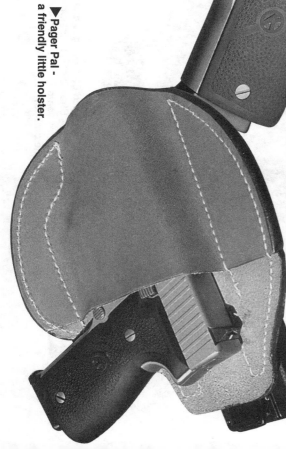

▲ PCS holster features a tunnel loop.

▶ Pager Pal - a friendly little holster.

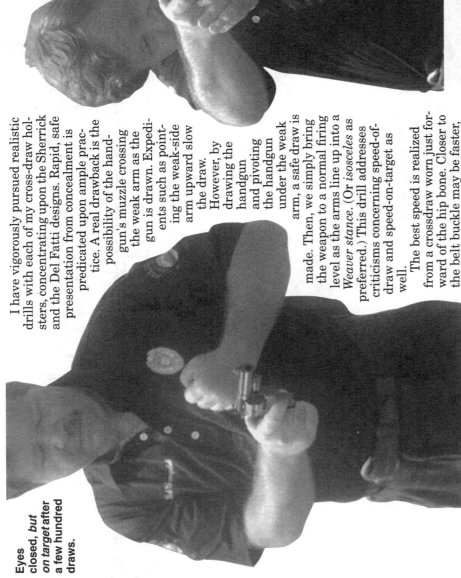

Eyes closed, *but on target* after a few hundred draws.

I have vigorously pursued realistic drills with each of my cross-draw holsters, concentrating upon the Sherrick and the Del Fatti designs. Rapid, safe presentation from concealment is predicated upon ample practice. A real drawback is the possibility of the handgun's muzzle crossing the weak arm as the gun is drawn. Expedients such as pointing the weak-side arm upward slow the draw. However, by drawing the handgun and pivoting the handgun under the weak arm, a safe draw is made. Then, we simply bring the weapon to a normal firing level as the arms line up into a *Weaver stance.* (Or *isosceles* as preferred.) This drill addresses criticisms concerning speed-of-draw and speed-on-target as well.

The best speed is realized from a crossdraw worn just forward of the hip bone. Closer to the belt buckle may be faster, but not practical or concealable. Further towards the rear of the hip, concealment may be better but the draw is slowed and may become awkward.

A little work is needed, but just forward of the hipbone is the best position for most of us.

Carrying spare ammunition is no problem for the revolver, since revolver loads are best carried on the strong side. But spare magazines are usually carried weak-side, and the crossdraw occupies this space. The best approach is to simply carry spare pistol magazines farther back on the belt; even over the rear hip pocket. You run out of time before you run out of bullets, but it is good to have spare ammunition available.

As you can see, I like my cross-draw holsters in certain situations. They should not be discounted out of hand although the strong-side holster is usually a better choice. Appropriate candidates for the cross-draw carry include mounted and airborne units.

For those who carry two handguns, the second handgun carried in a crossdraw is a good choice. After all, few of us gain real proficiency with the weak hand. Those who contemplate defending themselves with a gun in each hand should do so only after achieving

the Colt 45 Auto for some time. It is as rugged and tight as the day it was shipped. This holster holds the Colt high and tight against my side, exactly as a crossdraw should. However, this is one of few holsters versatile enough to be worn strong-side if desired.

I like this holster a great deal. I've worn it both on and off duty with complete satisfaction. The man with only one gun on a high-risk raid would be in the minority. The crossdraw offers access by either hand and will be more accessible to either hand than any other type of holster.

Another favorite is the Pocket Concealment Systems cross-draw, molded for my Kahr K 40 pistol. This holster is brilliantly fast, carrying the light 40-caliber pistol at a good angle for concealment.

There are a few other holsters that make excellent crossdraw choices. For those desiring deep concealment, the Pager Pal holster offers inside-the-pants wear in surprising comfort. Some users erroneously attempt to use this holster as a strong-side holster. Worn crossdraw, the weak hand grasps the fake pager as the strong hand draws the gun. A workable combination in troubled times.

Completing a fast crossdraw.

the same level of competence with each hand and hand/eye combination. Daunting? Thought so - it is to me!

The carrying of two guns allows a shooter to stay in operation by drawing a second gun. And, the gun may be drawn with the weak hand.

The cross-draw holster is a fine option under many circumstances. It is not the best holster for every situation—but a carry option I would not like to give up.

Holster Makers

Del Fatti
637 E Main St.
Greenwood, WI 54437

Rusty Sherrick
507 Mark Drive
Elizabethtown, PA 17022

Pocket Concealment Systems
PO 12071
Baltimore, MD 21234

Pager Pal
200 West Pleasantview
Hurst, TX 76054

VINTAGE ARMS

THE 7.62 NAGANT
GAS-SEAL REVOLVERS

by Bernard H. DiGiacobbe
and George E. Dvorchak Jr.

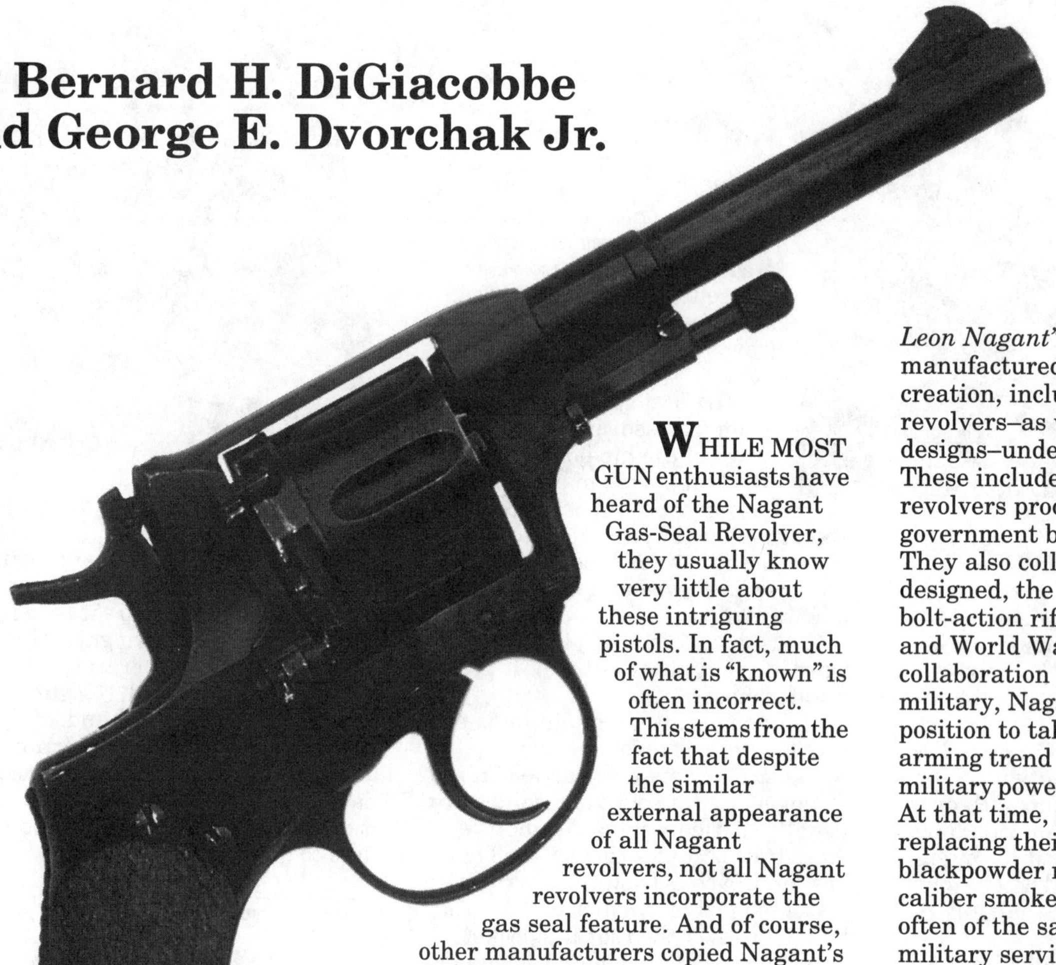

Nagant Model of 1895

W HILE MOST
GUN enthusiasts have
heard of the Nagant
Gas-Seal Revolver,
they usually know
very little about
these intriguing
pistols. In fact, much
of what is "known" is
often incorrect.
This stems from the
fact that despite
the similar
external appearance
of all Nagant
revolvers, not all Nagant
revolvers incorporate the
gas seal feature. And of course,
other manufacturers copied Nagant's
designs. To further complicate the
picture, not all gas-seal revolvers were
Nagants. There were, in fact, various
manufacturers and systems of gas-
seal revolvers dating back at least to
the era of percussion revolvers! What
assured Nagant's version its unique
status was that it was adopted by the
Russian army and, subsequently,
produced in enormous numbers.

Despite the long association of the
name Nagant with Russian small
arms, the name is actually Belgian, as
in Emile & Leon Nagant. Their
factory, "Fabrique d'Armes Emile et

Leon Nagant" of Liege, Belgium,
manufactured guns of their own
creation, including a line of military
revolvers—as well as other outside
designs–under licensing agreements.
These included thousands of Galand
revolvers produced for the Russian
government between 1874 and 1878.
They also collaborated on, and
designed, the Russian Mosin Nagant
bolt-action rifle used in World War I
and World War II. Because of this
collaboration with the Russian
military, Nagant was in an ideal
position to take advantage of the re-
arming trend sweeping the European
military powers during the late 1890s.
At that time, governments were
replacing their large-caliber
blackpowder revolvers with smaller-
caliber smokeless powder revolvers,
often of the same caliber as their
military service rifle. This was an
economic and practical consideration
since both arms could use the same
barrel-making machinery.

While 30-caliber may seem small
for a military revolver, remember
this was the era when aristocratic
officers used their pistols as a badge
of rank and to direct the fire of their
troops–rather than using those
pistols for the more mundane tasks
of warfare. By 1894, Nagant was
ready to offer their recently patented
(1894) gas-seal revolver to any
government looking for what was an
advanced handgun for the time.

Gun, ammo and holster.

What finally made the gas seal concept feasible was the unique cartridge designed and patented in 1886 by a rival Belgian designer/manufacturer by the name of Pieper. The significant feature of his design was that the cartridge utilized an extra-long case with the bullet seated entirely within. This radically-designed cartridge looked like a modern rimmed 30-caliber Carbine case with the bullet seated entirely within the case, and then some! This new cartridge was approximately 1.53-inches long and had a 108-grain jacketed bullet ahead of 12.3 grains of smokeless powder: all contained with a sharp taper-crimp to the case mouth. While the original 7.62mm (or 30-caliber) bullet was of conventional configuration, it was later given a flat nose to increase its effectiveness.

Why such a case was needed was that if the mouth of the "crimped" cartridge case protruded slightly ahead of the cylinder, it could be advanced into the rear of the barrel. Upon firing, the mouth of the cartridge case would expand and serve as a gasket, sealing the gap between the cylinder and barrel. If Pieper's cartridge was a good idea, his under-lever rifle, which retracted the barrel before firing the cartridge, wasn't. Fortunately, Leon Nagant's revolver was a better adaptation since he utilized the concept of a pistol with a fixed barrel—but with a sliding cylinder.

This cartridge is sometimes misnamed the 7.5 millimeter Nagant. It's worth noting at this point that because of the popularity of this cartridge, it was also used in conventional non-gas seal revolvers, adding to the confusion surrounding Nagant's gas-seal-revolvers.

Unlike other revolvers designed to fire the gas-seal cartridges, Leon Nagant's design, patented in 1894, was relatively simple and reliable, with the front of each chamber counter-bored. This allowed the cartridge mouth to project 1.5 millimeters. The design also featured a bottom-pivoting "T"-shaped component located behind the cylinder and ahead of a vertically-sliding wedge. In actual operation, the first part of the trigger pull, (which, with our specimen, took 18 pounds of pressure on the trigger), rotated the cylinder. The last part of the trigger pull, which then took 6 additional pounds, forced the vertically sliding wedge against the pivoting "T"-shaped component before the hammer dropped to fire the handgun. This, in turn, pushed the cartridge and cylinder forward while supporting the cartridge head. While the first half of the trigger pull rotates the cylinder to align it with the barrel, the second portion of the trigger pull pushed the counter-bored cylinder/chamber into the barrel. All of this took a total of 24 pounds of pressure on the trigger to fire double action—which obviously made accurate double-action firing extremely difficult, if not impossible.

When firing the revolver in the single-action mode, cocking the hammer would, of course, rotate the cylinder to activate the gas seal mechanism. Once cocked, it then takes an additional 11 pounds of pressure on the trigger to fire. After firing, the return spring cycles the trigger to its normal position, simultaneously retracting the vertically-sliding wedge. A coaxial coil spring around the cylinder pin will then push the cylinder—and thus the "T"-shaped component—to their normal rearward position. This coil spring, unfortunately, contributes to the heavy trigger pull. Replacing this spring with a weaker one should lighten the trigger pull. Yet, this might have reduced reliability, considering freezing lubricants from the notoriously cold Russian winters.

As with other revolvers of the era, the firing pin is attached—actually pivoted like that on a Smith & Wesson—to the hammer. The "T"-shaped component requires a particularly long and slender firing pin, which measures approximately .75-inch. While this may seem unduly fragile, Nagant revolvers, including their firing pins, were recognized for their reliability.

The gas seal mechanism also provides an ideal system for aligning the cylinder to the barrel. This illustrates why this system is sometimes used on Russian and Czech target revolvers. As with other Nagant revolvers, the spur on the top of the trigger protrudes into the bottom of the window of the frame and into the corresponding notches in the cylinder to maintain barrel/cylinder alignment when the gun is fired.

As these gas-seal revolvers are chambered for seven shots, the indexing notch is located - ideally - between the chambers. Remember, a conventional six-shot revolver requires that the indexing notches be placed over the chamber, a practice which reduces strength in this critical area. The cylinder, as do other European revolvers of the time, has a belt - or ridge - about the rear to further maintain strength under the notches.

Like other Nagant revolvers, the loading gate and cylinder are configured into a ratchet to prevent the cylinder from rotating when the trigger is in its normal forward position.

The ejector system of the Nagant gas-seal revolver is the same system used on other Nagant revolvers. While it looks similar to that found on a conventional double-action revolver with a swing-out cylinder, the Nagant's functions more like the ejector system of a single-action revolver. To operate it, the shooter rotates the ejector rod 180° counterclockwise—and then pulls the ejector rod forward. This allows the shooter to rotate the ejector rod housing around the base of the barrel and align the ejector rod with the chamber. The operator then pushes the spent shell out, withdraws the ejector rod (as there is no return spring like in a conventional single-action revolver) and rotates the cylinder, repeating this procedure six more times. The shooter needs to reposition the ejector rod housing, then push the ejector rod backward and rotate it clockwise 180°. If this description is long and cumbersome, so is the procedure, particularly for a military revolver. Reloading is significantly slower than even a conventional single-action revolver. However, like a traditional single-action revolver, the ejection system is inherently strong and eliminates the prospect of misalignment from an abused crane, not uncommon on conventional double-action revolvers.

Like other Nagant revolvers, the trigger guard pivots downward. However, unlike other Nagant

This target was the first group fired offhand by Dvorchak at 20 yards with the test gun. Each cylinder locks up on the barrel, ensuring alignment which contributes to accuracy. The recoil was a lot less than a 9mm or 38 Special; quite pleasant to fire—even with the heavy trigger pull.

The cartridge (*left*) is a modern factory round; (*center*) that factory round with the 98-grain FMJ bullet partially pulled. The fired case (*right*) which, by the shape, demonstrates how severe a crimp this ammo requires.

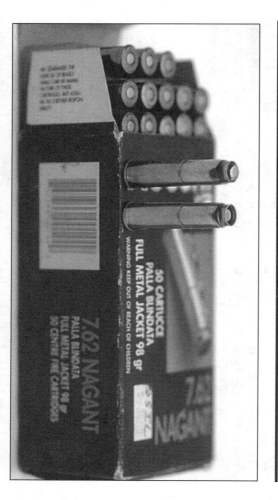

Although there should be military surplus ammo out there, we could not find any. Shown is what we used in our testing...which proved to be quite good.

▲ For a size comparison, the Nagant is shown above a S&W Model 66 with a 2.5-inch barrel.

▲ Shown are loaded cartridges in the cylinders. Note the flutes between the cylinders do not extend to the front of the cylinder. The cartridge case projects 1.5mm beyond the face of the counter-bored cylinder.

With the cylinder removed, a cartridge is inserted into the barrel to demonstrate the gas seal system.

revolvers, this does not compress the V-shaped mainspring for its easy removal. Incidentally, the bottom of this V-shaped mainspring serves as a trigger return spring which indirectly provides for rebound of the hammer and firing pin. As with other European revolvers of the time, these components are affixed to a thin flat plate, rather than housed in a thicker frame as is the case with American revolvers. Yet, like American revolvers, they do have a removable sideplate. These parallel plates comprise the grip portion of the frame. There is also a checkered wooden

insert to match the grips inlet into the back of the grip frame.

In addition to the early commercial versions manufactured by Nagant, the manufacturer supplied approximately 20,000 gas-seal revolvers to the Russian military by 1899. By that time, the company had sold all rights to Russia, which then manufactured revolvers at the Tula Arsenal until 1944. By the eve of World War I, the Russian army had acquired its goal of 436,210 revolvers.

As expected of a gun with a half-century production life, there were numerous variations, mainly in the

configuration of the front sight and frame markings. There was even a single-action model issued to noncoms, generally referred to as the Trooper Model. However, after the Russian Revolution, all comrades being equal, the single-action version was no longer produced. Another interesting model is a short-barrel version manufactured in 1924 for the *GPU* personnel (Russian Secret Police), with an 84-millimeter barrel replacing the standard 114-millimeter length barrel, shaving 57 grams (about 2 ounces/Ed.) from the weight.

When the Nagant factory ceased production of the commercial model in 1899, after selling all production rights to Russia, they went on to develop a model in 1910 with a "conventional" swing-out cylinder and crane. With this system, the crane and cylinder swung to the right side of the revolver rather than to the left as on conventional revolvers. The Grah Company manufactured a similar copy with the conventional pattern, having the cylinder and crane swing to the right of the frame. Contemporary Belgian manufacturer, Pieper, also offered a gas-seal revolver with a different mechanism. There were also many others, mostly Spanish copies.

There are reports of Nagant gas-seal revolvers having been

Notice the large cylinder gap on the gun with the hammer down in the 'normal' carry position (*right*). Now, with the hammer cocked, (below) notice how the cylinder telescopes onto the forcing cone of the barrel—increasing the gap between the rear of the cylinder and the frame. Note the necessarily-long firing pin on the hammer.

▲ The wooden grips are checkered as is the wooded backstrap. The wood-to-metal fit is quite good! Also notice the single action-style loading gate.

manufactured for the Austro-Hungarian Empire commencing in 1891, as well as for Romania and Serbia. These reports are most likely incorrect, since the patent date for the Nagant gas seal revolver was 1894! The Nagant factory did, however, in 1930, sell all rights and machinery to their 1910 model with its swing-out cylinder to Poland, where it was manufactured as the Radom Ng 30. This model remained in production until it was replaced by the VIS-35 autoloading pistol.

The question arises when discussing its gas seal and cartridge—was the velocity gained with the gas seal worth the mechanical complexity? Like just about everything else written about gas-seal revolvers, the opinions vary widely from author to

author. The problem arises in the difficulty of removing the gas seal feature from the revolver. One source compared the cartridge—fired in both a non-gas-seal revolver—to a gas-seal revolver—and reported a 357 fps increase in velocity. This seems plausible since when we fired and chronographed a 170-grain handloaded 357 Remington Maximum out of a Dan Wesson with an 8-inch barrel and then a T/C Contender with a 10-inch barrel, (the latter eliminates the gases escaping out of the cylinder gap as does the Nagant), the MV in the Contender was around 250 fps faster. When allowing for two additional inches of barrel in the Contender, we estimate a 200 fps increase in velocity with these rounds due to the elimination of the cylinder gap. Since velocity varies with different calibers, and obviously barrel length can affect these results, an increase of over 300

the complicated mechanism with a simpler firing mechanism and stronger frame would not only allow a much better double-action trigger pull but also the use of a much more powerful cartridge.

As you are aware, this is not how collectors see things. The ingenious gas-seal mechanism and unusual methods of construction (by American standards) puts these revolvers into the *"quite collectable"* category of unique and historic handguns.

Due to its production volume and wide array of models manufactured, there are more than enough of these guns available to satisfy any collector. Best of all, since prices are quite reasonable, the Nagant can be a historically significant handgun with which to begin a collection.

This was the pistol that the Czar's army carried during flamboyant cavalry charges and into the muddy trenches of WWI. It also served on both

Field-stripping the Nagant can be accomplished with a single screwdriver, needed only to remove the grips.

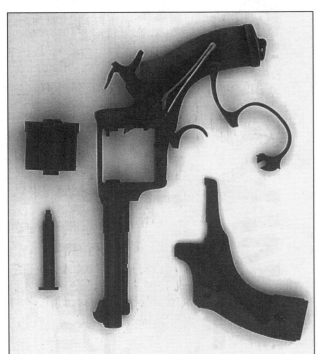

fps is not unreasonable, considering all is equal. Therefore, by eliminating the cylinder gap one can expect an increase in velocity!

As surplus military ammo is no longer available, in our test firing of the Nagant we used Fiocchi ammunition. As measured on a Chrony Chronograph (air temperature of 42 degrees F), the mean muzzle velocity for 7 shots was 876 fps with a high of 889 and low of 883 fps.

Despite the heavy trigger pull, we found the fixed military sights to be satisfactory. Once we felt comfortable with the handgun's "feel", using its

factory sights and with the issued military grips, offhand groups at 20 yards–surprisingly-averaged 2 inches. Certainly the cartridge's low recoil contributed to accurate shooting with this quite remarkable revolver.

The long production life indicates the satisfaction of the Russian military with this revolver. It was not only cheap to manufacture and quite reliable, but could also be readily maintained and repaired in the field. It was also appreciated by soldiers for its great adaptability, particularly when firing through the ports of armored vehicles. With the pistol's heavy trigger pull, slow loading and weak cartridge, this gun is of limited value for sporting or defense purposes by today's standards.

Hindsight has shown that replacing

► The indexing notch is located between the seven chambers in the cylinder. Also notice the ratchet-like arrangement of the single action-style loading gate. The loading gate spring is inlet into the frame, allowing it to function as a ratchet.

▼ Shown is a close-up view of the single action-style loading gate which also functions as a ratchet to maintain cylinder alignment during normal carry. Notice how the frame is notched to accommodate the loading of cartridges.

sides of the Russian Revolution and later on the side of the Russian Army during the Great Patriotic War, as the Russians are fond of calling WWII.

All of this in a handgun that can generally be had for less than the price of two boxes of ammo. How can you go wrong!

TRIVIA NOTE: For those infatuated with trivia, the French Saint Etienne 1892 revolver is one of the few other revolvers with a cylinder swinging out of the right side of the frame.

Muzzleloading Pistols for BIG GAME

by Wm. Hovey Smith

Thompson/Center's Sam Ricker took this New Hampshire buck with an Encore 209x50 muzzleloading pistol in 1998. In 1999, he killed a similar-sized deer with the same handgun.

I HAD PROBLEMS the first time I pointed a muzzleloading handgun at a deer. In theory, I knew the 50-caliber Thompson/Center Scout loaded with 85 grains of *FFg* and a 370-grain MaxiBall should have no difficulty making a killing shot on the small Cumberland Island deer at 7 yards. After all, I was shooting a rifle load out of this 12-inch barreled handgun.

Certainly the load was powerful enough. It developed the 500 foot/pounds of energy at 100 yards required under Georgia law for hunting big game with a pistol. Testing had shown the load would consistently shoot 4-inch groups at 50 yards - much more accurate than necessary for a 7-yard shot. So what was the problem?

My problems were more psychological and physiological, than technical. I had never taken a deer with a muzzleloading handgun and I knew, too well, that I had only one shot. There was also the problem of the *"shakes."* I was excited at the prospect of killing a deer with a blackpowder pistol and *"afeared"* of making a fool out of myself by missing this deer at 7 yards. I had practiced with the Scout out to 75 yards. Now, here was my deer at *spitball* range. No one could ask for a better opportunity, but I

was unnerved by the unexpected sight of this deer slowly walking beside the same trail I was on.

"Raise the pistol. Cock the pistol. Align the sights behind the shoulder. Take half a breath, and smoothly squeeze the trigger. Nothing to it." Or so I was telling myself.

Gripping the gun, I assumed the classic "Weaver" stance. My feet were set well apart, and my elbows were locked—which thrust the pistol away from the center of my body and brought the sights to eye level. This was as stable a shooting position as I

HANDGUN HUNTING

could assume. I aimed behind the shoulder and, reminding myself not to blow it, made the shot. Everything looked good. The front sight blade was 'square' in the notch of the rear sight, and there was nothing but brown deer hair around the front blade when the hammer fell.

After the smoke dissipated, I could see the deer had fallen in its tracks - cleanly shot through the spine. The heavy 50-caliber slug penetrated the deer just as if it had been fired from a rifle. I have killed deer and hogs with a variety of blackpowder handguns since, but the thrill of taking that first small buck with a muzzleloading pistol is hard to beat.

Muzzleloading handguns powerful enough to consistently take big game are a small subset of muzzleloaders intended for hunting. To comply with state laws, which often require that pistols used on big game develop 500 foot/pounds of energy at either 50 or 100 yards–depending on the state– these must be heavy guns with barrels from 12 to 16 inches long. No percussion revolver, not even the Colt Walker, comes close to developing this much energy; their chambers will simply not hold enough powder.

Such specialized hunting pistols are often offered late in a company's production history, enjoy only modest sales compared to rifles and are the first items to be cut when there is pressure to trim costs.

One traditional gun that meets some states' requirements is the replica of the Harper's Ferry Model 1855 single-shot pistol. This horse pistol was issued in pairs to dragoons and carried in holsters slung across the front of a saddle. It had a 58-caliber bore and a 11 7/8-inch barrel. As was the custom, it shot the same caliber ball as the issue rifle of the time. Sam Fadala, in his *Black Powder Loading Manual*, reported he developed loads using up to 60 grains *FFg* and a 500-grain Minie ball to yield nearly 700 foot/pounds of energy at 50 yards. A replica of this pistol was once imported by Navy Arms, but is not listed in their current catalogue.

Gonic Arms

Gonic Arms is a family business that makes, among other things, muzzleloading barrels for Thompson/Center Contenders. Gonic prides itself on its bullet design which uses multiple full-caliber driving bands–instead of only one groove-diameter band–which increases resistance and combustion efficiency. Gonic's barrels are priced at about $250 for a 16-inch barrel; forends start at $123.

Kahnke Gun Works

Kahnke's hunting handgun has a Peacemaker-style grip, an investment cast steel frame and features interchangeable 36- to 54-caliber barrels from 10 1/2 to 14 inches long. The 36 is a small game barrel, the 45 a transitional caliber and the 50 and 54 calibers are intended for big game. This gun uses a centrally-hung hammer and is fired using either No. 11 or Musket caps. Prices for the pistol start at $369 for the blued gun and $389 for stainless steel. Kahnke Gun Works has a web site at **www.powderandbow.com/kahnke.**

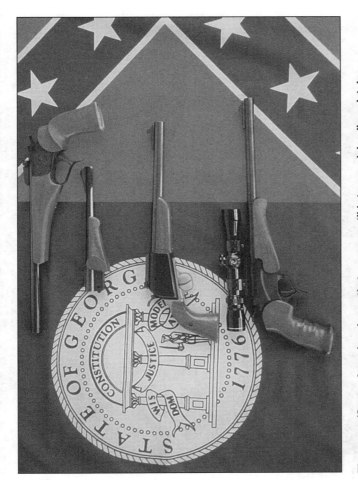

Thompson/Center Arms handguns that are convertible to muzzleloading pistols. Muzzleloading barrels for the Contender (*top*) are available from Gonic Arms. The now-discontinued Scout (*middle*), here in 50-caliber, and (*bottom*) the Encore which is offered with a 209x50 muzzleloading pistol replacement barrel or as a complete muzzleloading pistol.

A pair of Thompson/Center Arms pistols that took deer on consecutive days on Georgia's Cumberland Island. The Super 14 Contender (*top*) in 44 Remington Magnum killed a doe one day and the muzzleloading Scout killed a similar-size buck the next. Both deer were taken at close range, hit in very nearly the same place. There was no apparent difference in effective killing power between the two handguns. If anything, the 50-caliber Scout dropped its deer faster.

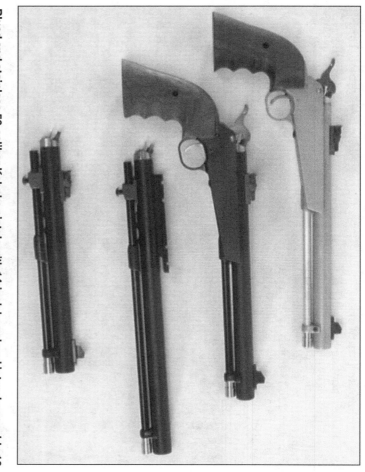

Blued and stainless 50-caliber Kahnke pistols with 14-inch barrel and interchangeable 10 1/2-inch barrels. The Kahnke pistol may be fired using either No. 11 or Musket caps.

range deer is 90 grains of *FFg* and a 320-grain T/C MaxiBall.

No deer presented themselves while I was hunting with the Encore, but I did take a beaver in a convincing fashion using a load of two Pyrodex pellets and a copper-plated 295-grain Black Belt bullet. My partner fired at the same animal with a 7mm-08 which resulted only in the bullet blowing up on the animal's water-saturated hide, the jacket penetrating a short distance beneath the skin.

Traditions Performance Firearms

Three variants of Traditions' Buckhunter Pro are now available. The basic gun is offered in 50 caliber with a 9 1/2-inch barrel in either blued or C-Nickel bright finish. A 12-inch version is also available with a blued finish. The newest variant is a 14 3/4-inch barreled pistol with a fluted barrel and muzzle brake. The retail prices of these guns range from $219 to $277. A 54-caliber Buckhunter Pro was formerly offered, but is no longer available.

▲ Gonic barrel and forend on Thompson/Center Encore frame.

Thompson/Center Arms

T/C's 209x50 Encore pistol ($569 for complete pistol, $225 for the barrel) has a 15-inch barrel, a hand-filling grip, massive forend and an attached ramrod. This gun uses a 209 shotgun primer in a closed breech for weather-resistant ignition. Given the choice of shooting the Encore in the 30/06 or in the muzzleloading version, I much prefer the muzzleloader. Two, 50-grain Pyrodex pellets and bullets weighing between 300 and 370 grains is about all I want to shoot in this pistol. A more pleasant load for close-

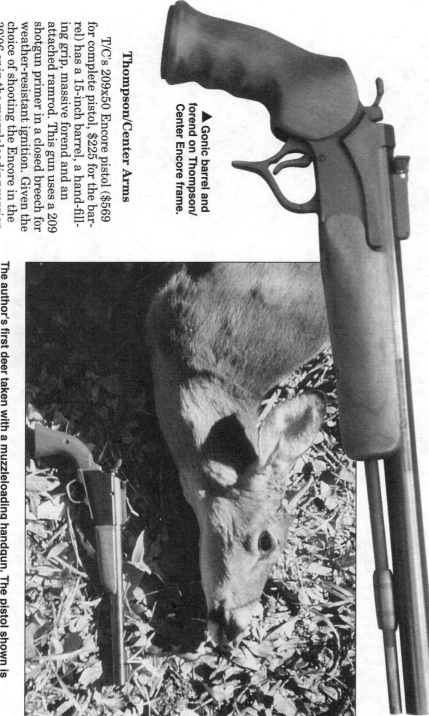

The author's first deer taken with a muzzleloading handgun. The pistol shown is Thompson/Center Arms' now-discontinued Scout in 50 caliber. This small buck was only one of seven deer taken by 60 hunters on a quota hunt at the Cumberland Island National Seashore. This hunt took place when temperatures dropped to 0 degrees Fahrenheit and hung in the low teens - the coldest winter on the Georgia coast in 70 years. The previous day the author took a similar-size doe with a cartridge handgun. For information about quota deer and hog hunts on the island call (912) 882-4336.

A beaver taken with the 50-caliber Thompson/Center Encore pistol firing two Pyrodex pellets and a Black-Belt bullet.

Although the least costly handgun in its class, the Buckhunter Pro is intrinsically accurate and, where allowable, is best fitted with a scope. I have taken a hog with the 12-inch, 50-caliber version of this pistol. The load I used was Traditions' saboted 275-grain Silver Lightning lead boattail bullet with a controlled-expansion plastic tip and 80 grains of *FFg*. The bullet performed well on the 50-pound animal. For heavier game, I prefer the 300-grain Spitzer Hollow Point for deeper penetration. The 12-inch barrel offers a significant improvement in velocity and shooting characteristics over the 9 1/2-inch barreled version of this handgun.

Recently, some appropriate models have been dropped by their manufacturers. The Thompson/Center Scout was discontinued after its tooling was destroyed during a fire at the Rochester, New Hampshire, plant. Modern Muzzleloading, the maker of the Knight Rifle and—until recently–the Hawkeye in-line pistol, has dropped this model. Markesbery Muzzleloaders has also indefinitely suspended production of it's big-game handgun.

Target visibility, bullet drop, delivered muzzle energy and bullet performance are the qualities that determine the technical side of taking big game with muzzleloading handguns. Looking at these qualities alone, there is no reason why appropriate loads used in any of the modern muzzleloading handguns

mentioned above cannot take deer at 100 yards.

The real limitations of these pistols are not technical considerations, but personal ones. The use of the best available rest is vital, as is taking

A tree stand is the safest place to be when hunting potentially dangerous animals with a muzzleloading single-shot pistol.

care the hands are supporting the gun - just like they did when the pistol was sighted in. I sight-in my pistols using a knee-braced sitting position because shots from sitting

either on the ground or from a tree stand, are my most common shots.

For the hunter who has some experience with pistol shooting but has not taken game with a muzzleloading pistol, the first try with an iron-sighted pistol on game should be at 35 yards or, if using a scope, out to perhaps 75 yards. Only with experience, and after determining the bullet's trajectory at longer ranges, should attempts to take big game be made at distances of 100 yards and beyond. For example, when the Encore pistol was zeroed at 25 yards with a load consisting of two Pyrodex pellets and a 295-grain Black Belt bullet, the bullet was shooting 2 inches low at 50 yards and 7 inches low at 100. Had I zeroed the gun to hit the point of aim at 50 yards, I would expect the bullet to be 2 to 3 inches high at 25 and 3 to 4 inches low at 100.

Although I have used Pyrodex pellets and saboted bullets with success in the Encore pistol, I prefer *FFg* blackpowder and Maxi-Balls or Black Belt bullets in these handguns. The Scout, designed for use with blackpowder, gives unreliable ignition with the new pellets. Except with reduced charges of about 40 grains for small game, round balls do not typically shoot well in these guns. In addition, round balls do not retain sufficient energy to meet my state's energy requirements. Even if they did, I like the typical *pass-through* performance offered by conical projectiles.

Heavier bullets, weighing between 320 and 380 grains in 50 caliber, or

Traditions' 50-caliber Buckhunter Pro with a 12-inch barrel and Thompson/Center scope. This is the least expensive blackpowder handgun that is capable of taking big game. Although the author found the 'issue' iron sights leave much to be desired, the gun shoots very well with a scope.

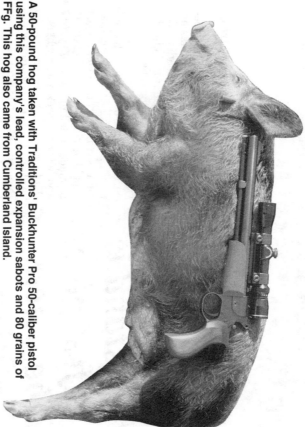

A 50-pound hog taken with Traditions' Buckhunter Pro 50-caliber pistol using this company's lead, controlled expansion sabots and 80 grains of FFg. This hog also came from Cumberland Island.

240/300-grain bullets in sabots, offer sufficient resistance to more completely burn heavy blackpowder charges in these 12 to 16-inch barrels. Depending on the gun, charges of between 80 (Traditions) and 110 grains (Encore) of *FFg* can be accommodated.

Two-handed holds are preferred with these long, heavy pistols. The most stable two-handed offhand grip is pulling on the handgrip while pushing forward on the forend, as if trying to stretch the pistol. With the Scout, which vents through the frame, the best stance is to hold the grip with one hand while supporting the wrist with the other.

Shooting these long-barreled guns from a rest is best of all. Firing from a rest reduces "wobble"-which not only increases confidence when making a shot, but also allows the shooter to pay more attention to trigger pull. One thing is absolutely certain. If I jerk the trigger, I will miss the deer -

even at 10 yards. Only practice will give a new shooter the skills needed to shoot fast while still retaining acceptable accuracy.

Toting these outsize handguns presents a unique set of problems. If holstered, they are slow and noisy to draw. If carried all day in the shooting hand, the hand and wrist become too fatigued to steadily support the gun when the time finally arrives to take a shot. The best carry for these guns is in the non-shooting hand with the gun reversed and the long barrel resting on the forearm and pointing away from the shooter. For some slim-gripped pistols, like the Scout, the thumb of the carrying hand can be hooked in the belt to take some of the weight off the arm. When it is time to fire, the pistol can be quickly and silently grasped by the shooting hand, raised to a two-handed firing position and discharged.

Holsters, slings and side-carried fanny packs can all be used to transport the gun to the hunting area, but when expecting to be in the presence of game the "on arm" carry described above is best of all.

Handguns, even those with 16-inch barrels, are easily pointed in unintended directions. Extra care must be taken to insure the gun is always pointed away from one's hunting companions.

Probably the most common unsafe act in handgun hunting is walking with a cocked pistol. The usual case is that game is sighted-the gun is cocked...then the game moves. In turn, the hunter moves to keep the animal in sight, forgetting for the moment he has a cocked pistol in his hand. *Never, ever* take a step while carrying a cocked handgun - even if it means passing up a shot. Similarly, do not sit with a cocked handgun in a tree stand. Should the gun fall, it has a very high probability of discharging.

Even though your quarry is down and apparently dead, reload and shoot the animal again in the spine at point-blank range. More than one "dead" hog, deer or bear has got up and done damage to the hunter because this safety shot was not taken. Lead is cheap, doctor bills aren't.

Of all types of blackpowder hunting arms, only the matchlock presents a greater challenge to taking game than a muzzleloading handgun. Consider: The game animal must be approached closely; only one opportunity exists to make a killing shot and a pistol is more difficult than a rifle to shoot well. With any muzzleloader, there is always the possibility the gun will not fire if weather conditions are poor or the pistol improperly loaded.

To circumvent these pitfalls and take any game at all with a black-powder pistol is an accomplishment. Not everyone has the opportunity, or desire, to shoot the biggest deer, hog etc. in the woods. Taking a nice doe for the freezer with a handgun returns the challenge to the hunt and elevates the commonplace to a memorable experience.

A selection of suitable handguns is available in a wide price range. The real challenge, as with all hunting, comes not so much from mastering the tools of the hunt and taking game, but from successfully overcoming our own physical shortcomings, mental lapses and fears. When a hunt is brought to a successful conclusion, the most lasting trophies are not those on the wall, but those in the mind - trophies that can be gathered by using a muzzleloading handgun. ●

CENTERFIRE HANDGUN CARTRIDGES — BALLISTICS & PRICES

Notes: Blanks are available in 32 S&W, 38 S&W and 38 Special. "V" after barrel length indicates test barrel was vented to produce ballistics similar to a revolver with a normal barrel-to-cylinder gap. Ammo prices are per 50 rounds except when marked with an ** which signifies a 20 round box; *** signifies a 25-round box. Not all loads are available from all ammo manufacturers. Listed loads are those made by Remington, Winchester, Federal, and others. DISC. is a discontinued load. Prices are rounded to nearest whole dollar and will vary with brand and retail outlet. † = new bullet weight this year; "c" indicates a change in data.

Cartridge	Bullet Wgt. Grs.	VELOCITY (fps)			ENERGY (ft. lbs.)			Mid-Range Traj. (in.)		Bbl. Lgth. (in).	Est. Price/box
		Muzzle	50 yds.	100 yds.	Muzzle	50 yds.	100 yds.	50 yds.	100 yds.		
221 Rem. Fireball	50	2650	2380	2130	780	630	505	0.2	0.8	10.5"	$15
25 Automatic	35	900	813	742	63	51	43	NA	NA	2"	$18
25 Automatic	45	815	730	655	65	55	40	1.8	7.7	2"	$21
25 Automatic	50	760	705	660	65	55	50	2.0	8.7	2"	$17
7.5mm Swiss	107	1010	NA	NA	240	NA	NA	NA	NA	NA	NEW
7.62mmTokarev	87	1390	NA	NA	365	NA	NA	0.6	NA	4.5"	NA
7.62 Nagant	97	1080	NA	NA	350	NA	NA	NA	NA	NA	NEW
7.63 Mauser	88	1440	NA	NA	405	NA	NA	NA	NA	NA	NEW
30 Luger	93†	1220	1110	1040	305	255	225	0.9	3.5	4.5"	$34
30 Carbine	110	1790	1600	1430	785	625	500	0.4	1.7	10"	$28
32 S&W	88	680	645	610	90	80	75	2.5	10.5	3"	$17
32 S&W Long	98	705	670	635	115	100	90	2.3	10.5	4"	$17
32 Short Colt	80	745	665	590	100	80	60	2.2	9.9	4"	$19
32 H&R Magnum	85	1100	1020	930	230	195	165	1.0	4.3	4.5"	$21
32 H&R Magnum	95	1030	940	900	225	190	170	1.1	4.7	4.5"	$19
32 Automatic	60	970	895	835	125	105	95	1.3	5.4	4"	$22
32 Automatic	60	1000	917	849	133	112	96	NA	NA	4"	NA
32 Automatic	65	950	890	830	130	115	100	1.3	5.6	NA	NA
32 Automatic	71	905	855	810	130	115	95	1.4	5.8	4"	$19
8mm Lebel Pistol	111	850	NA	NA	180	NA	NA	NA	NA	NA	NEW
8mm Steyr	112	1080	NA	NA	290	NA	NA	NA	NA	NA	NEW
8mm Gasser	126	850	NA	NA	200	NA	NA	NA	NA	NA	NEW
380 Automatic	60	1130	960	NA	170	120	NA	1.0	NA	NA	NA
380 Automatic	85/88	990	920	870	190	165	145	1.2	5.1	4"	$20
380 Automatic	90	1000	890	800	200	160	130	1.2	5.5	3.75"	$10
380 Automatic	95/100	955	865	785	190	160	130	1.4	5.9	4"	$20
38 Super Auto +P	115	1300	1145	1040	430	335	275	0.7	3.3	5"	$26
38 Super Auto +P	125/130	1215	1100	1015	425	350	300	0.8	3.6	5"	$26
38 Super Auto +P	147	1100	1050	1000	395	355	325	0.9	4.0	5"	NA
9x18mm Makarov	95	1000	NA	NA	240	NA	NA	NA	NA	NA	NEW
9x18mm Ultra	100	1050	NA	NA	240	NA	NA	NA	NA	NA	NEW
9x23mm Largo	124	1190	1055	966	390	306	257	0.7	3.7	4"	$21
9x23mm Win.	125	1450	1249	1103	583	433	338	0.6	2.8	NA	$23
9mm Steyr	115	1180	NA	NA	350	NA	NA	NA	NA	NA	NEW
9mm Luger	88	1500	1190	1010	440	275	200	0.6	3.1	4"	$24
9mm Luger	90	1360	1112	978	370	247	191	NA	NA	4"	$26
9mm Luger	95	1300	1140	1010	350	275	215	0.8	3.4	4"	NA
9mm Luger	100	1180	1080	NA	305	255	NA	0.9	NA	4"	NA
9mm Luger +P	115	1155	1045	970	340	280	240	0.9	3.9	4"	$21
9mm Luger +P	123/125	1110	1030	970	340	290	260	1.0	4.0	4"	$23
9mm Luger	140	935	890	850	270	245	225	1.3	5.5	4"	$23
9mm Luger	147	990	940	900	320	290	265	1.1	4.9	4"	$26
9mm Luger +P	90	1475	NA	NA	437	NA	NA	NA	NA	NA	NA
9mm Luger +P	115	1250	1113	1019	399	316	265	0.8	3.5	4"	$27
9mm Federal	115	1280	1130	1040	420	330	280	0.7	3.3	4"V	$24
9mm Luger Vector	115	1155	1047	971	341	280	241	NA	NA	4"V	NA
9mm Luger +P	124	1180	1089	1021	384	327	287	0.8	3.8	4"	NA
38 S&W	146	685	650	620	150	135	125	2.4	10.0	4"	$19
38 Short Colt	125	730	685	645	150	130	115	2.2	9.4	6"	$19
39 Special	100	950	900	NA	200	180	NA	1.3	NA	4"V	NA
38 Special	110	945	895	850	220	195	175	1.3	5.4	4"V	$23

CENTERFIRE HANDGUN CARTRIDGES — BALLISTICS & PRICES, continued

Notes: Blanks are available in 32 S&W, 38 S&W and 38 Special. "v" after barrel length indicates test barrel was vented to produce ballistics similar to a revolver with a normal barrel-to-cylinder gap. Ammo prices are per 50 rounds except when marked with an ** which signifies a 20 round box; *** signifies a 25-round box. Not all loads are available from all ammo manufacturers. Listed loads are those made by Remington, Winchester, Federal, and others. DISC. is a discontinued load. Prices are rounded to nearest whole dollar and will vary with brand and retail outlet. † = new bullet weight this year; "c" indicates a change in data.

Cartridge	Bullet Wgt. Grs.	VELOCITY (fps) Muzzle	50 yds.	100 yds.	ENERGY (ft. lbs.) Muzzle	50 yds.	100 yds.	Mid-Range Traj. (in.) 50 yds.	100 yds.	Bbl. Lgth. (in).	Est. Price/box
38 cont.											
38 Special	110	945	895	850	220	195	175	1.3	5.4	4"V	$23
38 Special	130	775	745	710	175	160	120	1.9	7.9	4"V	$22
38 Special Cowboy	140	800	767	735	199	183	168				NA
38 (Multi-Ball)	140	830	730	505	215	130	80	2.0	10.6	7.5"V	$10**
38 Special	148	710	635	565	165	130	105	2.4	10.6	4"V	$17
38 Special	158	755	725	690	200	185	170	2.0	8.3	4"V	$18
38 Special +P	95	1175	1045	960	290	230	195	0.9	3.9	4"V	$23
38 Special +P	110	995	925	870	240	210	185	1.2	5.1	4"V	$23
38 Special +P	125	975	929	885	264	238	218	1.2	5.2	4"	$23
38 Special +P	125	945	900	860	250	225	205	1.3	5.4	4"	#23
38 Special +P	129	945	910	870	255	235	215	1.3	5.3	4"V	$11
38 Special +P	130	925	887	852	247	227	210	1.3	5.50	4"V	$11
38 Special +P	147/150(c)	884	NA	NA	264	NA	NA	1.3	5.50	4"V	$27
38 Special +P	158	890	855	825	280	255	240	1.4	6.0	4"V	$20
357											
357 SIG	115	1520	NA	NA	593	NA	NA	NA	NA	4"V	NA
357 SIG	124	1450	NA	NA	578	NA	NA	NA	NA	4"V	NA
357 Mag., Super Clean	105	1650	NA	NA	NA	NA	NA	NA	NA	NA	NA
357 SIG	125	1350	1190	1080	510	395	325	0.7	3.1	4"	$25
357 SIG	150	1130	1030	970	420	355	310	0.9	4.0	NA	NA
357 Magnum	110	1295	1095	975	410	290	230	0.8	3.5	NA	NA
357 Magnum	125	1450	1240	1090	585	425	330	0.6	2.8	4"V	$25
357 (Multi-Ball)	140	1155	830	665	420	215	135	1.2	6.4	4"V	$11**
357 Magnum	140	1360	1195	1075	575	445	360	0.7	3.0	4"V	$25
357 Magnum	145	1290	1155	1060	535	430	360	0.8	3.5	4"V	$25
357 Magnum	150/158	1235	1105	1015	535	430	360	0.8	3.5	4"V	$25
357 Mag. Cowboy	158	800	761	725	225	203	185	0.8	3.5	NA	$25
357 Magnum	165	1290	1189	1108	610	518	450	0.7	3.1	8-3/8"	NA
357 Magnum	180	1145	1055	985	525	445	390	0.9	3.9	8"V	$25
357 Magnum	180	1180	1088	1020	557	473	416	0.8	3.6	8"V	NA
357 Mag. CorBon F.A.	180	1650	1512	1386	1088	913	767	0.0	1.66	NA	NA
357 Mag. CorBon	200	1200	1123	1061	640	560	500	0.0	3.19	NA	NA
357 Rem. Maximum	158	1825	1590	1380	1170	885	670	0.4	1.7	10.5"	$14**
40, 10mm											
40 S&W	135	1140	1070	NA	390	345	NA	0.9	NA	4"	NA
40 S&W	155	1140	1026	958	447	362	309	0.9	4.1	4"	$14***
40 S&W	165	1150	NA	NA	485	NA	NA	NA	NA	4"	$18***
40 S&W	180	985	936	893	388	350	319	1.4	5.0	4"	$14***
40 S&W	180	1015	960	914	412	368	334	1.3	4.5	4"	$14**
40 S&W	180	950	905	865	361	327	299	1.5	5.4	4"	$16**
400 Cor-Bon	135	1450	NA	NA	630	NA	NA	NA	NA	5"	$26
10mm Automatic	155	1125	1046	986	436	377	335	0.9	3.9	5"	NA
10mm Automatic	170	1340	1165	1145	680	510	415	0.7	3.2	5"	$31
10mm Automatic	175	1290	1140	1035	650	505	420	0.7	3.3	5.5"	$11**
10mm Auto. (FBI)	180	950	905	865	361	327	299	1.5	5.4	4"	$16**
10mm Automatic	180	1030	970	920	425	375	340	1.1	4.7	5"	$16**
10mm Automatic	180	1030	970	920	425	375	340	1.1	4.7	5"	$16**
10mm Auto H.V.	180†	1240	1124	1037	618	504	430	0.8	3.4	5"	$27
10mm Automatic	200	1160	1070	1010	598	510	430	0.9	3.8	5"	$14**
10.4mm Italian	177	950	NA	NA	360	NA	NA	NA	NA	NA	NEW

CENTERFIRE HANDGUN CARTRIDGES — BALLISTICS & PRICES, *continued*

Notes: Blanks are available in 32 S&W, 38 S&W and 38 Special. "V" after barrel length indicates test barrel was vented to produce ballistics similar to a revolver with a normal barrel-to-cylinder gap. Ammo prices are per 50 rounds except when marked with an ** which signifies a 20 round box; *** signifies a 25-round box. Not all loads are available from all ammo manufacturers. Listed loads are those made by Remington, Winchester, Federal, and others. DISC. is a discontinued load. Prices are rounded to nearest whole dollar and will vary with brand and retail outlet. † = new bullet weight this year; "c" indicates a change in data.

(Left-margin section tabs: "40, 10mm cont." · "44" · "45, 50")

Cartridge	Bullet Wgt. Grs.	VELOCITY (fps) Muzzle	50 yds.	100 yds.	ENERGY (ft. lbs.) Muzzle	50 yds.	100 yds.	Mid-Range Traj. (in.) 50 yds.	100 yds.	Bbl. Lgth. (in.)	Est. Price/box
41 Action Exp.	180	1000	947	903	400	359	326	0.5	4.2	5"	$13**
41 Rem. Magnum	170	1420	1165	1015	760	515	390	0.7	3.2	4"V	$33
41 Rem. Magnum	175	1250	1120	1030	605	490	410	0.8	3.4	4"V	$14**
41 (Med. Vel.)	210	965	900	840	435	375	330	1.3	5.4	4"V	$30
41 Rem. Magnum	210	1300	1160	1060	790	630	535	0.7	3.2	4"V	$33
44 S&W Russian	247	780	NA	NA	335	NA	NA	NA	NA	6.5"	NA
44 S&W Special	180	980	NA	NA	383	NA	NA	NA	NA	7.5"V	NA
44 S&W Special	180	1000	935	882	400	350	311	1.2	6.0	6"	$13**
44 S&W Special	200†	875	825	780	340	302	270	1.1	4.9	6.5"	$13**
44 S&W Special	200	1035	940	865	475	390	335	2.0	8.3	6.5"	$26
44 S&W Special	240/246	755	725	695	310	285	265	NA	NA	NA	NA
44-40 Win. Cowboy	225	750	723	695	281	261	242	0.5	2.3	NA	NA
44 Rem. Magnum	180	1610	1365	1175	1035	745	550	NA	NA	4"V	$18**
44 Rem. Magnum	200	1400	1192	1053	870	630	492	0.6	2.5	6.5"	$20
44 Rem. Magnum	210	1495	1310	1165	1040	805	635	0.6	2.5	6.5"	$18**
44 (Med. Vel.)	240	1000	945	900	535	475	435	1.1	4.8	6.5"	$17
44 R.M. (Jacketed)	240	1180	1080	1010	740	625	545	0.9	3.7	4"V	$18**
44 R.M. (Lead)	240	1350	1185	1070	970	750	610	0.7	3.1	4"V	$29
44 Rem. Magnum	250	1180	1100	1040	775	670	600	0.8	3.6	6.5"V	$21
44 Rem. Magnum	250	1230	1132	1057	840	711	620	0.8	2.9	6.5"V	NA
44 Rem. Magnum	275	1235	1142	1070	931	797	699	0.8	3.3	6.5"	NA
44 Rem. Magnum	300	1200	1100	1026	959	806	702	NA	NA	7.5"	$17
44 Rem. Magnum	330	1385	1297	1220	1406	1234	1090	1.83	0.00	NA	NA
440 CorBon	260	1700	1544	1403	1669	1377	1136	1.58	NA	10	NA
450 Short Colt/450 Revolver	226	830	NA	NA	350	NA	NA	NA	NA	NA	NEW
45 S&W Schofield	180	730	NA	NA	213	NA	NA	NA	NA	NA	NA
45 S&W Schofield	230	730	NA	NA	272	NA	NA	na	NA	NA	NA
45 Automatic	165	1030	930	890	385	315	290	1.2	4.9	5"	$28
45 Automatic	185	1000	940	890	410	360	325	1.1	8.7	5"	$28
45 Auto. (Match)	185	770	705	650	245	204	175	2.0	8.6	5"	$20
45 Auto. (Match)	200	940	890	840	392	352	312	2.0	5.0	5"	$18
45 Automatic	200	975	917	860	421	372	328	1.4	6.8	5"	$27
45 Automatic	230	830	800	775	355	325	300	1.6	6.1	5"	NA
45 Automatic	230	880	846	816	396	366	340	1.5	NA	5"	$31
45 Automatic +P	165	1250	NA	NA	573	NA	NA	0.9	4.0	5"	NA
45 Automatic +P	185	1140	1040	970	535	445	385	NA	NA	5"	NA
45 Automatic +P	200	1055	982	925	494	428	380	NA	NA	5"	$17
45 Super	185	1300	1190	1108	694	582	504	0.6	2.8	5"	$14**
45 Win. Magnum	230	1400	1230	1105	1000	775	635	0.8	3.3	5"	$16**
45 Win. Magnum	260	1250	1137	1053	902	746	640	NA	NA	5"	NA
45 Win. Mag. CorBon	320	1150	1080	1025	940	830	747	3.47	NA	NA	NA
455 Webley MKII	262	850	NA	NA	420	NA	NA	NA	NA	NA	$21
45 Colt	200	1000	938	889	444	391	351	1.3	4.8	5.5"	$22
45 Colt	225	960	890	830	460	395	345	1.3	5.5	5.5"	NA
45 Colt + P CorBon	265	1350	1225	1126	1073	884	746	2.65	0.0	5"	NA
45 Colt + P CorBon	300	1300	1197	1114	1126	956	827	2.78	0.0	5"	$18
45 Colt	250/255	860	820	780	410	375	340	1.6	6.6	5.5"	$27
454 Casull	250	1300	1151	1047	938	735	608	0.7	3.2	7.5"V	NA
454 Casull	260	1800	1577	1381	1871	1436	1101	0.4	1.8	7.5"V	NA
454 Casull	300	1625	1451	1308	1759	1413	1141	0.5	2.0	7.5"V	NA
454 Casull CorBon	360	1500	1387	1286	1800	1538	1323	2.01	0.0	NA	NA
475 Linebaugh	400	1350	1217	1119	1618	1315	1112	NA	NA	NA	NA
50 Action Exp.	325	1400	1209	1075	1414	1055	835	0.2	2.3	6"	$24**

COMPLETE COMPACT CATALOG

HANDGUNS 2001

REFERENCE

ACCESSORIES

HANDGUNS

GUNDEX

GUNDEX

GUNDEX

NEW!

BRILEY 1911-STYLE AUTO PISTOLS
Caliber: 9mm Para, 38 Super, 40 S&W, 10-shot magazine; 45 ACP, 8-shot magazine. **Barrel:** 3.6" or 5". **Weight:** NA. **Length:** NA. **Grips:** rosewood or rubber. **Sights:** Bo-Mar adjustable rear, Briley dovetail blade front. **Features:** Modular or Caspian alloy, carbon steel or stainless steel frame; match barrel and trigger group; lowered and flared ejection port; front and rear serrations on slide; beavertail grip safety; hot blue, hard chrome or stainless steel finish. Introduced 2000. Made in U.S. From Briley Manufacturing Inc.
Price: Fantom (3.6" bbl., fixed low-mount rear sight, armor coated lower receiver) . . . . from **$1,795.00**
Price: Fantom with two-port compensator . . . . from **$2,145.00**
Price: Advantage (5" bbl., adj. low-mount rear sight, checkered mainspring housing) . . . . from **$1,495.00**
Price: Versatility Plus (5" bbl., adj. low-mount rear sight, modular or Caspian frame) . . . . from **$1,695.00**
Price: Signature Series (5" bbl., adj. low-mount rear sight, 40 S&W only) . . . . from **$1,995.00**
Price: Plate Master (5" bbl. with compensator, lightened slide, Briley scope mount) . . . . from **$1,795.00**
Price: El Presidente (5" bbl. with Briley quad compensator, Briley scope mount) . . . . from **$2,195.00**

ED BROWN CLASSIC CUSTOM AND CLASS A LIMITED 1911-STYLE AUTO PISTOLS
Caliber: 45 ACP; 7-shot magazine; 40 S&W, 400 Cor-Bon, 38 Super, 9x23, 9mm Para. **Barrel:** 4.25", 5", 6". **Weight:** NA. **Length:** NA. **Grips:** Hogue exotic checkered wood. **Sights:** Bo-Mar or Novak rear, blade front. **Features:** Blued or stainless steel frame; ambidextrous safety; beavertail grip safety; checkered forestrap and mainspring housing; match-grade barrel; slotted hammer; long lightweight or Videki short steel trigger. Many options offered. Made in U.S. by Ed Brown Products.
Price: Classic Custom (45 ACP, 5" barrel) . . . . from **$2,499.00**

EUROPEAN AMERICAN ARMORY WITNESS AUTO PISTOLS
Caliber: 9mm Para, 9x21, 38 Super, 40 S&W, 45 ACP, 10mm; 10-shot magazine. **Barrel:** 3.55", 3.66", 4.25", 4.5", 4.75", 5.25". **Weight:** 26 to 38 oz. **Length:** 7.25" to 10.5" overall. **Sights:** three-dot, windage-adjustable or fully adjustable rear, blade front. **Grips:** Black rubber, smooth walnut, checkered walnut, ivory polymer. **Features:** Single and double action; polymer or forged steel frame; forged steel slide; field strips without tools; ergonomic grip angle; front and rear serrations on slide; matte blue and stainless steel finish. Frame can be converted to other calibers. Imported from Italy by European American Armory.
Price: Witness Full Size (4.5" bbl., three-dot sights, 8.1" overall) . . . . from **$399.00**
Price: Witness Compact (3.66" bbl., three-dot sights, 7.25" overall) . . . . from **$399.00**

Price: Class A Limited (all calibers; several bbl. lengths in competition and carry forms) . . . . from **$1,999.00**

Price: Carry-Comp (4.25" bbl. with compensator, three-dot sights, 8.1" overall) . . . . from **$439.00**
Price: Gold Team (5.25" bbl. with compensator, adjustable sights, 10.5" overall) . . . . from **$2,195.00**
Price: Silver Team (5.25" bbl. with compensator, adjustable sights, 9.75" overall) . . . . from **$999.00**
Price: Limited Class (4.75" barrel, adj. sights and trigger, drilled for scope mount) . . . . from **$999.00**
Price: P-Series (4.55" bbl., polymer frame in four colors, many porting and sight options) . . . . from **$379.00**

KIMBER CUSTOM 1911-STYLE AUTO PISTOLS
Caliber: 9mm Para, 38 Super, 9-shot magazines; 40 S&W, 8-shot magazine; 45 ACP, 7-shot magazine. **Barrel:** 5". **Weight:** 38 oz. **Length:** 8.7" overall. **Grips:** Black synthetic, smooth or double-diamond checkered rosewood, or double-diamond checkered walnut. **Sights:** McCormick low profile or Kimber adjustable rear, blade front. **Features:** Machined steel slide, frame and barrel; match-grade barrel; adjustable aluminum trigger; full-length button-rifled, match-grade barrel; adjustable beavertail safety; beveled guide rod; Commander-style hammer; high-ride beavertail safety; beveled magazine well. Other models available. Made in U.S. by Kimber Mfg. Inc.
Price: Custom (black matte finish) . . . . from **$723.00**
Price: Custom Royal (polished blue finish, checkered rosewood grips) **$745.00**
Price: Custom Stainless (satin-finished stainless steel frame and slide) **$825.00**
Price: Custom Target (matte black or stainless finish, Kimber adj. sight) **$935.00**

Ed Brown Classic

Ed Brown Classic Class A

Kimber Custom Compact CDP

SEMI-CUSTOM HANDGUNS — AUTOLOADERS

North American Arms Guardian with gold accents

Kimber Custom Pro CDP

Kimber Ultra CDP

Price: Custom Compact CDP (4" bbl., alum. frame, tritium three-dot sights, 28 oz.) **$1,109.00**

Price: Custom Pro CDP (4" bbl., alum. frame, tritium sights, full-length grip, 28 oz.) **$1,109.00**

Price: Ultra CDP (3" bbl., aluminum frame, tritium sights, 25 oz.) **$1,109.00**

Price: Gold Match (polished blue finish, hand-fitted barrel, ambid. safety) **$1,135.00**

Price: Stainless Gold Match (stainless steel frame and slide, hand-fitted bbl., amb. safety) **$1,277.00**

Price: Gold Combat (hand-fitted, stainless barrel; KimPro black finish, tritium sights) **$1,633.00**

Price: Gold Combat Stainless (stainless frame and slide, satin silver finish, tritium sights) **$1,576.00**

Price: Super Match (satin stainless frame, KimPro black finished, stainless slide) **$1,871.00**

LES BAER CUSTOM 1911-STYLE AUTO PISTOLS

Caliber: 9mm Para., 38 Super, 40 S&W, 45 ACP, 400 Cor-Bon; 7- or 8-shot magazine. **Barrel:** 4-1/4", 5", 6". **Weight:** 28 to 40 oz. **Length:** NA. **Grips:** Checkered cocobolo. **Sights:** Low-mount combat fixed, combat fixed with tritium inserts or low-mount adjustable rear, dovetail front. **Features:** Forged steel or aluminum frame; slide serrated front and rear; low-ered and flared ejection port; beveled magazine well; speed trigger with

4-pound pull; beavertail grip safety; ambidextrous safety. Other models available. Made in U.S. by Les Baer Custom.

Price: Baer 1911 Premier II 5" Model (5" bbl., optional stainless steel frame and slide) . . . . from **$1,428.00**

Price: Premier II 6" Model (6" barrel) . . . . from **$1,595.00**

Price: Premier II LW1 (forged aluminum frame, steel slide and barrel) . . . . from **$1,740.00**

Price: Custom Carry (4" or 5" barrel, steel frame) . . . from **$1,640.00**

Price: Custom Carry (4" barrel, aluminum frame) . . . . . from **$1,923.00**

Price: Swift Response Pistol (fixed tritium sights, Bear Coat finish) . . . . from **$2,495.00**

Price: Monolith (5" barrel and slide with extra-long dust cover) . . . . from **$1,599.00**

Price: Stinger (4-1/4" barrel, steel or aluminum frame) . . . from **$1,491.00**

Price: Thunder Ranch Special (tritium fixed combat sight, Thunder Ranch logo) . . . . from **$1,620.00**

Price: National Match Hardball (low-mount adj. sight; meets DCM rules) . . . . from **$1,335.00**

Price: Bullseye Wadcutter Pistol (Bo-Mar rib w/ adj. sight, guar. 2-1/2" groups) . . . . from **$1,495.00**

Price: Ultimate Master Combat (5" or 6" bbl., adj. sights, checkered front strap) . . . . from **$2,376.00**

Price: Ultimate Master Combat Compensated (four-port compensator, adj. sights) . . . . from **$2,476.00**

NORTH AMERICAN ARMS GUARDIAN AUTO PISTOL

Caliber: 32 ACP, 6-shot magazine. **Barrel:** 2.18". **Weight:** 13.57 oz. **Length:** 4.36" overall. **Grips:** Checkered or smooth; cocobolo, kingwood, winewood, goncalo alves, pau ferro, white or black simulated mother of pearl. **Sights:** White dot, fiber optics or tritium (nine models). **Features:** Double action only; stainless steel frame and slide; barrel porting; frame stippling; forward striped or scalloped slide serrations; meltdown (rounded edges) treatment; slide/frame finishes available in combinations that in-clude black titanium, stainless steel, gold titanium and highly polished or matte choices. From North American Arms Custom Shop.

Price: NAA-32 Guardian. **$359.00**

Price: Gold or black titanium finish. . . . . add **$120.00**

Price: High-polish finish . . . . add **$150.00**

Price: Ported barrel . . . . add **$90.00**

SEMI-CUSTOM HANDGUNS — AUTOLOADERS

**North American
Arms Guardian
with high polish finish**

**North American
Arms Guardian
with matte finish**

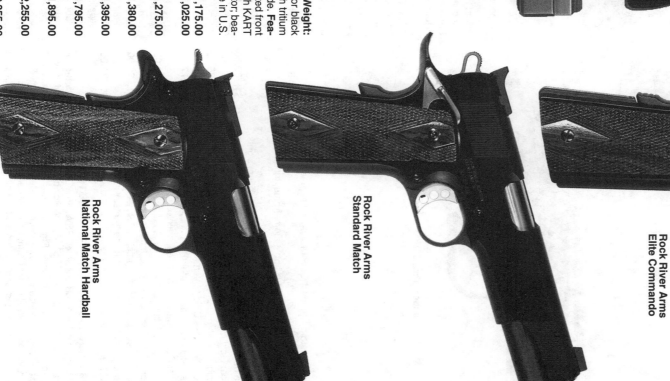

**Rock River Arms
National Match Hardball**

**Rock River Arms
Standard Match**

**Rock River Arms
Elite Commando**

ROCK RIVER ARMS 1911-STYLE AUTO PISTOLS

Caliber: 9mm Para., 38 Super, 40 S&W, 45 ACP. **Barrel:** 4" or 5". **Weight:** NA. **Length:** NA. **Grips:** Double-diamond, checkered cocobolo or black synthetic. **Sights:** Bo-Mar low-mount adjustable, Novak fixed with tritium inserts, Heine fixed or Rock River scope mount; dovetail front blade. **Features:** Chrome-moly, machined steel frame and slide; slide serrated front and rear; aluminum speed trigger with 3.5-4 lb. pull; national match KART barrel; lowered and flared ejection port; tuned and polished extractor; beavertail grip safety; beveled mag. well. Other frames offered. Made in U.S. by Rock River Arms Inc.

Price: Elite Commando (4" barrel, Novak tritium sights) . . from **$1,175.00**
Price: Standard Match (5" barrel, Heine fixed sights). . . . from **$1,025.00**
Price: National Match Hardball (5" barrel, Bo-Mar adj. sights)
. . . . from **$1,275.00**
Price: Bullseye Wadcutter (5" barrel, Rock River slide scope
mount) . . . . from **$1,380.00**
Price: Basic Limited Match (5" barrel, Bo-Mar adj. sights)
. . . . from **$1,395.00**
Price: Limited Match (5" barrel, guaranteed 1-1/2" groups
at 50 yards) . . . . from **$1,795.00**
Price: Hi-Cap Basic Limited (5" barrel, four frame choices)
. . . . from **$1,895.00**
Price: Ultimate Match Achiever (5" bbl. with compensator,
mount and Aimpoint) . . . . from **$2,255.00**
Price: Match Master Steel (5" bbl. with compensator,
mount and Aimpoint) . . . . from **$2,355.00**

SEMI-CUSTOM HANDGUNS — AUTOLOADERS

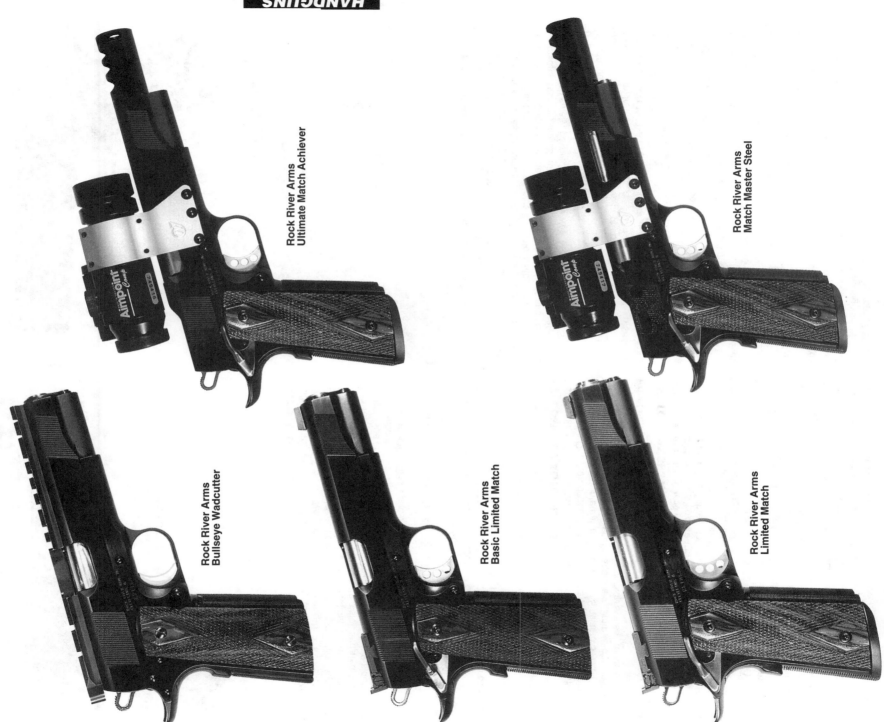

**Rock River Arms
Ultimate Match Achiever**

**Rock River Arms
Match Master Steel**

**Rock River Arms
Bullseye Wadcutter**

**Rock River Arms
Basic Limited Match**

**Rock River Arms
Limited Match**

SEMI-CUSTOM HANDGUNS — AUTOLOADERS

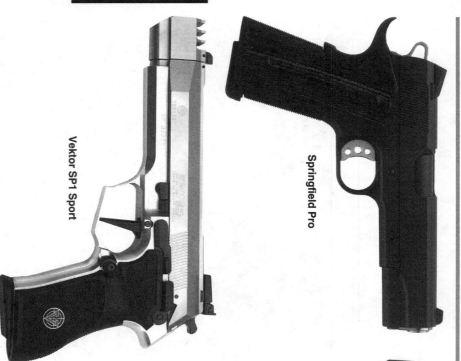

Vektor SP1 Sport

Springfield Pro

Vektor SP1 Target

SPRINGFIELD ARMORY 1911-STYLE AUTO PISTOLS

Caliber: 9mm Para., 8- or 9-shot magazine; 45 ACP, 7-, 8- or 10-shot magazine, 7-shot magazine. **Barrel:** 3.5", 3.9", 5", 6". **Weight:** 25 to 41 oz. **Length:** 7" to 9.5" overall. **Grips:** Checkered cocobolo or synthetic. **Sights:** Novak low-profile, Novak tritium or adjustable target rear; blade front. **Features:** Parkerized, blued, stainless steel or bi-tone frame and slide; lightweight Delta hammer; match trigger; front and rear slide serrations; hammer-forged, air-gauged barrel; beavertail grip safety; extended thumb safety; beveled magazine well. Made in U.S. From Springfield Inc.

Price: Mil-Spec 1911-A1 (5" barrel, fixed three-dot sights, parkerized finish) $610.00
Price: Full-Size 1911-A1 (5" bbl., Novak fixed or adj. sights, steel or alum. frame) $648.00
Price: Champion 1911-A1 (3.9" bbl., Novak fixed sights, steel or alum. frame) .... from $669.00
Price: Compact 1911-A1 (3.9" bbl., Novak fixed sights, alum. frame) .... from $678.00
Price: Ultra-Compact 1911-A1 (3.5" bbl., Novak fixed sights, steel or alum. frame) .... from $669.00
Price: Trophy Match 1911-A1 (5" or 6" bbl., adj. sights, blued or stainless) .... from $1,089.00
Price: Long Slide 1911-A1 (6" bbl., adj. sights, stainless, 45 ACP or 45 Super) .... from $849.00
Price: Full Size High Capacity (5" bbl., Novak fixed sights, two 10-shot magazines) .... from $733.00
Price: Ultra Compact High Capacity (3.5" bbl., Novak fixed sights, 10-shot mag.) .... from $759.00
Price: Tactical Response Pistol (3.9 or 5", Novak fixed sights, Teflon or stain.) .... from $1,289.00
Price: Professional Model (5" bbl., Novak three-dot tritium sights, Black-T finish) .... from $2,395.00

STI 2011 AUTO PISTOLS

Caliber: 9mm Para., 9x23, 38 Super, 40 S&W, 10mm, 45 ACP. **Barrel:** 3.4", 5", 5.5", 6". **Weight:** 28 to 44 oz. **Length:** 7" to 9-5/8" overall. **Grips:** Checkered, double-diamond rosewood or glass-filled nylon polymer (six colors). **Sights:** STI, Novak or Heine adjustable rear, blade front. **Features:** Updated version of 1911-style auto pistol; serrated slide, front and rear; STI skeletonized trigger; ambidextrous or single-sided thumb safety; blue or hard-chrome finish; etched logo and model name. From STI International.

Price: Competitor (38 Super, 5.5" barrel, C-More Rail Scope and mount) .... from $2,499.00
Price: Trojan (9mm, 45 ACP, 40 Super, 40 S&W; 5" or 6" barrel) .... from $970.00
Price: Edge 5.0" (40 S&W or 45 ACP; 5" barrel) .... from $1,776.00
Price: Eagle 5.0" (9mm, 9x23, 38 Super, 40 S&W, 10mm, 40 Super, 45 ACP; 5" bbl.) .... from $1,699.00
Price: Eagle 6.0" (9mm, 38 Super, 40 S&W, 10mm, 40 Super, 45 ACP; 6" bbl.) .... from $1,795.40
Price: BLS9/BLS40 (9mm, 40 S&W; 3.4" barrel, full-length grip) .... from $843.70

STI COMPACT AUTO PISTOLS

Caliber: 9mm Para., 40 S&W. **Barrel:** 3.4". **Weight:** 28 oz. **Length:** 7" overall. **Grips:** Checkered double-diamond rosewood. **Sights:** Heine Low Mount fixed rear, slide integral front. **Features:** Similar to STI 2011 models except has compact frame, 7-shot magazine in 9mm (6-shot in 40 cal.), single-sided thumb safety, linkless barrel lockup system, matte blue finish. From STI International.

Price: (9mm Para. or 40 S&W) .... from $746.50

VEKTOR SP1/SP2 AUTO PISTOLS

Caliber: 9mm Para., 40 S&W. 10-shot magazine. **Barrel:** 4", 4-5/8", 5", 5-7/8". **Weight:** 31.5 to 42 oz. **Length:** 7-1/2" to 11" overall. **Grips:** Black synthetic. **Sights:** Fixed, three-dot adjustable or scope mount; blade front. **Features:** Cold forged, polygon-rifled barrel; Aluminum alloy frame with machined steel slide; blued, anodized or nickel finish. Imported from South Africa by Vektor USA.

Price: SP1 Service Pistol (9mm Para., 4-5/8" barrel, fixed sights) .... from $619.95
Price: SP2 Service Pistol (40 S&W, 4-5/8" barrel, fixed sights) .... from $649.95
Price: SP1 Sport Pistol (9mm, 5" bbl. with compensator, combat sight, trigger stop) .... from $849.95
Price: SP1 Target Pistol (9mm, 5-7/8" bbl. with compensator, three-dot sights, adj. trigger) .... from $1,199.95
Price: SP1 Ultra Sport (9mm, 5-7/8" bbl. with comp., integral Weaver rail, polymer mount) $1,949.95

An American gunmaking legend . . . has returned.

Rekindle your love affair with one of the finest double guns ever built... the Ithaca N.I.D.

Grade 7E

Grade 4E

Special Field Grade

Ron Sauter

Ithaca
CLASSIC DOUBLES
The Legend Returns

The Old Station, #5 Railroad St.
Victor, NY 14564

A Classic American game gun with hand fitting, checkering and engraving available in 16, 20, 28 and .410 bore. Visit our custom shop by appointment, or contact one of our exclusive Dealers. Visit our website at http://gunshop.com/ithaca_classic.htm

Ithaca trademarks used under license of Ithaca Gun Company LLC.

Chadick's Ltd., Inc.	(972) 563-7577	The Gun Room	(401) 267-0102
Doug Turnbull Restoration	(716) 657-6338	Kittery Trading Post	(207) 439-2700
Fieldsport	(616) 933-0767	William Larkin Moore & Co.	(602) 951-8913
Firing Line	(303) 363-0041	Orvis Company	(802) 362-2580
Game Fair, Ltd.	(615) 353-0602	Sheldon Snyder & Co.	(843) 846-0408
The Gentleman Hunter, Inc.	(301) 907-4668	The Way It Was, Inc.	(609) 231-0111

Expert Firearms Information At Your Fingertips

GUNS ILLUSTRATED 2001
33rd ANNUAL EDITION

Edited by
Ken Ramage

EXPERT REPORTS:
• New Big Bore Hunting Handguns
• Titanium Arrives!
• Small Pistols
• Latest .22s
...and More!

Exclusive!
GUNDEX
catalog
gun finder

The
Standard
Reference
for Today's
Firearms

Expanded,
Illustrated
Complete
Sporting
Arms
Catalog

Handguns • Rifles • Shotguns
Muzzleloaders • Airguns
Directory of Arms Manufacturers

HANDGUNS 2001
13th Annual Edition

Latest Handguns For Sport & Personal Protection

Edited by
Ken Ramage

Test Reports:
• Taurus Big Bore Snubbies
• Magnum Research BFR
• SIG Pro Polymer
• Beretta 8045
...and more!

All New Expert Reports: Trends • Custom Guns
Ammunition • Reloading

Illustrated
Catalog
• Revolvers
• Autoloaders
• Single Shots
• Blackpowder
• Airguns

Accessories

Handguns 2001

13th Annual Edition
Edited by Ken Ramage

Virtually every current production handgun sold in America - plus a new section on semi-custom handguns- is found in this practical volume. Pistol and revolver specifications, features and prices are included. Shooting tests of new models, an expanded, illustrated section of sights and scopes, plus a showcase of engraved guns are all on target!

Softcover • 8-1/2 x 11 • 352 pages • 1,800 b&w photos
H2001 • $22.95

Guns Illustrated 2001

33rd Annual Edition
Edited by Ken Ramage

Inside this new edition, you'll find the latest news about today's handguns, rifles and shotguns from the top writers in the business. Plus cutting-edge articles on breaking arms technology, like the detailed report on Remington's brand new electronic rifle and ammunition! The illustrated arms catalog lists more than 3,000 commercially available firearms, including muzzleloaders and airguns. New to this edition - the catalog of Semi-Custom Firearms - found only in *Guns Illustrated!*

Softcover • 8-1/2 x 11 • 352 pages • 2,000+ b&w photos
GI2001 • $22.95

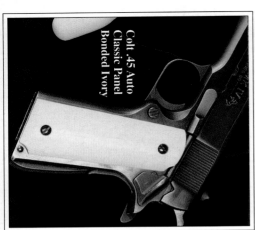
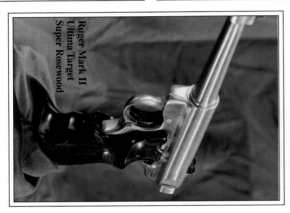

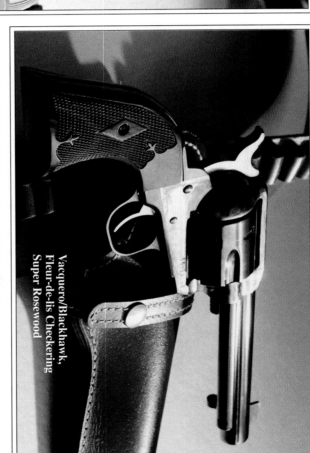

SEMI-CUSTOM HANDGUNS — AUTOLOADERS

Price: SP2 Ultra Sport (40 S&W, 5-7/8" bbl. with comp., integral Weaver rail, polymer mount) **$1,949.95**
Price: SP2 Competition (40 S&W, 5-7/8" bbl, combat sights, thickened frame for scope mount) **$999.95**
Price: SP1 General's Model (9mm, 4" barrel, fixed sights) . . . **$659.95**
Price: SP2 General's Model (40 S&W, 4" barrel, fixed sights) . . **$659.95**

VOLQUARTSEN CUSTOM 22 CALIBER AUTO PISTOLS

Caliber: 22 LR; 10-shot magazine. **Barrel:** 3.5" to 10"; stainless steel air gauge. **Weight:** 2-1/2 to 3 lbs. 10 oz. **Length:** NA. **Grips:** Finger-grooved plastic or walnut. **Sights:** Adjustable rear and blade front or Weaver-style scope mount. **Features:** Conversions of Ruger Mk. II Auto pistol. Variety of configurations featuring compensators, underlug barrels, etc. Stainless steel finish; black Teflon finish available for additional $85; target hammer, trigger. Made in U.S. by Volquartsen Custom.

Price: 3.5 Compact (3.5" barrel, T/L adjustable rear sight, scope base optional) **$640.00**
Price: Deluxe (barrel to 10", T/L adjustable rear sight) **$650.00**
Price: Deluxe with compensator **$721.50**
Price: Masters (6.5" barrel, finned underlug, T/L adjustable rear sight, compensator) **$924.00**
Price: Olympic (7" barrel, recoil-reducing gas chamber, T/L adjustable rear sight) **$845.00**
Price: Stingray (7.5" ribbed, ported barrel; red-dot sight) **$980.00**
Price: Terminator (7.5" ported barrel, grooved receiver, scope rings) **$705.00**
Price: Ultra-Light Match (6" tensioned barrel, Weaver mount, weighs 2-1/2 lbs.) **$795.00**
Price: V-6 (6", triangular, ventilated barrel with underlug, T/L adj. sight) **$1,007.50**
Price: V-2000 (6" barrel with finned underlug, T/L adj. sight) . . **$1,062.50**
Price: V-Magic II (7.5" barrel, red-dot sight) **$1,029.50**

Vektor SP2 Ultra

Volquartsen 3.5 Compact

Volquartsen Deluxe

Volquartsen Masters

Volquartsen Olympic

SEMI-CUSTOM HANDGUNS — AUTOLOADERS

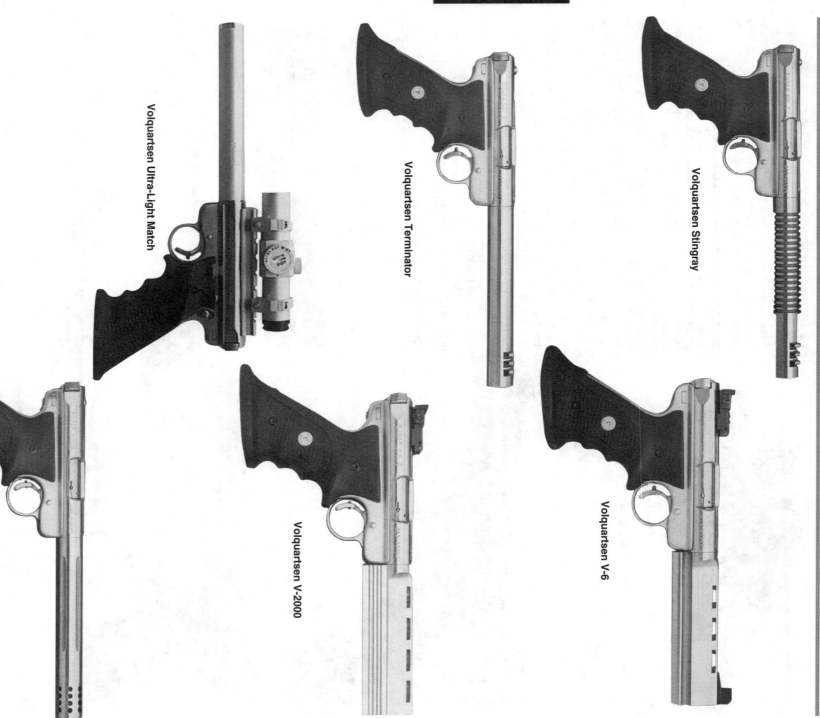

Volquartsen Ultra-Light Match

Volquartsen Terminator

Volquartsen Stingray

Volquartsen V-Magic II

Volquartsen V-2000

Volquartsen V-6

SEMI-CUSTOM HANDGUNS — REVOLVERS

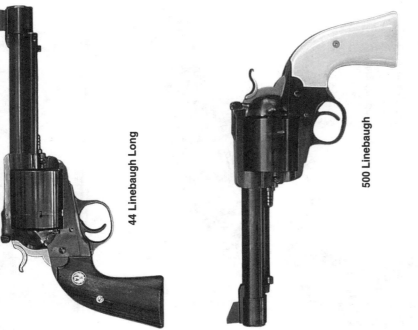

44 Linebaugh Long

500 Linebaugh

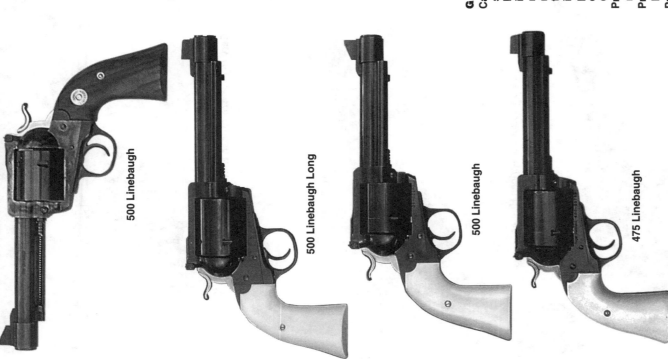

500 Linebaugh

500 Linebaugh Long

500 Linebaugh

475 Linebaugh

LINEBAUGH CUSTOM SIXGUNS REVOLVERS

Caliber: 45 Colt, 44 Linebaugh Long, 458 Linebaugh, 475 Linebaugh, 500 Linebaugh, 500 Linebaugh Long, 445 Super Mag. **Barrel:** 4-3/4", 5-1/2", 6", 7-1/2"; other lengths available. **Weight:** NA. **Length:** NA. **Grips:** Dustin Linebaugh Custom made to customer's specs. **Sights:** Bowen steel rear or factory Ruger; blade front. **Features:** Conversions using customer's Ruger Blackhawk Bisley and Vaquero Bisley frames. Made in U.S. by Linebaugh Custom Sixguns.

Price: Small 45 Colt conversion (rechambered cyl., new barrel)
. . . . from **$1,000.00**

Price: Large 45 Colt conversion (oversized cyl., new barrel, 5- or 6-shot) . . . . from **$1,500.00**

Price: 475 Linebaugh, 500 Linebaugh conversions . . . . from **$1,500.00**

Price: Linebaugh and 445 Super Mag calibers on 357 Maximum frame . . . . from **$2,700.00**

GARY REEDER CUSTOM GUNS REVOLVERS

Caliber: 357 Magnum, 45 Colt, 44-40, 41 Magnum, 44 Magnum, 454 Casull, 475 Linebaugh, 500 Linebaugh. **Barrel:** 2-1/2" to 12". **Weight:** Varies by model. **Length:** Varies by model. **Grips:** Black Cape buffalo horn, laminated walnut, simulated pearl, others. **Sights:** Notch fixed or adjustable rear, blade or ramp front. **Features:** Custom conversions of Ruger Vaquero, Blackhawk Bisley and Super Blackhawk frames. Jeweled hammer and trigger, tuned action, model name engraved on barrel, additional engraving on frame and cylinder, integral muzzle brake, finish available in high-polish or satin stainless steel or black Chromex finish. Also available on customer's gun at reduced cost. Other models available. Made in U.S. by Gary Reeder Custom Guns.

Price: Gamblers Classic (2-1/2" bbl., engraved cards and dice, no ejector rod housing) . . . . from **$995.00**

Price: Tombstone Classic (3-1/2" bbl. with gold bands, notch sight, birdshead grips) . . . . from **$750.00**

Price: Doc Holliday Classic (3-1/2" bbl., engraved cards and dice, white pearl grips) . . . . from **$750.00**

Price: Ultimate Vaquero (engraved barrel, frame and cylinder, made to customer specs) . . . . from **$750.00**

Price: Black Widow (4-5/8" bbl., black Chromex finish, black widow spider engraving) . . . . from **$995.00**

Price: Cowboy Classic (stainless finish, cattle brand engraved, limited to 100 guns) . . . . from **$995.00**

Price: African Hunter (6" bbl., with or without muzzle brake, 475 or 500 Linebaugh) . . . . from **$1,395.00**

Price: Alaskan Survivalist (3" bbl., Redhawk frame, engraved bear, 45 Colt or 44 Magnum) . . . . from **$995.00**

Price: Master Hunter (7-1/2" bbl. with muzzle brake, Super Redhawk frame, scope rings) . . . . from **$995.00**

Price: Ultimate Back-Up (3-1/2" bbl., fixed sights, choice of animal engraving, 454 Casull) . . . . from **$1,995.00**

SEMI-CUSTOM HANDGUNS — REVOLVERS

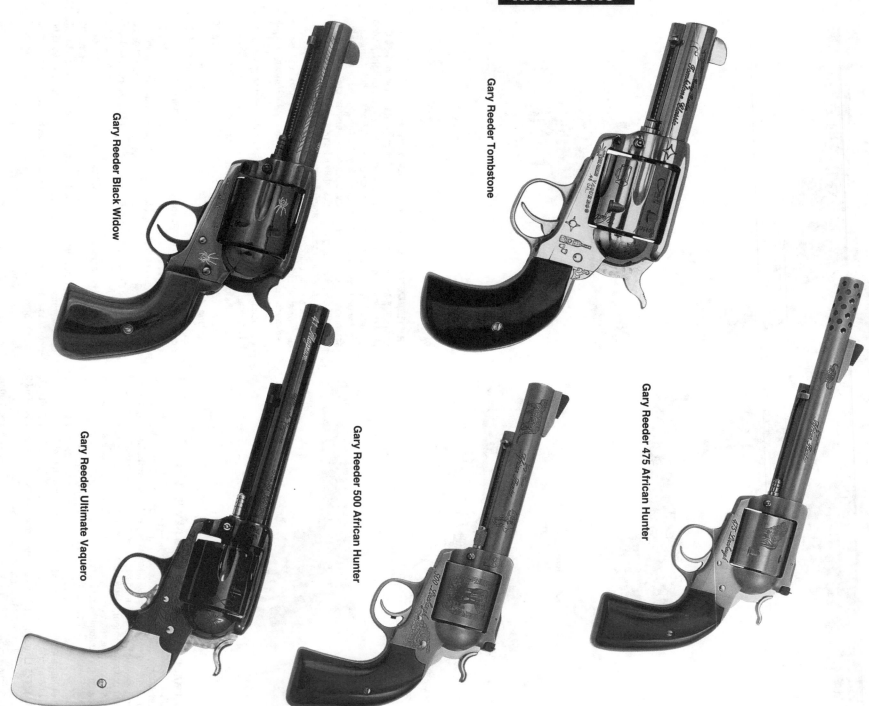

Gary Reeder Black Widow

Gary Reeder Tombstone

Gary Reeder Ultimate Vaquero

Gary Reeder 500 African Hunter

Gary Reeder 475 African Hunter

SEMI-CUSTOM HANDGUNS — REVOLVERS

**United States Fire-Arms
SAA Bisley**

**United States Fire-Arms
Omni-Snubnose**

**United States Fire-Arms
Omni-Potent Six Shooter**

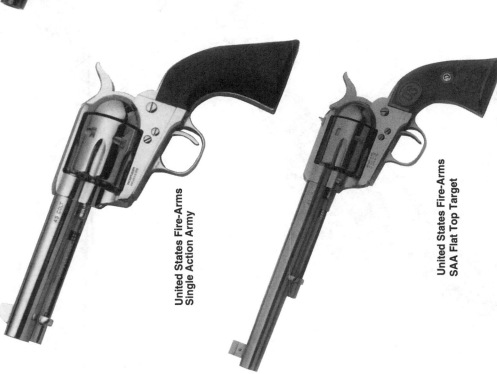

**United States Fire-Arms
Single Action Army**

**United States Fire-Arms
SAA Flat Top Target**

UNITED STATES FIRE-ARMS SINGLE-ACTION REVOLVERS

Caliber: 32 WCF, 38 Special, 38 WCF, 41 Colt, 44 WCF, 44 Special, 45 Colt, **Barrel:** 2", 3", 4-3/4", 5-1/2", 7-1/2", 16". **Weight:** NA. **Length:** NA. **Grips:** Hard rubber, rosewood, stag, pearl, ivory, ivory Micarta, smooth walnut, burled walnut and checkered walnut. **Sights:** Notch rear, blade front. **Features:** Hand-fitted replicas of Colt single-action revolvers. Full Dome Blue, Dome Blue, Armory Blue (gray-blue), Old Armory Bone Case (color casehardened) and nickel plate finishes. Carved and scrimshaw grips, engraving and gold inlays offered. Made in U.S. From United States Fire-Arms Mfg. Co.

Price: Single Action Army (32 WCF, 38 Spec., 38 WCF, 41 Colt, 45 Colt, 44 Spec., 44 WCF) **$919.00**

Price: SAA Flat Top Target (extended blade front, drift-adj. rear sights. . . . . from **$995.00**

Price: SAA Bisley (Bisley grip and hammer) . . . . from **$995.00**

Price: Omni-Snubnose (2" or 3" barrel, lanyard loop, 45 Colt only) . . . . from **$1,120.00**

Price: Omni-Potent Six Shooter (lanyard loop on grip). . . from **$1,125.00**

Price: New Buntline Special (16" bbl., skeleton shoulder stock, case, scabbard) . . . . from **$2,199.00**

Price: China Camp Cowboy Action Gun (4-3/4", 5-1/2" or 7-1/2" bbl., Silver Steel finish) . . . . from **$989.00**

Price: Henry Nettleton Cavalry Revolver (5-1/2" or 7-1/2" bbl., 45 Colt only) . . . . from **$1,125.00**

Price: U.S. 1851 Navy Conversion (7-1/2" bbl., color casehardened frame, 38 Spec. only). . . . . from **$1,499.00**

Price: U.S. Pre-War (SAA, Old Armory Bone Case or Armory Blue finish). . . . . from **$1,175.00**

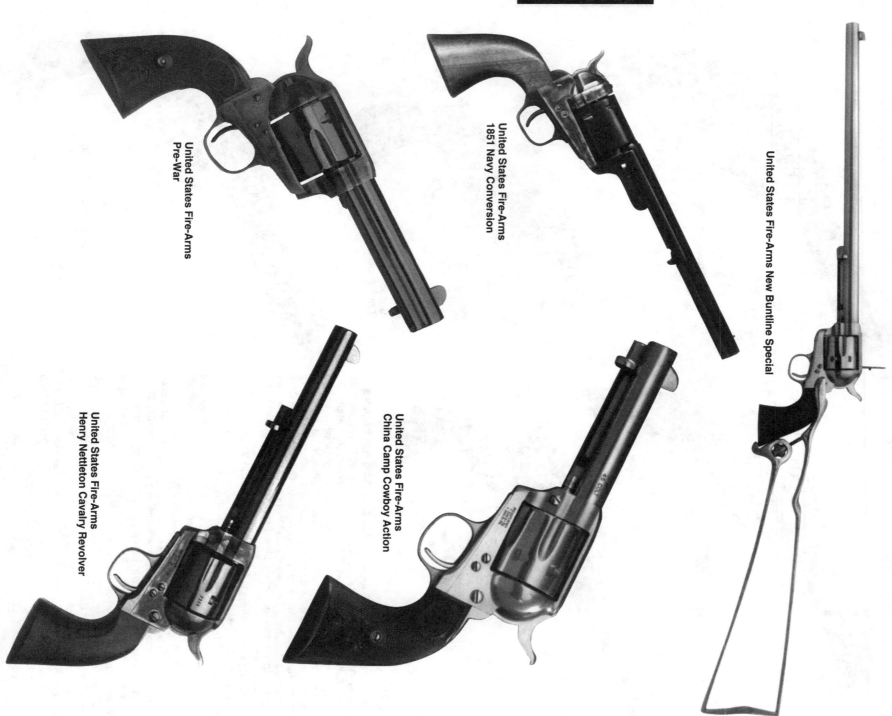

United States Fire-Arms
Pre-War

United States Fire-Arms
1851 Navy Conversion

United States Fire-Arms New Buntline Special

United States Fire-Arms
Henry Nettleton Cavalry Revolver

United States Fire-Arms
China Camp Cowboy Action

SEMI-CUSTOM HANDGUNS — REVOLVERS

SEMI-CUSTOM HANDGUNS — SINGLE SHOT

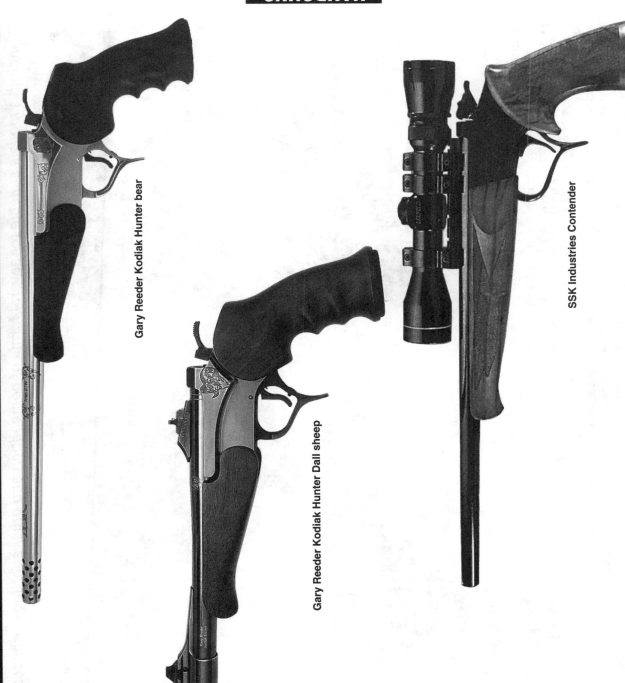

Gary Reeder Kodiak Hunter bear

Gary Reeder Kodiak Hunter Dall sheep

SSK Industries Contender

GARY REEDER CUSTOM GUNS
CONTENDER AND ENCORE PISTOLS

Caliber: 22 Cheetah, 218 Bee, 22 K-Hornet, 22 Hornet, 218 Mashburn Bee, 22-250 Improved, 6mm/284, 7mm STW, 7mm GNR, 30 GNR, 338 GNR, 300 Win. Magnum, 338 Win. Magnum, 350 Rem. Magnum, 358 STA, 375 H&H, 378 GNR, 416 Remington, 416 GNR, 450 GNR, 475 Linebaugh, 500 Linebaugh, 50 Alaskan, 50 AE, 454 Casull; others available. **Barrel:** 8" to 15" (others available). **Weight:** NA. **Length:** Varies with barrel length. **Grips:** Walnut fingergroove. **Sights:** Express-style adjustable rear and barrel band front (Kodiak Hunter); none furnished most models. **Features:** Offers complete guns and barrels in the T/C Contender and Encore. Integral muzzle brake, engraved animals and model name, tuned action, high-polish or satin stainless steel or black Chromex finish. Made in U.S. by Gary Reeder Custom Guns.

Price: Kodiak Hunter (50 AE or 454 Casull, Kodiak bear and Dall sheep engravings) . . . . from **$995.00**

Price: Ultimate Encore (15" bbl. with muzzle brake, grizzly bear engraving) . . . . from **$995.00**

SSK INDUSTRIES CONTENDER AND ENCORE PISTOLS

Caliber: More than 200, including most standard pistol and rifle calibers, as well as 226 JDJ, 6mm JDJ, 257 JDJ, 6.5mm JDJ, 7mm JDJ, 6.5mm Mini-Dreadnaught, 30-06 JDJ, 280 JDJ, 375 JDJ, 6mm Whisper, 300 Whisper and 338 Whisper. **Barrel:** 10" to 26"; blued or stainless; variety of configurations. **Weight:** Varies with barrel length and features. **Length:** Varies with barrel length. **Grips:** Pachmayr, wood models available. **Features:** Offers frames, barrels and complete guns in the T/C Contender and Encore. Fluted, diamond, octagon and round barrels; flatside Contender frames; chrome-plating; muzzle brakes; trigger jobs; variety of stocks and forends; sights and optics. Made in U.S. by SSK Industries.

Price: Blued Contender frame . . . . from **$263.00**
Price: Stainless Contender frame . . . . from **$290.00**
Price: Blued Encore frame . . . . from **$290.00**
Price: Stainless Encore frame . . . . from **$318.00**
Price: Contender barrels . . . . from **$315.00**
Price: Encore barrels . . . . from **$340.00**

HANDGUNS — AUTOLOADERS, SERVICE & SPORT

Includes models suitable for several forms of competition and other sporting purposes.

Accu-Tek BL-9

Accu-Tek AT-380

Accu-Tek HC-380

Accu-Tek CP-45

AA ARMS AP9 MINI PISTOL

Caliber: 9mm Para., 10-shot magazine. **Barrel:** 3". **Weight:** 3.5 lbs. **Length:** 12" overall. **Stocks:** Checkered black synthetic. **Sights:** Post front adjustable for elevation, rear adjustable for windage. **Features:** Ventilated barrel shroud; blue or electroless nickel finish. Made in U.S. by AA Arms.

Price: 3" barrel, blue $239.00
Price: 3" barrel, electroless nickel $259.00
Price: Mini/5, 5" barrel, blue $259.00
Price: Mini/5, 5" barrel, electroless nickel ... $279.00

ACCU-TEK BL-9 AUTO PISTOL

Caliber: 9mm Para., 5-shot magazine. **Barrel:** 3". **Weight:** 22 oz. **Length:** 5.6" overall. **Stocks:** Black pebble composition. **Sights:** Fixed. **Features:** Double action only; black finish. Introduced 1997. Price includes cleaning kit and gun lock, two magazines. Made in U.S. by Accu-Tek.

Price: $232.00

Accu-Tek Model AT-32SS Auto Pistol

Same as the AT-380SS except chambered for 32 ACP. Introduced 1991. Price includes cleaning kit and gun lock.

Price: Satin stainless $221.00

ACCU-TEK MODEL AT-380 AUTO PISTOL

Caliber: 380 ACP, 5-shot magazine. **Barrel:** 2.75". **Weight:** 20 oz. **Length:** 5.6" overall. **Stocks:** Grooved black composition. **Sights:** Blade front, rear adjustable for windage. **Features:** Stainless steel frame and slide. External hammer; manual thumb safety; firing pin block, trigger disconnect. Introduced 1991. Price includes cleaning kit and gun lock. Made in U.S. by Accu-Tek.

Price: Satin stainless $221.00

ACCU-TEK CP-45 AUTO PISTOL

Caliber: 45 ACP, 6-shot magazine. **Barrel:** 3-1/4 inches. **Weight:** 31 oz. **Length:** 6-3/8 inches overall. **Grips:** Checkered black nylon. **Sights:** Fully adjustable rear, three-dot; blade front. **Features:** Stainless steel frame and slide; single action with external hammer and firing pin block, manual thumb safety; last-shot hold open. Includes gun lock and cleaning kit. Introduced 2000. Made in U.S. by Excel Industries Inc.

Price: $425.00

ACCU-TEK MODEL HC-380 AUTO PISTOL

Caliber: 380 ACP, 10-shot magazine. **Barrel:** 2.75". **Weight:** 26 oz. **Length:** 6" overall. **Stocks:** Checkered black composition. **Sights:** Blade front, rear adjustable for windage. **Features:** External hammer; manual thumb safety with firing pin and trigger disconnect; bottom magazine release. Stainless steel construction. Introduced 1993. Price includes cleaning kit and gun lock. Made in U.S. by Accu-Tek.

Price: Satin stainless $231.00

ACCU-TEK XL-9 AUTO PISTOL

Caliber: 9mm Para., 5-shot magazine. **Barrel:** 3". **Weight:** 24 oz. **Length:** 5.6" overall. **Stocks:** Black pebble composition. **Sights:** Three-dot system; rear adjustable for windage. **Features:** Stainless steel construction; double-action-only mechanism. Introduced 1999. Price includes cleaning kit and gun lock, two magazines. Made in U.S. by Accu-Tek.

Price: $248.00

AMT Backup

Auto-Ordnance 1911A1 Standard

Accu-Tek XL9

American Derringer LM4 Simmerling

AMERICAN ARMS MATEBA AUTO/REVOLVER

Caliber: 357 Mag., 6-shot. **Barrel:** 4", 6", 8". **Weight:** 2.75 lbs. **Length:** 8.77" overall. **Stocks:** Smooth walnut. **Sights:** Blade on ramp front, adjustable rear. **Features:** Double or single action. Cylinder and slide recoil together upon firing. All-steel construction with polished blue finish. Introduced 1995. Imported from Italy by American Arms, Inc.

Price: $1,295.00
Price: 6" $1,349.00

AMERICAN DERRINGER LM4 SIMMERLING AUTO PISTOL

Caliber: 45 ACP, 4-shot magazine. **Barrel:** 3". **Weight:** 24 oz. **Length:** 5.2" overall. **Grips:** Plastic. **Sights:** Blade front, fixed notch rear. **Features:** Stainless steel frame and slide; 1" thick; one of the smallest 45 ACPs made. Made in U.S. From American Derringer.

Price: $2,500.00

AMT AUTOMAG II AUTO PISTOL

Caliber: 22 WMR, 9-shot magazine (7-shot with 3-3/8" barrel). **Barrel:** 3-3/8", 4-1/2", 6". **Weight:** About 32 oz. **Length:** 9-3/8" overall. **Stocks:** Grooved carbon fiber. **Sights:** Blade front, adjustable rear. **Features:** Made of stainless steel. Gas-assisted action. Exposed hammer. Slide flats have brushed finish, rest is sandblast. Squared trigger guard. Introduced 1986. From Galena Industries, Inc.

Price: $429.00

AMT AUTOMAG III PISTOL

Caliber: 30 Carbine, 8-shot magazine. **Barrel:** 6-3/8". **Weight:** 43 oz. **Length:** 10-1/2" overall. **Stocks:** Carbon fiber. **Sights:** Blade front, adjustable rear. **Features:** Stainless steel construction. Hammer-drop safety. Slide flats have brushed finish, rest is sandblasted. Introduced 1989. From Galena Industries, Inc.

Price: ....

AMT AUTOMAG IV PISTOL

Caliber: 45 Winchester Magnum, 6-shot magazine. **Barrel:** 6.5". **Weight:** 46 oz. **Length:** 10.5" overall. **Stocks:** Carbon fiber. **Sights:** Blade front, adjustable rear. **Features:** Made of stainless st3578eel with brushed finish. Introduced 1990. Made in U.S. by Galena Industries, Inc.

Price: $599.00

AMT 45 ACP HARDBALLER II

Caliber: 45 ACP. **Barrel:** 5". **Weight:** 39 oz. **Length:** 8-1/2" overall. **Stocks:** Wrap-around rubber. **Sights:** Adjustable. **Features:** Extended combat safety, serrated matte slide rib, loaded chamber indicator, long grip safety, beveled magazine well, adjustable target trigger. All stainless steel. From Galena Industries, Inc.

Price: $425.00
Price: Government model (as above except no rib, fixed sights). $399.00
Price: 400 Accelerator (400 Cor-Bon, 7" barrel). $549.00
Price: Commando (40 S&W, Government Model frame) $435.00

AMT 45 ACP HARDBALLER LONG SLIDE

Caliber: 45 ACP. **Barrel:** 7". **Length:** 10-1/2" overall. **Stocks:** Wrap-around rubber. **Sights:** Fully adjustable rear sight. **Features:** Slide and barrel are 2" longer than the standard 45, giving less recoil, added velocity, longer sight radius. Has extended combat safety, serrated matte rib, loaded chamber indicator, wide adjustable trigger. From Galena Industries, Inc.

Price: $529.00

AMT BACKUP PISTOL

Caliber: 357 SIG (5-shot); 38 Super, 9mm Para. (6-shot); 40 S&W, 400 Cor-Bon; 45 ACP (5-shot). **Barrel:** 3". **Weight:** 23 oz. **Length:** 5-3/4" overall. **Stocks:** Checkered black synthetic. **Sights:** None. **Features:** Stainless steel construction; double-action-only trigger; dust cover over the trigger transfer bar; extended magazine; titanium nitride finish. Introduced 1992. Made in U.S. by Galena Industries.

Price: 9mm, 40 S&W, 45 ACP $319.00
Price: 38 Super, 357 SIG, 400 Cor-Bon $369.00

HANDGUNS — AUTOLOADERS, SERVICE & SPORT

AMT 380 DAO Small Frame Backup

Similar to the DAO Backup except has smaller frame, 2-1/2" barrel, weighs 18 oz., and is 5" overall. Has 5-shot magazine, matte/stainless finish. Made in U.S. by Galena Industries.

Price: **$319.00**

AUTO-ORDNANCE 1911A1 AUTOMATIC PISTOL

Caliber: 45 ACP, 7-shot magazine. Barrel: 5". Weight: 39 oz. Length: 8-1/2" overall. Stocks: Checkered plastic with medallion. Sights: Blade front, rear adjustable for windage. Features: Same specs as 1911A1 military guns—parts interchangeable. Frame and slide blued; each radius has non-glare finish. Made in U.S. by Auto-Ordnance Corp.

Price: 45 ACP, blue **$447.00**
Price: 45 ACP, Parkerized **$462.00**
Price: 45 ACP Deluxe (three-dot sights, textured rubber wraparound grips) **$455.00**

Auto-Ordnance 1911A1 Custom High Polish Pistol

Similar to the standard 1911A1 except has a Videki speed trigger, extended thumb safety, flat mainspring housing, Acurod recoil spring guide system, rosewood grips, custom combat hammer, beavertail grip safety. High-polish blue finish. Introduced 1998. Made in U.S. by Auto-Ordnance Corp.

Price: **$585.00**

Auto-Ordnance ZG-51 Pit Bull Auto

Same as the 1911A1 except has 3-1/2" barrel, weighs 36 oz. and has an over-all length of 7-1/4". Available in 45 ACP only; 7-shot magazine. Introduced 1989.

Price: **$470.00**

Auto-Ordnance Deluxe

Auto-Ordnance Pit Bull

AUTAUGA 32 AUTO PISTOL

Caliber: 32 ACP, 6-shot magazine. Barrel: 2". Weight: 11.3 oz. Length: 4.3" overall. Stocks: Black polymer. Sights: Fixed. Features: Double-action-only mechanism. Stainless steel construction. Uses Winchester Silver Tip ammunition.

Price: .... **NA**

BAER 1911 CUSTOM CARRY AUTO PISTOL

Caliber: 45 ACP, 7- or 10-shot magazine. Barrel: 5". Weight: 37 oz. Length: 8.5" overall. Stocks: Checkered walnut. Sights: Baer improved ramp-style dovetailed front, Novak low-mount rear. Features: Baer forged NM frame, slide and barrel with stainless bushing; fitted slide to frame; double serrated slide (full-size only); Baer speed trigger with 4-lb. pull; Baer deluxe hammer and sear, tactical-style extended ambidextrous safety, beveled magazine well; polished feed ramp and throated barrel; tuned extractor; Baer extended ejector, checkered slide stop; lowered and flared ejection port, full-length recoil guide rod; recoil buff. Made in U.S. by Les Baer Custom, Inc.

Price: Standard size, blued **$1,620.00**
Price: Standard size, stainless **$1,690.00**
Price: Comanche size, blued **$1,640.00**
Price: Comanche size, stainless **$1,690.00**
Price: Comanche size, aluminum frame, blued slide **$1,890.00**
Price: Comanche size, aluminum frame, stainless slide .. **$1,995.00**

Baer 1911 Concept III Auto Pistol

Same as the Concept I except has forged stainless frame with blued steel slide. Bo-Mar rear sight, 30 lpi checkering on front strap. Made in U.S. by Les Baer Custom, Inc.

Price: Concept IV (with Baer adjustable rear sight) **$1,520.00**
Price: Concept IV (with Baer adjustable rear sight) **$1,499.00**
Price: Concept V (all stainless, Bo-Mar sight, checkered front strap) **$1,558.00**
Price: Concept VI (stainless, Baer adjustable sight, checkered front strap) **$1,558.00**

Baer Premium II

Baer Custom Carry

HANDGUNS — AUTOLOADERS, SERVICE & SPORT

Beretta 92FS

Beretta 96

BAER 1911 PREMIER II AUTO PISTOL

Caliber: 9x23, 38 Super, 400 Cor-Bon, 45 ACP, 7- or 10-shot magazine. **Barrel:** 5". **Weight:** 37 oz. **Length:** 8.5" overall. **Stocks:** Checkered rosewood, double diamond pattern. **Sights:** Baer dovetailed front, low-mount Bo-Mar rear with hidden leaf. **Features:** Baer NM forged steel frame and barrel with stainless bushing; slide fitted to frame; double serrated slide; lowered, flared ejection port; tuned, polished extractor; Baer extended ejector, checkered slide stop, aluminum speed trigger with 4-lb. pull, deluxe Commander hammer and sear, beavertail grip safety with pad, beveled magazine well, extended ambidextrous safety; flat mainspring housing; polished feed ramp and throated barrel; 30 lpi checkered front strap. Made in U.S. by Les Baer Custom, Inc.

Price: Blued $1,428.00
Price: Stainless $1,558.00
Price: 6" model, blued, from $1,595.00

BAER 1911 S.R.P. PISTOL

Caliber: 45 ACP. **Barrel:** 5". **Weight:** 37 oz. **Length:** 8.5" overall. **Stocks:** Checkered walnut. **Sights:** Trijicon night sights. **Features:** Similar to the F.B.I. contract gun except uses Baer forged steel frame. Has Baer match barrel with supported chamber, Wolff springs, complete tactical action job. All parts Mag-na-fluxed; deburred for tactical carry. Has Baer Ultra Coat finish. Tuned for reliability. Contact Baer for complete details. Introduced 1996. Made in U.S. by Les Baer Custom, Inc.

Price: Government or Comanche length $2,990.00

BAER 1911 CONCEPT I AUTO PISTOL

Caliber: 45 ACP, 7-shot magazine. **Barrel:** 5". **Weight:** 37 oz. **Length:** 8.5" overall. **Stocks:** Checkered rosewood. **Sights:** Baer dovetail front, Bo-Mar deluxe low-mount rear with hidden leaf. **Features:** Baer forged steel frame, slide and barrel with Baer stainless bushing; slide fitted to frame; double serrated slide; Baer beavertail grip safety, checkered slide stop, tuned extractor, extended ejector, deluxe hammer and sear, match disconnector; lowered and flared ejection port; fitted recoil link; polished feed ramp, throated barrel; Baer fitted speed trigger, flat serrated mainspring housing. Blue finish. Made in U.S. by Les Baer Custom, Inc.

Price: $1,390.00
Price: Concept II (with Baer adjustable rear sight) $1,390.00

Baer 1911 Concept VII Auto Pistol

Same as the Concept I except reduced Comanche size with 4.25" barrel, weighs 27.5 oz., 7.75" overall. Blue finish, checkered front strap. Made in U.S. by Les Baer Custom, Inc.

Price: $1,495.00
Price: Concept VIII (stainless frame and slide, Baer adjustable rear sight) $1,547.00

Baer 1911 Concept IX Auto Pistol

Same as the Comanche Concept VII except has Baer lightweight forged aluminum frame, blued steel slide, Baer adjustable rear sight. Chambered for 45 ACP, 7-shot magazine. Made in U.S. by Les Baer Custom, Inc.

Price: $1,655.00
Price: Concept X (as above with stainless slide) $1,675.00

Baer 1911 Prowler III Auto Pistol

Same as the Premier II except also has full-length guide rod, tapered cone stub weight and reverse recoil plug. Made in U.S. by Les Baer Custom, Inc.

Price: Standard size, blued. $1,795.00

BERETTA MODEL 92FS PISTOL

Caliber: 9mm Para., 10-shot magazine. **Barrel:** 4.9". **Weight:** 34 oz. **Length:** 8.5" overall. **Stocks:** Checkered black plastic. **Sights:** Blade front, rear adjustable for windage. Tritium night sights available. **Features:** Double action. Extractor acts as chamber loaded indicator, squared trigger guard, grooved front- and backstraps, inertia firing pin. Matte or blued finish. Introduced 1977. Made in U.S. and imported from Italy by Beretta U.S.A.

Price: With plastic grips $655.00
Price: Stainless, rubber grips $718.00

Beretta Model 92FS/96 Brigadier Pistols

Similar to the Model 92FS/96 except with a heavier slide to reduce felt recoil and allow mounting removable front sight. Wrap-around rubber grips. Three-dot sights dovetailed to the slide, adjustable for windage. Weighs 35.3 oz. Introduced 1999.

Price: 9mm or 40 S&W, 10-shot. $702.00

Beretta Model 92FS 470th Anniversary Limited Edition

Similar to the Model 92FS stainless except has mirror polish finish, smooth walnut grips with inlaid gold-plated medallions. Special and unique gold-filled engraving includes the signature of Beretta's president. The anniversary logo is engraved on the top of the slide and the back of the magazine. Each pistol identified by a "1 of 470" gold-filled number. Special chrome-plated magazine included. Deluxe lockable walnut case with teak inlays and engraving. Only 470 pistols will be sold. Introduced 1999.

Price: $2,082.00

Beretta Model 92FS Compact and Compact Type M Pistol

Similar to the Model 92FS except more compact and lighter: overall length 7.8"; 4.3" barrel; weighs 30.9 oz. Has Bruniton finish, chrome-lined bore, combat trigger guard, ambidextrous safety/decock lever. Single column 8-shot magazine (Type M), or double column 10-shot (Compact), 9mm only. Introduced 1998. Imported from Italy by Beretta U.S.A.

Price: Compact (10-shot) $655.00
Price: Compact Type M (8-shot) $655.00

Beretta Model 96 Pistol

Same as the Model 92FS except chambered for 40 S&W. Ambidextrous safety mechanism with passive firing pin catch, slide safety/decocking lever, trigger bar disconnect. Has 10-shot magazine. Available with three-dot sights. Introduced 1992.

Price: Model 96, plastic grips $655.00
Price: Stainless, rubber grips $718.00

HANDGUNS — AUTOLOADERS, SERVICE & SPORT

Beretta M8000/8040 Cougar

Beretta 950 Jetfire

Beretta 9000S Compact

Beretta M9 Special Edition Pistol

Copy of the U.S. M9 military pistol. Similar to the Model 92FS except has special M9 serial number range; one 15-round (pre-ban) magazine, dot-and-post sight system; special M9 military packaging; Army TM 9-1005-317-10 operator's manual; special M9 Special Edition patch; certificate of authenticity; Bianchi M12 holster, M1025 magazine pouch, and M1015 web pistol belt. Introduced 1998. From Beretta U.S.A.

Price: **$861.00**

BERETTA MODEL 80 CHEETAH SERIES DA PISTOLS

Caliber: 380 ACP. 10-shot magazine (M84); 8-shot (M85); 22 LR, 7-shot (M87). **Barrel:** 3.82". **Weight:** About 23 oz. (M84/85); 20.8 oz. (M87). **Length:** 6.8" overall. **Stocks:** Glossy black plastic (wood optional at extra cost). **Sights:** Fixed front, drift-adjustable rear. **Features:** Double action, quick takedown, convenient magazine release. Introduced 1977. Imported from Italy by Beretta U.S.A.

Price: Model 84 Cheetah, plastic grips **$565.00**
Price: Model 84 Cheetah, wood grips **$595.00**
Price: Model 84 Cheetah, wood grips, nickel finish .. **$639.00**
Price: Model 85 Cheetah, plastic grips, 8-shot **$533.00**
Price: Model 85 Cheetah, wood grips, 8-shot **$596.00**
Price: Model 85 Cheetah, wood grips, nickel, 8-shot . **$566.00**
Price: Model 87 Cheetah, wood, 22 LR, 7-shot **$565.00**

Beretta Model 86 Cheetah

Similar to the 380-caliber Model 85 except has tip-up barrel for first-round loading. Barrel length is 4.4", overall length of 7.33". Has 8-shot magazine, walnut grips. Introduced 1989.

Price: **$566.00**

BERETTA MODEL 950 JETFIRE AUTO PISTOL

Caliber: 25 ACP, 8-shot. **Barrel:** 2.4". **Weight:** 9.9 oz. **Length:** 4.7" overall. **Stocks:** Checkered black plastic or walnut. **Sights:** Fixed. **Features:**

Single action, thumb safety; tip-up barrel for direct loading/unloading, cleaning. From Beretta U.S.A.

Price: Jetfire plastic, blue **$220.00**
Price: Jetfire plastic, nickel **$300.00**
Price: Jetfire wood, EL **$337.00**
Price: Jetfire plastic, matte finish **$220.00**

Beretta Model 21 Bobcat Pistol

Similar to the Model 950 BS. Chambered for 22 LR or 25 ACP. Both double action. Has 2.4" barrel, 4.9" overall length; 7-round magazine on 22 cal.; 8 rounds in 25 ACP, 9.9 oz., available in nickel, matte, engraved or blue finish. Plastic or walnut grips. Introduced in 1985.

Price: Bobcat, 22-cal., blue **$279.00**
Price: Bobcat, nickel, 22-cal. **$322.00**
Price: Bobcat, 25-cal., blue **$279.00**
Price: Bobcat, nickel, 25-cal. **$322.00**
Price: Bobcat EL, 22 or 25 .... **$356.00**
Price: Bobcat plastic matte, 22 or 25 .... **$246.00**

BERETTA MODEL 3032 TOMCAT PISTOL

Caliber: 32 ACP, 7-shot magazine. **Barrel:** 2.45". **Weight:** 14.5 oz. **Length:** 5" overall. **Stocks:** Checkered black plastic. **Sights:** Blade front, drift-adjustable rear. **Features:** Double action with exposed hammer; tip-up barrel for direct loading/unloading; thumb safety; polished or matte blue finish. Imported from Italy by Beretta U.S.A. Introduced 1996.

Price: Blue **$362.00**
Price: Matte **$333.00**

BERETTA MODEL 8000/8040/8045 COUGAR PISTOL

Caliber: 9mm Para, 10-shot, 40 S&W, 10-shot magazine; 45 ACP, 8-shot. **Barrel:** 3.6". **Weight:** 33.5 oz. **Length:** 7" overall. **Stocks:** Checkered plastic. **Sights:** Blade front, rear drift adjustable for windage. **Features:** Slide-mounted safety; rotating barrel; exposed hammer. Matte black Bruniton finish. Announced 1994. Imported from Italy by Beretta U.S.A.

Price: **$695.00**
Price: D model, 9mm, 40 S&W **$672.00**
Price: D model, 45 ACP **$724.00**

BERETTA MODEL 9000S COMPACT PISTOL

Caliber: 9mm Para., 40 S&W. 10-shot magazine. **Barrel:** 3.4". **Weight:** 26.8 oz. **Length:** 6.6". **Grips:** Soft polymer. **Sights:** Windage-adjustable white-dot rear, white-dot blade front. **Features:** Glass-reinforced polymer frame; patented tilt-barrel, open-slide locking system; chrome-lined barrel; external serrated hammer; automatic firing pin and manual safeties. Introduced 2000. Imported from Italy by Beretta USA.

Price: 9000S Type F (single and double action, external hammer) **$551.00**
Price: 9000S Type D (double-action only, no external hammer or safety) **$551.00**

HANDGUNS — AUTOLOADERS, SERVICE & SPORT

**Browning Micro
Buck Mark Standard**

Bersa Thunder 380

Browning Capitan Hi-Power

windage and elevation. Also available with fixed rear (drift-adjustable for windage). **Features:** External hammer with half-cock and thumb safeties. A blow on the hammer cannot discharge a cartridge; cannot be fired with magazine removed. Fixed rear sight model available. Imported from Belgium by Browning.

Price: Fixed sight model, walnut grips $615.00
Price: 9mm with rear sight adj. for w. and e., walnut grips $668.00
Price: Mark III, standard matte black finish, fixed sight, moulded grips, ambidextrous safety $579.00
Price: Silver chrome, adjustable sight, Pachmayr grips $684.00

Browning 40 S&W Hi-Power Mark III Pistol

Similar to the standard Hi-Power except chambered for 40 S&W, 10-shot magazine, weighs 35 oz., and has 4-3/4" barrel. Comes with matte blue finish, low profile front sight blade, drift-adjustable rear sight, ambidextrous safety, moulded polyamide grips with thumb rest. Introduced 1993. Imported from Belgium by Browning.

Price: Mark III $579.00

Browning Capitan Hi-Power Pistol

Similar to the standard Hi-Power except has adjustable tangent rear sight authentic to the early-production model. Also has Commander-style hammer. Checkered walnut grips, polished blue finish. Reintroduced 1993. Imported from Belgium by Browning.

Price: 9mm only $728.00

Browning Hi-Power HP-Practical Pistol

Similar to the standard Hi-Power except has silver-chromed frame with blued slide, wrap-around Pachmayr rubber grips, round-style serrated hammer and removable front sight, fixed rear (drift-adjustable for windage). Available in 9mm Para. or 40 S&W. Introduced 1991.

Price: $662.00
Price: With fully adjustable rear sight $717.00

BROWNING BUCK MARK 22 PISTOL

Caliber: 22 LR, 10-shot magazine. **Barrel:** 5-1/2". **Weight:** 32 oz. **Length:** 9-1/2" overall. **Stocks:** Black moulded composite with checkering. **Sights:** Ramp front, Browning Pro Target rear adjustable for windage and elevation. **Features:** All steel, matte blue finish or nickel, gold-colored trigger. Buck Mark Plus has laminated wood grips. Made in U.S. Introduced 1985. From Browning.

Price: Buck Mark, blue $265.00
Price: Buck Mark, nickel finish with contoured rubber stocks. $312.00
Price: Buck Mark Plus $324.00

Browning Buck Mark Camper

Similar to the Buck Mark except 5-1/2" bull barrel. Weight is 34 oz. Available in matte blue. Introduced 1999. From Browning.

Price: $234.00

Browning Buck Mark Challenge, Challenge Micro

Similar to the Buck Mark except has a lightweight barrel and smaller grip diameter. Barrel length is 5-1/2", weight is 25 oz. Introduced 1999. From Browning.

Price: $296.00
Price: Challenge Micro (4" barrel) $296.00

Beretta Model 8000/8040/8040 Mini Cougar

Similar to the Model 8000/8040 Cougar except has shorter grip frame and weighs 27.6 oz. Introduced 1998. Imported from Italy by Beretta U.S.A.

Price: 9mm or 40 S&W. $695.00
Price: 9mm or 40 S&W, DAO. $672.00
Price: 45 ACP, 6-shot. $724.00
Price: 45 ACP DAO $724.00

BERSA THUNDER 380 AUTO PISTOLS

Caliber: 380 ACP, 7-shot (Thunder 380 Lite), 9-shot magazine (Thunder 380 DLX). **Barrel:** 3.5". **Weight:** 25.75 oz. **Length:** 6.6" overall. **Stocks:** Black polymer. **Sights:** Blade front, notch rear adjustable for windage; three-dot system. **Features:** Double action; firing pin and magazine safeties. Available in blue or nickel. Introduced 1995. Distributed by Eagle Imports, Inc.

Price: Thunder 380, 7-shot, deep blue finish $234.95

BROWNING FORTY-NINE AUTOMATIC PISTOL

Caliber: 40 S&W, 10-shot magazine. **Barrel:** 4.25". **Weight:** 26 oz. **Length:** 7.75" overall. **Stocks:** Integral; black nylon with pebble-grain texture. **Sights:** Dovetailed three-dot. **Features:** Has FN's patented RSS (Repeatable Secure Striker) firing system; extended modular slide rails; reversible magazine catch; stainless slide, black nylon frame. Introduced 1999. Imported by Browning.

Price: $440.00

BROWNING HI-POWER 9mm AUTOMATIC PISTOL

Caliber: 9mm Para., 40 S&W, 10-shot magazine. **Barrel:** 4-21/32". **Weight:** 32 oz. **Length:** 7-3/4" overall. **Stocks:** Walnut, hand checkered, or black Polyamide. **Sights:** 1/8" blade front; rear screw-adjustable for

HANDGUNS — AUTOLOADERS, SERVICE & SPORT

Calico M-110

Browning Buck Mark Varmint

Browning Buck Mark Challenge

Carbon-15

Charles Daly M-1911-A1P

Browning Micro Buck Mark

Same as the standard Buck Mark and Buck Mark Plus except has 4" barrel. Available in blue or nickel. Has 16-click Pro Target rear sight. Introduced 1992.

Price: Blue $265.00
Price: Nickel $312.00
Price: Buck Mark Micro Plus $324.00
Price: Buck Mark Micro Plus Nickel ... $354.00

Browning Buck Mark Varmint

Same as the Buck Mark except has 9-7/8" heavy barrel with .900" diameter and full-length scope base (no open sights); walnut grips with optional forend, or finger-groove walnut. Overall length is 14", weighs 48 oz. Introduced 1987.

Price: $403.00

CALICO M-110 AUTO PISTOL

Caliber: 22 LR. Barrel: 6". Weight: 3.7 lbs. (loaded). Length: 17.9" overall. Stocks: Moulded composition. Sights: Adjustable post front, notch rear. Features: Aluminum alloy frame; compensator; pistol grip compartment;

ambidextrous safety. Uses same helical-feed magazine as M-100 Carbine. Introduced 1986. Made in U.S. From Calico.

Price: $570.00

CARBON-15 (Type 97) PISTOL

Caliber: 223, 10-shot magazine. Barrel: 7.25". Weight: 46 oz. Length: 20" overall. Stock: Checkered composite. Sights: Ghost ring. Features: Semi-automatic, gas-operated, rotating bolt action. Carbon fiber upper and lower receiver; chromemoly bolt carrier; fluted stainless match barrel; mil. spec. optics mounting base; uses AR-15-type magazines. Introduced 1992. From Professional Ordnance, Inc.

Price: $1,600.00
Price: Type 20 pistol (light-profile barrel, no compensator, weighs 40 oz.) $1,500.00

CHARLES DALY M-1911-A1P AUTOLOADING PISTOL

Caliber: 45 ACP, 7- or 10-shot magazine. Barrel: 5". Weight: 38 oz. Length: 8-3/4" overall. Stocks: Checkered. Sights: Blade front, rear drift adjustable for windage; three-dot system. Features: Skeletonized combat hammer and trigger; beavertail grip safety; extended slide release; oversize thumb safety; Parkerized finish. Introduced 1996. Imported from the Philippines by K.B.I., Inc.

Price: $469.95

COLT MODEL 1991 MODEL O AUTO PISTOL

Caliber: 45 ACP, 7-shot magazine. Barrel: 5". Weight: 38 oz. Length: 8.5" overall. Stocks: Checkered black composition. Sights: Ramped blade front, fixed square notch rear, high profile. Features: Parkerized finish. Continuation of serial number range used on original G.I. 1911 A1 guns. Comes with one magazine and moulded carrying case. Introduced 1991.

Price: $573.00
Price: Stainless........................ $628.00

HANDGUNS — AUTOLOADERS, SERVICE & SPORT

Colt XS Lightweight Commander

Colt Lightweight Commander

Colt Defender

Colt 1991 Model O Compact

Colt XS Model O Commander

Colt Model 1991 Model O Compact Auto Pistol

Similar to the Model 1991 A1 except has 3-1/2" barrel. Overall length is 7", and gun is 3/8" shorter in height. Comes with one 6-shot magazine, moulded case. Introduced 1993.
Price: **$556.00**

COLT XS SERIES MODEL O AUTO PISTOLS

Caliber: 45 ACP, 8-shot magazine. **Barrel:** 4.25", 5". **Weight:** N/A. **Length:** N/A. **Grips:** Checkered, double diamond rosewood. **Sights:** Drift-adjustable three-dot combat. **Features:** Brushed stainless finish; adjustable, two-cut aluminum trigger; extended ambidextrous thumb safety; upswept beavertail with palm swell; elongated slot hammer; beveled magazine well. Introduced 1999. From Colt's Manufacturing Co., Inc.
Price: XS Government (5" barrel) **$750.00**
Price: XS Commander (4.25" barrel) **$750.00**

COLT XS LIGHTWEIGHT COMMANDER AUTO PISTOL

Caliber: 45 ACP, 8-shot. **Barrel:** 4-1/4". **Weight:** 26 oz. **Length:** 7-3/4" overall. **Stocks:** Double diamond checkered rosewood. **Sights:** Fixed, glare-proofed blade front, square notch rear; three-dot system. **Features:** Brushed stainless slide, nickeled aluminum frame; McCormick elongated-slot enhanced hammer, McCormick two-cut adjustable aluminum hammer. Made in U.S. by Colt's Mfg. Co., Inc.
Price: 45, stainless **$750.00**

Colt Model 1991 Model O Commander Auto Pistol

Similar to the Model 1991 Model O except has 4-1/4" barrel. Parkerized finish. 7-shot magazine. Comes in moulded case. Introduced 1993.
Price: **$556.00**

COLT DEFENDER

Caliber: 40 S&W, 45 ACP, 7-shot magazine. **Barrel:** 3". **Weight:** 22-1/2 oz. **Length:** 6-3/4" overall. **Stocks:** Pebble-finish rubber wraparound with fin-

ger grooves. **Sights:** White dot front, snag-free Colt competition rear. **Features:** Stainless finish; aluminum frame; combat-style hammer; Hi Ride grip safety, extended manual safety, disconnect safety. Introduced 1998. Made in U.S. by Colt's Mfg. Co.
Price: **$840.00**

HANDGUNS — AUTOLOADERS, SERVICE & SPORT

Coonan 357 Magnum

CZ 75B 9mm

CZ 75B Decocker

CZ 75D Compact

COONAN 357 MAGNUM, 41 MAGNUM PISTOLS

Caliber: 357 Mag., 41 Magnum, 7-shot magazine. **Barrel:** 5". **Weight:** 42 oz. **Length:** 8.3" overall. **Stocks:** Smooth walnut. **Sights:** Interchangeable ramp front, rear adjustable for windage. **Features:** Stainless steel construction. Unique barrel hood improves accuracy and reliability. Linkless barrel. Many parts interchange with Colt autos. Has grip, hammer, half-cock safeties, extended slide latch. Made in U.S. by Coonan Arms, Inc.

Price: Classic model (Teflon black two-tone finish, 8-shot magazine, fully adjustable rear sight, integral compensated barrel) $1,400.00
Price: 41 Magnum Model, from $825.00

Coonan Compact Cadet 357 Magnum Pistol

Similar to the 357 Magnum full-size gun except has 3.9" barrel, shorter frame, 6-shot magazine. Weight is 39 oz. overall length 7.8". Linkless bull barrel, full-length recoil spring guide rod, extended slide latch. Introduced 1993. Made in U.S. by Coonan Arms, Inc.

Price: $855.00

CZ 75B AUTO PISTOL

Caliber: 9mm Para., 40 S&W, 10-shot magazine. **Barrel:** 4.7". **Weight:** 34.3 oz. **Length:** 8.1" overall. **Stocks:** High impact checkered plastic. **Sights:** Square post front, rear adjustable for windage; three-dot system.

Price: 5" barrel, from $735.00
Price: 6" barrel, from $768.00
Price: With 6" compensated barrel $1,014.00

Features: Single action/double action design; firing pin block safety; choice of black polymer, matte or high-polish blue finishes. All-steel frame. Imported from the Czech Republic by CZ-USA.

Price: Black polymer $472.00
Price: Glossy blue $486.00
Price: Dual tone or satin nickel $486.00
Price: 22 LR conversion unit $279.00

CZ 75B Decocker

Similar to the CZ 75B except has a decocking lever in place of the safety lever. All other specifications are the same. Introduced 1999. Imported from the Czech Republic by CZ-USA.

Price: 9mm, black polymer $467.00

CZ 75B Compact Auto Pistol

Similar to the CZ 75 except has 10-shot magazine, 3.9" barrel and weighs 32 oz. Has removable front sight, non-glare ribbed slide top. Trigger guard is squared and serrated; combat hammer. Introduced 1993. Imported from the Czech Republic by CZ-USA.

Price: 9mm, black polymer $499.00
Price: Dual tone or satin nickel $513.00
Price: D Compact, black polymer $526.00

HANDGUNS — AUTOLOADERS, SERVICE & SPORT

CZ 97B

CZ 75/85 Kadet

CZ 85

CZ 83B

CZ 85B Auto Pistol

Same gun as the CZ 75 except has ambidextrous slide release and safety-levers; non-glare, ribbed slide top; squared, serrated trigger guard; trigger stop to prevent overtravel. Introduced 1986. Imported from the Czech Republic by CZ-USA.

Price: Black polymer. **$483.00**
Price: Combat, black polymer. **$540.00**
Price: Combat, dual tone **$487.00**
Price: Combat, glossy blue. **$499.00**

CZ 85 Combat

Similar to the CZ 85B (9mm only) except has an adjustable rear sight, adjustable trigger for overtravel, free-fall magazine, extended magazine catch. Does not have the firing pin block safety. Introduced 1999. Imported from the Czech Republic by CZ-USA.

Price: 9mm, black polymer. **$540.00**
Price: 9mm, glossy blue **$561.00**
Price: 9mm, dual tone or satin nickel **$561.00**

CZ 83B DOUBLE-ACTION PISTOL

Caliber: 9mm Makarov, 32 ACP, 380 ACP, 10-shot magazine. **Barrel:** 3.8". **Weight:** 26.2 oz. **Length:** 6.8" overall. **Stocks:** High impact checkered plastic. **Sights:** Removable square post front, rear adjustable for windage; three-dot system. **Features:** Single action/double action; ambidextrous magazine release and safety. Blue finish; non-glare ribbed slide top. Imported from the Czech Republic by CZ-USA.

Price: Blue **$378.00**
Price: Nickel **$378.00**

CZ 97B AUTO PISTOL

Caliber: 45 ACP, 10-shot magazine. **Barrel:** 4.85". **Weight:** 40 oz. **Length:** 8.34" overall. **Stocks:** Checkered walnut. **Sights:** Fixed. **Features:** Single action/double action; full-length slide rails; screw-in barrel bushing; linkless barrel; all-steel construction; chamber loaded indicator; dual transfer bars. Introduced 1999. Imported from the Czech Republic by CZ-USA.

Price: Black polymer. **$607.00**
Price: Glossy blue **$621.00**

CZ 75/85 KADET AUTO PISTOL

Caliber: 22 LR, 10-shot magazine. **Barrel:** 4.88". **Weight:** 36 oz. **Length:** NA. **Stocks:** High impact checkered plastic. **Sights:** Blade front, fully adjustable rear. **Features:** Single action/double action mechanism; all-steel construction. Duplicates weight, balance and function of the CZ 75 pistol. Introduced 1999. Imported from the Czech Republic by CZ-USA.

Price: Black polymer. **$486.00**

CZ 100 AUTO PISTOL

Caliber: 9mm Para, 40 S&W, 10-shot magazine. **Barrel:** 3.7". **Weight:** 24 oz. **Length:** 6.9" overall. **Stocks:** Grooved polymer. **Sights:** Blade front with dot, white outline rear drift adjustable for windage. **Features:** Double action only with firing pin block; polymer frame, steel slide; has laser sight mount. Introduced 1996. Imported from the Czech Republic by CZ-USA.

Price: 9mm Para. **$405.00**
Price: 40 S&W **$405.00**

HANDGUNS — AUTOLOADERS, SERVICE & SPORT

Davis P-380

Davis P-32

CZ 100

Desert Eagle Baby Eagle

Desert Eagle Mark XIX

DAVIS P-380 AUTO PISTOL

Caliber: 380 ACP, 5-shot magazine. **Barrel:** 2.8". **Weight:** 22 oz. **Length:** 5.4" overall. **Stocks:** Black composition. **Sights:** Fixed. **Features:** Choice of chrome or black Teflon finish. Introduced 1991. Made in U.S. by Davis Industries.
Price: $98.00

DAVIS P-32 AUTO PISTOL

Caliber: 32 ACP, 6-shot magazine. **Barrel:** 2.8". **Weight:** 22 oz. **Length:** 5.4" overall. **Stocks:** Laminated wood. **Sights:** Fixed. **Features:** Choice of black Teflon or chrome finish. Announced 1986. Made in U.S. by Davis Industries.
Price: $107.00

DESERT EAGLE MARK XIX PISTOL

Caliber: 357 Mag., 9-shot; 44 Mag., 8-shot; 50 Magnum, 7-shot. **Barrel:** 6", 10", interchangeable. **Weight:** 357 Mag.—62 oz.; 44 Mag.—69 oz.; 50 Mag.—72 oz. **Length:** 10-1/4" overall (6" bbl.). **Stocks:** Rubber. **Sights:** Blade on ramp front, combat-style rear. Adjustable available. **Features:** Interchangeable barrels; rotating three-lug bolt; ambidextrous safety; adjustable trigger. Military epoxy finish. Satin, bright nickel, hard chrome, polished and blued finishes available. 10" barrel extra. Imported from Israel by Magnum Research, Inc.
Price: 357, 6" bbl., standard pistol $1,199.00
Price: 44 Mag., 6" bbl., standard pistol $1,199.00
Price: 50 Magnum, 6" bbl., standard pistol $1,199.00
Price: 440 Cor-Bon, 6" bbl. $1,389.00

DESERT EAGLE BABY EAGLE PISTOLS

Caliber: 9mm Para., 40 S&W, 45 ACP, 10-round magazine. **Barrel:** 3.5", 3.7", 4.72". **Weight:** NA. **Length:** 7.25" to 8.25" overall. **Grips:** Polymer. **Sights:** Drift-adjustable rear, blade front. **Features:** Steel frame and slide; polygonal rifling to reduce barrel wear; slide safety; decocker. Reintroduced in 1999. Imported from Israel by Magnum Research Inc.
Price: Standard (9mm or 40 cal.; 4.72" barrel, 8.25" overall) ... $449.00
Price: Semi-Compact (9mm, 40 or 45 cal.; 3.7" barrel, 7.75" overall) $449.00
Price: Compact (9mm or 40 cal.; 3.5" barrel, 7.25" overall) ... $449.00
Price: Polymer (9mm or 40 cal; polymer frame; 3.25" barrel, 7.25" overall) $449.00

HANDGUNS — AUTOLOADERS, SERVICE & SPORT

Entréprise Boxer P500

Entréprise Tactical 500

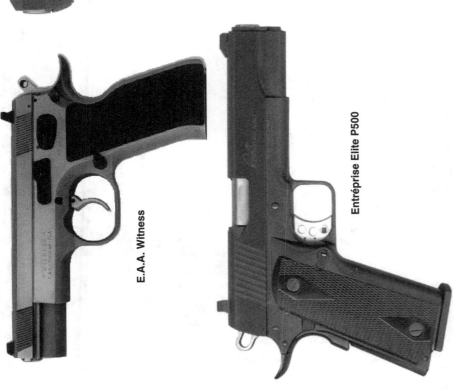

E.A.A. Witness

Entréprise Elite P500

E.A.A. WITNESS DA AUTO PISTOL

Caliber: 9mm Para., 9mm Super, 40 S&W, 10-shot magazine; 45 ACP, 10-shot overall. **Barrel:** 4.50". **Weight:** 35.33 oz. **Length:** 8.10" overall. **Stocks:** Checkered rubber. **Sights:** Undercut blade front, open rear adjustable for windage. **Features:** Double-action trigger system; round trigger guard; frame-mounted safety. Introduced 1991. Imported from Italy by European American Armory.

Price: 9mm, blue.	$351.00
Price: 9mm, Wonder finish.	$366.00
Price: 9mm Compact, blue, 10-shot.	$351.00
Price: As above, Wonder finish	$366.60
Price: 40 S&W, blue	$366.60
Price: As above, Wonder finish	$366.60
Price: 40 S&W Compact, 9-shot, blue	$366.60
Price: As above, Wonder finish	$351.00
Price: 45 ACP, blue	$366.60
Price: As above, Wonder finish	$351.00
Price: 45 ACP Compact, 8-shot, blue.	$366.60
Price: As above, Wonder finish	$366.60

E.A.A. EUROPEAN MODEL AUTO PISTOLS

Caliber: 32 ACP or 380 ACP, 7-shot magazine. **Barrel:** 3.88". **Weight:** 26 oz. **Length:** 7-3/8" overall. **Stocks:** European hardwood. **Sights:** Fixed blade front, rear drift-adjustable for windage. **Features:** Chrome or blue finish; magazine, thumb and firing pin safeties; external hammer; safety-lever takedown. Imported from Italy by European American Armory.

Price: Blue	$132.60
Price: Wonder finish	$163.80

ENTRÉPRISE ELITE P500 AUTO PISTOL

Caliber: 45 ACP, 10-shot magazine. **Barrel:** 5". **Weight:** 40 oz. **Length:** 8.5" overall. **Stocks:** Black ultra-slim, double diamond, checkered synthetic. **Sights:** Dovetailed blade front, rear adjustable for windage; three-

dot system. **Features:** Reinforced dust cover; lowered and flared ejection port; squared trigger guard; adjustable match trigger; bolstered front strap; high grip cut; high ride beavertail grip safety; steel flat mainspring housing; extended thumb lock; skeletonized hammer, match grade sear, disconnector; Wolff springs. Introduced 1998. Made in U.S. by Entréprise Arms.

Price: $739.90

Entréprise Boxer P500 Auto Pistol

Similar to the Medalist model except has adjustable Competizione "melded" rear sight with dovetailed Patridge front; high mass chiseled slide with sweep cut; machined slide parallel rails; polished breech face and barrel channel. Introduced 1998. Made in U.S. by Entréprise Arms.

Price: $1,399.00

Entréprise Medalist P500 Auto Pistol

Similar to the Elite model except has adjustable Competizione "melded" rear sight with dovetailed Patridge front; machined slide parallel rails with polished breech face and barrel channel; front and rear slide serrations; lowered and flared ejection port; full-length one-piece guide rod with plug; National Match barrel and bushing; stainless firing pin; tuned match extractor; oversize firing pin stop; throated barrel and polished ramp; slide lapped to frame. Introduced 1998. Made in U.S. by Entréprise Arms.

Price: 45 ACP. $979.00
Price: 40 S&W $1,099.00

Entréprise Tactical P500 Auto Pistol

Similar to the Elite model except has Tactical2 Ghost Ring sight or Novak lo-mount sight; ambidextrous thumb safety; front and rear slide serrations; full-length guide rod; throated barrel, polished ramp; tuned match extractor; fitted barrel and bushing; stainless firing pin; slide lapped to frame; dehorned. Introduced 1998. Made in U.S. by Entréprise Arms.

Price: $979.90
Price: Tactical Plus (full-size frame, Officer's slide) $1,049.00

HANDGUNS — AUTOLOADERS, SERVICE & SPORT

ERMA KGP68 AUTO PISTOL

Caliber: 32 ACP, 6-shot, 380 ACP, 5-shot. **Barrel:** 4". **Weight:** 22-1/2 oz. **Length:** 7-3/8" overall. **Stocks:** Checkered plastic. **Sights:** Fixed. **Features:** Toggle action similar to original "Luger" pistol. Action stays open after last shot. Has magazine and sear disconnect safety systems.
Price: **$499.95**

FEG PJK-9HP AUTO PISTOL

Caliber: 9mm Para., 10-shot magazine. **Barrel:** 4.75". **Weight:** 32 oz. **Length:** 8" overall. **Stocks:** Hand-checkered walnut. **Sights:** Blade front, rear adjustable for windage; three dot system. **Features:** Single action; polished blue or hard chrome finish; rounded combat-style serrated hammer. Comes with two magazines and cleaning rod. Imported from Hungary by K.B.I., Inc.
Price: Blue **$259.95**
Price: Hard chrome. **$259.95**

FEG SMC-380 AUTO PISTOL

Caliber: 380 ACP, 6-shot magazine. **Barrel:** 3.5". **Weight:** 18.5 oz. **Length:** 6.1" overall. **Stocks:** Checkered composition with thumbrest. **Sights:** Blade front, rear adjustable for windage. **Features:** Patterned after the PPK pistol. Alloy frame, steel slide; double action. Blue finish. Comes with two magazines, cleaning rod. Imported from Hungary by K.B.I., Inc.
Price: **$224.95**

FELK MTF 450 AUTO PISTOL

Caliber: 9mm Para. (10-shot); 40 S&W (8-shot); 45 ACP (9-shot magazine). **Barrel:** 3.5". **Weight:** 19.9 oz. **Length:** 6.4" overall. **Features:** Double-action only trigger, striker fired; polymer frame; trigger safety, firing pin safety, trigger

Felk MTF 450

FEG PJK-9HP

bar safety; adjustable trigger weight; fully interchangeable slide/barrel to change calibers. Introduced 1998. Imported by Felk Inc.
Price: **$395.00**
Price: 45 ACP pistol with 9mm and 40 S&W slide/barrel assemblies **$999.00**

GLOCK 17 AUTO PISTOL

Caliber: 9mm Para., 10-shot magazine. **Barrel:** 4.49". **Weight:** 22.04 oz. (without magazine). **Length:** 7.32" overall. **Stocks:** Black polymer. **Sights:** Dot on front blade, white outline rear adjustable for windage. **Features:** Polymer frame, steel slide; double-action trigger with "Safe Action" system; mechanical firing pin safety, drop safety; simple takedown without tools; locked breech, recoil operated action. Adopted by Austrian armed forces 1983. NATO approved 1984. Imported from Austria by Glock, Inc.
Price: Fixed sight, with extra magazine, magazine loader, cleaning kit **$641.00**
Price: Adjustable sight **$641.00**
Price: Model 17L (6" barrel) **$671.00**
Price: Model 17C, ported barrel (compensated) .. **$646.00**

Glock 19 Auto Pistol

Similar to the Glock 17 except has a 4" barrel, giving an overall length of 6.85" and weight of 20.99 oz. Magazine capacity is 10 rounds. Fixed or adjustable rear sight. Introduced 1988.
Price: Fixed sight **$641.00**
Price: Adjustable sight **$671.00**
Price: Model 19C, ported barrel **$646.00**

Glock 20 10mm Auto Pistol

Similar to the Glock Model 17 except chambered for 10mm Automatic cartridge. Barrel length is 4.60", overall length is 7.59" and weight is 26.3 oz. (without magazine). Magazine capacity is 10 rounds. Fixed or adjustable rear sight. Comes with an extra magazine, magazine loader, cleaning rod and brush. Introduced 1990. Imported from Austria by Glock, Inc.
Price: Fixed sight **$700.00**
Price: Adjustable sight **$730.00**

Glock 17L

Glock 17C

HANDGUNS

Glock 30

Glock 31

Glock 22

Glock 26

Glock 21 Auto Pistol

Similar to the Glock 17 except chambered for 45 ACP, 10-shot magazine. Overall length is 7.59", weight is 25.2 oz. (without magazine). Fixed or adjustable rear sight. Introduced 1991.

Price: Fixed sight $700.00
Price: Adjustable sight $730.00

Glock 22 Auto Pistol

Similar to the Glock 17 except chambered for 40 S&W, 10-shot magazine. Overall length is 7.28", weight is 22.3 oz. (without magazine). Fixed or adjustable rear sight. Introduced 1990.

Price: Fixed sight $641.00
Price: Adjustable sight $671.00
Price: Model 22C, ported barrel $646.00

Glock 23 Auto Pistol

Similar to the Glock 19 except chambered for 40 S&W, 10-shot magazine. Overall length is 6.85", weight is 20.6 oz. (without magazine). Fixed or adjustable rear sight. Introduced 1990.

Price: Fixed sight $641.00
Price: Model 23C, ported barrel $646.00
Price: Adjustable sight $671.00

GLOCK 26, 27 AUTO PISTOLS

Caliber: 9mm Para. (M26), 10-shot magazine; 40 S&W (M27), 9-shot magazine. **Barrel:** 3.46". **Weight:** 21.75 oz. **Length:** 6.29" overall. **Stocks:** Integral. Stippled polymer. **Sights:** Dot on front blade, fixed or fully adjustable white outline rear. **Features:** Subcompact size. Polymer frame,

steel slide; double-action trigger with "Safe Action" system, three safeties. Matte black Tenifer finish. Hammer-forged barrel. Imported from Austria by Glock, Inc. Introduced 1996.

Price: Fixed sight $641.00
Price: Adjustable sight $671.00

GLOCK 29, 30 AUTO PISTOLS

Caliber: 10mm (M29), 45 ACP (M30), 10-shot magazine. **Barrel:** 3.78". **Weight:** 24 oz. **Length:** 6.7" overall. **Stocks:** Integral. Stippled polymer. **Sights:** Dot on front, fixed or fully adjustable white outline rear. **Features:** Compact size. Polymer frame steel slide; double-recoil spring reduces recoil; Safe Action system with three safeties; Tenifer finish. Two magazines supplied. Introduced 1997. Imported from Austria by Glock, Inc.

Price: Fixed sight $700.00
Price: Adjustable sight $730.00

Glock 31/31C Auto Pistols

Similar to the Glock 17 except chambered for 357 Auto cartridge; 10-shot magazine. Overall length is 7.32", weight is 23.28 oz. (without magazine). Fixed or adjustable sight. Imported from Austria by Glock, Inc.

Price: Fixed sight $641.00
Price: Adjustable sight $671.00
Price: Model 31C, ported barrel $646.00

Glock 32/32C Auto Pistols

Similar to the Glock 19 except chambered for the 357 Auto cartridge; 10-shot magazine. Overall length is 6.85", weight is 21.52 oz. (without magazine). Fixed or adjustable sight. Imported from Austria by Glock, Inc.

Price: Fixed sight $616.00
Price: Adjustable sight $644.00
Price: Model 32C, ported barrel $646.00

HANDGUNS — AUTOLOADERS, SERVICE & SPORT

Glock 35

Glock 33

Heckler & Koch USP Compact

Hammerli Trailside PL 22

Glock 33 Auto Pistol
Similar to the Glock 26 except chambered for the 357 Auto cartridge; 9-shot magazine. Overall length is 6.29", weight is 19.75 oz. (without magazine). Fixed or adjustable sight. Imported from Austria by Glock, Inc.
Price: Fixed sight $641.00
Price: Adjustable sight $671.00

GLOCK 34, 35 AUTO PISTOLS
Caliber: 9mm Para. (M34), 40 S&W (M35), 10-shot magazine. **Barrel:** 5.32". **Weight:** 22.9 oz. **Length:** 8.15" overall. **Stocks:** Integral. Stippled polymer. **Sights:** Dot on front, fully adjustable white outline rear. **Features:** Polymer frame, steel slide; double-action trigger with "Safe Action" system; three safeties; Tenifer finish. Imported from Austria by Glock, Inc.
Price: Model 34, 9mm $770.00
Price: Model 35, 40 S&W $770.00

GLOCK 36 AUTO PISTOL
Caliber: 45 ACP, 6-shot magazine. **Barrel:** 3.78". **Weight:** 20.11 oz. **Length:** 6.77" overall. **Stocks:** Integral. Stippled polymer. **Sights:** Dot on front, fully adjustable white outline rear. **Features:** Polymer frame, steel slide; double-action trigger with "Safe Action" system; three safeties; Tenifer finish. Imported from Austria by Glock, Inc.
Price: Fixed sight $700.00
Price: Adj. sight $730.00

HAMMERLI TRAILSIDE PL 22 TARGET PISTOL
Caliber: 22 LR, 10-shot magazine. **Barrel:** 4.5", 6". **Weight:** 28 oz. (4.5" barrel). **Length:** 7.75" overall. **Stocks:** Wood target-style. **Sights:** Blade front, rear adjustable for windage. **Features:** One-piece barrel/frame unit; two-stage competition-style trigger; dovetail scope mount rail. Introduced 1999. Imported from Switzerland by SIGARMS, Inc.
Price: .... NA

HECKLER & KOCH USP AUTO PISTOL
Caliber: 9mm Para., 10-shot magazine, 40 S&W, 10-shot magazine. **Barrel:** 4.25". **Weight:** 28 oz. (USP40). **Length:** 6.9" overall. **Stocks:** Non-slip stippled black polymer. **Sights:** Blade front, rear adjustable for windage. **Features:** New HK design with polymer frame, modified Browning action with recoil reduction system, single control lever. Special "hostile environment" finish on all metal parts. Available in SA/DA, DAO, left- and right-hand versions. Introduced 1993. Imported from Germany by Heckler & Koch, Inc.
Price: Right-hand $699.00
Price: Left-hand $714.00
Price: Stainless steel, right-hand $749.00
Price: Stainless steel, left-hand $799.00

Heckler & Koch USP Compact Auto Pistol
Similar to the USP except has 3.58" barrel, measures 6.81" overall, and weighs 1.60 lbs. (9mm). Available in 9mm Para. or 40 S&W with 10-shot magazine. Introduced 1996. Imported from Germany by Heckler & Koch, Inc.
Price: Blue $719.00
Price: Blue with control lever on right $744.00
Price: Stainless steel $769.00
Price: Stainless steel with control lever on right ... $794.00

Heckler & Koch USP45 Auto Pistol
Similar to the 9mm and 40 S&W USP except chambered for 45 ACP, 10-shot magazine. Has 4.13" barrel, overall length of 7.87" and weighs 30.4 oz. Has adjustable three-dot sight system. Available in SA/DA, DAO, left- and right-hand versions. Introduced 1995. Imported from Germany by Heckler & Koch, Inc.
Price: Right-hand $759.00
Price: Left-hand $784.00
Price: Stainless steel right-hand $799.00
Price: Stainless steel left-hand $724.00

HANDGUNS — AUTOLOADERS, SERVICE & SPORT

Heckler & Koch USP Expert

Heckler & Koch P7M8

Heckler & Koch USP45

Heckler & Koch USP45 Tactical

Heckler & Koch USP45 Compact

Similar to the USP45 except has stainless slide; 8-shot magazine; modified and contoured slide and frame; extended slide release; 3.80" barrel, 7.09" overall length, weighs 1.75 lbs.; adjustable three-dot sights. Introduced 1998. Imported from Germany by Heckler & Koch, Inc.

Price: With control lever on left, stainless **$789.00**
Price: As above, blue **$739.00**
Price: With control lever on right, stainless **$814.00**
Price: As above, blue **$739.00**

HECKLER & KOCH USP45 TACTICAL PISTOL

Caliber: 45 ACP, 10-shot magazine. **Barrel:** 4.92". **Weight:** 2.24 lbs. **Length:** 8.64" overall. **Stocks:** Non-slip stippled polymer. **Sights:** Blade front, fully adjustable target rear. **Features:** Has extended threaded barrel with rubber O-ring; adjustable trigger; extended magazine floorplate; adjustable trigger stop; polymer frame. Introduced 1998. Imported from Germany by Heckler & Koch, Inc.

Price: **$999.00**

HECKLER & KOCH MARK 23 SPECIAL OPERATIONS PISTOL

Caliber: 45 ACP, 10-shot magazine. **Barrel:** 5.87". **Weight:** 43 oz. **Length:** 9.65" overall. **Stocks:** Integral with frame; black polymer. **Sights:** Blade front, rear drift adjustable for windage; three-dot. **Features:** Polymer frame; double action; exposed hammer; short recoil, modified Browning action. Civilian version of the SOCOM pistol. Introduced 1996. Imported from Germany by Heckler & Koch, Inc.

Price: **$2,169.00**

Heckler & Koch USP Expert Pistol

Combines features of the USP Tactical and HK Mark 23 pistols with a new slide design. Chambered for 45 ACP, 10-shot magazine. Has adjustable target sights. 5.20" barrel, 8.74" overall length, weighs 1.87 lbs. Matchgrade single- and double-action trigger pull with adjustable stop; ambi-

dextrous control levers; elongated target slide; barrel O-ring that seals and centers barrel. Suited to IPSC competition. Introduced 1999. Imported from Germany by Heckler & Koch, Inc.

Price: **$1,369.00**

HECKLER & KOCH P7M8 AUTO PISTOL

Caliber: 9mm Para., 8-shot magazine. **Barrel:** 4.13". **Weight:** 29 oz. **Length:** 6.73" overall. **Stocks:** Stippled black plastic. **Sights:** Blade front, adjustable rear; three dot system. **Features:** Unique "squeeze cocker" in frontstrap cocks the action. Gas-retarded action. Squared combat-type trigger guard. Blue finish. Compact size. Imported from Germany by Heckler & Koch, Inc.

Price: P7M8, blued **$1,229.00**

HERITAGE STEALTH AUTO PISTOL

Caliber: 9mm Para., 40 S&W, 10-shot magazine. **Barrel:** 3.9". **Weight:** 20.2 oz. **Length:** 6.3" overall. **Stocks:** Black polymer; integral. **Sights:** Blade front, rear drift adjustable for windage. **Features:** Gas retarded blowback action; polymer frame, 17-4 stainless slide; frame mounted ambidextrous trigger safety, magazine safety. Introduced 1996. Made in U.S. by Heritage Mfg., Inc.

Price: **$289.95**
Price: Stainless or stainless/black **$329.95**

HERITAGE H25S AUTO PISTOL

Caliber: 25 ACP, 6-shot magazine. **Barrel:** 2.25". **Weight:** 13.5 oz. **Length:** 4.5" overall. **Stocks:** Smooth hardwood. **Sights:** Fixed. **Features:** Frame-mounted trigger safety, magazine disconnect safety. Made in U.S. by Heritage Mfg. Inc.

Price: Blue **$149.95**
Price: Nickel **$159.95**

HANDGUNS — AUTOLOADERS, SERVICE & SPORT

Hi-Point 45 ACP

Heritage Stealth

HS America HS2000

Hi-Point 9MM Comp

HI-POINT FIREARMS 40 S&W AUTO
Caliber: 40 S&W, 8-shot magazine. **Barrel:** 4.5". **Weight:** 39 oz. **Length:** 7.72" overall. **Stocks:** Checkered acetal resin. **Sights:** Adjustable; low profile. **Features:** Internal drop-safe mechanism; alloy frame. Introduced 1991. From MKS Supply, Inc.
Price: Matte black...$159.00

HI-POINT FIREARMS 45 CALIBER PISTOL
Caliber: 45 ACP, 7-shot magazine. **Barrel:** 4.5". **Weight:** 39 oz. **Length:** 7.95" overall. **Stocks:** Checkered acetal resin. **Sights:** Adjustable; low profile. **Features:** Internal drop-safe mechanism; alloy frame. Introduced 1991. From MKS Supply, Inc.
Price: Matte black...$159.00
Price: Chrome slide, black frame...........................$169.00

HI-POINT FIREARMS 9MM COMP PISTOL
Caliber: 9mm, Para, 10-shot magazine. **Barrel:** 4". **Weight:** 39 oz. **Length:** 7.72" overall. **Stocks:** Textured acetal plastic. **Sights:** Adjustable; low profile. **Features:** Single-action design. Scratch-resistant, non-glare blue finish, alloy frame. Muzzle brake/compensator. Compensator is slotted for laser or flashlight mounting. Introduced 1998. From MKS Supply, Inc.
Price: Matte black...$159.00

HI-POINT FIREARMS MODEL 9MM COMPACT PISTOL
Caliber: 9mm Para., 8-shot magazine. **Barrel:** 3.5". **Weight:** 29 oz. **Length:** 6.7" overall. **Stocks:** Textured acetal plastic. **Sights:** Combat-style adjustable three-dot system; low profile. **Features:** Single-action design; frame-mounted magazine release; polymer or alloy frame. Scratch-resistant matte finish. Introduced 1993. From MKS Supply, Inc.
Price: Black, alloy frame..$137.00
Price: With polymer frame (29 oz.), non-slip grips.....$137.00
Price: Aluminum with polymer frame.........................$137.00

Hi-Point Firearms Model 380 Polymer Pistol
Similar to the 9mm Compact model except chambered for 380 ACP, 8-shot magazine, adjustable three-dot sights. Weighs 29 oz. Polymer frame. Introduced 1998. Made in U.S. From MKS Supply.
Price: $99.95

HS AMERICA HS2000 PISTOL
Caliber: 9mm Para., 357 SIG, 40 S&W, 10-shot magazine. **Barrel:** 4.08 inches. **Weight:** 22.88 oz. **Length:** 7.2 inches overall. **Stocks:** Integral black polymer. **Sights:** Drift-adjustable white dot rear, white dot blade front. **Features:** Incorporates trigger, firing pin, grip and out-of-battery safeties; firing-pin status and loaded chamber indicators; ambidextrous magazine release; dual-tension recoil spring with stand-off device; poly-mer frame; black finish with chrome-plated magazine. Imported from Croatia by HS America.
Price: $419.00

KAHR K9, K40 DA AUTO PISTOLS
Caliber: 9mm Para., 7-shot magazine. **Barrel:** 3.5". **Weight:** 25 oz. **Length:** 6" overall. 40 S&W, 6-shot magazine. **Stocks:** Wrap-around textured soft polymer. **Sights:** Blade front, rear drift adjustable for windage; bar-dot combat style. **Features:** Trigger-cocking double-action mechanism with passive firing pin block. Made of 4140 ordnance steel with matte black fin-ish. Contact maker for complete price list. Introduced 1994. Made in U.S. by Kahr Arms.
Price: E9, black matte finish.....................................$399.00
Price: Matte black, night sights 9mm.........................$640.00
Price: Matte stainless steel, 9mm.............................$580.00
Price: 40 S&W, matte black......................................$550.00
Price: 40 S&W, matte black, night sights.....................$640.00

HANDGUNS — AUTOLOADERS, SERVICE & SPORT

Kel-Tec P-11

Kel-Tec P-32

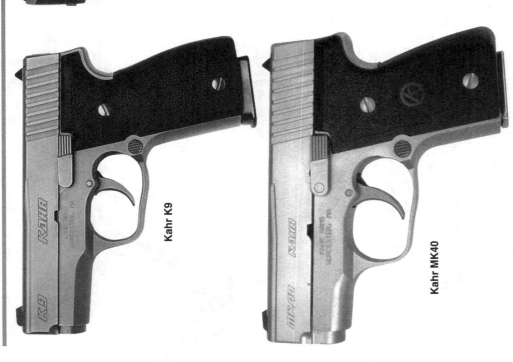

Kahr K9

Kahr MK40

Price: 40 S&W, matte stainless $580.00
Price: K9 Elite 98 (high-polish stainless slide flats, Kahr combat trigger), from $631.00
Price: As above, MK9 Elite 98, from.................. $631.00
Price: As above, K40 Elite 98, from $631.00

Kahr K9 9mm Compact Polymer Pistol

Similar to K9 steel frame pistol except has polymer frame, matte stainless steel slide. Barrel length 3.5", overall length 6"; weighs 17.9 oz. Includes two 7-shot magazines, hard polymer case, trigger lock. Introduced 2000. Made in U.S. by Kahr Arms.
Price: $527.00

Kahr MK9/MK40 Micro Pistol

Similar to the K9/K40 except is 5.5" overall, 4" high, has a 3" barrel. Weighs 22 oz. Has snag-free bar-dot sights, polished feed ramp, dual recoil spring system, DA-only trigger. Comes with 6- and 7-shot magazines. Introduced 1998. Made in U.S. by Kahr Arms.
Price: Matte stainless $580.00
Price: Elite 98, polished stainless, tritium night sights $721.00

KEL-TEC P-11 AUTO PISTOL

Caliber: 9mm Para., 10-shot magazine. **Barrel:** 3.1". **Weight:** 14 oz. **Length:** 5.6" overall. **Stocks:** Checkered black polymer. **Sights:** Blade front, rear adjustable for windage. **Features:** Ordnance steel slide, aluminum frame. Double-action-only trigger mechanism. Introduced 1995. Made in U.S. by Kel-Tec CNC Industries, Inc.
Price: Blue $309.00
Price: Hard chrome. $363.00
Price: Parkerized $350.00

KEL-TEC P-32 AUTO PISTOL

Caliber: 32 ACP, 7-shot magazine. **Barrel:** 2.68". **Weight:** 6.6 oz. **Length:** 5.07" overall. **Stocks:** Checkered composite. **Sights:** Fixed. **Features:** Double-action-only mechanism with 6-lb. pull; internal slide stop. Textured composite grip/frame. Made in U.S. by Kel-Tec CNC Industries, Inc.
Price: $295.00

KIMBER CUSTOM AUTO PISTOL

Caliber: 45 ACP, 7-shot magazine. **Barrel:** 5", match grade. **Weight:** 38 oz. **Length:** 8.7" overall. **Stocks:** Checkered black rubber (standard), or rosewood. **Sights:** McCormick dovetailed front, low combat rear. **Features:** Slide, frame and barrel machined from steel forgings; match-grade barrel, chamber, trigger; extended thumb safety; beveled magazine well; beveled front and rear slide serrations; high-ride beavertail safety; checkered flat mainspring housing; kidney cut under trigger guard; high cut grip design; match-grade stainless barrel bushing; Commander-style hammer; lowered and flared ejection port; Wolff springs; bead blasted black oxide finish. Made in U.S. by Kimber Mfg., Inc.
Price: Custom................................... $723.00
Price: Custom Walnut (double-diamond walnut grips) $745.00
Price: Custom Stainless. $823.00
Price: Custom Stainless 40 S&W $861.00
Price: Custom Stainless Target 45 ACP (stainless, adj. sight)... $935.00
Price: Custom Stainless Target 40 S&W $968.00

Kimber Compact Auto Pistol

Similar to the Custom model except has 4" bull barrel fitted directly to the slide without a bushing; full-length guide rod; grip is .400" shorter than full-size gun; no front serrations. Steel frame models weigh 34 oz., aluminum 28 oz. Introduced 1998. Made in U.S. by Kimber Mfg., Inc.

HANDGUNS — AUTOLOADERS, SERVICE & SPORT

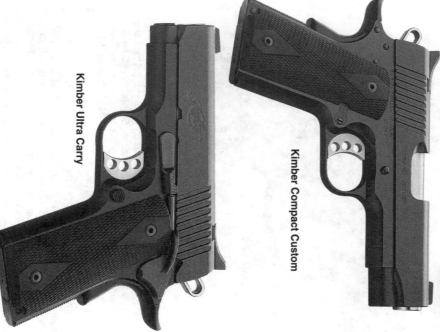

Kimber Custom 45

Kimber Compact Custom

Kimber Ultra Carry

Kimber High Capacity Polymer

Price: 45 ACP, matte black $757.00
Price: Compact Stainless 45 ACP $863.00
Price: Compact Stainless 40 S&W $893.00
Price: Compact Stainless Aluminum 45 ACP (aluminum frame, stainless slide) $829.00
Price: Compact Stainless Aluminum 40 S&W $864.00

Kimber Pro Carry Auto Pistol

Similar to the Compact model except has aluminum frame with full-length grip. Has 4" bull barrel fitted directly to the slide without bushing. Introduced 1998. Made in U.S. by Kimber Mfg., Inc.
Price: 40 S&W $758.00
Price: 45 ACP $792.00
Price: Stainless Pro Carry 45 ACP $829.00
Price: Stainless Pro Carry 40 S&W $864.00

Kimber Gold Match Auto Pistol

Similar to the Custom model except has Kimber adjustable sight with rounded and blended edges; stainless steel match-grade barrel hand-fitted to spherical barrel bushing; premium aluminum trigger; extended ambidextrous thumb safety; hand-checkered double diamond rosewood grips. Hand-fitted by Kimber Custom Shop. Made in U.S. by Kimber Mfg., Inc.
Price: Gold Match 45 ACP $1,135.00
Price: Stainless Gold Match 45 ACP (highly polished flats) $1,277.00
Price: Stainless Gold Match 40 S&W $1,306.00

Kimber Polymer Gold Match Auto Pistol

Similar to the Polymer model except has Kimber adjustable sight with rounded and blended edges; stainless steel match-grade barrel hand-fitted to spherical barrel bushing; premium aluminum trigger; extended ambidextrous thumb safety. Hand-fitted by Kimber Custom Shop. Introduced 1999. Made in U.S. by Kimber Mfg., Inc.
Price: $1,183.00
Price: Polymer Stainless Gold Match (polished stainless slide). $1,337.00

Kimber Gold Combat Auto Pistol

Similar to the Gold Match except designed for concealed carry. Has two-piece extended and beveled magazine well, tritium night sights; premium aluminum trigger; 30 lpi front strap checkering; special Custom Shop markings; Kim Pro black finish. Introduced 1999. Made in U.S. by Kimber Mfg., Inc.
Price: 45 ACP $1,633.00
Price: Gold Combat Stainless (satin-finished stainless frame and slide, special Custom Shop markings) $1,576.00

Kimber Ultra Carry Auto Pistol

Similar to the Compact Aluminum model except has 3" balljoint spherical bushingless cone barrel; aluminum frame; beveling at front and rear of ejection port; relieved breech face; tuned ejector; special slide stop; dual captured low-effort spring system. Weighs 25 oz. Introduced 1999, made in U.S. by Kimber Mfg., Inc.
Price: 45 ACP $792.00
Price: 40 S&W $822.00
Price: Stainless, 45 ACP $868.00
Price: Stainless, 40 S&W $904.00

KIMBER HIGH CAPACITY POLYMER PISTOL

Caliber: 45 ACP, 14-shot magazine. Barrel: 5". Weight: 34 oz. Length: 8.7" overall. Stocks: Integral; checkered black polymer. Sights: McCormick low profile front and rear. Features: Polymer frame with steel insert. Comes with pre-ban magazine. Checkered front strap and mainspring housing; polymer trigger; stainless high ride beavertail grip safety; hooked trigger guard. Introduced 1997. Made in U.S. by Kimber Mfg., Inc.
Price: Matte black finish $904.00
Price: Polymer Stainless (satin-finish stainless slide) $973.00
Price: Polymer Pro Carry (compact slide, 4" bull barrel) $924.00
Price: Polymer Pro Carry Stainless $993.00

HANDGUNS — AUTOLOADERS, SERVICE & SPORT

Llama Micromax

Llama Minimax

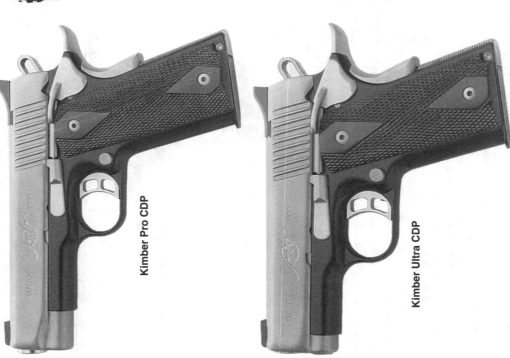

Kimber Pro CDP

Kimber Ultra CDP

KIMBER PRO CDP AUTO PISTOL

Caliber: 45 ACP, 7-shot magazine. **Barrel:** 4". **Weight:** 28 oz. **Length:** 7.7" overall. **Grips:** Hand-checkered. double diamond rosewood. **Sights:** Tritium three-dot. **Features:** Matte black, machined aluminum frame; satin stainless steel slide; match-grade barrel and chamber; beveled magazine well; extended ejector; high-ride beavertail grip safety; match-grade trigger group; ambidextrous safety; checkered frontstrap; meltdown treatment. Introduced 2000. Made in U.S. by Kimber.

Price: **$1,086.00**

KIMBER ULTRA CDP AUTO PISTOL

Caliber: 45 ACP, 6-shot magazine. **Barrel:** 3". **Weight:** 25 oz. **Length:** 6.8" overall. **Grips:** Hand-checkered. double diamond rosewood. **Sights:** Tritium three-dot. **Features:** Matte black, machined aluminum frame; beveled magazine well. Similar to the Pro CDP except has 3" barrel. Introduced 2000. Made in U.S. by Kimber.

Price: **$1,086.00**

LLAMA MICROMAX 380 AUTO PISTOL

Caliber: 32 ACP, 8-shot, 380 ACP, 7-shot magazine. **Barrel:** 3-11/16". **Weight:** 23 oz. **Length:** 6-1/2" overall. **Stocks:** Checkered high impact polymer. **Sights:** 3-dot combat. **Features:** Single-action design. Mini custom extended slide release; mini custom extended beavertail grip safety; combat-style hammer. Introduced 1997. Imported from Spain by Import Sports, Inc.

Price: Matte blue **$246.95**
Price: Satin chrome (380 only) **$281.95**

LLAMA MINIMAX SERIES

Caliber: 9mm Para., 8-shot; 40 S&W, 7-shot; 45 ACP, 6-shot magazine. **Barrel:** 3-1/2". **Weight:** 35 oz. **Length:** 7-1/3" overall. **Stocks:** Checkered rubber. **Sights:** Three-dot combat. **Features:** Single action, skeletonized combat-style hammer, extended slide release, cone-style barrel, flared ejection port. Introduced 1996. Imported from Spain by Import Sports, Inc.

Price: Blue **$308.95**
Price: Duo-Tone finish (45 only) **$314.95**
Price: Satin chrome **$314.95**

Llama Minimax Sub Compact Auto Pistol

Similar to the Minimax except has 3.14" barrel, weighs 31 oz.; 6.8" overall length; has 10-shot magazine with finger extension; beavertail grip safety. Introduced 1999. Imported from Spain by Import Sports, Inc.

Price: 9mm Para., 40 S&W, 45 ACP, matte blue **$314.95**
Price: As above, satin chrome **$324.95**
Price: Duo-Tone finish (45 only) **$341.95**

LLAMA MAX-I AUTO PISTOLS

Caliber: 45 ACP, 7-shot. **Barrel:** 5-1/8". **Weight:** 36 oz. **Length:** 8-1/2" overall. **Stocks:** Black rubber. **Sights:** Blade front, rear adjustable for windage; three-dot system. **Features:** Single-action trigger; skeletonized combat-style hammer; steel frame; extended manual and grip safeties. Introduced 1995. Imported from Spain by Import Sports, Inc.

Price: 45 ACP, 7-shot, Government model **$298.95**
Price: As above, satin chrome finish **$314.95**

13th EDITION **155**

HANDGUNS — AUTOLOADERS, SERVICE & SPORT

One Pro .45

Llama Max-1

Para-Ordnance P12.45

NORTH AMERICAN ARMS GUARDIAN PISTOL
Caliber: 32 ACP, 6-shot magazine. **Barrel:** 2.1". **Weight:** 13.5 oz. **Length:** 4.36" overall. **Stocks:** Black polymer. **Sights:** Fixed. **Features:** Double-action-only mechanism. All stainless steel construction; snag-free. Introduced 1998. Made in U.S. by North American Arms.
Price: **$359.00**

OLYMPIC ARMS OA-96 AR PISTOL
Caliber: 223. **Barrel:** 6", 8", 4140 chrome-moly steel. **Weight:** 5 lbs. **Length:** 15-3/4" overall. **Stocks:** A2 stowaway pistol grip; no buttstock or receiver tube. **Sights:** Flat-top upper receiver, cut-down front sight base. **Features:** AR-15-type receivers with special bolt carrier; short aluminum hand guard; Vortex flash hider. Introduced 1996. Made in U.S. by Olympic Arms, Inc.
Price: **$858.00**

Olympic Arms OA-98 AR Pistol
Similar to the OA-93 except has removable 7-shot magazine, weighs 3 lbs. Introduced 1999. Made in U.S. by Olympic Arms, Inc.
Price: **$990.00**

ONE PRO .45 AUTO PISTOL
Caliber: 45 ACP or 400 Cor-Bon, 10-shot magazine. **Barrel:** 3.75". **Weight:** 31.1 oz. **Length:** 7.04" overall. **Stocks:** Textured composition. **Sights:** Blade front, drift-adjustable rear; three-dot system. **Features:** All-steel construction; decocking lever and automatic firing pin lock; DA or DAO operation. Introduced 1997. Imported from Switzerland by Magnum Research, Inc.
Price: **$649.00**
Price: Conversion kit, 45 ACP/400, 400/45 ACP **$249.00**

ONE PRO 9 AUTO PISTOL
Caliber: 9mm Para., 10-shot magazine. **Barrel:** 3.01". **Weight:** 25.1 oz. **Length:** 6.06" overall. **Stocks:** Smooth wood. **Sights:** Blade front, rear adjustable for windage. **Features:** Rotating barrel; short slide; double recoil springs; double-action mechanism; decocking lever. Introduced 1998. Imported from Switzerland by Magnum Research.
Price: **$649.00**

PARA-ORDNANCE P-SERIES AUTO PISTOLS
Caliber: 9mm Para., 40 S&W, 45 ACP, 10-shot magazine. **Barrel:** 3", 3-1/2", 4-1/4", 5". **Weight:** From 24 oz. (alloy frame). **Length:** 8.5" overall. **Stocks:** Textured composition. **Sights:** Blade front, rear adjustable for windage. High visibility three-dot system. **Features:** Available with alloy, steel or stainless steel frame with black finish (silver or stainless gun). Steel and stainless steel frame guns weigh 40 oz. (P14.45), 36 oz. (P13.45), 34 oz. (P12.45). Grooved match trigger, rounded combat-style hammer. Beveled magazine well. Manual thumb, grip and firing pin lock safeties. Solid barrel bushing. Contact maker for full details. Introduced 1990. Made in Canada by Para-Ordnance.
Price: P14.45ER (steel frame) **$775.00**
Price: P14.45RR (alloy frame) **$740.00**
Price: P12.45RR (3-1/2" bbl., 24 oz., alloy) **$740.00**
Price: P13.45RR (4-1/4" barrel, 28 oz., alloy) **$740.00**
Price: P12.45ER (steel frame) **$750.00**
Price: P16.40ER (steel frame) **$875.00**
Price: P10-9RR (9mm, alloy frame) **$740.00**

Para-Ordnance Limited Pistols
Similar to the P-Series pistols except with full-length recoil guide system; fully adjustable rear sight; tuned trigger with overtravel stop; beavertail grip safety; competition hammer; front and rear slide serrations; ambidextrous safety; lowered ejection port; ramped match-grade barrel; dovetailed front sight. Introduced 1998. Made in Canada by Para-Ordnance.
Price: 9mm, 40 S&W, 45 ACP .... **$865.00 to $899.00**

Para-Ordnance LDA Auto Pistols
Similar to the P-series except has double-action trigger mechanism. Steel frame with matte black finish, checkered composition grips. Available in 9mm Para., 40 S&W, 45 ACP. Introduced 1999. Made in Canada by Para-Ordnance.
Price: **$775.00**

PETERS STAHL AUTOLOADING PISTOLS
Caliber: 9mm Para., 45 ACP. **Barrel:** 5" or 6". **Weight:** NA. **Length:** NA. **Grips:** Walnut or walnut with rubber wrap. **Sights:** Fully adjustable rear, blade front. **Features:** Stainless steel extended slide stop, safety and extended magazine release button; speed trigger with stop and approx. 3-lb. pull; polished ramp. Introduced 2000. Imported from Germany by Phillips & Rogers.

HANDGUNS — AUTOLOADERS, SERVICE & SPORT

Peters Stahl Millenium

Phoenix Arms HP22

PSA-25 Auto

Para-Ordnance LDA

Peters Stahl High Capacity

Peters Stahl Trophy Master

Price: High Capacity (accepts 15-shot magazines in 45 cal.; includes 10-shot magazine) **$1,695.00**
Price: Trophy Master (blued or stainless, 7-shot in 45, 8-shot in 9mm) **$1,995.00**
Price: Millenium Model (titanium coating on receiver and slide). **$2,195.00**

PHOENIX ARMS HP22, HP25 AUTO PISTOLS

Caliber: 22 LR, 10-shot (HP22), 25 ACP, 10-shot (HP25). **Barrel:** 3".
Weight: 20 oz. **Length:** 5-1/2" overall. **Stocks:** Checkered composition.
Sights: Blade front, adjustable rear. **Features:** Single action, exposed
hammer; manual hold-open; button magazine release. Available in satin
nickel, polished blue finish. Introduced 1993. Made in U.S. by Phoenix
Arms.
Price: With gun lock **$116.00**

PSA-25 AUTO POCKET PISTOL

Caliber: 25 ACP, 6-shot magazine. **Barrel:** 2-1/8". **Weight:** 9.5 oz. **Length:**
4-1/8" overall. **Stocks:** Checkered black polymer, ivory, checkered transparent carbon fiber-filled polymer. **Sights:** Fixed. **Features:** All steel con-
struction; striker fired; single action only; magazine disconnector; cocking
indicator. Introduced 1987. Made in U.S. by Precision Small Arms, Inc.
Price: Traditional (polished black oxide) **$269.00**
Price: Nouveau - Satin (brushed nickel) **$269.00**
Price: Nouveau - Mirror (highly polished nickel) **$309.00**
Price: Featherweight (aluminum frame, nickel slide) **$405.00**
Price: Diplomat (black oxide with gold highlights, ivory grips) . . **$625.00**
Price: Montreaux (gold plated, ivory grips) **$692.00**
Price: Renaissance (hand engraved nickel, ivory grips) **$1,115.00**
Price: Imperiale (inlaid gold filigree over blue, scrimshawed
ivory grips) **$3,600.00**

HANDGUNS — AUTOLOADERS, SERVICE & SPORT

Republic Patriot

Rock River Standard Match

Ruger P89

REPUBLIC PATRIOT PISTOL

Caliber: 45 ACP, 6-shot magazine. **Barrel:** 3". **Weight:** 20 oz. **Length:** 6" overall. **Stocks:** Checkered. **Sights:** Blade front, drift-adjustable rear. **Features:** Black polymer frame, stainless steel slide; double-action-only trigger system; squared trigger guard. Introduced 1997. Made in U.S. by Republic Arms, Inc.
Price: About $325.00

ROCK RIVER ARMS STANDARD MATCH AUTO PISTOL

Caliber: 45 ACP. **Barrel:** NA. **Weight:** NA. **Length:** NA. **Grips:** Cocobolo, checkered. **Sights:** Heine fixed rear, blade front. **Features:** Chrome-moly steel frame and slide; beavertail grip safety with raised pad; checkered slide stop; ambidextrous safety; polished feed ramp and extractor; aluminum speed trigger with 3.5 lb. pull. Made in U.S. From Rock River Arms.
Price: $1,025.00

ROCKY MOUNTAIN ARMS PATRIOT PISTOL

Caliber: 223, 10-shot magazine. **Barrel:** 7", with muzzle brake. **Weight:** 5 lbs. **Length:** 20.5" overall. **Stocks:** Black composition. **Sights:** None furnished. **Features:** Milled upper receiver with enhanced Weaver base; milled lower receiver from billet plate; machined aluminum National Match handguard. Finished in DuPont Teflon-S matte black or NATO green. Comes with black nylon case, one magazine. Introduced 1993. From Rocky Mountain Arms, Inc.
Price: With A-2 handle top . . . . $2,500.00 to $2,800.00
Price: Flat top model . . . . $3,000.00 to $3,500.00

RUGER P89 AUTOLOADING PISTOL

Caliber: 9mm Para., 10-shot magazine. **Barrel:** 4.50". **Weight:** 32 oz. **Length:** 7.84" overall. **Stocks:** Grooved black Xenoy composition. **Sights:** Square post front, square notch rear adjustable for windage, both with white dot inserts. **Features:** Double action with ambidextrous slide-mounted safety-levers. Slide is 4140 chrome-moly steel or 400-series stainless steel, frame is a lightweight aluminum alloy. Ambidextrous magazine release. Blue or stainless steel. Introduced 1986; stainless introduced 1990.
Price: P89, blue, with extra magazine and magazine loading tool, plastic case with lock $430.00
Price: KP89, stainless, with extra magazine and magazine loading tool, plastic case with lock $475.00

Ruger P89D Decocker Autoloading Pistol

Similar to the standard P89 except has ambidextrous decocking levers in place of the regular slide-mounted safety. The decocking levers move the firing pin inside the slide where the hammer can not reach it, while simultaneously blocking the firing pin from forward movement—allows shooter to decock a cocked pistol without manipulating the trigger. Conventional thumb decocking procedures are therefore unnecessary. Blue or stainless steel. Introduced 1990.
Price: P89D, blue with extra magazine and loader, plastic case with lock $430.00
Price: KP89D, stainless, with extra magazine, plastic case with lock $475.00

Ruger P89 Double-Action-Only Autoloading Pistol

Same as the KP89 except operates only in the double-action mode. Has a spurless hammer, gripping grooves on each side of the rear of the slide; no external safety or decocking lever. An internal safety prevents forward movement of the firing pin unless the trigger is pulled. Available in 9mm Para., stainless steel only. Introduced 1991.
Price: With lockable case, extra magazine, magazine loading tool $475.00

RUGER P90 MANUAL SAFETY MODEL AUTOLOADING PISTOL

Caliber: 45 ACP, 7-shot magazine. **Barrel:** 4.50". **Weight:** 33.5 oz. **Length:** 7.87" overall. **Stocks:** Grooved black Xenoy composition. **Sights:** Square post front, square notch rear adjustable for windage, both with white dot inserts. **Features:** Double action with ambidextrous slide-mounted safety-levers which move the firing pin inside the slide where the hammer can not reach it, while simultaneously blocking the firing pin from forward movement. Stainless steel only. Introduced 1991.
Price: KP90 with extra magazine, loader, plastic case with lock $513.00
Price: P90 (blue) $476.00

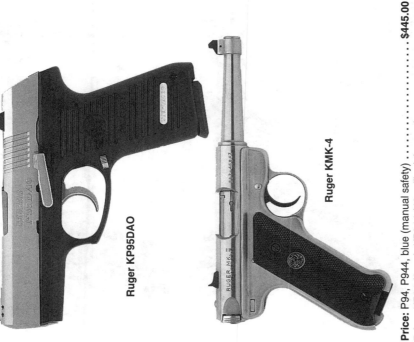

Ruger KP95DAO

Ruger KMK-4

Ruger P90

Ruger P93DAO

Ruger KP90 Decocker Autoloading Pistol

Similar to the P90 except has a manual decocking system. The ambidextrous decocking levers move the firing pin inside the slide where the hammer can not reach it, while simultaneously blocking the firing pin from forward movement—allows shooter to decock a cocked pistol without manipulating the trigger. Available only in stainless steel. Overall length 7.87", weighs 34 oz. Introduced 1991.

Price: KP90D with lockable case, extra magazine, and magazine loading tool **$513.00**

RUGER P93 COMPACT AUTOLOADING PISTOL

Caliber: 9mm Para., 10-shot magazine. **Barrel:** 3.9". **Weight:** 31 oz. **Length:** 7.3" overall. **Stocks:** Grooved black Xenoy composition. **Sights:** Square post front, square notch rear adjustable for windage. **Features:** Front of slide is crowned with a convex curve; slide has seven finger grooves; trigger guard bow is higher for a better grip; 400-series stainless slide, lightweight alloy frame; also in blue. Decocker-only or DAO-only. Introduced 1993. Made in U.S. by Sturm, Ruger & Co.

Price: KP93DAO, double-action-only **$520.00**
Price: KP93D ambidextrous decocker, stainless **$520.00**
Price: P93D, ambidextrous decocker, blue **$445.00**

Ruger KP94 Autoloading Pistol

Sized midway between the full-size P-Series and the compact P93. Has 4.25" barrel, 7.5" overall length and weighs about 33 oz. KP94 is manual safety model; KP94DAO is double-action-only (both 9mm Para., 10-shot magazine); KP94D is decocker-only in 40-caliber with 10-shot magazine. Slide gripping grooves roll over top of slide. KP94 has ambidextrous safety-levers; KP94DAO has no external safety, full-cock hammer position or decocking lever; KP94D has ambidextrous decocking levers. Matte finish stainless slide, barrel, alloy frame. Also available in blue. Introduced 1994. Made in U.S. by Sturm, Ruger & Co.

Price: P94, P944, blue (manual safety) **$445.00**
Price: KP94 (9mm), KP944 (40-caliber) (manual safety-stainless) **$520.00**
Price: KP94DAO (9mm), KP944DAO (40-caliber) **$520.00**
Price: KP94D (9mm), KP944D (40-caliber) - decock only **$520.00**

RUGER P95 AUTOLOADING PISTOL

Caliber: 9mm Para., 10-shot magazine. **Barrel:** 3.9". **Weight:** 27 oz. **Length:** 7.3" overall. **Stocks:** Grooved; integral with frame. **Sights:** Blade front, rear drift adjustable for windage; three-dot system. **Features:** Moulded polymer grip frame, stainless steel or chrome-moly slide. Suitable for +P+ ammunition. Decocker or DAO. Introduced 1996. Made in U.S. by Sturm, Ruger & Co. Comes with lockable plastic case, spare magazine, loading tool.

Price: P95 DAO double-action-only **$388.00**
Price: P95D decocker only **$388.00**
Price: KP95 stainless steel **$431.00**
Price: KP95DAO double-action only, stainless steel **$431.00**

RUGER P97 AUTOLOADING PISTOL

Caliber: 45ACP, 8-shot magazine. **Barrel:** 4-1/8". **Weight:** 30-1/2 oz. **Length:** 7-1/4" overall. **Grooved:** Integral with frame. **Sights:** Blade front, rear drift adjustable for windage; three dot system. **Features:** Moulded polymer grip frame, stainless steel slide. Decocker or DAO. Introduced 1997. Made in U.S. by Sturm, Ruger & Co. Comes with lockable plastic case, spare magazine, loading tool. .

Price: (KP97D decock-only) **$460.00**
Price: (KP97DAO double-action only) **$460.00**

RUGER MARK II STANDARD AUTOLOADING PISTOL

Caliber: 22 LR, 10-shot magazine. **Barrel:** 4-3/4" or 6". **Weight:** 25 oz. (4-3/4" bbl.). **Length:** 8-5/16" (4-3/4" bbl.). **Stocks:** Checkered plastic. **Sights:** Fixed, wide blade front, fixed rear. **Features:** Updated design of the original Standard Auto. Has new bolt hold-open latch. 10-shot magazine, magazine catch, safety, trigger and new receiver contours. Introduced 1982.

Price: Blued (MK 4, MK 6) **$278.00**
Price: In stainless steel (KMK 4, KMK 6) **$364.00**

HANDGUNS — AUTOLOADERS, SERVICE & SPORT

Ruger 22/45

Ruger KP512

Safari Arms Cohort

Ruger 22/45 Mark II Pistol

Similar to the other 22 Mark II autos except has grip frame of Zytel that matches the angle and magazine latch of the Model 1911 45 ACP pistol. Available in 4", 4-3/4" standard and 5-1/2" bull barrel. Comes with extra magazine, plastic case, lock. Introduced 1992.
Price: P4, 4", adjustable sights $265.00
Price: KP 4 (4-3/4" barrel), fixed sights $294.00
Price: KP512 (5-1/2" bull barrel), stainless steel, adj. sights $347.00
Price: P512 (5-1/2" bull barrel, all blue), adj. sights $265.00

SAFARI ARMS ENFORCER PISTOL

Caliber: 45 ACP, 6-shot magazine. **Barrel:** 3.8", stainless. **Weight:** 36 oz. **Length:** 7.3" overall. **Stocks:** Smooth walnut with etched black widow spider logo. **Sights:** Ramped blade front, LPA adjustable rear. **Features:** Extended safety, extended slide release; Commander-style hammer; beavertail grip safety; throated, polished, tuned. Parkerized matte black or satin stainless steel finishes. Made in U.S. by Safari Arms.
Price: $630.00

SAFARI ARMS GI SAFARI PISTOL

Caliber: 45 ACP, 7-shot magazine. **Barrel:** 5", 416 stainless. **Weight:** 39.9 oz. **Length:** 8.5" overall. **Stocks:** Checkered walnut. **Sights:** G.I.-style blade front, drift-adjustable rear. **Features:** Beavertail grip safety; extended thumb safety and slide release; Commander-style hammer. Parkerized finish. Reintroduced 1996.
Price: $439.00

SAFARI ARMS CARRIER PISTOL

Caliber: 45 ACP, 7-shot magazine. **Barrel:** 6", 416 stainless steel. **Weight:** 30 oz. **Length:** 9.5" overall. **Stocks:** Wood. **Sights:** Ramped blade front, LPA adjustable rear. **Features:** Beavertail grip safety; extended controls; full-length recoil spring guide; Commander-style hammer. Throated, polished and tuned. Satin stainless steel finish. Introduced 1999. Made in U.S. by Safari Arms, Inc.
Price: $714.00

SAFARI ARMS COHORT PISTOL

Caliber: 45 ACP, 7-shot magazine. **Barrel:** 3.8", 416 stainless. **Weight:** 37 oz. **Length:** 8.5" overall. **Stocks:** Smooth walnut with laser-etched black

widow logo. **Sights:** Ramped blade front, LPA adjustable rear. **Features:** Combines the Enforcer model, slide and MatchMaster frame. Beavertail grip safety; extended thumb safety and slide release; Commander-style hammer. Throated, polished and tuned. Satin stainless finish. Introduced 1996. Made in U.S. by Safari Arms, Inc.
Price: $654.00

SAFARI ARMS MATCHMASTER PISTOL

Caliber: 45 ACP, 7-shot. **Barrel:** 5" or 6", 416 stainless steel. **Weight:** 38 oz. (5" barrel). **Length:** 8.5" overall. **Stocks:** Smooth walnut. **Sights:** Ramped blade, LPA adjustable rear. **Features:** Beavertail grip safety; extended controls; Commander-style hammer; throated, polished, tuned. Parkerized matte-black or satin stainless steel. Made in U.S. by Olympic Arms, Inc.
Price: 5" barrel $594.00
Price: 6" barrel $654.00

Safari Arms Carry Comp Pistol

Similar to the Matchmaster except has Wil Schueman-designed hybrid compensator system. Made in U.S. by Olympic Arms, Inc.
Price: $1,067.00

SEECAMP LWS 32 STAINLESS DA AUTO

Caliber: 32 ACP Win. Silvertip, 6-shot magazine. **Barrel:** 2", integral with frame. **Weight:** 10.5 oz. **Length:** 4-1/8" overall. **Stocks:** Glass-filled nylon. **Sights:** Smooth, no-snag, contoured slide and barrel top. **Features:** Aircraft quality 17-4 PH stainless steel. Inertia-operated firing pin. Hammer fired double-action-only. Hammer automatically follows slide down to safety rest position after each shot—no manual safety needed. Magazine safety disconnector. Polished stainless. Introduced 1985. From L.W. Seecamp.
Price: $425.00

SIG SAUER P220 SERVICE AUTO PISTOL

Caliber: 45 ACP, (7- or 8-shot magazine). **Barrel:** 4-3/8". **Weight:** 27.8 oz. **Length:** 7.8" overall. **Stocks:** Checkered black plastic. **Sights:** Blade front, drift adjustable rear for windage. Optional Siglite nightsights. **Features:** Double action. Decocking lever permits lowering hammer onto locked firing pin. Squared combat-type trigger guard. Slide stays open after last shot. Imported from Germany by SIGARMS, Inc.
Price: Blue SA/DA or DAO $790.00
Price: Blue, Siglite night sights $880.00
Price: K-Kote or nickel slide $830.00
Price: K-Kote or nickel slide with Siglite night sights $930.00

HANDGUNS — AUTOLOADERS, SERVICE & SPORT

SIG Arms Pro 2009

SIG Sauer P229S

SIG Sauer P220

SIG Arms P245 Compact

SIG Sauer P220 Sport Auto Pistol

Similar to the P220 except has 4.9" barrel, ported compensator, all-stainless steel frame and slide, factory-tuned trigger, adjustable sights, extended competition controls. Overall length is 9.9", weighs 43.5 oz. Introduced 1999. From SIGARMS, Inc.

Price: $1,320.00

SIG Sauer P245 Compact Auto Pistol

Similar to the P220 except has 3.9" barrel, shorter grip, 6-shot magazine, 7.28" overall length, and weighs 27.5 oz. Introduced 1999. From SIG-ARMS, Inc.

Price: Blue $780.00
Price: Blue, with Siglite sights............................ $850.00
Price: Two-tone $830.00
Price: Two-tone with Siglite sights $930.00
Price: With K-Kote finish....................................... $830.00
Price: K-Kote with Siglite sights $930.00

SIG Sauer P229 DA Auto Pistol

Similar to the P228 except chambered for 9mm Para., 40 S&W, 357 SIG. Has 3.86" barrel, 7.08" overall length and 3.35" height. Weight is 30.5 oz. Introduced 1991. Frame made in Germany, stainless steel slide assembly made in U.S.; pistol assembled in U.S. From SIGARMS, Inc.

Price: $795.00
Price: With nickel slide $890.00
Price: Nickel slide Siglite night sights................. $935.00

SIG PRO AUTO PISTOL

Caliber: 9mm Para., 40 S&W, 10-shot magazine. **Barrel:** 3.86". **Weight:** 27.2 oz. **Length:** 7.36" overall. **Stocks:** Composite and rubberized one-piece. **Sights:** Blade front, rear adjustable for windage. Optional Siglite night sights. **Features:** Polymer frame, stainless steel slide; integral frame accessory rail; replaceable steel frame rails; left- or right-handed magazine release. Introduced 1999. From SIGARMS, Inc.

Price: SP2340 (40 S&W) $596.00
Price: SP2009 (9mm Para.) $596.00
Price: As above with Siglite night sights................. $655.00

SIG Sauer P226 Service Pistol

Similar to the P220 pistol except has 4.4" barrel, and weighs 28.3 oz. 357 SIG or 40 S&W. Imported from Germany by SIGARMS, Inc.

Price: Blue SA/DA or DAO.................................... $830.00
Price: With Siglite night sights $930.00
Price: Blue, SA/DA or DAO 357 SIG $830.00
Price: With Siglite night sights $930.00
Price: K-Kote finish, 40 S&W only or nickel slide $830.00
Price: K-Kote or nickel slide Siglite night sights $930.00
Price: Nickel slide 357 SIG.................................... $875.00
Price: Nickel slide, Siglite night sights $930.00

SIG Sauer P229 Sport Auto Pistol

Similar to the P229 except available in 357 SIG only; 4.8" heavy barrel; 8.6" overall length; weighs 40.6 oz.; vented compensator; adjustable target sights; rubber grips; extended slide latch and magazine release. Made of stainless steel. Introduced 1998. From SIGARMS, Inc.

Price: $1,320.00

HANDGUNS — AUTOLOADERS, SERVICE & SPORT

Smith & Wesson 457

SIG Sauer P232

Smith & Wesson 4013 TSW

SIG SAUER P232 PERSONAL SIZE PISTOL

Caliber: 380 ACP, 7-shot. **Barrel:** 3-3/4". **Weight:** 16 oz. **Length:** 6-1/2" overall. **Stocks:** Checkered black composite. **Sights:** Blade front, rear adjustable for windage, stationary barrel. **Features:** Double action/single action or DAO. Blowback operation, stationary barrel. Introduced 1997. Imported from Germany by SIGARMS, Inc.

Price: Blue SA/DA or DAO $505.00
Price: In stainless steel $545.00
Price: With stainless steel slide, blue frame $525.00
Price: Stainless steel, Siglite night sights, Hogue grips $585.00

SIG SAUER P239 PISTOL

Caliber: 9mm Para., 8-shot. 357 SIG 40 S&W, 7-shot magazine. **Barrel:** 3.6". **Weight:** 25.2 oz. **Length:** 6.6" overall. **Stocks:** Checkered black composite. **Sights:** Blade front, rear adjustable for windage. Optional Siglite night sights. **Features:** SA/DA or DAO; blackened stainless steel slide, aluminum alloy frame. Introduced 1996. Made in U.S. by SIGARMS, Inc.

Price: SA/DA or DAO $620.00
Price: SA/DA or DAO with Siglite night sights $720.00
Price: Two-tone finish $665.00
Price: Two-tone finish, Siglite sights $765.00

SMITH & WESSON MODEL 22A SPORT PISTOL

Caliber: 22 LR, 10-shot magazine. **Barrel:** 4", 5-1/2", 7". **Weight:** 29 oz. **Length:** 8" overall. **Stocks:** Two-piece polymer. **Sights:** Patridge front, fully adjustable rear. **Features:** Comes with a sight bridge with Weaver-style integral optics mount; alloy frame; .312" serrated trigger; stainless

steel slide and barrel with matte blue finish. Introduced 1997. Made in U.S. by Smith & Wesson.

Price: 4" $230.00
Price: 5-1/2" $255.00
Price: 7" $289.00

SMITH & WESSON MODEL 457 TDA AUTO PISTOL

Caliber: 45 ACP, 7-shot magazine. **Barrel:** 3-3/4". **Weight:** 29 oz. **Length:** 7-1/4" overall. **Stocks:** One-piece Xenoy, wrap-around with straight backstrap. **Sights:** Post front, fixed rear, three-dot system. **Features:** Aluminum alloy frame, matte blue carbon steel slide; bobbed hammer; smooth trigger. Introduced 1996. Made in U.S. by Smith & Wesson.

Price: $563.00

SMITH & WESSON MODEL 908 AUTO PISTOL

Caliber: 9mm Para., 8-shot magazine. **Barrel:** 3-1/2". **Weight:** 26 oz. **Length:** 6-13/16". **Stocks:** One-piece Xenoy, wrap-around with straight backstrap. **Sights:** Post front, fixed rear, three-dot system. **Features:** Aluminum alloy frame, matte blue carbon steel slide; bobbed hammer; smooth trigger. Introduced 1996. Made in U.S. by Smith & Wesson.

Price: $509.00

SMITH & WESSON 9MM RECON AUTO PISTOL MODEL

Caliber: 9mm Para. **Barrel:** 3-1/2". **Weight:** 27 oz. **Length:** 7" overall. **Stocks:** Hogue wrap-around, finger-groove rubber. **Sights:** Three-dot Novak Low Mount, drift adjustable. **Features:** Traditional double-action mechanism. Tuned action, hand-crowned muzzle, polished feed ramp, hand-lapped slide, spherical barrel bushing. Checkered frontstrap. Introduced 1999. Made by U.S. by Smith & Wesson.

Price: $1,150.00

SMITH & WESSON MODEL 2213, 2214 SPORTSMAN AUTOS

Caliber: 22 LR, 8-shot magazine. **Barrel:** 3". **Weight:** 18 oz. **Length:** 6-1/8" overall. **Stocks:** Checkered black polymer. **Sights:** Patridge front, fixed rear, three-dot system. **Features:** Internal hammer; serrated trigger; single action. Model 2213 is stainless with alloy frame, Model 2214 is blued carbon steel with alloy frame. Introduced 1990. Made in U.S. by Smith & Wesson.

Price: Model 2213 .... $340.00
Price: Model 2214 .... $292.00

SMITH & WESSON MODEL 4013, 4053 TSW AUTOS

Caliber: 40 S&W, 9-shot magazine. **Barrel:** 3-1/2". **Weight:** 26.4 oz. **Length:** 6-7/8" overall. **Stocks:** Xenoy one-piece wrap-around. **Sights:** Novak three-dot system. **Features:** Traditional double-action system; stainless slide, alloy frame; fixed barrel bushing; ambidextrous decocker; reversible magazine catch. Introduced 1997. Made in U.S. by Smith & Wesson.

Price: Model 4013 TSW $844.00
Price: Model 4053 TSW, double-action-only $844.00

Smith & Wesson 3913 LadySmith

Smith & Wesson 3913 TSW

Smith & Wesson Model 22S Sport Pistols

Similar to the Model 22A Sport except with stainless steel frame. Available only with 5-1/2" or 7" barrel. Introduced 1997. Made in U.S. by Smith & Wesson.

Price: 5-1/2" standard barrel. $312.00
Price: 5-1/2" bull barrel, wood target stocks with thumbrest. $379.00
Price: 7" standard barrel. $344.00
Price: 5-1/2" bull barrel, two-piece target stocks with thumbrest . . $353.00

SMITH & WESSON MODEL 410 DA AUTO PISTOL

Caliber: 40 S&W, 10-shot magazine. **Barrel:** 4". **Weight:** 28.5 oz. **Length:** 7.5 oz. **Stocks:** One-piece Xenoy, wrap-around with straight backstrap. **Sights:** Post front, fixed rear; three-dot system. **Features:** Aluminum alloy frame; blued carbon steel slide; traditional double action with left-side slide-mounted decocking lever. Introduced 1996. Made in U.S. by Smith & Wesson.

Price: $563.00

SMITH & WESSON MODEL 910 DA AUTO PISTOL

Caliber: 9mm Para., 10-shot magazine. **Barrel:** 4". **Weight:** 28 oz. **Length:** 7-3/8" overall. **Stocks:** One-piece Xenoy, wrap-around with straight backstrap. **Sights:** Post front with white dot, fixed two-dot rear. **Features:** Alloy frame, blue carbon steel slide. Slide-mounted decocking lever. Introduced 1995.

Price: Model 910. . . . . $509.00

SMITH & WESSON
MODEL 3913 TRADITIONAL DOUBLE ACTION

Caliber: 9mm Para., 8-shot magazine. **Barrel:** 3-1/2". **Weight:** 26 oz. **Length:** 6-13/16" overall. **Stocks:** One-piece Delrin wrap-around, textured surface. **Sights:** Post front with white dot, Novak LoMount Carry with two dots, adjustable for windage. **Features:** Aluminum alloy frame, stainless slide (M3913) or blue steel slide (M3914). Bobbed hammer with no half-cock notch; smooth .304" trigger with rounded edges. Straight backstrap. Extra magazine included. Introduced 1989.

Price: $662.00

Smith & Wesson Model 3913-LS LadySmith Auto

Similar to the standard Model 3913 except has frame that is upswept at the front, rounded trigger guard. Comes in frosted stainless steel with matching gray grips. Grips are ergonomically correct for a woman's hand. Novak LoMount Carry rear sight adjustable for windage, smooth edges for snag resistance. Extra magazine included. Introduced 1990.

Price: $744.00

Smith & Wesson Model 3953 DAO Pistol

Same as the Model 3913 except double-action-only. Model 3953 has stainless slide with alloy frame. Overall length 7"; weighs 25.5 oz. Extra magazine included. Introduced 1990.

Price: $724.00

Smith & Wesson Model 3913TSW/3953TSW Auto Pistols

Similar to the Model 3913 and 3953 except TSW guns have tighter tolerances, ambidextrous manual safety/decocking lever, flush-fit magazine, delayed-unlock firing system; magazine disconnector. Compact alloy frame, stainless steel slide. Straight backstrap. Introduced 1998. Made in U.S. by Smith & Wesson.

Price: Single action/double action $724.00
Price: Double action only $724.00

SMITH & WESSON MODEL 4006 TDA AUTO

Caliber: 40 S&W, 10-shot magazine. **Barrel:** 4". **Weight:** 38.5 oz. **Length:** 7-7/8" overall. **Stocks:** Xenoy wrap-around with checkered panels. **Sights:** Replaceable post front with white dot, Novak LoMount Carry fixed rear with two white dots, or micro. click adjustable rear with two white dots. **Features:** Stainless steel construction with non-reflective finish. Straight back-strap. Extra magazine included. Introduced 1990.

Price: With adjustable sights $899.00
Price: With fixed sight. $864.00
Price: With fixed night sights $991.00

Smith & Wesson Model 4043, 4046 DA Pistols

Similar to the Model 4006 except is double-action-only. Has a semi-bobbed hammer, smooth trigger, 4" barrel; Novak LoMount Carry rear sight, post front with white dot. Overall length is 7-1/2", weighs 28 oz. Model 4043 has alloy frame. Extra magazine included. Introduced 1991.

Price: Model 4043 (alloy frame) $844.00
Price: Model 4046 (stainless frame). $864.00
Price: Model 4046 with fixed night sights $991.00

SMITH & WESSON MODEL 4500 SERIES AUTOS

Caliber: 45 ACP, 8-shot magazine. **Barrel:** 5" (M4506). **Weight:** 41 oz. (4506). **Length:** 8-1/2" overall. **Stocks:** Xenoy one-piece wrap-around, arched or straight backstrap. **Sights:** Post front with white dot, adjustable or fixed Novak LoMount Carry on M4506. **Features:** M4506 has serrated hammer spur. All have two magazines. Contact Smith & Wesson for complete data. Introduced 1989.

Price: Model 4506, fixed sight $822.00
Price: Model 4506, adjustable sight $855.00
Price: Model 4566 (stainless, 4-1/4", traditional DA, ambidextrous safety, fixed sight). $897.00
Price: Model 4586 (stainless, 4-1/4", DA only). $897.00

SMITH & WESSON MODEL 4513TSW/4553TSW PISTOLS

Caliber: 45 ACP, 6-shot magazine. **Barrel:** 3-3/4". **Weight:** 28 oz. (M4513TSW). **Length:** 6-7/8 overall. **Stocks:** Checkered Xenoy; straight backstrap. **Sights:** White dot front, Novak Lo Mount Carry 2-Dot rear. **Features:** Model 4513TSW is traditional double action, Model 4553TSW is double action only. TSW series has tighter tolerances, ambidextrous manual safety/decocking lever, flush-fit magazine, delayed-unlock firing system; magazine disconnector. Compact alloy frame, stainless steel slide. Introduced 1998. Made in U.S. by Smith & Wesson.

Price: Model 4513TSW $880.00
Price: Model 4553TSW $837.00

HANDGUNS — AUTOLOADERS, SERVICE & SPORT

Smith & Wesson 4553 TSW

Smith & Wesson 4506

Smith & Wesson SW99

Smith & Wesson Sigma SW40V

SMITH & WESSON MODEL 5900 SERIES AUTO PISTOLS
Caliber: 9mm Para., 10-shot magazine. **Barrel:** 4". **Weight:** 28-1/2 to 37-1/2 oz. (fixed sight); 38 oz. (adjustable sight). **Length:** 7-1/2" overall. **Stocks:** Xenoy wrap-around with curved backstrap. **Sights:** Post front with white dot, fixed or fully adjustable with two white dots. **Features:** All stainless, stainless and alloy or carbon steel and alloy construction. Smooth .304" trigger, .260" serrated hammer. Introduced 1989.
Price: Model 5906 (stainless, traditional DA, adjustable sight, ambidextrous safety) $861.00
Price: As above, fixed sight $822.00
Price: With fixed night sights $948.00
Price: Model 5946 DAO (as above, stainless frame and slide) ... $822.00

SMITH & WESSON ENHANCED SIGMA SERIES PISTOLS
Caliber: 9mm Para., 40 S&W, 10-shot magazine. **Barrel:** 4". **Weight:** 26 oz. **Length:** 7.4" overall. **Stocks:** Integral. **Sights:** White dot front, fixed rear; three-dot system. Tritium night sights available. **Features:** Ergonomic polymer frame; low barrel centerline; internal striker firing system; corrosion-resistant slide; Teflon-filled, electroless-nickel coated magazine. Introduced 1994. Made in U.S. by Smith & Wesson.
Price: SW9E, 9mm, 4" barrel, black finish, fixed sights $657.00
Price: SW9V, 9mm, 4" barrel, satin stainless, fixed night sights . $447.00
Price: SW40E, 40 S&W, 4" barrel, black finish, fixed night sights . $657.00
Price: SW40V, 40 S&W, 4" barrel, black polymer, fixed sights .. $447.00

SMITH & WESSON SW99 AUTO PISTOL
Caliber: 9mm Para., 40 S&W, 10-shot magazine. **Barrel:** 4" (9mm); 4-1/8" (40 cal.). **Weight:** 25.4 oz. **Length:** 7-1/4" overall. **Grips:** Integral polymer. **Sights:** White-dot post front, adjustable two-dot rear. **Features:** Polymer frame made by Walther of Germany, black Melonite slide and barrel made by Smith & Wesson; traditional double-action with striker firing system; slide-mounted decocking lever; three interchangeable grip backstraps to accommodate different hand sizes. Introduced 2000. From Smith & Wesson.
Price: Adjustable sights $771.00
Price: Night sights $881.00

SMITH & WESSON SIGMA SW380 AUTO
Caliber: 380 ACP, 6-shot magazine. **Barrel:** 3". **Weight:** 14 oz. **Length:** 5.8" overall. **Stocks:** Integral. **Sights:** Fixed groove in the slide. **Features:** Polymer frame; double-action-only trigger mechanism; grooved/serrated front and rear straps; two passive safeties. Introduced 1995. Made in U.S. by Smith & Wesson.
Price: $328.00

Smith & Wesson Model 6906 Double-Action Auto
Similar to the Model 5906 except with 3-1/2" barrel, 10-shot magazine, fixed rear sight, .260" bobbed hammer. Extra magazine included. Introduced 1989.
Price: Model 6906, stainless $720.00
Price: Model 6906 with fixed night sights $836.00
Price: Model 6946 (stainless, DA only, fixed sights) $720.00

HANDGUNS — AUTOLOADERS, SERVICE & SPORT

Springfield 1911A1 Standard

Springfield N.R.A. PPC

Springfield Full-Size 1911A1

Springfield TRP

SMITH & WESSON MODEL CS9 CHIEFS SPECIAL AUTO

Caliber: 9mm Para., 7-shot magazine. **Barrel:** 3". **Weight:** 20.8 oz. **Length:** 6-1/4" overall. **Stocks:** Hogue wrap-around rubber. **Sights:** White dot front, fixed two-dot rear. **Features:** Traditional double-action trigger mechanism. Alloy frame, stainless or blued slide. Introduced 1999. Made in U.S. by Smith & Wesson.
Price: Blue or stainless. **$648.00**

Smith & Wesson Model CS40 Chiefs Special Auto

Similar to the CS9 except chambered for 40 S&W (7-shot magazine), has 3-1/4" barrel, weighs 24.2 oz., and measures 6-1/2" overall. Introduced 1999. Made in U.S. by Smith & Wesson.
Price: Blue or stainless. **$683.00**

Smith & Wesson Model CS45 Chiefs Special Auto

Similar to the CS40 except chambered for 45 ACP, 6-shot magazine, weighs 23.9 oz. Introduced 1999. Made in U.S. by Smith & Wesson.
Price: Blue or stainless. **$683.00**

SPRINGFIELD, INC. FULL-SIZE 1911A1 AUTO PISTOL

Caliber: 9mm Para., 9-shot; 38 Super, 9-shot; 45 ACP, 8-shot. **Barrel:** 5". **Weight:** 35.6 oz. **Length:** 8-5/8" overall. **Stocks:** Checkered plastic or walnut. **Sights:** Fixed three-dot system. **Features:** Beveled magazine well; lowered and flared ejection port. All forged parts, including frame, barrel, slide. All new production. Introduced 1990. From Springfield, Inc.
Price: Mil-Spec 45 ACP, Parkerized. **$610.00**
Price: Standard, 45 ACP, blued **$669.00**
Price: Standard, 45 ACP, stainless **$719.00**
Price: Lightweight (28.6 oz., matte finish)............ **$695.00**
Price: Standard, 9mm, 38 Super, blued **$549.00**
Price: Standard, 9mm, stainless steel **$599.00**

Springfield, Inc. N.R.A. PPC Pistol

Specifically designed to comply with NRA rules for PPC competition. Has custom slide-to-frame fit; polished feed ramp; throated barrel; total internal honing; tuned extractor; recoil buffer system; fully checkered walnut grips; two fitted magazines; factory test target; custom carrying case. Introduced 1995. From Springfield, Inc.
Price: **$1,469.00**

Springfield, Inc. TRP Pistols

Similar to the 1911A1 except 45 ACP only; has checkered front strap and mainspring housing; Novak combat rear sight and matching dovetailed front sight; tuned, polished extractor; oversize barrel link; lightweight speed trigger and combat action job; match barrel and bushing; extended ambidextrous thumb safety and fitted beavertail grip safety; Carry bevel on entire pistol; checkered cocobolo wood grips; comes with two Wilson 8-shot magazines. Frame is engraved "Tactical," both sides of frame with "TRP." Introduced 1998. From Springfield, Inc.
Price: Standard with Armory Kote finish.............. **$1,299.00**
Price: Standard, stainless steel **$1,289.00**
Price: Champion, Armory Kote....................... **$1,349.00**

Springfield, Inc. 1911A1 High Capacity Pistol

Similar to the Standard 1911A1 except available in 45 ACP with 10-shot magazine. Has Commander-style hammer, walnut grips, beveled magazine well, plastic carrying case. Introduced 1993. From Springfield, Inc.
Price: Mil-Spec 45 ACP **$733.00**
Price: 45 ACP Factory Comp **$1,198.00**
Price: 45 ACP Compact, Ultra **$759.00**
Price: As above, stainless steel **$859.00**

HANDGUNS — AUTOLOADERS, SERVICE & SPORT

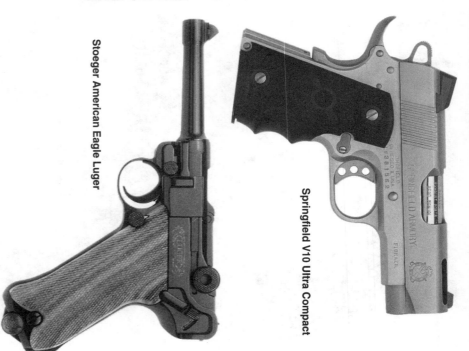

Stoeger American Eagle Luger

Springfield V10 Ultra Compact

Taurus PT 22

Springfield, Inc. 1911A1 Custom Carry Gun

Similar to the standard 1911A1 except has Novak low-mount sights, Videki speed trigger, match barrel and bushing; extended thumb safety, beavertail grip safety; beveled, polished magazine well, polished feed ramp and throated barrel; match Commander hammer and sear, tuned extractor; lowered and flared ejection port; recoil buffer system, full-length spring guide rod; walnut grips. Comes with two magazines with slam pads, plastic carrying case. Available in all popular calibers. Introduced 1992. From Springfield, Inc.

Price: **$1,299.00**

Springfield, Inc. 1911A1 Factory Comp

Similar to the standard 1911A1 except comes with bushing-type dual-port compensator, adjustable rear sight, extended thumb safety, Videki speed trigger, and beveled magazine well. Checkered walnut grips standard. Available in 45 ACP, blue only. Introduced 1992.

Price: 45 ACP **$1,158.00**

Springfield, Inc. 1911A1 Champion Pistol

Similar to the standard 1911A1 except slide is 4.025". Novak sight system. Comes with Delta hammer and cocogrips. Available in 45 ACP only. Parkerized or stainless. Introduced 1989.

Price: Parkerized **$669.00**
Price: Stainless. **$739.00**

Springfield, Inc. V10 Ultra Compact Pistol

Similar to the 1911A1 Compact except has shorter slide, 3.5" barrel, recoil reducing compensator built into the barrel and slide. Beavertail grip safety, beveled magazine well, "hi-viz" combat sights, Videki speed trigger, flared ejection port, stainless steel frame, blued slide, match grade barrel, walnut grips. Introduced 1996. From Springfield, Inc.

Price: V10 45 ACP **$769.00**
Price: Ultra Compact (no compensator), 45 ACP. **$1069.00**

STEYR M & S SERIES AUTO PISTOLS

Caliber: 9mm Para., 40 S&W, 357 SIG; 10-shot magazine. **Barrel:** 4" (3.58" for Model S). **Weight:** 28 oz. (22.5 oz. for Model S). **Length:** 7.05" overall (6.53" for Model S). **Grips:** Ultra-rigid polymer. **Sights:** Drift-adjustable, white-outline rear; white-triangle blade front. **Features:** Polymer frame; trigger-drop firing pin, manual and key-lock safeties; loaded chamber indicator; 5.5-lb. trigger pull; 111-degree grip angle enhances natural pointing. Introduced 2000. Imported from Austria by GSI Inc.

Price: Model M (full-sized frame with 4" barrel) **$609.95**
Price: Model S (compact frame with 3.58" barrel) **$609.95**
Price: Extra 10-shot magazines (Model M or S) **$39.00**

STOEGER AMERICAN EAGLE LUGER

Caliber: 9mm Para. **Barrel:** 4", 6". **Weight:** 32 oz. **Length:** 9.6" overall. **Stocks:** Checkered walnut. **Sights:** Blade front, fixed rear. **Features:** Recreation of the American Eagle Luger pistol in stainless steel. Chamber loaded indicator. Introduced 1994. From Stoeger Industries.

Price: 4", or 6" Navy Model **$720.00**
Price: With matte black finish. **$798.00**

TAURUS MODEL PT 22/PT 25 AUTO PISTOLS

Caliber: 22 LR, 8-shot (PT 22); 25 ACP, 9-shot (PT 25). **Barrel:** 2.75". **Weight:** 12.3 oz. **Length:** 5.25" overall. **Stocks:** Smooth rosewood. **Sights:** Blade front, fixed rear. **Features:** Double action. Tip-up barrel for loading, cleaning. Blue or stainless. Introduced 1992. Made in U.S. by Taurus International.

Price: 22 LR or 25 ACP, blue, nickel or with duo-tone finish with rosewood grips **$203.00**
Price: 22 LR or 25 ACP, blue with gold trim, rosewood grips. ... **$219.00**
Price: 22 LR or 25 ACP, blue, nickel or duo-tone finish with checkered wood grips **$180.00**
Price: 22 LR or 25 ACP, blue with gold trim, mother of pearl grips **$219.00**

TAURUS MODEL PT92B AUTO PISTOL

Caliber: 9mm Para., 15-shot magazine. **Barrel:** 5". **Weight:** 34 oz. **Length:** 8.5" overall. **Stocks:** Black rubber. **Sights:** Fixed notch rear. Three-dot sight system. **Features:** Double action, exposed hammer, chamber loaded indicator, ambidextrous safety, inertia firing pin. Imported by Taurus International.

Price: Blue **$508.00**
Price: Stainless steel **$523.00**
Price: Blue with gold trim, rosewood grips **$550.00**
Price: Stainless steel with gold trim, rosewood grips **$570.00**

HANDGUNS — AUTOLOADERS, SERVICE & SPORT

Taurus PT-945

Taurus PT-957

Taurus PT92B

Taurus PT-911

Taurus Model PT99 Auto Pistol

Similar to the PT92 except has fully adjustable rear sight, smooth Brazilian walnut stocks and is available in stainless steel or polished blue. Introduced 1983.

Price: Blue **$531.00**
Price: Stainless steel **$547.00**

TAURUS MODEL PT-111 MILLENNIUM AUTO PISTOL

Caliber: 9mm Para., 10-shot magazine. **Barrel:** 3.25". **Weight:** 18.7 oz. **Length:** 6.0" overall. **Stocks:** Polymer. **Sights:** Fixed. Low profile, three-dot combat. **Features:** Double action only. Firing pin lock; polymer frame; striker fired; push-button magazine release. Introduced 1998. Imported by Taurus International.

Price: Blue **$367.00**
Price: Stainless **$383.00**

Taurus Model PT-111 Millennium Titanium Pistol

Similar to the PT-111 except with titanium slide, night sights.

Price: **$547.00**

TAURUS MODEL PT-911 AUTO PISTOL

Caliber: 9mm Para., 10-shot magazine. **Barrel:** 4". **Weight:** 28.2 oz. **Length:** 7" overall. **Stocks:** Black rubber. **Sights:** Fixed. Low profile, three-dot combat. **Features:** Double action, exposed hammer; ambidextrous hammer drop; chamber loaded indicator. Introduced 1997. Imported by Taurus International.

Price: Blue **$453.00**
Price: Stainless **$469.00**
Price: Blue with gold accents **$504.00**
Price: Stainless with gold accents **$508.00**

Taurus Model PT-138 Auto Pistol

Similar to the PT-911 except chambered for 380 ACP, with 10-shot magazine. Double-action-only mechanism. Has black polymer frame with blue or stainless slide. Introduced 1999. Imported by Taurus International.

Price: Blue **$367.00**
Price: Stainless **$383.00**

TAURUS MODEL PT-945 AUTO PISTOL

Caliber: 45 ACP, 8-shot magazine. **Barrel:** 4.25". **Weight:** 29.5 oz. **Length:** 7.48" overall. **Stocks:** Black rubber. **Sights:** Drift-adjustable front and rear, three-dot system. **Features:** Double-action mechanism. Has manual ambidextrous hammer drop safety, intercept notch, firing pin block, chamber loaded indicator, last-shot hold-open. Introduced 1995. Imported by Taurus International.

Price: Blue **$484.00**
Price: Stainless **$500.00**
Price: Blue, ported **$523.00**
Price: Stainless, ported **$539.00**

TAURUS MODEL PT-957 AUTO PISTOL

Caliber: 357 SIG, 10-shot magazine. **Barrel:** 3-5/8". **Weight:** 28 oz. **Length:** 7" overall. **Stocks:** Checkered rubber. **Sights:** Fixed, low profile, three-dot combat. **Features:** Double action mechanism; exposed hammer; ported barrel/slide; three-position safety with decocking lever and ambidextrous safety. Introduced 1999. Imported by Taurus International.

Price: Blue **$508.00**
Price: Stainless **$523.00**
Price: Blue with gold accents, rosewood grips **$553.00**
Price: Stainless with gold accents, rosewood grips ... **$568.00**

TAURUS MODEL PT-938 AUTO PISTOL

Caliber: 380 ACP, 10-shot magazine. **Barrel:** 3.72". **Weight:** 27 oz. **Length:** 6.5" overall. **Stocks:** Black rubber. **Sights:** Fixed. Low profile, three-dot combat. **Features:** Double-action only. Chamber loaded indicator; firing pin block; ambidextrous hammer drop. Introduced 1997. Imported by Taurus International.

Price: Blue $453.00
Price: Stainless. $469.00

TAURUS MODEL PT-940 AUTO PISTOL

Caliber: 40 S&W, 10-shot magazine. **Barrel:** 3.35". **Weight:** 28.2 oz. **Length:** 7.05" overall. **Stocks:** Black rubber. **Sights:** Drift-adjustable front and rear; three-dot combat. **Features:** Double action, exposed hammer; manual ambidextrous hammer-drop; inertia firing pin; chamber loaded indicator. Introduced 1996. Imported by Taurus International.

Price: Blue $469.00
Price: Stainless steel $484.00
Price: Blue with gold accents, rosewood grips $540.00
Price: Stainless with gold accents, rosewood grips ... $555.00

VEKTOR SP1 SPORT PISTOL

Caliber: 9mm Para., 10-shot magazine. **Barrel:** 5 ". **Weight:** 38 oz. **Length:** 9-3/8" overall. **Stocks:** Checkered black composition. **Sights:** Combat-type blade front, adjustable rear. **Features:** Single action only with adjustable trigger stop; three-chamber compensator; extended magazine release. Introduced 1999. Imported from South Africa by Vektor USA.

Price: $829.95

Vektor SP1 Tuned Sport Pistol

Similar to the Vektor Sport except has fully adjustable straight trigger, LPA three-dot sight system, and hard nickel finish. Introduced 1999. Imported from South Africa by Vektor USA.

Price: $1,199.95

Taurus PT-940

Taurus PT-938

VEKTOR SP1 Target Pistol

Similar to the Vektor Sport except has 5-7/8" barrel without compensator; weighs 40-1/2 oz.; has fully adjustable straight match trigger; black slide, bright frame. Introduced 1999. Imported from South Africa by Vektor USA.

Price: $1,299.95

Vektor SP1, SP2 Ultra Sport Pistols

Similar to the Vektor Target except has three-chamber compensator with three jet ports; strengthened frame with integral beavertail; lightweight polymer scope mount (Weaver rail). Overall length is 11", weighs 41-1/2 oz. Model SP2 is in 40 S&W. Introduced 1999. Imported from South Africa by Vektor USA.

Price: SP1 (9mm) $2,149.95
Price: SP2 (40 S&W) $2,149.95

VEKTOR SP1 AUTO PISTOL

Caliber: 9mm Para., 40 S&W (SP2), 10-shot magazine. **Barrel:** 4-5/8". **Weight:** 35 oz. **Length:** 8-1/4" overall. **Stocks:** Checkered black composition. **Sights:** Combat-type fixed. **Features:** Alloy frame, steel slide; traditional double-action mechanism; matte black finish. Introduced 1999. Imported from South Africa by Vektor USA.

Price: SP1 (9mm) $599.95
Price: SP1 with nickel finish $629.95
Price: SP2 (40 S&W) $649.95

Vektor SP1, SP2 Compact General's Model Pistol

Similar to the 9mm Para. Vektor SP1 except has 4" barrel, weighs 31-1/2 oz., and is 7-1/2" overall. Recoil operated. Traditional double-action mechanism, SP2 model is chambered for 40 S&W. Introduced 1999. Imported from South Africa by Vektor USA.

Price: SP1 (9mm Para.) $649.95
Price: SP2 (40 S&W) $649.95

Vektor SP1

Vektor Ultra with Tasco Scope

HANDGUNS — AUTOLOADERS, SERVICE & SPORT

Walther PPK

Walther P99

Walther TPH

Walther PP

Walther PPK/S

VEKTOR CP-1 COMPACT PISTOL

Caliber: 9mm Para., 10-shot magazine. **Barrel:** 4". **Weight:** 25.4 oz. **Length:** 7" overall. **Stocks:** Textured polymer. **Sights:** Blade front adjustable for windage, fixed rear; adjustable sight optional. **Features:** Ergonomic grip frame shape; stainless steel barrel; delayed gas-buffered blowback action. Introduced 1999. Imported from South Africa by Vektor USA.

Price: With black slide $479.95
Price: With nickel slide $499.95
Price: With black slide, adjustable sight $509.95
Price: With nickel slide, adjustable sight $529.95

WALTHER PP AUTO PISTOL

Caliber: 380 ACP, 7-shot magazine. **Barrel:** 3.86". **Weight:** 23-1/2 oz. **Length:** 6.7" overall. **Stocks:** Checkered plastic. **Sights:** Fixed, white markings. **Features:** Double action; manual safety blocks firing pin and drops hammer; chamber loaded indicator on 32 and 380; extra finger rest magazine provided. Imported from Germany by Carl Walther USA.

Price: 380 .... $999.00

Walther PPK/S American Auto Pistol

Similar to Walther PP except made entirely in the United States. Has 3.27" barrel with 6.1" length overall. Introduced 1980.

Price: 380 ACP only, blue $540.00
Price: As above, 32 ACP or 380 ACP, stainless $540.00

Walther PPK American Auto Pistol

Similar to Walther PPK/S except weighs 21 oz., has 6-shot capacity. Made in the U.S. Introduced 1986.

Price: Stainless, 32 ACP or 380 ACP $540.00
Price: Blue, 380 ACP only $540.00

WALTHER MODEL TPH AUTO PISTOL

Caliber: 22 LR, 25 ACP, 6-shot magazine. **Barrel:** 2-1/4". **Weight:** 14 oz. **Length:** 5-3/8" overall. **Stocks:** Checkered black composition. **Sights:** Blade front, rear drift-adjustable for windage. **Features:** Made of stainless steel. Scaled-down version of the Walther PP/PPK series. Made in U.S. Introduced 1987. From Carl Walther USA.

Price: Blue or stainless steel, 22 or 25 .... $440.00

WALTHER P88 COMPACT PISTOL

Caliber: 9mm Para., 10-shot magazine. **Barrel:** 3.93". **Weight:** 28 oz. **Length:** NA. **Stocks:** Checkered black polymer. **Sights:** Blade front, drift adjustable rear. **Features:** Double action with ambidextrous decocking lever and magazine release; alloy frame; loaded chamber indicator; matte blue finish. Imported from Germany by Carl Walther USA.

Price: $900.00

WALTHER P99 AUTO PISTOL

Caliber: 9mm Para., 9x21, 40 S&W, 10-shot magazine. **Barrel:** 4". **Weight:** 25 oz. **Length:** 7" overall. **Stocks:** Textured polymer. **Sights:** Blade front (comes with three interchangeable blades for elevation adjustment), micrometer rear adjustable for windage. **Features:** Double-action mechanism with trigger safety, decock safety, internal striker safety; chamber loaded indicator; ambidextrous magazine release levers; polymer frame with interchangeable backstrap inserts. Comes with two magazines. Introduced 1997. Imported from Germany by Carl Walther USA.

Price: $799.00

HANDGUNS — AUTOLOADERS, SERVICE & SPORT

Dan Wesson Pointman Seven

Dan Wesson Pointman Major

Wilkinson Sherry

Dan Wesson Pointman Guardian

Walther P990 QA Auto Pistol
Similar to the P990 pistol except has "Quick Action" trigger that provides the same trigger pull effort (about 6.5 lbs.) for all shots. Striker is in a pre-cocked position, with the gun fully cocking, then firing when the trigger is pulled. Available in 9mm Para. and 40 S&W. Introduced 2000. From Walther USA.
Price: $749.00

Walther P990 Auto Pistol
Similar to the P990 except is double action only. Available in blue or silver tenifer finish. Introduced 1999. Imported from Germany by Carl Walther USA.
Price: $698.52

WALTHER P-5 AUTO PISTOL
Caliber: 9mm Para, 8-shot magazine. Barrel: 3.62". Weight: 28 oz. Length: 7.10" overall. Stocks: Checkered plastic. Sights: Blade front, adjustable rear. Features: Uses the basic Walther P-38 double-action mechanism. Blue finish. Imported from Germany by Carl Walther USA.
Price: $900.00

DAN WESSON POINTMAN MAJOR AUTO PISTOL
Caliber: 45 ACP. Barrel: 5". Weight: NA. Length: NA. Grips: Rosewood checkered. Sights: Features: Stainless steel frame and serrated slide; Chip McCormick match-grade trigger group, sear and disconnect; match-grade barrel; high-ride beavertail safety; checkered slide release; high rib; interchangeable sight system; laser engraved. Introduced 2000. Made in U.S. by Dan Wesson Firearms.
Price: Model PM1 .... $779.00

Dan Wesson Pointman Minor Auto Pistol
Similar to Pointman Major except has blued frame and slide with fixed rear sight. Introduced 2000. Made in U.S. by Dan Wesson Firearms.
Price: Model PM2 .... $599.00

Dan Wesson Pointman Seven Auto Pistols
Similar to Pointman Major except has dovetail adjustable target rear sight and dovetail target front sight. Available in blued or stainless finish. Introduced 2000. Made in U.S. by Dan Wesson Firearms.
Price: PM7 (blued frame and slide) $999.00
Price: PM7S (stainless finish) $1,099.00

Dan Wesson Pointman Guardian Auto Pistols
Similar to Pointman Major except has a more compact frame with 4.25" barrel. Available in blued or stainless finish with fixed or adjustable sights. Introduced 2000. Made in U.S. by Dan Wesson Firearms.
Price: PMG-FS (blued frame and slide, fixed sights) $769.00
Price: PMG-AS (blued frame and slide, adjustable sights) $779.00
Price: PMGD-FS Guardian Duce (stainless frame and blued slide, fixed sights) $829.00
Price: PMGD-AS Guardian Duce (stainless frame and blued slide, adj. sights) $839.00

WILKINSON SHERRY AUTO PISTOL
Caliber: 22 LR, 8-shot magazine. Barrel: 2-1/8". Weight: 9-1/4 oz. Length: 4-3/8" overall. Stocks: Checkered black plastic. Sights: Fixed, groove. Features: Cross-bolt safety locks the sear into the hammer. Available in all blue finish or blue slide and trigger with gold frame. Introduced 1985.
Price: $195.00

WILKINSON LINDA AUTO PISTOL
Caliber: 9mm Para. Barrel: 8-5/16". Weight: 4 lbs., 13 oz. Length: 12-1/4" overall. Stocks: Checkered black plastic pistol grip, walnut forend. Sights: Protected blade front, aperture rear. Features: Fires from closed bolt. Semi-auto only. Straight blowback action. Cross-bolt safety. Removable barrel. From Wilkinson Arms.
Price: $533.33

HANDGUNS — COMPETITION HANDGUNS

Includes models suitable for several forms of competition and other sporting purposes.

Beretta Model 89

Beretta Model 96 Combat

Baer 1911 Ultimate Master

Baer 1911 Bullseye Wadcutter

BAER 1911 ULTIMATE MASTER COMBAT PISTOL

Caliber: 9x23, 38 Super, 400 Cor-Bon 45 ACP (others available), 10-shot magazine. **Barrel:** 5", 6", Baer NM. **Weight:** 37 oz. **Length:** 8.5" overall. **Stocks:** Checkered rosewood. **Sights:** Baer dovetail front, low-mount Bo-Mar rear with hidden leaf. **Features:** Full-house competition gun. Baer forged NM blued steel frame and double serrated slide; Baer triple port, tapered cone compensator; fitted slide to frame; lowered, flared ejection port; Baer reverse recoil plug; full-length guide rod; recoil buff; beveled magazine well; Baer Commander hammer, sear; Baer extended ambidextrous safety, extended ejector, checkered slide stop, beavertail grip safety with pad, extended magazine release button; Baer speed trigger. Made in U.S. by Les Baer Custom, Inc.

Price: Compensated, open sights. **$2,560.00**
Price: 6" Model 400 Cor-Bon **$2,590.00**
Price: Compensated, with Baer optics mount. **$3,195.00**

Baer 1911 Ultimate Master Steel Special Pistol

Similar to the Ultimate Master except chambered for 38 Super with supported chamber (other calibers available), lighter slide, bushing-type compensator; two-piece guide rod. Designed for maximum 150 power factor. Comes without sights—scope and mount only. Hard chrome finish. Made in U.S. by Les Baer Custom, Inc.

Price: **$2,980.00**

BAER 1911 NATIONAL MATCH HARDBALL PISTOL

Caliber: 45 ACP, 7-shot magazine. **Barrel:** 5". **Weight:** 37 oz. **Length:** 8.5" overall. **Stocks:** Checkered walnut. **Sights:** Baer dovetail front with undercut post, low-mount Bo-Mar rear with hidden leaf. **Features:** Baer NM forged steel frame, double serrated slide and barrel with stainless bushing; slide fitted to frame; Baer match trigger with 4-lb. pull; polished feed ramp, throated barrel; checkered front strap, arched mainspring housing; Baer beveled magazine well; lowered, flared ejection port; tuned extractor; Baer extended ejector, checkered slide stop; recoil buff. Made in U.S. by Les Baer Custom, Inc.

Price: **$1,335.00**

Baer 1911 Bullseye Wadcutter Pistol

Similar to the National Match Hardball except designed for wadcutter loads only. Has polished feed ramp and barrel throat; Bo-Mar rib on slide;

full-length recoil rod; Baer speed trigger with 3-1/2-lb. pull; Baer deluxe hammer and sear; Baer beavertail grip safety with pad; flat mainspring housing checkered 20 lpi. Blue finish; checkered walnut grips. Made in U.S. by Les Baer Custom, Inc.

Price: From. **$1,495.00**
Price: With 6" barrel, from **$1,690.00**

BENELLI MP90S WORLD CUP PISTOL

Caliber: 22 Long Rifle, 6- or 9-shot magazine. **Barrel:** 4.4" **Weight:** 2.5 lbs. **Length:** 11.75". **Grip:** Walnut. **Sights:** Blade front, fully adjustable rear. **Features:** Single-action target pistol with fully adjustable trigger and adjustable heel rest; integral scope rail mount; attachment system for optional external weights.

Price: **$1,190.00**

Benelli MP95E Atlanta Pistol

Similar to MP90S World Cup Pistol, but available in blue finish with walnut grip or chrome finish with laminate grip. Overall length 11.25". Trigger overtravel adjustment only.

Price: (blue finish, walnut grip). **$740.00**
Price: (chrome finish, laminate grip) **$810.00**

BERETTA MODEL 89 GOLD STANDARD PISTOL

Caliber: 22 LR, 8-shot magazine. **Barrel:** 6". **Weight:** 41 oz. **Length:** 9.5" overall. **Stocks:** Target-type walnut with thumbrest. **Sights:** Interchangeable blade front, fully adjustable rear. **Features:** Single action target pistol. Matte black, Bruniton finish. Imported from Italy by Beretta U.S.A.

Price: **$802.00**

BERETTA MODEL 96 COMBAT PISTOL

Caliber: 40 S&W, 10-shot magazine. **Barrel:** 4.9" (5.9" with weight). **Weight:** 34.4 oz. **Length:** 8.5" overall. **Stocks:** Checkered black plastic. **Sights:** Blade front, fully adjustable target rear. **Features:** Uses heavier Brigadier slide with front and rear serrations; extended frame-mounted safety; extended, reversible magazine release; single-action-only with competition-tuned trigger with extra-short let-off and over-travel

Browning Buck Mark Target 5.5

BF Ultimate

Browning Buck Mark Bullseye

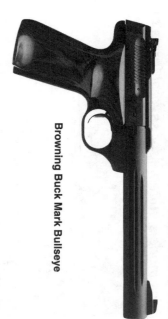

Colt Gold Cup Trophy

adjustment. Comes with tool kit. Introduced 1997. Imported from Italy by Beretta U.S.A.

Price: **$1,593.00**
Price: 4.9" barrel. **$1,341.00**
Price: 5.9" barrel. **$1,634.00**
Price: Combo **$1,599.00**

Beretta Model 96 Stock Pistol

Similar to the Model 96 Combat except is single/double action, with half-cock notch. Has front and rear slide serrations, rubber magazine bumper, replaceable accurizing barrel bushing, ultra-thin fine-checkered grips (aluminum optional), checkered front and back straps, radiused back strap, fitted case. Weighs 35 oz., 8.5" overall. Introduced 1997. Imported from Italy by Beretta U.S.A.

Price: ......

BF ULTIMATE SINGLE SHOT PISTOL

Caliber: 7mm U.S., 22 LR Match and 100 other chamberings. **Barrel:** 10.75" Heavy Match Grade with 11"target crown. **Length:** 16" overall. **Stocks:** Thumbrest target style. **Sights:** BoMar/Bond ScopeRib I Combo with hooded post front adjustable for height and width, rear notch available in .032", .062", .080" and .100" widths; 1/2-MOA clicks. **Features:** Designed to meet maximum rules for IHMSA Production Gun. Falling block action gives rigid barrel-receiver mating. Hand fitted and headspaced. Etched receiver; gold-colored trigger. Introduced 1988. Made in U.S. by E.A. Brown Mfg.

Price: **$1,700.00**

BROWNING BUCK MARK SILHOUETTE

Caliber: 22 LR, 10-shot magazine. **Barrel:** 9-7/8". **Weight:** 53 oz. **Length:** 14" overall. **Stocks:** Smooth walnut stocks and forend, or finger-groove walnut. **Sights:** Post-type hooded front adjustable for blade width and height; Pro Target rear fully adjustable for windage and elevation. **Features:** Heavy barrel with .900" diameter; 12-1/2" sight radius. Special sighting plane forms scope base. Introduced 1987. Made in U.S. From Browning.

Price: **$895.00**

Browning Buck Mark Target 5.5

Same as the Buck Mark Silhouette except has a 5-1/2" barrel with .900" diameter. Has hooded sights mounted on a scope base that accepts an optical or reflex sight. Rear sight is a Browning fully adjustable Pro Target, front sight is an adjustable post that customizes to different widths, and

Price: **$448.00**

can be adjusted for height. Contoured walnut grips with thumbrest, or finger-groove walnut. Matte blue finish. Overall length is 9-5/8", weighs 35-1/2 oz. Has 10-shot magazine. Introduced 1990. From Browning.

Price: Target 5.5 Gold (as above with gold anodized frame and top rib) **$477.00**
Price: Target 5.5 Nickel (as above with nickel frame and top rib) **$477.00**

Browning Buck Mark Field 5.5

Same as the Target 5.5 except has hoodless ramp-style front sight and low profile rear sight. Matte blue finish, contoured or finger-groove walnut stocks. Introduced 1991.

Price: **$425.00**

Browning Buck Mark Bullseye

Similar to the Buck Mark Silhouette except has 7-1/4" heavy barrel with three flutes per side; trigger is adjustable from 2-1/2 to 5 lbs.; specially designed rosewood target or three-finger-groove stocks with competition-style heel rest, or with contoured rubber grip. Overall length is 11-5/16", weighs 36 oz. Introduced 1996. Made in U.S. From Browning.

Price: With ambidextrous moulded composite stocks **$389.00**
Price: With rosewood stocks, or wrap-around finger groove **$500.00**

COLT GOLD CUP TROPHY MK IV/SERIES 80

Caliber: 45 ACP, 8-shot magazine. **Barrel:** 5", with new design bushing. **Weight:** 39 oz. **Length:** 8-1/2". **Stocks:** Checkered rubber composite with silver-plated medallion. **Sights:** Patridge-style front, Colt-Elliason rear adjustable for windage and elevation, sight radius 6-3/4". **Features:** Arched or flat housing; wide, grooved trigger with adjustable stop; ribbed-top slide, hand fitted, with improved ejection port.

Price: Blue **$1,224.00**
Price: Stainless. **$1,300.00**

COLT NATIONAL MATCH PISTOL

Caliber: 45 ACP, 8-shot magazine. **Barrel:** 5". **Weight:** 39 oz. **Length:** 8-1/2" overall. **Stocks:** Double-diamond checkered rosewood. **Sights:** Dovetailed Patridge front, fully adjustable rear; three-dot system. **Features:** Adjustable two-cut aluminum trigger; Defender grip safety; ambidextrous manual safety. Introduced 1999. Made in U.S. by Colt's Mfg., Inc.

Price: ...... **NA**

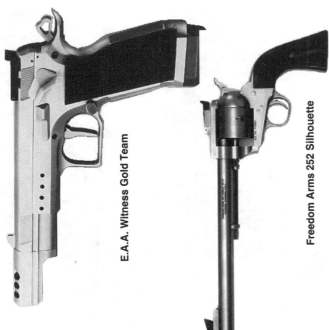

E.A.A. Witness Gold Team

Freedom Arms 252 Silhouette

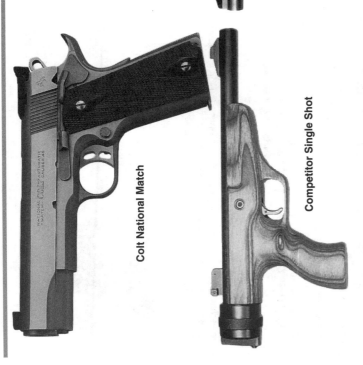

Colt National Match

Competitor Single Shot

COMPETITOR SINGLE SHOT PISTOL

Caliber: 22 LR through 50 Action Express, including belted magnums. **Barrel:** 14" standard; 10.5" silhouette; 16" optional. **Weight:** About 59 oz. (14" bbl.). **Length:** 15.12" overall. **Stocks:** Ambidextrous; synthetic (standard) or laminated or natural wood. **Sights:** Ramp front, adjustable rear. **Features:** Rotary canon-type action cocks on opening; cammed ejector; interchangeable barrels, ejectors. Adjustable single stage trigger, sliding thumb safety and trigger safety. Matte blue finish. Introduced 1988. From Competitor Corp., Inc.

Price: 14", standard calibers, synthetic grip $414.95
Price: Extra barrels, from $159.95

CZ 75 CHAMPION COMPETITION PISTOL

Caliber: 9mm Para., 9x21, 40 S&W, 10-shot magazine. **Barrel:** 4.49". **Weight:** 35 oz. **Length:** 9.44" overall. **Stocks:** Black rubber. **Sights:** Blade front, fully adjustable rear. **Features:** Single-action trigger mechanism; three-port compensator (40 S&W, 9mm have two port) full-length guide rod; extended magazine release; ambidextrous safety; flared magazine well; fully adjustable match trigger. Introduced 1999. Imported from the Czech Republic by CZ USA.

Price: 9mm Para., 9x21, 40 S&W, dual-tone finish $1,484.00

CZ 75 ST IPSC AUTO PISTOL

Caliber: 40 S&W, 10-shot magazine. **Barrel:** 5.12". **Weight:** 2.9 lbs. **Length:** 8.86" overall. **Stocks:** Checkered walnut. **Sights:** Fully adjustable rear. **Features:** Single-action mechanism; extended slide release and ambidextrous safety; full-length slide rail; double slide serrations. Introduced 1999. Imported from the Czech Republic by CZ-USA.

Price: Dual-tone finish $1,038.00

EAA/BAIKAL IZH35 AUTO PISTOL

Caliber: 22 LR, 5-shot magazine. **Barrel:** 6". **Weight:** NA. **Length:** NA. **Grips:** Walnut; fully adjustable right-hand target-style. **Sights:** Fully adjustable rear, blade front; detachable scope mount. **Features:** Hammer-forged target barrel; machined steel receiver; adjustable trigger; manual slide hold back, grip and manual trigger-bar disconnect safeties; cocking indicator. Introduced 2000. Imported from Russia by European American Armory.

Price: Blued finish $519.00

E.A.A. WITNESS GOLD TEAM AUTO

Caliber: 9mm Para., 9x21, 38 Super, 40 S&W, 45 ACP. **Barrel:** 5.1". **Weight:** 41.6 oz. **Length:** 9.6" overall. **Stocks:** Checkered walnut, competition style. **Sights:** Square post front, fully adjustable rear. **Features:** Triple-chamber cone compensator; competition SA trigger; extended safety and magazine release; competition hammer; beveled magazine well; beavertail grip. Hand-fitted major components. Hard chrome finish. Match-grade barrel. From E.A.A. Custom Shop. Introduced 1992. From European American Armory.

Price: $2,150.00

E.A.A. Witness Silver Team Auto

Similar to the Witness Gold Team except has double-chamber compensator, oval magazine release, black rubber grips, double-dip blue finish. Comes with Super Sight and drilled and tapped for scope mount. Built for the intermediate competition shooter. Introduced 1992. From European American Armory Custom Shop.

Price: 9mm Para., 9x21, 38 Super, 40 S&W, 45 ACP $968.00

ENTRÉPRISE TOURNAMENT SHOOTER MODEL I

Caliber: 45 ACP, 10-shot magazine. **Barrel:** 6". **Weight:** 40 oz. **Length:** 8.5" overall. **Stocks:** Black ultra-slim double diamond checkered synthetic. **Sights:** Dovetailed Patridge front, adjustable Competizione "melded" rear. **Features:** Oversized magazine release button; flared magazine well; fully machined parallel slide rails; front and rear slide serrations; serrated top of slide; stainless ramped bull barrel with fully supported chamber; full-length guide rod with plug; stainless firing pin; match extractor; polished ramp; tuned match extractor; black oxide. Introduced 1998. Made in U.S. by Entréprise Arms.

Price: $2,300.00
Price: TSMIII (Satin chrome finish, two-piece guide rod) $2,700.00

FREEDOM ARMS CASULL MODEL 252 SILHOUETTE

Caliber: 22 LR, 5-shot cylinder. **Barrel:** 10". **Weight:** 63 oz. **Length:** 15.5" overall. **Stocks:** Black micarta, western style. **Sights:** Adjustable front with bead, Iron Sight Gun Works silhouette rear, click adjustable for windage and elevation. **Features:** Stainless steel. Built on the Model 83. Two-point firing pin, lightened hammer for fast lock time. Trigger pull is 3 to 5 lbs. with pre-set overtravel screw. Introduced 1991. From Freedom Arms.

Price: Silhouette Class $1,578.00
Price: Extra fitted 22 WMR cylinder $264.00

GAUCHER GP SILHOUETTE PISTOL

Caliber: 22 LR, single shot. **Barrel:** 10". **Weight:** 42.3 oz. **Length:** 15.5" overall. **Stocks:** Stained hardwood. **Sights:** Hooded post on ramp front, open rear adjustable for windage and elevation. **Features:** Matte chrome barrel, blued bolt and sights. Other barrel lengths available on special order. Introduced 1991. Imported by Mandall Shooting Supplies.

Price: $425.00

HANDGUNS — COMPETITION HANDGUNS

Hammerli SP 20

High Standard Victor

High Standard Trophy

HAMMERLI SP 20 TARGET PISTOL
Caliber: 22 LR, 32 S&W. Barrel: 4.6". Weight: 34.6-41.8 oz. Length: 11.8" overall. Stocks: Anatomically shaped synthetic Hi-Grip available in five sizes. Sights: Integral front in three widths, adjustable rear with changeable notch widths. Features: Extremely low-level sight line; anatomically shaped trigger; adjustable JPS buffer system for different recoil characteristics. Receiver available in red, blue, gold, violet or black. Introduced 1998. Imported from Switzerland by SIGARMS, Inc and Hammerli Pistols USA.
Price: .... NA

HARRIS GUNWORKS SIGNATURE JR. LONG RANGE PISTOL
Caliber: Any suitable caliber. Barrel: To customer specs. Weight: 5 lbs. Stock: Gunworks fiberglass. Sights: None furnished; comes with scope rings. Features: Right- or left-hand benchrest action of titanium or stainless steel; single shot or repeater. Comes with bipod. Introduced 1992. Made in U.S. by Harris Gunworks, Inc.
Price: $2,700.00

HIGH STANDARD TROPHY TARGET PISTOL
Caliber: 22 LR, 10-shot magazine. Barrel: 5-1/2" bull or 7-1/4" fluted. Weight: 44 oz. Length: 9.5" overall. Stock: Checkered hardwood with thumbrest. Sights: Undercut ramp front, frame-mounted micro-click rear adjustable for windage and elevation; drilled and tapped for scope mounting. Features: Gold-plated trigger, slide lock, safety-lever and magazine release; stippled front grip and backstrap; adjustable trigger and sear. Barrel weights optional. From High Standard Manufacturing Co., Inc.
Price: 5-1/2", scope base $510.00
Price: 7.25" $650.00
Price: 7.25", scope base $591.00

HIGH STANDARD VICTOR TARGET PISTOL
Caliber: 22 LR, 10-shot magazine. Barrel: 4-1/2" or 5-1/2"; push-button takedown. Weight: 46 oz. Length: 9.5" overall. Stock: Checkered hardwood with thumbrest. Sights: Undercut ramp front, micro-click rear adjustable for windage and elevation. Also available with scope mount, rings, no sights. Features: Stainless steel construction. Full-length vent rib. Gold-plated trigger, slide lock, safety-lever and magazine release; stippled front grip and backstrap; polished slide; adjustable trigger and sear. Comes with barrel weight. From High Standard Manufacturing Co., Inc.
Price: $591.00
Price: With Weaver rib $532.00

KIMBER SUPER MATCH AUTO PISTOL
Caliber: 45 ACP, 7-shot magazine. Barrel: 5". Weight: 38 oz. Length: 8.7" overall. Sights: Blade front, Kimber fully adjustable rear. Features: Guaranteed to have shot 3" group at 50 yards. Stainless steel frame, black KimPro slide; two-piece magazine well; premium aluminum match-grade trigger; 30 lpi front strap checkering; stainless match-grade barrel; ambidextrous safety; special Custom Shop markings. Introduced 1999. Made in U.S. by Kimber Mfg., Inc.
Price: $1,871.00

MORINI MODEL 84E FREE PISTOL
Caliber: 22 LR, single shot. Barrel: 11.4". Weight: 43.7 oz. Length: 19.4" overall. Stocks: Adjustable match type with stippled surfaces. Sights: Interchangeable blade front, match-type fully adjustable rear. Features: Fully adjustable electronic trigger. Introduced 1995. Imported from Switzerland by Nygord Precision Products.
Price: $1,450.00

PARDINI MODEL SP, HP TARGET PISTOLS
Caliber: 22 LR, 32 S&W, 5-shot magazine. Barrel: 4.7". Weight: 38.9 oz. Length: 11.6" overall. Stocks: Adjustable; stippled walnut; match type. Sights: Interchangeable, fully adjustable rear. Features: Fully adjustable match trigger. Introduced 1995. Imported from Italy by Nygord Precision Products.
Price: Model SP (22 LR) $950.00
Price: Model HP (32 S&W) $1,050.00

PARDINI GP RAPID FIRE MATCH PISTOL
Caliber: 22 Short, 5-shot magazine. Barrel: 4.6". Weight: 43.3 oz. Length: 11.6" overall. Stocks: Wrap-around stippled walnut. Sights: Interchangeable post front, fully adjustable match rear. Features: Model GP Schuman has extended rear sight for longer sight radius. Introduced 1995. Imported from Italy by Nygord Precision Products.
Price: Model GP $1,095.00
Price: Model GP Schuman $1,595.00

PARDINI K22 FREE PISTOL
Caliber: 22 LR, single shot. Barrel: 9.8". Weight: 34.6 oz. Length: 18.7" overall. Stocks: Wrap-around walnut; adjustable match type. Sights: Interchangeable post front, fully adjustable match open rear. Features: Removable, adjustable match trigger. Barrel weights mount above the barrel. New model introduced in 1999. Imported from Italy by Nygord Precision Products.
Price: $1,295.00

RUGER MARK II TARGET MODEL AUTOLOADING PISTOL
Caliber: 22 LR, 10-shot magazine. Barrel: 6-7/8". Weight: 42 oz. Length: 11-1/8" overall. Stocks: Checkered hard plastic. Sights: .125" blade front, micro-click rear, adjustable for windage and elevation. Sight radius 9-3/8". Comes with lockable plastic case with lock. Features: Introduced 1982.
Price: Blued (MK-678) $326.00
Price: Stainless (KMK-678) $408.00

Ruger Mark II Government Target Model
Same gun as the Mark II Target Model except has 6-7/8" barrel, higher sights and is roll marked "Government Target Model" on the right side of the receiver below the rear sight. Identical in all aspects to the military model used for training U.S. Armed Forces except for markings. Comes with lockable plastic case with lock. Introduced 1987.
Price: Blued (MK-678G) $393.00
Price: Stainless (KMK-678G) $470.00

HANDGUNS — COMPETITION HANDGUNS

Ruger Mark II Bull Barrel

Smith & Wesson Model 41

Springfield 1911A1 Trophy Match

Safari Arms Big Deuce

Ruger Stainless Competition Model Pistol

Similar to the Mark II Government Target Model stainless pistol except has 6-7/8" slab-sided barrel; the receiver top is fitted with a Ruger scope base of blued, chrome moly steel; comes with Ruger 1" stainless scope rings for mounting a variety of optical sights; has checkered laminated grip panels with right-hand thumbrest. Has blued open sights with 9-1/4" radius. Overall length is 11-1/8", weight 45 oz. Comes with lockable plastic case with lock. Introduced 1991.

Price: KMK-678GC **$486.00**

Ruger Mark II Bull Barrel

Same gun as the Target Model except has 5-1/2" or 10" heavy barrel (10" meets all IHMSA regulations). Weight with 5-1/2" barrel is 42 oz., with 10" barrel, 51 oz. Comes with lockable plastic case with lock.

Price: Blued (MK-512) **$326.00**
Price: Blued (MK-10) **$330.00**
Price: Stainless (KMK-10) **$413.00**
Price: Stainless (KMK-512) **$408.00**

SAFARI ARMS BIG DEUCE PISTOL

Caliber: 45 ACP, 7-shot magazine. **Barrel:** 6", 416 stainless steel. **Weight:** 40.3 oz. **Length:** 9.5" overall. **Stocks:** Smooth walnut. **Sights:** Ramped blade front, LPA adjustable rear. **Features:** Beavertail grip safety; extended thumb safety and slide release; Commander-style hammer. Throated, polished and tuned. Parkerized matte black slide with satin stainless steel frame. Introduced 1995. Made in U.S. by Safari Arms, Inc.

Price: **$714.00**

SMITH & WESSON MODEL 41 TARGET

Caliber: 22 LR, 10-shot clip. **Barrel:** 5-1/2" 7". **Weight:** 44 oz. (5-1/2" barrel). **Length:** 9" overall (5-1/2" barrel). **Stocks:** Checkered walnut with modified thumbrest, usable with either hand. **Sights:** 1/8" Patridge on ramp base; micro-click rear adjustable for windage and elevation. **Features:** 3/8" wide, grooved trigger; adjustable trigger stop.

Price: S&W Bright Blue, either barrel **$801.00**

SMITH & WESSON MODEL 22A TARGET PISTOL

Caliber: 22 LR, 10-shot magazine. **Barrel:** 5-1/2" bull. **Weight:** 38.5 oz. **Length:** 9-1/2" overall. **Stocks:** Dymondwood with ambidextrous thumbrests and flared bottom or rubber soft touch with thumbrest. **Sights:** Patridge front, fully adjustable rear. **Features:** Sight bridge with Weaver-style integral optics mount; alloy frame, stainless barrel and slide; matte black finish. Introduced 1997. Made in U.S. by Smith & Wesson.

Price: **$320.00**

Smith & Wesson Model 22S Target Pistol

Similar to the Model 22A except has stainless steel frame. Introduced 1997. Made in U.S. by Smith & Wesson.

Price: **$379.00**

Springfield, Inc. 1911A1 Trophy Match Pistol

Similar to the 1911A1 except factory accurized, Videki speed trigger, skeletonized hammer; has 4- to 5-1/2-lb. trigger pull, click adjustable rear sight, match-grade barrel and bushing. Comes with cocobolo grips. Introduced 1994. From Springfield, Inc.

Price: Blue **$1,089.00**
Price: Stainless steel **$1,149.00**
Price: High Capacity (stainless steel, 10-shot magazine, front slide serrations, checkered slide serrations) **$1,118.00**

Springfield, Inc. Expert Pistol

Similar to the Competition Pistol except has triple-chamber tapered cone compensator on match barrel with dovetailed front sight; lowered and flared ejection port; fully tuned for reliability; fitted slide to frame; extended ambidextrous thumb safety, extended magazine release button; beavertail grip safety; Pachmayr wrap-around grips. Comes with two magazines, plastic carrying case. Introduced 1992. From Springfield, Inc.

Price: 45 ACP, Duotone finish **$1,724.00**
Price: Expert Ltd. (non-compensated) **$1,624.00**

Springfield, Inc. Distinguished Pistol

Has all the features of the 1911A1 Expert except is full-house pistol with deluxe Bo-Mar low-mounted adjustable rear sight; full-length recoil spring guide rod and recoil spring retainer; checkered frontstrap; S&A magazine well; walnut grips. Hard chrome finish. Comes with two magazines with slam pads, plastic carrying case. From Springfield, Inc.

Price: 45 ACP **$2,445.00**
Price: Distinguished Limited (non-compensated) **$2,345.00**

SPRINGFIELD, INC. 1911A1 BULLSEYE WADCUTTER PISTOL

Caliber: 38 Super, 45 ACP. **Barrel:** 5". **Weight:** 45 oz. **Length:** 8.59" overall (5" barrel). **Stocks:** Checkered walnut. **Sights:** Bo-Mar rib with undercut blade front, fully adjustable rear. **Features:** Built for wadcutter loads only. Has full-length recoil spring guide rod, fitted Videki speed trigger with 3.5-lb. pull; match Commander hammer and sear; beavertail grip safety; lowered and flared ejection port; tuned extractor; fitted slide to frame; recoil buffer system; beveled and polished magazine well; checkered front strap and steel mainspring housing (flat housing standard); polished and throated National Match barrel and bushing. Comes with two magazines with slam pads, plastic carrying case, test target. Introduced 1992. From Springfield, Inc.

Price: **$1,499.00**

Springfield, Inc. Basic Competition Pistol

Has low-mounted Bo-Mar adjustable rear sight, undercut blade front; match throated barrel and bushing; polished feed ramp; lowered and flared ejection port; fitted Videki speed trigger with tuned 3.5-lb. pull; fitted slide to frame; recoil buffer system; checkered walnut grips; serrated, arched mainspring housing. Comes with two magazines with slam pads, plastic carrying case. Introduced 1992. From Springfield, Inc.
Price: 45 ACP, blue, 5" only **$1,295.00**

Springfield, Inc. 1911A1 N.M. Hardball Pistol

Has Bo-Mar adjustable rear sight with undercut front blade; fitted match Videki trigger with 4-lb. pull; fitted slide to frame; throated National Match barrel and bushing, polished feed ramp; recoil buffer system; tuned extractor; Herrett walnut grips. Comes with two magazines, plastic carrying case, test target. Introduced 1992. From Springfield, Inc.
Price: 45 ACP, blue **$1,336.00**

STI EAGLE 5.1 PISTOL

Caliber: 9mm Para., 38 Super, 40 S&W, 45 ACP, 10-ACP, 10-shot magazine. **Barrel:** 5", bull. **Weight:** 34 oz. **Length:** 8.62" overall. **Stocks:** Checkered polymer. **Sights:** Bo-Mar fully adjustable rear. **Features:** Modular frame design; adjustable match trigger, skeletonized hammer; extended grip safety with locator pad; adjustable fit of all parts. Many options available. Introduced 1994. Made in U.S. by STI International.
Price: **$1,792.00**

THOMPSON/CENTER SUPER 14 CONTENDER

Caliber: 22 LR, 222 Rem., 223 Rem., 7-30 Waters, 30-30 Win., 357 Rem. Maximum, 44 Mag., single shot. **Barrel:** 14". **Weight:** 45 oz. **Length:** 17-1/4" overall. **Stocks:** T/C "Competitor Grip" (walnut and rubber). **Sights:** Fully adjustable target-type. **Features:** Break-open action with auto safety. Interchangeable barrels for both rimfire and centerfire calibers. Introduced 1978.
Price: Blued **$520.24**
Price: Stainless steel **$578.40**
Price: Extra barrels, blued **$251.06**
Price: Extra barrels, stainless steel **$278.68**

Thompson/Center Super 16 Contender

Same as the T/C Super 14 Contender except has 16-1/4" barrel. Rear sight can be mounted at mid-barrel position (10-3/4" radius) or moved to the rear (using scope mount position) for 14-3/4" radius. Overall length is 20-1/4". Comes with T/C Competitor Grip of walnut and rubber. Available in, 223 Rem., 45-70 Gov't. Also available with 16" vent rib barrel with internal choke, caliber 45 Colt/410 shotshell.
Price: Blue **$525.95**
Price: 45-70 Gov't., blue **$531.52**
Price: Super 16 Vent Rib, blued **$559.70**

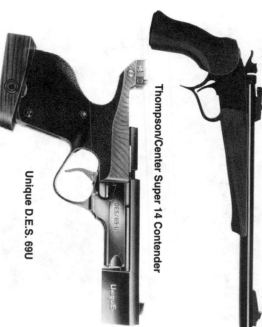

Thompson/Center Super 14 Contender

Unique D.E.S. 69U

UNIQUE D.E.S. 32U TARGET PISTOL

Caliber: 32 S&W Long wadcutter. **Barrel:** 5.9". **Weight:** 40.2 oz. **Stocks:** Anatomically shaped, adjustable stippled French walnut. **Sights:** Blade front, micrometer click rear. **Features:** Trigger adjustable for weight and position; dry firing mechanism; slide stop catch. Optional sleeve weights. Introduced 1990. Imported from France by Nygord Precision Products.
Price: Right-hand, about **$1,350.00**
Price: Left-hand, about **$1,380.00**

UNIQUE D.E.S. 69U TARGET PISTOL

Caliber: 22 LR, 5-shot magazine. **Barrel:** 5.91". **Weight:** 35.3 oz. **Length:** 10.5" overall. **Stocks:** French walnut target-style with thumbrest and adjustable shelf; hand-checkered panels. **Sights:** Ramp front, micro. adjustable rear mounted on frame; 8.66" sight radius. **Features:** Meets U.I.T. standards. Comes with 260-gram barrel weight; 100, 150, 350-gram weights available. Fully adjustable match trigger; dry-firing safety device. Imported from France by Nygord Precision Products.
Price: Right-hand, about **$1,250.00**
Price: Left-hand, about **$1,290.00**

UNIQUE MODEL 96U TARGET PISTOL

Caliber: 22 LR, 5- or 6-shot magazine. **Barrel:** 5.9". **Weight:** 40.2 oz. **Length:** 11.2" overall. **Stocks:** French walnut. Target style with thumbrest and adjustable shelf. **Sights:** Blade front, micrometer rear mounted on frame. **Features:** Designed for Sport Pistol and Standard U.I.T. shooting. External hammer; fully adjustable and movable trigger; dry-firing device. Introduced 1997. Imported from France by Nygord Precision Products.
Price: **$1,350.00**

WALTHER GSP MATCH PISTOL

Caliber: 22 LR, 32 S&W Long (GSP-C), 5-shot magazine. **Barrel:** 4.22". **Weight:** 44.8 oz. (22 LR) 49.4 oz. (32) **Length:** 11.8" overall. **Stocks:** Walnut. **Sights:** Post front, match rear adjustable for windage and elevation. **Features:** Available with either 2.2-lb. (1000 gm) or 3-lb. (1360 gm) trigger. Spare magazine, barrel weight, tools supplied. Imported from Germany by Nygord Precision Products.
Price: GSP, with case **$1,495.00**
Price: GSP-C, with case **$1,595.00**

WICHITA SILHOUETTE PISTOL

Caliber: 308 Win. F.L., 7mm IHMSA, 7mm-308. **Barrel:** 14-15/16". **Weight:** 4-1/2 lbs. **Length:** 21-3/8" overall. **Stock:** American walnut with oil finish. Glass bedded. **Sights:** Wichita Multi-Range sight system. **Features:** Comes with left-hand action with right-hand grip. Round receiver and barrel. Fluted bolt, flat bolt handle. Wichita adjustable trigger. Introduced 1979. From Wichita Arms.
Price: Center grip stock **$1,800.00**
Price: As above except with Rear Position Stock and target-type Lightpull trigger **$1,800.00**

WICHITA CLASSIC SILHOUETTE PISTOL

Caliber: All standard calibers with maximum overall length of 2.800". **Barrel:** 11-1/4". **Weight:** 3 lbs., 15 oz. **Stocks:** AAA American walnut with oil finish, checkered grip. **Sights:** Hooded post front; open adjustable rear. **Features:** Three locking lug bolt, three gas ports; completely adjustable Wichita trigger. Introduced 1981. From Wichita Arms.
Price: **$3,450.00**

Wichita Silhouette

Price: Extra 16" barrel, blued **$245.61**
Price: Extra 45-70 barrel, blued **$251.08**
Price: Extra Super 16 vent rib barrel, blue **$278.73**

HANDGUNS — DOUBLE ACTION REVOLVERS, SERVICE & SPORT

Includes models suitable for hunting and competitive courses of fire, both police and international.

Ruger GP161

Ruger KSP-931

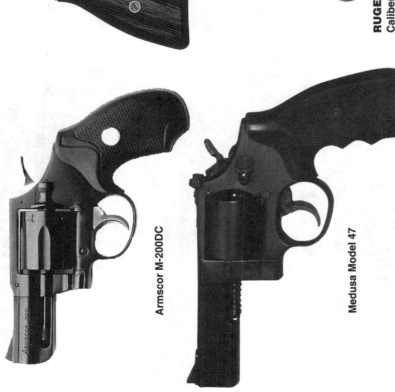

Armscor M-200DC

Medusa Model 47

ARMSCOR M-200DC REVOLVER

Caliber: 38 Spec., 6-shot cylinder. **Barrel:** 2-1/2", 4" **Weight:** 22 oz. (2-1/2" barrel). **Length:** 7-3/8" overall (2-1/2" barrel). **Stocks:** Checkered rubber. **Sights:** Blade front, fixed notch rear. **Features:** All-steel construction; floating firing pin, transfer bar ignition; shrouded ejector rod; blue finish. Reintroduced 1996. Imported from the Philippines by K.B.I., Inc.

Price: 2-1/2" $199.99
Price: 4" $205.00

ARMSPORT MODEL 4540 REVOLVER

Caliber: 38 Special. **Barrel:** 4". **Weight:** 32 oz **Length:** 9" overall. **Sights:** Fixed rear, blade front. **Features:** Ventilated rib; blued finish. Imported from Argentina by Armsport Inc.

Price: $140.00

E.A.A. WINDICATOR

Caliber: 38 Spec., 6-shot; 357 magnum, 6-shot. **Barrel:** 2", 4". **Weight:** 38 oz. **Length:** 8.8" overall (4" bbl.). **Stocks:** Rubber with finger grooves. **Sights:** Blade front, fixed rear. **Features:** Swing-out cylinder; hammer block safety; blue finish. Introduced 1991. Imported from Germany by European American Armory.

Price: 38 Special 2" bbl $198.00
Price: 38 Special, 4" bbl $229.00
Price: 357 Magnum, 2" bbl $229.00
Price: 357 Magnum, 4" bbl $239.00

MEDUSA MODEL 47 REVOLVER

Caliber: Most 9mm, 38 and 357 caliber cartridges; 6-shot cylinder. **Barrel:** 2-1/2", 3", 4", 5", 6"; fluted. **Weight:** 39 oz. **Length:** 10" overall (4" barrel). **Stocks:** Gripper-style rubber. **Sights:** Changeable front blades, fully adjustable rear. **Features:** Patented extractor allows gun to chamber, fire and extract over 25 different cartridges in the .355- to .357 range, without half-moon clips. Steel frame and cylinder; match quality barrel. Matte blue finish. Introduced 1996. Made in U.S. by Phillips & Rogers, Inc.

Price: $899.00

RUGER GP-100 REVOLVERS

Caliber: 38 Spec., 357 Mag., 6-shot. **Barrel:** 3", 3" full shroud, 4", 4" full shroud, 6", 6" full shroud. **Weight:** 3" barrel—35 oz., 3" full shroud—36 oz., 4" barrel—37 oz., 4" full shroud—38 oz. **Sights:** Fixed; adjustable on 4" full shroud and all 6" barrels. **Stocks:** Ruger Santoprene Cushioned Grip with Goncalo Alves inserts. **Features:** Uses action and frame incorporating improvements and features of both the Security-Six and Redhawk revolvers. Full length and short ejector shroud. Satin blue and stainless steel.

Price: GP-141 (357, 4" full shroud, adj. sights, blue) $462.00
Price: GP-160 (357, 6", adj. sights, blue) $462.00
Price: GP-161 (357, 6" full shroud, adj. sights, blue), 46 oz. $462.00
Price: GPF-331 (357, 3" full shroud) $445.00
Price: GPF-340 (357, 4") $445.00
Price: GPF-341 (357, 4" full shroud) $445.00
Price: KGP-141 (357, 4" full shroud, adj. sights, stainless) $498.00
Price: KGP-160 (357, 6", adj. sights, stainless), 43 oz. $498.00
Price: KGP-161 (357, 6" full shroud, adj. sights, stainless) 46 oz. .. $498.00
Price: KGPF-330 (357, 3", stainless) $480.00
Price: KGPF-331 (357, 3" full shroud, stainless) $480.00
Price: KGPF-340 (357, 4", stainless), KGPF-840 (38 Spec.) $480.00
Price: KGPF-341 (357, 4" full shroud, stainless) $480.00

Ruger SP101 Double-Action-Only Revolver

Similar to the standard SP101 except is double-action-only with no single-action sear notch. Has spurless hammer for snag-free handling, floating firing pin and Ruger's patented transfer bar safety system. Available with 2-1/4" barrel in 357 Magnum. Weighs 25-1/2 oz., overall length 7.06". Natural brushed satin or high-polish stainless steel. Introduced 1993.

Price: KSP321XL (357 Mag.) $458.00

RUGER SP101 REVOLVERS

Caliber: 22 LR, 32 H&R Mag., 6-shot; 9mm Para., 38 Spec. +P, 357 Mag., 5-shot. **Barrel:** 2-1/4", 3-1/16", 4". **Weight:** (38 & 357 mag models) 2-1/4"—25 oz.; 3-1/16"—27 oz. **Sights:** Adjustable on 22, 32, fixed on others. **Stocks:** Ruger Santoprene Cushioned Grip with Xenoy inserts. **Features:** Incorporates improvements and features found in the GP-100

Ruger KSRH-7

revolvers into a compact, small frame, double-action revolver. Full-length ejector shroud. Stainless steel only. Introduced 1988.

Price: KSP-821 (2-1/2", 38 Spec.) $458.00
Price: KSP-831 (3-1/16", 38 Spec.) $458.00
Price: KSP-221 (2-1/4", 22 LR) $458.00
Price: KSP-240 (4", 22 LR), 32 oz. $458.00
Price: KSP-241 (4" heavy bbl, 22 LR), 34 oz. . $458.00
Price: KSP-3231 (3-1/16", 32 H&R) $458.00
Price: KSP-921 (2-1/4", 9mm Para.) $458.00
Price: KSP-931 (3-1/16", 9mm Para.) $458.00
Price: KSP-321 (2-1/4", 357 Mag.) $458.00
Price: KSP331X (3-1/16", 357 Mag.) $458.00

RUGER REDHAWK

Caliber: 44 Rem. Mag., 45 Colt, 6-shot. **Barrel:** 5-1/2", 7-1/2". **Weight:** About 54 oz. (7-1/2" bbl.). **Length:** 13" overall (7-1/2" barrel). **Stocks:** Square butt Goncalo Alves. **Sights:** Interchangeable Patridge-type front, rear adjustable for windage and elevation. **Features:** Stainless steel, brushed satin finish, or blued ordnance steel. Has a 9-1/2" sight radius. Introduced 1979.

Price: Blued, 44 Mag., 5-1/2" RH-445, 7-1/2" RH-44 .... $545.00
Price: Blued, 44 Mag., 7-1/2" RH44R, with scope mount, rings . $578.00
Price: Stainless, 44 Mag., 5-1/2", 7-1/2" KRH-445 .... $603.00
Price: Stainless, 44 Mag., 7-1/2", with scope mount, rings KRH-44 . $603.00
Price: Stainless, 45 Colt, 5-1/2", 7-1/2" KRH-455 .... $629.00
Price: Stainless, 45 Colt, 7-1/2", with scope mount KRH-45 . $629.00

Ruger Super Redhawk Revolver

Similar to the standard Redhawk except has a heavy extended frame with the Ruger Integral Scope Mounting System on the wide topstrap. Also available in 454 Casull. The wide hammer spur has been lowered for better scope clearance. Incorporates the mechanical design features and improvements of the GP-100. Choice of 7-1/2" or 9-1/2" barrel, both with ramp front sight base with Redhawk-style Interchangeable Insert sight blades, adjustable rear sight. Comes with Ruger "Cushioned Grip" panels of Santoprene with Goncalo Alves wood panels. Satin stainless steel. Introduced 1987.

Price: KSRH-7 (7-1/2"), KSRH-9 (9-1/2") $629.00
Price: KSRH-7454 (7-1/2") 454 Casull $629.00

Ruger Super Redhawk 454 Casull Revolver

Similar to the Ruger Super Redhawk except chambered for 454 Casull (also accepts 45 Colt cartridges). Unfluted cylinder, 7" barrel, weighs 53 ounces. Comes with 1" stainless scope rings. Introduced 2000.

Price: (satin or target gray stainless steel finishes) $745.00

SMITH & WESSON MODEL 10 M&P HB REVOLVER

Caliber: 38 Spec., 6-shot. **Barrel:** 4". **Weight:** 33.5 oz. **Length:** 9-5/16" overall. **Stocks:** Uncle Mike's Combat soft rubber; square butt. **Sights:** Fixed; ramp front, square notch rear.

Price: Blue $458.00

SMITH & WESSON MODEL 14 FULL LUG REVOLVER

Caliber: 38 Spec., 6-shot. **Barrel:** 6", full lug. **Weight:** 47 oz. **Length:** 11-1/8" overall. **Stocks:** Hogue soft rubber. **Sights:** Pinned Patridge front,

adjustable micrometer click rear. **Features:** Has .500" target hammer, .312" smooth combat trigger. Polished blue finish. Reintroduced 1991. Limited production.

Price: $450.00

SMITH & WESSON MODEL 15 COMBAT MASTERPIECE

Caliber: 38 Spec., 6-shot. **Barrel:** 4". **Weight:** 32 oz. **Length:** 9-5/16" (4" bbl.). **Stocks:** Uncle Mike's Combat soft rubber. **Sights:** Serrated ramp front, micro-click rear adjustable for windage and elevation.

Price: Blued $498.00

SMITH & WESSON MODEL 19 COMBAT MAGNUM

Caliber: 357 Mag. and 38 Spec., 6-shot. **Barrel:** 4". **Weight:** 36 oz. **Length:** 9-9/16" (4" bbl.). **Stocks:** Uncle Mike's Combat soft rubber; wood optional. **Sights:** Red ramp front, micro-click rear adjustable for windage and elevation.

Price: 4" $457.00

SMITH & WESSON MODEL 629 REVOLVERS

Caliber: 44 Magnum, 6-shot. **Barrel:** 5", 6", 8-3/8". **Weight:** 47 oz. (6" bbl.). **Length:** 11-3/8" overall (6" bbl.). **Stocks:** Soft rubber; wood optional. **Sights:** 1/8" red ramp front, micro-click rear, adjustable for windage and elevation.

Price: Model 629 (stainless steel), 5" $625.00
Price: Model 629, 6" $631.00
Price: Model 629, 8-3/8" barrel $646.00

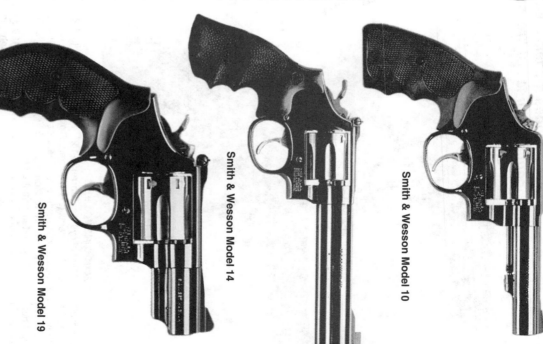

Smith & Wesson Model 19

Smith & Wesson Model 14

Smith & Wesson Model 10

HANDGUNS — DOUBLE ACTION REVOLVERS, SERVICE & SPORT

Smith & Wesson Model 65LS

Has a speedloader cutout. Comes in a fitted carry/storage case. Introduced 1989.

Price: Model 36LS **$478.00**
Price: Model 60LS, as above except in stainless, 357 Magnum . **$539.00**

SMITH & WESSON MODEL 60 357 MAGNUM

Caliber: 357 Magnum, 5-shot. **Barrel:** 2-1/8" or 3". **Weight:** 24 oz. **Length:** 7-1/2 overall (3" barrel). **Stocks:** Uncle Mike's Combat. **Sights:** Fixed, serrated ramp front, square notch rear. **Features:** Stainless steel construction. Made in U.S. by Smith & Wesson.

Price: 2-1/8" barrel **$505.00**
Price: 3" barrel **$536.00**

SMITH & WESSON MODEL 65

Caliber: 357 Mag. and 38 Spec., 6-shot. **Barrel:** 3", 4". **Weight:** 34 oz. **Length:** 9-5/16" overall (4" bbl.). **Stocks:** Uncle Mike's Combat. **Sights:** 1/8" serrated ramp front, fixed square notch rear. **Features:** Heavy barrel. Stainless steel construction.

Price: **$501.00**

SMITH & WESSON
MODEL 317 AIRLITE, 317 LADYSMITH REVOLVERS

Caliber: 22 LR, 8-shot. **Barrel:** 1-7/8" 3". **Weight:** 9.9 oz. **Length:** 6-3/16" overall. **Stocks:** Dymondwood Boot or Uncle Mike's Boot. **Sights:** Serrated ramp front, fixed notch rear. **Features:** Aluminum alloy, carbon and stainless steels, and titanium construction. Short spur hammer, smooth combat trigger. Clear Cote finish. Introduced 1997. Made in U.S. by Smith & Wesson.

Price: With Uncle Mike's Boot grip **$508.00**
Price: With DymondWood Boot grip, 3" barrel **$537.00**
Price: Model 317 LadySmith (DymondWood only, comes with display case) **$568.00**

Smith & Wesson Model 637 Airweight Revolver

Similar to the Model 37 Airweight except has alloy frame, stainless steel barrel, cylinder and yoke; rated for 38 Spec. +P; Uncle Mike's Boot Grip. Weighs 15 oz. Introduced 1996. Made in U.S. by Smith & Wesson.

Price: **$459.00**

SMITH & WESSON MODEL 64 STAINLESS M&P

Caliber: 38 Spec., 6-shot. **Barrel:** 2", 3", 4". **Weight:** 34 oz. **Length:** 9-5/16" overall. **Stocks:** Soft rubber. **Sights:** Fixed, 1/8" serrated ramp front, square notch rear. **Features:** Satin finished stainless steel, square butt.

Price: 2" **$487.00**
Price: 3", 4" **$496.00**

SMITH & WESSON MODEL 65LS LADYSMITH

Caliber: 357 Magnum, 6-shot. **Barrel:** 3". **Weight:** 31 oz. **Length:** 7.94" overall. **Stocks:** Rosewood, round butt. **Sights:** Serrated ramp front, fixed notch rear. **Features:** Stainless steel with frosted finish. Smooth combat trigger, service hammer, shrouded ejector rod. Comes with case. Introduced 1992.

Price: **$539.00**

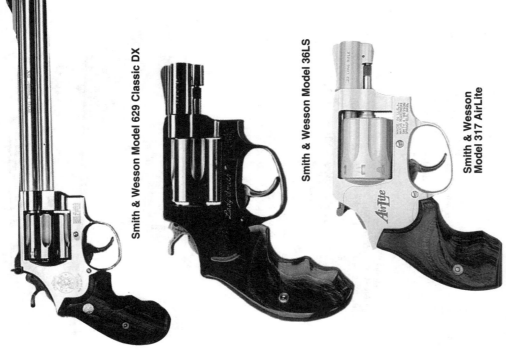

Smith & Wesson Model 629 Classic DX

Smith & Wesson Model 36LS

Smith & Wesson Model 317 AirLite

Smith & Wesson Model 629 Classic Revolver

Similar to the standard Model 629 except has full-lug 5", 6-1/2" or 8-3/8" barrel; chamfered front of cylinder; interchangeable red ramp front sight with adjustable white outline rear; Hogue grips with S&W monogram; the frame is drilled and tapped for scope mounting. Factory accurizing and endurance packages. Overall length with 5" barrel is 10-1/2"; weighs 51 oz. Introduced 1990.

Price: Model 629 Classic (stainless), 5", 6-1/2" **$670.00**
Price: As above, 8-3/8" **$691.00**

Smith & Wesson Model 629 Classic DX Revolver

Similar to the Model 629 Classic except offered only with 6-1/2" or 8-3/8" full-lug barrel; comes with five front sights: red ramp; black Patridge; black Patridge with gold bead; black ramp; and black Patridge with white dot. Comes with Hogue combat-style and wood round butt grip. Introduced 1991.

Price: Model 629 Classic DX, 6-1/2" **$860.00**
Price: As above, 8-3/8" **$888.00**

SMITH & WESSON
MODEL 36, 37 CHIEFS SPECIAL & AIRWEIGHT

Caliber: 38 Spec.+P, 5-shot. **Barrel:** 1-7/8". **Weight:** 19-1/2 oz. (2" bbl.); 13-1/2 oz. (Airweight). **Length:** 6-1/2" (round butt). **Stocks:** Round butt soft rubber. **Sights:** Fixed, serrated ramp front, square notch rear.

Price: Blue, standard Model 36 .... **$406.00**
Price: Blue, Airweight Model 37 .... **$483.00**

Smith & Wesson Model 36LS, 60LS LadySmith

Similar to the standard Model 36. Available with 1-7/8" barrel, 38 Special. Comes with smooth, contoured rosewood grips with the S&W monogram.

Smith & Wesson Model 586,
686 Distinguished Combat

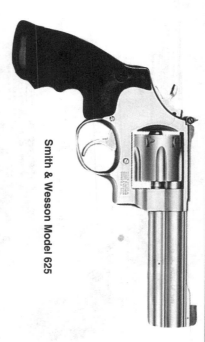

Smith & Wesson Model 625

SMITH & WESSON MODEL 66 STAINLESS COMBAT MAGNUM

Caliber: 357 Mag. and 38 Spec., 6-shot. **Barrel:** 2-1/2", 4". **Weight:** 36 oz. (4" barrel). **Length:** 9-9/16" overall. **Stocks:** Soft rubber. **Sights:** Red ramp front, micro-click rear adjustable for windage and elevation. **Features:** Satin finish stainless steel.
Price: 2-1/2" $545.00
Price: 4", 6" $551.00

SMITH & WESSON MODEL 67 COMBAT MASTERPIECE

Caliber: 38 Special, 6-shot. **Barrel:** 4". **Weight:** 32 oz. **Length:** 9-5/16" overall. **Stocks:** Soft rubber. **Sights:** Red ramp front, micro-click rear adjustable for windage and elevation. **Features:** Stainless steel with satin finish. Smooth combat trigger, semi-target hammer. Introduced 1994.
Price: $546.00

SMITH & WESSON MODEL 242 AIRLITE TI REVOLVER

Caliber: 38 Special, 7-shot. **Barrel:** 2-1/2". **Weight:** 18.9 oz. **Length:** 7-3/8" overall. **Stocks:** Uncle Mike's Boot grip. **Sights:** Serrated ramp front, fixed notch rear. **Features:** Alloy frame, yoke and barrel shroud; titanium cylinder; stainless steel barrel insert. Medium, L-frame size. Introduced 1999. Made in U.S. by Smith & Wesson.
Price: $658.00

SMITH & WESSON MODEL 296 AIRLITE TI REVOLVER

Caliber: 44 Spec. **Barrel:** 2-1/2". **Weight:** 18.9 oz. **Length:** 7-3/8" overall. **Stocks:** Uncle Mike's Boot grip. **Sights:** Serrated ramp front, fixed notch rear. **Features:** Alloy frame, yoke and barrel shroud; titanium cylinder; stainless steel barrel insert. Medium, L-frame size. Introduced 1999. Made in U.S. by Smith & Wesson.
Price: $718.00

SMITH & WESSON MODEL 586, 686 DISTINGUISHED COMBAT MAGNUMS

Caliber: 357 Magnum. **Barrel:** 4", 6" (M 586), 2-1/2", 4" (M 686). **Weight:** 46 oz. (6"), 41 oz. (4"). **Stocks:** Soft rubber. **Sights:** Red ramp front, S&W micrometer click rear. Drilled and tapped for scope mount. **Features:** Uses L-frame, but takes all K-frame grips. Full-length ejector rod shroud. Smooth combat-type trigger, semi-target type hammer. Also available in stainless as Model 686. Introduced 1981.
Price: Model 586, blue, 4", from $494.00
Price: Model 586, blue, 6" $499.00
Price: Model 686, 6", ported barrel. $564.00
Price: Model 686, 8-3/8". $550.00
Price: Model 686, 2-1/2". $514.00

Smith & Wesson Model 686 Magnum PLUS Revolver

Similar to the Model 686 except has 7-shot cylinder, 2-1/2", 4" or 6" barrel. Weighs 34-1/2 oz., overall length 7-1/2" (2-1/2" barrel). Hogue rubber grips. Introduced 1996. Made in U.S. by Smith & Wesson.
Price: 2-1/2" barrel $534.00
Price: 4" barrel $542.00
Price: 6" barrel $550.00

SMITH & WESSON MODEL 625 REVOLVER

Caliber: 45 ACP, 6-shot. **Barrel:** 5". **Weight:** 46 oz. **Length:** 11.375" overall. **Stocks:** Soft rubber, wood optional. **Sights:** Patridge front on ramp, S&W micrometer click rear adjustable for windage and elevation. **Features:** Stainless steel construction with .400" semi-target hammer, .312" smooth combat trigger; full lug barrel. Introduced 1989.
Price: $636.00

SMITH & WESSON MODEL 640 CENTENNIAL

Caliber: 357 Mag., 5-shot. **Barrel:** 2-1/8". **Weight:** 25 oz. **Length:** 6-3/4" overall. **Stocks:** Uncle Mike's Boot Grip. **Sights:** Serrated ramp front, fixed notch rear. **Features:** Stainless steel. Fully concealed hammer, snag-proof smooth edges. Introduced 1995 in 357 Magnum.
Price: $502.00

SMITH & WESSON MODEL 617 FULL LUG REVOLVER

Caliber: 22 LR, 6- or 10-shot. **Barrel:** 4", 6", 8-3/8". **Weight:** 42 oz. (4" barrel). **Length:** NA. **Stocks:** Soft rubber. **Sights:** Patridge front, adjustable rear. Drilled and tapped for scope mount. **Features:** Stainless steel with satin finish; 4" has .312" smooth trigger, .375" semi-target hammer; 6" has either .312" combat or .400" serrated trigger, .375" semi-target or .500" target hammer; 8-3/8" with .400" serrated trigger, .500" target hammer. Introduced 1990.
Price: 4" $534.00
Price: 6", target hammer, target trigger $524.00
Price: 6", 10-shot $566.00
Price: 8-3/8", 10 shot $578.00

SMITH & WESSON MODEL 610 CLASSIC HUNTER REVOLVER

Caliber: 10mm, 6-shot cylinder. **Barrel:** 6-1/2" full lug. **Weight:** 52 oz. **Length:** 12" overall. **Stocks:** Hogue rubber combat. **Sights:** Interchangeable blade front, micro-click rear adjustable for windage and elevation. **Features:** Stainless steel construction; target hammer, target trigger; unfluted cylinder; drilled and tapped for scope mounting. Introduced 1998.
Price: $684.00

SMITH & WESSON MODEL 331, 332 AIRLITE TI REVOLVERS

Caliber: 32 H&R Mag., 6-shot. **Barrel:** 1-7/8". **Weight:** 11.2 oz. (with wood grip). **Length:** 6-15/16" overall. **Stocks:** Uncle Mike's Boot or Dymondwood Boot. **Sights:** Black serrated ramp front, fixed notch rear. **Features:** Aluminum alloy frame, barrel shroud and yoke; titanium cylinder; stainless steel barrel liner. Matte finish. Introduced 1999. Made in U.S. by Smith & Wesson.
Price: Model 331 Chiefs $682.00
Price: Model 332 .... $699.00

SMITH & WESSON MODEL 337 CHIEFS SPECIAL AIRLITE TI

Caliber: 38 Spec., 5-shot. **Barrel:** 1-7/8". **Weight:** 11.2 oz. (Dymondwood grips). **Length:** 6-5/16" overall. **Stocks:** Uncle Mike's Boot or Dymondwood Boot. **Sights:** Black serrated front, fixed notch rear. **Features:** Aluminum alloy frame, barrel shroud and yoke; titanium cylinder; stainless steel barrel liner. Matte finish. Introduced 1999. Made in U.S. by Smith & Wesson.
Price: $682.00

HANDGUNS — DOUBLE ACTION REVOLVERS, SERVICE & SPORT

Smith & Wesson Model 442

Smith & Wesson Model 649

Smith & Wesson Model 337PD

Smith & Wesson Model 342

Smith & Wesson Model 337PD AirLite Ti Chiefs Special Revolver

Similar to the Model 337 Chiefs Special AirLite Ti except has a black-gray finish and Hogue Bantam lightweight grips. Overall weight 10.7 oz.; overall length 6-5/16". Introduced 2000. From Smith & Wesson.

Price: **$704.00**

SMITH & WESSON MODEL 342 CENTENNIAL AIRLITE Ti

Caliber: 38 Spec., 5-shot. **Barrel:** 1-7/8". **Weight:** 11.3 oz. (Dymondwood stocks). **Length:** 6-15/16" overall. **Stocks:** Uncle Mike's Boot or Dymondwood Boot. **Sights:** Black serrated ramp front, fixed notch rear. **Features:** Aluminum alloy frame, barrel shroud and yoke; titanium cylinder; stainless steel barrel liner. Shrouded hammer. Matte finish. Introduced 1999. Made in U.S. by Smith & Wesson.

Price: **$699.00**

Smith & Wesson Model 342PD AirLite Ti Centennial

Similar to the Model 342 AirLite Ti Centennial except has a black-gray finish and Hogue Bantam lightweight grips. Overall weight 10.8 oz.; overall length 6-5/16". Introduced 2000. From Smith & Wesson.

Price: .... **NA**

Smith & Wesson Model 442 Centennial Airweight

Similar to the Model 640 Centennial except has alloy frame giving weight of 15.8 oz. Chambered for 38 Special, 1-7/8" carbon steel barrel; carbon steel cylinder; concealed hammer; Uncle Mike's Boot grip. Fixed square notch rear sight, serrated ramp front. Introduced 1993.

Price: Blue **$459.00**

SMITH & WESSON MODEL 638 AIRWEIGHT BODYGUARD

Caliber: 38 Spec., 5-shot. **Barrel:** 1-7/8". **Weight:** 15 oz. **Length:** 6-15/16" overall. **Stocks:** Uncle Mike's Boot grip. **Sights:** Serrated ramp front, fixed notch rear. **Features:** Alloy frame, stainless cylinder and barrel; shrouded hammer. Introduced 1997. Made in U.S. by Smith & Wesson.

Price: With Uncle Mike's Boot grip **$492.00**

Smith & Wesson Model 642 Airweight Revolver

Similar to the Model 442 Centennial Airweight except has stainless steel barrel, cylinder and yoke with matte finish; Uncle Mike's Boot Grip; weighs 15.8 oz. Introduced 1996. Made in U.S. by Smith & Wesson.

Price: **$474.00**

Smith & Wesson Model 642LS LadySmith Revolver

Same as the Model 642 except has smooth combat wood grips, and comes with case; aluminum alloy frame, stainless cylinder, barrel and yoke; frosted matte finish. Weighs 15.8 oz. Introduced 1996. Made in U.S. by Smith & Wesson.

Price: **$505.00**

SMITH & WESSON MODEL 649 BODYGUARD REVOLVER

Caliber: 357 Mag., 5-shot. **Barrel:** 2-1/8". **Weight:** 20 oz. **Length:** 6-5/16" overall. **Stocks:** Uncle Mike's Combat. **Sights:** Black pinned ramp front, fixed notch rear. **Features:** Stainless steel construction; shrouded hammer; smooth combat trigger. Made in U.S. by Smith & Wesson.

Price: **$502.00**

SMITH & WESSON MODEL 657 REVOLVER

Caliber: 41 Mag., 6-shot. **Barrel:** 6". **Weight:** 48 oz. **Length:** 11-3/8" overall. **Stocks:** Soft rubber. **Sights:** Pinned 1/8" red ramp front, micro-click rear adjustable for windage and elevation. **Features:** Stainless steel construction.

Price: **$564.00**

HANDGUNS — DOUBLE ACTION REVOLVERS, SERVICE & SPORT

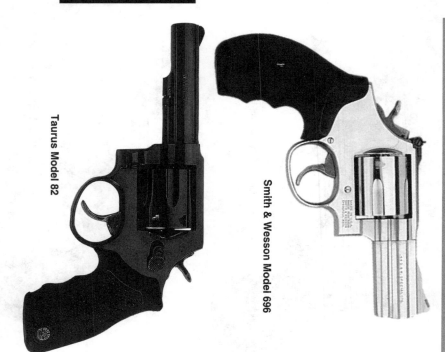

Smith & Wesson Model 696

Taurus Model 82

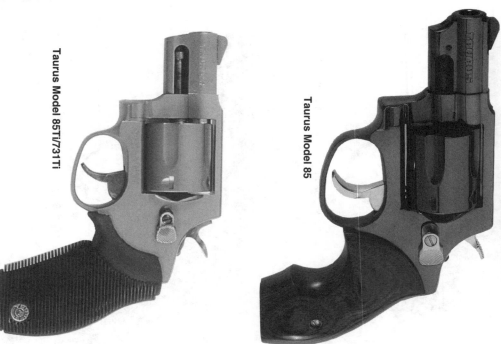

Taurus Model 85TI/731TI

Taurus Model 85

SMITH & WESSON MODEL 696 REVOLVER

Caliber: 44 Spec., 5-shot. **Barrel:** 3". **Weight:** 35.5 oz. **Length:** 8-1/4" overall. **Stocks:** Uncle Mike's Combat. **Sights:** Red ramp front, click adjustable white outline rear. **Features:** Stainless steel construction; round butt frame; satin finish. Introduced 1997. Made in U.S. by Smith & Wesson.
Price: $525.00

TAURUS MODEL 65 REVOLVER

Caliber: 357 Mag., 6-shot. **Barrel:** 4". **Weight:** 38 oz. **Length:** 10-1/2" overall. **Stocks:** Soft rubber. **Sights:** Serrated front, notch rear. **Features:** Solid rib barrel; +P rated. Imported by Taurus International.
Price: Blue $313.00
Price: Stainless. $359.00

Taurus Model 66 Revolver

Same to the Model 65 except with 4" or 6" barrel, 7-shot cylinder, adjustable rear sight. Imported by Taurus International.
Price: Blue $359.00
Price: Stainless $406.00

TAURUS MODEL 82 HEAVY BARREL REVOLVER

Caliber: 38 Spec., 6-shot. **Barrel:** 4", heavy. **Weight:** 34 oz. (4" bbl.). **Length:** 9-1/4" overall (4" bbl.). **Stocks:** Soft black rubber. **Sights:** Serrated ramp front, square notch rear. **Features:** Imported by Taurus International.
Price: Blue $297.00
Price: Polished, stainless. $344.00

TAURUS MODEL 85 REVOLVER

Caliber: 38 Spec., 5-shot. **Barrel:** 2", 3". **Weight:** 21 oz. **Stocks:** Black rubber, boot grip. **Sights:** Ramp front, square notch rear. **Features:** Blue finish or stainless steel. Introduced 1980. Imported by Taurus International.
Price: Blue, 2", 3". $286.00
Price: Stainless steel $327.00
Price: Blue, 2", ported barrel $305.00
Price: Stainless, 2", ported barrel. $345.00

Price: Blue, Ultra-Lite (17 oz.), 2" $311.00
Price: Stainless, Ultra-Lite (17 oz.), 2" $342.00
Price: Blue with gold trim, ported $350.00

Taurus Model 85ULTi Revolver

Similar to the Model 85 except has titanium cylinder, aluminum alloy frame, and ported aluminum barrel with stainless steel sleeve. Weight is 13.5 oz.
Price: .... International. $515.00

Taurus Model 85Ti, Model 731Ti Revolvers

Similar to the 2" Model 85 except has titanium frame, cylinder and ported barrel with stainless steel liner; yoke detent and extended ejector rod. Weight is 15.4 oz. Comes with soft, ridged Ribber grips. Available in Bright and Matte Spectrum blue, Matte Spectrum gold, and Steel Gray colors. Introduced 1999. Imported by Taurus International.
Price: Model 85Ti. $529.00
Price: Model 731Ti (32 H&R mag., 6-shot) $529.00

Taurus Model 85CH Revolver

Same as the Model 85 except has 2" barrel only and concealed hammer. Double aciton only. Soft rubber boot grip. Introduced 1991. Imported by Taurus International.
Price: Blue $286.00
Price: Stainless. $327.00
Price: Blue, ported barrel $305.00
Price: Stainless, ported barrel $345.00

Taurus Model 44

Taurus Model 415

TAURUS MODEL 44 REVOLVER

Caliber: 44 Mag., 6-shot. **Barrel:** 4", 6-1/2", 8-3/8" **Weight:** 44-3/4 oz. (4" barrel). **Length:** NA. **Stocks:** Soft black rubber. **Sights:** Serrated ramp front, micro-click rear adjustable for windage and elevation. **Features:** Heavy solid rib on 4", vent rib on 6-1/2", 8-3/8". Compensated barrel. Blued model has color case-hardened hammer and trigger. Introduced 1994. Imported by Taurus International.

Price: Blue, 4"	$447.00
Price: Blue, 6-1/2", 8-3/8"	$466.00
Price: Stainless, 4"	$508.00
Price: Stainless, 6-1/2", 8-3/8"	$530.00

TAURUS MODEL 415 REVOLVER

Caliber: 41 Mag., 5-shot. **Barrel:** 2-1/2". **Weight:** 30 oz. **Length:** 7-1/8" overall. **Stocks:** Soft, ridged Ribber. **Sights:** Serrated front, notch rear. **Features:** Stainless steel construction; matte finish; ported barrel. Introduced 1999. Imported by Taurus International.

Price:	$452.00

TAURUS MODEL 445, 445CH REVOLVERS

Caliber: 44 Special, 5-shot. **Barrel:** 2". **Weight:** 28.25 oz. **Length:** 6-3/4" overall. **Stocks:** Soft black rubber. **Sights:** Serrated ramp front, notch rear. **Features:** Blue or stainless steel. Standard or concealed hammer. Introduced 1997. Imported by Taurus International.

Price: Blue	$323.00
Price: Blue, ported	$342.00
Price: Stainless	$370.00
Price: Stainless, ported	$389.00
Price: M445CH, concealed hammer, blue, DAO	$323.00
Price: M445CH, blue, ported	$342.00
Price: M445CH, stainless	$370.00
Price: M445CH, stainless, ported	$389.00
Price: M445CH, Ultra-Lite, stainless, ported	$483.00

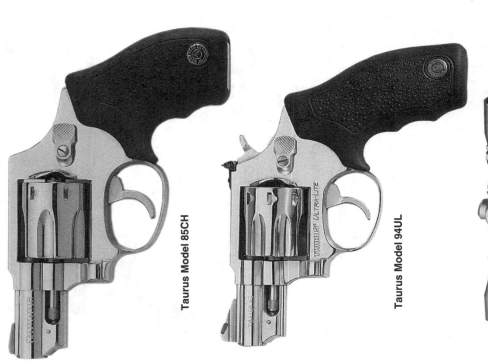

Taurus Model 85CH

Taurus Model 94UL

Taurus Model 22H Raging Hornet

TAURUS MODEL 94 REVOLVER

Caliber: 22 LR, 9-shot cylinder. **Barrel:** 2", 4", 5". **Weight:** 25 oz. **Stocks:** Soft black rubber. **Sights:** Serrated ramp front, click-adjustable rear for windage and elevation. **Features:** Floating firing pin, color case-hardened hammer and trigger. Introduced 1989. Imported by Taurus International.

Price: Blue	$308.00
Price: Stainless	$356.00
Price: Model 94 UL, blue, 2", fixed sight, weighs 14 oz.	$342.00
Price: As above, stainless	$391.00

TAURUS MODEL 22H RAGING HORNET REVOLVER

Caliber: 22 Hornet, 8-shot cylinder. **Barrel:** 10". **Weight:** 50 oz. **Length:** 6.5" overall. **Stocks:** Soft black rubber. **Sights:** Patridge front, micrometer click adjustable rear. **Features:** Ventilated rib; 1:10: twist rifling; comes with scope base; stainless steel construction with matte finish. Introduced 1999. Imported by Taurus International.

Price:	$898.00

HANDGUNS — DOUBLE ACTION REVOLVERS, SERVICE & SPORT

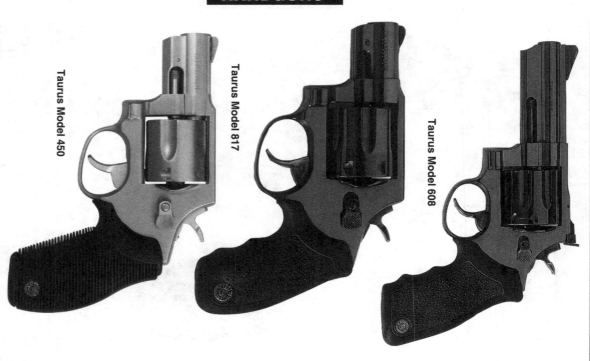

Taurus Model 450

Taurus Model 817

Taurus Model 608

Taurus Model 454 Raging Bull

TAURUS MODEL 605 REVOLVER

Caliber: 357 Mag., 5-shot. **Barrel:** 2-1/4", 3". **Weight:** 24.5 oz. **Length:** NA. **Stocks:** Soft black rubber. **Sights:** Serrated ramp front, fixed notch rear. **Features:** Heavy, solid rib barrel; floating firing pin. Blue or stainless. Introduced 1995. Imported by Taurus International.

Price: Blue $303.00
Price: Stainless $344.00
Price: Model 605CH (concealed hammer) 2-1/4", blue, DAO $303.00
Price: Model 605CH, stainless, 2-1/4" $344.00
Price: Blue, 2-1/4", ported barrel $322.00
Price: Stainless, 2-1/4", ported barrel $363.00
Price: Blue, 2-1/4", ported barrel, concealed hammer, DAO $322.00
Price: Stainless, 2-1/4", ported barrel, concealed hammer, DAO $363.00

TAURUS MODEL 608 REVOLVER

Caliber: 357 Mag., 8-shot. **Barrel:** 4", 6-1/2", 8-3/8". **Weight:** 44 oz. **Length:** 9-3/8" overall. **Stocks:** Soft black rubber. **Sights:** Serrated ramp front, fully adjustable rear. **Features:** Built-in compensator. Available in blue or stainless. Introduced 1995. Imported by Taurus international.

Price: Blue, 4", solid rib $447.00
Price: Blue, 6-1/2", 8-3/8", vent rib $466.00
Price: Stainless, 4", solid rib $508.00
Price: Stainless, 6-1/2", 8-3/8", vent rib ... $530.00

TAURUS MODEL 817 REVOLVER

Caliber: 38 Spec., 7-shot. **Barrel:** 2". **Weight:** 21 oz. **Length:** 6-1/2" overall. **Stocks:** Soft rubber. **Sights:** Serrated front, notch rear. **Features:** Compact alloy frame. Introduced 1999. Imported by Taurus International.

Price: Blue $350.00
Price: Blue, ported $369.00
Price: Matte, stainless $389.00
Price: Matte, stainless, ported $408.00

TAURUS MODEL 450 REVOLVER

Caliber: 45 Colt, 5-shot cylinder. **Barrel:** 2". **Weight:** 28 oz. **Length:** 6-5/8" overall. **Stocks:** Soft, ridged rubber. **Sights:** Serrated front, notch rear. **Features:** Stainless steel construction; ported barrel. Introduced 1999. Imported by Taurus International.

Price: $452.00
Price: Ultra-Lite (alloy frame) $483.00

TAURUS MODEL 45, 444, 454 RAGING BULL REVOLVER

Caliber: 454 Casull, 5-shot. **Barrel:** 5", 6-1/2", 8-3/8". **Weight:** 53 oz. (6-1/2" barrel). **Length:** 12" overall (6-1/2" barrel). **Stocks:** Soft black rubber. **Sights:** Patridge front, micrometer click adjustable rear. **Features:** Ventilated rib; integral compensating system. Introduced 1997. Imported by Taurus International.

Price: 6-1/2", 8-3/8", blue $750.00
Price: 6-1/2", polished, stainless $820.00
Price: 5", 6-1/2", 8-3/8", matte stainless .. $820.00
Price: 5", 6-1/2", 8-3/8", color case-hardened frame $845.00
Price: Model 45 (45 Colt), blue, 6-1/2", 8-3/8" $545.00
Price: Model 45, stainless, 6-1/2", 8-3/8" .. $608.00
Price: Model 444 (44 Mag.), blue, 6-1/2", 8-3/8" $545.00
Price: Model 444, matte, stainless, 6-1/2", 8-3/8" $608.00

TAURUS MODEL 617, 606CH REVOLVER

Caliber: 357 Magnum, 7-shot. **Barrel:** 2". **Weight:** 29 oz. **Length:** 6-3/4" overall. **Stocks:** Soft black rubber. **Sights:** Serrated ramp front, notch rear. **Features:** Heavy, solid barrel rib, ejector shroud. Available with porting, concealed hammer. Introduced 1998. Imported by Taurus International.

Price: Blue, regular or concealed hammer ... $355.00
Price: Stainless, regular or concealed hammer $402.00
Price: Blue, ported $373.00
Price: Stainless, ported $420.00
Price: Blue, concealed hammer, ported $373.00
Price: Stainless, concealed hammer, ported .. $420.00

Taurus Model 415Ti, 445Ti, 450Ti, 617Ti Revolvers

Similar to the Model 617 except has titanium frame, cylinder, and ported barrel with stainless steel liner; yoke detent and extended ejector rod; +P rated; ridged Ribber grips. Available in Bright and Matte Spectrum Blue, Matte Spectrum Gold, and Stealth Gray. Introduced 1999. Imported by Taurus International.

Price: Model 617Ti, (357 Mag., 7-shot, 19.9 oz.) $599.00
Price: Model 415Ti (41 Mag., 5-shot, 20.9 oz.) $599.00
Price: Model 450Ti (45 Colt, 5-shot, 19.2 oz.) $599.00
Price: Model 445Ti (44 Spec., 5-shot, 19.8 oz.) $599.00

Taurus Model 941

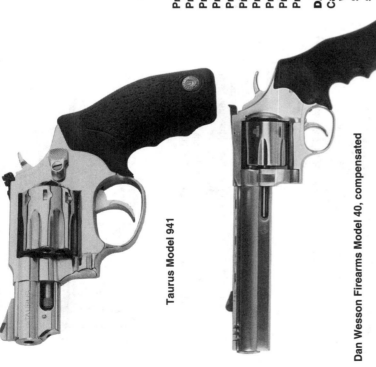

Dan Wesson Firearms Model 40, compensated

**Dan Wesson Firearms
Model 445 Supermag**

Price: Blue, 4"		$702.00
Price: Blue, 6"		$749.00
Price: Blue, 8"		$795.00
Price: Blue, 10"		$858.00
Price: Stainless, 4"		$834.00
Price: Stainless, 6"		$892.00
Price: Stainless, 8" slotted		$1,024.00
Price: Stainless, 10"		$998.00
Price: 4", 6", 8" Compensated, blue		$749.00 to $885.00
Price: As above, stainless		$893.00 to $1,061.00

DAN WESSON FIREARMS MODEL 22 REVOLVER

Caliber: 22 LR, 22 WMR, 6-shot. **Barrel:** 2-1/2", 4", 6", 8"; interchangeable. **Weight:** 36 oz. (2-1/2"), 44 oz. (6"). **Length:** 9-1/4" overall (4" barrel). **Stocks:** Checkered; undercover, service or over-size target. **Sights:** 1/8" serrated, interchangeable front, white outline rear adjustable for windage and elevation. **Features:** Built on the same frame as the Wesson 357; smooth, wide trigger with over-travel adjustment, wide spur hammer, with short double-action travel. Available in Brite blue or stainless steel. Reintroduced 1997. Contact Dan Wesson Firearms for complete price list.

Price: 2-1/2" bbl., blue		$489.00
Price: As above, stainless		$509.00
Price: With 4", vent heavy, blue		$509.00
Price: As above, stainless		$539.00
Price: Blue Pistol Pac, 22 LR		$1,199.00

Dan Wesson Firearms Model 414, 445 SuperMag Revolvers

Similar size and weight as the Model 40 revolvers. Chambered for the 445 SuperMag cartridge, a longer version of the 44 Magnum and 414 SuperMag. Barrel lengths of 4", 6", 8", 10". Contact maker for complete price list. Reintroduced 1997. Made in the U.S. by Dan Wesson Firearms.

Price: 4", vent heavy, blue		$797.00
Price: As above, stainless		$829.00
Price: 8", vent heavy, blue		$899.00
Price: As above, stainless		$929.00
Price: 10", vent heavy, blue		$959.00
Price: As above, stainless		$995.00
Price: 8", vent slotted, blue		$987.00
Price: As above, stainless		$1,134.00
Price: 10", vent slotted, blue		$1,195.00
Price: As above, stainless		$1,285.00
Price: 4", 6", 8" Compensated, blue		$859.00 to $979.00
Price: As above, stainless		$899.00 to $995.00

DAN WESSON FIREARMS MODEL 15 & 32 REVOLVERS

Caliber: 32-20, 32 H&R Mag. (Model 32), 357 Mag. (Model 15). **Barrel:** 2-1/2", 4", 6", 8" (M32), 2-1/2", 4", 6", 8", 10" (M15); vent heavy. **Weight:** 36 oz. (2-1/2" barrel). **Length:** 9-1/4" overall (4" barrel). **Stocks:** Checkered, interchangeable. **Sights:** 1/8" serrated front, fully adjustable rear. **Features:** New Generation Series. Interchangeable barrels; wide, smooth trigger, wide hammer spur; short double-action travel. Available in blue or stainless. Reintroduced 1997. Made in U.S. by Dan Wesson Firearms. Contact maker for full list of models.

Price: Model 15, blue, 2-1/2"		$489.00
Price: Model 15, blue, 8"		$569.00

TAURUS MODEL 941 REVOLVER

Caliber: 22 WMR, 8-shot. **Barrel:** 2", 4", 5". **Weight:** 27.5 oz. (4" barrel). **Length:** NA. **Stocks:** Soft black rubber. **Sights:** Serrated ramp front, rear adjustable for windage and elevation. **Features:** Solid rib heavy barrel with full-length ejector rod shroud. Blue or stainless steel. Introduced 1992. Imported by Taurus International.

Price: Blue		$331.00
Price: Stainless		$384.00
Price: Model 941 Ultra Lite, blue, 2", fixed sight, weighs 8.5 oz.		$366.00
Price: As above, stainless		$419.00

DAN WESSON FIREARMS MODEL 22 SILHOUETTE REVOLVER

Caliber: 22 LR, 6-shot. **Barrel:** 10"; regular vent or vent heavy. **Weight:** 53 oz. **Stocks:** Combat style. **Sights:** Patridge-style front, .080" narrow notch rear. **Features:** Single action only. Available in blue or stainless. Reintroduced 1997. Made in U.S. by Dan Wesson Firearms.

Price: Blue, regular vent		$474.00
Price: Blue, vent heavy		$492.00
Price: Stainless, regular vent		$504.00
Price: Stainless, vent heavy		$532.00

DAN WESSON FIREARMS MODEL 322/7322 TARGET REVOLVER

Caliber: 32-20, 6-shot. **Barrel:** 2.5", 4", 6", 8", standard vent, vent heavy. **Weight:** 43 oz. (6" VH). **Length:** 11.25" overall. **Stocks:** Checkered walnut. **Sights:** Red ramp interchangeable front, fully adjustable rear. **Features:** Bright blue or stainless. Reintroduced 1997. Made in U.S. by Dan Wesson Firearms.

Price: 6", vent heavy, blue		$619.00
Price: 6", vent heavy, stainless		$659.00
Price: 8", vent heavy, blue		$649.00
Price: 8", vent heavy, stainless		$699.00

DAN WESSON FIREARMS MODEL 40 SILHOUETTE

Caliber: 357 Maximum, 6-shot. **Barrel:** 4", 6", 8", 10". **Weight:** 64 oz. (8" bbl.). **Length:** 14.3" overall (8" bbl.). **Stocks:** Smooth walnut, target-style. **Sights:** 1/8" serrated front, fully adjustable rear. **Features:** Meets criteria for IHMSA competition with 8" slotted barrel. Blue or stainless steel. Made in U.S. by Dan Wesson Firearms.

Dan Wesson Firearms Silhouette

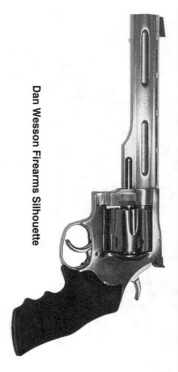

Dan Wesson Firearms Super Ram Silhouette

Price: Model 15, stainless, 4" $539.00
Price: Model 15, stainless, 6" $569.00
Price: Model 15, blue, compensated $579.00
Price: Model 15, stainless, compensated .... $619.00 to $699.00
Price: Model 32, blue, 4" $589.00
Price: Model 32, blue, 8" $649.00
Price: Model 32, stainless, 2-1/2" $589.00
Price: Model 32, stainless, 6" $659.00

DAN WESSON FIREARMS MODEL 41V, 44V, 45V REVOLVERS
Caliber: 41 Mag., 44 Mag., 45 Colt, 6-shot. **Barrel:** 4", 6", 8", 10"; interchangeable; 4", 6", 8" Compensated. **Weight:** 48 oz. (4"). **Length:** 12" overall (6" bbl.) **Stocks:** Smooth. **Sights:** 1/8" serrated front, white outline rear adjustable for windage and elevation. **Features:** Available in blue or stainless steel. Smooth, wide trigger with adjustable over-travel; wide hammer spur. Available in Pistol Pac set also. Reintroduced 1997. Contact Dan Wesson Firearms for complete price list.
Price: 41 Mag., 4", vent heavy $579.00
Price: As above except in stainless $599.00
Price: 44 Mag., 4", blue $579.00
Price: As above except in stainless $599.00
Price: 45 Colt, 4", vent heavy $599.00
Price: As above except in stainless $619.00
Price: Model 41, 44, 45, blue, 4", 6", 8" compensated .... $633.00 to $727.00
Price: As above in stainless .... $752.00 to $868.00

DAN WESSON FIREARMS MODEL 360 REVOLVER
Caliber: 357 Mag. **Barrel:** 4", 6", 8", 10", vent heavy. **Weight:** 64 oz. (8" barrel). **Length:** NA. **Stocks:** Hogue rubber finger groove. **Sights:** Interchangeable ramp or Patridge front, fully adjustable rear. **Features:** New Generation Large Frame Series. Interchangeable barrels and grips; smooth trigger, wide hammer spur. Blue or stainless. Introduced 1999. Made in U.S. by Dan Wesson Firearms.
Price: Blue, from $639.00
Price: Stainless, from $669.00

DAN WESSON FIREARMS MODEL 460 REVOLVER
Caliber: 45 ACP and 460 Rowland. **Barrel:** 4", 6", 8", 10", vent heavy. **Weight:** 49 oz. (4" barrel). **Length:** NA. **Stocks:** Hogue rubber finger groove; interchangeable. **Sights:** Interchangeable ramp or Patridge front, fully adjustable rear. **Features:** New Generation Large Frame Series. Shoots 45 ACP and 460 Rowland. Interchangeable barrels and grips. Available with non-fluted cylinder and Slotted Lightweight barrel shroud. Introduced 1999. Made in U.S. by Dan Wesson Firearms.
Price: .... NA

DAN WESSON FIREARMS STANDARD SILHOUETTE REVOLVER
Caliber: 357 SuperMag/Maxi, 41 Mag., 414 SuperMag, 445 SuperMag. **Barrel:** 8", 10". **Weight:** 64 oz. (8" barrel). **Length:** 14.3" overall (8" barrel). **Stocks:** Hogue rubber finger groove; interchangeable. **Sights:** Patridge front, fully adjustable rear. **Features:** Interchangeable barrels and grips; fluted or non-fluted cylinder; blue or stainless. Introduced 1999. Made in U.S. by Dan Wesson Firearms.
Price: 357 SuperMag/Maxi, 8", blue or stainless $949.00
Price: 41 Mag., 10", blue or stainless $229.00
Price: 414 SuperMag, 8", blue or stainless $949.00
Price: 445 SuperMag, 8", blue or stainless $949.00

Dan Wesson Firearms Super Ram Silhouette Revolver
Similar to the Standard Silhouette except has 10 land and groove Laser Coat barrel, Bo-Mar target sights with hooded front, and special laser engraving. Fluted or non-fluted cylinder. Introduced 1999. Made in U.S. by Dan Wesson Firearms.
Price: 357 SuperMag/Maxi, 414 SuperMag, 445 SuperMag, 8", blue or stainless $1,195.00
Price: 41 Magnum, 44 Magnum, 8", blue or stainless $1,099.00
Price: 41 Magnum, 44 Magnum, 10", blue or stainless $1,139.00

HANDGUNS — SINGLE ACTION REVOLVERS

Both classic six-shooters and modern adaptations for hunting and sport.

American Frontier 1871-1872 Open-Top

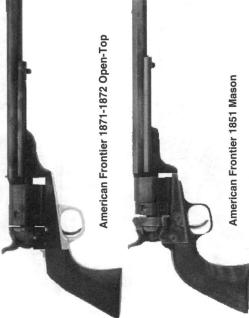

American Frontier 1851 Mason

American Western Arms Peacekeeper

Century Model 100

AMERICAN FRONTIER 1851 NAVY CONVERSION

Caliber: 38, 44. **Barrel:** 5-1/2", 7-1/2", octagon. **Weight:** NA. **Length:** NA. **Stocks:** Varnished walnut, Navy size. **Sights:** Blade front, fixed rear. **Features:** Shoots metallic cartridge ammunition. Non-rebated cylinder; blued steel backstrap and trigger guard; color case-hardened hammer, trigger, ramrod, plunger; no ejector rod assembly. Introduced 1996.
Price: $795.00

AMERICAN FRONTIER 1871-1872 OPEN-TOP REVOLVERS

Caliber: 38, 44. **Barrel:** 5-1/2", 7-1/2", 8" round. **Weight:** NA. **Length:** NA. **Stocks:** Varnished walnut. **Sights:** Blade front, fixed rear. **Features:** Reproduction of the early cartridge conversions from percussion. Made for metallic cartridges. High polish blued steel, silver-plated brass backstrap and trigger guard, color case-hardened hammer; straight non-rebated cylinder with or without ejector assembly. Rebated cylinder; available with naval engagement engraving; stamped with original patent dates. Does not have conversion breechplate.
Price: $795.00

AMERICAN FRONTIER RICHARDS 1860 ARMY

Caliber: 38, 44. **Barrel:** 5-1/2", 7-1/2", 8" round. **Weight:** NA. **Length:** NA. **Stocks:** Varnished walnut, Army size. **Sights:** Blade front, fixed rear. **Features:** Shoots metallic cartridge ammunition. Rebated cylinder; high-polish blue including backstrap; silver-plated trigger guard; color case-hardened hammer and trigger. Introduced 1996.
Price: $795.00

American Frontier 1851 Navy Richards & Mason Conversion
Similar to the 1851 Navy Conversion except has Mason ejector assembly. Introduced 1996. Imported from Italy by American Frontier Firearms Mfg.
Price: $695.00

AMERICAN WESTERN ARMS LONGHORN REVOLVERS

Caliber: 32-20, 38/357 Magnum, 44/40, 45 Colt. **Barrel:** 3-1/2", 4", 4-3/4", 5-1/2", 7-1/2", 10", 12". **Weight:** NA. **Grips:** One-piece walnut. **Sights:** Blade front. **Features:** Color case-hardened frame; precision-broached steel barrel; exact first-generation cylinder pin and bushing; historically correct trigger-guard configuration; period-correct checkered hammer; 3-1/2 lb. trigger pull. Introduced 2000. From American Western Arms Inc.

Price: Longhorn SSA $395.00
Price: Longhorn Bisley $425.00
Price: Longhorn Sheriff (3" bbl. only) $425.00
Price: Longhorn (bright nickel finish) $549.00
Price: Longhorn Model buntline (10" or 12" bbl.) $425.00

AMERICAN WESTERN ARMS PEACEKEEPER REVOLVERS

Caliber: 32-20, 38/357 Magnum, 44/40, 45 Colt. **Barrel:** 3-1/2", 4", 4-3/4", 5-1/2", 7-1/2", 10", 12". **Weight:** NA. **Length:** NA. **Grips:** Hard rubber.

Sights: Blade front. **Features:** Historically correct first-generation Single Action Army replica. Bone/charcoal color case-hardened frame; correct first-generation hammer, firing pin, cylinder pin, bushing and enlarged cylinder flutes; hand-checkered hammer; hammer-forged steel barrel; factory-tuned action; 3-1/2 lb. trigger pull. Introduced 2000. From American Western Arms Inc.

Price: Peacekeeper Model SSA $750.00
Price: Peacekeeper Sheriff.................................... $795.00
Price: Peacekeeper Birds head $795.00
Price: Peacekeeper Thunderer $795.00
Price: Peacekeeper Buntline (10" or 12" bbl.) $795.00
Price: Peacekeeper (nickel finish) $850.00
Price: Peacekeeper (nickel finish, "D" engraved) $1,450.00

CENTURY GUN DIST. MODEL 100 SINGLE-ACTION

Caliber: 30-30, 375 Win., 444 Marlin, 45-70, 50-70. **Barrel:** 6-1/2" (standard), 8", 10". **Weight:** 6 lbs. (loaded). **Length:** 15" overall (8" bbl.). **Stocks:** Smooth walnut. **Sights:** Ramp front, Millett adjustable square notch rear. **Features:** Highly polished high tensile strength manganese bronze frame, blue cylinder and barrel; coil spring trigger mechanism. Contact maker for full price information. Introduced 1975. Made in U.S. From Century Gun Dist., Inc.
Price: 6-1/2" barrel, 45-70 .... $2,000.00

CIMARRON U.S. CAVALRY MODEL SINGLE-ACTION

Caliber: 45 Colt. **Barrel:** 7-1/2". **Weight:** 42 oz. **Length:** 13-1/2" overall. **Stocks:** Walnut. **Sights:** Fixed. **Features:** Has "A.P. Casey" markings; "U.S." plus patent dates on frame, serial number on backstrap, trigger guard, frame and cylinder; "APC" cartouche on left grip; color case-hardened frame and hammer, rest charcoal blue. Exact copy of the original. Imported by Cimarron F.A. Co.
Price: $499.00

Cimarron Rough Rider Artillery Model Single-Action
Similar to the U.S. Cavalry model except has 5-1/2" barrel, weighs 39 oz., and is 11-1/2" overall. U.S. markings and cartouche, case-hardened frame and hammer; 45 Colt only.
Price: $499.00

HANDGUNS — SINGLE ACTION REVOLVERS

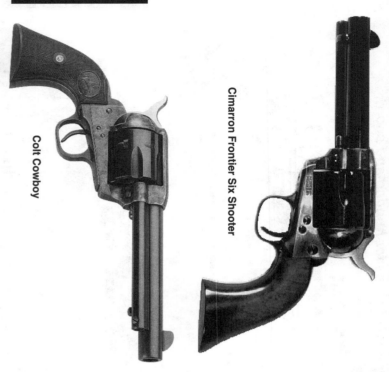

Colt Cowboy

Cimarron Frontier Six Shooter

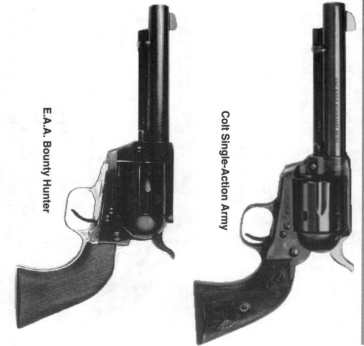

E.A.A. Bounty Hunter

Colt Single-Action Army

CIMARRON 1873 FRONTIER SIX SHOOTER

Caliber: 38 WCF, 357 Mag., 44 WCF, 44 Spec., 45 Colt. **Barrel:** 4-3/4", 5-1/2", 7-1/2". **Weight:** 39 oz. **Length:** 10" overall (4" barrel). **Stocks:** Walnut. **Sights:** Blade front, fixed or adjustable rear. **Features:** Uses "old model" blackpowder frame with "Bullseye" ejector or New Model frame. Imported by Cimarron F.A. Co.

Price: 4-3/4" barrel $469.00
Price: 5-1/2" barrel $469.00
Price: 7-1/2" barrel $469.00

Cimarron Bisley Model Single-Action Revolvers

Similar to the 1873 Frontier Six Shooter except has special grip frame and trigger guard, knurled wide-spur hammer, curved trigger. Available in 357 Mag., 44 WCF, 45 Schofield, 45 Colt. Introduced 1999. Imported by Cimarron F.A. Co.

Price: $499.00

Cimarron Flat Top Single-Action Revolvers

Similar to the 1873 Frontier Six Shooter except has flat top strap with windage-adjustable rear sight, elevation-adjustable front sight. Available in 357 Mag., 44 WCF, 45 Schofield, 45 Colt; 4-3/4", 5-1/2", 7-1/2" barrel. Introduced 1999. Imported by Cimarron F.A. Co.

Price: $479.00

Cimarron Bisley Flat Top Revolver

Similar to the Flat Top revolver except has special grip frame and trigger guard, wide spur hammer, curved trigger. Introduced 1999. Imported by Cimarron F.A. Co.

Price: $509.00

CIMARRON THUNDERER REVOLVER

Caliber: 357 Mag., 44 WCF, 44 Spec., 45 Colt, 6-shot. **Barrel:** 3-1/2", 4-3/4", 5-1/2", 7-1/2", with ejector. **Weight:** 38 oz. (3-1/2" barrel). **Length:** NA. **Stocks:** Smooth walnut. **Sights:** Blade front, notch rear. **Features:** Thunderer grip; color case-hardened frame with balance blued. Introduced 1993. Imported by Cimarron F.A. Co.

Price: 3-1/2", 4-3/4", smooth grips $489.00
Price: As above, checkered grips $524.00
Price: 5-1/2", 7-1/2", smooth grips $529.00
Price: As above, checkered grips $564.00

CIMARRON 1872 OPEN-TOP REVOLVER

Caliber: 38 Spec., 38 Colt, 44 Colt, 44 Russian, 45 Schofield, 45 Colt. **Barrel:** 7-1/2". **Weight:** NA. **Length:** NA. **Stocks:** Smooth walnut. **Sights:** Blade front, fixed rear. **Features:** Replica of the original production. Color case-hardened frame, rest blued, including grip frame. Introduced 1999. Imported from Italy by Cimarron F.A. Co.

Price: $579.00

COLT COWBOY SINGLE-ACTION REVOLVER

Caliber: 45 Colt, 6-shot. **Barrel:** 5-1/2". **Weight:** 42 oz. **Stocks:** Black composition, first generation style. **Sights:** Blade front, notch rear. **Features:** Dimensional replica of Colt's original Peacemaker with medium-size color case-hardened frame; transfer bar safety system; half-cock loading. Introduced 1998. Made in U.S. by Colt's Mfg. Co.

Price: About $599.00

COLT SINGLE-ACTION ARMY REVOLVER

Caliber: 44-40, 45 Colt, 6-shot. **Barrel:** 4-3/4", 5-1/2", 7-1/2". **Weight:** 40 oz. (4-3/4" barrel). **Length:** 10-1/4" overall (4-3/4" barrel). **Stocks:** Black Eagle composite. **Sights:** Blade front, notch rear. **Features:** Available in full nickel finish with nickel grip medallions, or Royal Blue with color case-hardened frame, gold grip medallions. Reintroduced 1992.

Price: $1,900.00

E.A.A. BOUNTY HUNTER SA REVOLVERS

Caliber: 22 LR/22 WMR, 357 Mag., 44 Mag., 45 Colt, 6-shot. **Barrel:** 4-1/2", 7-1/2". **Weight:** 2.5 lbs. **Length:** 11" overall (4-5/8" barrel). **Stocks:** Smooth walnut. **Sights:** Blade front, grooved topstrap rear. **Features:** Transfer bar safety; three position hammer; hammer forged barrel. Introduced 1992. Imported by European American Armory.

Price: Blue or case-hardened $280.00
Price: Nickel $298.00
Price: 22LR/22WMR, blue $187.20
Price: As above, nickel $204.36

EMF HARTFORD SINGLE-ACTION REVOLVERS

Caliber: 22 LR, 357 Mag., 32-20, 38-40, 44-40, 44 Spec., 45 Colt. **Barrel:** 4-3/4", 5-1/2", 7-1/2". **Weight:** 45 oz. **Length:** 13" overall (7-1/2" barrel). **Stocks:** Smooth walnut. **Sights:** Blade front, fixed rear. **Features:** Identical to the original Colts with inspector cartouche on left grip, original patent dates and U.S. markings. All major parts serial numbered using original numbering. Bullseye ejector head and color case-hardening on frame and hammer. Introduced 1990. From E.M.F.

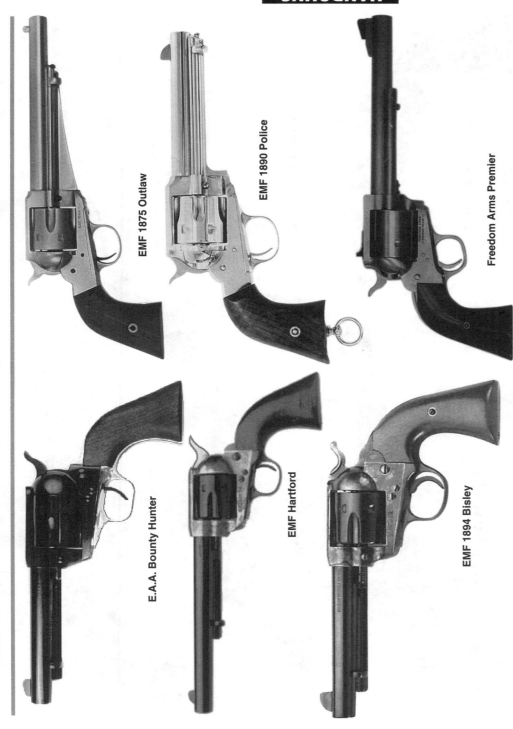

EMF 1875 Outlaw

EMF 1890 Police

Freedom Arms Premier

E.A.A. Bounty Hunter

EMF Hartford

EMF 1894 Bisley

Price: $600.00
Price: Cavalry or Artillery $655.00
Price: Nickel plated $725.00
Price: Engraved, nickel plated $840.00

EMF 1894 Bisley Revolver

Similar to the Hartford single-action revolver except has special grip frame and trigger guard, wide spur hammer; available in 45 Colt only, 5-1/2" or 7-1/2" barrel. Introduced 1995. Imported by E.M.F.

Price: Blue $680.00
Price: Nickel $805.00

EMF Hartford Pinkerton Single-Action Revolver

Same as the regular Hartford except has 4" barrel with ejector tube and birds head grip. Calibers 32-20, 38-40, 44-40, 44 Special, 45 Colt. Introduced 1997. Imported by E.M.F.

Price: $475.00

EMF Hartford Express Single-Action Revolver

Same as the regular Hartford model except uses grip of the Colt Lightning revolver. Barrel lengths of 4", 4-3/4", 5-1/2". Introduced 1997. Imported by E.M.F.

Price: $475.00

EMF 1875 OUTLAW REVOLVER

Caliber: 357 Mag., 44-40, 45 Colt. **Barrel:** 7-1/2". **Weight:** 46 oz. **Length:** 13-1/2" overall. **Stocks:** Smooth walnut. **Sights:** Blade front, fixed groove rear. **Features:** Authentic copy of 1875 Remington with firing pin in hammer; color case-hardened frame, blue cylinder, barrel, steel backstrap and brass trigger guard. Also available in nickel, factory engraved. Imported by E.M.F.

Price: All calibers $465.00
Price: Nickel $550.00
Price: Engraved $600.00
Price: Engraved nickel $710.00

EMF 1890 Police Revolver

Similar to the 1875 Outlaw except has 5-1/2" barrel, weighs 40 oz., with 12-1/2" overall length. Has lanyard ring in butt. No web under barrel. Calibers 357, 44-40, 45 Colt. Imported by E.M.F.

Price: All calibers $470.00
Price: Nickel $560.00
Price: Engraved $620.00
Price: Engraved nickel $725.00

FREEDOM ARMS MODEL 83 454 SINGLE-ACTION REVOLVER

Caliber: 357 Mag., 41 Rem. Mag., 44 Rem. Mag., 454 Casull, 50 AE, 5-shot. **Barrel:** 4-3/4", 6", 7-1/2", 10". **Weight:** 50 oz. **Length:** 14" overall (7-1/2" bbl.). **Stocks:** Impregnated hardwood (Premier grade), or Pachmayr (Field Grade). **Sights:** Blade front, notch or adjustable rear. **Features:** All stainless steel construction; sliding bar safety system. Lifetime warranty. Made in U.S. by Freedom Arms, Inc.

Price: Premier Grade, 454 Casull, 50 AE, adj. sight $1,958.00
Price: Premier Grade, 454 Casull, fixed sight $1,894.00
Price: Field Grade, 454 Casull, 50 AE, adj. sight $1,519.00
Price: Field Grade, 454 Casull, fixed sight $1,484.00
Price: Premier Grade, 357 Mag., 41 Rem. Mag., 44 Rem. Mag., adj. sight $1,882.00
Price: Premier Grade, 44 Rem. Mag., fixed sight $1,816.00
Price: Field Grade, 357 Mag., 41 Rem. Mag., 44 Rem. Mag., adj. sight $1,442.00

HANDGUNS — SINGLE ACTION REVOLVERS

Freedom Arms Model 83 353 Revolver
Made on the Model 83 frame. Chambered for 357 Magnum with 5-shot cylinder. 4-3/4", 6", 7-1/2" or 9" barrel. Weighs 59 oz. with 7-1/2" barrel. Field grade model has adjustable sights, matte finish, Pachmayr grips. Silhouette has 9" barrel, adjustable front sight blade with hood, Iron Sight Gun Works Silhouette adjustable rear, Pachmayr grips, trigger over-travel adjustment screw. All stainless steel. Introduced 1992.
Price: Field Grade **$1,340.00**
Price: Premier Grade (brushed finish, impregnated hardwood grips, Premier Grade sights) **$1,760.00**
Price: Silhouette (9", 357 Mag., 10", 44 Mag.) **$1,448.00**

Freedom Arms Model 83 654 Revolver
Made on the Model 83 frame. Chambered for 41 Magnum with 5-shot cylinder. Introduced 1998. Made in U.S. by Freedom Arms.
Price: Field Grade, adjustable sights **$1,400.00**
Price: Premier Grade, adjustable sights **$1,820.00**
Price: Silhouette **$1,448.00**

FREEDOM ARMS MODEL 83 475 LINEBAUGH REVOLVER
Caliber: 475 Linebaugh, 5-shot. **Barrel:** 4.75", 6", 7.5". **Weight:** NA. **Length:** NA. **Stocks:** Impregnated hardwood (Premier Grade) or Pachmayr (Field Grade). **Sights:** Removable ramp front, fully adjustable notch rear. **Features:** All stainless steel construction with brushed finish (Premier Grade) or matte finish (Field Grade); patented slide bar safety. Introduced 1999. Made in U.S. by Freedom Arms.
Price: Premier Grade **$1,958.00**
Price: Field Grade **$1,519.00**

Freedom Arms Model 83 555 Revolver
Made on the Model 83 frame. Chambered for the 50 A.E. (Action Express) cartridge. Offered in Premier and Field Grades with adjustable sights, 4-3/4", 6", 7-1/2" or 10" barrel. Introduced 1994. Made in U.S. by

Freedom Arms Model 555

Freedom Arms Model 83 475 Linebaugh

Freedom Arms Model 353

IAR Model 1873 Six Shooter

Heritage Rough Rider

Freedom Arms Model 252 Varmint

Freedom Arms, Inc.
Price: Premier Grade **$1,820.00**
Price: Field Grade **$1,400.00**

FREEDOM ARMS MODEL 97 MID FRAME REVOLVER
Caliber: 357 Mag., 6-shot cylinder; 45 Colt, 5-shot. **Barrel:** 5-1/2", 7-1/2". **Weight:** 40 oz. (5-1/2" barrel). **Length:** 10-3/4"overall (5-1/2" barrel). **Stocks:** Impregnated hardwood or black micanta optional. **Sights:** Blade on ramp front, fixed or fully adjustable rear. **Features:** Made of stainless steel; brushed finish. Introduced 1997. Made in U.S. by Freedom Arms.
Price: Adjustable sight **$1,492.00**
Price: Fixed sight **$1,500.00**

FREEDOM ARMS MODEL 252 VARMINT CLASS REVOLVER
Caliber: 22 LR, 5-shot. **Barrel:** 5.125", 7.5". **Weight:** 58 oz. (7.5" barrel). **Length:** NA. **Stocks:** Black and green laminated hardwood. **Sights:** Brass bead express front, express rear with shallow V-notch. **Features:** All stainless steel construction. Dual firing pins; lightened hammer; pre-set trigger stop. Built on Model 83 frame and accepts Model 83 Freedom Arms sights and/or scope mounts. Introduced 1991. Made in U.S. by Freedom Arms.
Price: **$1,527.00**
Price: Extra fitted 22 WMR cylinder **$264.00**

HERITAGE ROUGH RIDER REVOLVER
Caliber: 22 LR, 22 LR/22 WMR combo, 6-shot. **Barrel:** 2-3/4", 3-1/2", 4-3/4", 6-1/2", 9". **Weight:** 31 to 38 oz. **Length:** NA. **Stocks:** Exotic hardwood. **Sights:** Blade front, fixed rear. Adjustable sight on 6-1/2" only. **Features:** Hammer block safety. High polish blue or nickel finish. Introduced 1993. Made in U.S. by Heritage Mfg., Inc.
Price: . . . . **$119.95 to $174.95**
Price: 2-3/4", 3-1/2", 4-3/4" bird's-head grip . . . . **$139.95 to $174.95**

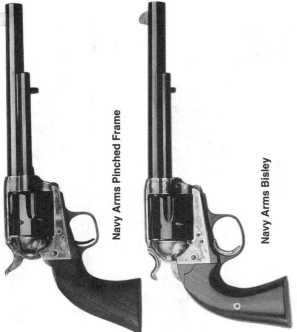

Navy Arms Pinched Frame

Navy Arms Bisley

MAGNUM RESEARCH BFR SINGLE-ACTION REVOLVER

Caliber: 22 Hornet, 45 Colt +P, 454 Casull, 50 A.E. (Little Max, standard cylinder). **Barrel:** 7-1/2", 10". **Weight:** 4 lbs. **Length:** 11" overall with 7-1/2" barrel. **Stocks:** Uncle Mike's checkered rubber. **Sights:** Orange blade on ramp front, fully adjustable rear. **Features:** Stainless steel construction. Optional pearl and finger-groove grips available. Introduced 1997. Made in U.S. From Magnum Research, Inc.

Price: $999.00

MAGNUM RESEARCH LITTLE MAX REVOLVER

Caliber: 22 Hornet, 45 Colt, 454 Casull, 50 A.E. **Barrel:** 6-1/2", 7-1/2", 10". **Weight:** 45 oz. **Length:** 13" overall (7-1/2" barrel). **Stocks:** Rubber. **Sights:** Ramp front, adjustable rear. **Features:** Single action; stainless steel construction. Announced 1998. Made in U.S. From Magnum Research.

Price: $999.00
Price: Maxline model (7-1/2", 10", 45 Colt, 45-70, 444 Marlin) .. $999.00

NAVY ARMS FLAT TOP TARGET MODEL REVOLVER

Caliber: 45 Colt, 6-shot cylinder. **Barrel:** 7-1/2". **Weight:** 40 oz. **Length:** 13-1/4" overall. **Stocks:** Smooth walnut. **Sights:** Spring-loaded German silver front, rear adjustable for windage. **Features:** Replica of Colt's Flat Top Frontier target revolver made from 1888 to 1896. Blue with color case-hardened frame. Introduced 1997. Imported by Navy Arms.

Price: $425.00

NAVY ARMS "PINCHED FRAME" SINGLE-ACTION REVOLVER

Caliber: 45 Colt, 6-shot. **Barrel:** 7-1/2". **Weight:** 37 oz. **Length:** 13" overall. **Stocks:** Smooth walnut **Sights:** German silver blade, notch rear. **Features:** Replica of Colt's original Peacemaker. Color case-hardened frame, hammer, rest charcoal blued. Introduced 1997. Imported by Navy Arms.

Price: $415.00

NAVY ARMS BISLEY MODEL SINGLE-ACTION REVOLVER

Caliber: 44-40 or 45 Colt, 6-shot cylinder. **Barrel:** 4-3/4", 5-1/2", 7-1/2". **Weight:** 40 oz. **Length:** 12-1/2" overall (7-1/2" barrel). **Stocks:** Smooth walnut. **Sights:** Blade front, notch rear. **Features:** Replica of Colt's Bisley Model. Polished blue finish, color case-hardened frame. Introduced 1997. Imported by Navy Arms.

Price: $405.00

Navy Arms Bisley Model Flat Top Target Revolver

Similar to the standard Bisley model except with flat top strap, 7-1/2" barrel only, and a spring-loaded German silver front sight blade, standing leaf rear sight adjustable for windage. Polished blue finish, color case-hardened frame. Introduced 1998. Imported by Navy Arms.

Price: $435.00

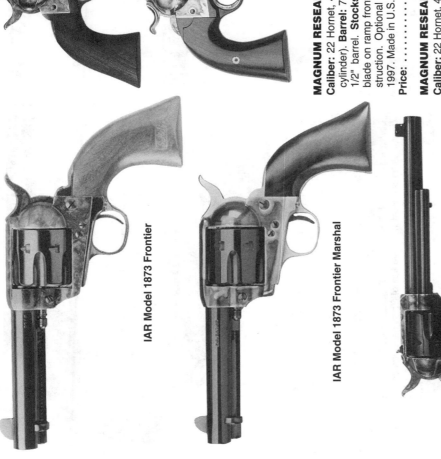

IAR Model 1873 Frontier

IAR Model 1873 Frontier Marshal

Navy Arms Flat Top

IAR MODEL 1873 SIX SHOOTER

Caliber: 22 LR/22 WMR combo. **Barrel:** 5-1/2". **Weight:** 36-1/2" oz. **Length:** 11-3/8" overall. **Stocks:** One-piece walnut. **Sights:** Blade front, notch rear. **Features:** A 3/4-scale reproduction. Color case-hardened frame, blued barrel. All-steel construction. Made by Uberti. Imported from Italy by IAR, Inc.

Price: $360.00

IAR MODEL 1873 FRONTIER REVOLVER

Caliber: 22 RL, 22 LR/22 WMR. **Barrel:** 4-3/4". **Weight:** 45 oz. **Length:** 10-1/2" overall. **Stocks:** One-piece walnut with inspector's cartouche. **Sights:** Blade front, notch rear. **Features:** Color case-hardened frame, blued barrel, black nickel-plated brass trigger guard and backstrap. Bright nickel and engraved versions available. Introduced 1997. Imported from Italy by IAR, Inc.

Price: $395.00
Price: Nickel-plated. $485.00
Price: 22 LR/22WMR combo $425.00

IAR MODEL 1873 FRONTIER MARSHAL

Caliber: 357 Mag., 45 Colt. **Barrel:** 4-3/4, 5-1/2, 7-1/2". **Weight:** 39 oz. **Length:** 10-1/2" overall. **Stocks:** One-piece walnut. **Sights:** Blade front, notch rear. **Features:** Bright brass trigger guard and backstrap, color case-hardened frame, blued barrel and cylinder. Introduced 1998. Imported from Italy by IAR, Inc.

Price: $395.00

HANDGUNS — SINGLE ACTION REVOLVERS

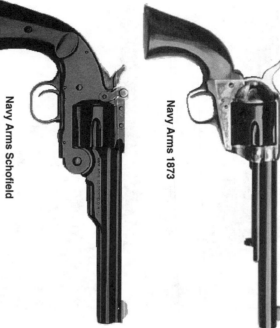

Navy Arms 1873

Navy Arms Schofield

North American Mini

Navy Arms New Model Russian

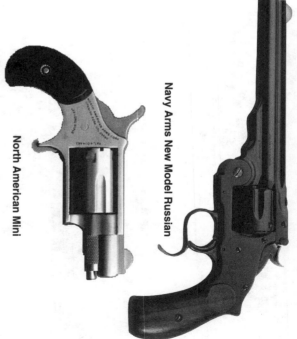

NAVY ARMS 1872 OPEN TOP REVOLVER

Caliber: 38 Spec., 6-shot. **Barrel:** 5-1/2" or 7-1/2". **Weight:** 2 lbs., 12 oz. **Length:** 11" or 13". **Stocks:** Smooth walnut. **Sights:** Blade front, notch rear. **Features:** Replica of Colt's first production cartridge "six shooter." Polished blue finish with color case hardened frame, silver plated trigger guard and backstrap Introduced 2000. Imported by Navy Arms.
Price: $390.00

NAVY ARMS 1873 SINGLE-ACTION REVOLVER

Caliber: 357 Mag., 44-40, 45 Colt, 6-shot cylinder. **Barrel:** 4-3/4", 5-1/2", 7-1/2". **Weight:** 36 oz. **Length:** 10-3/4" overall (5-1/2" barrel). **Stocks:** Smooth walnut. **Sights:** Blade front, notch rear. **Features:** Blue with color case-hardened frame. Introduced 1991. Imported by Navy Arms.
Price: 1873 U.S. Cavalry Model (7-1/2", 45 Colt, arsenal markings) $385.00
Price: 1895 U.S. Artillery Model (as above, 5-1/2" barrel) $455.00

NAVY ARMS SHOOTIST MODEL SINGLE-ACTION REVOLVER

Caliber: 357 Mag., 44-40, 45 Colt, 6-shot cylinder. **Barrel:** 4-3/4", 5-1/2", 7-1/2". **Weight:** 36 oz. **Length:** 11-1/4" overall (5-1/2" barrel). **Stocks:** Smooth walnut. **Sights:** Blade front, notch rear. **Features:** Replica of Colt's Single Action Army. Parts interchange with first and second generation Colts. Polished blue, color case-hardened frame. Introduced 1999. Imported by Navy Arms.
Price: $385.00

NAVY ARMS 1875 SCHOFIELD REVOLVER

Caliber: 44-40, 45 Colt, 6-shot cylinder. **Barrel:** 3-1/2", 5", 7". **Weight:** 39 oz. **Length:** 10-3/4" overall (5" barrel). **Stocks:** Smooth walnut. **Sights:** Blade front, notch rear. **Features:** Replica of Smith & Wesson Model 3 Schofield. Single-action, top-break with automatic ejection. Polished blue finish. Introduced 1994. Imported by Navy Arms.
Price: Hideout Model, 3-1/2" barrel $695.00
Price: Wells Fargo, 5" barrel $695.00
Price: U.S. Cavalry model, 7" barrel, military markings $695.00

Navy Arms Deluxe 1875 Schofield Revolver

Similar to standard Schofield except has hand-cut "A" engraving and gold inlays, charcoal blue finish. Available in either Wells Fargo (5" barrel) or Cavalry (7" barrel) model. Introduced 1999.
Price: $1,875.00

NAVY ARMS NEW MODEL RUSSIAN REVOLVER

Caliber: 44 Russian, 6-shot cylinder. **Barrel:** 6-1/2". **Weight:** 40 oz. **Length:** 12" overall. **Stocks:** Smooth walnut. **Sights:** Blade front, notch

rear. **Features:** Replica of the S&W Model 3 Russian Third Model revolver. Spur trigger guard, polished blue finish. Introduced 1999. Imported by Navy Arms.
Price: $745.00

NAVY ARMS 1851 NAVY CONVERSION REVOLVER

Caliber: 38 Spec., 38 Long Colt. **Barrel:** 5-1/2", 7-1/2". **Weight:** 44 oz. **Length:** 14" overall (7-1/2" barrel). **Stocks:** Smooth walnut. **Sights:** Bead front, notch rear. **Features:** Replica of Colt's cartridge conversion revolver. Polished blue finish with color case-hardened frame, silver plated trigger guard and backstrap. Introduced 1999. Imported by Navy Arms.
Price: $365.00

NAVY ARMS 1860 ARMY CONVERSION REVOLVER

Caliber: 38 Spec., 38 Long Colt. **Barrel:** 5-1/2", 7-1/2". **Weight:** 44 oz. **Length:** 13-1/2" overall (7-1/2" barrel). **Stocks:** Smooth walnut. **Sights:** Blade front, notch rear. **Features:** Replica of Colt's cartridge conversion revolver. Polished blue finish with color case-hardened frame, full-size 1860 Army grip with blued steel backstrap. Introduced 1999. Imported by Navy Arms.
Price: $365.00

NAVY ARMS 1861 NAVY CONVERSION REVOLVER

Caliber: 38 Spec., 38 Long Colt. **Barrel:** 5-1/2", 7-1/2". **Weight:** 44 oz. **Length:** 13-1/2" overall (7-1/2" barrel). **Stocks:** Smooth walnut. **Sights:** Blade front, notch rear. **Features:** Replica of Colt's cartridge conversion. Polished blue finish with color case-hardened frame, silver plated trigger guard and backstrap. Introduced 1999. Imported by Navy Arms.
Price: $365.00

NORTH AMERICAN MINI-REVOLVERS

Caliber: 22 Short, 22 LR, 22 WMR, 5-shot. **Barrel:** 1-1/8", 1-5/8". **Weight:** 4 to 6.6 oz. **Length:** 3-5/8" to 6-1/8" overall. **Stocks:** Laminated wood. **Sights:** Blade front, notch fixed rear. **Features:** All stainless steel construction. Polished satin and matte finish. Engraved models available. From North American Arms.
Price: 22 Short, 22 LR $176.00
Price: 22 WMR, 1-5/8" bbl. $194.00
Price: 22 WMR, 1-1/8" or 1-5/8" bbl. with extra 22 LR cylinder . . . $231.00

NORTH AMERICAN MINI-MASTER

Caliber: 22 LR, 22 WMR, 5-shot cylinder. **Barrel:** 4". **Weight:** 10.7 oz. **Length:** 7.75" overall. **Stocks:** Checkered hard black rubber. **Sights:** Blade front, white outline rear adjustable for elevation, or fixed. **Features:** Heavy vent barrel; full-size grips. Non-fluted cylinder. Introduced 1989.
Price: Adjustable sight, 22 WMR or 22 LR $299.00
Price: As above with extra WMR/LR cylinder $336.00
Price: Fixed sight, 22 WMR or 22 LR $281.00
Price: As above with extra WMR/LR cylinder $318.00

HANDGUNS — SINGLE ACTION REVOLVERS

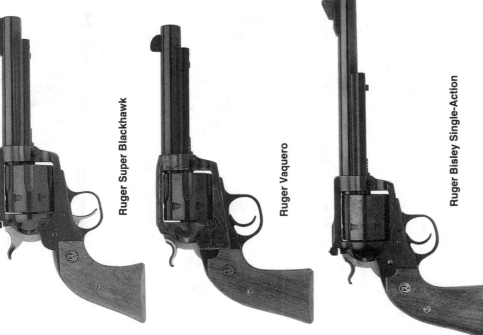

Ruger Super Blackhawk

Ruger Vaquero

Ruger Bisley Single-Action

North American Mini-Master

North American Black Widow

Ruger Blackhawk

North American Black Widow Revolver
Similar to the Mini-Master except has 2" heavy vent barrel. Built on the 22 WMR frame. Non-fluted cylinder, black rubber grips. Available with either Millett Low Profile fixed sights or Millett sight adjustable for elevation only. Overall length 5-7/8", weighs 8.8 oz. From North American Arms.
Price: Adjustable sight, 22 LR or 22 WMR **$269.00**
Price: As above with extra WMR/LR cylinder **$306.00**
Price: Fixed sight, 22 LR or 22 WMR **$251.00**
Price: As above with extra WMR/LR cylinder **$288.00**

RUGER NEW MODEL BLACKHAWK REVOLVER
Caliber: 30 Carbine, 357 Mag./38 Spec., 41 Mag., 45 Colt, 6-shot. **Barrel:** 4-5/8" or 5-1/2" either caliber; 7-1/2" (30 Carbine and 45 Colt). **Weight:** 42 oz. (6-1/2" bbl.). **Length:** 12-1/4" overall (5-1/2" bbl.). **Stocks:** American walnut. **Sights:** 1/8" ramp front, micro-click rear adjustable for windage and elevation. **Features:** Ruger transfer bar safety system, independent firing pin, hardened chrome-moly steel frame, music wire springs throughout. Comes with plastic lockable case and lock.
Price: Blue 30 Carbine, 7-1/2" (BN31) **$399.00**
Price: Blue, 357 Mag., 4-5/8", 6-1/2" (BN34, BN36) **$399.00**
Price: As above, stainless (KBN34, KBN36) **$489.00**
Price: Blue, 357 Mag./9mm Convertible, 4-5/8", 6-1/2" (BN34X, BN36X) **$449.00**
Price: Blue, 41 Mag., 4-5/8", 6-1/2" (BN41, BN42) **$399.00**
Price: Blue, 45 Colt, 4-5/8", 5-1/2", 7-1/2" (BN44, BN455, BN45) . **$399.00**
Price: Stainless, 45 Colt, 4-5/8", 7-1/2" (KBN44, KBN45) **$489.00**
Price: Blue, 45 Colt/45 ACP Convertible, 4-5/8", 5-1/2" (BN44X, BN455X) **$449.00**

RUGER NEW MODEL SUPER BLACKHAWK
Caliber: 44 Mag., 6-shot. Also fires 44 Spec. **Barrel:** 4-5/8", 5-1/2", 7-1/2", 10-1/2" bull. **Weight:** 48 oz. (7-1/2" bbl.), 51 oz. (10-1/2" bbl.). **Length:** 13-3/8" overall (7-1/2" bbl.). **Stocks:** American walnut. **Sights:** 1/8" ramp front, micro-click rear adjustable for windage and elevation. **Features:** Ruger transfer bar safety system, fluted or un-fluted cylinder, steel grip and cylinder frame, round or square back trigger guard, wide serrated trigger and wide spur hammer. Comes with plastic lockable case and lock.
Price: Blue, 4-5/8", 5-1/2", 7-1/2" (S458N, S45N, S47N) **$478.00**
Price: Blue, 10-1/2" bull barrel (S411N) **$485.00**
Price: Stainless, 4-5/8", 5-1/2", 7-1/2" (KS458N, KS45N, KS47N) . **$499.00**
Price: Stainless, 10-1/2" bull barrel (KS411N) **$505.00**

RUGER VAQUERO SINGLE-ACTION REVOLVER
Caliber: 357 Mag., 44-40, 44 Mag., 45 Colt, 6-shot. **Barrel:** 4-5/8", 5-1/2", 7-1/2". **Weight:** 41 oz. **Length:** 13-1/8" overall (7-1/2" barrel). **Stocks:** Smooth rosewood with Ruger medallion. **Sights:** Blade front, fixed notch rear. **Features:** Uses Ruger's patented transfer bar safety system and loading gate interlock with classic styling. Blued model has color case-hardened finish on the frame, the rest polished and blued. Stainless model has high-gloss polish. Introduced 1993. From Sturm, Ruger & Co.
Price: 357 Mag. BNV34 (4-5/8"), BNV35 (5-1/2") **$498.00**
Price: 357 Mag. KBNV34 (4-5/8"), KBNV35 (5-1/2") stainless . . . **$498.00**
Price: BNV44 (4-5/8"), BNV445 (5-1/2"), BNV45 (7-1/2"), blue . . **$498.00**
Price: KBNV44 (4-5/8"), KBNV455 (5-1/2"), KBNV45 (7-1/2"), stainless **$498.00**
Price: 45 Colt BNV455, all blue finish, 4-5/8" or 5-1/2" **$498.00**
Price: 45 Colt KBNV455, stainless, 5-1/2" **$498.00**

HANDGUNS — SINGLE ACTION REVOLVERS

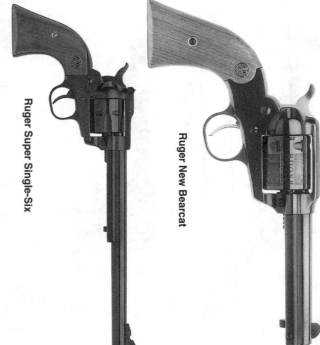

Ruger Super Single-Six

Ruger New Bearcat

Ruger Bisley-Vaquero Single-Action Revolver

Similar to the Vaquero except has Bisley-style hammer, grip and trigger and is available in 357 Magnum, 44 Magnum and 45 Colt only, with 4-5/8" or 5-1/2" barrel. Has smooth rosewood grips with Ruger medallion. Roll-engraved, unfluted cylinder. Introduced 1997. From Sturm, Ruger & Co.

Price: Color case-hardened frame, blue grip frame, barrel and cylinder, RBNV-475, RBNV-455 . . . . **$498.00**

Price: High-gloss stainless steel, KRBNV-475, KRBNV-455 . . . **$529.00**

Price: For simulated ivory grips add **$36.00**

Price: 44-40 BNV40 (4-5/8"), BNV405 (5-1/2"), BNV407 (7-1/2") **$498.00**

Price: 44-40 KBNV40 (4-5/8"), KBNV405 (5-1/2"), KBNV407 (7-1/2") stainless **$498.00**

RUGER NEW BEARCAT SINGLE-ACTION

Caliber: 22 LR, 6-shot. **Barrel:** 4". **Weight:** 24 oz. **Length:** 8-7/8" overall. **Stocks:** Smooth rosewood with Ruger medallion. **Sights:** Blade front, fixed notch rear. **Features:** Reintroduction of the Ruger Bearcat with slightly lengthened frame, Ruger patented transfer bar safety system. Available in blue only. Introduced 1993. Comes with plastic lockable case and lock. From Sturm, Ruger & Co.

Price: SBC4, blue **$347.00**

RUGER SINGLE-SIX AND SUPER SINGLE-SIX CONVERTIBLE

Caliber: 22 LR, 6-shot; 22 WMR in extra cylinder. **Barrel:** 4-5/8", 5-1/2", 6-1/2", 9-1/2" (6-groove). **Weight:** 35 oz. (6-1/2" bbl.). **Length:** 11-13/16" overall (6-1/2" bbl.). **Stocks:** Smooth American walnut. **Sights:** Improved Patridge front on ramp, fully adjustable rear protected by integral frame ribs (Super Single-Six); or fixed sight (Single Six). **Features:** Ruger transfer bar safety system, loading gate interlock, hardened chrome-moly steel frame, wide trigger, music wire springs throughout, independent firing pin.

Price: 4-5/8", 5-1/2", 6-1/2", 9-1/2" barrel, blue, adjustable sight NR4, NR6, NR9, NR5 . . . . **$352.00**

Price: 5-1/2", 6-1/2" bbl. only, stainless steel, adjustable sight KNR5, KNR6 . . . . **$436.00**

Price: 5-1/2", 6-1/2" barrel, blue fixed sights **$347.00**

Ruger Bisley Small Frame Revolver

Similar to the Single-Six except frame is styled after the classic Bisley "flat-top." Most mechanical parts are unchanged. Hammer is lower and smoothly curved with a deeply checkered spur. Trigger is strongly curved with a wide smooth surface. Longer grip frame designed with a hand-filling shape, and the trigger guard is a large oval. Adjustable dovetail rear sight; front sight base accepts interchangeable square blades of various heights and styles. Has an unfluted cylinder and roll engraving. Weighs

41 oz. Chambered for 22 LR, 6-1/2" barrel only. Comes with plastic lockable case and lock. Introduced 1985.

Price: RB-22AW **$402.00**

Ruger Bisley Single-Action Revolver

Similar to standard Blackhawk except the hammer is lower with a smooth-ly curved, deeply checkered wide spur. The trigger is strongly curved with a wide smooth surface. Longer grip frame has a hand-filling shape. Ad-justable rear sight, ramp-style front. Has an unfluted cylinder and roll en-graving, adjustable sights. Chambered for 357, 44 Mags. and 45 Colt; 7-1/2" barrel; overall length of 13"; weighs 48 oz. Comes with plastic lock-able case and lock. Introduced 1985.

Price: RB-35W, 357Mag, R3-44W, 44Mag, RB-45W, 45 Colt. . . **$498.00**

Traditions 1861 Navy

Traditions 1851 Navy

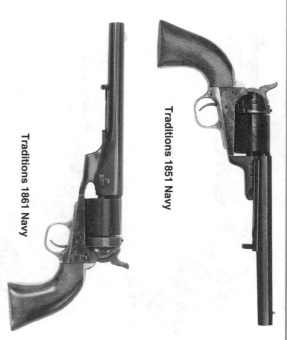

TRADITIONS 1851 NAVY CONVERSION REVOLVER

Caliber: 38 Spec. **Barrel:** 7-1/2". **Weight:** 40 oz. **Length:** 14-1/2" overall. **Stocks:** Smooth walnut. **Sights:** Post front, hammer-notch rear. **Features:** Steel frame, brass trigger guard. Introduced 1998. From Traditions.

Price: **$395.00**

TRADITIONS 1858 REMINGTON CONVERSION REVOLVER

Caliber: 38 Spec. **Barrel:** 7-1/2". **Weight:** 2 lbs., 8 oz. **Length:** 14-1/2" overall. **Stocks:** Smooth walnut. **Sights:** Post front, notch rear. **Features:** Replica of converted Remington. Blued steel grip frame and trigger guard. Introduced 1999. Imported by Traditions.

Price: **$425.00**

TRADITIONS 1860 ARMY CONVERSION REVOLVER

Caliber: 38 Spec. **Barrel:** 7-1/2". **Weight:** 44 oz. **Length:** 14-1/2" overall. **Stocks:** Smooth walnut. **Sights:** Blade front, notch rear. **Features:** Replica of Colt's conversion revolver. Polished blue finish with color case-hardened frame, full-size 1860 Army grip with blued steel backstrap. Intro-duced 1999. Imported by Traditions.

Price: **$410.00**

TRADITIONS 1861 NAVY CONVERSION REVOLVER

Caliber: 38 Spec. **Barrel:** 7-1/2". **Weight:** 44 oz. **Length:** 14-1/2" overall. **Stocks:** Smooth walnut. **Sights:** Blade front, fixed rear. **Features:** Rep-lica of Colt's cartridge conversion. Polished blue finish with color case-hardened frame, brass trigger guard and backstrap. Introduced 1999. Im-ported by Traditions.

Price: **$410.00**

TRADITIONS 1872 OPEN-TOP CONVERSION REVOLVER

Caliber: 38 Spec. **Barrel:** 8". **Weight:** 2 lbs. 8 oz. **Length:** 14-1/2" overall. **Stocks:** Smooth walnut. **Sights:** Blade front, fixed rear. **Features:** Repli-ca of the original production. Color case-hardened frame, rest blued, in-cluding grip frame. Introduced 1999. Imported from Italy by Traditions.

Price: **$410.00**

HANDGUNS — SINGLE ACTION REVOLVERS

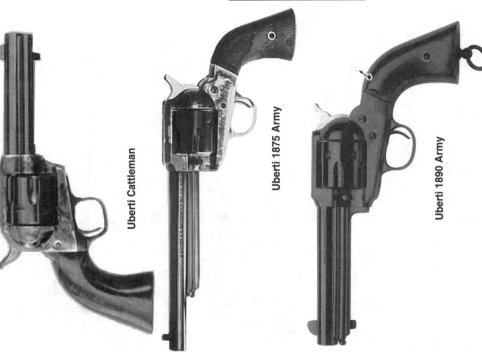

Uberti Cattleman

Uberti 1875 Army

Uberti 1890 Army

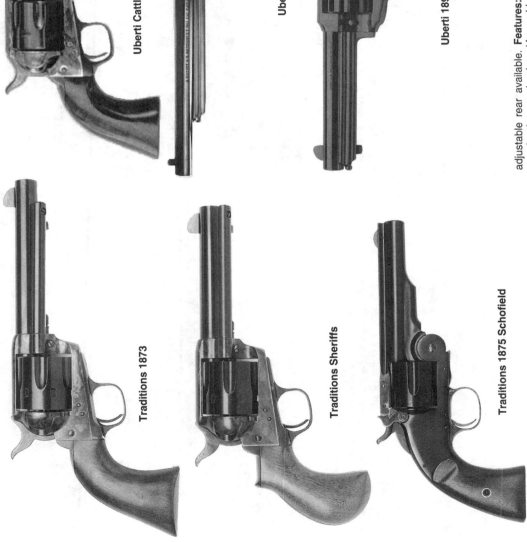

Traditions 1873

Traditions Sheriffs

Traditions 1875 Schofield

TRADITIONS 1873 SINGLE-ACTION REVOLVER

Caliber: 22 LR, 357 Mag., 44-40, 45 Colt, 6-shot cylinder. **Barrel:** 4-3/4", 5-1/2", 7-1/2". **Weight:** 44 oz. **Length:** 10-3/4" overall (5-1/2" barrel). **Stocks:** Walnut. **Sights:** Blade front, groove in topstrap rear. **Features:** Blued barrel, cylinder, color case-hardened frame, blue or brass trigger guard. Nickel-plated frame with polished brass trigger guard available in 357 Mag, 44-40, 45 Colt. Introduced 1998. From Traditions.
Price: .... **$300.00** to **$395.00**

Traditions Sheriffs Revolver

Similar to the 1873 single-action revolver except has special birds-head grip with spur, and smooth or checkered walnut grips. Introduced 1998. From Traditions.
Price: With smooth walnut grips **$370.00**

TRADITIONS 1875 SCHOFIELD REVOLVER

Caliber: 44-40, 45 Schofield, 45 Colt, 6-shot cylinder. **Barrel:** 5-1/2". **Weight:** 40 oz. **Length:** 11-1/4" overall. **Stocks:** Walnut. **Sights:** Blade front, notch rear. **Features:** Blue finish, case-hardened frame, hammer, trigger. Introduced 1998. From Traditions.
Price: **$659.00**

UBERTI 1873 CATTLEMAN SINGLE-ACTION

Caliber: 22 LR/22 WMR, 38 Spec., 357 Mag., 44 Spec., 44-40, 45 Colt/45 ACP, 6-shot. **Barrel:** 4-3/4", 5-1/2", 7-1/2", 44-40, 45 Colt also with 3", 3-1/2", 4". **Weight:** 38 oz. (5-1/2" bbl.). **Length:** 10-3/4" overall (5-1/2" bbl.). **Stocks:** One-piece smooth walnut. **Sights:** Blade front, groove rear; fully

adjustable rear available. **Features:** Steel or brass backstrap, trigger guard; color case-hardened frame, blued barrel, cylinder. Imported from Italy by Uberti U.S.A.
Price: Steel backstrap, trigger guard, fixed sights **$435.00**
Price: Brass backstrap, trigger guard, fixed sights **$365.00**
Price: Bisley model **$435.00**

Uberti 1873 Buckhorn Single-Action

A slightly larger version of the Cattleman revolver. Available in 44 Magnum or 44 Magnum/44-40 convertible, otherwise has same specs.
Price: Steel backstrap, trigger guard, fixed sights **$410.00**
Price: Convertible (two cylinders) **$475.00**

UBERTI 1875 SA ARMY OUTLAW REVOLVER

Caliber: 357 Mag., 44-40, 45 Colt, 45 Colt/45 ACP convertible, 6-shot. **Barrel:** 5-1/2", 7-1/2". **Weight:** 44 oz. **Length:** 13-3/4" overall. **Stocks:** Smooth walnut. **Sights:** Blade front, notch rear. **Features:** Replica of the 1875 Remington S.A. Army revolver. Brass trigger guard, color case-hardened frame, rest blued. Imported by Uberti U.S.A.
Price: **$435.00**
Price: 45 Colt/45 ACP convertible **$475.00**

UBERTI 1890 ARMY OUTLAW REVOLVER

Caliber: 357 Mag., 44-40, 45 Colt, 45 Colt/45 ACP convertible, 6-shot. **Barrel:** 5-1/2", 7-1/2". **Weight:** 37 oz. **Length:** 12-1/2" overall. **Stocks:** American walnut. **Sights:** Blade front, groove rear. **Features:** Replica of the 1890 Remington single-action. Brass trigger guard, rest is blued. Imported by Uberti U.S.A.
Price: **$435.00**
Price: 45 Colt/45 ACP convertible **$475.00**

UBERTI NEW MODEL RUSSIAN REVOLVER
Caliber: 44 Russian, 6-shot cylinder. **Barrel:** 6-1/2". **Weight:** 40 oz. **Length:** 12" overall. **Stocks:** Smooth walnut. **Sights:** Blade front, notch rear. **Features:** Replica of the S&W Model 3 Russian Third Model revolver. Spur trigger guard, polished blue finish. Introduced 1999. Imported by Uberti USA.
Price: $775.00

UBERTI 1875 SCHOFIELD REVOLVER
Caliber: 44-40, 45 Colt, 6-shot cylinder. **Barrel:** 5", 7". **Weight:** 39 oz. **Length:** 10-3/4" overall (5" barrel). **Stocks:** Smooth walnut. **Sights:** Blade front, notch rear. **Features:** Replica of Smith & Wesson Model 3 Schofield. Single-action, top-break with automatic ejection. Polished blue finish. Introduced 1994. Imported by Uberti USA.
Price: $700.00

UBERTI BISLEY MODEL SINGLE-ACTION REVOLVER
Caliber: 38-40, 357 Mag., 44 Spec., 44-40 or 45 Colt, 6-shot cylinder. **Barrel:** 4-3/4", 5-1/2", 7-1/2". **Weight:** 40 oz. **Length:** 12-1/2" overall (7-1/2" barrel). **Stocks:** Smooth walnut. **Sights:** Blade front, notch rear. **Features:** Replica of Colt's Bisley Model. Polished blue finish, color case-hardened frame. Introduced 1997. Imported by Uberti USA.
Price: 435.00

Uberti Bisley Model Flat Top Target Revolver
Similar to the standard Bisley model except with flat top strap, 7-1/2" barrel only, and a spring-loaded German silver front sight blade, standing leaf rear sight adjustable for windage. Polished blue finish, color case-hardened frame. Introduced 1998. Imported by Uberti USA.
Price: $455.00

U.S. PATENT FIRE-ARMS SINGLE ACTION ARMY REVOLVER
Caliber: 22 LR, 22 WMR, 357 Mag., 44 Russian, 38-40, 44-40, 45 Colt, 6-shot cylinder. **Barrel:** 3", 4", 4-3/4", 5-1/2", 7-1/2", 10". **Weight:** 37 oz. **Length:** NA. **Stocks:** Smooth walnut. **Sights:** Blade front, notch rear. **Features:** Recreation of original guns; 3" and 4" have no ejector. Available with all-blue, blue with color case-hardening, or full nickel-plate finish. Made in Italy; available from United States Patent Fire-Arms Mfg. Co.
Price: 3" blue $600.00
Price: 4-3/4", blue/cased-colors $732.00
Price: 7-1/2", blue/case-colors $739.00
Price: 10", nickel.......................... $847.50

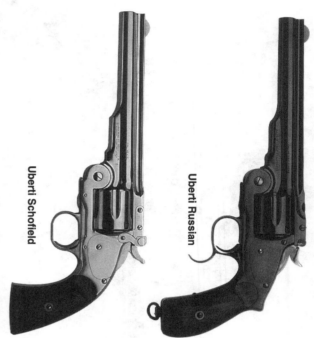

Uberti Schofield

Uberti Russian

U.S. Patent Fire-Arms Nettleton Cavalry Revolver
Similar to the Single Action Army, except in 45 Colt only, with 7-1/2" barrel, color case-hardened/blue finish, and has old-style hand numbering, exact cartouche branding and correct inspector hand-stamp markings. Made in Italy; available from United States Patent Fire-Arms Mfg. Co.
Price: $950.00
Price: Artillery Model, 5-1/2" barrel. $950.00

U.S. Patent Fire-Arms Bird Head Model Revolver
Similar to the Single Action Army except has bird's-head grip and comes with 3-1/2", 4" or 4-1/2" barrel. Made in Italy; available from United States Patent Fire-Arms Mfg. Co.
Price: 3-1/2", blue........................ $635.50
Price: 4", blue with color case-hardening .. $735.00
Price: 4-1/2", nickel-plated $795.50

U.S. Patent Fire-Arms Flattop Target Revolver
Similar to the Single Action Army except 4-3/4", 5-1/2" or 7-1/2" barrel, two-piece hard rubber stocks, flat top frame, adjustable rear sight. Made in Italy; available from United States Patent Fire-Arms Mfg. Co.
Price: 4-3/4", blue, polished hammer. $690.00
Price: 4-3/4", blue, case-colored hammer ... $813.00
Price: 5-1/2", blue, case-colored hammer ... $816.00
Price: 5-1/2", blue, nickel-plated $765.00
Price: 7-1/2", blue, polished hammer. $717.00
Price: 7-1/2", blue, case-colored hammer ... $822.00

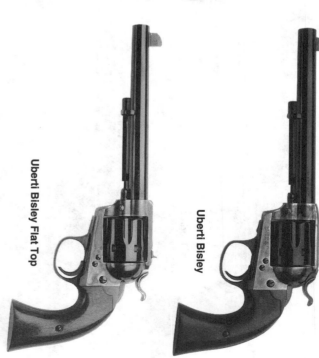

Uberti Bisley Flat Top

Uberti Bisley

U.S. PATENT FIRE-ARMS BISLEY MODEL REVOLVER
Caliber: 4 Colt, 6-shot cylinder. **Barrel:** 4-3/4", 5-1/2", 7-1/2", 10". **Weight:** 38 oz. (5-1/2" barrel). **Length:** NA. **Stocks:** Smooth walnut. **Sights:** Blade front, notch rear. **Features:** Available in all-blue, blue with color case-hardening, or full nickel plate finish. Made in Italy; available from United States Patent Fire-Arms Mfg. Co.
Price: 4-3/4", blue........................ $652.00
Price: 5-1/2", blue/case-colors $750.50
Price: 7-1/2", blue/case-colors $756.00
Price: 10", nickel.......................... $862.50

HANDGUNS — MISCELLANEOUS

Specially adapted single-shot and multi-barrel arms.

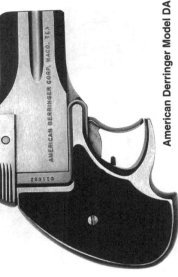

American Derringer Model 1

AMERICAN DERRINGER MODEL 1

Caliber: 22 LR, 22 WMR, 30 Carbine, 30 Luger, 30-30 Win., 32 H&R Mag., 32-20, 380 ACP, 38 Super, 38 Spec., 38 Spec. shotshell, 38 Spec. +P, 9mm Para., 357 Mag., 357 Mag./45/410, 357 Maximum, 10mm, 40 S&W, 41 Mag, 38-40, 44-40 Win., 44 Spec., 44 Mag., 45 Colt, 45 Win. Mag., 45 ACP, 45 Colt/410, 45-70 single shot. **Barrel:** 3". **Weight:** 15-1/2 oz. (38 Spec.). **Length:** 4.82" overall. **Stocks:** Rosewood, Zebra wood. **Sights:** Blade front. **Features:** Made of stainless steel with high-polish or satin finish. Two-shot capacity. Manual hammer block safety. Introduced 1980. Available in almost any pistol caliber. Contact the factory for complete list of available calibers and prices. From American Derringer Corp.

Price: 22 LR $260.00
Price: 38 Spec. $285.00
Price: 357 Maximum $310.00
Price: 357 Mag. $300.00
Price: 9mm, 380 . . . . $285.00
Price: 40 S&W $300.00
Price: 44 Spec. $363.00
Price: 44-40 Win. $363.00
Price: 45 Colt $350.00
Price: 30-30, 45 Win. Mag. $425.00
Price: 41, 44 Mags. $400.00
Price: 45-70, single shot $352.00
Price: 45 Colt, 410, 2-1/2" $363.00
Price: 45 ACP, 10mm Auto $300.00

American Derringer Model 4

Similar to the Model 1 except has 4.1" barrel, overall length of 6", and weighs 16-1/2 oz.; chambered for 357 Mag., 357 Maximum, 45-70, 3" 410-bore shotshells or 45 Colt or 44 Mag. Made of stainless steel. Manual hammer block safety. Introduced 1985.

Price: 3" 410/45 Colt $390.00
Price: 45-70 (Alaskan Survival model) . . $440.00
Price: 44 Mag. with oversize grips $480.00
Price: Alaskan Survival model (45-70 upper barrel, 410 or 45 Colt lower) $400.00

American Derringer Model 6

Similar to the Model 1 except has 6" barrel chambered for 3" 410 shotshells or 22 WMR, 357 Mag., 45 ACP, 45 Colt; rosewood stocks; 8.2" o.a.l. and weighs 21 oz. Shoots either round for each barrel. Manual hammer block safety. Introduced 1986.

Price: 22 WMR $405.00
Price: 357 Mag. $405.00
Price: 45 Colt/410 . . . . $415.00
Price: 45 ACP $405.00

American Derringer Model 7 Ultra Lightweight

Similar to Model 1 except made of high strength aircraft aluminum. Weighs 7-1/2 oz., 4.82" o.a.l., rosewood stocks. Available in 22 LR, 22 WMR, 32 H&R Mag, 380 ACP, 38 Spec., 44 Spec. Introduced 1986.

Price: 22 LR, WMR $290.00

Price: 38 Spec. $290.00
Price: 380 ACP $290.00
Price: 32 H&R Mag/32 S&W Long $290.00
Price: 44 Spec. $530.00

American Derringer Model 8

Similar to Model 1 except has 8" barrels chambered in 357 Magnum or 45 ACP. Overall length 10"; weighs 26 oz. Satin or high-polish stainless steel finish; rosewood, walnut or black grips.

Price: $425.00

American Derringer Model 10 Ultra Light

Similar to the Model 1 except frame is of aluminum, giving weight of 10 oz. Stainless barrels. Available in 38 Spec., 45 Colt or 45 ACP only. Matte gray finish. Introduced 1989.

Price: 45 Colt $350.00
Price: 45 ACP $295.00
Price: 38 Spec. $270.00

American Derringer Model 11 Ultra Light

Similar dimensions as the Model 10 except weighs 11 oz. Barrels made of aircraft aluminum; frame is stainless steel. Chambered in 22 LR, 22 WMR, 38 Special, 380 or 32 Magnum.

Price: $250.00

American Derringer Lady Derringer

Same as the Model 1 except has tuned action, is fitted with scrimshawed synthetic ivory grips; chambered for 32 H&R Mag. and 38 Spec.; 357 Mag., 45 Colt, 45/410. Deluxe Grade is highly polished; Deluxe Engraved is engraved in a pattern similar to that used on 1880s derringers. All come in a French fitted jewelry box. Introduced 1991.

Price: 32 H&R Mag. $340.00
Price: 357 Mag. $370.00
Price: 38 Spec. $325.00
Price: 45 Colt, 45/410 . . . . $400.00

American Derringer Texas Commemorative

A Model 1 Derringer with solid brass frame, stainless steel barrel and rosewood grips. Available in 38 Spec., 44-40 Win., or 45 Colt. Introduced 1987.

Price: 38 Spec. $330.00
Price: 44-40 . . . . $385.00
Price: Brass frame, 45 Colt $415.00

AMERICAN DERRINGER DA 38 MODEL

Caliber: 22 LR, 9mm Para., 38 Spec., 357 Mag., 40 S&W. **Barrel:** 3". **Weight:** 14.5 oz. **Length:** 4.8" overall. **Stocks:** Rosewood, walnut or other hardwoods. **Sights:** Fixed. **Features:** Double-action only; two-shots. Manual safety. Made of satin-finished stainless steel and aluminum. Introduced 1989. From American Derringer Corp.

Price: 22 LR, 38 Spec. $400.00
Price: 9mm Para. $410.00
Price: 357 Mag. $415.00
Price: 40 S&W $440.00

American Derringer Model DA 38

HANDGUNS — MISCELLANEOUS

Bond Arms C2K Defender

Davis Big-Bore

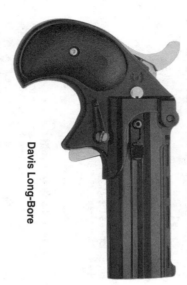

Davis Long-Bore

American Derringer Model DS

Similar to DA except is 5-1/8" overall, weighs 15 oz. Stainless steel finish; 22 WMR only

Price: **$300.00**

ANSCHUTZ MODEL 64P SPORT/TARGET PISTOL

Caliber: 22 LR, 22 WMR, 5-shot magazine. **Barrel:** 10". **Weight:** 3 lbs, 8 oz. **Length:** 18-1/2" overall. **Stock:** Choate Rynite. **Sights:** None furnished; grooved for scope mounting. **Features:** Right-hand bolt; polished blue finish. Introduced 1998. Imported from Germany by AcuSport.

Price: 22 LR **$455.95**
Price: 22 WMR **$479.95**

BOND ARMS TEXAS DEFENDER DERRINGER

Caliber: 9mm Para, 38 Spec./357 Mag., 40 S&W, 44 Spec./44 Mag., 45 Colt/410 shotshell. **Barrel:** 3", 3-1/2". **Weight:** 21 oz. **Length:** 5" overall. **Stocks:** Laminated black ash or rosewood. **Sights:** Blade front, fixed rear. **Features:** Interchangeable barrels; retracting firing pins; rebounding firing pins; cross-bolt safety; removable trigger guard; automatic extractor for rimmed calibers. Stainless steel construction with blasted/polished and ground combination finish. Introduced 1997. Made in U.S. by Bond Arms, Inc.

Price: **$349.00**
Price: Century 2000 Defender (410-bore, 3-1/2" barrels) **$369.00**

BROWN CLASSIC SINGLE SHOT PISTOL

Caliber: 17 Ackley Hornet through 45-70 Govt. **Barrel:** 15" airgauged match grade. **Weight:** About 3 lbs., 7 oz. **Stocks:** Walnut, thumbrest target style. **Sights:** None furnished; drilled and tapped for scope mounting. **Features:** Falling block action gives rigid barrel-receiver mating; hand-fitted and headspaced. Introduced 1998. Made in U.S. by E.A. Brown Mfg.

Price: **$499.00**

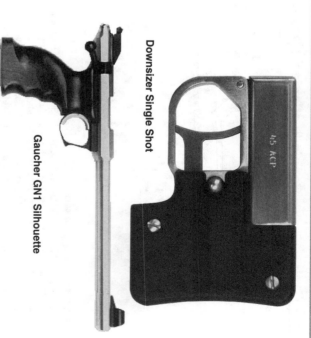

Downsizer Single Shot

Gaucher GN1 Silhouette

DAVIS BIG-BORE DERRINGERS

Caliber: 22 WMR, 38 Spec., 9mm Para. **Barrel:** 2.75". **Weight:** 11.5 oz. **Length:** 4.65" overall. **Stocks:** Textured black synthetic. **Sights:** Blade front, fixed notch rear. **Features:** Alloy frame, steel-lined barrels, steel breech block. Plunger-type safety with integral hammer block. Chrome or black Teflon finish. Introduced 1992. Made in U.S. by Davis Industries.

Price: 9mm Para. **$104.00**
Price: 9mm Para. **$104.00**

DAVIS LONG-BORE DERRINGERS

Caliber: 22 WMR, 38 Spec., 9mm Para. **Barrel:** 3.5". **Weight:** 13 oz. **Length:** 5.65" overall. **Stocks:** Textured black synthetic. **Sights:** Fixed. **Features:** Chrome or black Teflon finish. Larger than Davis D-Series models. Introduced 1995. Made in U.S. by Davis Industries.

Price: 9mm Para. **$110.00**
Price: Big-Bore models (same calibers, 3/4" shorter barrels)..... **$98.00**

DAVIS D-SERIES DERRINGERS

Caliber: 22 LR, 22 WMR, 25 ACP, 32 ACP. **Barrel:** 2.4". **Weight:** 9.5 oz. **Length:** 4" overall. **Stocks:** Laminated wood or pearl. **Sights:** Blade front, fixed notch rear. **Features:** Choice of black Teflon or chrome finish; spur trigger. Introduced 1986. Made in U.S. by Davis Industries.

Price: **$99.50**

DOWNSIZER WSP SINGLE SHOT PISTOL

Caliber: 9mm Para, 357 Magnum, 40 S&W, 45 ACP. **Barrel:** 2.10". **Weight:** 11 oz. **Length:** 3.25" overall. **Stocks:** Black polymer. **Sights:** None. **Features:** Single shot, tip-up barrel. Double action only. Stainless steel construction. Measures .900" thick. Introduced 1997. From Downsizer Corp.

Price: **$354.00**

GAUCHER GN1 SILHOUETTE PISTOL

Caliber: 22 LR, single shot. **Barrel:** 10". **Weight:** 2.4 lbs. **Length:** 15.5" overall. **Stocks:** European hardwood. **Sights:** Blade front, adjustable rear. **Features:** Bolt action, adjustable trigger. Introduced 1990. Imported from France by Mandall Shooting Supplies.

Price: About **$525.00**
Price: Model GP Silhouette **$425.00**

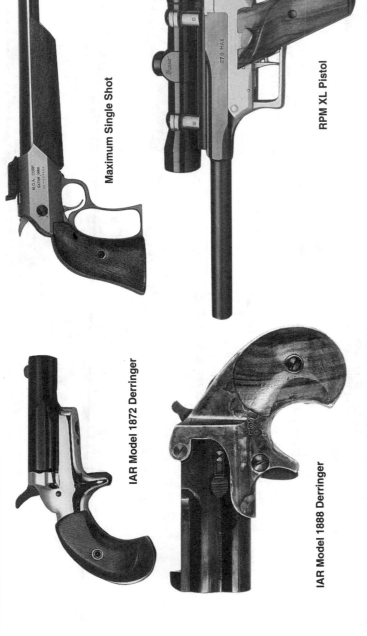

Maximum Single Shot

IAR Model 1872 Derringer

IAR Model 1888 Derringer

Magnum Research Lone Eagle

RPM XL Pistol

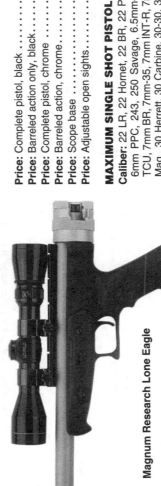

Price: Complete pistol, black	$438.00
Price: Barreled action only, black	$319.00
Price: Complete pistol, chrome	$478.00
Price: Barreled action, chrome	$359.00
Price: Scope base	$14.00
Price: Adjustable open sights	$35.00

MAXIMUM SINGLE SHOT PISTOL

Caliber: 22 LR, 22 Hornet, 22 BR, 22 PPC, 223 Rem., 22-250, 6mm BR, 6mm PPC, 243, 250 Savage, 6.5mm-35M, 270 MAX, 270 Win., 7mm TCU, 7mm BR, 7mm-35, 7mm INT-R, 7mm-08, 7mm Rocket, 7mm Super-Mag., 30 Herrett, 30 Carbine, 30-30, 308 Win., 30x39, 32-20, 350 Rem. Mag., 357 Mag., 357 Maximum, 358 Win., 375 H&H, 44 Mag., 454 Casull. **Barrel:** 8-3/4", 10-1/2", 14". **Weight:** 61 oz. (10-1/2" bbl.); 78 oz. (14" bbl.). **Length:** 15", 18-1/2" overall (with 10-1/2" and 14" bbl., respectively). **Stocks:** Smooth walnut stocks and forend. Also available with 17" finger groove grip. **Sights:** Ramp front, fully adjustable open rear. **Features:** Falling block action; drilled and tapped for M.O.A. scope mounts; integral grip frame/receiver; adjustable trigger; Douglas barrel (interchangeable). Introduced 1983. Made in U.S. by M.O.A. Corp.

Price: Stainless receiver, blue barrel	$799.00
Price: Stainless receiver, stainless barrel	$883.00
Price: Extra blued barrel	$254.00
Price: Extra stainless barrel	$317.00
Price: Scope mount	$60.00

RPM XL SINGLE SHOT PISTOL

Caliber: 22 LR through 45-70. **Barrel:** 8", 10-3/4", 12", 14". **Weight:** About 60 oz. **Length:** NA. **Stocks:** Smooth Goncalo Alves with thumb and heel rests. **Sights:** Hooded front with interchangeable post, or Patridge; ISGW rear adjustable for windage and elevation. **Features:** Barrel drilled and tapped for scope mount. Visible cocking indicator. Spring-loaded barrel lock, positive hammer-block safety. Trigger adjustable for weight of pull and over-travel. Contact maker for complete price list. Made in U.S. by RPM.

Price: Hunter model (stainless frame, 5/16" underlug, latch lever and positive extractor)	$1,295.00
Price: Extra barrel, 8" through 10-3/4"	$387.50
Price: Extra barrel with positive extractor, add	$100.00
Price: Muzzle brake	$100.00

IAR MODEL 1872 DERRINGER

Caliber: 22 Short. **Barrel:** 2-3/8". **Weight:** 7 oz. **Length:** 5-1/8" overall. **Stocks:** Smooth walnut. **Sights:** Blade front, notch rear. **Features:** Gold or nickel frame with blue barrel. Reintroduced 1996 using original Colt designs and tooling for the Colt Model 4 Derringer. Made in U.S. by IAR, Inc.

Price:	$99.00
Price: Single cased gun	$125.00
Price: Double cased set	$215.00

IAR MODEL 1888 DOUBLE DERRINGER

Caliber: 38 Special. **Barrel:** 2-3/4". **Weight:** 16 oz. **Length:** NA. **Stocks:** Smooth walnut. **Sights:** Blade front, notch rear. **Features:** All steel construction. Blue barrel, color case-hardened frame. Uses original designs and tooling for the Uberti New Maverick Derringer. Introduced 1999. Made in U.S. by IAR, Inc.

Price:	$395.00

MAGNUM RESEARCH LONE EAGLE SINGLE SHOT PISTOL

Caliber: 22 Hornet, 223, 22-250, 243, 260 Rem., 7mm BR, 7mm-08, 30-30, 7.62x39, 308, 30-06, 357 Max, 35 Rem., 358 Win., 44 Mag., 444 Marlin, 440 Cor-Bon. **Barrel:** 14", interchangeable. **Weight:** 4 lbs., 3 oz. to 4 lbs., 7 oz. **Length:** 15" overall. **Stocks:** Ambidextrous. **Sights:** None furnished; drilled and tapped for scope mounting and open sights. Open sights optional. **Features:** Cannon-type rotating breech with spring-activated ejector. Ordnance steel with matte blue finish. Cross-bolt safety. External cocking lever on left side of gun. Muzzle brake optional. Introduced 1991. Available from Magnum Research, Inc.

HANDGUNS — MISCELLANEOUS

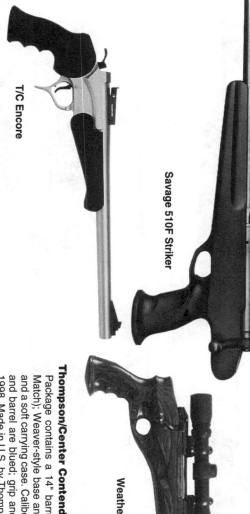

T/C Encore

Savage 510F Striker

Weatherby Mark V CFP

SAVAGE STRIKER BOLT-ACTION HUNTING HANDGUN
Caliber: 223, 22-250, 243, 206, 7mm-08, 308, 2-shot magazine. **Barrel:** 14". **Weight:** About 5 lbs. **Length:** 22-1/2" overall. **Stock:** Black composite ambidextrous mid-grip; grooved forend; "Dual Pillar" bedding. **Sights:** None furnished; drilled and tapped for scope mounting. **Features:** Short left-hand bolt with right-hand ejection; free-floated barrel; uses Savage Model 110 rifle scope rings/bases. Introduced 1998. Made in U.S. by Savage Arms, Inc.
Price: Model 510F (blued barrel and action) $425.00
Price: Model 516FSS (stainless barrel and action) $462.00
Price: Model 516FSAK (stainless, adjustable muzzle brake) $512.00

Savage Sport Striker Bolt-Action Hunting Handgun
Similar to the Striker, but chambered in 22 LR and 22 WMR. Detachable, 10-shot magazine (5-shot magazine for 22 WMR). Overall length 19", weighs 4 lbs. Ambidextrous fiberglass/graphite composite rear grip. Drilled and tapped, scope mount installed. Introduced 2000. Made in U.S. by Savage Arms Inc.
Super Striker
Price: $512.00
Price: Model 501F (blue finish, 22LR) $201.00
Price: Model 502F (blue finish, 22 WMR) $221.00

THOMPSON/CENTER ENCORE PISTOL
Caliber: 22-250, 223, 260 Rem., 7mm-08, 243, 308, 270, 30-06, 44 Mag., 454 Casull, 444 Marlin single shot. **Barrel:** 12", 15", tapered round. **Weight:** NA. **Length:** 21" overall with 12" barrel. **Stocks:** American walnut with finger grooves, walnut forend. **Sights:** Blade on ramp front, adjustable rear, or none. **Features:** Interchangeable barrels; action opens by squeezing the trigger guard; drilled and tapped for scope mounting; blue finish. Announced 1996. Made in U.S. by Thompson/Center Arms.
Price: $554.06
Price: Extra 12" barrels $240.68
Price: Extra 15" barrels $248.14
Price: 45 Colt/410 barrel, 12" $263.24
Price: 45 Colt/410 barrel, 15" $280.39

Thompson/Center Stainless Encore Pistol
Similar to the blued Encore except made of stainless steel and available with 15" barrel in 223, 22-250 7mm-08, 308. Comes with black rubber grip and forend. Made in U.S. by Thompson/Center Arms.
Price: $620.99

Thompson/Center Stainless Super 14
Same as the standard Super 14 and Super 16 except they are made of stainless steel with blued sights. Both models have black Rynite forend and finger-groove, ambidextrous grip with a built-in rubber recoil cushion that has a sealed-in air pocket. Receiver has a different cougar etching. Available in 22 LR Match, .223 Rem., 30-30 Win., 35 Rem. (Super 14), 45 Colt/410. Introduced 1993.
Price: $578.40
Price: 45 Colt/410, 14" $613.94

Thompson/Center Contender Shooter's Package
Package contains a 14" barrel without iron sights (10" for the 22 LR Match); Weaver-style base and rings; 2.5x-7x Recoil Proof pistol scope; and a soft carrying case. Calibers 22 LR, 223, 7-30 Waters, 30-30. Frame and barrel are blued; grip and forend are black composite. Introduced 1998. Made in U.S. by Thompson/Center Arms.
Price: $735.00

THOMPSON/CENTER CONTENDER
Caliber: 7mm TCU, 30-30 Win., 22 LR, 22 WMR, 22 Hornet, 223 Rem., 270 Rem., 7-30 Waters, 32-20 Win., 357 Rem. Max., 44 Mag., 10mm Auto, 445 SuperMag, 45/410, single shot. **Weight:** 43 oz. (10" bbl.). **Length:** 13-1/4" (10" bbl.). **Stock:** T/C "Competitor Grip." Right or left hand. **Sights:** Under-cut blade ramp front, rear adjustable for windage and elevation. **Features:** Break-open action with automatic safety. Single-action only. Interchangeable bbls., both caliber (rim & centerfire), and length. Drilled and tapped for scope. Engraved frame. See T/C catalog for exact barrel/caliber availability.
Price: Blued (rimfire cals.) $509.03
Price: Blued (centerfire cals.) $509.03
Price: Extra bbls. $229.02
Price: 45/410, internal choke bbl. $235.11

Thompson/Center Stainless Contender
Same as the standard Contender except made of stainless steel with blued sights, black Rynite forend and ambidextrous finger-groove grip with a built-in rubber recoil cushion that has a sealed-in air pocket. Receiver has a different cougar etching. Available with 10" bull barrel in 22 LR, 22 LR Match, 22 Hornet, 223 Rem., 30-30 Win., 357 Mag., 44 Mag., 45 Colt/410. Introduced 1993.
Price: $566.59
Price: 45 Colt/410. .... $590.44
Price: With 22 LR match chamber $578.40

UBERTI ROLLING BLOCK TARGET PISTOL
Caliber: 22 LR, 22 WMR, 22 Hornet, 357 Mag., 45 Colt, single shot. **Barrel:** 9-7/8", half-round, half-octagon. **Weight:** 44 oz. **Length:** 14" overall. **Stock:** Walnut grip and forend. **Sights:** Blade front, fully adjustable rear. **Features:** Replica of the 1871 rolling block target pistol. Brass trigger guard, color case-hardened frame, blue barrel. Imported by Uberti U.S.A.
Price: $410.00

WEATHERBY MARK V CFP PISTOL
Caliber: 22-250, 243, 7mm-08, 308. **Barrel:** 15" fluted stainless. **Weight:** NA. **Length:** NA. **Stock:** Brown laminate with ambidextrous rear grip. **Sights:** None furnished; drilled and tapped for scope mounting. **Features:** Uses Mark V lightweight receiver of chrome-moly steel, matte blue finish. Introduced 1998. Made in U.S. From Weatherby.
Price: $1,049.00

WEATHERBY MARK V ACCUMARK CFP PISTOL
Caliber: 223, 22-250, 243, 7mm-08, 308, 3-shot magazine. **Barrel:** 15", 1:12" twist (223). **Weight:** 5 lbs. **Length:** 26-1/2" overall. **Stock:** Kevlar-fiberglass composite. **Sights:** None; drilled and tapped for scope mounting. **Features:** Molded-in aluminum bedding plate; fluted stainless steel barrel; fully adjustable trigger. Introduced 2000. From Weatherby.
Price: .... NA

BLACKPOWDER SINGLE SHOT PISTOLS — FLINT & PERCUSSION

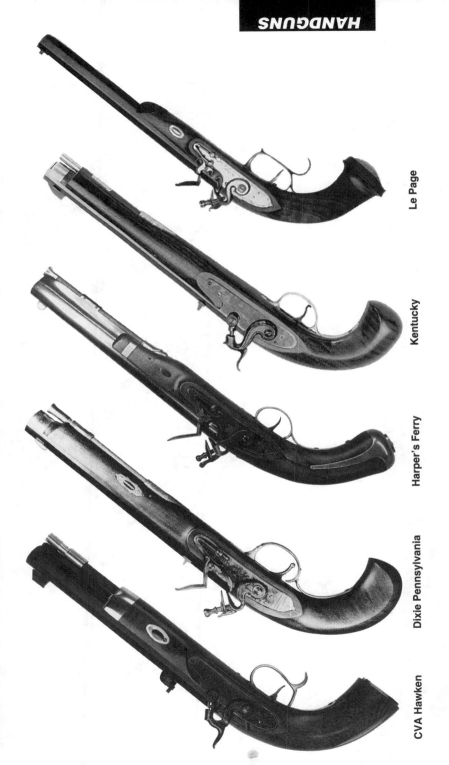

CVA Hawken

Dixie Pennsylvania

Harper's Ferry

Kentucky

Le Page

CVA HAWKEN PISTOL
Caliber: 50. **Barrel:** 9-3/4", 15/16" flats. **Weight:** 50 oz. **Length:** 16-1/2" overall. **Stocks:** Select hardwood. **Sights:** Beaded blade front, fully adjustable open rear. **Features:** Color case-hardened lock, polished brass wedge plate, instep, ramrod thimble, trigger guard, grip cap. Imported by CVA.

Price: $149.95
Price: Kit $119.95

DIXIE PENNSYLVANIA PISTOL
Caliber: 44 (.430" round ball). **Barrel:** 10" (7/8" octagon). **Weight:** 2-1/2 labs. **Stocks:** Walnut-stained hardwood. **Sights:** Blade front, open rear drift-adjustable for windage; brass. **Features:** Available in flint only. Brass trigger guard, thimbles, instep, wedge plates; high-luster blue barrel. Imported from Italy by Dixie Gun Works.

Price: Finished $195.00
Price: Kit $185.00

FRENCH-STYLE DUELING PISTOL
Caliber: 44. **Barrel:** 10". **Weight:** 35 oz. **Length:** 15-3/4" overall. **Stocks:** Carved walnut. **Sights:** Fixed. **Features:** Comes with velvet-lined case and accessories. Imported by Mandall Shooting Supplies.

Price: $295.00

HARPER'S FERRY 1806 PISTOL
Caliber: 58 (.570" round ball). **Barrel:** 10". **Weight:** 40 oz. **Length:** 16" overall. **Stocks:** Walnut. **Sights:** Fixed. **Features:** Case-hardened lock, brass-mounted browned barrel. Replica of the first U.S. Gov't.-made flintlock pistol. Imported by Navy Arms, Dixie Gun Works.

Price: .... $275.00 to $405.00
Price: Kit (Dixie) $249.00

KENTUCKY FLINTLOCK PISTOL
Caliber: 44, 45. **Barrel:** 10-1/8". **Weight:** 32 oz. **Length:** 15-1/2" overall. **Stocks:** Walnut. **Sights:** Fixed. **Features:** Specifications, including cali-

ber, weight and length may vary with importer. Case-hardened lock, blued barrel; available also as brass barrel flint Model 1821. Imported by Navy Arms, The Armoury.

Price: .... $145.00 to $235.00
Price: In kit form, from .... $90.00 to $112.00
Price: Single cased set (Navy Arms) $360.00
Price: Double cased set (Navy Arms) $590.00

Kentucky Percussion Pistol
Similar to flint version but percussion lock. Imported by The Armoury, Navy Arms, CVA (50-cal.).

Price: .... $129.95 to $225.00
Price: Steel barrel (Armoury) $179.00
Price: Single cased set (Navy Arms) $355.00
Price: Double cased set (Navy Arms) $600.00

LE PAGE PERCUSSION DUELING PISTOL
Caliber: 44. **Barrel:** 10", rifled. **Weight:** 40 oz. **Length:** 16" overall. **Stocks:** Walnut, fluted butt. **Sights:** Blade front, notch rear. **Features:** Double-set triggers. Blued barrel; trigger guard and buttcap are polished silver. Imported by Dixie Gun Works.

Price: $259.95

LYMAN PLAINS PISTOL
Caliber: 50 or 54. **Barrel:** 8"; 1:30" twist, both calibers. **Weight:** 50 oz. **Length:** 15" overall. **Stocks:** Walnut half-stock. **Sights:** Blade front, square notch rear adjustable for windage. **Features:** Polished brass trigger guard and ramrod tip, color case-hardened coil spring lock, spring-loaded trigger, stainless steel nipple, blackened iron furniture. Hooked patent breech, detachable belt hook. Introduced 1981. From Lyman Products.

Price: Finished $229.95
Price: Kit $184.95

BLACKPOWDER SINGLE SHOT PISTOLS — FLINT & PERCUSSION

Lyman Plains Pistol

Pedersoli Mang

Queen Anne

Traditions Pioneer

Traditions William Parker

Traditions Buckhunter Pro

PEDERSOLI MANG TARGET PISTOL
Caliber: 38. Barrel: 10.5", octagonal; 1:15" twist, Weight: 2.5 lbs. Length: 17.25" overall. Stocks: Walnut with fluted grip. Sights: Blade front, open rear adjustable for windage.
Features: Browned barrel, polished breech plug, rest color case-hardened. Imported from Italy by Dixie Gun Works.
Price: **$786.00**

QUEEN ANNE FLINTLOCK PISTOL
Caliber: 50 (.490" round ball). Barrel: 7-1/2", smoothbore. Stocks: Walnut. Sights: None. Features: Browned steel barrel, fluted brass trigger guard, brass mask on butt. Lockplate left in the white. Made by Pedersoli in Italy. Introduced 1983. Imported by Dixie Gun Works.
Price: **$225.00**
Price: Kit **$175.00**

THOMPSON/CENTER ENCORE 209x50 MAGNUM PISTOL
Caliber: 50, 54. Barrel: 15"; 1:20" twist. Weight: About 4 lbs. Grips: American walnut grip and forend. Sights: Click-adjustable, steel rear, ramp front. Features: Uses 209 shotgun primer for closed-breech ignition; accepts charges up to 110 grains of FFg black powder or two, 50-grain Pyrodex pellets. Introduced 2000.
Price: **$569.47**

TRADITIONS BUCKHUNTER PRO IN-LINE PISTOL
Caliber: 50, 54. Barrel: 9-1/2", round. Weight: 48 oz. Length: 14" overall. Stocks: Smooth walnut or black epoxy coated grip and forend. Sights: Beaded blade front, folding adjustable rear. Features: Thumb safety; removable stainless steel breech plug; adjustable trigger, barrel drilled and tapped for scope mounting. From Traditions.
Price: With walnut grip **$219.00**
Price: Nickel with black grip **$234.00**
Price: With walnut grip and 12-1/2" barrel **$234.00**

TRADITIONS KENTUCKY PISTOL
Caliber: 50. Barrel: 10"; octagon with 7/8" flats; 1:20" twist. Weight: 40 oz. Length: 15" overall. Stocks: Stained beech. Sights: Blade front, fixed rear. Features: Birds-head grip; brass thimbles; color case-hardened lock. Percussion only. Introduced 1995. From Traditions.
Price: Finished **$138.00**
Price: Kit **$109.00**

TRADITIONS PIONEER PISTOL
Caliber: 45. Barrel: 9-5/8", 13/16" flats, 1:16" twist. Weight: 31 oz. Length: 15" overall. Stocks: Beech. Sights: Blade front, fixed rear. Features: V-type mainspring. Single trigger. German silver furniture, blackened hardware. From Traditions.
Price: **$140.00**
Price: Kit **$116.00**

TRADITIONS TRAPPER PISTOL
Caliber: 50. Barrel: 9-3/4", 7/8" flats; 1:20" twist. Weight: 2-3/4 lbs. Length: 16" overall. Stocks: Beech. Sights: Blade front, adjustable rear. Features: Double-set triggers; brass buttcap, trigger guard, wedge plate, forend tip, thimble. From Traditions.
Price: Percussion **$189.00**
Price: Flintlock **$204.00**
Price: Kit **$145.00**

TRADITIONS WILLIAM PARKER PISTOL
Caliber: 50. Barrel: 10-3/8"; 15/16" flats; polished steel. Weight: 37 oz. Length: 17-1/2" overall. Stocks: Walnut with checkered grip. Sights: Brass blade front, fixed rear. Features: Replica dueling pistol with 1:20" twist, hooked breech. Brass wedge plate, trigger guard, cap guard; separate ramrod. Double-set triggers. Polished steel barrel, lock. Imported by Traditions.
Price: **$262.00**

BLACKPOWDER REVOLVERS

Baby Dragoon 1848

Army 1860

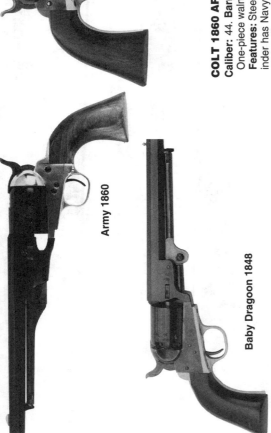

Colt 1860 Army

ARMY 1851 PERCUSSION REVOLVER
Caliber: 44, 6-shot. **Barrel:** 7-1/2". **Weight:** 45 oz. **Length:** 13" overall. **Stocks:** Walnut finish. **Sights:** Fixed. **Features:** 44-caliber version of the 1851 Navy. Imported by The Armoury, Armsport.
Price: **$129.00**

ARMY 1860 PERCUSSION REVOLVER
Caliber: 44, 6-shot. **Barrel:** 8". **Weight:** 40 oz. **Length:** 13-5/8" overall. **Stocks:** Walnut. **Sights:** Fixed. **Features:** Engraved Navy scene on cylinder; brass trigger guard; case-hardened frame, loading lever and hammer. Some importers supply pistol cut for detachable shoulder stock, have accessory stock available. Imported by Cabela's (1860 Lawman), E.M.F., Navy Arms, The Armoury, Cimarron, Dixie Gun Works (half-fluted cylinder, not roll engraved), Euroarms of America (brass or steel model), Armsport, Traditions (brass or steel), Uberti U.S.A. Inc, United States Patent Fire-Arms.
Price: About .... **$92.95 to $395.00**
Price: Hartford model, steel frame, German silver trim,
cartouches (E.M.F.) **$215.00**
Price: Single cased set (Navy Arms) **$300.00**
Price: Cased set (Navy Arms) **$490.00**
Price: 1861 Navy: Same as Army except 36-cal., 7-1/2" bbl., weighs 41 oz., cut for shoulder stock; round cylinder (fluted available), from Cabela's, CVA (brass frame, 44-cal.), United States Patent Fire-Arms
.... **$99.95 to $385.00**
Price: Steel frame kit (E.M.F., Euroarms).. **$125.00 to $216.25**
Price: Colt Army Police, fluted cyl., 5-1/2", 36-cal. (Cabela's) ... **$124.95**
Price: With nickeled frame, barrel and backstrap, gold-tone fluted cylinder, trigger and hammer, simulated ivory grips (Traditions) **$199.00**

BABY DRAGOON 1848, 1849 POCKET, WELLS FARGO
Caliber: 31. **Barrel:** 3", 4", 5", 6"; seven-groove; RH twist. **Weight:** About 21 oz. **Stocks:** Varnished walnut. **Sights:** Brass pin front, hammer notch rear. **Features:** No loading lever on Baby Dragoon or Wells Fargo models. Unfluted cylinder with stagecoach holdup scene; cupped cylinder pin; no grease grooves; one safety pin on cylinder and slot in hammer face; straight (flat) mainspring. From Armsport, Cimarron F.A. Co., Dixie Gun Works, Uberti U.S.A. Inc.
Price: 6" barrel, with loading lever (Dixie Gun Works) **$254.95**
Price: 4" (Uberti USA Inc.) **$335.00**

CABELA'S STARR PERCUSSION REVOLVERS
Caliber: 44. **Barrel:** 6", 8". **Weight:** N/A. **Length:** N/A. **Grips:** Walnut. **Sights:** Blade front. **Features:** Replicas of government-contract revolvers made by Ebenezer T. Starr. Knurled knob allows quick removal and replacement of cylinder. Introduced 2000. From Cabela's.
Price: Starr 1858 Army double action, 6" barrel **$349.99**
Price: Starr 1863 Army single action, 8" barrel **$349.99**

COLT 1860 ARMY PERCUSSION REVOLVER
Caliber: 44. **Barrel:** 8", 7-groove, left-hand twist. **Weight:** 42 oz. **Stocks:** One-piece walnut. **Sights:** German silver front sight, hammer notch rear. **Features:** Steel backstrap cut for shoulder stock; brass trigger guard. Cylinder has Navy scene. Color case-hardened frame, hammer, loading lever. Reproduction of original gun with all original markings. From Colt Blackpowder Arms Co.
Price: **$449.95**

COLT 1848 BABY DRAGOON REVOLVER
Caliber: 31, 5-shot. **Barrel:** 4". **Weight:** About 21 oz. **Stocks:** Smooth walnut. **Sights:** Brass pin front, hammer notch rear. **Features:** Color case-hardened frame; no loading lever; square-back trigger guard; round bolt cuts; octagonal barrel; engraved cylinder scene. Imported by Colt Blackpowder Arms Co.
Price: **$429.95**

Colt 1860 "Cavalry Model" Percussion Revolver
Similar to the 1860 Army except has fluted cylinder. Color case-hardened frame, hammer, loading lever and plunger; blued barrel, backstrap and cylinder, brass trigger guard. Has four-screw frame cut for optional shoulder stock. From Colt Blackpowder Arms Co.
Price: **$399.95**

COLT 1851 NAVY PERCUSSION REVOLVER
Caliber: 36. **Barrel:** 7-1/2", octagonal; 7-groove left-hand twist. **Weight:** 40-1/2 oz. **Stocks:** One-piece oiled American walnut. **Sights:** Brass pin front, hammer notch rear. **Features:** Faithful reproduction of the original gun. Color case-hardened frame, loading lever, plunger, hammer and latch. Blue cylinder, trigger, barrel, screws, wedge. Silver-plated brass backstrap and square-back trigger guard. From Colt Blackpowder Arms Co.
Price: **$449.95**

COLT 1861 NAVY PERCUSSION REVOLVER
Caliber: 36. **Barrel:** 7-1/2". **Weight:** 42 oz. **Length:** 13-1/8" overall. **Stocks:** One-piece walnut. **Sights:** Blade front, hammer notch rear. **Features:** Color case-hardened frame, loading lever, plunger; blued barrel, backstrap, trigger guard; roll-engraved cylinder and barrel. From Colt Blackpowder Arms Co.
Price: **$449.95**

COLT 1849 POCKET DRAGOON REVOLVER
Caliber: 31. **Barrel:** 4". **Weight:** 24 oz. **Length:** 9-1/2" overall. **Stocks:** One-piece walnut. **Sights:** Fixed. Brass pin front, hammer notch rear. **Features:** Color case-hardened frame. No loading lever. Unfluted cylinder with engraved scene. Exact reproduction of original. From Colt Blackpowder Arms Co.
Price: **$429.95**

COLT 1862 POCKET POLICE "TRAPPER MODEL" REVOLVER
Caliber: 36. **Barrel:** 3-1/2". **Weight:** 20 oz. **Length:** 8-1/2" overall. **Stocks:** One-piece walnut. **Sights:** Blade front, hammer notch rear. **Features:** Has separate 4-5/8" brass ramrod. Color case-hardened frame and hammer; silver-plated backstrap and trigger guard; blued semi-fluted cylinder, blued barrel. From Colt Blackpowder Arms Co.
Price: **$429.95**

BLACKPOWDER REVOLVERS

Dixie Wyatt Earp

Colt 1847 Walker

Le Mat Revolver

Griswold & Gunnison

COLT THIRD MODEL DRAGOON
Caliber: 44. **Barrel:** 7-1/2". **Weight:** 66 oz. **Length:** 13-3/4" overall. **Stocks:** One-piece walnut. **Sights:** Blade front, hammer notch rear. **Features:** Color case-hardened frame, hammer, lever and plunger; round trigger guard; flat mainspring; hammer roller; rectangular bolt cuts. From Colt Blackpowder Arms Co.
Price: Three-screw frame with brass grip straps $499.95
Price: First Dragoon (oval bolt cuts in cylinder, square-back trigger guard) $499.95
Price: Second Dragoon (rectangular bolt cuts in cylinder, square-back trigger guard) $499.95

Colt Walker 150th Anniversary Revolver
Similar to the standard Walker except has original-type "A Company No. 1" markings embellished in gold. Serial numbers begin with 221, a continuation of A Company numbers. Imported by Colt Blackpowder Arms Co.
Price: $699.95

COLT 1847 WALKER PERCUSSION REVOLVER
Caliber: 44. **Barrel:** 9", 7-groove; right-hand twist. **Weight:** 73 oz. **Stocks:** One-piece walnut. **Sights:** German silver front sight, hammer notch rear. **Features:** Made in U.S. Faithful reproduction of the original gun, including markings. Color case-hardened frame, hammer, loading lever and plunger. Blue steel backstrap, brass square-back trigger guard. Blue barrel, cylinder, trigger and wedge. From Colt Blackpowder Arms Co.
Price: $499.95

DIXIE WYATT EARP REVOLVER
Caliber: 44. **Barrel:** 12", octagon. **Weight:** 46 oz. **Length:** 18" overall. **Stocks:** Two-piece walnut. **Sights:** Fixed. **Features:** Highly polished brass frame, backstrap and trigger guard; blued barrel and cylinder; case-hardened hammer, trigger and loading lever. Navy-size shoulder stock ($45) will fit with minor fitting. From Dixie Gun Works.
Price: $150.00

GRISWOLD & GUNNISON PERCUSSION REVOLVER
Caliber: 36 or 44, 6-shot. **Barrel:** 7-1/2". **Weight:** 44 oz (36-cal.). **Length:** 13" overall. **Stocks:** Walnut. **Sights:** Fixed. **Features:** Replica of famous Confederate pistol. Brass frame, backstrap and trigger guard; case-hardened loading lever, rebated cylinder (44-cal. only). Rounded Dragoon-type barrel. Imported by Navy Arms as Reb Model 1860.
Price: $115.00
Price: Kit $90.00
Price: Single cased set $235.00
Price: Double cased set $365.00

LE MAT REVOLVER
Caliber: 44/65. **Barrel:** 6-3/4" (revolver); 4-7/8" (single shot). **Weight:** 3 lbs., 7 oz. **Stocks:** Hand-checkered walnut. **Sights:** Post front, hammer notch rear. **Features:** Exact reproduction with all-steel construction; 44-cal. 9-shot cylinder, 65-cal. single barrel; color case-hardened hammer with selector; spur trigger guard; ring at butt; lever-type barrel release. From Navy Arms.
Price: Cavalry model (lanyard ring, spur trigger guard) $595.00
Price: Army model (round trigger guard, pin-type barrel release) ... $595.00
Price: Naval-style (thumb selector on hammer) $595.00
Price: Engraved 18th Georgia cased set $795.00
Price: Engraved Beauregard cased set $1,000.00

NAVY ARMS NEW MODEL POCKET REVOLVER
Caliber: 31, 5-shot. **Barrel:** 3-1/2", octagon. **Weight:** 15 oz. **Length:** 7-3/4". **Stocks:** Two-piece walnut. **Sights:** Fixed. **Features:** Replica of the Remington New Model Pocket. Available with polisehd brass frame or nickel plated finish. Introduced 2000. Imported by Navy Arms.
Price: Brass frame $165.00
Price: Nickel plated $175.00

NAVY ARMS DELUXE 1858 REMINGTON-STYLE REVOLVER
Caliber: 44. **Barrel:** 6". **Weight:** 3 lbs. **Length:** 11-3/4". **Stocks:** Smooth walnut. **Sights:** Blade front, notch rear. **Features:** Replica of the famous percussion double action revolver. Polished blue finish. Introduced 1999. Imported by Navy Arms.
Price: $355.00

NAVY ARMS STARR SINGLE ACTION MODEL 1863 ARMY REVOLVER
Caliber: 44. **Barrel:** 8". **Weight:** 3 lbs. **Length:** 13-3/4". **Stocks:** Smooth walnut. **Sights:** Blade front, notch rear. **Features:** Replica of the third most popular revolver used by Union forces during the Civil War. Polished blue finish. Introduced 1999. Imported by Navy Arms.
Price: $355.00

NAVY ARMS STARR DOUBLE ACTION MODEL 1858 ARMY REVOLVER
Caliber: 44. **Barrel:** 8". **Weight:** 2 lbs., 13 oz. **Stocks:** Smooth walnut. **Sights:** Dovetailed blade front. **Features:** First exact reproduction—correct in size and weight to the original, with progressive rifling; highly polished with blue finish. From Navy Arms.
Price: Deluxe model $415.00

BLACKPOWDER REVOLVERS

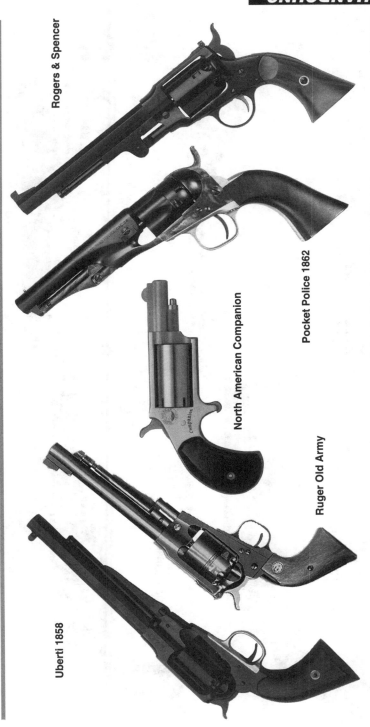

Rogers & Spencer

Pocket Police 1862

North American Companion

Ruger Old Army

Uberti 1858

NAVY MODEL 1851 PERCUSSION REVOLVER

Caliber: 36, 44, 6-shot. **Barrel:** 7-1/2". **Weight:** 44 oz. **Length:** 13" overall. **Stocks:** Walnut finish. **Sights:** Post front, hammer notch rear. **Features:** Brass backstrap and trigger guard; some have 1st Model squareback trigger guard, engraved cylinder with navy battle scene; case-hardened frame, hammer, loading lever. Imported by The Armoury, Cabela's, Cimarron F.A. Co, Navy Arms, E.M.F., Dixie Gun Works, Euroarms of America, Armsport, CVA (44-cal. only), Traditions (44 only) Uberti U.S.A. Inc., United States Patent Fire-Arms.

Price: Brass frame	$99.95 to $385.00
Price: Steel frame	$130.00 to $285.00
Price: Kit form	$110.00 to $123.95
Price: Engraved model (Dixie Gun Works)	$159.95
Price: Single cased set, steel frame (Navy Arms)	$280.00
Price: Double cased set, steel frame (Navy Arms)	$455.00
Price: Confederate Navy (Cabela's)	$89.99
Price: Hartford model, steel frame, German silver trim, cartouche (E.M.F.)	$190.00

NEW MODEL 1858 ARMY PERCUSSION REVOLVER

Caliber: 36 or 44, 6-shot. **Barrel:** 6-1/2" or 8". **Weight:** 38 oz. **Length:** 13-1/2" overall. **Stocks:** Walnut. **Sights:** Blade front, groove-in-frame rear. **Features:** Replica of Remington Model 1858. Also available from some importers as Army Model Belt Revolver in 36-cal., a shortened and lightened version of the 44. Target Model (Uberti U.S.A. Inc., Navy Arms) has fully adjustable target rear sight, target front, 36 or 44. Imported by Cabela's, Cimarron F.A. Co., CVA (as 1858 Army, brass frame, 44 only), Dixie Gun Works, Navy Arms, The Armoury, E.M.F., Euroarms of America (engraved, stainless and plain), Armsport, Traditions (44 only), Uberti U.S.A. Inc.

Price: Steel frame, about	$99.95 to $280.00
Price: Steel frame kit (Euroarms, Navy Arms)	$115.95 to $150.00
Price: Single cased set (Navy Arms)	$290.00
Price: Double cased set (Navy Arms)	$480.00
Price: Stainless steel Model 1858 (Euroarms, Uberti U.S.A. Inc., Cabela's, Navy Arms, Armsport, Traditions)	$169.95 to $380.00
Price: Target Model, adjustable rear sight (Cabela's, Euroarms, Uberti U.S.A. Inc., Stone Mountain Arms)	$95.95 to $399.00
Price: Brass frame (CVA, Cabela's, Traditions, Navy Arms)	$79.95 to $144.95
Price: As above, kit (Dixie Gun Works, Navy Arms)	$145.00 to $188.95

| Price: Buffalo model, 44-cal. (Cabela's) | $119.99 |
| Price: Hartford model, steel frame, German silver trim, cartouche (E.M.F.) | $215.00 |

NORTH AMERICAN COMPANION PERCUSSION REVOLVER

Caliber: 22. **Barrel:** 1-1/8". **Weight:** 5.1 oz. **Length:** 4-5/10" overall. **Stocks:** Laminated wood. **Sights:** Blade front, notch fixed rear. **Features:** All stainless steel construction. Uses standard #11 percussion caps. Comes with bullets, powder measure, bullet seater, leather clip holster, gun rag. Long Rifle or Magnum frame size. Introduced 1996. Made in U.S. by North American Arms.

| Price: Long Rifle frame | $191.00 |

North American Magnum Companion Percussion Revolver

Similar to the Companion except has larger frame. Weighs 7.2 oz., has 1-5/8" barrel, measures 5-7/16" overall. Comes with bullets, powder measure, bullet seater, leather clip holster, gun rag. Introduced 1996. Made in U.S. by North American Arms.

| Price: | $209.00 |

POCKET POLICE 1862 PERCUSSION REVOLVER

Caliber: 36, 5-shot. **Barrel:** 4-1/2", 5-1/2", 6-1/2", 7-1/2". **Weight:** 26 oz. **Length:** 12" overall (6-1/2" bbl.). **Stocks:** Walnut. **Sights:** Fixed. **Features:** Round tapered barrel; half-fluted and rebated cylinder; case-hardened frame, loading lever and hammer; silver or brass trigger guard and backstrap. Imported by Dixie Gun Works, Navy Arms (5-1/2" only), Uberti U.S.A. Inc. (5-1/2", 6-1/2" only), United States Patent Fire-Arms and Cimarron F.A. Co.

Price: About	$139.95 to $335.00
Price: Single cased set with accessories (Navy Arms)	$365.00
Price: Hartford model, steel frame, German silver trim, cartouche (E.M.F.)	$215.00

ROGERS & SPENCER PERCUSSION REVOLVER

Caliber: 44. **Barrel:** 7-1/2". **Weight:** 47 oz. **Length:** 13-3/4" overall. **Stocks:** Walnut. **Sights:** Cone front, integral groove in frame for rear. **Features:** Accurate reproduction of a Civil War design. Solid frame; extra large nipple cut-out on rear of cylinder; loading lever and cylinder easily removed for cleaning. From Dixie Gun Works, Euroarms of America (standard blue, engraved, burnished, target models), Navy Arms.

| Price: | $160.00 to $299.95 |
| Price: Nickel-plated | $215.00 |

BLACKPOWDER REVOLVERS

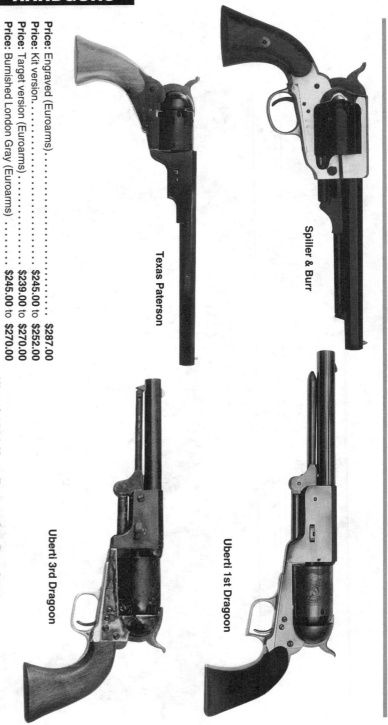

Texas Paterson

Spiller & Burr

Uberti 3rd Dragoon

Uberti 1st Dragoon

RUGER OLD ARMY PERCUSSION REVOLVER
Caliber: 45, 6-shot. Uses .457" dia. lead bullets. **Barrel:** 7-1/2" (6-groove, 16" twist). **Weight:** 46 oz. **Length:** 13-3/4" overall. **Stocks:** Smooth walnut. **Sights:** Ramp front, rear adjustable for windage and elevation; or fixed (groove). **Features:** Stainless steel; standard size nipples, chrome-moly steel cylinder and frame, same lockwork as in original Super Blackhawk. Also available in stainless steel. Made in USA. From Sturm, Ruger & Co.
Price: Stainless steel (Model KBP-7) $499.00
Price: Blued steel (Model BP-7) $478.00
Price: Blued steel, fixed sight (BP-7F) $478.00
Price: Stainless steel, fixed sight (KBP-7F) $499.00

SHERIFF MODEL 1851 PERCUSSION REVOLVER
Caliber: 36, 44, 6-shot. **Barrel:** 5". **Weight:** 40 oz. **Length:** 10-1/2" overall. **Stocks:** Walnut. **Sights:** Fixed. **Features:** Brass backstrap and trigger guard; engraved navy scene; case-hardened frame, hammer, loading lever. Imported by E.M.F.
Price: Steel frame $172.00
Price: Brass frame $140.00

SPILLER & BURR REVOLVER
Caliber: 36 (.375" round ball). **Barrel:** 7", octagon. **Weight:** 2-1/2 lbs. **Length:** 12-1/2" overall. **Stocks:** Two-piece walnut. **Sights:** Fixed. **Features:** Reproduction of the C.S.A. revolver. Brass frame and trigger guard. Also available as a kit. From Dixie Gun Works, Navy Arms.
Price: $145.00
Price: Kit form (Dixie) $149.95
Price: Single cased set (Navy Arms) $270.00
Price: Double cased set (Navy Arms) $430.00

TEXAS PATERSON 1836 REVOLVER
Caliber: 36 (.375" round ball). **Barrel:** 7-1/2". **Weight:** 42 oz. **Stocks:** One-piece walnut. **Sights:** Fixed. **Features:** Copy of Sam Colt's first commercially-made revolving pistol. Has no loading lever but comes with loading tool. From Cimarron F.A. Co., Dixie Gun Works, Navy Arms, Uberti U.S.A. Inc.
Price: About .... $310.00 to $395.00
Price: With loading lever (Uberti U.S.A. Inc.) $450.00
Price: Engraved (Navy Arms). $485.00

Uberti 1861 Navy Percussion Revolver
Similar to Colt 1851 Navy except has round 7-1/2" barrel, rounded trigger guard, German silver blade front sight, "creeping" loading lever. Available with fluted or round cylinder. Imported by Uberti U.S.A. Inc.
Price: Steel backstrap, trigger guard, cut for stock............. $300.00

1ST U.S. MODEL DRAGOON
Caliber: 44. **Barrel:** 7-1/2", part round, part octagon. **Weight:** 64 oz. **Stocks:** One-piece walnut. **Sights:** German silver blade front, hammer notch rear. **Features:** First model has oval bolt cuts in cylinder, square-back flared trigger guard, V-type mainspring, short trigger. Ranger and Indian scene roll-engraved on cylinder. Color case-hardened frame, loading lever, plunger and hammer; blue barrel, cylinder, trigger and wedge. Available with old-time charcoal blue or standard blue-black finish. Polished brass backstrap and trigger guard. From Cimarron F.A. Co., Uberti U.S.A. Inc., United States Patent Fire-Arms, Navy Arms.
Price: .... $325.00 to $435.00

2nd U.S. Model Dragoon Revolver
Similar to the 1st Model except distinguished by rectangular bolt cuts in the cylinder. From Cimarron F.A. Co., Uberti U.S.A. Inc., United States Patent Fire-Arms, Navy Arms.
Price: .... $325.00 to $435.00

3rd U.S. Model Dragoon Revolver
Similar to the 2nd Model except for oval trigger guard, long trigger, modifications to the loading lever and latch. Imported by Cimarron F.A. Co., Uberti U.S.A. Inc., United States Patent Fire-Arms.
Price: Military model (frame cut for shoulder stock, steel backstrap) .... $330.00 to $435.00
Price: Civilian (brass backstrap, trigger guard) $325.00

1862 POCKET NAVY PERCUSSION REVOLVER
Caliber: 36, 5-shot. **Barrel:** 5-1/2", 6-1/2", octagonal, 7-groove, LH twist. **Weight:** 27 oz. (5-1/2" barrel). **Length:** 10-1/2" overall (5-1/2" bbl.). **Stocks:** One-piece varnished walnut. **Sights:** Brass pin front, hammer notch rear. **Features:** Rebated cylinder, hinged loading lever, brass or silver-plated backstrap and trigger guard, color-cased frame, hammer, loading lever, plunger and latch, rest blued. Has original-type markings. From Cimarron F.A. Co. and Uberti U.S.A. Inc.
Price: With brass backstrap, trigger guard $310.00

Price: Engraved (Euroarms) $287.00
Price: Kit version (Euroarms) .... $245.00 to $252.00
Price: Target version (Euroarms) .... $239.00 to $270.00
Price: Burnished London Gray (Euroarms) ...... $245.00 to $270.00

BLACKPOWDER REVOLVERS

Uberti 1862 Pocket Navy

Walker Revolver

1861 Navy Percussion Revolver

Similar to Colt 1851 Navy except has round 7-1/2" barrel, rounded trigger guard, German silver blade front sight, "creeping" loading lever. Fluted or round cylinder. Imported by Cimarron F.A. Co., Uberti U.S.A. Inc.
Price: Steel backstrap, trigger guard, cut for stock............ **$300.00**

U.S. PATENT FIRE-ARMS 1862 POCKET NAVY

Caliber: 36. **Barrel:** 4-1/2", 5-1/2", 6-1/2". **Weight:** 27 oz. (5-1/2" barrel). **Length:** 10-1/2" overall (5-1/2" barrel). **Stocks:** Smooth walnut. **Sights:** Brass pin front, hammer notch rear. **Features:** Blued barrel and cylinder, color case-hardened frame, hammer, lever; silver-plated backstrap and trigger guard. Imported from Italy; available from United States Patent Fire-Arms Mfg. Co.
Price: **$335.00**

WALKER 1847 PERCUSSION REVOLVER

Caliber: 44, 6-shot. **Barrel:** 9". **Weight:** 84 oz. **Length:** 15-1/2" overall. **Stocks:** Walnut. **Sights:** Fixed. **Features:** Case-hardened frame, loading lever and hammer; iron backstrap; brass trigger guard; engraved cylinder. Imported by Cabela's, Cimarron F.A. Co., Navy Arms, Dixie Gun Works, Uberti U.S.A. Inc., E.M.F., Cimarron, Traditions, United States Patent Fire-Arms.
Price: About .... **$225.00** to **$445.00**
Price: Single cased set (Navy Arms) **$405.00**
Price: Deluxe Walker with French fitted case (Navy Arms) **$540.00**
Price: Hartford model, steel frame, German silver trim, cartouche (E.M.F.) **$295.00**

AIRGUNS

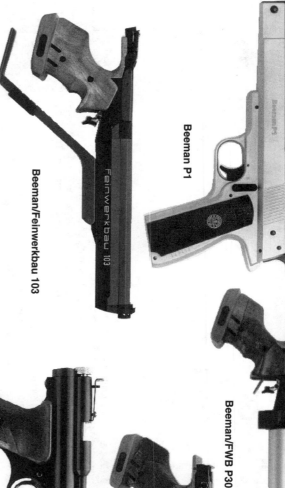

Beeman P1

Beeman/Feinwerkbau 103

Benjamin Sheridan CO2

Beeman/FWB P30

Beeman/FWB C55

BEEMAN P1 MAGNUM AIR PISTOL

Caliber: 177, 5mm, single shot. **Barrel:** 8.4". **Weight:** 2.5 lbs. **Length:** 11" overall. **Power:** Top lever cocking; spring-piston. **Stocks:** Checkered walnut. **Sights:** Blade front, square notch rear with click micrometer adjustments for windage and elevation. Grooved for scope mounting. **Features:** Dual power for 177 and 20-cal.; low setting gives 350-400 fps; high setting 500-600 fps. Rearward expanding mainspring simulates firearm recoil. All Colt 45 auto grips fit gun. Dry-firing feature for practice. Optional wooden shoulder stock. Introduced 1985. Imported by Beeman.

Price: 177, 5mm $415.00

Beeman P2 Match Air Pistol

Similar to the Beeman P1 Magnum except shoots only 177 pellets; completely recoilless single-stroke pneumatic action. Weighs 2.2 lbs. Choice of thumbrest match grips or standard style. Introduced 1990.

Price: 177, 5mm, standard grip $385.00

Price: 177, match grip $455.00

BEEMAN P3 AIR PISTOL

Caliber: 177 pellet, single shot. **Barrel:** N/A. **Weight:** 1.7 lbs. **Length:** 9.6" overall. **Power:** Single-stroke pneumatic; overlever barrel cocking. **Grips:** Reinforced polymer. **Sights:** Adjustable rear, blade front. **Features:** Velocity 410 fps. Polymer frame; automatic safety; two-stage trigger; built-in muzzle brake. Introduced 1999 by Beeman.

Price: $159.00

BEEMAN/FEINWERKBAU 65 MKII AIR PISTOL

Caliber: 177, single shot. **Barrel:** 6.1", removable bbl. wgt. available. **Weight:** 42 oz. **Length:** 13.3" overall. **Power:** Spring, sidelever cocking. **Stocks:** Walnut, stippled thumbrest; adjustable or fixed. **Sights:** Front, interchangeable post element system, open rear, click adjustable for windage and elevation and for sighting notch width. Scope mount available. **Features:** New shorter barrel for better balance and control. Cocking effort 9 lbs. Two-stage trigger, four adjustments. Quiet firing, 525 fps. Programs instantly for recoil or recoilless operation. Permanently lubricated. Steel piston ring. Imported by Beeman.

Price: Right-hand $1,070.00

BEEMAN/FEINWERKBAU 103 PISTOL

Caliber: 177, single shot. **Barrel:** 10.1", 12-groove rifling. **Weight:** 2.5 lbs. **Length:** 16.5" overall. **Power:** Single-stroke pneumatic, underlever cocking. **Stocks:** Stippled walnut with adjustable palm shelf. **Sights:** Blade front, open rear adjustable for windage and elevation. Notch size adjustable for width. Interchangeable front blades. **Features:** Velocity 510 fps. Fully adjustable trigger. Cocking effort of 2 lbs. Imported by Beeman.

Price: Right-hand ....
Price: Left-hand ....

BEEMAN/FWB P30 MATCH AIR PISTOL

Caliber: 177, single shot. **Power:** Pre-charged pneumatic. **Stocks:** Stippled walnut; ad-

justable match type. **Sights:** Undercut blade front, fully adjustable match rear. **Features:** Velocity to 525 fps; up to 200 shots per CO2 cartridge. Fully adjustable trigger; built-in muzzlebrake. Introduced 1995. Imported from Germany by Beeman.

Price: Right-hand $1,275.00

Price: Left-hand $1,350.00

BEEMAN/FWB C55 CO2 RAPID FIRE PISTOL

Caliber: 177, single shot or 5-shot magazine. **Barrel:** 7.3". **Weight:** 2.5 lbs. **Length:** 15" overall. **Power:** Special CO2 cylinder. **Stocks:** Anatomical, adjustable. **Sights:** Interchangeable front, fully adjustable open micro-click rear with adjustable notch size. **Features:** Velocity 510 fps. Has 11.75" sight radius. Built-in muzzlebrake. Introduced 1993. Imported by Beeman Precision Airguns.

Price: Right-hand $1,460.00

Price: Left-hand $1,520.00

BEEMAN HW70A AIR PISTOL

Caliber: 177, single shot. **Barrel:** 6-1/4", rifled. **Weight:** 38 oz. **Length:** 12-3/4" overall. **Power:** Spring, barrel cocking. **Stocks:** Plastic, with thumbrest. **Sights:** Hooded post front, square notch rear adjustable for windage and elevation. Comes with scope mount base. **Features:** Adjustable trigger, 31-lb. cocking effort, 440 fps MV; automatic barrel safety. Imported by Beeman.

Price: $185.00

Price: HW70S, black grip, silver finish $210.00

BEEMAN/WEBLEY TEMPEST AIR PISTOL

Caliber: 177, 22, single shot. **Barrel:** 6-7/8". **Weight:** 32 oz. **Length:** 8.9" overall. **Power:** Spring-piston, break barrel. **Stocks:** Checkered black plastic with thumbrest. **Sights:** Blade front, adjustable rear. **Features:** Velocity to 500 fps (177), 400 fps (22). Aluminum frame; black epoxy finish; manual safety. Imported from England by Beeman.

Price: $225.00

Beeman/Webley Hurricane Air Pistol

Similar to the Tempest except has extended frame in the rear for a click-adjustable rear sight; hooded front sight; comes with scope mount. Imported from England by Beeman.

Price: $180.00

BENJAMIN SHERIDAN CO2 PELLET PISTOLS

Caliber: 177, 20, 22, single shot. **Barrel:** 6-3/8", rifled brass. **Weight:** 29 oz. **Length:** 9.8" overall. **Power:** 12-gram CO2 cylinder. **Stocks:** Walnut. **Sights:** High ramp front, fully adjustable notch rear. **Features:** Velocity to 500 fps. Bolt action with cross-bolt safety. Gives about 40 shots per CO2 cylinder. Black or nickel finish. Made in U.S. by Benjamin Sheridan Co.

Price: Black finish, EB17 (177), EB20 (20), about $115.23

AIRGUNS

BRNO TAU-7

Crosman Auto Air II

Crosman Model 1377

Daisy/Power Line 717

(pellets). Spring-fed magazine; cross-bolt safety. Introduced 1996. Made in U.S. by Crosman Corp.
Price: About **$20.00**

CROSMAN BLACK FANG PISTOL
Caliber: 177 BB, 17-shot magazine. **Barrel:** 4.75" smoothbore. **Weight:** 10 oz. **Length:** 10.8" overall. **Power:** Spring. **Stocks:** Checkered. **Sights:** Blade front, fixed notch rear. **Features:** Velocity to 250 fps. Spring-fed magazine; cross-bolt safety. Introduced 1996. Made in U.S. by Crosman Corp.
Price: About **$16.00**

CROSMAN MODEL 1322, 1377 AIR PISTOLS
Caliber: 177 (M1377), 22 (M1322), single shot. **Barrel:** 8", rifled steel. **Weight:** 39 oz. **Length:** 13-5/8". **Power:** Hand pumped. **Sights:** Blade front, rear adjustable for windage and elevation. **Features:** Bolt action moulded plastic grip, hand size pump forearm. Cross-bolt safety. From Crosman.
Price: About **$60.00**

CROSMAN AUTO AIR II PISTOL
Caliber: BB, 17-shot magazine, 177 pellet, single shot. **Barrel:** 8-5/8" steel, smoothbore. **Weight:** 13 oz. **Length:** 10-3/4" overall. **Power:** CO$_2$ Powerlet. **Stocks:** Grooved plastic. **Sights:** Blade front, adjustable rear; highlighted system. **Features:** Velocity to 480 fps (BBs), 430 fps (pellets). Semi-automatic action with BBs, single shot with pellets. Silvered finish. Introduced 1991. From Crosman.
Price: About **$38.00**

CROSMAN MODEL 357 SERIES AIR PISTOL
Caliber: 177 10-shot pellet clips. **Barrel:** 4" (Model 3574GT), 6" (Model 3576GT). **Weight:** 32 oz. (6"). **Length:** 11-3/8" overall (357-6). **Power:** CO$_2$ Powerlet. **Stocks:** Average 430 fps (Model 3574GT). Break-open barrel for easy loading. Single or double action. Vent. rib barrel. Wide, smooth trigger. Two cylinders come with each gun. Black finish. From Crosman.
Price: 4" or 6", about **$65.00**

CROSMAN MODEL 1008 REPEAT AIR
Caliber: 177, 8-shot pellet clip. **Barrel:** 4.25", rifled steel. **Weight:** 17 oz. **Length:** 8.625" overall. **Power:** CO$_2$ Powerlet. **Stocks:** Checkered black plastic. **Sights:** Post front, adjustable rear. **Features:** Velocity about 430 fps. Break-open barrel for easy loading; single or double semi-automatic action; two 8-shot clips included. Optional carrying case available. Introduced 1992. From Crosman.
Price: About **$60.00**
Price: With case, about **$70.00**
Price: Model 1008SB (silver and black finish), about **$60.00**

DAISY MODEL 2003 PELLET PISTOL
Caliber: 177 pellet, 35-shot clip. **Barrel:** Rifled steel. **Weight:** 2.2 lbs. **Length:** 11.7" overall. **Power:** CO$_2$. **Stocks:** Checkered plastic. **Sights:** Blade front, open rear. **Features:** Velocity to 400 fps. Crossbolt trigger-block safety. Made in U.S. by Daisy Mfg. Co.
Price: About **$67.95**

DAISY MODEL 454 AIR PISTOL
Caliber: 177 BB, 20-shot clip. **Barrel:** Smoothbore steel. **Weight:** 1.6 lbs. **Length:** 10.4" overall. **Power:** CO$_2$. **Stocks:** Moulded black, ribbed composition. **Sights:** Blade front, fixed rear. **Features:** Velocity to 420 fps. Semi-automatic action; cross-bolt safety; black finish. Introduced 1998. Made in U.S. by Dairy Mfg. Co.
Price: **$61.95**

DAISY/POWERLINE 717 PELLET PISTOL
Caliber: 177, single shot. **Barrel:** 9.61". **Weight:** 2.25 lbs. **Length:** 13-1/2" overall. **Stocks:** Moulded wood-grain plastic, with thumbrest. **Sights:** Blade and ramp front, micro-adjustable notch rear. **Features:** Single pump pneumatic pistol. Rifled steel barrel. Cross-bolt trigger block. Muzzle velocity 385 fps. From Daisy Mfg. Co. Introduced 1979.
Price: About **$71.95**

BENJAMIN SHERIDAN PNEUMATIC PELLET PISTOLS
Caliber: 177, 20, 22, single shot. **Barrel:** 9-3/8", rifled brass. **Weight:** 38 oz. **Length:**13-1/8" overall. **Power:** Underlever pnuematic, hand pumped. **Stocks:** Walnut stocks and pump handle. **Sights:** High ramp front, fully adjustable notch rear. **Features:** Velocity to 525 fps (variable). Bolt action with cross-bolt safety. Choice of black or nickel finish. Made in U.S. by Benjamin Sheridan Co.
Price: Black finish, HB17 (177), HB20 (20), HB22 (22), about **$129.50**

BERETTA 92 FS/CO$_2$ AIR PISTOLS
Caliber: 177 pellet, 8-shot magazine. **Barrel:** 4.9". **Weight:** 44.4 oz. **Length:** 8.2" (10.2" with compensator). **Power:** CO2 cartridge. **Grips:** plastic or wood. **Sights:** Adjustable rear, blade front. **Features:** Velocity 375 fps. Replica of Beretta 92 FS pistol. Single- and double-action trigger; ambidextrous safety; black or nickel-plated finish. Made by Umarex for Beretta USA.
Price: Starting at **$200.00**

BRNO TAU-7 CO$_2$ MATCH PISTOL
Caliber: 177. **Barrel:** 10.24". **Weight:** 37 oz. **Length:** 15.75" overall. **Power:** 12.5-gram CO$_2$ cartridge. **Stocks:** Stippled hardwood with adjustable palm rest. **Sights:** Blade front, open fully adjustable rear. **Features:** Comes with extra seals and counterweight. Blue finish. Imported by Great Lakes Airguns.
Price: About **$299.50**

BSA 240 MAGNUM AIR PISTOL
Caliber: 177, 22, single shot. **Barrel:** 6". **Weight:** 2 lbs. **Length:** 9" overall. **Power:** Spring-air, top-lever cocking. **Stocks:** Walnut. **Sights:** Blade front, micrometer adjustable rear. **Features:** Velocity 510 fps (177), 420 fps (22); crossbolt safety. Combat autoloader styling. Imported from U.K. by Precision Sales International, Inc.
Price: **$259.99**

COLT GOVERNMENT 1911 A1 AIR PISTOL
Caliber: 177, 8-shot cylinder magazine. **Barrel:** 5", rifled. **Weight:** 38 oz. **Length:** 8-1/2" overall. **Power:** CO$_2$ cylinder. **Stocks:** Checkered black plastic or smooth wood. **Sights:** Post front, adjustable rear. **Features:** Velocity to 393 fps. Quick-loading cylinder magazine; single and double action; black or silver finish. Introduced 1998. Imported by Colt's Mfg. Co., Inc.
Price: Black finish. **$199.00**
Price: Silver finish. **$209.00**

CROSMAN BLACK VENOM PISTOL
Caliber: 177 pellets, BB, 17-shot magazine; darts, single shot. **Barrel:** 4.75" smoothbore. **Weight:** 16 oz. **Length:** 10.8" overall. **Power:** Spring. **Stocks:** Checkered. **Sights:** Blade front, adjustable rear. **Features:** Velocity to 270 fps (BBs), 250 fps

AIRGUNS

"GAT" AIR PISTOL
Caliber: 177, single shot. Barrel: 7-1/2" cocked, 9-1/2" extended. Weight: 22 oz. Power: Spring-piston. Stocks: Cast checkered metal. Sights: Fixed. Features: Shoots pellets, corks or darts. Matte black finish. Imported from England by Stone Enterprises, Inc.
Price: $24.95

EAA/BAIKAL MP-651K AIR PISTOL/RIFLE
Caliber: 177 pellet (8-shot magazine); 177 BB (23-shot). Barrel: 5.9" (17.25" with rifle attachment). Weight: 1.54 lbs. (3.3 lbs. with rifle attachment) Power: CO2 cartridge, semi-automatic. Stock: Plastic. Sights: Notch rear/blade front (pistol); periscopic sighting system (rifle). Features: Velocity 328 fps. Unique pistol/rifle combination allows the pistol to be inserted into the rifle shell. Imported from Russia by European American Armory.
Price: ....

EAA/BAIKAL MP-654K AIR PISTOL
Caliber: 177 BB, detachable 13-shot magazine. Barrel: 3.75". Weight: 1.6 lbs. Power: CO2 cartridge. Grips: Black checkered plastic. Sights: Notch rear, blade front. Features: Velocity about 380 fps. Double-action trigger, slide safety; metal slide and frame. Replica of Makarov pistol. Imported from Russia by European American Armory.
Price: $110.00

EAA/BAIKAL IZH-46 TARGET AIR PISTOL
Caliber: 177, single shot. Barrel: 11.02". Weight: 2.87 lbs. Length: 16.54" overall. Power: Underlever single-stroke pneumatic. Grips: Adjustable wooden target. Sights: Micrometer fully adjustable rear, blade front. Features: Velocity about 420 fps. Hammer-forged, rifled barrel. Imported from Russia by European American Armory.
Price: $275.00

DAISY/POWERLINE 1270 CO2 AIR PISTOL
Caliber: BB, 60-shot magazine. Barrel: Smoothbore steel. Weight: 17 oz. Length: 11.1" overall. Power: CO2 pump action. Stocks: Moulded black polymer. Sights: Blade on ramp front, adjustable rear. Features: Velocity to 420 fps. Crossbolt trigger block safety; plated finish. Introduced 1997. Made in U.S. by Daisy Mfg. Co.
Price: About $39.95

DAISY/POWERLINE 44 REVOLVER
Caliber: 177 pellets, 6-shot. Barrel: 6". rifled steel; interchangeable 4" and 8". Weight: 2.7 lbs. Length: 13.1" overall. Power: CO2. Stocks: Moulded plastic with checkering. Sights: Blade on ramp front, fully adjustable notch rear. Features: Velocity up to 400 fps. Replica of 44 Magnum revolver. Has swingout cylinder and interchangeable barrels. Introduced 1987. From Daisy Mfg. Co.
Price: About $59.95

DAISY/POWERLINE 1140 PELLET PISTOL
Caliber: 177, single shot. Barrel: Rifled steel. Weight: 1.3 lbs. Length: 11.7" overall. Power: Single-stroke barrel cocking. Stocks: Checkered resin. Sights: Hooded post front, open adjustable rear. Features: Velocity of 360 fps. Manual cross-bolt safety; weight engineering resin. Introduced 1995. From Daisy.
Price: About $38.95

Daisy/PowerLine 747 Pistol
Caliber: 177, single shot. Similar to the 717 pistol except has a 12-groove rifled steel barrel by Lothar Walther, and adjustable trigger pull weight. Velocity of 360 fps.
Price: About $140.00

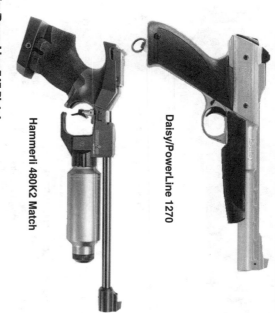

Daisy/PowerLine 1270

Hammerli 480K2 Match

HAMMERLI 480 MATCH AIR PISTOL.
Caliber: 177, single shot. Barrel: 9.8". Weight: 37 oz. Length: 16.5" overall. Power: Air or CO2. Stocks: Walnut with 7-degree rake adjustment. Stippled grip area. Sights: Undercut blade front, fully adjustable open match rear. Features: Under-barrel cannister charges with air or CO2 for power supply; gives 320 shots per filling. Trigger adjustable for position. Introduced 1994. Imported from Switzerland by Hammerli Pistols U.S.A.
Price: $1,325.00

Hammerli 480K2 Match Air Pistol
Caliber: 177, single shot. Similar to the 480 except has a short, detachable aluminum air cylinder for use only with compressed air; can be filled while on the gun or off; special adjustable barrel weights. Muzzle velocity of 470 fps, gives about 180 shots. Has stippled black composition grip with adjustable palm shelf and rake angle. Comes with air pressure gauge. Introduced 1996. Imported from Switzerland by SIGARMS, Inc.
Price: $1,112.50

MARKSMAN 1010 REPEATER PISTOL
Caliber: 177, 18-shot BB repeater. Barrel: 2-1/2", smoothbore. Weight: 24 oz. Power: Spring. Features: Velocity to 200 fps. Thumb safety. Black finish. Uses BBs, darts, bolts or pellets. Repeats with BBs only. From Marksman Products.
Price: Matte black finish $26.00
Price: Model 2000 (as above except silver-chrome finish) $27.00

MARKSMAN 2005 LASERHAWK SPECIAL EDITION AIR PISTOL
Caliber: 177, 24-shot magazine. Barrel: 3.8", smoothbore. Weight: 22 oz. Length: 10.3" overall. Power: Spring-air. Stocks: Checkered. Sights: Fixed fiber optic front sight. Features: Velocity to 300 fps with Hyper-Velocity pellets. Square trigger guard with skeletonized trigger; extended barrel for greater velocity and accuracy. Shoots BBs, pellets, darts or bolts. Made in the U.S. From Marksman Products.
Price: $32.00

MORINI 162E MATCH AIR PISTOL
Caliber: 177, single shot. Barrel: 9.4". Weight: 32 oz. Length: 16.1" overall. Power: Scuba air. Stocks: Adjustable match type. Sights: Interchangeable blade front, fully adjustable match-type rear. Features: Power mechanism shuts down when pressure drops to a pre-set level. Adjustable electronic trigger. Introduced 1995. Imported from Switzerland by Nygord Precision Products.
Price: $995.00

PARDINI K58 MATCH AIR PISTOL
Caliber: 177, single shot. Barrel: 9.0". Weight: 37.7 oz. Length: 15.5" overall. Power: Pre-charged compressed air; single-stroke cocking. Stocks: Adjustable match type; stippled walnut. Sights: Interchangeable post front, fully adjustable match rear. Features: Fully adjustable trigger. Introduced 1995. Imported from Italy by Nygord Precision Products.
Price: $750.00

RWS/DIANA MODEL 5G AIR PISTOL
Caliber: 177, single shot. Barrel: 7". Weight: 2-3/4 lbs. Length: 15" overall. Power: Spring-air, barrel cocking. Stocks: Plastic, thumbrest design. Sights: Tunnel front, micro-click open rear. Features: Velocity of 450 fps. Adjustable two-stage trigger with automatic safety. Imported from Germany by Dynamit Nobel-RWS, Inc.
Price: $260.00

RWS C-225 AIR PISTOLS
Caliber: 177, 8-shot rotary magazine. Barrel: 4", 6". Weight: NA. Length: NA. Power: CO2. Stocks: Checkered black plastic. Sights: Post front, rear adjustable for windage. Features: Velocity to 385 fps. Semi-automatic fire; decocking lever. Imported from Germany by Dynamit Nobel-RWS.
Price: 4" blue $210.00
Price: 4" nickel $220.00
Price: 6" blue $220.00
Price: 6" nickel $245.00

Marksman 2005 Laserhawk

AIRGUNS

Walther CP99

Walther CP88

Walther PPK/S

STEYR LP 5CP MATCH AIR PISTOL
Caliber: 177, 5-shot magazine. **Barrel:** NA. **Weight:** 40.7 oz. **Length:** 15.2" overall. **Power:** Pre-charged air cylinder. **Stocks:** Adjustable match type. **Sights:** Interchangeable blade front, fully adjustable match rear. **Features:** Adjustable sight radius; fully adjustable trigger. Has barrel compensator. Introduced 1995. Imported from Austria by Nygord Precision Products.
Price: **$1,150.00**

STEYR LP10P MATCH PISTOL
Caliber: 177, single shot. **Barrel:** 9". **Weight:** 38.7 oz. **Length:** 15.3" overall. **Power:** Scuba air. **Stocks:** Fully adjustable Morini match with palm shelf; stippled walnut. **Sights:** Interchangeable blade in 4mm, 4.5mm or 5mm widths, fully adjustable open rear with interchangeable 3.5mm or 4mm leaves. **Features:** Velocity about 500 fps. Adjustable trigger; adjustable sight radius from 12.4" to 13.2". With compensator. Imported from Austria by Nygord Precision Products.
Price: **$1,195.00**

TECH FORCE SS2 OLYMPIC COMPETITION AIR PISTOL
Caliber: 177 pellet, single shot. **Barrel:** 7.4". **Weight:** 2.8 lbs. **Length:** 16.5" overall. **Power:** Spring piston, underlever. **Grips:** Hardwood. **Sights:** Extended adjustable rear, blade front accepts inserts. **Features:** Velocity 520 fps. Recoilless design; adjustments allow duplication of a firearm's feel. Match-grade, adjustable trigger; includes carrying case. Imported from China by Compasseco Inc.
Price: **$295.00**

TECH FORCE 35 AIR PISTOL
Caliber: 177 pellet, single shot. **Barrel:** N/A. **Weight:** 2.86 lbs. **Length:** 14.9" overall. **Power:** Spring piston, underlever. **Grips:** Hardwood. **Sights:** Micrometer adjustable rear, blade front. **Features:** Velocity 400 fps. Grooved for scope mount; trigger safety. Imported from China by Compasseco Inc.
Price: **$49.95**

Tech Force 8 Air Pistol
Similar to Tech Force 35, but with break-barrel action, ambidextrous polymer grips. From Compasseco Inc.
Price: **$59.95**

Tech Force S2-1 Air Pistol
Similar to Tech Force 8, but more basic grips and sights for plinking. From Compasseco Inc.
Price: **$29.95**

WALTHER CP88 PELLET PISTOL
Caliber: 177, 8-shot rotary magazine. **Barrel:** 4", 6". **Weight:** 37 oz. (4" barrel) **Length:** 7" (4" barrel). **Power:** CO_2. **Stocks:** Checkered plastic. **Sights:** Blade front, fully adjustable rear. **Features:** Faithfully replicates size, weight and trigger pull of the 9mm Walther P88 compact pistol. Has SA/DA trigger mechanism; ambidextrous safety, levers. Comes with two magazines, 500 pellets, one CO2 cartridge. Introduced 1997. Imported from Germany by Interarms.
Price: Blue **$179.00**
Price: Nickel **$189.00**

WALTHER LP20I MATCH PISTOL
Caliber: 177, single shot. **Barrel:** 8.66". **Weight:** NA. **Length:** 15.1" overall. **Power:** Scuba air. **Stocks:** Orthopaedic target type. **Sights:** Undercut blade front, open match rear fully adjustable for windage and elevation. **Features:** Adjustable velocity;

matte finish. Introduced 1995. Imported from Germany by Nygord Precision Products.
Price: **$1,095.00**

Walther CP88 Competition Pellet Pistol
Similar to the standard CP88 except has 6" match-grade barrel, muzzle weight, wood or plastic stocks. Weighs 41 oz., has overall length of 9". Introduced 1997. Imported from Germany by Interarms.
Price: Blue, plastic grips **$170.00**
Price: Nickel, plastic grips **$195.00**
Price: Blue, wood grips **$205.00**
Price: Nickel, wood grips **$232.00**

WALTHER CP99 AIR PISTOL
Caliber: 177 pellet, 8-shot rotary magazine. **Barrel:** 3". **Weight:** 26 oz. **Length:** 7.1" overall. **Power:** CO2 cartridge. **Grip:** Polymer. **Sights:** Drift-adjustable rear, blade front. **Features:** Velocity 320 fps. Replica of Walther P99 pistol. Trigger allows single and double action; ambidextrous magazine release; interchangeable backstraps to fit variety of hand sizes. Introduced 2000. From Walther USA.
Price: **$149.00**

WALTHER PPK/S AIR PISTOL
Caliber: 177 BB. **Barrel:** N/A. **Weight:** 20 oz. **Length:** 6.3" overall. **Power:** CO2 cartridge. **Grip:** Plastic. **Sights:** Fixed rear, blade front. **Features:** Replica of Walther PPK pistol. Blow back system moves slide when fired; trigger allows single and double action. Introduced 2000. From Walther USA.
Price: **$89.00**

GRIPS

AJAX CUSTOM GRIPS

Grip materials include ivory polymer, ivory, white and black Pearlite, Indian Sambar stag, walnut, cherrywood, black silverwood, simulated buffalo horn and pewter. Smooth, fingergroove and checkered designs offered for some models. Available for most single- and double-action revolvers and automatics. Made in U.S. by Ajax Custom Grips Inc.

Prices: $35 to $145 (ivory is by special order only)

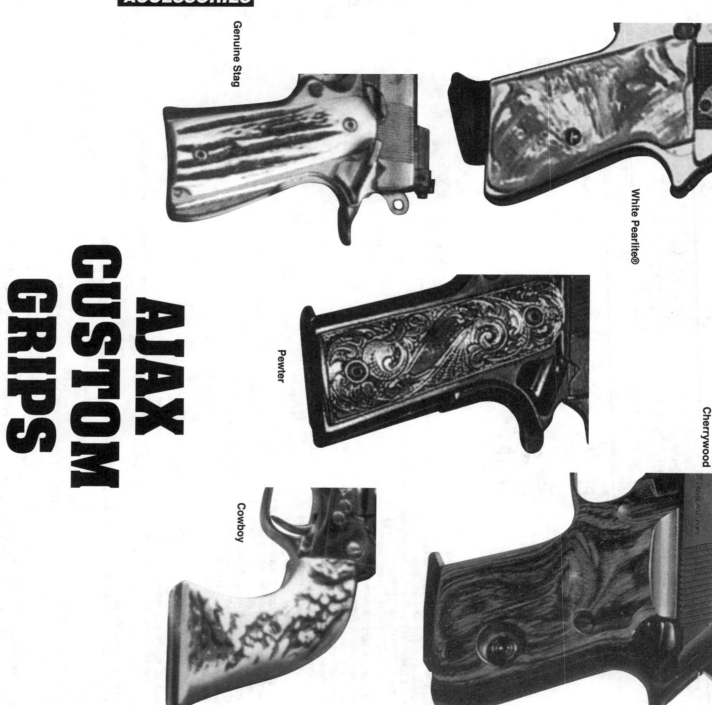

Genuine Stag

White Pearlite®

Pewter

Cowboy

Cherrywood

GRIPS

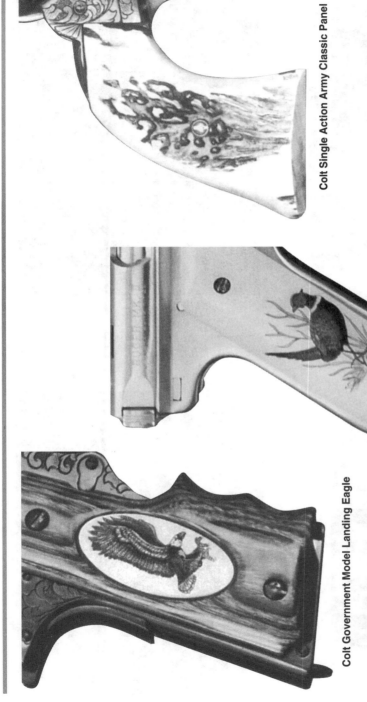

Colt Single Action Army Classic Panel

Ruger Pheasant

Colt Government Model Landing Eagle

Beretta Super Rosewood

ALTAMONT CUSTOM GRIPS

Colt Government Model Facing Buck

Grip materials include bonded ivory, laminated rosewood, fancy walnut, laminated walnut, laminated silver-black hardwood, black ebony, bocote, rosewood, hard black epoxy, imitation pearl, Asian Sambar stag and ivory. Scrimshaw designs, inlays, carvings and personalization available. Smooth, fingergroove and checkered designs offered. Grips made for most single- and double-action revolvers and automatics. Made in U.S. by Altamont.

Prices: $21 to $85 (ivory and other exotics at additional cost)

GRIPS

Slip-on Grips for Autoloaders

Grips for Pistols

Boot Grips for Revolvers

BUTLER CREEK (UNCLE MIKE'S)

CUSTOM GRADE SYNTHETIC MOLDED GRIPS

These Uncle Mike's polymer grips are designed by custom handgun grip maker Craig Spegel. They are designed to fill the hand without a spongy feel. Double-action revolver grips feature finger grooves for improved control. From Butler Creek.

Price: Revolver Grips (for most Ruger, Smith & Wesson and Taurus single- and double-action revolvers) **$19.95**
Price: Revolver Boot Grips (for small-frame Ruger, Smith & Wesson and Taurus double-action revolvers) **$19.95**
Price: Slip-on Grips (for most small, medium, compact large-frame and full-size large frame automatics that do not have grip safeties) . . . **$19.95**
Price: Pistol Grips (for most Ruger, Smith & Wesson Beretta, Colt, Sig-Sauer, Taurus and CZ-75 autos) **$19.95**

GRIPS

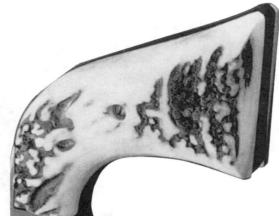

Rosewood Checkered

Indian Sambar Stag

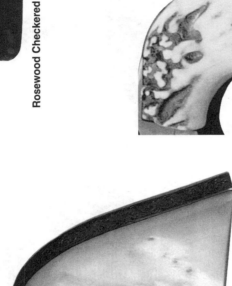

Mother-of-Pearl

EAGLE GRIPS

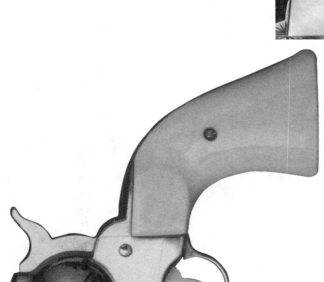

Ultra Imitation Ivory

Buffalo Horn

Grip materials include imitation ivory, rosewood, buffalo horn, ebony, mother of pearl and Indian Sambar stag. Smooth, fingergroove and checkered designs offered. Grips made for most single- and double-action revolvers and automatics. Made in U.S. by Eagle Grips.

Prices: $39.95 to $195.00 (checkering at additional cost)

HOGUE GRIPS

Cocobolo

Beretta

Lamo Camo

Kingwood

Pau Ferro

Hogue offers its patented revolver Monogrip one-piece grip and automatic pistol grips in soft, synthetic rubber, rubber-nylon composite and pure nylon, as well as a synthetic rubber sleeve-type Handall grip that fits more than 50 automatic pistols. In addition, the company offers hardwood grips in smooth, checkered and fingergroove designs in rosewood laminate, Lamo Camo, rosewood, kingwood, tulipwood, cocobolo, pau ferro, goncalo alves, walnut, white pearlized polymer, black pearlized polymer, white paper micarta, black paper micarta and ivory polymer. Grips made for most single- and double-action revolvers and automatics. Made in U.S. by Hogue Inc.

Prices: $9.95 to $69.95 (checkering and other options at additional cost)

GRIPS

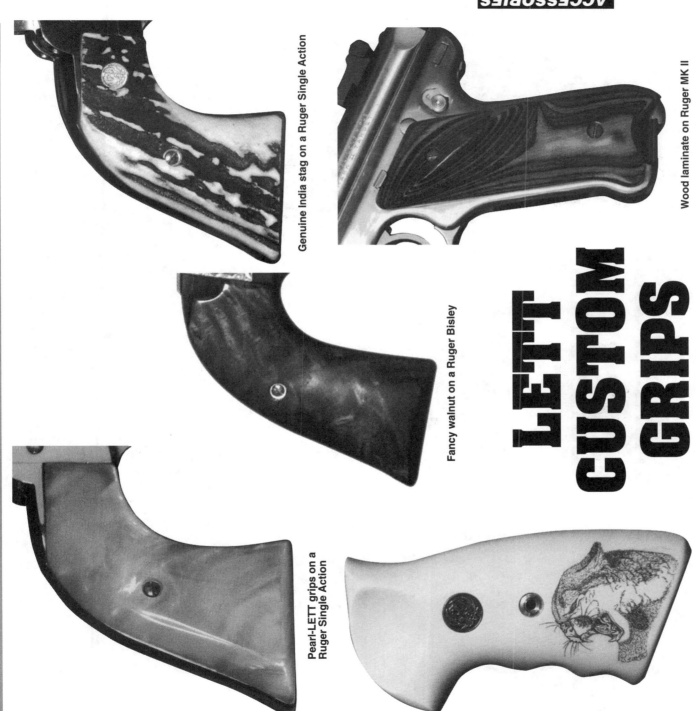

Genuine India stag on a Ruger Single Action

Wood laminate on Ruger MK II

Fancy walnut on a Ruger Bisley

LETT CUSTOM GRIPS

Pearl-LETT grips on a
Ruger Single Action

Scrimshaw on micarta
for Ruger Double Action

Grip materials offered include imitation ivory, Pearl-Lett (imitation mother of pearl), Bolivian rosewood, zebrawood, fancy walnut, goncalo alves, charcoal burgundy laminate, silver black laminate, charcoal ruby laminate, hawkeye laminate, winewood laminate, camouflage laminate, ivory micarta and black micarta. Checkering and scrimshaw designs, as well as custom scrimshaw, available. Grips made for most single- and double-action revolvers and automatics. Made in U.S. by W.F. Lett Mfg. Inc.

Prices: $26 to $98.50

UNITED STATES FIRE-ARMS GRIPS

Grip materials include hard rubber, American walnut, Turkish burl, bastone burl, English burl, African rosewood, stag, pearl, bone, ivory micarta and ivory. Checkering, scrimshaw and carved figuring also available. Grips available for single-action revolvers. Made in U.S. by United States Fire-Arms Manu. Co. Inc.

Prices: $75 to $550

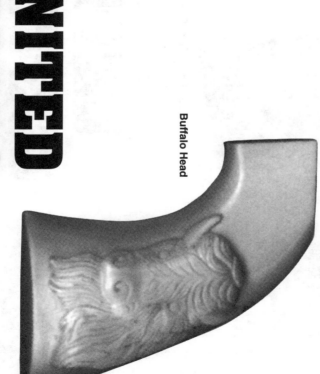

Fancy American
Diamond Checkered

Buffalo Head

Double Scrimshaw with border

METALLIC CARTRIDGE PRESSES

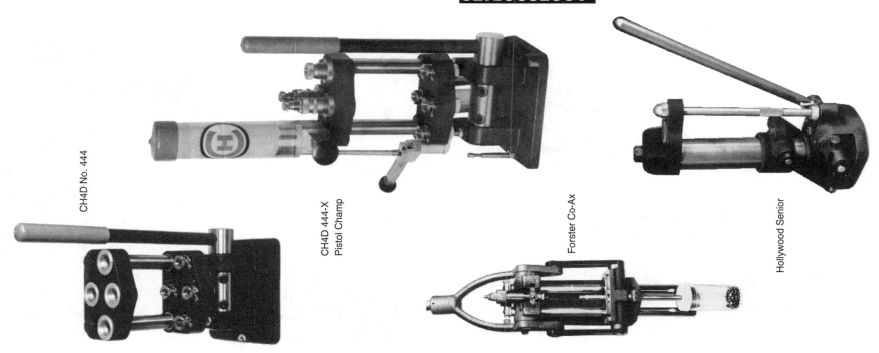

CH4D No. 444

CH4D 444-X
Pistol Champ

Forster Co-Ax

Hollywood Senior

CH4D Heavyweight Champion

Frame: Cast iron
Frame Type: O-frame
Die Thread: 7/8-14 or 1-14
Avg. Rounds Per Hour: NA
Ram Stroke: 3-1/4"
Weight: 26 lbs.
Features: 1.185" diameter ram with 16 square inches of bearing surface; ram drilled to allow passage of spent primers; solid steel handle; toggle that slightly breaks over the top dead center. Includes universal primer arm with large and small punches. From CH Tool & Die/4D Custom Die.
Price: **$220.00**

CH4D No. 444

Frame: Aluminum alloy
Frame Type: H-frame
Die Thread: 7/8-14
Avg. Rounds Per Hour: 200
Ram Stroke: 3-3/4"
Weight: 12 lbs.
Features: Two 7/8' solid steel shaft "H" supports; platen rides on permanently lubed bronze bushings; loads smallest pistol to largest magnum rifle cases and has strength to full-length resize. Includes four rams, large and small primer arm and primer catcher. From CH Tool & Die/4D Custom Die, Co.
Price: **$195.00**

CH4D No. 444-X Pistol Champ

Frame: Aluminum alloy
Frame Type: H-frame
Die Thread: 7/8-14
Avg. Rounds Per Hour: 200
Ram Stroke: 3-3/4"
Weight: 12 lbs.
Features: Tungsten carbide sizing die; Speed Seater seating die with tapered entrance to automatically align bullet on case mouth; automatic primer feed for large or small primers; push-button powder measure with easily changed bushings for 215 powder/load combinations; taper crimp die. Conversion kit for caliber changeover available. From CH Tool & Die/4D Custom Die, Co.
Price: .... **$292.00-$316.50**

FORSTER Co-Ax Press B-2

Frame: Cast iron
Frame Type: Modified O-frame
Die Thread: 7/8-14
Avg. Rounds Per Hour: 120
Ram Stroke: 4"
Weight: 18 lbs.
Features: Snap in/snap out die change; spent primer catcher with drop tube threaded into carrier below shellholder; automatic, handle-activated, cammed shellholder with opposing spring-loaded jaws to contact extractor groove; floating guide rods for alignment and reduced friction; no torque on the head due to design of linkage and pivots; shellholder jaws that float with die permitting case to center in the die; right- or left-hand operation; priming device for seating to factory specifications. "S" shellholder jaws included. From Forster Products.
Price: **$298.00**
Price: Extra shellholder jaws **$26.00**

HOLLYWOOD Senior Press

Frame: Ductile iron
Frame Type: O-frame
Die Thread: 7/8-14
Avg. Rounds Per Hour: 50-100
Ram Stroke: 6-1/2"
Weight: 50 lbs.
Features: Leverage and bearing surfaces ample for reloading cartridges or swaging bullets. Precision ground one-piece 2-1/2" pillar with base; operating

METALLIC CARTRIDGE PRESSES

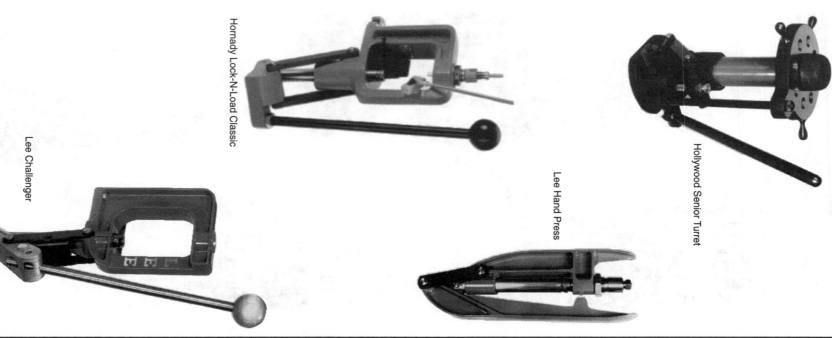

Hornady Lock-N-Load Classic

Lee Challenger

Lee Hand Press

Hollywood Senior Turret

HOLLYWOOD Senior Turret Press

Frame: Ductile iron
Frame Type: H-frame
Die Thread: 7/8-14
Avg. Rounds Per Hour: 50-100
Ram Stroke: 6-1/2"
Weight: 50 lbs.
Features: Same features as Senior press except has three-position turret head; holes in turret may be tapped 1-1/2" or 7/8" or four of each. Height, 15". Comes complete with one turret indexing handle; one 1-1/2" to 7/8" die hole bushing; one 5/8" tie down bar for swaging. From Hollywood Engineering.
Price: **$600.00**

handle of 3/4" steel and 15" long; 5/8" steel tie-down rod fro added strength when swaging; heavy steel toggle and camming arms held by 1/2" steel pins in reamed holes. The 1-1/2" steel die bushing takes standard threaded dies; removed, it allows use of Hollywood shotshell dies. From Hollywood Engineering.
Price: **$500.00**

HORNADY Lock-N-Load Classic

Frame: Die cast heat-treated aluminum alloy
Frame Type: O-frame
Die Thread: 7/8-14
Avg. Rounds Per Hour: NA
Ram Stroke: 3-5/8"
Weight: 14 lbs.
Features: Features Lock-N-Load bushing system that allows instant die changeovers. Solid steel linkage arms that rotate on steel pins; 30° angled frame design for improved visibility and accessibility; primer arm automatically moves in and out of ram for primer pickup and solid seating; two primer arms for large and small primers; long offset handle for increased leverage and unobstructed reloading; lifetime warranty. Comes as a package with primer catcher, PPS automatic primer feed and three Lock-N-Load die bushings. Dies and shellholder available separately or as a kit with primer catcher, positive priming system, automatic primer feed, three die bushings and reloading accessories. From Hornady Mfg. Co.
Price: Classic Reloading Package **$99.95**
Price: Classic Reloading Kit **$239.95**

LEE Hand Press

Frame: ASTM 380 aluminum
Frame Type: NA
Die Thread: 7/8-14
Avg. Rounds Per Hour: 100
Ram Stroke: 3-1/4"
Weight: 1 lb., 8 oz.
Features: Small and lightweight for portability; compound linkage for handling up to 375 H&H and case forming. Dies and shellholder not included. From Lee Precision, Inc.
Price: **$22.98**

LEE Challenger Press

Frame: ASTM 380 aluminum
Frame Type: O-frame
Die Thread: 7/8-14
Avg. Rounds Per Hour: 100
Ram Stroke: 3-1/2"
Weight: 4 lbs., 1 oz.
Features: Larger than average opening with 30° offset for maximum hand clearance; steel connecting pins; spent primer catcher; handle adjustable for start and stop positions; handle repositions for left- or right-hand use; shortened handle travel to prevent springing the frame from alignment. Dies and shellholders not included. From Lee Precision, Inc.
Price: **$39.98**

METALLIC CARTRIDGE PRESSES

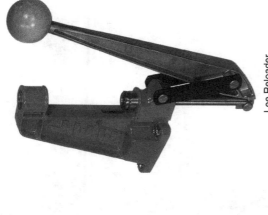

Lee Reloader

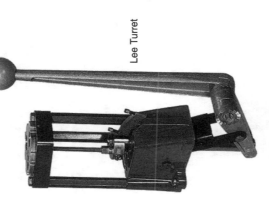

Lee Turret

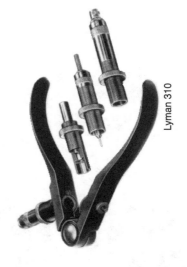

Lyman 310

LEE Loader

Kit consists of reloading dies to be used with mallet or soft hammer. Neck sizes only. Comes with powder charge cup. From Lee Precision, Inc.

Price: **$19.98**

LEE Reloader Press

Frame: ASTM 380 aluminum
Frame Type: C-frame
Die Thread: 7/8-14
Avg. Rounds Per Hour: 100
Ram Stroke: 3"
Weight: 1 lb., 12 oz.
Features: Balanced lever to prevent pinching fingers; unlimited hand clearance; left- or right-hand use. Dies and shellholders not included. From Lee Precision, Inc.

Price: **$22.98**

LEE Turret Press

Frame: ASTM 380 aluminum
Frame Type: O-frame
Die Thread: 7/8-14
Avg. Rounds Per Hour: 300
Ram Stroke: 3"
Weight: 7 lbs., 2 oz.
Features: Replaceable turret lifts out by rotating 30°; T-primer arm reverses for large or small primers; built-in primer catcher; adjustable handle for right- or left-hand use or changing angle of down stroke; accessory mounting hole for Lee Auto-Disk powder measure. Optional Auto-Index rotates die turret to next station for semi-progressive use. Safety override prevents overstressing should turret not turn. From Lee Precision, Inc.

Price: **$69.98**
Price: With Auto-Index **$83.98**
Price: Extra turret **$10.98**

LYMAN 310 Tool

Frame: Stainless steel
Frame Type: NA
Die Thread: 7/8-14
Avg. Rounds Per Hour: NA
Ram Stroke: NA
Weight: 10 oz.
Features: Compact, portable reloading tool for pistol or rifle cartridges. Adapter allows loading rimmed or rimless cases. Die set includes neck resizing/decapping die, primer seating chamber; neck expanding die; bullet seating die; and case head adapter. From Lyman Products Corporation.

Price: Dies **$39.95**
Price: Press **$44.95**
Price: Carrying pouch **$9.95**

LYMAN AccuPress

Frame: Die cast
Frame Type: C-frame
Die Thread: 7/8-14
Avg. Rounds Per Hour: 75
Ram Stroke: 3.4"
Weight: 4 lbs.
Features: Reversible, contoured handle for bench mount or hand-held use; for rifle or pistol; compound leverage; Delta frame design. Accepts all standard powder measures. From Lyman Products Corporation.

Price: **$33.25**

METALLIC CARTRIDGE PRESSES

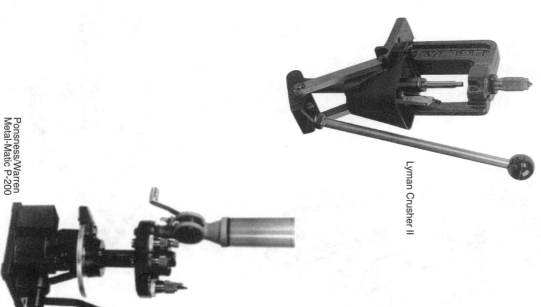

Lyman Crusher II

Turret handle disconnector

Lyman T-Mag II

Ponsness/Warren
Metal-Matic P-200

LYMAN Crusher II

Frame: Cast iron
Frame Type: O-frame
Die Thread: 7/8-14
Avg. Rounds Per Hour: 75
Ram Stroke: 3-7/8"
Weight: 19 lbs.
Features: Reloads both pistol and rifle cartridges; 1" diameter ram; 4-1/2" press opening for loading magnum cartridges; direct torque design; right- or left-hand use. New base design with 14 square inches of flat mounting surface with three bolt holes. Comes with priming arm and primer catcher. Dies and shellholders not included. From Lyman Products Corporation.
Price: **$112.50**

LYMAN T-Mag II

Frame: Cast iron with silver metalflake powder finish
Frame Type: Turret
Die Thread: 7/8-14
Avg. Rounds Per Hour: 125
Ram Stroke: 3-13/16"
Weight: 18 lbs.
Features: Reengineered and upgraded with new turret system for ease of indexing and tool-free turret removal for caliber changeover; new flat machined base for bench mounting; new nickel-plated non-rust handle and links; and new silver hammertone powder coat finish for durability. Right- or left-hand operation; handles all rifle or pistol dies. Comes with priming arm and primer catcher. Dies and shellholders not included. From Lyman Products Corporation.
Price: **$154.95**
Price: Extra turret **$36.00**

PONSNESS/WARREN Metal-Matic P-200

Frame: Die cast aluminum
Frame Type: Unconventional
Die Thread: 7/8-14
Avg. Rounds Per Hour: 200+
Weight: 18 lbs.
Features: Designed for straight-wall cartridges; die head with 10 tapped holes for holding dies and accessories for two calibers at one time; removable spent primer box; pivoting arm moves case from station to station. Comes with large and small primer tool. Optional accessories include primer feed, extra die head, primer speed feeder, powder measure extension and dust cover. Dies, powder measure and shellholder not included. From Ponsness/Warren.
Price: **$199.00**
Price: Extra die head. **$44.95**
Price: Powder measure extension **$26.95**
Price: Primer feed. **$42.95**
Price: Primer speed feed. **$13.95**
Price: Dust cover. **$20.95**

RCBS Partner

Frame: Aluminum
Frame Type: O-frame
Die Thread: 7/8-14
Avg. Rounds Per Hour: 50-60
Ram Stroke: 3-5/8"
Weight: 5 lbs.
Features: Designed for the beginning reloader. Comes with primer arm equipped with interchangeable primer plugs and sleeves for seating large and small primers. Shellholder and dies not included. Available in kit form (see Metallic Presses—Accessories). From RCBS.
Price: **$54.95**

METALLIC CARTRIDGE PRESSES

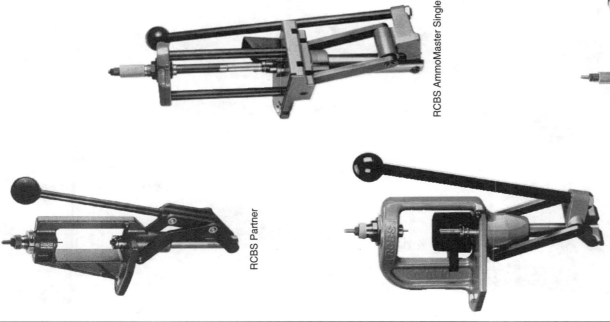

RCBS AmmoMaster Single

RCBS Rock Chucker

RCBS Partner

RCBS Reloader Special-5

RCBS AmmoMaster Single

Frame: Aluminum base; cast iron top plate connected by three steel posts.

Frame Type: NA

Die Thread: 1-1/4"-12 bushing; 7/8-14 threads

Avg. Rounds Per Hour: 50-60

Ram Stroke: 5-1/4"

Weight: 19 lbs.

Features: Single-stage press convertible to progressive. Will form cases or swage bullets. Case detection system to disengage powder measure when no case is present in powder charging station; five-station shellplate; Uniflow Powder measure with clear powder measure adaptor to make bridged powders visible and correctable. 50-cal. conversion kit allows reloading 50 BMG. Kit includes top plate to accommodate either 1-3/8" x 12 or 1-1/2" x 12 reloading dies. Piggyback die plate for quick caliber change-overs available. Reloading dies not included. From RCBS.

Price: **$186.95**

Price: 50 conversion kit **$74.95**

Price: Piggyback/AmmoMaster die plate **$22.95**

Price: Piggyback/AmmoMaster shellplate **$27.95**

Price: Press cover **$10.95**

RCBS Reloader Special-5

Frame: Aluminum

Frame Type: 30° offset O-frame

Die Thread: 1-1/4"-12 bushing; 7/8-14 threads

Avg. Rounds Per Hour: 50-60

Ram Stroke: 3-1/16"

Weight: 7.5 lbs.

Features: Single-stage press convertible to progressive with RCBS Piggyback II. Primes cases during resizing operation. Will accept RCBS shotshell dies. From RCBS.

Price: **$103.95**

RCBS Rock Chucker

Frame: Cast iron

Frame Type: O-frame

Die Thread: 1-1/4"-12 bushing; 7/8-14 threads

Avg. Rounds Per Hour: 50-60

Ram Stroke: 3-1/16"

Weight: 17 lbs.

Features: Designed for heavy-duty reloading, case forming and bullet swaging. Provides 4" of ram-bearing surface to support 1" ram and ensure alignment; ductile iron toggle blocks; hardened steel pins. Comes standard with Universal Primer Arm and primer catcher. Can be converted from single-stage to progressive with Piggyback II conversion unit. From RCBS.

Price: **$130.95**

REDDING Turret Press

Frame: Cast iron

Frame Type: Turret

Die Thread: 7/8-14

Avg. Rounds Per Hour: NA

Ram Stroke: 3.4"

Weight: 23 lbs., 2 oz.

Features: Strength to reload pistol and magnum rifle, case form and bullet swage; linkage pins heat-treated, precision ground and in double shear; hollow ram to collect spent primers; removable turret head for caliber changes; progressive linkage for increased power as ram nears die; slight frame tilt for comfortable operation; rear turret support for stability and precise alignment; six-station turret head; priming arm for both large and small primers. Also available in kit form with shellholder, primer catcher and one die set. From

METALLIC CARTRIDGE PRESSES

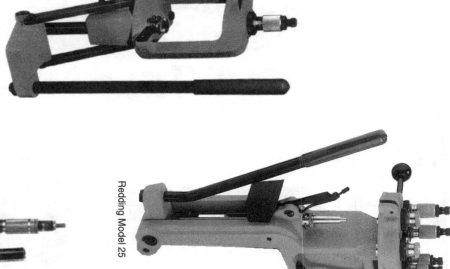

Redding Ultramag

Redding Boss

Redding Model 25

Rock Crusher

Redding Reloading Equipment.

Price: $298.50
Price: Kit $334.50

REDDING Boss

Frame: Cast iron
Frame Type: O-frame
Die Thread: 7/8-14
Avg. Rounds Per Hour: NA
Ram Stroke: 3.4"
Weight: 11 lbs., 8 oz.
Features: 36° frame offset for visibility and accessibility; primer arm positioned at bottom ram travel; positive ram travel stop machined to hit exactly top-dead-center. Also available in kit form with shellholder and set of Redding A dies. From Redding Reloading Equipment.

Price: $129.00
Price: Kit $165.00

REDDING Ultramag

Frame: Cast iron
Frame Type: Non-conventional
Die Thread: 7/8-14
Avg. Rounds Per Hour: NA
Ram Stroke: 4-1/8"
Weight: 23 lbs., 6 oz.
Features: Unique compound leverage system connected to top of press for tons of ram pressure; large 4-3/4" frame opening for loading outsized cartridges; hollow ram for spent primers. Kit available with shellholder and one set Redding A dies. From Redding Reloading Equipment.

Price: $298.50
Price: Kit $334.50

ROCK CRUSHER Press

Frame: Cast iron
Frame Type: O-frame
Die Thread: 2-3/4"-12 with bushing reduced to 1-1/2"-12
Avg. Rounds Per Hour: 50
Ram Stroke: 6"
Weight: 67 lbs.
Features: Designed to load and form ammunition from 50 BMG up to 23x115 Soviet. Frame opening of 8-1/2"x3-1/2"; 1-1/2"x12"; bushing can be removed and bushings of any size substituted; ram pressure can exceed 10,000 lbs. with normal body weight; 40mm diameter ram. Angle block for bench mounting and reduction bushing for RCBS dies available. Accessories for Rock Crusher include powder measure, dies, shellholder, bullet puller, priming tool, case gauge and other accessories found elsewhere in this catalog. From The Old Western Scrounger.

Price: $785.00
Price: Angle block $57.95
Price: Reduction bushing $21.00
Price: Shellholder, 50 BMG, 12.7, 55 Boyes $36.75
Price: Shellholder, 23 Soviet $65.00
Price: Shellholder, all others $47.95
Price: Priming tool, 50 BMG, 20 Lahti $65.10

PROGRESSIVE PRESSES

DILLON AT 500

Frame: Aluminum alloy
Frame Type: NA
Die Thread: 7/8-14
Avg. Rounds Per Hour: 200-300
Ram Stroke: 3-7/8"
Weight: NA
Features: Four stations; removable tool head to hold dies in alignment and allow caliber changes without die adjustment; manual indexing; capacity to be upgraded to progressive RL 550B. Comes with universal shellplate to accept

METALLIC CARTRIDGE PRESSES

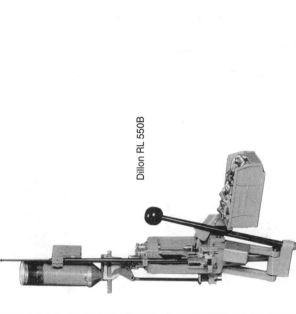

Dillon RL 550B

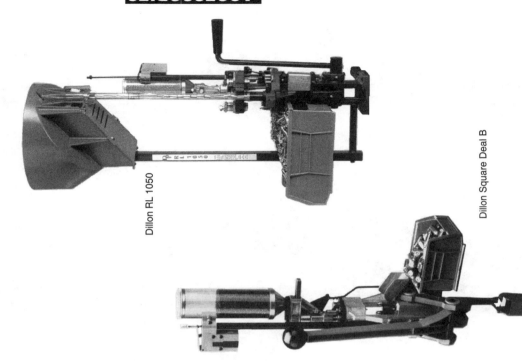

Dillon RL 1050

Dillon Square Deal B

223, 22-250, 243, 30-06, 9mm, 38/357, 40 S&W, 45 ACP. Dies not included. From Dillon Precision Products.
Price: **$193.95**

DILLON RL 550B

Frame: Aluminum alloy
Frame Type: NA
Die Thread: 7/8-14
Avg. Rounds Per Hour: 500-600
Ram Stroke: 3-7/8"
Weight: 25 lbs.
Features: Four stations; removable tool head to hold dies in alignment and allow caliber changes without die adjustment; auto priming system that emits audible warning when primer tube is low; a 100-primer capacity magazine contained in DOM steel tube for protection; new auto powder measure system with simple mechanical connection between measure and loading platform for positive powder bar return; a separate station for crimping with star-indexing system; 220 ejected-round capacity bin; 3/4-lb. capacity powder measure. Height above bench, 35"; requires 3/4" bench overhang. Will reload 120 different rifle and pistol calibers. Comes with one caliber conversion kit. Dies not included. From Dillon Precision Products, Inc.
Price: **$325.95**

DILLON RL 1050

Frame: Ductile iron
Frame Type: Platform type
Die Thread: 7/8-14
Avg. Rounds Per Hour: 1000-1200
Ram Stroke: 2-5/16"
Weight: 62 lbs.
Features: Eight stations; auto case feed; primer pocket swager for military cartridge cases; auto indexing; removable tool head; auto prime system with 100-primer capacity; low primer supply alarm; positive powder bar return; auto powder measure; 515 ejected round bin capacity; 500-600 case feed capacity; 3/4-lb. capacity powder measure. Loads all pistol rounds as well as 30 M1 Carbine, 223, and 7.62x39 rifle rounds. Height above the bench, 43". Dies not included. From Dillon Precision Products, Inc.
Price: **$1,199.95**

DILLON Square Deal B

Frame: Zinc alloy
Frame Type: NA
Die Thread: None (unique Dillon design)
Avg. Rounds Per Hour: 400-500
Ram Stroke: 2-5/16"
Weight: 17 lbs.
Features: Four stations; auto indexing; removable tool head; auto prime system with 100-primer capacity; low primer supply alarm; auto powder measure; positive powder bar return; 170 ejected round capacity bin; 3/4-lb. capacity powder measure. Height above the bench, 34". Comes complete with factory adjusted carbide die set. From Dillon Precision Products, Inc.
Price: **$252.95**

DILLON XL 650

Frame: Aluminum alloy
Frame Type: NA
Die Thread: 7/8-14
Avg. Rounds Per Hour: 800-1000
Ram Stroke: 4-9/16"
Weight: 46 lbs.
Features: Five stations; auto indexing; auto case feed; removable tool head; auto prime system with 100-primer capacity; low primer supply alarm; auto

METALLIC CARTRIDGE PRESSES

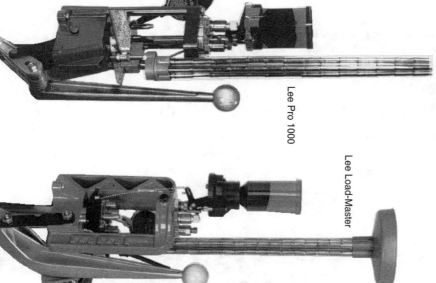

Lee Pro 1000

Hornady Lock-N-Load AP

Lee Load-Master

Dillon XL 650

powder measure; positive powder bar return; 220 ejected round capacity bin; 3/4-lb. capacity powder measure. 500-600 case feed capacity with optional auto case feed. Loads all pistol/rifle calibers less than 3-1/2" in length. Height above the bench, 44"; 3/4" bench overhang required. From Dillon Precision Products, Inc.

Price: Less dies. **$443.95**

HORNADY Lock-N-Load AP

Frame: Die cast heat-treated aluminum alloy
Frame Type: O-frame
Die Thread: 7/8-14
Avg. Rounds Per Hour: NA
Ram Stroke: 3-3/4"
Weight: 26 lbs.
Features: Features Lock-N-Load bushing system that allows instant die changeovers; five-station die platform with option of seating and crimping separately or adding taper-crimp die; auto prime with large and small primer tubes with 100-primer capacity and protective housing; brass kicker to eject loaded rounds into 80-round capacity cartridge catcher; offset operating handle for leverage and unobstructed operation; 2" diameter ram driven by heavy-duty cast linkage arms rotating on steel pins. Comes with five Lock-N-Load die bushings, shellplate, deluxe powder measure, auto powder drop, and auto primer feed and shut-off, brass kicker and primer catcher. Lifetime warranty. From Hornady Mfg. Co.

Price: **$367.65**

LEE Load-Master

Frame: ASTM 380 aluminum
Frame Type: O-frame
Die Thread: 7/8-14
Avg. Rounds Per Hour: 600
Ram Stroke: 3-1/4"
Weight: 8 lbs., 4 oz.
Features: Available in kit form only. A 1-3/4" diameter hard chrome ram for handling largest magnum cases; loads rifle or pistol rounds; five station press to factory crimp and post size; auto indexing with wedge lock mechanism to hold one ton; auto priming; removable turrets; four-tube case feeder with optional case collator and bullet feeder (late 1995); loaded round ejector with chute to optional loaded round catcher; quick change shellplate; primer catcher. Dies and shellholder for one caliber included. From Lee Precision, Inc.

Price: Rifle **$320.00**
Price: Pistol **$330.00**
Price: Extra turret **$10.98**
Price: Adjustable charge bar. **$9.98**

LEE Pro 1000

Frame: ASTM 380 aluminum and steel
Frame Type: O-frame
Die Thread: 7/8-14
Avg. Rounds Per Hour: 600
Ram Stroke: 3-1/4"
Weight: 8 lbs., 7 oz.
Features: Optional transparent large/small or rifle case feeder; deluxe auto-disk case-activated powder measure; case sensor for primer feed. Comes complete with carbide die set (steel dies for rifle) for one caliber. Optional accessories include: case feeder for large/small pistol cases or rifle cases; shell plate carrier with auto prime, case ejector, auto-index with spare parts; case collator for case feeder. From Lee Precision, Inc.

Price: **$199.98**

METALLIC CARTRIDGE PRESSES

RCBS AmmoMaster

Fully-automated Star Universal

PONSNESS/WARREN Metallic II

Frame: Die cast aluminum
Frame Type: H-frame
Die Thread: 7/8-14
Avg. Rounds Per Hour: 150+
Ram Stroke: NA
Weight: 32 lbs.
Features: Die head with five tapped 7/8-14 holes for dies, powder measure or other accessories; pivoting die arm moves case from station to station; depriming tube for removal of spent primers; auto primer feed; interchangeable die head. Optional accessories include additional die heads, powder measure extension tube to accommodate any standard powder measure, primer speed feeder to feed press primer tube without disassembly. Comes with small and large primer seating tools. Dies, powder measure and shellholder not included. From Ponsness/Warren.
Price: $359.00
Price: Extra die head $54.95
Price: Primer speed feeder $13.95
Price: Powder measure extension $26.95
Price: Dust cover $27.95

RCBS AmmoMaster-Auto

Frame: Aluminum base; cast iron top plate connected by three steel posts.
Frame Type: NA
Die Thread: 1-1/4-12 bushing; 7/8-14 threads
Avg. Rounds Per Hour: 400-500
Ram Stroke: 5-1/4"
Weight: 19 lbs.
Features: Progressive press convertible to single-stage. Features include: 1-1/2" solid ram; automatic indexing, priming, powder charging and loaded round ejection. Case detection system disengages powder measure when no case is present in powder charging station. Comes with five-station shellplate and Uniflow powder measure with clear powder measure adaptor to make bridged powders visible and correctable. Piggyback die plate for quick caliber change-over available. Reloading dies not included. From RCBS.
Price: $394.95
Price: Piggyback/AmmoMaster die plate $22.95
Price: Piggyback/AmmoMaster shellplate $27.95
Price: Press cover $10.95

STAR Universal Pistol Press

Frame: Cast iron with aluminum base
Frame Type: Unconventional
Die Thread: 11/16-24 or 7/8-14
Avg. Rounds Per Hour: 300
Ram Stroke: NA
Weight: 27 lbs.
Features: Four or five-station press depending on need to taper crimp; handles all popular handgun calibers from 32 Long to 45 Colt. Comes completely assembled and adjusted with carbide dies (except 30 Carbine) and shellholder to load one caliber. Prices slightly higher for 9mm and 30 Carbine. From Star Machine Works.
Price: With taper crimp $950.00
Price: Without taper crimp $925.00
Price: Extra tool head, taper crimp $381.00
Price: Extra tool head, w/o taper crimp. $356.00

METALLIC SIGHTS

Open Sights

MILLETT SCOPE-SITE Open, adjustable or fixed rear sights dovetails into a base integral with the top scope-mounting ring. Blaze orange front ramp sight is integral with the front ring half. Rear sights have white outline aperture. Provides fast, short-radius, Patridge-type open sights on the top of the scope. Can be used with all Millett rings, Ruger Ranch Rifle, No. 1, No. 3, Rem. 870, 1100; 77 (also fits Redhawk), Ruger Ranch Rifle, No. 1, No. 3, Rem. 870, 1100; Burris, Leupold and Redfield bases.
Price: Scope-Site top only, windage only **$31.15**
Price: As above, fully adjustable **$66.10**
Price: Scope-Site Hi-Turret, fully adjustable, low, medium, high . . . **$66.10**

P-T NIGHT SIGHTS Made to fit a variety of handguns, shotguns and rifles. Machined steel sights made from 4140 steel. Sight variations include a 3-dot style (green/green, green/red, green/yellow, green/orange, and green/blue) with several bar configurations available. All 3-dot configurations come with a bold white outline for easier daytime acquisition. **P-T Night Sights** come standard with a full 15-year warranty on all sight systems. From Innovative Weaponry Inc.
Price: **$85.00/set**

WICHITA MULTI RANGE SIGHT SYSTEM Designed for silhouette shooting. System allows you to adjust the rear sight to four repeatable range settings, once it is pre-set. Sight clicks to any of the settings by turning a serrated wheel. Front sight is adjustable for weather and light conditions with one adjustment. Specify gun when ordering.
Price: Rear sight **$120.00**
Price: Front sight **$90.00**

WILLIAMS DOVETAIL OPEN SIGHT (WDOS) Open rear sight with windage and elevation adjustment. Furnished with "U" notch or choice of blades. Slips into dovetail and locks with gib lock. Heights from .281" to .531".
Price: Less blade **$16.85**
Price: Extra blades, each **$6.50**

Front Sights

ERA FRONT SIGHTS European-type front sights inserted from the front. Various heights available. From New England Custom Gun Service.
Price: With blade **$16.35**
Price: Less Blade **$10.25**

WILLIAMS GUIDE OPEN SIGHT (WGOS) Open rear sight with windage and elevation adjustment. Bases to fit most military and commercial barrels. Choice of square "U" or "V" notch blade, 3/16", 1/4", 5/16", or 3/8" high.
Price: Less blade **$11.95**
Price: Sourdough bead **$16.00**
Price: Fiber Optic **$22.00**
Price: Folding night sight with ivory bead **$39.50**

Globe Target Front Sights

LYMAN 20 MJT TARGET FRONT Has 7/8" diameter, one-piece steel globe with 3/8" dovetail base. Height is .700" from bottom of dovetail to center of aperture; height on 20 LJT is .750". Comes with seven Anschutz-size steel inserts—two posts and five apertures .126" through .177".
Price: 20 MJT or 20 LJT **$32.50**

LYMAN No. 17A TARGET Includes seven interchangeable inserts: four apertures, one transparent amber and two posts .50" and .100" in width.
Price: Insert set **$12.00**

Lyman 17AEU

LYMAN 17AEU Similar to the Lyman 17A except has a special dovetail design to mount easily onto European muzzleloaders such as CVA, Traditions and Investarm. All steel, comes with eight inserts.
Price: **$26.50**

Ashley Express Big Dot

ASHLEY EXPRESS SIGHTS Low-profile, snag-free express-type sights. Shallow V rear with white vertical line, white dot/front. All-steel, matte black finish. Rear is available in different heights. Made for most pistols, many with double set-screws. From Ashley Outdoors, Inc.
Price: Standard Set, front and rear **$60.00**
Price: Big Dot Set, front and rear **$60.00**
Price: Tritium Set, Standard or Big Dot **$90.00**

Ashley Pro Express

ASHLEY PRO EXPRESS SIGHTS Big Dot Tritium or Standard Dot Tritium Front Sight incorporating a new vertical Tritium Bar within the Rear of Express Sights. Provides enchanced low-light sight acquisition with speed set-screw style for easier installation. Rear sights available in fitted or double set-screw style for easier installation. From Ashley Outdoors Sight Systems.
Price: Pro Express Big Dot Tritium **$120.00**
Price: Pro Express Standard Dot Tritium **$120.00**

Ashley Adjustable

ASHLEY ADJUSTABLE EXPRESS SIGHT SETS Incorporates Adjustable Rear Express Sight with a white stripe rear, or Pro Express Rear with a Vertical Tritium Bar., fits either a Bomar style cut, LPA style cut, or a Kimber Tgt cut rear sight. Affords same Express Sight principles as fixed sight models.

METALLIC SIGHTS

BO-MAR DELUXE BMCS Gives 3/8" windage and elevation adjustment at 50 yards on Colt Gov't 45; sight radius under 7". For GM and Commander models only. Uses existing dovetail slot. Has shield-type rear blade.
Price: $65.95
Price: BMCS-2 (for GM and 9mm) $68.95
Price: Flat bottom $65.95
Price: BMGC (for Colt Gold Cup), angled serrated blade, rear.... $68.95
Price: BMGC front sight. $12.95

BO-MAR FRONT SIGHTS Dovetail style for S&W 4506, 4516, 1076; undercut style (.250", .280", 5/16" high); Fast Draw style (.210", .250", .230" high).
Price $12.95

BO-MAR BMU XP-100/T/C CONTENDER No gunsmithing required; has .080" notch.
Price: $77.00

BO-MAR BMML For muzzleloaders; has .062" notch, flat bottom.
Price: $65.95
Price: With 3/8" dovetail $65.95

BO-MAR RUGER "P" ADJUSTABLE SIGHT Replaces factory front and rear sights.
Price: Rear sight. $65.95
Price: Front sight. $12.00

BO-MAR BMR Fully adjustable rear sight for Ruger MKI, MKII Bull barrel autos.
Price: Rear. $65.95
Price: Undercut front sight. $12.00

BO-MAR GLOCK Fully adjustable, all-steel replacement sights. Sight fits factory dovetail. Longer sight radius. Uses Novak Glock .275" high, .135" wide front, or similar.
Price: Rear sight. $68.95
Price: Front sight. $20.95

BO-MAR LOW PROFILE RIB & ACCURACY TUNER Streamlined rib with front and rear sights; 7 1/8" sight radius. Brings sight line closer to the bore than standard or extended sight and ramp. Weight 5 oz. Made for Colt Gov't 45, Super 38, and Gold Cup 45 and 38.
Price: $140.00

BO-MAR COMBAT RIB For S&W Model 19 revolver with 4" barrel. Sight radius 5 3/4", weight 5 1/2 oz.
Price: $127.00

Price: Adjustable Express w/White Stripe Rear and Big Dot Front or Standard Dot Front $90.00
Price: Adjustable Express w/White Stripe Rear and Big Dot Tritium or Standard Dot Tritium Front $150.00
Price: Adjustable Pro Express w/Tritium Rear and Big Dot Tritium or Standard Dot Tritium Front $150.00

BO-MAR WINGED RIB For S&W 4" and 6" length barrels—K-38, M10, HB 14 and 19. Weight for the 6" model is about 7 1/4 oz.
Price: $140.00

BO-MAR COVER-UP RIB Adjustable rear sight, winged front guards. Fits right over revolver's original front sight. For S&W 4" M-10HB, M-13, M-58, M-64 & 65, Ruger 4" models SDA-34, SS-34, SDA-34, SS-84, GF-34, GF-84.
Price: $130.00

C-MORE SIGHTS Replacement front sight blades offered in two types and five styles. Made of Du Pont Acetal, they come in a set of five high-contrast colors: blue, green, pink, red and yellow. Easy to install. Patridge style for Colt Python (all barrels), Ruger Super Blackhawk (7 1/2"), Ruger Blackhawk (4 5/8"); ramp style for Python (all barrels), Blackhawk (4 5/8"), Super Blackhawk (7 1/2" and 10 1/2"). From C-More Systems.
Price: Per set. $19.95

JP GHOST RING Replacement bead front, ghost ring rear for Glock and M1911 pistols. From JP Enterprises.
Price: $79.95
Price: Bo-Mar replacement leaf with JP dovetail front bead $99.95

MMC TACTICAL ADJUSTABLE SIGHTS Low-profile, snag free design. Twenty-two click positions for elevation, drift adjustable for windage. Machined from 4140 steel and heat treated to 40 RC. Tritium and non-tritium. Ten different configurations and colors. Three different finishes. For 1911s, all Glock, HK USP, S&W, Browning Hi-Power.
Price: Sight set, tritium $147.90
Price: Sight set, white outline or white dot $101.90
Price: Sight set, black $95.90

MEPROLIGHT TRITIUM NIGHT SIGHTS Replacement sight assemblies for use in low-light conditions. Available for rifles, shotguns, handguns and bows. **TRU-DOT** models carry a 12-year warranty on the useable illumination, while non-**TRU-DOT** have a 5-year warranty. Contact Hesco, Inc. for complete list of available models.
Price: Kahr K9, K40, fixed, **TRU-DOT** $100.00
Price: Ruger P85, P89, P94, adjustable, **TRU-DOT** $140.00
Price: Ruger Mini-14R sights $140.00
Price: SIG Sauer P220, P225, P226, P228, adjustable, **TRU-DOT** $156.00
Price: Smith&Wesson autos, fixed or adjustable, **TRU-DOT** $100.00
Price: Taurus PT92, PT100, adjustable, **TRU-DOT** $156.00
Price: Walther P-99, fixed, **TRU-DOT** $100.00
Price: Shotgun bead $32.00
Price: Beretta M92, Cougar, Brigadier, fixed, **TRU-DOT** $100.00
Price: Browning Hi-Power, adjustable, **TRU-DOT** $156.00
Price: Colt M1911 Govt., adjustable, **TRU-DOT** $156.00

MILLETT SERIES 100 REAR SIGHTS All-steel highly visible, click adjustable. Blades in white outline, target black, silhouette, 3-dot, and tritium bars. Fit most popular revolvers and autos.
Price: .... $49.30 to $80.00

Colt 1911 Govt. Commander Pistol

Taurus Model 44 & 608 Revolvers

Meprolight Night Sights

Beretta Pistol

H&K USP

Glock Pistol

Ruger P85, P85MKII & P89 Pistol

METALLIC SIGHTS

Millett Series 100

MILLETT BAR-DOT-BAR TRITIUM NIGHT SIGHTS Replacement front and rear combos fit most automatics. Horizontal tritium bars on rear, dot front sight.
Price: **$145.00**

MILLETT 3-DOT SYSTEM SIGHTS The 3-Dot System sights use a single white dot on the front blade and two dots flanking the rear notch. Fronts available in Dual-Crimp and Wide Stake-On styles, as well as special applications. Adjustable rear sight available for most popular auto pistols and revolvers.
Price: Front, from **$16.00**
Price: Adjustable rear **$55.60**

MILLETT REVOLVER FRONT SIGHTS All-steel replacement front sights with either white or orange bar. Easy to install. For Ruger GP-100, Redhawk, Security-Six, Speed-Six, Colt Trooper, Diamondback, King Cobra, Peacemaker, Python, Dan Wesson 22 and 15-2.
Price: . . . . **$13.60** to **$16.00**

MILLETT DUAL-CRIMP FRONT SIGHT Replacement front sight for automatic pistols. Dual-Crimp uses an all-steel, two-point hollow rivet system. Available in eight heights and four styles. Has a skirted base that covers the front sight pad. Easily installed with the Millet Installation Tool Set. Available in Blaze Orange Bar, White Bar, Serrated Ramp, Plain Post.
Price: **$16.00**

MILLETT STAKE-ON FRONT SIGHT Replacement front sight for automatic pistols. Stake-On sights have skirted base that covers the front sight pad. Easily installed with the Millet Installation Tool Set. Available in seven heights and four styles—Blaze Orange Bar, White Bar, Serrated Ramp, Plain Post.
Price: **$16.00**

OMEGA OUTLINE SIGHT BLADES Replacement rear sight blades for Colt and Ruger single action guns and the Interarms Virginian Dragoon. Standard Outline available in gold or white notch outline on blue metal. From Omega Sales, Inc.
Price: **$16.00**

OMEGA MAVERICK SIGHT BLADES Replacement "peep-sight" blades for Colt, Ruger SAs, Virginian Dragoon. Three models available—No. 1, Plain; No. 2, Single Bar; No. 3, Double Bar Rangefinder. From Omega Sales, Inc.
Price: Each **$8.95**

Pachmayr Accu-Set

PACHMAYR ACCU-SET Low-profile, fully adjustable rear sight to be used with existing front sight. Available with target, white outline or 3-dot blade. Blue finish. Uses factory dovetail and locking screw. For Browning, Colt, Glock, SIG Sauer, S&W and Ruger autos. From Pachmayr.
Price: . . . . **NA**

P-T TRITIUM NIGHT SIGHTS Self-luminous tritium sights for most popular handguns, Colt AR-15, H&K rifles and shotguns. Replacement handgun sight sets available in 3-Dot style (green/green, green/yellow, green/orange) with bold outlines around inserts; Bar-Dot available in green/green with or without white outline rear sight. Functional life exceeds 15 years. From Innovative Weaponry, Inc.
Price: Handgun sight sets **$99.95**
Price: Rifle sight sets **$99.95**
Price: Rifle, front only **$49.95**
Price: Shotgun, front only **$49.95**

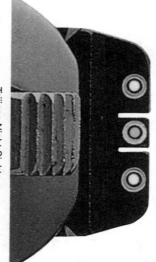

Trijicon Night Sights

TRIJICON NIGHT SIGHTS Three-dot night sight system uses tritium lamps in the front and rear sights. Tritium "lamps" are mounted in silicone rubber inside a metal cylinder. A polished crystal sapphire provides protection and clarity. Inlaid white outlines provide 3-dot aiming in daylight also. Available for most popular handguns. From Trijicon, Inc.
Price: . . . . **$50.00** to **$249.00**

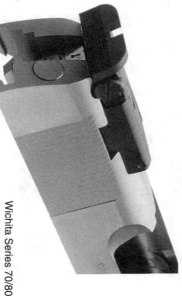

Wichita Series 70/80

WICHITA SERIES 70/80 SIGHT Provides click windage and elevation adjustments with precise repeatability of settings. Sight blade is grooved and angled back at the top to reduce glare. Available in Low Mount Combat or Low Mount Target styles for Colt 45s and their copies, S&W 645, Hi-Power, CZ 75 and others.
Price: Rear sight, target or combat **$75.00**
Price: Front sight, Patridge or ramp **$15.00**

WICHITA GRAND MASTER DELUXE RIBS Ventilated rib has wings machined into it for better sight acquisition and is relieved for Mag-Na-Porting. Milled to accept Weaver see-thru-style rings. Made of stainless or blued steel; front and rear sights blued. Has Wichita Multi-Range rear sight system, adjustable front sight. Made for revolvers with 6" barrel.
Price: Model 301S, 301B (adj. sight K frames with custom bbl. of 1" to 1.032" dia. L and N frame with 1.062" to 1.100" dia. bbl.) **$189.00**
Price: Model 303S, 303B (adj. sight K, L, N frames with factory barrel) **$189.00**

METALLIC SIGHTS

Williams Fire Sight Ruger MKII Sights

WILLIAMS FIRE SIGHT SETS Red fiber optic metallic sight replaces the original. Rear sight has two green fiber optic elements. Made of CNC-machined aluminum. Fits all Glocks, Ruger P-Series (except P-85), S&W 910, Colt Gov't. Model Series 80, Ruger GP 100 and Redhawk, and SIG Sauer (front only).
Price: Front and rear set **$39.95**
Price: SIG Sauer front **$19.95**

Sight Attachments

MERIT ADJUSTABLE APERTURES Eleven clicks give 12 different apertures. No. 3 Disc and Master, primarily target types, 0.22" to .125"; No. 4, 1/2" dia. hunting type, .025" to .155". Available for all popular sights. The Master, with flexible rubber light shield, is particularly adapted to extension, scope height, and tang sights. All models have internal click springs; are hand fitted to minimum tolerance.
Price: No. 3 Master Disk **$66.00**
Price: No. 3 Target Disc (Plain Face) **$56.00**
Price: No. 4 Hunting Disc **$48.00**

Merit Optical Attachment

MERIT LENS DISC Similar to Merit Iris Shutter (Model 3 or Master) but incorporates provision for mounting prescription lens integrally. Lens may be obtained locally from your optician. Sight disc is 7/16" wide (Model 3), or 3/4" wide (Master).
Price: No. 3 Target Lens Disk **$68.00**
Price: No. 3 Master Lens Disk. **$78.00**

MERIT OPTICAL ATTACHMENT For iron sight shooting with handgun or rifle. Instantly attached by rubber suction cup to prescription or shooting glasses. Swings aside. Aperture adjustable from .020" to .156".
Price: **$65.00**

WILLIAMS APERTURES Standard thread, fits most sights. Regular series 3/8" to 1/2" O.D., .050" to .125" hole. "Twilight" series has white reflector ring.
Price: Regular series **$5.15**
Price: Twilight series **$7.55**
Price: Wide open 5/16" aperture for shotguns fits 5-D or Foolproof sights (specify model) **$9.05**

MUZZLE BRAKES

Gentry Quiet Muzzle Brake

Developed by gunmaker David Gentry, the "Quiet Muzzle Brake" is said to reduce recoil by up to 85 percent with no loss of accuracy or velocity. There is no increase in noise level because the noise and gases are directed away from the shooter. The barrel is threaded for installation and the unit is blued to match the barrel finish. Price, installed, is **$150.00**. Add **$15.00** for stainless steel, **$45.00** for knurled cap to protect threads. Shipping extra.

JP Muzzle Brake

Designed for single shot handguns, AR-15, Ruger Mini-14, Ruger Mini Thirty and other sporting rifles, the JP Muzzle Brake redirects high pressure gases against a large frontal surface which applies forward thrust to the gun. All gases are directed up, rearward and to the sides. Priced at **$79.95** (AR-15 or sporting rifles), **$89.95** (bull barrel and SKS, AK models), **$89.95** (Ruger Minis), Dual Chamber model **$79.95**. From JP Enterprises, Inc.

JP Muzzle Brake

KDF Slim Line Muzzle Brake

This threaded muzzle brake has 30 pressure ports that direct combustion gases in all directions to reduce felt recoil up to a claimed 80 percent without affecting accuracy or ballistics. It is said to reduce felt recoil of a 30-06 to that of a 243. Price, installed, is **$179.00**. From KDF, Inc.

Mag-Na-Port

Electrical Discharge Machining works on any firearm except those having non-conductive shrouded barrels. EDM is a metal erosion technique using carbon electrodes that control the area to be processed. The Mag-Na-Port venting process

utilizes small trapezoidal openings to direct powder gases upward and outward to reduce recoil. No effect is had on bluing or nickeling outside the Mag-Na-Port area so no refinishing is needed. Rifle-style porting on single shot or large caliber handguns with barrels 7 1/2" or longer is **$110.00**; Dual Trapezoidal porting on most handguns with minimum barrel length of 3", **$100.00**; standard revolver porting, **$78.50**; porting through the slide and barrel for semi-autos, **$115.00**; traditional rifle porting, **$125.00**. Prices do not include shipping, handling and insurance. From Mag-Na-Port International.

Mag-Na-Brake

A screw-on brake under 2" long with progressive integrated exhaust chambers to neutralize expanding gases. Gases dissipate with an opposite twist to prevent the brake from unscrewing, and with a 5-degree forward angle to minimize sound pressure level. Available in blue, satin blue, bright or satin stainless. Standard and Light Contour installation cost **$179.00** for bolt-action rifles, many single action and single shot handguns. A knurled thread protector supplied at extra cost. Also available in Varmint style with exhaust chambers covering 220 degrees for prone-position shooters. From Mag-Na-Port International.

SSK Arrestor Brake

This is a true muzzle brake with an expansion chamber. It takes up about 1" of barrel and reduces velocity accordingly. Some Arrestors are added to a barrel, increasing its length. Said to reduce the felt recoil of a 458 to that approaching a 30-06. Can be set up to give zero muzzle rise in any caliber, and can be added to most guns. For handgun or rifle. Prices start at **$95.00**. Contact SSK Industries for full data.

SSK Arrestor Muzzle Brakes

SCOPES / HUNTING, TARGET & VARMINT

Maker and Model	Magn.	Field at 100 Yds. (feet)	Eye Relief (in.)	Length (in.)	Tube Dia. (in.)	W & E Adjustments	Weight (ozs.)	Price	Other Data
ADCO									
Magnum 45 mm⁵	0	—	—	4.1	45 mm	Int.	6.8	$279.00	¹Multi-Color Dot system changes from red to green. ²For airguns, paintball, rimfires. Uses common lithium water battery. ³Comes with standard dovetail mount, 4.75" dovetail mount; poly body; adj. intensity diode, 510 MOA dot; black or nickel. ⁶Square format; with mount battery. From ADCO Sales.
MIRAGE Ranger 1"¹	0	—	—	5.2	1	Int.	3.9	159.00	
MIRAGE Ranger 30mm	0	—	—	5.5	30mm	Int.	5	179.00	
MIRAGE Sportsman¹	0	—	—	5.2	1	Int.	4.5	229.00	
MIRAGE Competitor	0	—	—	5.5	30mm	Int.	5.5	229.00	
IMP Sight²	0	—	—	4.5	—	Int.	1.3	17.95	
Square Shooter³	0	—	—	5	—	Int.	5	125.00	
MIRAGE Eclipse¹	0	—	—	5.5	30mm	Int.	5.5	229.00	
MIRAGE Champ	0	—	—	6.25	—	Int.	2	33.95	
Red Dot	0	—	—	4.5	—	Int.	—	—	
AIMPOINT									
Comp	0	—	—	4.6	30mm	Int.	4.3	331.00	Illuminates red dot in field of view. Noparallax (dot does not need to be centered). Unlimited field of view and eye relief. On/off, adj. intensity. Dot covers 3' @100 yds. ¹Comes with 30mm rings, battery, lens cloth. ²Requires 1" rings. Black finish, AP Comp avail. in black, blue, SS, camo. ³Black finish (AP 5000-B) avail. with regular 3-min. or 10-min. Mag Dot as B2 or S2. ⁴Band pass reflection coating for compatibility with night vision equipment; U.S. Army contract model; with anti-reflex coated lenses (Comp ML), $359.00. From Aimpoint U.S.A.
Comp M4	0	—	—	5	30mm	Int.	6.1	409.00	
Series 5000³	0	—	—	6	30mm	Int.	6	297.00	
Series 3000 Universal²	0	—	—	6.25	1	Int.	6	232.00	
Series 5000/2x¹	2	—	—	7	30mm	Int.	9	388.00	
Vantage 1"	0	—	—	3.9	1	Int.	3.9	129.00	
Vantage 30mm	0	—	—	4.2	30mm	Int.	4.9	132.00	
Vision 2000⁶	0	60	—	4.7	—	Int.	6.2	79.00	
ARMSON O.E.G.									
Standard	0	—	—	5.125	1	Int.	4.3	202.00	Shown red dot aiming point. No batteries needed. Standard model fits 1" ring mounts (not incl.). From Trijicon, Inc.
BEEMAN									
Pistol Scopes									
5021	2	19	10-24	9.1	1	Int.	7.4	79.95	Imported by Beeman.
5020	1.5	14	11-16	8.3	.75	Int.	3.6	NA	
BSA									
Pistol Scopes									
P52x20	2	N/A	N/A	N/A	N/A	Int.	N/A	85.50	All scopes have 5 point reticle, all glass fully coated lenses. Imported by BSA. ¹Red dot sights also available in 42mm and 50mm versions.
P54x28	4	N/A	N/A	N/A	N/A	Int.	N/A	NA	
Red Dot									
RD30¹	1	88	unlimited	3.8	30mm	Int.	5	59.95	
BURRIS									
Speeddot 135¹³									¹Dot reticle on some models. ²Matte satin finish. ³Available with parallax adjustment (standard on 10x, 12x, 4-12x, 6-12x, 6-18x, 6x HBR and 3-12x Signature). ⁵Silver matte finish extra. ⁶Target knobs extra, standard on silhouette models. LER and XER with P.A. 6x HBR. ⁹Available with Heavy Plex reticle. ¹⁰Available with Posi-Lock. ¹³Selected models available with camo finish. **Signature Series:** LER=Long Eye Relief; XER=Extra Eye Relief. **Speeddot 135:** ¹³Waterproof, fogproof, coated lenses, 11 brightness settings;3-MOA or 11-MOA dot size; includes Weaver-style rings and battery. **Partial listing shown.** Contact Burris for complete details.
Red Dot	1	—	—	4.85	35mm	Int.	5	291.00	
Handgun									
1.50-4x LER¹,⁵,¹⁰	1.6-3.7	16-11	11-25	10.25	1	Int.	11	363.00	
2-7x LER²,³,⁵,¹⁰	2.6-6.5	21-7	7-27	9.5	1	Int.	12.6	401.00	
3-9x LER³,⁵,¹⁰	3.4-8.4	12-5	22-14	11	1	Int.	14	453.00	
2x LER³,⁵,⁶	1.7	21	10-24	8.75	1	Int.	6.8	265.00	
4x LER¹,³,⁵,⁶,¹⁰	3.7	11	10-22	9.625	1	Int.	9	296.00	
10x LER¹,⁴,⁶	9.5	4	8-12	13.5	1	Int.	14	460.00	
Scout Scope									
1xXER²,⁹	1.5	32	4-24	9	1	Int.	7.0	290.00	
2.75xXER²,⁹	2.7	15	7-14	9.375	1	Int.	7.0	319.00	

Reticle Legend

 Plex

 Fine Plex

 Heavy Plex & Electro-Dot Plex

 Peep Plex

Ballistic Mil-Dot

Target Dot

 Mil-Dot

SCOPES / HUNTING, TARGET & VARMINT

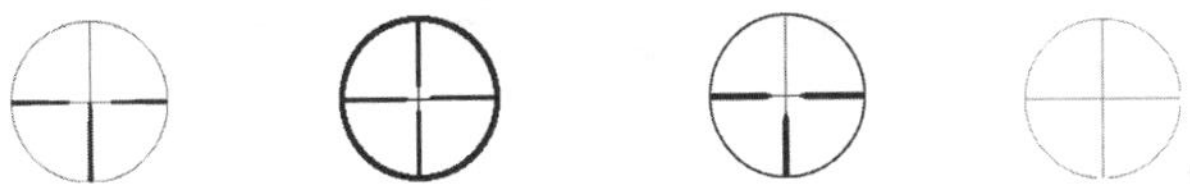

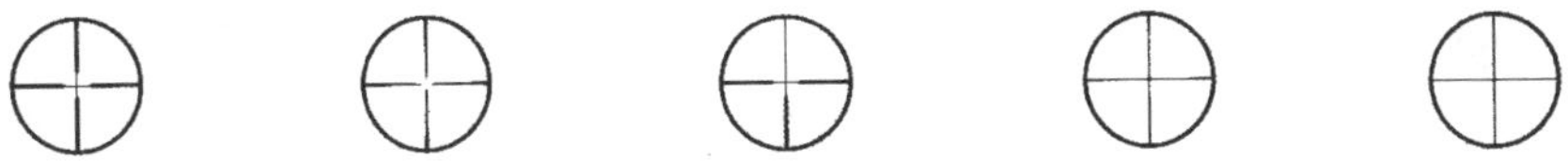

Maker and Model	Magn.	Field at 100 Yds. (feet)	Eye Relief (in.)	Length (in.)	Tube Dia. (in.)	W & E Adjustments	Weight (ozs.)	Price	Other Data
BUSHNELL									(Bausch & Lomb Elite)
Elite 3200 Handgun									[1]Adj. objective, sunshade; also in matte and with 1/4-MOA dot reticle. [2]Also in matte and silver finish. [3]Only in matte finish. [4]Also in matte and silver finish. [5]Adjustable objective. [6]50mm objective; also in matte finish. [7]Also in silver finish. **Partial listings shown. Contact Bushnell Sports Optics for details.**
32-2632G7	2-6	10-4	20	9	1	Int.	10	444.95	
32-2632G	2-6	10-4	20	9	1	Int.	10	444.95	
HOLOsight Model[8]	1	—	—	6	—	Int.	8.7	562.95	(Bushnell)
Trophy Handgun									[2]Also silver finish. [3]Also silver finish. [7]Adj. obj. [8]Variable intensity. $111.95; fits Weaver-style base. Comp model 430 with diamond reticle and 1911 No-hole or 5-hole pattern mount, or STI mount, $631.00. (2x magnification adapter $248.95).
73-0232[2]	2	20	9-26	8.7	1	Int.	7.7	218.95	
73-2632[3]	2-6	21-7	9-26	9.1	1	Int.	9.6	287.95	
Red Dot									
79-0130 6 MOA Dot	1	60	unlim.	5.5	1	Int.	4.9	212.95	
C-MORE SYSTEMS									[1]All Weaver and Picatinny-style rail mounts. [2]Most popular auto pistols. [3]Mounts to any flat surface, custom mounts, shotgun ribs; Glock adapter plate for direct slide mounting. From C-More Systems, Inc.
Handgun 1.5x20	1.5	183	11-22	5.4	1	Int.	6.8	159.00	
Handgun 4x32	4	91	11-22	8.6	1	Int.	7.6	165.00	
Handgun 1.5-4.5x20	1.5-4.5	190-88	11-22	7.7	1	Int.	7.6	215.00	
Handgun 2.5-7x28	2.5-7	135-52	11-22	9.3	1	Int.	8.6	245.00	
Red Dots									
Railway[1]	1	—	—	4.8	—	Int.	5	299.00	
Serendipity[2]	1	—	—	5.3	—	Int.	3.75	299.00	
Slide Ride[3]	1	—	—	4.8	—	Int.	3	249.00	
KILHAM									Unlimited eye relief; internal click adjustments; crosshair reticle. Fits Thompson/Center rail mounts, for S&W K, N, Ruger Blackhawk, Super, Super Single-Six, Contender.
Hutson Handgunner II	1.7	8	—	5.5	.875	Int.	5.1	119.95	
Hutson Handgunner	3	8	10-12	6	.875	Int.	5.3	119.95	
LEUPOLD									Constantly centered reticles, choice of Duplex, tapered CPC, Leupold Dot, Crosshair and Dot. CPC and Dot reticles extra. [1]2x and 4x scopes have from 12"-24" of eye relief and are suitable for handguns, top ejection arms and muzzleloaders. [2]3x9 Compact, 6x Compact, 12x, 3x9, and 6.5x20 come with adjustable objective. Sunshade available for all adjustable objective scopes, $23.20-$41.10. [3]Silver finish about $25.00 extra. [4]Long Range scopes have side focus parallax adjustment, additional windage and elevation travel. Partial listing shown. **Contact Leupold for complete details.** *Models available with illuminated reticle for additional cost.
M8-2X EER[1]	1.7	21.2	12-24	7.9	1	Int.	6	312.50	
M8-2X EER Silver[1]	1.7	21.2	12-24	7.9	1	Int.	6	337.50	
M8-4X EER[1]	3.7	9	12-24	8.4	1	Int.	7	425.00	
M8-4X EER Silver[1]	3.7	9	12-24	8.4	1	Int.	7	425.00	
Vari-X 2.5-8 EER	2.5-8	13-4.3	11.7-12	9.7	1	Int.	10.9	608.90	
MEPROLIGHT									[1]Also available with 4.2 MOA dot. Uses tritium and fiber optics-no batteries required. From Hesco, Inc.
Meprolight Reflex Sights 14-21 5.5 MOA 1x30[1]	1	—	—	4.4	30mm	Int.	5.2	335.00	

HOLOSIGHT RETICLES

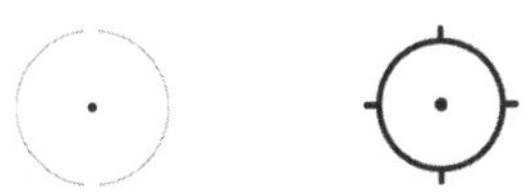

MOA Dot · Standard

SCOPE RETICLES

CP2 · Multi · Euro · Circle-X

Duplex · CPC · Post & Duplex · Leupold Dot · Dot

SCOPES / HUNTING, TARGET & VARMINT

Maker and Model	Magn.	Field at 100 Yds. (feet)	Eye Relief (in.)	Length (in.)	Tube Dia. (in.)	W & E Adjustments	Weight (ozs.)	Price	Other Data
MILLETT									
SP-1 Compact[1] Red Dot	1	36.65	—	4.1	1	Int.	3.2	149.95	[1]3-MOA dot. [2]5-MOA dot. [3]3-, 5-, 8-, 10-MOA dots. [4]10-MOA dot. All have click adjustments; waterproof, shockproof; 11 dot intensity settings. All avail. in matte/black or silver finish. From Millett Sights.
SP-2 Compact[2] Red Dot	1	58	—	4.5	30mm	Int.	4.3	149.95	
MultiDot SP[3]	1	50	—	4.8	30mm	Int.	5.3	289.95	
30mm Wide View[4]	1	60	—	5.5	30mm	Int.	5	289.95	
NIKON									
Monarch UCC 2x20 EER	2	22	26.4	8.1	1	Int.	6.3	248.95	Super multi-coated lenses and blackening of all internal metal parts for maximum light gathering capability; positive .25-MOA; fogproof; waterproof; shockproof; luster and matte finish. From Nikon, Inc.
SIGHTRON									
Pistol									
SII 1x28P	1	30	9-24	9.49	1	Int.	8.46	135.95	
SII 2x28P	2	16-10	9-24	9.49	1	Int.	8.28	135.95	
SIMMONS									
Prohunter Handgun									
7732[1]	2	22	9-17	8.75	1	Int.	7	139.99	[1]Black matte finish; also available in silver. [2]With dovetail rings. [3]With 3V lithium battery, extension tube, polarizing filter, Weaver rings. Contact Simmons Outdoor Corp. for complete details.
7738[1]	4	15	11.8-17.6	8.5	1	Int.	8	149.99	
Red Dot									
510042	1	—	—	4.8	25mm	Int.	4.7	59.99	
51112[3]	1	—	—	5.25	30mm	Int.	6	99.99	
SWIFT									
667 Fire-Fly[2]	1	40	—	5.4	30mm	Int.	5	220.00	All Swift scopes have Quadraplex reticles and are fogproof and waterproof. Available in regular matte black or silver finish. [2]Comes with ring mounts, wrench, lens caps, extension tubes, filter, battery.
TASCO									
Propoint									
PDP2[1,2]	1	40	Unltd.	5	30mm	Int.	5	109.99	[1]Also matte aluminum finish. [2]Available with 5-min, or 10-min. dot. [3]Has 4, 8, 12, 16MOA dots (switchable). **Contact Tasco for details on complete line.**
PDP3[10,17]	1	52	Unltd.	5	30mm	Int.	5	129.99	
PDP3CMP	1	68	Unltd.	4.75	33mm	Int.	—	144.99	
PDP5CMP[22]	1	82	Unltd.	4	47mm	Int.	8	204.99	
Optima 2000									
OPP2000-3.5[3,20]	1	—	—	1.5	—	Int.	1/2	249.99	
OPP2000-7[3,20]	1	—	—	1.5	—	Int.	1.2	249.99	
Pistol Scopes									
PX20[10]	2	21	10-23	8	1	Int.	6.5	69.99	
P1.25x4[10]	1.25-4	23-9	15-23	9.25	1	Int.	8.2	109.99	
THOMPSON/CENTER RECOIL PROOF SERIES									
Pistol Scopes									
8315[1]	2.5-7	15-5	8-21,8-11	9.25	1	Int.	9.2	308.99	[1]Black; lighted reticle. From Thompson/Center Arms.
8326	2.5-7	15-5	8-21,8-11	9.25	1	Int.	10.5	360.49	
TRIJICON									
Reflex II 1x24	1	—	—	4.25	1	Int.	4.6	379.00	
ULTRA DOT									
Ultra-Dot Sights[1]									[1]Ultra Dot sights include rings, battery, polarized filter, and 5-year warranty. All models available in black or satin finish. [2]Illuminated red dot has eleven brightness settings. Shock-proof aluminum tube. From Ultra Dot Distribution.
Ultra-Dot 25[2]	1	—	5.1	1	Int.	3.9	159.00	
Ultra-Dot 30[2]	1	—	5.1	30mm	Int.	4	179.00	
WEAVER									
Handgun									
H2[1-3]	2	21	4-29	8.5	1	Int.	6.7	212.99-224.99	[1]Gloss black, [2]Matte black, [3]Silver. All scopes are shock-proof, waterproof, and fogproof. From Weaver Products.
H4[1-3]	4	18	11.5-18	8.5	1	Int.	6.7	234.99	
VH4[1-3]	1.5-4	13.6-5.8	11-17	8.6	1	Int.	8.1	289.99	
VHB1[1-2,3]	2.5-8	8.5-3.7	12.16	9.3	1	Int.	8.3	299.99	

Hunting scopes in general are furnished with a choice of reticle—crosshairs, post with crosshairs, tapered or blunt post, or dot crosshairs, etc. W—Windage E—Elevation MOA—Minute of Angle or 1" (approx.) at 100 yards, etc.

LASER SIGHTS

Laseraim LA5X

Laseraim LAX

Alpec Mini Shot

Lasergrips LG-206

Laser Devices ULS 2001 with TLS 8R light

Maker and Model	Wavelen gth (nm)	Beam Color	Lens	Operating Temp. (degrees F.)	Weight (ozs.)	Price	Other Data
ALPEC							
Power Shot[1]	635	Red	Glass	NA	2.5	$199.95	[1]Range 1000 yards. [2]Range 300 yards. Mini Shot II range 500 yards, output 650mm, **$129.95**. [3]Range 300 yards; Laser Shot II 500 yards; Super Laser Shot 1000 yards. Black or stainless finish aluminum; removable pressure or push-button switch. Mounts for most handguns, many rifles and shotguns. From Alpec Team, Inc.
Mini Shot[2]	670	Red	Glass	NA	2.5	99.95	
Laser Shot[3]	670	Red	Glass	NA	3.0	99.95	
BEAMSHOT							
1000[1]	670	Red	Glass	—	3.8	NA	[1]Black or silver finish; adj. for windage and elevation; 300-yd. range; also M1000/S (500-yd. range), M1000/u (800-yd.). [2]Black finish; 300-, 500-, 800-yd. models. All come with removable touch pad switch, 5" cable. Mounts to fit virtually any firearm. From Quarton USA Co.
3000[2]	635/670	Red	Glass	—	2	NA	
1001/u	635	Red	Glass	—	3.8	NA	
780	780	Red	Glass	—	3.8	NA	
BSA							
LS650[1]	N/A	Red	N/A	N/A	N/A	69.95	[1]Comes with mounts for 22/air rifle and Weaver-style bases.
LASERAIM							
LA5X Handgun Sight[1]	—	Red	—	—	1 oz.	129.95	[1].5-mile range; 1" dot at 100 yds.; 20+ hrs. batt. life. [2]Laser projects 2" dot at 100 yds.: with rotary switch; with Hotdot $237.00; with Hotdot touch switch **$357.00**. [3]For Glock 17-27; G1 Hotdot **$299.00**; price installed. All have w&e adj.; black or satin silver finish. From Laseraim Technologies, Inc.
LAX[1]	—	Red	—	—	2 oz.	79.00	
LA10 Hotdot[1]	—	—	—	—	NA	199.00	
MA-35RB Mini Aimer[2]	—	—	—	—	1.0	129.00	
G1 Laser[3]	—	—	—	—	2.0	229.00	

LASER SIGHTS

BA-3 on Smith & Wesson

BA-5

Sig Pro Laser & Tactical Light

Maker and Model	Wavelength (nm)	Beam Color	Lens	Operating Temp. (degrees F.)	Weight (ozs.)	Price	Other Data
LASER DEVICES							1For S&W P99 semi-auto pistols; also BA-2, 5 oz., **$339.00**. 2For revolvers. 3For HK, Walther P99. 4For semi-autos. 5For rifles; also FA-4/ULS, 2.5 oz., **$325.00**. 6For HK sub guns. 7For military rifles. 8For shotguns. 9For SIG-Pro pistol. 10Universal, semi-autos. 11For AR-15 variants. All avail. with Magnum Power Point (632nM) or daytime-visible Super Power Point (650nM) diode. Infrared diodes avail. for law enforcement. From Laser Devices, Inc.
BA-1[1]	632	Red	Glass	—	2.4	372.00	
BA-3[2]	632	Red	Glass	—	3.3	332.50	
BA-5[3]	632	Red	Glass	—	3.2	372.00	
Duty-Grade[4]	632	Red	Glass	—	3.5	372.00	
FA-4[5]	632	Red	Glass	—	2.6	358.00	
LasTac[1]	632	Red	Glass	—	5.5	298.00 to 477.00	
MP-5[6]	632	Red	Glass	—	2.2	495.00	
MR-2[7]	632	Red	Glass	—	6.3	485.00	
SA-2[8]	632	Red	Glass	—	3.0	360.00	
SIG-Pro[9]	632	Red	Glass	—	2.6	372.00	
ULS-2001[10]	632	Red	Glass	—	4.5	210.95	
Universal AR-2A	632	Red	Glass	—	4.5	445.00	
LASERGRIPS							Replaces existing grips with built-in laser high in the right grip panel. Integrated pressure sensitive pad in grip activates the laser. Also has master on/off switch. 1For Beretta 92, 96, Colt 1911/Commander, Ruger MkII, S&W J-frames, SIG Sauer P228, P229. 2For all Glock models. Option on/off switch. Requires factory installation. 3For S&W K, L, N frames, round or square butt (LG-207); 4For Taurus small-frame revolvers. 5For Ruger SP-101. 6For SIG Sauer P226. From Crimson Trace Corp.
LG-201[1]	633	Red-Orange	Glass	NA	—	349.00	
LG-206[3]	633	Red-Orange	Glass	NA	—	289.00	
LG-085[4]	633	Red-Orange	Glass	NA	—	279.00	
LG-101[5]	633	Red-Orange	Glass	NA	—	289.00	
LG-226[6]	633	Red-Orange	Glass	NA	—	379.00	
GLS-630[2]	633	Red-Orange	Glass	NA	—	595.00	
LASERLYTE							1Dot/circle or dot/crosshair projection; black or stainless. 2Also 635/645mm model. From TacStar Laserlyte.
LLX-0006-140/090[1]	635/645	Red	—	—	1.4	159.95	
WPL-0004-140/090[2]	670	Red	—	—	1.2	109.95	
TPL-0004-140/090[2]	670	Red	—	—	1.2	109.95	
T7S-0004-140[2]	670	Red	—	—	0.8	109.95	
LASERMAX							Replaces the recoil spring guide rod; includes a customized take-down lever that serves as the laser's instant on/off switch. For Glock, Smith & Wesson, Sigarms, Beretta and select Taurus models. Installs in most pistols without gunsmithing. Battery life 1/2 hour to 2 hours in continuous use. From LaserMax.
LMS-1000 Guide Rod Internal	635	Red-Orange	Glass	40-120	2.46	From 394.95	
NIGHT STALKER							Waterproof; LCD panel displays power remaining; programmable blink rate; constant or memory on. From Wilcox Industries Corp.
S0 Smart	635	Red	NA	NA	2.46	515.00	

SCOPE MOUNTS

Maker, Model, Type	Adjust.	Scopes	Price
AIMTECH			
Handguns			
AMT Auto Mag II 22 Mag.	No	Weaver rail	$56.99
AMT Auto Mag III 30 Carb.	No	Weaver rail	64.95
Auto Mag IV 45WM	No	Weaver rail	64.95
Astra 44 Mag Revolver	No	Weaver rail	63.25
Beretta/Taurus 92/99	No	Weaver rail	63.25
Browning Buckmark/Challenger II	No	Weaver rail	56.99
Browning Hi-Power	No	Weaver rail	63.25
CZ75	No	Weaver rail	63.25
EA9/P9 Tanfoglio frame	No	Weaver rail	63.25
Glock 17, 17L, 19, 22, 23	No	Weaver rail	63.25
Glock 20, 21	No	Weaver rail	63.25
Govt. 45 Auto/38 Super	No	Weaver rail	69.95
Hi-Standard 22 all makes	No	Weaver rail	63.25
Rossi 85/851/951 Revolvers	No	Weaver rail	63.25
Ruger Mk I, Mk II	No	Weaver rail	49.95
Ruger P89	No	Weaver rail	63.25
S&W K, L, N frames	No	Weaver rail	63.25
S&W K, L, N with tapped top strap[1]	No	Weaver rail	69.95
S&W Model 41 Target 22	No	Weaver rail	63.25
S&W Model 52 Target 38	No	Weaver rail	63.25
S&W 2nd Gen. 59/459/659	No	Weaver rail	56.99
S&W 3rd Gen. 59 Series	No	Weaver rail	69.95
S&W 422/622/2206/2206TGT	No	Weaver rail	63.25
S&W 645/745	No	Weaver rail	56.99
S&W Sigma	No	Weaver rail	64.95
Taurus PT908	No	Weaver rail	63.25
Taurus 44 6.5" bbl.	No	Weaver rail	69.95

All mounts no-gunsmithing, see-through/iron sight usable. All mounts accommodate standard split rings of all makes. From Aimtech, L&S Technologies, Inc. [1]3-blade sight and mount combination.

Maker, Model, Type	Adjust.	Scopes	Price
B-SQUARE			
Pistols (centerfire)			
Beretta 92/Taurus 99	No	Weaver rail	64.95
Colt M1911	E only	Weaver rail	64.95
Desert Eagle	No	Weaver rail	64.95
Glock	No	Weaver rail	64.95
H&K USP, 9mm and 40 S&W	No	Weaver rail	64.95
Ruger P85/89	E only	Weaver rail	64.95
SIG Sauer P226	E only	Weaver rail	64.95
Pistols (rimfire)			
Browning Buck Mark	No	Weaver rail	49.95
Colt 22	No	Weaver rail	49.95
Ruger Mk I/II, bull or taper	No	Weaver rail	49.95
Smith & Wesson 41, 2206	No	Weaver rail	49.95
Revolvers			

Maker, Model, Type	Adjust.	Scopes	Price
B-SQUARE (cont.)			
Colt Anaconda/Python	No	Weaver rail	64.95
Ruger Single-Six	No	Weaver rail	64.95
Ruger GP-100	No	Weaver rail	64.95
Ruger Blackhawk, Super	No	Weaver rail	64.95
Ruger Redhawk, Super	No	Weaver rail	64.95
Smith & Wesson K, L, N	No	Weaver rail	64.95
Taurus 66, 669, 689	No	Weaver rail	64.95
BURRIS			
L.E.R. (LU) Mount Bases[1]	W only	1" split rings	24.00-52.00
L.E.R. No Drill-No Tap Bases[1,2,3]	W only	1" split rings	48.00-52.00

[1]Universal dovetail; accepts Burris, Universal, Redfield, Leupold rings. For Dan Wesson, S&W, Virginian, Ruger Blackhawk, Win. 94. [2]Selected rings and bases available with matte Safari or silver finish. [3]For S&W K, L, N frames, Colt Python, Dan Wesson with 6" or longer barrels.

Maker, Model, Type	Adjust.	Scopes	Price
CONETROL			
Pistol Bases, 2-or 3-ring[1]	W only	—	99.96-149.88
Daptar base for Weaver-type mount			49.98 (Huntur grade)
			59.94 (Gunnur grade)
			74.94 (Custum grade)

[1]For XP-100, T/C Contender, Colt SAA, Ruger Blackhawk, S&W and nearly all others. Three-ring mount for T/C Contender and other pistols in Conetrol's three grades. Any Conetrol mount available in stainless or Teflon for double regular cost of grade.

Maker, Model, Type	Adjust.	Scopes	Price
IRONSIGHTER			
Ironsighter Handguns[1]	No	1" split rings	83.95

[1]For 1" dia. extended eye relief scopes. From Ironsighter Co.

Maker, Model, Type	Adjust.	Scopes	Price
KRIS MOUNTS			
One Piece (T)[1]	No	1", 26mm split rings	12.98

[1]Blackhawk revolver. Mounts have oval hole to permit use of iron sights.

Maker, Model, Type	Adjust.	Scopes	Price
LASER AIM			
Laser Aim	No	Laser Aim	19.99-69.00

Mounts Laser Aim above or below barrel. Avail. for most popular handguns, rifles, shotguns, including militaries. From Laser Aim Technologies, Inc.

Maker, Model, Type	Adjust.	Scopes	Price
LEUPOLD			
STD Bases[1]	W only	One- or two-piece bases	24.20

Base and two rings; Casull, Ruger, S&W, T/C; add $5.00 for silver finish.

Maker, Model, Type	Adjust.	Scopes	Price
MILLETT			
One-Piece Bases[2]	Yes	1"	23.95
Handgun Bases, Rings[1]	—	1"	34.60-69.15
30mm Rings[3]	—	30mm	37.75-42.95

[1]Two- and three-ring sets for Colt Python, Trooper, Diamondback, Peacekeeper, Dan Wesson, Ruger Redhawk, Super Redhawk. [2]Turn-in bases and Weaver-style for most popular rifles and T/C Contender, XP-100 pistols. [3]Both Weaver and turn-in styles; three heights. From Millett Sights.

Maker, Model, Type	Adjust.	Scopes	Price
REDFIELD			
American Widefield See-Thru[2]	No	1"	15.95

SCOPE MOUNTS

Maker, Model, Type	Adjust.	Scopes	Price
REDFIELD			
Three-Ring Pistol System SMP[1]	No	1", split rings (three)	49.95-52.95

[1]Used with MP scopes for: S&W K, L or N frame, XP-100, T/C Contender, Ruger receivers. [2]Fits American or Weaver-style base. Non-Gunsmithing mount system. For many popular shotguns, rifles, handguns and blackpowder rifles. Uses existing screw holes.

Maker, Model, Type	Adjust.	Scopes	Price
SSK INDUSTRIES			
T'SOB	No	1"	65.00-145.00
Quick Detachable	No	1"	From 160.00

Custom installation using from two to four rings (included). For T/C Contender, most 22 auto pistols, Ruger and other S.A. revolvers, Ruger, Dan Wesson, S&W, Colt DA revolvers. Black or white finish. Uses Kimber rings in two- or three-ring sets. In blue or SSK chrome. For T/C Contender or most popular revolvers. Standard, non-detachable model also available, from $65.00.

Maker, Model, Type	Adjust.	Scopes	Price
TASCO			
World Class	No	1"	28.00-39.00
Aluminum Ringsets	Yes	1", 30mm	12.00-17.00

From Tasco.

Maker, Model, Type	Adjust.	Scopes	Price
THOMPSON/CENTER			
Duo-Ring Mount[1]	No	1"	60.00
Weaver-Style Rings[2]	No	1"	28.00-39.00

[1]Attaches directly to T/C Contender bbl., no drilling/tapping; also for T/C M/L rifles, needs base adapter; blue or stainless; for M/L guns $59.80. [2]Medium and high; blue or silver finish. From Thompson/Center.

Maker, Model, Type	Adjust.	Scopes	Price
WARNE			
Premier Series (all steel)	No	1", 4 heights 30mm, 2 heights	78.00
T.P.A. (Permanently Attached)	No	1", 4 heights 30mm, 2 heights	87.60
Premier Series Rings fit Premier Series Bases			
Premier Series (all-steel Q.D. rings)			
Premier Series (all steel). Quick detachable lever.	No	1", 4 heights 26mm, 2 heights 30mm, 3 heights	111.00 115.50 121.50
Maxima Series (fits all Weaver-style bases)			
Permanently Attached[1]	No	1", 3 heights 30mm, 3 heights	31.40 45.50

Vertically split rings with dovetail clamp, precise return to zero. Fit most popular rifles, handguns. Regular blue, matte blue, silver finish. [1]All-Steel, non-Q.D. rings. From Warne Mfg. Co.

Maker, Model, Type	Adjust.	Scopes	Price
WEAVER			
Complete Mount Systems			
Pistol	No	1"	75.00-105.00

Nearly all modern rifles, pistols, and shotguns. Detachable rings in standard, See-Thru, and extension styles, in Low, Medium, High or X-High heights; gloss (blued), silver and matte finishes to match scopes. Extension rings are only available in 1" High style and See-Thru X-tensions only in gloss finish. No Drill & Tap Pistol systems in gloss or silver for: Colt Python, Trooper, 357, Officer's Model; Ruger Single-Six, Security-Six (gloss finish only); Blackhawk, Super Blackhawk, Blackhawk SRM 357, Redhawk, Ruger 22 Auto Pistols, Mark II; Smith & Wesson I- and current K-frames with adj. rear sights. From Weaver.

Maker, Model, Type	Adjust.	Scopes	Price
WEIGAND			
Browning Buck Mark[1]	No	—	29.95
Colt 22 Automatic[1]	No	—	19.95
Integra Mounts[2]	No	—	39.95-69.00
S&W Revolver[3]	No	—	29.95
Ruger 10/22[4]	No	—	14.95-39.95
Ruger Revolver[5]	No	—	29.95
Taurus Revolver[4]	No	—	29.95-65.00
T/C Encore Monster Mount	No	—	69.00
T/C Contender Monster Mount	No	—	69.00
Lightweight Rings	No	1", 30mm	29.95-39.95
1911, P-9 Scopemounts	No	—	
SM3[6]	No	Weaver rail	99.95
SRS 1911-2[7]	No	30mm	59.95
APCMNT[8]	No	—	69.95

[1]No gunsmithing. [2]S&W K, L, N frames; Taurus, vent rib models; Colt Anaconda/Python; Ruger Redhawk, Ruger 10/22; 3K, L, N frames. [4]Three models. [5]Redhawk, Blackhawk, GP-100. [6]3rd Gen.; drill and tap; without slots $59.95. [7]Ringless design, silver only. [8]For Aimpoint Comp. Red Dot scope, silver only. From Weigand Combat Handguns, Inc.

Maker, Model, Type	Adjust.	Scopes	Price
WILLIAMS			
Guideline Handgun[1]	No	1" split rings	61.75

[1]No drilling, tapping required; heat treated alloy. For Ruger Mk II Bull Barrel ($61.75); Streamline Top Mount for T.C Contender ($14.15); From Williams Gunsight Co.

SPOTTING SCOPES

BAUSCH & LOMB PREMIER HDR 60mm objective, 15x-45x zoom. Straight or 45° eyepiece. Field at 1000 yds. 125 ft. (15x), 68 ft. (45x). Length 13.0″; weight 38 oz. Interchangeable bayonet-style eyepieces.
Price: Straight, 15-45x **$590.95**
Price: Angled, 15-45x with 45° eyepiece **$638.95**
Price: 22x wide angle eyepiece **$86.95**
Price: 30x long eye relief eyepiece **$136.95**

BAUSCH & LOMB DISCOVERER 15x to 60x zoom, 60mm objective. Constant focus throughout range. Field at 1000 yds. 38 ft (60x), 150 ft. (15x). Comes with lens caps. Length 17 1/2″; weight 48.5 oz.
Price: **$391.95**

BAUSCH & LOMB ELITE 15x to 45x zoom, 60mm objective. Field at 1000 yds., 125-65 ft. Length is 12.2″; weight, 26.5 oz. Waterproof, armored. Tripod mount. Comes with black case.
Price: **$766.95**

BAUSCH & LOMB ELITE ZOOM 20x-60x, 70mm objective. Roof prism. Field at 1000 yds. 90-50 ft. Length is 16″; weight 40 oz. Waterproof, armored. Tripod mount. Comes with black case.
Price: **$921.95**

BAUSCH & LOMB 80MM ELITE 20x-60x zoom, 80mm objective. Field of view at 1000 yds. 108-62 ft. (zoom). Weight 51 oz. (20x, 30x), 54 oz. (zoom); length 16.8″. Interchangeable bayonet-style eyepieces. Built-in peep sight.
Price: With EDPrime Glass.............................. **$1,212.95**

Burris 18-45x-60mm

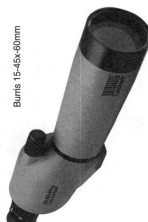

Burris 15-45x-60mm

BURRIS 18-45x SIGNATURE SPOTTER 60mm objective, 18x-45x, constant focus, Field at 1000 yds. 112-63 ft.; weighs 29oz.; length 12.6″. Camera adapters available.
Price: **$819.00**

BURRIS LANDMARK SPOTTER 15-45x, 60mm objective. Straight type. Field at 100 yds. 146-72 ft. Length 12.7″; weight 24 oz. Rubber armor coating, multi-coated lenses, 22mm eye relief. Recessed focus adjustment. Nitrogen filled.
Price: 30x 60mm **$644.00**

BUSHNELL TROPHY 63mm objective, 20x-60x zoom. Field at 1000 yds. 90ft. (20x), 45 ft. (60x). Length 12.7″; weight 20 oz. Black rubber armored, waterproof. Case included.
Price: **$421.95**

BUSHNELL COMPACT TROPHY 50mm objective, 20x-50x zoom. Field at 1000 yds. 92 ft. (20x), 52 ft. (50x). Length 12.2″; weight 17 oz. Black rubber armored, waterproof. Case included.
Price: **$337.95**

Bushnell Banner Sentry

BUSHNELL BANNER SENTRY 18x-36x zoom, 50mm objective. Field at 1000 yds. 115-78 ft. Length 14.5″; weight 27 oz. Black rubber armored. Built-in peep sight. Comes with tripod and hardcase.
Price: **$180.95**
Price: With 45 field eyepiece, includes tripod **$202.95**

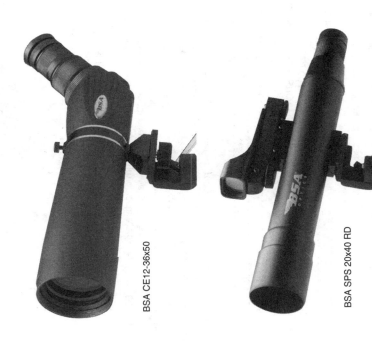

BSA CE12-36x50

BSA SPS 20x40 RD

BSA Spotting Scopes Offset 45-degree or straight body; offered in 40mm, 50mm and 60mm objective lenses and 20x, 12-36x, 20-40x, 15-45x and 20-60x. Field of view at 100 yards: 16.9 feet (12-36x). Length 11″, weight 24 oz. (12-36x).
Price: 20x40m with red dot viewfinder **$59.95**
Price: 20-40x40mm with red dot viewfinder **$69.95**
Price: 15-45x50mm Zoom **$79.95**
Price: 20-60x60mm Zoom **$89.95**
Price: 12-36x50mm Zoom **$119.95**
Price: 15-45 x50mm Zoom **$139.95**
Price: 15-45x60mm Zoom **$199.95**
Price: 20-60x60mm Zoom **$249.95**

SPOTTING SCOPES

BUSHNELL SPACEMASTER 20x-45x zoom. Long eye relief. Rubber armored, prismatic. 60mm objective. Field at 1000 yds. 98-58 ft. Minimum focus 20 ft. Length 12.7"; weight 43 oz.
Price: With tripod, carrying case and 20x-45x LER eyepiece. **$560.95**

BUSHNELL SPORTVIEW 12x-36x 200m, 50mm objective. Field at 100 yds. 160 ft. (12x), 90 ft. (36x). Length 14.6"; weight 25 oz.
Price: With tripod and carrying case. **$159.95**

HERMES 1 70mm objective, 16x, 25x, 40x. Field at 1000 meters 160 ft. (16x), 75ft. (40x). Length 12.2"; weight 33 oz. From CZ-USA.
Price: Body. **$359.00**
Price: 25x eyepiece **$86.00**
Price: 40x eyepiece **$128.00**

Kowa TSN-823

KOWA TSN SERIES Offset 45 or straight body. 77mm objective, 20x WA, 25x, 25x LER, 30x WA, 40x, 60x, 77x and 20-60x zoom. Field at 1000 yds. 179 ft. (20xWA), 52 ft. (60x). Available with flourite lens.
Price: TSN-1 (without eyepiece) 45 offset scope. **$696.00**
Price: TSN-2 (without eyepiece) Straight scope. **$660.00**
Price: 20x W.A. (wide angle) eyepiece. **$230.00**
Price: 25x eyepiece **$143.00**
Price: 25x LER (long eye relief) eyepiece **$214.00**
Price: 30x W.A. (wide angle) eyepiece. **$266.00**
Price: 40x eyepiece **$159.00**
Price: 60x W.A. (wide angle) eyepiece. **$230.00**
Price: 77x eyepiece **$235.00**
Price: 20-60x zoom eyepiece **$302.00**

Kowa TS-611

Kowa TS-612

KOWA TS-610 SERIES Offset 45 or straight body. 60mm objective, 20x WA, 25x, 25x LER, 27x WA, 40x and 20x-60x zoom. Field at 1000 yds. 162 ft. (20x WA), 51 ft. (60x). Available with ED lens.
Price: TS-611 (without eyepiece) 45 offset scope. **$510.00**
Price: TS-612 (without eyepiece) Straight scope **$462.00**
Price: 20x W.A. (wide angle) eyepiece. **$111.00**
Price: 25x eyepiece **$95.00**
Price: 25x LER (long eye relief) eyepiece **$214.00**
Price: 27x W.A. (wide angle) eyepiece **$166.00**
Price: 40x eyepiece **$98.00**
Price: 20-60x zoom eyepiece **$207.00**

KOWA TS-9 SERIES Offset 45, straight or rubber armored (straight only). 50mm objective, 15x, 20x and 11-33x zoom. Field at 1000 yds. 188 ft. (15x), 99 ft. (33x).
Price: TS-9B (without eyepiece) 45 offset scope. **$223.00**
Price: TS-9C (without eyepiece) straight scope **$176.00**
Price: TS-9R (without eyepiece) straight rubber armored scope/black **$197.00**
Price: 15x eyepiece **$38.00**
Price: 20x eyepiece **$36.00**
Price: 11-33x zoom eyepiece **$122.00**

LEUPOLD 12-40x60 VARIABLE 60mm objective, 12-40x. Field at 100 yds. 17.5-5.3 ft.; eye relief 1.2" (20x). Overall length 11.5", weight 32 oz. Rubber armored.
Price: **$848.20**

LEUPOLD 25x50 COMPACT 50mm objective, 25x. Field at 100 yds. 8.3 ft.; eye relief 1"; length overall 9.4"; weight 20.5 oz.
Price: Armored model. **$1,217.90**
Price: Packer Tripod. **$96.40**

Leupold 12-40x60mm

MIRADOR TTB SERIES Draw tube armored spotting scopes. Available with 75mm or 80mm objective. Zoom model (28x-62x, 80mm) is 11 7/8" (closed), weighs 50 oz. Field at 1000 yds. 70-42 ft. Comes with lens covers.
Price: 28-62x80mm **$1,133.95**
Price: 32x80mm **$971.95**
Price: 26-58x75mm **$989.95**
Price: 30x75mm **$827.95**

MIRADOR SSD SPOTTING SCOPES 60mm objective, 15x, 20x, 22x, 25x, 40x, 60x, 20-60x; field at 1000 yds. 37 ft.; length 10 1/4"; weight 33 oz.
Price: 22x Wide Angle **$809.95**
Price: 25x **$827.95**
Price: 20-60x Zoom **$980.95**

MIRADOR SIA SPOTTING SCOPES Similar to the SSD scopes except with 45° eyepiece. Length 12 1/4"; weight 39 oz.
Price: 25x **$575.95**
Price: 22x Wide Angle **$746.95**
Price: 20-60x Zoom **$944.95**

MIRADOR SSR SPOTTING SCOPES 50mm or 60mm objective. Similar to SSD except rubber armored in black or camouflage. Length 11 1/8"; weight 31 oz.
Price: Black, 20x **$521.95**
Price: Black, 18x Wide Angle **$539.95**
Price: Black, 16-48x Zoom **$593.95**
Price: Black, 20x **$692.95**
Price: Black, 60mm **$701.95**
Price: Black, 22x Wide Angle, 60mm **$854.95**
Price: Black, 20-60x Zoom . . . . . .

SPOTTING SCOPES

MIRADOR SSF FIELD SCOPES Fixed or variable power, choice of 50mm, 60mm, 75mm objective lens. Length 9 3/4"; weight 20 oz. (15-32x50).

Price: 20x50mm	$359.95
Price: 25x60mm	$440.95
Price: 30x75mm	$584.95
Price: 15-32x50mm Zoom	$548.95
Price: 18-40x60mm Zoom	$629.95
Price: 22-47x75mm Zoom	$773.95

MIRADOR SRA MULTI ANGLE SCOPES Similar to SSF Series except eyepiece head rotates for viewing from any angle.

Price: 20x50mm	$503.95
Price: 25x60mm	$647.95
Price: 30x75mm	$764.95
Price: 15-32x50mm Zoom	$692.95
Price: 18-40x60mm Zoom	$836.95
Price: 22-47x75mm Zoom	$953.95

MIRADOR SIB FIELD SCOPES Short-tube, 45° scopes with porro prism design. 50mm and 60mm objective. Length 10 1/4"; weight 18.5 oz. (15-32x50mm); field at 1000 yds. 129-81 ft.

Price: 20x50mm	$386.95
Price: 25x60mm	$449.95
Price: 15-32x50mm Zoom	$575.95
Price: 18-40x60mm Zoom	$638.95

Nikon
Fieldscope 78mm

NIKON FIELDSCOPES 60mm and 78mm lens. Field at 1000 yds. 105 ft. (60mm, 20x), 126 ft. (78mm, 25x). Length 12.8" (straight 60mm), 12.6" (straight 78mm); weight 34.5-47.5 oz. Eyepieces available separately.

Price: 60mm straight body	$690.95
Price: 60mm angled body	$796.95
Price: 60mm straight ED body	$1,200.95
Price: 60mm angled ED body	$1,314.95
Price: 78mm straight ED body	$2,038.95
Price: 78mm angled ED body	$2,170.95
Price: Eyepieces (15x to 60x)	$146.95 to $324.95
Price: 20-45x eyepiece (25-56x for 78mm)	$318.95

NIKON SPOTTING SCOPE 60mm objective, 20x fixed power or 15-45x zoom. Field at 1000 yds. 145 ft. (20x). Gray rubber armored. Straight or angled eyepiece. Weighs 44.2 oz., length 12.1" (20x).

Price: 20x60 fixed (with eyepiece)	$368.95
Price: 15-45x zoom (with case, tripod, eyepiece)	$578.95

SIGHTRON SII 2050X63 63mm objective lens, 20x-50x zoom. Field at 1000 yds 91.9 ft. (20x), 52.5 ft. (50x). Length 14"; weight 30.8 oz. Black rubber finish. Also available with 80mm objective lens.

Price: 63mm or 80mm	$339.95

SIMMONS 1280 50mm objective, 15-45x zoom. Black matte finish. Ocular focus. Peep finder sight. Waterproof. FOV 95-51 ft. @ 1000 yards. Wgt. 33.5 oz., length 12".

Price: With tripod	$267.99

SIMMONS 1281 60mm objective, 20-60x zoom. Black matte finish. Ocular focus. Peep finder sight. Waterproof. FOV 78-43 ft. @ 1000 yards. Wgt. 34.5 oz. Length 12".

Price: With tripod	$295.99

SIMMONS 77206 PROHUNTER 50mm objectives, 25x fixed power. Field at 1000 yds. 113 ft.; length 10.25"; weighs 33.25 oz. Black rubber armored.

Price: With tripod case	$160.60

SIMMONS 41200 REDLINE 50mm objective, 15-45x zoom. Field at 1000 yds. 104-41 ft.; length 16.75"; weighs 32.75 oz.

Price: With hard case and tripod	$99.99
Price: 20-60x, Model 41201	$129.99

STEINER FIELD TELESCOPE 24x, 80mm objective. Rubber armored.

Price:	$1,299.00

SWAROVSKI CT EXTENDIBLE SCOPES 75mm or 85mm objective, 20-60x zoom, or fixed 15x, 22x, 30x, 32x eyepieces. Field at 1000 yds. 135 ft. (15x), 99 ft. (22x), 99 ft. (32x), 5.2 ft. (60x) for zoom. Length 12.4" (closed), 17.2" (open) for the CT75; 9.7"/17.2" for CT85. Weight 40.6 oz. (CT75); 49.4 oz. (CT85). Green rubber armored.

Price: CT75 body	$765.56
Price: CT85 body	$1,094.44
Price: 20-60x eyepiece	$343.33
Price: 15x, 22x eyepiece	$232.22
Price: 30x eyepiece	$265.55

SWAROVSKI AT-80/ST-80 SPOTTING SCOPES 80mm objective, 20-60x zoom, or fixed 15x, 22x, 30x, 32x eyepieces. Field at 1000 yds. 135 ft. (15x), 99 ft. (32x), 99 ft. (20x), 52.5 ft. (60x) for zoom. Length 16" (AT-80), 15.6" (ST-80); weight 51.8 oz. Available with HD (high density) glass.

Price: AT-80 (angled) body	$1,094.44
Price: ST-80 (straight) body	$1,094.44
Price: With HD glass	$1,555.00
Price: 20-60x eyepiece	$343.33
Price: 15x, 22x eyepiece	$232.22
Price: 30x eyepiece	$265.55

SWIFT LYNX M836 15x-45x zoom, 60mm objective. Weight 7 lbs., length 14". Has 45° eyepiece, sunshade.

Price:	$315.00

SWIFT NIGHTHAWK M849U 80mm objective, 20-60x zoom, or fixed 19, 25x, 31x, 50x, 75x eyepieces. Has rubber armored body, 1.8x optical finder, retractable lens hood, 45° eyepiece. Field at 1000 yds. 60 ft. (28x), 41 ft. (75x). Length 13.4 oz.; weight 39 oz.

Price: Body only	$870.00
Price: 20-68x eyepiece	$370.00
Price: Fixed eyepieces	$130.00 to $240.00
Price: Model 849 (straight) body	$795.00

SWIFT NIGHTHAWK M850U 65mm objective, 16x-48x zoom, or fixed 19x, 20x, 25x, 40x, 60x eyepieces. Rubber armored with a 1.8x optical finder, retractable lens hood. Field at 1000 yds. 83 ft. (22x), 52 ft. (60x). Length 12.3"; weight 30 oz. Has 45° eyepiece.

Price: Body only	$650.00
Price: 16x-48x eyepiece	$370.00
Price: Fixed eyepieces	$130.00 to $240.00
Price: Model 850 (straight) body	$575.00

SWIFT LEOPARD M837 50mm objective, 25x. Length 9 11/16" to 10 1/2". Weight with tripod 28 oz. Rubber armored. Comes with tripod.

Price:	$160.00

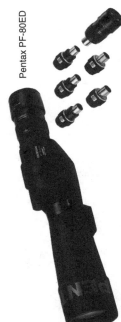

Pentax PF-80ED

PENTAX PF-80ED spotting scope 80mm objective lens available in 18x, 24x, 36x, 48x, 72x and 20-60x. Length 15.6", weight 11.9 to 19.2 oz.

Price:	$1,320.00

SPOTTING SCOPES

SWIFT TELEMASTER M841 60mm objective. 15x to 60x variable power. Field at 1000 yds. 160 feet (15x) to 40 feet (60x). Weight 3.25 lbs.; length 18" overall.
Price: **$399.50**

SWIFT PANTHER M844 15x-45x zoom or 22x WA, 15x, 20x, 40x, 60mm objective. Field at 1000 yds. 141 ft. (15x), 68 ft. (40x), 95-58 ft. (20x-45x).
Price: Body only **$380.00**
Price: 15x-45x zoom eyepiece **$120.00**
Price: 20x-45x zoom (long eye relief) eyepiece **$140.00**
Price: 15x, 20x, 40x eyepiece **$65.00**
Price: 22x WA eyepiece **$80.00**

Swift M700T Scout

SWIFT M700T 12x-36x, 50mm objective. Field of view at 100 yds. 16 ft. (12x), 9 ft. (36x). Length 14"; weight with tripod 3.22 lbs.
Price: **$225.00**

SWIFT SEARCHER M839 60mm objective, 20x, 40x. Field at 1000 yds. 118 ft. (30x), 59 ft. (40x). Length 12.6"; weight 3 lbs. Rotating eyepiece head for straight or 45° viewing.
Price: **$580.00**
Price: 30x, 50x eyepieces, each. **$67.00**

TASCO 29TZBWP WATERPROOF SPOTTER 60mm objective lens, 20x-60x zoom. Field at 100 yds. 7 ft., 4 in. to 3 ft., 8 in. Black rubber armored. Comes with tripod, hard case.
Price: **$356.50**

TASCO WC28TZ WORLD CLASS SPOTTING SCOPE 50mm objective, 12-36x zoom. Field at 100 yds. World Class. 13-3.8 ft. Comes with tripod and case.
Price: **$220.00**

TASCO CW5001 COMPACT ZOOM 50mm objective, 12x-36x zoom. Field at 100 yds. 16 ft., 9 in. Includes photo adapter tube, tripod with panhead lever, case.
Price: **$280.00**

TASCO 3700WP WATERPROOF SPOTTER 50mm objective, 18x-36x zoom. Field at 100 yds. 12ft., 6 in. to 7 ft., 9 in. Black rubber armored. Comes with tripod, hard case.
Price: **$288.60**

TASCO 3700, 3701 SPOTTING SCOPE 50mm objective. 18x-36x zoom. Field at 100 yds. 12 ft., 6 in. to 7 ft., 9 in. Black rubber armored.
Price: Model 3700 (black, with tripod, case) **$237.00**
Price: Model 3701 (as above, brown camo) **$237.00**

TASCO 21EB ZOOM 50mm objective lens, 15x-45x zoom. Field at 100 yds. 11 ft. (15x). Weight 22 oz.; length 18.3" overall. Comes with panhead lever tripod.
Price: **$119.00**

TASCO 22EB ZOOM 60mm objective lens, 20x-60x zoom. Field at 100 yds. 7 ft., 2 in. (20x). Weight 28 oz.; length 21.5" overall. Comes with micro-adjustable tripod.
Price: **$183.00**

UNERTL "FORTY-FIVE" 54mm objective, 20x (single fixed power). Field at 100 yds. 10'.10"; eye relief 1"; focusing range infinity to 33 ft. Weight about 32 oz.; overall length 153/4". With lens covers.
Price: **$515.00**

UNERTL 20x STRAIGHT PRISMATIC 54mm objective, 20x. Field at 100 yds. 8.5 ft. Relative brightness 6.1. Eye relief 1/2". Weight 36 oz.; length closed 13 1/2". Complete with lens covers.
Price: **$477.00**

UNERTL TEAM SCOPE 100mm objective. 15x, 24x, 32x eyepieces. Field at 100 yds. 13 to 7.5 ft. Relative brightness, 39.06 to 9.79. Eye relief 2" to 11/2". Weight 13 lbs.; length 29 7/8" overall. Metal tripod, yoke and wood carrying case furnished (total weight 80 lbs.).
Price: **$2,810.00**

UNERTL STRAIGHT PRISMATIC 63.5mm objective, 24x. Field at 100 yds., 7 ft. Relative brightness, 6.96. Eye relief 1/2". Weight 40 oz.; length closed 19". Push-pull and screw-focus eyepiece. 16x and 32x eyepieces $125.00 each.
Price: **$662.00**
Price: **$572.00**

WEAVER 20x50 50mm objective. Field of view 124 ft. at 100 yds. Eye relief .85"; weighs 21 oz.; overall length 10". Waterproof, armored.
Price: **$368.99**

WEAVER 15-40x60 ZOOM 60mm objective. 15x-40x zoom. Field at 100 yds. 119 ft. (15x), 66 ft. (60x). Overall length 12.5"; weighs 26 oz. Waterproof, armored.
Price: **$551.99**

NRA - RIGHT-TO-CARRY RECIPROCITY GUIDE

This guide is not to be considered as legal advice or a restatement of the law. It is important to remember that state carry laws vary considerably. Be sure to check with local authorities outside your home state for a complete listing of restrictions on carrying concealed in that state. Many states restrict carrying in bars, restaurants (where alcohol is served), establishments where packaged alcohol is sold, schools, colleges, universities, churches, parks, sporting events, correctional facilities, courthouses, federal and state government offices/buildings, banks, airport terminals, police stations, polling places, any posted private property restricting the carrying of concealed firearms, etc. In addition to state restrictions, federal law prohibits carrying on military bases, in national parks and the sterile area of airports. National Forests usually follow laws of the state wherein the forest is located.

NOTE: Vermont does not issue permits, but allows carrying of concealed firearms if there is no intent to commit a crime.

Important note: Reciprocity status is changing rapidly. This data was the best available at the time of publication, however, to ensure compliance with the law, it is important to contact legal authorities before carrying a concealed weapon across state lines.

State	ISSUING AUTHORITY	These states also recognize your permit	Contact agency for out-of-state permits if granted	Grants out-of-state permits
Alabama	County Sheriff	Idaho, Indiana, Kentucky, Michigan	Permits not granted	No
Alaska	State Trooper	Idaho, Indiana, Kentucky, Michigan, Wyoming, Utah	Permits not granted	No
Arizona	Dept. of Public Safety	Alaska, Idaho, Indiana, Kentucky, Michigan, Wyoming, Tennessee, Utah	Permits not granted	No
Arkansas	State Police	Alaska, Idaho, Indiana, Kentucky, Michigan, Wyoming, Oklahoma, Tennessee, Utah, Texas	Permits not granted	No
California	County Sheriff	Idaho, Indiana, Kentucky, Michigan	Permits not granted	No
Colorado	Chief of Police / County Sheriff	Idaho, Indiana, Kentucky, Michigan	Permits not granted	No
Connecticut	Commissioner of State Police	Alaska, Idaho, Indiana, Kentucky, Michigan, Wyoming	State Police Special Licensing Division: (860) 685-8290	Yes
Delaware	Prothonotary of Superior Court	Idaho, Indiana, Kentucky, Michigan, Wyoming	Permits not granted	
Florida	Dept. of State	Alaska, Idaho, Indiana, Kentucky, Michigan, Wyoming	Dept. of State, Division of Licensing: (904) 488-5381	
Georgia	County Probate Judge	Idaho, Indiana, Kentucky, Michigan, Tennessee	Permits not granted	
Hawaii	Chief of Police	Idaho, Indiana, Kentucky, Michigan, Utah	Permits not granted	
Idaho	County Sheriff	Georgia, Indiana, Kentucky, Michigan	Any Sheriff's Department	
Illinois	n/a	n/a	Permits not granted	

NRA - RIGHT-TO-CARRY RECIPROCITY GUIDE

State	ISSUING AUTHORITY	These states also recognize your permit	Contact agency for out-of-state permits if granted	Grants out-of-state permits
Indiana	Chief Law Enforcement Officer of Municipality	Idaho, Kentucky, Michigan	Permits not granted	
Iowa	(resident) Sheriff (non-resident) Commissioner of Public Safety	Idaho, Indiana, Kentucky, Michigan	Commissioner of Public Safety: (515) 281-7610	
Kansas	n/a	n/a	Permits not granted	
Kentucky	State Police	Idaho, Indiana, Michigan, Wyoming, Tennessee	Permits not granted	
Louisiana	Chief Law Enforcement Officer of Parish	Alaska, Idaho, Indiana, Kentucky, Michigan, Texas, Utah	Permits not granted	
Maine	County Sheriff/Chief of Police	Alaska, Idaho, Indiana, Kentucky, Michigan, Wyoming	Chief of State Police: (207) 624-8775	
Maryland	Superintendent of State Police	Idaho, Indiana, Kentucky, Michigan, Wyoming	Permits not granted	
Massachusetts	Chief of Police	Idaho, Indiana, Kentucky, Michigan	Permits not granted	
Michigan	County Gun Board/Sheriff	Georgia, Idaho, indiana, Kentucky	Permits not granted	
Minnesota	Chief of Police.County Sheriff	Idaho, Indiana, Kentucky, Michigan	Permits not granted	
Mississippi	Dept. of Public Safety	Idaho, Indiana, Kentucky, Michigan, Wyoming, Georgia, Tennessee	Permits not granted	
Missouri	n/a	n/a	Permits not granted	
Montana	County Sheriff	Idaho, Indiana, Kentucky, Michigan	Permits not granted	
Nebraska	n/a	n/a	Permits not granted	
Nevada	County Sheriff	Alaska, Idaho, Indiana, Kentucky, Michigan, Oklahoma, Utah	Permits not granted	
New Hampshire	Selectman/Mayor or Chief of Police	Idaho, Indiana, Kentucky, Michigan, Georgia	Director of State Police: (603) 271-3575	
New Jersey	Chief of Police/Superintendent of State Police	Alaska, Idaho, Indiana, Kentucky, Michigan, Wyoming	Superintendent of State Police: (609) 882-2000, ext. 2664	
New Mexico	n/a	n/a	Permits not granted	
New York	Varies by county	Idaho, Indiana, Kentucky, Michigan	Permits not granted	
North Carolina	County Sheriff	Alaska, Idaho, Indiana, Kentucky, Michigan, Oklahoma, Utah	Permits not granted	
North Dakota	Chief of the Bureau of Criminal Investigation	Alaska, Idaho, Indiana, Kentucky, Michigan, Wyoming	Permits not granted	
Ohio	n/a	n/a	Permits not granted	

NRA - RIGHT-TO-CARRY RECIPROCITY GUIDE

State	ISSUING AUTHORITY	These states also recognize your permit	Contact agency for out-of-state permits if granted	Grants out-of-state permits
Oklahoma	State Bureau of Investigation	Alaska, Arkansas, Idaho, Indiana, Kentucky, Michigan, Wyoming, Tennessee, Texas, Utah	Permits not granted	
Oregon	County Sheriff	Alaska, Idaho, Indiana, Kentucky, Michigan	Permits not granted	
Pennsylvania	County Sheriff	Idaho, Indiana, Kentucky, Michigan	Any Sheriff's Department	
Rhode Island	Attorney General	Idaho, Indiana, Kentucky, Michigan, Wyoming	mail only (no phone calls) send self-addressed stamped envelope to: Dept. of Attorney General, 150 South Main Street, Providence, RI 02903 ATTN: Bureau of Criminal Identification.	
South Carolina	S.C. Law Enforcement Division	Alaska, Arkansas, Idaho, Indiana, Kentucky, Michigan, Wyoming, Oklahoma, Utah	Permits not granted	
South Dakota	Chief of Police/Count Sheriff	Idaho, Indiana, Kentucky, Michigan	Permits not granted	
Tennessee	Dept. of Public Safety	Alaska, Arkansas, Idaho, Indiana, Kentucky, Michigan, Wyoming, Virginia, Utah	Permits not granted	
Texas	Dept. of Public Safety	Alaska, Arkansas, Idaho, Indiana, Kentucky, Louisiana, Michigan, Wyoming, Oklahoma, Georgia, Utah	Permits granted by DPS to qualified non-residents from states with no concealed carry permit system. Call (800) 224-5744 or (512) 424-7293.	
Utah	Dept. of Public Safety	Alaska, Arkansas, Idaho, Indiana, Kentucky, Michigan, Oklahoma, Wyoming	Dept. of Public Safety: (801) 965-4484	
Vermont	Vermont allows concealed carry without a permit and issues no official permit	n/a	No permit required	
Virginia	Clerk of Circuit Court	Idaho, Indiana, Kentucky, Michigan, Tennessee	Permits not granted	
Washington	Chief of Police/Sheriff	Idaho, Indiana, Kentucky, Michigan	Any Sheriff's Department	
West Virginia	Sheriff	Kentucky, Michigan, Tennessee	Permits not granted	
Wisconsin	n/a	n/a	Permits not granted	
Wyoming	Attorney General	Alaska, Idaho, Indiana, Kentucky, Michigan, Oklahoma	Permits not granted	

Courtesy of the National Rifle Association, 11250 Waples Mill Road, Fairfax, VA 22030 / 703-267-1000. 1999 data.

ARMS ASSOCIATIONS

UNITED STATES

ALABAMA

Alabama Gun Collectors Assn., Inc.
Secretary, P.O. Box 70965, Tuscaloosa, AL 35407

ALASKA

Alaska Gun Collectors Assn., Inc.
C.W. Floyd, Pres., 5240 Little Tree, Anchorage, AK 99507

ARIZONA

Arizona Arms Assn.
Don DeBusk, President, 4837 Bryce Ave., Glendale, AZ 85301

CALIFORNIA

California Cartridge Collectors Assn.
Rick Montgomery, 1729 Christina, Stockton, CA 95204/209-463-7216 evs.

California Waterfowl Assn.
4630 Northgate Blvd., #150, Sacramento, CA 95834

Greater Calif. Arms & Collectors Assn.
Donald L. Bullock, 8291 Carburton St., Long Beach, CA 90808-3302

Los Angeles Gun Ctg. Collectors Assn.
F.H. Ruffra, 20810 Amie Ave., Apt. #9, Torrance, CA 90503

Stock Gun Players Assn.
6038 Appian Way, Long Beach, CA, 90803

COLORADO

Colorado Gun Collectors Assn.
L.E.(Bud) Greenwald, 2553 S. Quitman St., Denver, CO 80219/303-935-3850

Rocky Mountain Cartridge Collectors Assn.
John Roth, P.O. Box 757, Conifer, CO 80433

CONNECTICUT

Ye Connecticut Gun Guild, Inc.
Dick Fraser, P.O. Box 425, Windsor, CT 06095

FLORIDA

Unified Sportsmen of Florida
P.O. Box 6565, Tallahassee, FL 32314

GEORGIA

Georgia Arms Collectors Assn., Inc.
Michael Kindberg, President, P.O. Box 277, Alpharetta, GA 30239-0277

ILLINOIS

Illinois State Rifle Assn.
P.O. Box 637, Chatsworth, IL 60921

Mississippi Valley Gun & Cartridge Coll. Assn.
Bob Filbert, P.O. Box 61, Port Byron, IL 61275/309-523-2593

Sauk Trail Gun Collectors
Gordell M. Matson, P.O. Box 1113, Milan, IL 61264

Wabash Valley Gun Collectors Assn., Inc.
Roger L. Dorsett, 2601 Willow Rd., Urbana, IL 61801/217-384-7302

INDIANA

Indiana State Rifle & Pistol Assn.
Thos. Glancy, P.O. Box 552, Chesterton, IN 46304

Southern Indiana Gun Collectors Assn., Inc.
Sheila McClary, 309 W. Monroe St., Boonville, IN 47601/812-897-3742

IOWA

Beaver Creek Plainsmen Inc.
Steve Murphy, Secy., P.O. Box 298, Bondurant, IA 50035

Central States Gun Collectors Assn.
Dennis Greischar, Box 841, Mason City, IA 50402-0841

KANSAS

Kansas Cartridge Collectors Assn.
Bob Linder, Box 84, Plainville, KS 67663

KENTUCKY

Kentuckiana Arms Collectors Assn.
Charles Billips, President, Box 1776, Louisville, KY 40201

Kentucky Gun Collectors Assn., Inc.
Ruth Johnson, Box 64, Owensboro, KY 42302/502-729-4197

LOUISIANA

Washitaw River Renegades
Sandra Rushing, P.O. Box 256, Main St., Grayson, LA 71435

MARYLAND

Baltimore Antique Arms Assn.
Mr. Cillo, 1034 Main St., Darlington, MD 21304

MASSACHUSETTS

Bay Colony Weapons Collectors, Inc.
John Brandt, Box 111, Hingham, MA 02043

Massachusetts Arms Collectors
Bruce E. Skinner, P.O. Box 31, No. Carver, MA 02355/508-866-5259

MICHIGAN

Association for the Study and Research of .22 Caliber Rimfire Cartridges
George Kass, 4512 Nakoma Dr., Okemos, MI 48864

MINNESOTA

Sioux Empire Cartridge Collectors Assn.
Bob Cameron, 14597 Glendale Ave. SE, Prior Lake, MN 55372

MISSISSIPPI

Mississippi Gun Collectors Assn.
Jack E. Swinney, P.O. Box 16323, Hattiesburg, MS 39402

MISSOURI

Greater St. Louis Cartridge Collectors Assn.
Don MacChesney, 634 Scottsdale Rd., Kirkwood, MO 63122-1109

Mineral Belt Gun Collectors Assn.
D.F. Saunders, 1110 Cleveland Ave., Monett, MO 65708

Missouri Valley Arms Collectors Assn., Inc.
Dean E. Yearout, Sr., Exec. Secy., P.O. Box 33033, Kansas City, MO 64114

MONTANA

Montana Arms Collectors Assn.
Dean E. Yearout, Sr., Exec. Secy., 1516 21st Ave. S., Great Falls, MT 59405

Weapons Collectors Society of Montana
R.G. Schipf, Ex. Secy., 3100 Bancroft St., Ex. Secy., 3100 Missoula, MT 59801/406-728-2995

NEBRASKA

Nebraska Cartridge Collectors Club
Gary Muckel, P.O. Box 84442, Lincoln, NE 68501

NEW HAMPSHIRE

New Hampshire Arms Collectors, Inc.
James Stamatelos, Secy., P.O. Box 5, Cambridge, MA 02139

NEW JERSEY

Englishtown Benchrest Shooters Assn.
Michael Toth, 64 Cooke Ave., Carteret, NJ 07008

Jersey Shore Antique Arms Collectors
Joe Sisia, P.O. Box 100, Bayville, NJ 08721-0100

New Jersey Arms Collectors Club, Inc.
Angus Laidlaw, Vice President, 230 Valley Rd., Montclair, NJ 07042/201-746-0939; e-mail: acclaid-law@juno.com

NEW YORK

Iroquois Arms Collectors Assn.
Bonnie Robinson, Show Secy., P.O. Box 142, Ransomville, NY 14131/716-791-4096

Mid-State Arms Coll. & Shooters Club
Jack Ackerman, 24 S. Mountain Terr., Binghamton, NY 13903

NORTH CAROLINA

North Carolina Gun Collectors Assn.
Jerry Ledford, 3231-7th St. Dr. NE, Hickory, NC 28601

OHIO

Ohio Gun Collectors Assn.
P.O. Box 9007, Maumee, OH 43537-9007/419-897-0861; Fax:419-897-0860

Shotshell Historical and Collectors Society
Madeline Bruemmer, 3886 Dawley Rd., Ravenna, OH 44266

OREGON

Oregon Arms Collectors Assn., Inc.
Phil Bailey, P.O. Box 13000-A, Portland, OR 97213-0017/503-281-6864; off.:503-281-0918

Oregon Cartridge Collectors Assn.
Boyd Northrup, P.O. Box 285, Rhododendron, OR 97049

PENNSYLVANIA

Presque Isle Gun Collectors Assn.
James Welch, 156 E. 37 St., Erie, PA 16504

SOUTH CAROLINA

Belton Gun Club, Inc.
J.K. Phillips, 195 Phillips Dr., Belton, SC 29627

Gun Owners of South Carolina
Membership Div.: William Strozier, Secretary, P.O. Box 70, Johns Island, SC 29457-0070/803-762-3240; Fax:803-795-0711; e-mail:76053.222@com-puserve.com

SOUTH DAKOTA

Dakota Territory Gun Coll. Assn., Inc.
Curt Carter, Castlewood, SD 57223

TENNESSEE

Smoky Mountain Gun Coll. Assn., Inc.
Hugh W. Yabro, President, P.O. Box 23225, Knoxville, TN 37933

Tennessee Gun Collectors Assn., Inc.
M.H. Parks, 3556 Pleasant Valley Rd., Nashville, TN 37204-3419

TEXAS

Houston Gun Collectors Assn., Inc.
P.O. Box 741429, Houston, TX 77274-1429

Texas Cartridge Collectors Assn., Inc.
Robert Mellichamp, Memb. Contact, 907 Shirkmere, Houston, TX 77008/713-869-0558

The Stark Gun Collectors, Inc.
William I. Gann, 5666 Waynesburg Dr., Waynesburg, OH 44688

ARMS ASSOCIATION

Texas Gun Collectors Assn.
Bob Eder, Pres., P.O. Box 12067, El Paso, TX 79913/915-584-8183

Texas State Rifle Assn.
1131 Rockingham Dr., Suite 101, Richardson, TX 75080-4326

VIRGINIA

Virginia Gun Collectors Assn., Inc.
Addison Hurst, Secy., 38802 Charlestown Height, Waterford, VA 20197/540-882-3543

WASHINGTON

Association of Cartridge Collectors on the Pacific Northwest
Robert Jardin, 14214 Meadowlark Drive KPN, Gig Harbor, WA 98329

Washington Arms Collectors, Inc.
Joyce Boss, P.O. Box 389, Renton, WA, 98057-0389/206-255-8410

WISCONSIN

Great Lakes Arms Collectors Assn., Inc.
Edward C. Warnke, 2913 Woodridge Lane, Waukesha, WI 53188

Wisconsin Gun Collectors Assn., Inc.
Lulita Zellmer, P.O. Box 181, Sussex, WI 53089

WYOMING

Wyoming Weapons Collectors
P.O. Box 284, Laramie, WY 82073/307-745-4652 or 745-9530

NATIONAL ORGANIZATIONS

Amateur Trapshooting Assn.
David D. Bopp, Exec. Director, 601 W. National Rd., Vandalia, OH 45377/937-898-4638; Fax:937-898-5472

American Airgun Field Target Assn.
5911 Cherokee Ave., Tampa, FL 33604

American Coon Hunters Assn.
Opal Johnston, P.O. Cadet, Route 1, Box 492, Old Mines, MO 63630

American Custom Gunmakers Guild
Jan Billeb, Exec. Director, P.O. Box 812, Burlington, IA 52601-0812/319-752-6114 (Phone or Fax)

American Defense Preparedness Assn.
Two Colonial Place, 2101 Wilson Blvd., Suite 400, Arlington, VA 22201-3061

American Paintball League
P.O. Box 3561, Johnson City, TN 37602/800-541-9169

American Pistolsmiths Guild
Alex B. Hamilton, Pres., 1449 Blue Crest Lane, San Antonio, TX 78232/210-494-3063

American Police Pistol & Rifle Assn.
3801 Biscayne Blvd., Miami, FL 33137

American Single Shot Rifle Assn.
Gary Staup, Secy., 709 Carolyn Dr., Delphos, OH 45833/419-692-3866. Website: www.assra.com

American Society of Arms Collectors
George E. Weatherly, P.O. Box 2567, Waxahachie, TX 75165

American Tactical Shooting Assn.(A.T.S.A.)
c/o Skip Gochenour, 2600 N. Third St., Harrisburg, PA 17110/717-233-0402; Fax:717-233-5340

Association of Firearm and Tool Mark Examiners
Lannie G. Emanuel, Secy., Southwest Institute of Forensic Sciences, P.O. Box 35728, Dallas, TX 75235/214-920-5979; Fax:214-920-5928; Membership Secy., Ann D. Jones, VA Div. of Forensic Science, P.O. Box 999, Richmond, VA 23208/804-786-4706; Fax:804-371-8328

Boone & Crockett Club
250 Station Dr., Missoula, MT 59801-2753

Browning Collectors Assn.
Secretary:Scherrie L. Brennac, 2749 Keith Dr., Villa Ridge, MO 63089/314-742-0571

The Cast Bullet Assn., Inc.
Ralland J. Fortier, Editor, 4103 Foxcraft Dr., Traverse City, MI 49684

Citizens Committee for the Right to Keep and Bear Arms
Natl. Hq., Liberty Park, 12500 NE Tenth Pl., Bellevue, WA 98005

Colt Collectors Assn.
25000 Highland Way, Los Gatos, CA 95030/408-353-2658.

Ducks Unlimited, Inc.
Natl. Headquarters, One Waterfowl Way, Memphis, TN 38120/901-758-3937

Fifty Caliber Shooters Assn.
PO Box 111, Monroe UT 84754-0111

Firearms Coalition/Neal Knox Associates
Box 6537, Silver Spring, MD 20906/301-871-3006

Firearms Engravers Guild of America
Rex C. Pedersen, Secy., 511 N. Rath Ave., Lundington, MI 49431/616-845-7695(Phone and Fax)

Foundation for North American Wild Sheep
720 Allen Ave., Cody, WY 82414-3402/web site: http://ligi.com/os/non/fnaws/fnaw s.htm; e-mail: fnaws@wyoming.com

Freedom Arms Collectors Assn.
P.O. Box 160302, Miami, FL 33116-0302

Garand Collectors Assn.
P.O. Box 181, Richmond, KY 40475

Golden Eagle Collectors Assn. (G.E.C.A.)
Chris Showler, 11144 Slate Creek Rd., Grass Valley, CA 95945

Gun Owners of America
8001 Forbes Place, Suite 102, Springfield, VA 22151/703-321-8585

Handgun Hunters International
J.D. Jones, Director, P.O. Box 357 MAG, Bloomingdale, OH 43910

Harrington & Richardson Gun Coll. Assn.
George L. Cardet, 330 S.W. 27th Ave., Suite 603, Miami, FL 33135

High Standard Collectors' Assn.
John J. Stimson, Jr., Pres., 540 W. 92nd St., Indianapolis, IN 46260

Hopkins & Allen Arms & Memorabilia Society (HAAMS)
P.O. Box 187, 1309 Pamela Circle, Delphos, OH 45833

International Ammunition Association, Inc.
C.R. Punnett, Secy., 8 Hillock Lane, Chadds Ford, PA 19317/610-358-1285;Fax:6 10-3 58-1560

International Benchrest Shooters
Joan Borden, RR1, Box 250BB, Springville, PA 18844/717-965-2366

International Blackpowder Hunting Assn.
P.O. Box 1180, Glenrock, WY 82637/307-436-9817

IHMSA (Intl. Handgun Metallic Silhouette Assn.)
PO Box 368, Burlington, IA 52601 Website: www.ihmsa.cor

International Society of Mauser Arms Collectors
Michael Kindberg, Pres., P.O. Box 277, Alpharetta, GA 30239-0277

Jews for the Preservation of Firearms Ownership (JPFO) 501(c)(3)
2872 S. Wentworth Ave., Milwaukee, WI 53207/414-769-0760; Fax:414-483-8435

The Mannlicher Collectors Assn., Ltd.
Dick Paterson, Secy., 407 Lincoln Bldg., 44 Main St., Champaign, IL 61820

Marlin Firearms Collectors Assn., Ltd.
Membership Office: P.O. Box1249, The Dalles, Oregon 97058

Merwin Hulbert Association,
2503 Kentwood Ct., High Point, NC 27265

Miniature Arms Collectors/Makers Society, Ltd.
Ralph Koebbeman, Pres., 4910 Kilburn Ave., Rockford, IL 61101/815-964-2569

M1 Carbine Collectors Assn. (M1-CCA)
623 Apaloosa Ln., Gardnerville, NV 89410-7840

National Association of Buckskinners (NAB)
Territorial Dispatch—1800s Historical Publication, 4701 Marion St., Suite 324, Livestock Exchange Bldg., Denver, CO 80216/303-297-9671

The National Association of Derringer Collectors
P.O. Box 20572, San Jose, CA 95160

National Assn. of Federally Licensed Firearms Dealers
Andrew Molchan, 2455 E. Sunrise, Ft. Lauderdale, FL 33304

National Association to Keep and Bear Arms
P.O. Box 78336, Seattle, WA 98178

National Automatic Pistol Collectors Assn.
Tom Knox, P.O. Box 15738, Tower Grove Station, St. Louis, MO 63163

National Bench Rest Shooters Assn., Inc.
Pat Ferrell, 2835 Guilford Lane, Oklahoma City, OK 73120-4404/405-842-9585; Fax: 405-842-9575

National Muzzle Loading Rifle Assn.
Box 67, Friendship, IN 47021 / 812-667-5131. Website: www.NMLRA@nmlra.org

National Professional Paintball League (NPPL)
540 Main St., Mount Kisco, NY 10549/914-241-7400

National Reloading Manufacturers Assn.
One Centerpointe Dr., Suite 300, Lake Oswego, OR 97035

National Rifle Assn. of America
11250 Waples Mill Rd., Fairfax, VA 22030 / 703-267-1000. Website: www.nra.org

National Shooting Sports Foundation, Inc.
Robert T. Delfay, President, Flintlock Ridge Office Center, 11 Mile Hill Rd., Newtown, CT 06470-2359/203-426-1320; FAX: 203-426-1087

National Skeet Shooting Assn.
Dan Snyuder, Director, 5931 Roft Road, San Antonio, TX 78253-9261/800-877-5338. Website: nssa-nsca.com

National Sporting Clays Association
Ann Myers, Director, 5931 Roft Road, San Antonio, TX 78253-9261/800-877-5338. Website: nssa-nsca.com

ARMS ASSOCIATIONS

National Wild Turkey Federation, Inc.
P.O. Box 530, 770 Augusta Rd., Edgefield, SC 29824

North American Hunting Club
P.O. Box 3401, Minnetonka, MN 55343/612-936-9333; FAX: 612-936-9755

North American Paintball Referees Association (NAPRA)
584 Cestaric Dr., Milpitas, CA 95035

North-South Skirmish Assn., Inc.
Stevan F. Meserve, Exec. Secretary, 507 N. Brighton Court, Sterling, VA 20164-3919

Remington Society of America
Gordon Fosburg, Secretary, 11900 North Brinton Road, Lake, MI 48623

Rocky Mountain Elk Foundation
P.O. Box 8249, Missoula, MT 59807-8249/406-523-4500; Fax: 406-523-4581 Website: www.rmef.org

Ruger Collector's Assn., Inc.
P.O. Box 240, Greens Farms, CT 06436

Safari Club International
4800 W. Gates Pass Rd., Tucson, AZ 85745/520-620-1220

Sako Collectors Assn., Inc.
Jim Lutes, 202 N. Locust, Whitewater, KS 67154

Second Amendment Foundation
James Madison Building, 12500 NE 10th Pl., Bellevue, WA 98005

Single Action Shooting Society (SASS)
23255-A La Palma Avenue, Yorba Linda, CA 92887/714-694/1800; FAX: 714-694-1815/email: sasseot@aol.com Website: www.sassnet.com

Smith & Wesson Collectors Assn.
Cally Plett, Admin. Asst.,PO Box 444, Afton, NY 13730

The Society of American Bayonet Collectors
P.O. Box 234, East Islip, NY 11730-0234

Southern California Schuetzen Society
Dean Lillard, 34657 Ave. E., Yucaipa, CA 92399

Sporting Arms and Ammunition Manufacturers' Institute (SAAMI)
Flintlock Ridge Office Center, 11 Mile Hill Rd., Newtown, CT 06470-2359/203-426-4358; FAX: 203-426-1087

Sporting Clays of America (SCA)
Ron L. Blosser, Pres., 9257 Buckeye Rd., Sugar Grove, OH 43155-9632/614-746-8334; Fax: 614-746-8605

The Thompson/Center Assn.
Joe Wright, President, Box 792, Northboro, MA 01532/508-845-6960

U.S. Practical Shooting Assn./IPSC
Dave Thomas, P.O. Box 811, Sedro Woolley, WA 98284/360-855-2245

U.S. Revolver Assn.
Brian J. Barer, 40 Larchmont Ave., Taunton, MA 02780/508-824-4836

U.S. Shooting Team
U.S. Olympic Shooting Center, One Olympic Plaza, Colorado Springs, CO 80909/719-578-4670

The Varmint Hunters Assn., Inc.
Box 759, Pierre, SD 57501/Member Services 800-528-4868

Weatherby Collectors Assn., Inc.
P.O. Box 888, Ozark, MO 65721

The Wildcatters
P.O. Box 170, Greenville, WI 54942

Winchester Arms Collectors Assn.
P.O. Box 230, Brownsboro, TX 75756/903-852-4027

The Women's Shooting Sports Foundation (WSSF)
4620 Edison Avenue, Ste. C, Colorado Springs, CO 80915/719-638-1299; FAX: 719-638-1271/email: wssf@worldnet.att.net

ARGENTINA
Asociacion Argentina de Coleccionistas de Armes y Municiones
Castilla de Correos No. 28, Succursal I B, 1401 Buenos Aires, Republica Argentina

AUSTRALIA
Antique & Historical Arms Collectors of Australia
P.O. Box 5654, GCMC Queensland 9726, Australia

The Arms Collector's Guild of Queensland Inc.
Ian Skennerton, P.O. Box 433, Ashmore City 4214, Queensland, Australia

Australian Cartridge Collectors Assn., Inc.
Bob Bennett, 126 Landscape Dr., E. Doncaster 3109, Victoria, Australia

Sporting Shooters Assn. of Australia, Inc.
P.O. Box 2066, Kent Town, SA 5071, Australia

CANADA
Canadian Historical Arms Society
P.O. Box 901, Edmonton, Alb., Canada T5J 2L8

ALBERTA
National Firearms Assn.
Natl. Hq: P.O. Box 1779, Edmonton, Alb., Canada T5J 2P1

BRITISH COLUMBIA
Historical Arms Collectors of B.C. (Canada)
Harry Moon, Pres., P.O. Box 50117, South Slope RPO, Burnaby, BC V5J 5G3, Canada/604-438-0950; Fax:604-277-3646

ONTARIO
Association of Canadian Cartridge Collectors
Monica Wright, RR 1, Millgrove, ON, LOR IVO, Canada

Tri-County Antique Arms Fair
P.O. Box 122, RR #1, North Lancaster, Ont., Canada K0C 1Z0

EUROPE

BELGIUM
European Cartridge Research Assn.
Graham Irving, 21 Rue Schaltin, 4900 Spa, Belgium/32.87.77.43.40; Fax:32.87.77.27.51

GERMANY
Bund Deutscher Sportschützen e.v. (BDS)
Borsigallee 10, 53125 Bonn 1, Germany

CZECHOSLOVAKIA
Spolecnost Pro Studium Naboju (Czech Cartridge Research Assn.)
JUDr. Jaroslav Bubak, Pod Homolko 1439, 26601 Beroun 2, Czech Republic

DENMARK
Aquila Dansk Jagtpatron Historic Forening (Danish Historical Cartridge Collectors Club)
Steen Elgaard Møller, Ulriksdalsvej 7, 4840 Nr. Alsley, Denmark 10045-53846218;Fax:00455 384 6209

ENGLAND
Arms and Armour Society
Hon. Secretary A. Dove, P.O. Box 10232, London, 5W19 2ZD, England

Dutch Paintball Federation
Aceville Publ., Castle House 97 High Street, Colchester, Essex C01 1TH, England/011-44-206-564840

European Paintball Sports Foundation
c/o Aceville Publ., Castle House 97 High St., Colchester, Essex, C01 1TH, England

Historical Breechloading Smallarms Assn.
D.J. Penn M.A., Secy., P.O. Box 12778, London SE1 6BX, England. Journal and newsletter are $23 a yr., including airmail.

National Rifle Assn. (Great Britain) Bisley Camp, Brookwood, Woking Surrey GU24 OPB, England/01483.797777.; Fax: 01473068627

United Kingdom Cartridge Club
Ian Southgate, 20 Millfield, Elmley Castle, Nr. Pershore, Worcestershire, WR10 3HR, England

FRANCE
STAC-Western Co.
3 Ave. Paul Doumer (N.311); 78360 Montesson, France/01.30.53-43-65; Fax: 01.30.53.19.10

Deutscher Schützenbund
Lahnstrasse 120, 65195 Wiesbaden, Germany

SPAIN
Asociacion Espanola de Coleccionistas de Cartuchos (A.E.C.C.)
Secretary: Apdo. Correos No. 1086, 2880-Alcala de Henares (Madrid), Spain. President: Apdo. Correos No. 682, 50080 Zaragoza, Spain

SWEDEN
Scandinavian Ammunition Research Assn.
Box 107, 77622 Hedemora, Sweden

NEW ZEALAND
New Zealand Cartridge Collectors Club
Terry Castle, 70 Tiraumea Dr., Pakuranga, Auckland, New Zealand

New Zealand Deerstalkers Assn.
P.O. Box 6514 TE ARO, Wellington, New Zealand

SOUTH AFRICA
Historical Firearms Soc. of South Africa
P.O. Box 145, 7725 Newlands, Republic of South Africa

Republic of South Africa Cartridge Collectors Assn.
Arno Klee, 20 Eugene St., Malanshof Randburg, Gauteng 2194, Republic of South Africa

S.A.A.C.A. (Southern Africa Arms and Ammunition Assn.)
Gauteng Office: P.O. Box 7597, Weltevreden Park, 1715, Republic of South Africa/011-679-1151; Fax: 011-679-1131; e-mail: saaaca@iafrica.com.

Kwa-Zulu Natal office: P.O. Box 4065, Northway, Kwazulu-Natal 4065, Republic of South Africa

SAGA (S.A. Gunowners' Assn.)
P.O. Box 35203, Northway, Kwazulu-Natal 4065, Republic of South Africa

PERIODICAL PUBLICATIONS

AAFTA News (M)
5911 Cherokee Ave., Tampa, FL 33604. Official newsletter of the American Airgun Field Target Assn.

Action Pursuit Games Magazine (M)
CFW Enterprises, Inc., 4201 W. Vanowen Pl., Burbank, CA 91505 818-845-2656. $4.99 single copy U.S., $5.50 Canada. Editor: Dan Reeves. World's leading magazine of paintball sports.

Air Gunner Magazine
4 The Courtyard, Denmark St., Wokingham, Berkshire RG11 2AZ, England/011-44-734-771677. $U.S. $44 for 1 yr. Leading monthly airgun magazine in U.K.

Airgun Ads
Box 33, Hamilton, MT 59840/406-363-3805; Fax: 406-363-4117. $35 1 yr. (for first mailing; $20 for second mailing; $35 for Canada and foreign orders.) Monthly tabloid with extensive For Sale and Wanted airgun listings.

The Airgun Letter
Gapp, Inc., 4614 Woodland Rd., Ellicott City, MD 21042-6329/410-730-5496; Fax: 410-730-9544; e-mail: staff@airgnltr.net; http://www.airgunletter.com. $21 U.S., $24 Canada, $27 Mexico and $33 other foreign orders, 1 yr. Monthly newsletter for airgun users and collectors.

Airgun World
4 The Courtyard, Denmark St., Wokingham, Berkshire RG40 2AZ, England/011-44-734-771677. Call for subscription rates. Oldest monthly airgun magazine in the U.K., now a sister publication to *Air Gunner.*

Alaska Magazine
Morris Communications, 735 Broad Street, Augusta, GA 30901/706-722-6060. Hunting, Fishing and Life on the Last Frontier articles of Alaska and western Canada.

American Firearms Industry
Nat'l. Assn. of Federally Licensed Firearms Dealers, 2455 E. Sunrise Blvd., Suite 916, Ft. Lauderdale, FL 33304. $35.00 yr. For firearms retailers, distributors and manufacturers.

American Guardian
NRA, 11250 Waples Mill Rd., Fairfax, VA 22030. Publications division. $15.00 1 yr. Magazine features personal protection; home-self-defense; family recreation shooting; women's issues; etc.

American Gunsmith
Belvoir Publications, Inc., 75 Holly Hill Lane, Greenwich, CT 06836-2626/203-661-6111. $49.00 (12 issues). Technical journal of firearms repair and maintenance.

American Handgunner*
Publisher's Development Corp., 591 Camino de la Reina, Suite 200, San Diego, CA 92108/800-537-3006 $16.95 yr. Articles for handgun enthusiasts, competitors, police and hunters.

American Hunter (M)
National Rifle Assn., 11250 Waples Mill Rd., Fairfax, VA 22030 (Same address for both.) Publications Div. $35.00 yr. Wide scope of hunting articles.

American Rifleman (M)
National Rifle Assn., 11250 Waples Mill Rd., Fairfax, VA 22030 (Same address for both.) Publications Div. $35.00 yr. Firearms articles of all kinds.

American Single Shot Rifle News* (M)
Membership Secy. Tim Mather, 1180 Easthill SE, N. Canton, Ohio. Annual dues $20 for 6 issues. Official journal of the American Single Shot Rifle Assn.

American Survival Guide
McMullen Angus Publishing, Inc., 774 S. Placentia Ave., Placentia, CA 92670-6846. 12 issues $19.95/714-572-2255; FAX: 714-572-1864.

Arms Collecting (Q)
Museum Restoration Service, P.O. Box 70, Alexandria Bay, NY 13607-0070. $22.00 yr.; $62.00 3 yrs.; $112.00 5 yrs.

Australian Shooters Journal
Sporting Shooters' Assn. of Australia, Inc., P.O. Box 2066, Kent Town SA 5071, Australia. $45.00 yr. locally; $55.00 yr. overseas surface mail only. Hunting and shooting articles.

The Backwoodsman Magazine
P.O. Box 627, Westcliffe, CO 81252. $16.00 for 6 issues per yr.; $30.00 for 2 yrs.; sample copy $2.75. Subjects include muzzle-loading, woodslore, primitive survival, trapping, homesteading, blackpowder cartridge guns, 19th century how-to.

Black Powder Cartridge News (Q)
SPG, Inc., P.O. Box 761, Livingston, MT 59047/Phone/Fax: 406-222-8416. $17 yr. (4 issues) ($6 extra 1st class mailing). For the blackpowder cartridge enthusiast.

Blackpowder Hunting (M)
Intl. Blackpowder Hunting Assn., P.O. Box 1180Z, Glenrock, WY 82637/307-436-9817. $20.00 1 yr., $36.00 2 yrs. How-to and where-to features by experts on hunting; shooting; ballistics; traditional and modern blackpowder rifles, shotguns, pistols and cartridges.

Black Powder Times
P.O. Box 234, Lake Stevens, WA 98258. $20.00 yr.; add $5 per year for Canada, $10 per year other foreign. Tabloid newspaper for blackpowder activities; test reports.

Blade Magazine
Krause Publications, 700 East State St., Iola, WI 54990-0001. $25.98 for 12 issues. Foreign price (including Canada-Mexico) $50.00. A magazine for all enthusiasts of handmade, factory and antique knives.

Caliber
GFI-Verlag, Theodor-Heuss Ring 62, 50668 K"lln, Germany. For hunters, target shooters and reloaders.

The Caller (Q) (M)
National Wild Turkey Federation, P.O. Box 530, Edgefield, SC 29824. Tabloid newspaper for members; 4 issues per yr. (membership fee $25.00)

Cartridge Journal (M)
Robert Mellichamp, 907 Shirkmere, Houston, TX 77008/713-869-0558. Dues $12 for U.S. and Canadian members (includes the newsletter); 6 issues.

The Cast Bullet*(M)
Official journal of The Cast Bullet Assn. Director of Membership, 203 E. 2nd St., Muscatine, IA 52761. Annual membership dues $14, includes 6 issues.

COLTELLI, che Passione (Q)
Casella postale N.519, 20101 Milano, Italy/Fax:02-48402857. $15 1 yr., $27 2 yrs. Covers all types of knives—collecting, combat, historical. Italian text.

Combat Handguns*
Harris Publications, Inc., 1115 Broadway, New York, NY 10010.

Deer & Deer Hunting Magazine
Krause Publications, 700 E. State St., Iola, WI 54990-0001. $19.95 yr. (9 issues). For the serious deer hunter. Website: www.krause.com

The Derringer Peanut (M)
The National Association of Derringer Collectors, P.O. Box 20572, San Jose, CA 95160. A newsletter dedicated to developing the best derringer information. Write for details.

Deutsches Waffen Journal
Journal-Verlag Schwend GmbH, Postfach 100340, D-74503 Schwäbisch Hall, Germany/0791-404-500; FAX:0791-404-505 and 404-424. DM102 p. yr. (interior); DM125.30 (abroad), postage included. Antique and modern arms and equipment. German text.

Double Gun Journal
P.O. Box 550, East Jordan, MI 49727/800-447-1658. $35 for 4 issues.

Ducks Unlimited, Inc. (M)
1 Waterfowl Way, Memphis, TN 38120

The Engraver (M) (Q)
P.O. Box 4365, Estes Park, CO 80517/970-586-2388; Fax: 970-586-0394. Mike Dubber, editor. The journal of firearms engraving.

The Field
King's Reach Tower, Stamford St., London SE1 9LS England. £36.40 U.K. 1 yr.; 49.90 (overseas, air mail) yr.; £82.00 (overseas, surface mail) yr.; Monthly shooting column. Articles on hunting and fishing, and all country sports.

Field & Stream
Times Mirror Magazines, Two Park Ave., New York, NY 10016/212-779-5000. Monthly shooting column. Articles on hunting and fishing. Website: www.timesmirror.com

Field Tests
Belvoir Publications, Inc., 75 Holly Hill Lane; P.O. Box 2626, Greenwich, CT 06836-2626/203-661-6111; 800-829-3361 (subscription line). U.S. & Canada $29 1 yr., $58 2 yrs.; all other countries $45 1 yr., $90 2 yrs. (air).

Fur-Fish-Game
A.R. Harding Pub. Co., 2878 E. Main St., Columbus, OH 43209. $15.95 yr. Practical guidance regarding trapping, fishing and hunting.

Gray's Sporting Journal
Gray's Sporting Journal, P.O. Box 1207, Augusta, GA 30903. $36.95 per yr. for 6 issues. Hunting and fishing journals. Expeditions and Guides Book (Annual Travel Guide).

The Gottlieb-Tartaro Report
Second Amendment Foundation, James Madison Bldg., 12500 NE 10th Pl., Bellevue, WA 98005/206-454-7012;Fax:206-451-3959. $30 for 12 issues. An insiders guide for gun owners.

Gun List†
700 E. State St., Iola, WI 54990. $36.98 yr. (26 issues); $65.98 2 yrs. (52 issues). Indexed market publication for firearms collectors and active shooters; guns, supplies and services. Website: www.krause.com

Gun News Digest (Q)
Second Amendment Fdn., P.O. Box 488, Station C, Buffalo, NY 14209/716-885-6408;Fax:716-884-4471. $10 U.S.; $20 foreign.

The Gun Report
World Wide Gun Report, Inc., Box 38, Aledo, IL 61231-0038. $33.00 yr. For the antique and collectable gun dealer and collector.

Gunmaker (M) (Q)
ACGG, P.O. Box 812, Burlington, IA 52601-0812. The journal of custom gunmaking.

The Gunrunner
Div. of Kexco Publ. Co. Ltd., Box 565G, Lethbridge, Alb., Canada T1J 3Z4. $23.00 yr., sample $2.00. Monthly newspaper, listing everything from antiques to artillery.

Gun Show Calendar (Q)
700 E. State St., Iola, WI 54990. $14.95 yr. (4 issues). Gun shows listed; chronologically and by state. Write for information. www.krause.com

Gun Tests
11 Commerce Blvd., Palm Coast, FL 32142. The consumer resource for the serious shooter. Write for information.

Gun Trade News
Bruce Publishing Ltd., P.O. Box 82, Wantage, Ozon OX12 7A8, England/44-1-235-771770; Fax: 44-1-235-771848. Britain's only "trade only" magazine exclusive to the gun trade.

Gun Week†
Second Amendment Foundation, P.O. Box 488, Station C, Buffalo, NY 14209. $35.00 yr. U.S. and possessions; $45.00 yr. other countries. Tabloid paper on guns, hunting, shooting and collecting (36 issues).

Gun World
Y-Visionary Publishing, LP 265 South Anita Drive, Ste. 120, Orange, CA 92868. $21.97 yr.; $34.97 2 yrs. For the hunting, reloading and shooting enthusiast.

Guns
Publishers Development Corporation, P.O. Box 85201, San Diego, CA 92138/800-537-3006. $19.95 yr. In-depth articles on a wide range of guns, shooting equipment and related accessories for gun collectors, hunters and shooters.

Guns & Ammo
EMAP USA, 6420 Wilshire Blvd., Los Angeles, CA 90048/213-782-2780. $23.94 yr. Guns, shooting, and technical articles.

Guns Review
Ravenhill Publishing Co. Ltd., Box 35, Standard House, Bonhill St., London EC 2A 4DA, England. £20.00 sterling (approx. U.S. $38 USA & Canada) yr. For collectors and shooters.

H.A.C.S. Newsletter (M)
Harry Moon, Pres., P.O. Box 50117, South Slope RPO, Burnaby BC, V5J 5G3, Canada/604-438-0950;Fax:604-277-364 6. $25 p. yr. U.S. and Canada. Official newsletter of The Historical Arms Collectors of B.C. (Canada).

Handgunner*
Richard A.J. Munday, Seychelles house, Brightlingsen, Essex CO7 0NN, England/012063-305201. £18.00 (sterling).

Handguns
EMAP USA, 6420 Wilshire Blvd., Los Angeles, CA 90048/323-782-2868. $23/94 yr. For the handgunning and shooting enthusiast. Website: www.petersenco.com

Man At Arms*
P.O. Box 460, Lincoln, RI 02865. $27.00 yr.; $52.00 2 yrs. plus $8.00 for foreign subscribers. The N.R.A. magazine of arms collecting-investing, with excellent articles for the collector of antique arms and militaria.

Knife World
Knife World Publications, P.O. Box 3395, Knoxville, TN 37927. $15.00 yr.; $25.00 2 yrs. Published monthly for knife enthusiasts and collectors. Articles on custom and factory knives; other knife-related interests, monthly column on knife identification, military knives.

Journal of the Historical Breechloading Smallarms Assn.
Published annually. P.O. Box 12778, London, SE1 6XB, England. £21.00 yr. Articles for the collector plus short articles on specific arms, reprints, newsletters, etc.

The Journal of the Arms & Armour Society (M)
A. Dove, P.O. Box 10232, London, SW19 2ZD England. £15.00 surface mail for 10 airmail sterling only yr. Articles for the historian and collector.

Internationales Waffen-Magazin
Habegger-Verlag Zürich, Postfach 9230, CH-8036 Zürich, Switzerland. SF 105.00 (approx. U.S. $73.00) surface mail for 10 issues. Modern and antique arms, self-defense. German text; English summary of contents.

International Shooting Sport*/UIT Journal
International Shooting Union (UIT), Bavariaring 21, D-80336 Munich, Germany. Europe: (Deutsche Mark) DM44.00 yr., 2 yrs. DM83.00; outside Europe: DM50.00 yr., 2 yrs. DM95.00 (air mail postage included.) For international sport shooting.

International Arms & Militaria Collector (Q)
Arms & Militaria Press, P.O. Box 80, Labrador, Qld. 4215, Australia. A$39.50 yr. (U.S. & Canada), 2 yrs. A$77.50; A$37.50 (others), 1 yr., 2 yrs. $73.50 all air express mail; surface mail is less. Editor: Ian D. Skennerton.

INSIGHTS*
NRA, 11250 Waples Mill Rd., Fairfax, VA 22030. Editor, John E. Robbins. $15.00 yr., which includes NRA junior membership; $10.00 for adult subscriptions (12 issues). Plenty of details for the young hunter and target shooter; emphasizes gun safety, marksmanship training, hunting skills.

Handloader*
Wolfe Publishing Co., 6471 Airpark Dr., Prescott, AZ 86301/520-445-7810;Fax:520-778-5124. $22.00 yr. The journal of ammunition reloading.

PERIODICAL PUBLICATIONS

The Mannlicher Collector (Q)(M)
Mannlicher Collectors Assn., Inc., P.O. Box 7144, Salem Oregon 97303. $20/ yr. subscription included in membership.

MAN/MAGNUM
S.A. Man (Pty) Ltd., P.O. Box 35204, Northway, Durban 4065, Republic of South Africa. SA Rand 200.00 for 12 issues. Africa's only publication on hunting, shooting, firearms, bushcraft, knives, etc.

The Marlin Collector (M)
R.W. Paterson, 407 Lincoln Bldg., 44 Main St., Champaign, IL 61820.

Muzzle Blasts (M)
National Muzzle Loading Rifle Assn., P.O. Box 67, Friendship, IN 47021/812-667-5131. $35.00 yr. annual membership. For the blackpowder shooter.

Muzzleloader Magazine*
Scurlock Publishing Co., Inc., Dept. Gun, Route 5, Box 347-M, Texarkana, TX 75501. $18.00 U.S.; $22.50 U.S./yr. for foreign subscribers. The publication for blackpowder shooters.

National Defense (M)*
American Defense Preparedness Assn., Two Colonial Place, Suite 400, 2101 Wilson Blvd., Arlington, VA 22201-3061/703-522-1820; FAX: 703-522-1885. $35.00 yr. Articles on both military and civil defense field, including weapons, materials technology management.

National Knife Magazine (M)
Natl. Knife Coll. Assn., 7201 Shallowford Rd., P.O. Box 21070, Chattanooga, TN 37424-0070. Membership $35 yr.; $65.00 International yr.

National Rifle Assn. Journal (British) (Q)
Natl. Rifle Assn. (BR.), Bisley Camp, Brookwood, Woking, Surrey, England. GU24, OPB. £24.00 Sterling including postage.

National Wildlife*
Natl. Wildlife Fed., 1400 16th St. NW, Washington, DC 20036. $16.00 yr. (6 issues); *International Wildlife*, 6 issues, $16.00 yr. Both, $22.00 yr., includes all membership benefits. Write attn.: Membership Services Dept., for more information.

New Zealand GUNS*
Waitekauri Publishing, P.O. 45, Waikino 3060, New Zealand. $NZ90.00 (6 issues) yr. Covers the hunting and firearms scene in New Zealand.

New Zealand Wildlife (Q)
New Zealand Deerstalkers Assoc., Inc., P.O. Box 6514, Wellington, N.Z. $30.00 (N.Z.). Hunting, shooting and firearms/game research articles.

North American Hunter* (M)
P.O. Box 3401, Minnetonka, MN 55343/612-936-9333; e-mail: huntingclub@pclink.com. $18.00 yr. (7 issues). Articles on all types of North American hunting.

Outdoor Life
Times Mirror Magazines, Two Park Ave., New York, NY 10016. $16.95/yr. Extensive coverage of hunting and shooting. Shooting column by Jim Carmichel. Website: www.timesmirror.com

La Passion des Courteaux (Q)
Phenix Editions, 25 rue Mademoiselle, 75015 Paris, France. French text.

Paintball Games International Magazine
Aceville Publications, Castle House, 97 High St., Colchester, Essex, England CO1 1TH/011-44-206-564840. Write for subscription rates. Leading magazine in the U.K. covering competitive paintball activities.

Paintball News
PBN Publishing, P.O. Box 1608, 24 Henniker St., Hillsboro, NH 03244/603-464-6080. $35 U.S. 1 yr. Bi-weekly. Newspaper covering the sport of paintball, new product reviews and industry features.

Paintball Sports (Q)
Paintball Publications, Inc., 540 Main St., Mount Kisco, NY 10549/941-241-7400. $24.75 U.S. 1 yr., $32.75 foreign. Covering the competitive paintball scene.

Performance Shooter
Belvoir Publications, Inc., 75 Holly Hill Lane, Greenwich, CT 06836-2626/203-661-6111. $45.00 yr. (12 issues). Techniques and technology for improved rifle and pistol accuracy.

Petersen's HUNTING Magazine
EMAP USA, 6420 Wilshire Blvd., Los Angeles, CA 90048. $19.94 yr.; Canada $29.34 yr.; foreign countries $29.94 yr. Hunting articles for all game; test reports.

P.I. Magazine
America's Private Investigation Journal, 755 Bronx Dr., Toledo, OH 43609. Chuck Klein, firearms editor with column about handguns.

Pirsch
BLV Verlagsgesellschaft mbH, Postfach 400320, 80703 Munich, Germany/089-12704-0;Fax:089-12705-3 54. German text.

Point Blank
Citizens Committee for the Right to Keep and Bear Arms (sent to contributors), Liberty Park, 12500 NE 10th Pl., Bellevue, WA 98005

POINTBLANK (M)
Natl. Firearms Assn., Box 4384 Stn. C, Calgary, AB T2T 5N2, Canada. Official publication of the NFA.

The Police Marksman*
6000 E. Shirley Lane, Montgomery, AL 36117. $17.95 yr. For law enforcement personnel.

Police Times (M)
3801 Biscayne Blvd., Miami, FL 33137/305-573-0070.

Popular Mechanics
Hearst Corp., 224 W. 57th St., New York, NY 10019. Firearms, camping, outdoor oriented articles.

Precision Shooting
Precision Shooting, Inc., 222 McKee St., Manchester, CT 06040. $32.00 yr. U.S. Journal of the International Benchrest Shooters, and target shooting in general. Also considerable coverage of varmint shooting, as well as big bore, small bore, schuetzen, lead bullet, wildcats and precision reloading.

Rifle*
Wolfe Publishing Co., 6471 Airpark Dr., Prescott, AZ 86301/520-445-7810; Fax: 520-778-5124. $19.00 yr. The sporting firearms journal.

Rifle's Hunting Annual
Wolfe Publishing Co., 6471 Airpark Dr., Prescott, AZ 86301/520-445-7810; Fax: 520-778-5124. $4.99 Annual. Dedicated to the finest pursuit of the hunt.

Rod & Rifle Magazine
Lithographic Serv. Ltd., P.O. Box 38-138, Wellington, New Zealand. $50.00 yr. (6 issues). Hunting, shooting and fishing articles.

Safari* (M)
Safari Magazine, 4800 W. Gates Pass Rd., Tucson, AZ 85745/602-620-1220. $55.00 (6 times). The journal of big game hunting, published by Safari Club International. Also publish *Safari Times*, a monthly newspaper, included in price of $55.00 national membership.

Second Amendment Reporter
Second Amendment Foundation, James Madison Bldg., 12500 NE 10th Pl., Bellevue, WA 98005. $15.00 yr. (non-contributors).

Shooter's News
23146 Lorain Rd., Box 349, North Olmsted, OH 44070/216-979-5258;Fax:216-979-5259. $29 U.S. 1 yr., $54 2 yrs.; $52 foreign surface. A journal dedicated to precision riflery.

Shooting Industry
Publisher's Dev. Corp., 591 Camino de la Reina, Suite 200, San Diego, CA 92108. $50.00 yr. To the trade. $25.00.

PERIODICAL PUBLICATIONS

Shooting Sports USA
National Rifle Assn. of America, 11250 Waples Mill Road, Fairfax, VA 22030. Annual subscriptions for NRA members are $5 for classified shooters and $10 for non-classified shooters. Non-NRA member subscriptions are $15. Covering events, techniques and personalities in competitive shooting.

Shooting Sportsman*
P.O. Box 11282, Des Moines, IA 5034/800-666-4955 (for subscriptions). Editorial: P.O. Box 1357, Camden, ME 04843. $19.95 for six issues. The magazine of wingshooting and fine guns.

The Shooting Times & Country Magazine (England)†
IPC Magazines Ltd. King's Reach Tower, Stamford St, 1 London SE1 9LS, England/0171-261-6180;Fax:0171-261-7 179. £65 (approx. $98.00) yr.; £79 yr. overseas (52 issues). Game shooting, wild fowling, hunting, game fishing and firearms articles. Britain's best selling field sports magazine.

Shooting Times
Primedia, News Plaza, P.O. Box 1790, Peoria, IL 61656/309-682-6626. $16.97 yr. Guns, shooting, reloading; articles on every gun activity.

The Shotgun News‡
Primedia, News Plaza, P.O. Box 1790, Peoria, IL 61656/800-495-8362. $28.95 yr.; foreign subscription call for rates. Sample copy $4.00. Gun ads of all kinds.

SHOT Business
Flintlock Ridge Office Center, 11 Mile Hill Rd., Newtown, CT 06470-2359/203-426-1320; FAX: 203-426-1087. For the shooting, hunting and outdoor trade retailer.

Shotgun Sports
P.O. Box 6810, Auburn, CA 9604/916-889-2220; FAX:916-889-9106. $31.00 yr. Trapshooting how-to's, shotshell reloading, shotgun patterning, shotgun tests and evaluations, Sporting Clays action, waterfowl/upland hunting. Call 1-800-676-8920 for a free sample copy.

The Sixgunner (M)
Handgun Hunters International, P.O. Box 357, MAG, Bloomingdale, OH 43910

The Skeet Shooting Review
National Skeet Shooting Assn., 5931 Roft Rd., San Antonio, TX 78253. $20.00 yr. (Assn. membership includes mag.) Competition results, personality profiles of top Skeet shooters, how-to articles, technical, reloading information.

Soldier of Fortune
Subscription Dept., P.O. Box 348, Mt. Morris, IL 61054. $29.95 yr.; $39.95 Canada; $50.95 foreign.

Sporting Clays Magazine
Patch Communications, 5211 South Washington Ave., Titusville, FL 32780/407-268-5010; FAX: 407-267-7216. $29.95 yr. (12 issues). Official publication of the National Sporting Clays Association.

Sporting Goods Business
Miller Freeman, Inc., One Penn Plaza, 10th Fl., New York, NY 10119-0004. Trade journal.

Sporting Goods Dealer
Two Park Ave., New York, NY 10016. $100.00 yr. Sporting goods trade journal.

Sporting Gun
Bretton Court, Bretton, Peterborough PE3 8DZ, England. £27.00 (approx. U.S. $36.00), airmail £35.50 yr. For the game and clay enthusiasts.

Sports Afield
11650 Riverside Drive, North Hollywood, CA 91602-1066/818-904-9981.

The Squirrel Hunter
P.O. Box 368, Chireno, TX 75937. $14.00 yr. Articles about squirrel hunting.

Stott's Creek Calendar
Stott's Creek Printers, 2526 S 475 W, Morgantown, IN 46160/317-878-5489. 1 yr. (3 issues) $11.50; 2 yrs. (6 issues) $20.00. Lists all gun shows everywhere in convenient calendar form; call for information.

Super Outdoors
2695 Aiken Road, Shelbyville, KY 40065/502-722-9463;800-404-6064; Fax: 502-722-8093. Mark Edwards, publisher. Contact for details.

TACARMI
Via E. De Amicis, 25; 20123 Milano, Italy. $100.00 yr. approx. Antique and modern guns. (Italian text.)

Territorial Dispatch—1800s Historical Publication (M)
National Assn. of Buckskinners, 4701 Marion St., Suite 324, Livestock Exchange Bldg., Denver, CO 80216. Michael A. Nester & Barbara Wyckoff, editors. 303-297-9671.

Trap & Field
1000 Waterway Blvd., Indianapolis, IN 46202. $25.00 yr. Official publ. Amateur Trapshooting Assn. Scores, averages, trapshooting articles.

Turkey Call* (M)
Natl. Wild Turkey Federation, Inc., P.O. Box 530, Edgefield, SC 29824. $25.00 with membership (6 issues per yr.)

Turkey & Turkey Hunting*
Krause Publications, 700 E. State St., Iola, WI 54990-0001. $13.95 (6 issue p. yr.). Magazine with leading-edge articles on all aspects of wild turkey behavior, biology and the successful ways to hunt better with that info. Learn the proper techniques to calling, the right equipment, and more.

The U.S. Handgunner* (M)
U.S. Revolver Assn., 40 Larchmont Ave., Taunton, MA 02780. $10.00 yr. General handgun and competition articles. Bi-monthly sent to members.

U.S. Airgun Magazine
P.O. Box 2021, Benton, AR 72018/800-247-4867; Fax: 501-316-8549. 10 issues a yr. Cover the sport from hunting, 10-meter, field target and collecting. Write for details.

The Varmint Hunter Magazine (Q)
The Varmint Hunters Assn., Box 759, Pierre, SD 57501/800-528-4868. $24.00 yr.

Waffenmarkt-Intern
GFI-Verlag, Theodor-Heuss Ring 62, 50668 K˝ln, Germany. Only for gunsmiths, licensed firearms dealers and their suppliers in Germany, Austria and Switzerland.

Wild Sheep (M) (Q)
Foundation for North American Wild Sheep, 720 Allen Ave., Cody, WY 82414. Website: http://iigi.com/os/non/fnaws.htm; e-mail: fnaws@wyoming.com. Official journal of the foundation.

Wisconsin Outdoor Journal
Krause Publications, 700 E. State St., Iola, WI 54990-0001. $17.97 yr. (8 issues). For Wisconsin's avid hunters and fishermen, with features from all over that state with regional reports, legislative updates, etc. Website: www.krause.com

Women & Guns
P.O. Box 488, Sta. C, Buffalo, NY 14209. $24.00 yr. U.S.; $72.00 foreign (12 issues). Only magazine edited by and for women gun owners.

World War II*
Cowles History Group, 741 Miller Dr., SE, Suite D-2, Leesburg, VA 20175-8920. Annual subscriptions $19.95 U.S.; $25.95 Canada; 43.95 foreign. The title says it—WWII; good articles, ads, etc.

*Published bi-monthly
†Published weekly
‡Published three times per month. All others are published monthly.

THE HANDGUNNER'S LIBRARY

FOR COLLECTOR ◆ HUNTER ◆ SHOOTER ◆ OUTDOORSMAN

IMPORTANT NOTICE TO BOOK BUYERS

Books listed here may be bought from Ray Riling Arms Books Co., 6844 Gorsten St., P.O. Box 18925, Philadelphia, PA 19119, phone 215/438-2456; FAX: 215/438-5395. Joe Riling is the researcher and compiler of "The Arms Library" and a seller of gun books for over 30 years.

The Riling stock includes books classic and modern, many hard-to-find items, and many not obtainable elsewhere. These pages list a portion of the current stock. They offer prompt, complete service, with delayed shipments occurring only on out-of-print or out-of-stock books.

NOTICE FOR ALL CUSTOMERS: Remittance in U.S. funds must accompany all orders. For U.S. add $2.00 per book for postage and insurance. Minimum order $10.00. For UPS add 50% to mailing costs.

All foreign countries add $5.00 per book. All foreign orders are shipped at the buyer's risk unless an additional $5 for insurance is included.

Payments in excess of order or for "Backorders" are credited or fully refunded at request. Books "As-Ordered" are not returnable except by permission and a handling charge on these of $2.00 per book is deducted from refund or credit. Only Pennsylvania customers must include current sales tax.

A full variety of arms books also available from Rutgers Book Center, 127 Raritan Ave., Highland Park, NJ 08904/908-545-4344; FAX: 908-545-6686 or I.D.S.A. Books, 1324 Stratford Drive, Piqua, OH 45356/937-773-4203; FAX: 937-778-1922.

BALLISTICS AND HANDLOADING

ABC's of Reloading, 6th Edition, by C. Rodney James and the editors of *Handloader's Digest*, DBI Books, a division of Krause Publications, Iola, WI, 1997. 288 pp., illus. Paper covers. $21.95.
The definitive guide to every facet of cartridge and shotshell reloading.

Ammunition Making, by George E. Frost, National Rifle Association of America, Washington, D.C., 1990. 160 pp., illus. Paper covers. $17.95.
Reflects the perspective of "an insider" with half a century's experience in successful management of ammunition manufacturing operations.

Barnes Reloading Manual #1, Barnes Bullets, American Fork, UT, 1995. 350 pp., illus. $24.95.
Data for more than 65 cartridges from 243 to 50 BMG.

Basic Handloading, by George C. Nonte, Jr., Outdoor Life Books, New York, NY, 1982. 192 pp., illus. Paper covers. $6.95.
How to produce high-quality ammunition using the safest, most efficient methods.

Big Bore Rifles And Cartridges, Wolfe Publishing Co., Prescott, AZ, 1991. Paper covers. $26.00.
This book covers cartridges from 8mm to .600 Nitro with loading tables.

Black Powder Guide, 2nd Edition, by George C. Nonte, Jr., Stoeger Publishing Co., So. Hackensack, NJ, 1991. 288 pp., illus. Paper covers. $14.95.
How-to instructions for selection, repair and maintenance of muzzleloaders, making your own bullets, restoring and refinishing, shooting techniques.

Blackpowder Loading Manual, 3rd Edition, by Sam Fadala, DBI Books, a division of Krause Publications, Iola, WI, 1995. 368 pp., illus. Paper covers. $19.95.
Revised and expanded edition of this landmark blackpowder loading book. Covers hundreds of loads for most of the popular blackpowder rifles, handguns and shotguns.

The Bullet Swage Manual. by Ted Smith, Corbin Manufacturing and Supply Co., White City, OR, 1988. 45 pp., illus. Paper covers. $10.00.
A book that fills the need for information on bullet swaging.

Cartridges of the World, 8th Edition, by Frank Barnes, edited by M. L. McPherson, DBI Books, a division of Krause Publications, Iola, WI, 1997. 480 pp., illus. Paper covers. $24.95.
Completely revised edition of the general purpose reference work for which collectors, police, scientists and laymen reach first for answers to cartridge identification questions.

Cartridge Reloading Tools of the Past, by R.H. Chamberlain and Tom Quigley, Tom Quigley, Castle Rock, WA, 1998. 167 pp., illustrated. Paper covers. $25.00.
A detailed treatment of the extensive Winchester and Ideal line of handloading tools and bullet molds, plus Remington, Marlin, Ballard, Browning, Maynard, and many others.

Cast Bullets for the Black Powder Rifle, by Paul A. Matthews, Wolfe Publishing Co., Prescott, AZ, 1996. 133 pp., illus. Paper covers. $22.50.
The tools and techniques used to make your cast bullet shooting a success.

Complete Blackpowder Handbook, 3rd Edition, by Sam Fadala, DBI Books, a division of Krause Publications, Iola, WI, 1997. 400 pp., illus. Paper covers. $21.95.
Expanded and completely rewritten edition of the definitive book on the subject of blackpowder.

The Complete Handloader for Rifles, Handguns and Shotguns, by John Wootters, Stackpole Books, Harrisburg, PA, 1988. 214 pp., $29.95.
Loading-bench know-how.

Complete Reloading Guide, by Robert & John Traister, Stoeger Publishing Co., Wayne, NJ, 1997. 608 pp., illus. Paper covers $34.95
Perhaps the finest, most comprehensive work ever published on the subject of reloading.

Designing and Forming Custom Cartridges, by Ken Howell, Ken Howell, Stevensville, MT, 1995. 596 pp., illus. $59.95.
Covers cartridge dimensions and includes complete introductory material on cartridge manufacture and appendices on finding loading data and equipment.

Game Loads and Practical Ballistics for the American Hunter, by Bob Hagel, Wolfe Publishing Co., Prescott, AZ, 1992. 310 pp., illus. $27.90.
Hagel's knowledge gained as a hunter, guide and gun enthusiast is gathered in this informative text.

Handbook of Bullet Swaging No. 7, by David R. Corbin, Corbin Manufacturing and Supply Co., White City, OR, 1986. 199 pp., illus. Paper covers. $10.00.
This handbook explains the most precise method of making quality bullets.

Handbook for Shooters and Reloaders, by P.O. Ackley, Salt Lake City, UT, 1970. (Vol. I), 567 pp., illus. (Vol. II), a new printing with specific new material. 495 pp., illus. $18.95 each.

Handbook of Metallic Cartridge Reloading, by Edward Matunas, Winchester Press, Piscataway, NJ, 1981. 272 pp., illus. $19.95.
Up-to-date, comprehensive loading tables prepared by four major powder manufacturers.

Handgun Reloading, The Gun Digest Book of, by Dean A. Grennell and Wiley M. Clapp, DBI Books, a division of Krause Publications, Iola, WI, 1987. 256 pp., illus. Paper covers. $16.95.
Detailed discussions of all aspects of reloading for handguns, from basic to complex. New loading data.

Handloader's Digest, 17th Edition, edited by Bob Bell, DBI Books, a division of Krause Publications, Iola, WI, 1997. 480 pp., illustrated. Paper covers. $27.95.
Top writers in the field contribute helpful information on techniques and components. Greatly expanded and fully indexed catalog of all currently available tools, accessories and components for metallic, blackpowder cartridge, shotgun reloading and swaging.

Handloader's Guide, by Stanley W. Trzoniec, Stoeger Publishing Co., So. Hackensack, NJ, 1985, 256 pp., illus. Paper covers. $14.95.
The complete step-by-step fully illustrated guide to handloading ammunition.

Handloader's Manual of Cartridge Conversions, by John J. Donnelly, Stoeger Publishing Co., So. Hackensack, NJ, 1986. Unpaginated. $49.95.
From 14 Jones to 70-150 Winchester in English and American cartridges, and from 4.85 U.K. to 15.2x28R Gevelot in metric cartridges. Over 900 cartridges described in detail.

Handloading, by Bill Davis, Jr., NRA Books, Wash., D.C., 1980. 400 pp., illus. Paper covers. $15.95.
A complete update and expansion of the NRA Handloader's Guide.

Handloading for Hunters, by Don Zutz, Winchester Press, Piscataway, NJ, 1977. 288 pp., illus. $30.00.
Precise mixes and loads for different types of game and for various hunting situations with rifle and shotgun.

Hatcher's Notebook, by S. Julian Hatcher, Stackpole Books, Harrisburg, PA, 1992. 488 pp., illus. $39.95.
A reference work for shooters, gunsmiths, ballisticians, historians, hunters and collectors.

Hodgdon Data Manual No. 26, Hodgdon Powder Co., Shawnee Mission, KS, 1993. 797 pp. $25.00.
Includes Hercules, Winchester and Dupont powders; data on cartridge cases; loads; silhouette; shotshell; pyrodex and blackpowder; conversion factors; weight equivalents, etc.

The Home Guide to Cartridge Conversions, by Maj. George C. Nonte Jr., The Gun Room Press, Highland Park, NJ, 1976. 404 pp., illus. $24.95.
Revised and updated version of Nonte's definitive work on the alteration of cartridge cases for use in guns for which they were not intended.

THE HANDGUNNER'S LIBRARY

REFERENCE

Hornady Handbook of Cartridge Reloading, 4th Edition, Vol. I and II, Hornady Mfg. Co., Grand Island, NE, 1991. 1200 pp. illus. $34.95.
New edition of this famous reloading handbook. Latest loads, ballistic information, etc.

Hornady Handbook of Cartridge Reloading, Abridged Edition, Hornady Mfg. Co., Grand Island, NE, 1991. $19.95.
Ballistic data for 25 of the most popular cartridges.

Hornady Load Notes, Hornady Mfg. Co., Grand Island, NE, 1991. $4.95.
Complete load data and ballistics for a single caliber. Eight pistol 9mm-45ACP; 16 rifle, 222-45-70.

How-To's for the Black Powder Cartridge Rifle Shooter, by Paul A. Matthews, Wolfe Publishing Co., Prescott, AZ, 1995. 45 pp. Paper covers, $22.50.
Covers lube recipes, good bore cleaners and over-powder wads. Tips include compressing powder charges, combating wind resistance, improving ignition and much more.

The Illustrated Reference of Cartridge Dimensions, edited by Dave Scovill, Wolfe Publishing Co., Prescott, AZ, 1994. 343 pp. illus. Paper covers, $19.00
A comprehensive volume with over 300 cartridges. Standard and metric dimensions have been taken from SAAMI drawings and/or fired cartridges.

Loading the Black Powder Rifle Cartridge, by Paul A Matthews, Wolfe Publishing Co., Prescott, AZ, 1993. 121 pp. illus. Paper covers, $22.50.
Author Matthews brings the blackpowder cartridge shooter valuable information on the basics, including cartridge care, lubes and moulds, powder charges and developing and testing loads in his usual authoritative style.

Loading the Peacemaker—Colt's Model P, by C. Kenneth Ramage, Lyman Products for Shooters, Middlefield, CT, 1996. 227 pp. illus. Paper covers, $24.95.
A comprehensive work about the history, maintenance and repair of the most famous revolver ever made, including the most extensive load data ever published.

Lyman Cast Bullet Handbook, 3rd Edition, edited by C. Kenneth Ramage, Lyman Publications, Middlefield, CT, 1980. 416 pp. illus. Paper covers, $19.95.
Information on more than 5000 tested cast bullet loads and 19 pages of trajectory and wind drift tables for cast bullets.

Lyman Black Powder Handbook, edited by C. Kenneth Ramage, Lyman Products for Shooters, Middlefield, CT, 1975. 239 pp. illus. Paper covers, $14.95.
Comprehensive load information for the modern blackpowder shooter.

Lyman Pistol & Revolver Handbook, 2nd Edition, edited by Thomas J. Griffin, Lyman Products Co., Middlefield, CT, 1996. 287 pp. illus. Paper covers, $18.95.
The most up-to-date loading data available including the hottest new calibers, like 40 S&W, 9x21,9mm Makarov, 9x25 Dillon and 454 Casull.

Lyman Reloading Handbook No. 47, edited by Edward A. Matunas, Lyman Publications, Middlefield, CT, 1992. 480 pp. illus. Paper covers, $24.95.
A comprehensive reloading manual complete with all the newest rifle and pistol information. Expanded data section with all the newest rifle and pistol calibers.

Lyman Shotshell Handbook, 4th Edition, edited by Edward A. Matunas, Lyman Products Co., Middlefield, CT, 1996. 330 pp., illus. Paper covers, $24.95.
Has 9000 loads, including slugs and buckshot, plus feature articles and a full color I.D. section.

Lyman's Guide to Big Game Cartridges & Rifles, by Edward Matunas, Lyman Publishing Corporation, Middlefield, CT, 1994. 287 pp. illus. Paper covers, $17.95.
A selection guide to cartridges and rifles for big game—antelope to elephant.

Making Loading Dies and Bullet Molds, by Harold Hoffman, H&P Publishing, San Angelo, TX, 1993. 230 pp. illus. Paper covers. $24.95.
A good book for learning tool and die making.

Metallic Cartridge Reloading, 3rd Edition, by M.L. McPherson, DBI Books, a division of Krause Publications, Iola, WI, 1996. 352 pp. illus. Paper covers, $21.95.
A true reloading manual with over 10,000 loads for all popular metallic cartridges and a wealth of invaluable technical data provided by a recognized expert.

Modern Handloading, by Maj. Geo. C. Nonte, Winchester Press, Piscataway, NJ, 1972. 416 pp. illus. $15.00.
Covers all aspects of metallic and shotshell ammunition loading, plus more loads than any book in print.

Modern Reloading, by Richard Lee, Inland Press, 1996. 510 pp., illus. $24.98.
The how-tos of rifle, pistol and shotgun reloading plus load data for rifle and pistol calibers.

Modern Practical Ballistics, by Art Pejsa, Pejsa Ballistics, Minneapolis, MN, 1990. 150 pp., illus. $24.95.
Covers all aspects of ballistics and new, simplified methods. Clear examples illustrate new, easy but very accurate formulas.

Mr. Single Shot's Cartridge Handbook, by Frank de Haas, Mark de Haas, Orange City, IA, 1996. 116 pp., illus. Paper covers, $21.50.
This book covers most of the cartridges, both commercial and wildcat, that the author has known and used.

Nick Harvey's Practical Reloading Manual, by Nick Harvey, Australian Print Group, Maryborough, Victoria, 1996. 235 pp., illus. Paper covers. $24.95.
Contains data for rifle and handgun including many popular wildcat and improved cartridges. Tools, powders, components and techniques for assembling optimum reloads with particular application to North America.

Nosler Reloading Manual #4, edited by Gail Root, Nosler Bullets, Inc., Bend, OR, 1996. 516 pp., illus. $24.99.
Combines information on their Ballistic Tip, Partition and Handgun bullets with traditional powders and new powders never before used, plus trajectory information from 100 to 500 yards.

The Paper Jacket, by Paul Matthews, Wolfe Publishing Co., Prescott, AZ, 1991. Paper covers, $13.50.
Up-to-date and accurate information about paper-patched bullets.

Precision Handloading, by John Withers, Stoeger Publishing Co., So. Hackensack, NJ, 1985. 224 pp. illus. Paper covers, $14.95.
An entirely new approach to handloading ammunition.

Propellant Profiles New and Expanded, 3rd Edition, Wolfe Publishing Co., Prescott, AZ, 1991. Paper covers, $16.95.

Reloader's Guide, 3rd Edition, by R.A. Steindler, Stoeger Publishing Co., So. Hackensack, NJ, 1984. 224 pp., illus. Paper covers. $11.95.
Complete, fully illustrated step-by-step guide to handloading ammunition.

Reloading for Shotgunners, 4th Edition, by Kurt D. Fackler and M.L. McPherson, DBI Books, a division of Krause Publications, Iola, WI, 1997. 320 pp. illus. Paper covers. $19.95.
Expanded reloading tables with over 11,000 loads, Bushing charts for every major press and component maker. All new presentation on all aspects of shotshell reloading by two of the top experts in the field.

Sierra 50th Anniversary, 4th Edition Handgun Manual, edited by Ken Ramage, Sierra Bullets, Santa Fe, 1997. 700 pp. illus. $21.99
Histories, reloading recommendations, bullets, powders and sections on the reloading process, etc.

Sierra 50th Anniversary, 4th Edition Rifle Manual, edited by Ken Ramage, Sierra Bullets, Santa Fe Springs, CA, 1997. 800 pp. illus. $26.99.
New cartridge introductions, etc.

Sixgun Cartridges and Loads, by Elmer Keith, The Gun Room Press, Highland Park, NJ, 1986. 151 pp. illus. $24.95.
A manual covering the selection, uses and loading of the most suitable and popular revolver cartridges. Originally published in 1936. Reprint.

Speer Reloading Manual Number 12, edited by the editors of the Speer research staff, Omark Industries, Lewiston, ID, 1987. 621 pp. illus. $18.95.
Reloading manual for rifles and pistols.

Understanding Ballistics, by Robert A. Rinker, Mulberry House Publishing Co., Corydon, IN, 1997. 373 pp. illus Paper covers, $19.95.
Explains basic to advanced firearm ballistics in understandable terms.

Why Not Load Your Own?, by Col. T. Whelen, A. S. Barnes, New York, 1957, 4th ed., rev. 237 pp., illus. $20.00.
A basic reference on handloading, describing each step, materials and equipment. Includes loads for popular cartridges.

Wildcat Cartridges Volumes 1 & 2 Combination, by the editors of Handloaders magazine, Wolfe Publishing Co., Prescott, AZ, 1997. 350 pp. illus. Paper covers, $39.95.
A profile of the most popular information on wildcat cartridges that appeared in the Handloader magazine.

The Winchester Lever Legacy, by Clyde "Snooky" Williamson, Buchary, LA, 1988. 664 pp. illustrated, $39.95.
A book on reloading for the different calibers of the Winchester lever action rifle.

Yours Truly, Harvey Donaldson, by Harvey Donaldson, Wolfe Publ. Co., Inc., Prescott, AZ, 1980. 288 pp. illus. $19.50.
Reprint of the famous columns by Harvey Donaldson which appeared in "Handloader" from May 1966 through December 1972.

COLLECTORS

Air Guns, by Eldon G. Wolff, Duckett's Publishing Co., Tempe, AZ, 1997. 204 pp., illus Paper covers, $35.00
Historical reference covering many makers, European and American guns, canes and more.

The American B.B. Gun, by Arni Dunathan, R&R Books, Livonia, N.Y. 1997. 154 pp., illus. $30.00.
A collector's guide.

The American Cartridge, by Charles R. Suydam, Borden Publishing Co., Alhambra, CA, 1986. 184 pp., illus. $24.95.
An illustrated study of the rimfire cartridge in the United States.

Ammunition: Grenades and Projectile Munitions, by Ian V. Hogg, Stackpole Books, Mechanicsburg, PA, 1998. 144 pp. illus. $22.95
Concise guide to modern ammunition. International coverage with detailed specifications and illustrations.

Antique Guns, the Collector's Guide, 2nd Edition, edited by John Traister, Stoeger Publishing Co., So. Hackensack, NJ, 1994. 320 pp. illus. Paper covers, $19.95.
Covers a vast spectrum of pre-1900 firearms: those manufactured by U.S. gunmakers as well as Canadian, French, German, Belgian, Spanish and other foreign firms.

Arms & Accoutrements of the Mounted Police 1873-1973, by Roger F. Phillips and Donald J. Klancher, Museum Restoration Service, Ont., Canada, 1982. 224 pp., illus. $49.95.
A definitive history of the revolvers, rifles, machine guns, cannons, ammunition, swords, etc. used by the NWMP, the RNWMP and the RCMP during the first 100 years of the Force.

Arms Makers of Maryland, by Daniel D. Hartzler, George Shumway, York, PA, 1975. 200 pp. illus. $50.00.
A thorough study of the gunsmiths of Maryland who worked during the late 18th and early 19th centuries.

THE HANDGUNNER'S LIBRARY

Arming the Dragon, Mauser Rifle Production in China 1895-1950, by Dolf L. Goldsmith, San Antonio, TX, 1998. 47 pp., illustrated. Spiral bound Paper covers. $15.00.
Details the manufacture and history of the Mauser rifle China.

Artistry in Arms: The Guns of Smith & Wesson, by Roy G. Jinks, Smith & Wesson, Springfield, MA, 1991. 85 pp., illus. Paper covers. $19.95.
Catalog of the Smith & Wesson International Museum Tour 1991-1995 organized by the Connecticut Valley Historical Museum and Springfield Library and Museum Association.

Assault Weapons, 4th Edition, The Gun Digest Book of, edited by Jack Lewis, DBI Books, a division of Krause Publications, Iola, WI, 1996. 256 pp. illus. Paper covers. $19.95.
An in-depth look at the history and uses of these arms.

Astra Automatic Pistols, by Leonardo M. Antaris, FIRAC Publishing Co., Sterling, CO, 1989. 248 pp., illus. $45.00.
Charts, tables, serial ranges, etc. The definitive work on Astra pistols.

Basic Documents on U.S. Martial Arms, commentary by Col. B. R. Lewis, reissue by Ray Riling, Phila., PA, 1956 and 1960. *Rifle Musket Model 1855*. The first issue rifle of musket caliber, a muzzle loader equipped with the Maynard Primer, 32 pp. *Breech-Loading Rifle Musket Model 1866*. The first of our 50-caliber breechloading rifles, 12 pp. *Remington Navy Rifle Model 1870*. A commercial type breech-loader made at Springfield, 16 pp. *Lee Straight Pull Navy Rifle Model 1895*. A magazine cartridge arm of 6mm caliber. 23 pp. *Breech-Loading Arms* (five models) 27 pp. *Ward-Burton Rifle Musket 1871-16* pp. Each $10.00.

Battle Weapons of the American Revolution, by George C. Neuman, Scurlock Publishing Co., Texarkana, TX, 1998. 400 pp. Illus. $65.00.
The most extensive photographic collection of Revolutionary War weapons ever in one volume. More than 1,600 photos of over 500 muskets, rifles, swords, bayonets, knives and other arms used by both sides in America's War for Independence.

Behold, the Longrifle Again, by James B. Whisker, Old Bedford Village Press, Bedford, PA, 1997. 176 pp., illus. $45.00
Excellent reference work for the collector profusely illustrated with photographs of some of the finest Kentucky rifles showing front and back profiles and overall view.

Beretta Automatic Pistols, by J.B. Wood, Stackpole Books, Harrisburg, PA, 1985. 192 pp., illus. $24.95.
Only English-language book devoted to the Beretta line. Includes all important models.

Birmingham Gunmakers, by Douglas Tate, Safari Press, Inc., Huntington Beach, CA, 1997. 300 pp., illus. $50.00.
An invaluable work for anybody interested in the fine sporting arms crafted in this famous British gunmakers' city.

Blacksmith Guide to Ruger Flat-Top & Super Blackhawks, by H.W. Ross, Jr., Blacksmith Corp., Chino Valley, AZ, 1990. 96 pp., illus. Paper covers. $9.95.
A key source on the extensively collected Ruger Blackhawk revolvers.

Blue Book of Gun Values, 19th Edition, edited by S.P. Fjestad, Blue Book Publications, Inc., Minneapolis, MN, 1998. 1301 pp., illus. Paper covers. $29.95
Covers all new 1998 firearm prices. Gives technical data on both new and discontinued domestic and foreign commercial and military guns.

The Blunderbuss 1500-1900, by James D. Forman, Museum Restoration Service, Bloomfield, Ont., Canada, 1995. 40 pp., illus. Paper covers. $4.95.
The guns that had no peer as an anti-personal weapon throughout the flintlock era.

Boarders Away, Volume II: Firearms of the Age of Fighting Sail, by William Gilkerson, Andrew Mowbray, Inc. Publishers, Lincoln, RI, 1993. 331 pp., illus. $65.00.
Covers the pistols, muskets, combustibles and small cannon used aboard American and European fighting ships, 1626-1826.

Boothroyd's Revised Directory of British Gunmakers, by Geoffrey and Susan Boothroyd, Sand Lake Press, Amity, OR, 1997. 412 pp., illus. $34.95.
A new revised and enlarged edition. Lists all makers in alphabetical order.

Breech-Loading Carbines of the United States Civil War Period, by Brig. Gen. John Pitman, Armory Publications, Tacoma, WA, 1987. 94 pp., illus. $29.95.
The first in a series of previously unpublished manuscripts originated by the late Brigadier General John Putnam. Exploded drawings showing parts actual size follow each sectioned illustration.

The Breech-Loading Single-Shot Rifle, by Major Ned H. Roberts and Kenneth L. Waters, Wolfe Publishing Co, Prescott, AZ, 1995. 333 pp., illus. $28.50.
A comprehensive and complete history of the evolution of the Schutzen and single-shot rifle.

The British Enfield Rifles, Volume 1, The SMLE Mk I and Mk III Rifles, by Charles R. Stratton, North Cape Publications, Tustin, CA, 1997. 150 pp., illus. Paper covers. $19.95.
A systematic and thorough examination on a part-by-part basis of the famous British battle rifle that endured for nearly 70 years as the British Army's number one battle rifle.

The British Falling Block Breechloading Rifle from 1865, by Jonathan Kirton, Tom Rowe Books, Maynardsville, TN, 2nd edition, 1997. 380 pp., illus. $70.00.
Expanded 2nd edition of a comprehensive work on the British falling block rifle.

British Military Firearms 1650-1850, by Howard L. Blackmore, Stackpole Books, Mechanicsburg, PA, 1994. 224 pp., illus. $50.00.
The definitive work on British military firearms.

British Service Rifles and Carbines 1888-1900, by Alan M. Petrillo, Excaliber Publications, Latham, NY, 1994. 72 pp., illus. Paper covers. $11.95.
A complete review of the Lee-Metford and Lee-Enfield rifles and carbines.

British Single Shot Rifles, Volume 1, Alexander Henry, by Wal Einfer, Tom Rowe, Manardville, TN, 1998, 200 pp., illus. $50.00.
Detailed description of the single shot rifles made by Henry. Illustrated with hundreds of photographs and drawings.

British Single Shot Rifles Volume 2, George Gibbs, by Wal Winfer, Tom Rowe, Maynardville, TN, 1998. 177 pp., illus. $50.00
Detailed study of the Farquharson as made by Gibbs. Hundreds of photos.

British Single Shot Rifles, Volume 3, Jeffery, by Wal Winfer, Rowe Publications, Rochester, N.Y., 1999. 260 pp., illustrated. $60.00.
The Farquharson as made by Jeffery and his competitors, H&H Bland, Westley, Manton, etc. Large section on the development of nitro cartridges including the .600.

The British Soldier's Firearms from Smoothbore to Rifled Arms, 1850-1864, by Dr. C.H. Roads, R&R Books, Livonia, NY, 1994. 332 pp., illus. $49.00.
A reprint of the classic text covering the development of British military hand and shoulder firearms in the crucial years between 1850 and 1864.

British Sporting Guns & Rifles, compiled by George Hoyem, Armory Publications, Coeur d'Alene, ID, 1997. 1024 pp., illus. In two volumes. $240.00.
Eighteen old sporting firearms trade catalogs and a rare book reproduced with their color covers in a limited, signed and numbered edition.

British Sporting Rifle Cartridges, by Bill Fleming, Armory Publications, Oceanside, CA, 1994. 302 pp., illus. $75.00.
An expanded study of volume three of *The History & Development of Small Arms Ammunition*. Includes pertinent trade catalog pages, etc.

Browning Dates of Manufacture, compiled by George Madis, Art and Reference House, Brownsboro, TX, 1989. 48 pp. $5.00.
Gives the date codes and product codes for all models from 1824 to the present.

Browning Sporting Arms of Distinction 1903-1992, by Matt Eastman, Matt Eastman Publications, Fitzgerald, GA, 1995. 450 pp., illus. $49.95.
The most recognized publication on Browning sporting arms; covers all models.

Bullard Arms, by G. Scott Jamieson, The Boston Mills Press, Ontario, Canada, 1989. 244 pp., illus. $35.00.
The story of a mechanical genius whose rifles and cartridges were the equal to any made in America in the 1880s.

Burning Powder, compiled by Major D.B. Wesson, Wolfe Publishing Company, Prescott, AZ, 1992. 110 pp. Soft cover. $10.95.
A rare booklet from 1932 for Smith & Wesson collectors.

The Burnside Breech Loading Carbines, by Edward A. Hull, Andrew Mowbray, Inc., Lincoln, RI, 1986. 95 pp., illus. $16.00.
No. 1 in the "Man at Arms Monograph Series." A model-by-model historical/technical examination of one of the most widely used cavalry weapons of the American Civil War based upon important and previously unpublished research.

California Gunsmiths 1846-1900, by Lawrence P. Sheldon, Far Far West Publ., Fair Oaks, CA, 1977. 289 pp., illus. $30.00.
A study of early California gunsmiths and the firearms they made.

Canadian Military Handguns 1855-1985, by Clive M. Law, Museum Restoration Service, Bloomfield, Ont. Canada, 1994. 130pp., illus. $40.00.
A long-awaited and important history for arms historians and pistol collectors.

Cap Guns, by James Dundas, Schiffer Publishing, Atglen, PA, 1996. 160 pp., illus. Paper covers. $29.95.
Over 600 full-color photos of cap guns and gun accessories with a current value guide.

Carbines of the Civil War, by John D. McAulay, Pioneer Press, Union City, TN, 1981. 123 pp., illus. Paper covers. $7.95.
A guide for the student and collector of the colorful arms used by the Federal cavalry.

Carbines of the U.S. Cavalry 1861-1905, by John D. McAulay, Andrew Mowbray Publishers, Lincoln, RI, 1996. $35.00.
Covers the crucial use of carbines from the beginning of the Civil War to the end of the cavalry carbine era in 1905.

Cartridge Catalogues, compiled by George Hoyem, Armory Publications, Coeur d'Alene, ID, 1997. 504 pp., illus. $125.00.
Fourteen old ammunition makers' and designers' catalogs reproduced with their color covers in a limited, signed and numbered edition.

Cartridges for Breechloading Rifles, by A. Mattenheimer, Armory Publications, Oceanside, CA, 1989. 90 pp. with two 15"x19" color lithos containing 163 drawings of cartridges and firearms mechanisms. $29.95.
Reprinting of this German work on cartridges. Text in German and English.

Cartridges of the World, 8th Edition, by Frank Barnes, edited by M. L. McPherson, DBI Books, a division of Krause Publications, Iola, WI, 1997. 480 pp., illus. Paper covers. $24.95.
Completely revised edition of the general purpose reference work for which collectors, police, scientists and laymen reach first for answers to cartridge identification questions. Available October, 1996.

Civil War Arms Makers and Their Contracts, edited by Stuart C. Mowbray and Jennifer Heroux, Andrew Mowbray Publishing, Lincoln, RI, 1998. 595 pp. $39.50.
A facsimile reprint of the Report by the Commissioner of Ordnance and Ordnance Stores, 1862.

Civil War Breech Loading Rifles, by John D. McAulay, Andrew Mowbray, Inc., Lincoln, RI, 1991. 144 pp. illus. Paper covers. $15.00.
All the major breech-loading rifles of the Civil War and most, if not all, of the obscure types are detailed, illustrated and set in their historical context.

THE HANDGUNNER'S LIBRARY

Civil War Carbines Volume 2: The Early Years, by John D. McAulay, Andrew Mowbray, Inc., Lincoln, RI, 1991. 144 pp. illus. Paper covers, $15.00. Covers the carbines made during the exciting years leading up to the outbreak of war and used by the North and South in the conflict.

Civil War Cartridge Boxes of the Union Infantryman, by Paul Johnson, Andrew Mowbray, Inc., Lincoln, RI, 1998. 352 pp. illustrated. $45.00. There were four patterns of infantry cartridge boxes used by Union forces during the Civil War. The author describes the development and subsequent pattern changes to these cartridge boxes.

Civil War Firearms, by Joseph G. Bilby, Combined Books, Conshohocken, PA, 1996. 252 pp. illus. $34.95. The complete story of Federal and Confederate small arms; design, manufacture, identifications, procurement, issue, employment, effectiveness, and postwar disposal by the recognized expert.

Civil War Guns, by William B. Edwards, Thomas Publications, Gettysburg, PA, 1997. 444 pp. illus. $40.00. The complete story of the firearms including short histories of specific serial numbers and the soldiers who received them.

Civil War Pistols, by John D. McAulay, Andrew Mowbray Inc., Lincoln, RI, 1992. 166 pp. illus. $38.50. A survey of the handguns used during the American Civil War.

Civil War Sharps Carbines and Rifles, by Earl J. Coates and John D. McAulay, Thomas Publications, Gettysburg, PA, 1996. 108 pp. illus. Paper covers, $12.95. Traces the history and development of the firearms including short histories of specific serial numbers.

The W.F. Cody Buffalo Bill Collector's Guide with Values, by James W. Wojtowicz, Collector Books, Paducah, KY, 1998. 271 pp. illustrated. $24.95. A profusion of colorful collectibles including lithographs, programs, photographs, books, medals, sheet music, guns, etc. and today's values.

Col. Burton's Spiller & Burr Revolver, by Matthew W. Norman, Mercer University Press, Macon, GA, 1997. 152 pp. illus. $22.95. A remarkable archival research project on the establishment and running of the factory, comprehensive story of the...

Collecting Western Toy Guns Identification and Value Guide, by Jim Schleyer, Books of Americana, Krause Publications, Iola, WI, 1996. 452 pp. illus. Paper covers, $29.95. Includes toy pistols, rifles, boxes, derringers, holsters, spurs, wrist cuffs, kerchiefs, hats, gloves, clothing, lariats, ammunition, badges, rubber knives and cowboy character sets.

Collector's Guide to Colt .45 Service Pistols Models of 1911 and 1911A1, by Charles W. Clawson, Clawson Publications, Fort Wayne, IN, 1998. 130 pp., illustrated. $29.95. Complete military identification, including all contractors from 1911 to the end of production in 1945.

A Collector's Guide to United States Combat Shotguns, by Bruce N. Canfield, Andrew Mowbray Inc., Lincoln, RI, 1992. 184 pp. illus. Paper covers, $22.00. Complete coverage of combat shotguns, from the earliest examples right up to the Gulf War and beyond.

A Collector's Guide to Winchester in the Service, by Bruce N. Canfield, Andrew Mowbray, Inc., Lincoln, RI, 1991. 192 pp. illus. Paper covers, $22.00. The firearms produced by Winchester for the national defense. From the Hotchkiss to the M14, each firearm is examined and illustrated.

A Collector's Guide to the M1 Garand and the M1 Carbine, by Bruce N. Canfield, Andrew Mowbray, Inc., Publisher, Lincoln, RI, 1988. 144 pp., illus., paper covers. $22.00. A comprehensive guide to the most important and ubiquitous American arms of WWII and Korea.

A Collector's Guide to the '03 Springfield, by Bruce N. Canfield, Andrew Mowbray Inc., Lincoln, RI, 1989. 160 pp. illus. Paper covers, $22.00. A comprehensive guide follows the '03 through its unparalleled tenure of service. Covers all of the interesting variations, modifications and accessories of this highly collectible military rifle.

Collector's Illustrated Encyclopedia of the American Revolution, by George C. Neumann and Frank J. Kravic, Rebel Publishing Co., Inc., Texarkana, TX, 1989. 286 pp., illus. $29.95. A showcase of more than 2,300 artifacts made, worn, and used by those who fought in the War for Independence.

Colonial Frontier Guns, by T.M. Hamilton, Pioneer Press, Union City, TN, 1988. 176 pp., illus. Paper covers, $13.95. A complete study of early flint muskets of this country.

Colt .45 Government Models (Commercial Series), by Charles W. Clawson, Charles W. Clawson, Fort Wayne, IN, 1996. 230 pp., illustrated. $45.00. A study of Colt's caliber .45 Government Model and other pistols built on the same size receiver.

The Colt Armory, by Ellsworth Grant, Man-at-Arms Bookshelf, Lincoln, RI, 1996. 232 pp., illus. $35.00. A history of Colt's Manufacturing Company.

Colt Heritage, by R.L. Wilson, Simon & Schuster, 1979. 358 pp. illus. $75.00. The official history of Colt firearms 1836 to the present.

Colt Memorabilia Price Guide, by John Ogle, Krause Publications, Iola, WI, 1998. 256 pp., illus. Paper covers, $29.95. The first book ever compiled about the vast array of non-gun merchandise produced by Sam Colt's companies, and other companies using the Colt name.

The Colt Model 1905 Automatic Pistol, by John Potocki, Andrew Mowbray Publishing, Lincoln, RI, 1998. 191 pp., illus. $28.00. Covers all aspects of the Colt Model 1905 Automatic Pistol, from its invention by the legendary John Browning to its numerous production variations.

Colt Peacemaker British Model, by Keith Cochran, Cochran Publishing Co., Rapid City, SD, 1989. 160 pp., illus. $35.00. Covers those revolvers Colt squeezed in while completing a large order of revolvers for the U.S. Cavalry in early 1874, to those magnificent cased target revolvers used in the pistol competitions at Bisley Commons in the 1890s.

Colt Peacemaker Encyclopedia, by Keith Cochran, Keith Cochran, Rapid City, SD, 1986. 434 pp., illus. $65.00. A must book for the Peacemaker collector.

Colt Peacemaker Encyclopedia, Volume 2, by Keith Cochran, Cochran Publishing Co., SD, 1992. 416 pp., illus. $60.00. The complete collector's guide to the identification of Colt percussion accoutrements; including Colt conversions and their values.

Colt Percussion Accoutrements 1834-1873, by Robin Rapley, Robin Rapley, Newport Beach, CA, 1994. 432 pp., illus. Paper covers. $39.95. Included in this volume are extensive notes on engraved, inscribed, historical and noted revolvers, as well as those revolvers used by outlaws, lawmen, movie and television stars.

Colt Pocket Hammerless Pistols, by Dr. John W. Brunner, Phillips Publications, Williamstown, NJ, 1998. 212 pp., illustrated. $59.95. You will never again have to question a .25, .32 or .380 with this well illustrated, definitive reference guide at hand.

Colt Revolvers and the Tower of London, by Joseph G. Rosa, Royal Armouries of the Tower of London, London, England, 1988. 72 pp. illus. Soft covers, $15.00. Details the story of Colt in London through the early cartridge period.

Colt Rifles and Muskets from 1847-1870, by Herbert Houze, Krause Publications, Iola, WI, 1996. 192 pp., illus. $34.95. Discover previously unknown Colt models along with an extensive list of production figures for all models.

Colt's SAA Post War Models, by George Garton, The Gun Room Press, Highland Park, NJ, 1995. 166 pp., illus. $39.95. Complete facts on the post-war Single Action revolvers. Information on calibers, production numbers and variations taken from factory records.

Colt Single Action Army Revolvers and the London Agency, by C. Kenneth Moore, Andrew Mowbray Publishers, Lincoln, RI, 1990. 144 pp. illus. $35.00. Drawing on vast documentary sources, this work chronicles the relationship between the London Agency and the Hartford home office.

The Colt U.S. General Officers' Pistols, by Horace Greeley IV, Andrew Mowbray Inc., Lincoln, RI, 1990. 199 pp. illus. $38.00. These unique weapons, issued as a badge of rank to General Officers in the U.S. Army from WWII onward, remain highly personal artifacts of the military leaders who carried them. Includes serial numbers and dates of issue.

Colts from the William M. Locke Collection, by Frank Sellers, Andrew Mowbray Publishers, Lincoln, RI, 1996. 192 pp. illus. $55.00. This important book illustrates all of the famous Locke Colts, with captions by arms authority Frank Sellers.

Colt's Dates of Manufacture 1837-1978, by R.L. Wilson, published by Maurie Albert, Coburg, Australia; N.A. distributor I.D.S.A. Books, Hamilton, OH, 1983. 61 pp. $10.00. An invaluable pocket guide to the dates of manufacture of Colt firearms up to 1978.

Colt's 100th Anniversary Firearms Manual 1836-1936: A Century of Achievement, Wolfe Publishing Co., Prescott, AZ, 1992. 100 pp., illus. Paper covers, $12.95. Originally published by the Colt Patent Firearms Co., this booklet covers the history, manufacturing procedures and the guns of the genius of Samuel Colt.

Complete Guide to the M1 Garand and the M1 Carbine, by Bruce N. Canfield, Andrew Mowbray Publishing, Lincoln, RI, 1998. 296 pp., illus. $39.50. Expanded and updated coverage of both the M1 Garand and the M1 Carbine, with more than twice as much information as the author's previous book on this topic.

The Complete Guide to U.S. Infantry Weapons of World War Two, by Bruce Canfield, Andrew Mowbray, Publisher, Lincoln, RI, 1995. 303 pp., illus. $35.00. A definitive work on the weapons used by the United States Armed Forces in WWII.

Compliments of Col. Ruger: A Study of Factory Engraved Single Action Revolvers, by John C. Dougan, Taylor Publishing Co., El Paso, TX, 1992. 238 pp., illus. $46.50. Clearly detailed black and white photographs and a precise text present an accurate history of the Sturm, Ruger & Co. single-action revolver engraving project.

Cowboy Collectibles and Western Memorabilia, by Bob Bell and Edward Vebell, Schiffer Publishing, Atglen, PA, 1992. 160 pp., illus. Paper covers. $29.95. A photographic encyclopedia with price guide and makers' index.

Cowboy Hero Cap Pistols, by Rudy D'Angelo, Antique Trader Books, Dubuque, IA, 1998. 196 pp., illus. Paper covers. $34.95. Aimed at collectors of cap pistols created and named for famous film and television cowboy heros, this in-depth guide hits all the marks. Current values are given.

Cowboy and Gunfighter Collectible, by Bill Mackin, Mountain Press Publishing Co., Missoula, MT, 1995. 178 pp., illus. Paper covers, $25.00. A photographic encyclopedia of the cowboy and the wild west collectibles including rifles, pistols, gun rigs, etc.

Czech Firearms and Ammunition Past and Present, 1919-1995, by Vladimir Dolinek & V. Karlicky, 190 pp., illus. in black & white and color. $49.95. Covers Czech firearms from the earliest to the present day.

The Deringer in America, Volume 1, The Percussion Period, by R.L. Wilson and L.D. Eberhart, Andrew Mowbray Inc., Lincoln, RI, 1985. 271 pp., illus. $48.00. A long awaited book on the American percussion deringer.

THE HANDGUNNER'S LIBRARY

The Deringer in America, Volume 2, The Cartridge Period, by L.D. Eberhart and R.L. Wilson, Andrew Mowbray Inc., Publishers, Lincoln, RI, 1993. 284 pp., illus. $65.00.

Comprehensive coverage of cartridge deringers organized alphabetically by maker. Includes all types of deringers known by the authors to have been offered to the American market.

The Devil's Paintbrush: Sir Hiram Maxim's Gun, by Dolf Goldsmith, 2nd Edition, expanded and revised, Collector Grade Publications, Toronto, Canada, 1993. 384 pp., illus. $69.95.

The classic work on the world's first true automatic machine gun.

Dr. Josephus Requa Civil War Dentist and the Billinghurst-Requa Volley Gun, by John M. Hyson, Jr., & Margaret Requa DeFrancisco, Museum Restoration Service, Bloomfield, Ont., Canada, 1999. 36 pp., illus. Paper covers. $6.95.

The story of the inventor of the first practical rapid-fire gun to be used during the American Civil War.

Drums A'beating Trumpets Sounding, by William H. Guthman, The Connecticut Historical Society, Westport, CT, 1993. 232 pp., illus. $75.00.

Artistically carved powder horns in the provincial manner, 1746-1781.

The Dutch Luger (Parabellum) A Complete History, by Bas J. Martens and Guus de Vries, Ironside International Publishers, Inc., Alexandria, VA, 1995. 268 pp., illus. $49.95.

The history of the Luger in the Netherlands. An extensive description of the Dutch pistol and trials and the different models of the Luger in the Dutch service.

The Eagle on U.S. Firearms, by John W. Jordan, Pioneer Press, Union City, TN, 1992. 140 pp., illus. Paper covers. $14.95.

Stylized eagles have been stamped on government owned or manufactured firearms in the U.S. since the beginning of our country. This book lists and illustrates these various eagles in an informative and refreshing manner.

Early Indian Trade Guns: 1625-1775, by T.M. Hamilton, Museum of the Great Plains, Lawton, OK, 1968. 34 pp., illus. Paper covers. $12.95.

Detailed descriptions of subject arms, compiled from early records and from the study of remnants found in Indian country.

Encyclopedia of Rifles & Handguns, edited by Sean Connolly, Book Sales, Inc., Edison, NJ, 1997. 160 pp., illus. $12.95.

A lavishly illustrated book providing a comprehensive history of military and civilian personal firepower.

Encyclopedia of Ruger Rimfire Semi-Automatic Pistols: 1949-1992, by Chad Hiddleson, Krause Publications, Iola, WI, 1993. 250 pp., illus. $29.95.

Covers all physical aspects of Ruger 22-caliber pistols including important features such as boxes, grips, muzzlebrakes, instruction manuals, serial numbers, etc.

Encyclopedia of Ruger Semi-Automatic Rimfire Pistols 1949-1992, by Chad Hiddleson, Krause Publications, Iola, WI, 1994. 304 pp., illus. $29.95.

This book is a compilation of years of research, outstanding photographs and technical data on Ruger.

Eprouvettes: A Comprehensive Study of Early Devices for the Testing of Gunpowder, by R.T.W. Kempers, Royal Armouries Museum, Leeds, England, 1998. 352 pp., illustrated with 240 black & white and 28 color plates. $125.00.

A survey of gunpowder testing through the ages precedes a proposal for an eprouvette typology, and the core of the book is an illustrated survey of types.

European Firearms in Swedish Castles, by Kaa Wennberg, Bohuslaningens Boktryckeri AB, Uddevalla, Sweden, 1986. 156 pp., illus. $50.00.

The famous collection of Count Keller, the Ettersburg Castle collection, and others. English text.

European Sporting Cartridges, Part 1, by W.B. Dixon, Armory Publications, Inc., Coeur d'Alene, ID, 1997. 250 pp., illus. $63.00

Photographs and drawings of over 550 centerfire cartridge case types in 1,300 illustrations produced in German and Austria from 1875 to 1995.

Fifteen Years in the Hawken Lode, by John D. Baird, The Gun Room Press, Highland Park, NJ, 1976. 120 pp., illus. $24.95.

A collection of thoughts and observations gained from many years of intensive study of the guns from the shop of the Hawken brothers.

'51 Colt Navies, by Nathan L. Swayze, The Gun Room Press, Highland Park, NJ, 1993. 243 pp., illus. $59.95.

The Model 1851 Colt Navy, its variations and markings.

Firearms and Tackle Memorabilia, by John Delph, Schiffer Publishing, Ltd., West Chester, PA, 1991. 124 pp., illus. $39.95.

A collector's guide to signs and posters, calendars, trade cards, boxes, envelopes, and other highly sought after memorabilia. With a value guide.

Firearms of the American West 1803-1865, by Louis A. Garavaglia and Charles G. Worman, University of Colorado Press, Niwot, CO, 1998. 402 pp., illustrated. $59.95.

Traces the development and uses of firearms on the frontier during this period.

Firearms of the American West 1866-1894, by Louis A. Garavaglia and Charles G. Worman, University of Colorado Press, Niwot, CO, 1998. 416 pp., illus. $59.95.

A monumental work that offers both technical information on all of the important firearms used in the West during this period and a highly entertaining history of how they were used, who used them, and why.

Flayderman's Guide to Antique American Firearms and Their Values, 7th Edition, edited by Norm Flayderman, DBI books, a division of Krause Publications, Iola, WI, 1998. 656 pp., illus. Paper covers. $32.95.

A completely updated and new edition with more than 3,600 models and variants extensively described with all marks and specifications necessary for quick identification.

The .45-70 Springfield, by Joe Poyer and Craig Riesch, North Cape Publications, Tustin, CA, 1996. 150 pp., illus. Paper covers. $15.95.

A revised and expanded second edition of a best-selling reference work organized by serial number and date of production to aid the collector in identifying popular "Trapdoor" rifles and carbines.

Frank and George Freund and the Sharps Rifle, by Gerald O. Kelver, Gerald O. Kelver, Brighton, CO, 1986. 60 pp., illus. Paper covers. $12.00.

Pioneer gunmakers of Wyoming Territory and Colorado.

The French 1935 Pistols, by Eugene Medlin and Colin Doane, Eugene Medlin, El Paso, TX, 1995. 172 pp., illus. Paper covers. $25.95.

The development and identification of successive models, fakes and variants, holsters and accessories, and serial numbers by dates of production.

Freund & Bro. Pioneer Gunmakers to the West, by F.J. Pablo Balentine, Graphic Publishers, Newport Beach, CA, 1997. 380 pp., illustrated $69.95.

The story of Frank W. and George Freund, skilled German gunsmiths who plied their trade on the Western American frontier during the final three decades of the nineteenth century.

From the Kingdom of Lilliput: The Miniature Firearms of David Kucer, by K. Corey Keeble and **The Making of Miniatures,** by David Kucer, Museum Restoration Service, Ontario, Canada, 1994. 51 pp., illus. $25.00.

An overview of the subject of miniatures in general combined with an outline by the artist himself on the way he makes a miniature firearm.

Frontier Pistols and Revolvers, by Dominique Venner, Book Sales Inc., Edison, N.J., 1998. 144 pp., illus. $19.95.

Colt, Smith & Wesson, Remington and other early-brand revolvers which tamed the American frontier are shown amid vintage photographs, etchings and paintings to evoke the wild West.

The Fusil de Tulole in New France, 1691-1741, by Russel Bouchard, Museum Restorations Service, Bloomfield, Ontario, Canada, 1997. 36 pp., illus. Paper covers. $6.95

The development of the company and the identification of their arms.

Game Guns & Rifles: Percussion to Hammerless Ejector in Britain, by Richard Akehurst, Trafalgar Square, N. Pomfret, VT, 1993. 192 pp., illus. $39.95.

Long considered a classic this important reprint covers the period of British gunmaking between 1830-1900.

George Schreyer, Sr. and Jr., Gunmakers of Hanover, Pennsylvania, by George Shumway, George Shumway Publishers, York, PA, 1990. 160pp., illus. $50.00.

This monograph is a detailed photographic study of almost all known surviving long rifles and smoothbore guns made by highly regarded gunsmiths George Schreyer, Sr. and Jr.

The German Assault Rifle 1935-1945, by Peter R. Senich, Paladin Press, Boulder, CO, 1987. 328 pp., illus. $49.95.

A complete review of machine carbines, machine pistols and assault rifles employed by Hitler's Wehrmacht during WWII.

The German K98k Rifle, 1934-1945: The Backbone of the Wehrmacht, by Richard D. Law, Collector Grade Publications, Inc., Toronto, Canada, 1993. 336 pp., illus. $69.95.

The most comprehensive study ever published on the 14,000,000 bolt-action K98k rifles produced in Germany between 1934 and 1945.

German Machineguns, by Daniel D. Musgrave, Revised edition, Ironside International Publishers, Inc. Alexandria, VA, 1992. 586 pp., 650 illus. $49.95.

The most definitive book ever written on German machineguns. Covers the introduction and development of machineguns in Germany from 1899 to the rearmament period after WWII.

German Military Rifles and Machine Pistols, 1871-1945, by Hans Dieter Gotz, Schiffer Publishing Co., West Chester, PA, 1990. 245 pp., illus. $35.00.

This book portrays in words and pictures the development of the modern German weapons and their ammunition including the scarcely known experimental types.

German 7.9mm Military Ammunition, by Daniel W. Kent, Daniel W. Kent, Ann Arbor, MI, 1991. 244 pp., illus. $35.00.

The long-awaited revised edition of a classic among books devoted to ammunition.

German Pistols and Holsters, 1934-1945, Volume 4, by Lt. Col. Robert D. Whittington, 3rd, U.S.A.R., Brownlee Books, Hooks, TX, 1991. 208 pp. $30.00.

Pistols and holsters issued in 412 selected armed forces, army and Waffen-SS units including information on personnel, other weapons and transportation.

The Golden Age of Remington, by Robert W.D. Ball, Krause publications, Iola, WI, 1995. 194 pp., illus. $29.95.

For Remington collectors or firearms historians, this book provides a pictorial history of Remington through World War I. Includes value guide.

The Government Models, by William H.D. Goddard, Andrew Mowbray Publishing, Lincoln, RI, 1998. 296 pp., illustrated. $58.50.

The most authoritative source on the development of the Colt model of 1911.

A Guide to Ballard Breechloaders, by George J. Layman, Pioneer Press, Union City, TN, 1997. 261 pp., illus. Paper covers $19.95

Documents the saga of this fine rifle from the first models made by Ball & Williams of Worchester, to its production by the Marlin Firearms Co, to the cessation of 19th century manufacture in 1891, and finally to the modern reproductions made in the 1990's.

A Guide to the Maynard Breechloader, by George J. Layman, George J. Layman, Ayer, MA, 1993. 125 pp., illus. Paper covers. $17.95.

The first book dedicated entirely to the Maynard family of breech-loading firearms. Coverage of the arms is given from the 1850s through the 1880s.

Guide to Ruger Single Action Revolvers Production Dates, 1953-73, by John C. Dougan, Blacksmith Corp., Chino Valley, AZ, 1991. 22 pp., illus. Paper covers. $9.95.

A unique pocket-sized handbook providing production information for the popular Ruger single-action revolvers manufactured during the first 20 years.

Gun Collecting, by Geoffrey Boothroyd, Sportsman's Press, London, 1989. 208 pp., illus. $29.95.

The most comprehensive list of 19th century British gunmakers and gunsmiths ever published.

Gun Collector's Digest, 5th Edition, edited by Joseph J. Schroeder, DBI Books, a division of Krause Publications, Iola, WI, 1989. 224 pp., illus. Paper covers. $17.95.

The latest edition of this sought-after series.

Gunmakers of Illinois, 1683-1900, Vol. 1, by Curtis L. Johnson, George Shumway Publisher, York, PA, 1997. 200 pp., illus. $50.00.

This first volume covering the alphabet from A to F of a projected three-volume series, records the available names, dates, biographical details, and illustrates the work undertaken, by almost 1600 Illinois gunsmiths and gunmakers.

Gunmakers of London 1350-1850, by Howard L. Blackmore, George Shumway Publisher, York, PA, 1986. 222 pp., illus. $35.00.

A listing of all the known workmen of gun making in the first 500 years, plus a history of the guilds, cutlers, armourers, founders, blacksmiths, etc.

Gunsmiths of Illinois, by Curtis L. Johnson, George Shumway Publishers, York, PA, 1995. 160 pp., illus. $49.95.

Genealogical information is provided for nearly one thousand gunsmiths. Contains hundreds of illustrations of rifles and other guns, of handmade origin, from Illinois.

The Gunsmiths of Manhattan, 1625-1900: A Checklist of Tradesmen, by Michael H. Lewis, Museum Restoration Service, Bloomfield, Ont., Canada, 1991. 40 pp., illus. Paper covers. $4.95.

This listing of more than 700 men in the arms trade in New York City prior to about the end of the 19th century will provide a guide for identification and further research.

The Guns of Dagenham: Lanchester, Patchett, Sterling, by Peter Laidler and David Howroyd, Collector Grade Publications, Inc., Cobourg, Ont., Canada, 1995. 310 pp., illus. $39.95.

An in-depth history of the small arms made by the Sterling Company of Dagenham, Essex, England, from 1940 until Sterling was purchased by British Aerospace in 1989 and closed.

Guns of the Western Indian War, by R. Stephen Dorsey, Collector's Library, Eugene, OR, 1997. 220 pp., illus. Paper covers. $30.00.

The full story of the guns and ammunition that made western history in the turbulent period of 1865-1890.

Gun Powder Cans & Kegs, by Ted & David Bacyk and Tom Rowe, Rowe Publications, Rochester, NY, 1999. 150 pp., illus. $65.00.

The first book devoted to powder tins and kegs. All cans and kegs in full color. With a price guide and rarity scale.

Gun Tools, Their History and Identification by James B. Shaffer, Lee A. Rutledge and R. Stephen Dorsey, Collector's Library, Eugene, OR, 1992. 375 pp., illus. $32.00.

Written history of foreign and domestic gun tools from the flintlock period to WWII.

Gun Tools, Their History and Identifications, Volume 2, by Stephen Dorsey and James B. Shaffer, Collector's Library, Eugene, OR, 1997. 396 pp., illus. Paper covers. $30.00.

Gun tools from the Royal Armouries Museum in England, Pattern Room, Royal Ordnance Reference Collection in Nottingham and from major private collections.

The Guns of Remington: Historic Firearms Spanning Two Centuries, compiled by Howard M. Madaus, Biplane Productions, Publisher, in cooperation with Buffalo Bill Historical Center, Cody, WY, 1998. 352 pp., illustrated with over 800 color photos. $79.95.

A complete catalog of the firearms in the exhibition, "It Never Failed Me: The Arms & Art of Remington Arms Company" at the Buffalo Bill Historical Center, Cody, Wyoming.

Gunsmiths of Maryland, by Daniel D. Hartzler and James B. Whisker, Old Bedford Village Press, Bedford, PA, 1998. 208 pp., illustrated. $45.00.

Covers firelock Colonial period through the breech-loading patent models. Featuring longrifles.

Hall's Military Breechloaders, by Peter A. Schmidt, Andrew Mowbray Publishers, Lincoln, RI, 1996. 232 pp., illus. $55.00.

The whole story behind these bold and innovative firearms.

Handbook of Military Rifle Marks 1870-1950, by Richard A. Hoffman and Noel P. Schott, Mapleleaf Militaria Publishing, St. Louis, MO, 1995. 42 pp., illus. Spiral bound. $15.00.

An illustrated guide to identifying military rifle and marks.

The Handgun, by Geoffrey Boothroyd, David and Charles, North Pomfret, VT, 1989. 566 pp., illus. $60.00.

Every chapter deals with an important period in handgun history from the 14th century to the present.

The Handgun in History, by Charles E. Hanson, Jr., The Fur Press, Chadron, NE, 1979. 104 pp., illus. Paper covers. $15.00.

A definitive work on this famous rifle.

Hawken Rifles, The Mountain Man's Choice, by John D. Baird, The Gun Room Press, Highland Park, NJ, 1976. 95 pp., illus. $29.95.

Covers the rifles developed for the Western fur trade. Numerous specimens are described and shown in photographs.

High Standard: A Collector's Guide to the Hamden & Hartford Target Pistols, by Tom Dance, Andrew Mowbray Inc., Lincoln, RI, 1991. 192 pp., illus. Paper covers. $24.00.

From Citation to Supermatic, all of the production models and specials made from 1951 to 1984 are covered according to model number or series.

Historic Pistols: The American Martial Flintlock 1760-1845, by Samuel E. Smith and Edwin W. Bitter, The Gun Room Press, Highland Park, NJ, 1986. 353 pp., illus. $45.00.

Covers over 70 makers and 163 models of American martial arms.

Historical Hartford Hardware, by William W. Dalrymple, Colt Collector Press, Rapid City, SD, 1976. 42 pp., illus. Paper covers. $10.00.

Historically associated Colt revolvers.

The History and Development of Small Arms Ammunition, Volume 1, by George A. Hoyem, Armory Publications, Oceanside, CA, 1991. 230 pp., illus. $65.00.

18th and 19th centuries, rifle, carbine and primitive machine gun cartridges of the 18th and 19th centuries, together with the firearms that chambered them.

The History and Development of Small Arms Ammunition, Volume 2, by George A. Hoyem, Armory Publications, Oceanside, CA, 1991. 303 pp., illus. $65.00.

Covers the blackpowder military centerfire rifle, carbine, machine gun and volley gun ammunition used in 28 nations and dominions, together with the firearms that chambered them.

The History and Development of Small Arms Ammunition, Volume 4, by George A. Hoyem, Armory Publications, Seattle, WA, 1998. 200 pp., illustrated $60.00.

A comprehensive book on American black powder and early smokeless rifle cartridges.

The History of Smith and Wesson, by Roy G. Jinks, Willowbrook Enterprises, Springfield, MA, 1988. 290 pp., illus. $27.95.

The History of Modern U.S. Military Small Arms Ammunition. Volume 1, 1880-1939, revised by F.W. Hackley, W.H. Woodin and E.L. Scranton, Thomas Publications, Gettysburg, PA, 1998. 328 pp., illus. $49.95.

Revised 10th Anniversary edition of the definite book on S&W firearms.

The History of Winchester Firearms 1866-1992, sixth edition, updated, expanded, and revised by Thomas Henshaw, New Win Publishing, Clinton, NJ, 1993. 280 pp., illus. $27.95.

This revised edition incorporates all publicly available information concerning military small arms ammunition for the period 1880 through 1939 in a single volume.

History of Winchester Repeating Arms Company, by Herbert G. Houze, Krause Publications, Iola, WI, 1994. 800 pp., illus. $50.00.

This classic is the standard reference for all collectors and others seeking the facts about any Winchester firearm, old or new.

Honour Bound: The Chauchat Machine Rifle, by Gerard Demaison and Yves Buffetaut, Collector Grade Publications, Inc., Cobourg, Ont., Canada, 1995. $39.95.

The complete Winchester history from 1856-1981.

Hopkins & Allen Revolvers & Pistols, by Charles E. Carder, Avil Onze Publishing, Delphos, OH, 1998, illustrated. Paper covers. $24.95.

The story of the CSRG (Chauchat) machine rifle, the most manufactured automatic weapon of World War One.

How to Buy and Sell Used Guns, by John Traister, Stoeger Publishing Co., So. Hackensack, NJ, 1984. 192 pp., illus. Paper covers. $10.95.

Covers over 165 photos, graphics and patent drawings.

Identification Manual on the .303 British Service Cartridge, No. 1-Ball Ammunition, by B.A. Temple, I.D.S.A. Books, Piqua, OH, 1986. 84 pp., 57 illus. $12.50.

A new guide to buying and selling guns.

Identification Manual on the .303 British Service Cartridge, No. 2-Blank Ammunition, by B.A. Temple, I.D.S.A. Books, Piqua, OH, 1986. 95 pp., 59 illus. $12.50.

Identification Manual on the .303 British Service Cartridge, No. 3-Special Purpose Ammunition, by B.A. Temple, I.D.S.A. Books, Piqua, OH, 1987. 82 pp., 49 illus. $12.50.

Identification Manual on the .303 British Service Cartridge, No. 4-Dummy Cartridges Henry 1869-c.1900, by B.A. Temple, I.D.S.A. Books, Piqua, OH, 1988. 84 pp., 70 illus. $12.50.

Identification Manual on the .303 British Service Cartridge, No. 5-Dummy Cartridges (2), by B.A. Temple, I.D.S.A. Books, Piqua, OH, 1994. 78 pp. $12.50.

The Illustrated Encyclopedia of Civil War Collectibles, by Chuck Lawliss, Henry Holt and Co., New York, NY, 1997. 316 pp., illus. Paper covers. $22.95.

A comprehensive guide to Union and Confederate arms, equipment, uniforms, and other memorabilia.

Illustrations of United States Military Arms 1776-1903 and Their Inspector's Marks, compiled by Turner Kirkland, Pioneer Press, Union City, TN, 1988. 37 pp., illus. Paper covers. $4.95.

Reprinted from the 1949 Bannerman catalog. Valuable information for both the advanced and beginning collector.

Indian War Cartridge Pouches, Boxes and Carbine Boots, by R. Stephen Dorsey, Collector's Library, Eugene, OR, 1993. 156 pp., illus. Paper Covers, $25.00.

The key reference work to the cartridge pouches, boxes, carbine sockets and boots of the Indian War period 1865-1890.

An Introduction to the Civil War Small Arms, by Earl J. Coates and Dean S. Thomas, Thomas Publishing Co., Gettysburg, PA, 1990. 96 pp., illus. Paper covers. $10.00.

The small arms carried by the individual soldier during the Civil War.

Iver Johnson's Arms & Cycle Works Handguns, 1871-1964, by W.E. "Bill" Goforth, Blacksmith Corp., Chino Valley, AZ, 1991. 160 pp., illus. Paper covers. $14.95.

Covers all of the famous Iver Johnson handguns from the early solid-frame pistols and revolvers to optional accessories, special orders and patents.

THE HANDGUNNER'S LIBRARY

Jaeger Rifles, by George Shumway, George Shumway Publisher, York, PA, 1994. 108 pp., illus. Paper covers. $30.00.
Thirty-six articles previously published in *Muzzle Blasts* are reproduced here. They deal with late-17th, and 18th century rifles from Vienna, Carlsbad, Bavaria, Saxony, Brandenburg, Suhl, North-Central Germany, and the Rhine Valley.

Japanese Rifles of World War Two, by Duncan O. McCollum, Excalibur Publications, Latham, NY, 1996. 64 pp., illus. Paper covers. $18.95.
A sweeping view of the rifles and carbines that made up Japan's arsenal during the conflict.

Kalashnikov Arms, compiled by Alexei Nedelin, Design Military Parade, Ltd., Moscow, Russia, 1997. 240 pp., illus. $49.95.
Weapons versions stored in the St. Petersburg Military Historical Museum of Artillery, Engineer Troops and Communications and in the Izhmash JSC.

The Kentucky Pistol, by Roy Chandler and James Whisker, Old Bedford Village Press, Bedford, PA, 1997. 225 pp., illus. $45.00
A photographic study of Kentucky pistols from famous collections.

The Kentucky Rifle, by Captain John G.W. Dillin, George Shumway Publisher, York, PA, 1993. 221 pp., illus. $50.00.
This well-known book was the first attempt to tell the story of the American longrifle. This edition retains the original text and illustrations with supplemental footnotes provided by Dr. George Shumway.

The Kentucky Rifle, a True American Heritage in Picture, by the Kentucky Rifle Associations, Washington, D.C., 1997. Published by the Forte Group, Alexandria, VA. 109 pp., illus. $35.00.
This photographic essay reveals both the beauty and the decorative nature of the Kentucky by providing detailed photos of some of the most significant examples of American rifles, pistols and accoutrements.

Know Your Broomhandle Mausers, by R.J. Berger, Blacksmith Corp., Southport, CT, 1985. 96 pp., illus. Paper covers. $9.95.
An interesting story on the big Mauser pistol and its variations.

Krag Rifles, by William S. Brophy, The Gun Room Press, Highland Park, NJ, 1980. 200 pp., illus. $50.00.
The first comprehensive work detailing the evolution and various models, both military and civilian.

The Krieghoff Parabellum, by Randall Gibson, Midland, TX, 1988. 279 pp., illus. $40.00.
A comprehensive text pertaining to the Lugers manufactured by H. Krieghoff Waffenfabrik.

Las Pistolas Espanolas Tipo "Mauser," by Artemio Mortera Perez, Quiron Ediciones, Valladolid, Spain, 1998. 71 pp., illustrated. Paper covers. $34.95.
This book covers in detail Spanish machine pistols and C96 copies made in Spain. Covers all Astra "Mauser" pistol series and the complete line of Beistegui C96 type pistols. Spanish text.

Levine's Guide to Knives And Their Values, 4th Edition, by Bernard Levine, DBI Books, a division of Krause Publications, Iola, WI, 1997. 512 pp., illus. Paper covers. $27.95
All the basic tools for identifying, valuing and collecting folding and fixed blade knives.

LeMat, the Man, the Gun, by Valmore J. Forgett and Alain F. and Marie-Antoinette Serpette, Navy Arms Co., Ridgefield, NJ, 1996. 218 pp., illus. $49.95.
The first definitive study of the Confederate revolvers invention, development and delivery by Francois Alexandre LeMat.

Les Pistolets Automatiques Francaise 1890-1990, by Jean Huon, Combined Books, Inc., Conshohocken, PA, 1997. 160 pp., illus. French text. $34.95
French automatic pistols from the earliest experiments through the World Wars and Indo-China to modern security forces.

The Lee-Enfield Story, by Ian Skennerton, Ian Skennerton, Ashmore City, Australia, 1993. 503 pp., illus. $59.95.
The Lee-Metford, Lee-Enfield, S.M.L.E. and No. 4 series rifles and carbines from 1880 to the present.

The London Gunmakers and the English Duelling Pistol, 1770-1830, by Keith R. Dill, Museum Restoration Service, Bloomfield, Ontario, Canada, 1997. 36 pp., illus. Paper covers. $6.95
Ten gunmakers made London one of the major gunmaking centers of the world. This book examines how the design and construction of their pistols contributed to that reputation and how these characteristics may be used to date flintlock arms.

Longrifles of North Carolina, by John Bivens, George Shumway Publisher, York, PA, 1988. 256 pp., illus. $50.00.
Covers art and evolution of the rifle, immigration and trade movements. Committee of Safety gunsmiths, characteristics of the North Carolina rifle.

Longrifles of Pennsylvania, Volume 1, Jefferson, Clarion & Elk Counties, by Russel H. Harringer, George Shumway Publisher, York, PA, 1984. 200 pp., illus. $50.00.
First in series that will treat in great detail the longrifles and gunsmiths of Pennsylvania.

The Luger Handbook, by Aarron Davis, Krause Publications, Iola, WI, 1997. 112 pp., illus. Paper covers. $9.95.
Quick reference to classify Luger models and variations with complete details including proofmarks.

Lugers at Random, by Charles Kenyon, Jr., Handgun Press, Glenview, IL, 1990. 420 pp., illus. $49.95.
A new printing of this classic, comprehensive reference for all Luger collectors.

The Luger Story, by John Walter, Stackpole Books, Mechanicsburg, PA, 1995. 256 pp., illus. $39.95.
The standard history of the world's most famous handgun.

The M1 Garand Serial Numbers and Data Sheets, by Scott A. Duff, Export, PA, 1995. 101 pp., illus. Paper covers. $9.95.
Provides the reader with serial numbers related to dates of manufacture and a large sampling of data sheets to aid in identification or restoration.

The M1 Garand: Owner's Guide, by Scott A. Duff, Scott A. Duff, Export, PA, 1997. 126 pp., illus. Paper covers. $16.95.
This book answers the questions M1 owners most often ask concerning maintenance activities not encountered by military users.

Machine Guns of World War 1, by Robert Bruce, Combined Publishing, Conshohocken, PA, 1998. 128 pp., illus. $39.95.
Live firing classic military weapons in color photographs.

Maine Made Guns and Their Makers, by Dwight B. Demeritt Jr., Maine State Museum, Augusta, ME, 1998. 209 pp., illustrated. $55.00.
An authoritative, biographical study of Maine gunsmiths.

Marlin Firearms: A History of the Guns and the Company That Made Them, by Lt. Col. William S. Brophy, USAR, Ret., Stackpole Books, Harrisburg, PA, 1989. 672 pp., illus. $75.00.
The definitive book on the Marlin Firearms Co. and their products.

Martini-Henry .450 Rifles & Carbines, by Dennis Lewis, Excalibur Publications, Latham, NY, 1996. 72 pp., illus. Paper covers. $11.95.
The stories of the rifles and carbines that were the mainstay of the British soldier through the Victorian wars.

Matt Eastman's Guide to Browning Belgium Firearms 1903-1994, by Matt Eastman, Matt Eastman Publications, Fitzgerald, GA, 1995. 150 pp. Paper covers. $14.95.
Covers all Belgium models through 1994. Manufacturing production figures on the Auto-5 and Safari rifles.

Mauser Bolt Rifles, by Ludwig Olson, F. Brownell & Son, Inc., Montezuma, IA, 1976. 364 pp., illus. $51.95.
The most complete, detailed, authoritative and comprehensive work ever done on Mauser bolt rifles.

Mauser Military Rifles of the World, by Robert W.D. Ball, Krause Publications, Iola, WI, 1996. 272 pp., illus. $39.95.
The rifles produced by the Mauser Co. for their international market with complete production quantities, rarity and technical specifications.

Military Handguns of France 1858-1958, by Eugene Medlin and Jean Huon, Excalibur Publications, Latham, NY, 1994. 124 pp., illus. Paper covers. $24.95.
The first book written in English that provides students of arms with a thorough history of French military handguns.

Military Holsters of World War 2, by Eugene J. Bender, Rowe Publications, Rochester, NY, 1998. 200 pp., illustrated. $45.00.
A revised edition with a new price guide of the most definitive book on this subject.

Military Pistols of Japan, by Fred L. Honeycutt, Jr., Julin Books, Palm Beach Gardens, FL, 1991. 168 pp., illus. $42.00.
Covers every aspect of military pistol production in Japan through WWII.

The Military Remington Rolling Block Rifle, by George Layman, George Layman, Ayer, MA, 1996. 146 pp., illus. Paper covers. $24.95.
A standard reference for those with an interest in the Remington rolling block family of firearms.

Military Rifles of Japan, 4th Edition, by F.L. Honeycutt, Julin Books, Lake Park, FL, 1989. 208 pp., illus. $42.00.
A new revised and updated edition. Includes the early Murata-period markings, etc.

Military Small Arms of the 20th Century, 6th Edition, by Ian V. Hogg, DBI Books, a division of Krause Publications, Iola, WI, 1991. 352 pp., illus. Paper covers. $20.95.
Fully revised and updated edition of the standard reference in its field.

M1 Carbine, by Larry Ruth, Gun room Press, Highland Park, NJ, 1987. 291 pp., illus. Paper $19.95.
The origin, development, manufacture and use of this famous carbine of World War II.

The M1 Garand 1936 to 1957, by Joe Poyer and Craig Riesch, North Cape Publications, Tustin, CA, 1996. 216 pp., illus. Paper covers. $19.95.
Describes the entire range of M1 Garand production in text and quick-scan charts.

The M1 Garand: Post World War, by Scott A. Duff, Scott A. Duff, Export, PA, 1990. 139 pp., illus. Soft covers. $19.95.
A detailed account of the activities at Springfield Armory through this period. International Harvester, H&R, Korean War production and quantities delivered. Serial numbers.

The M1 Garand: World War 2, by Scott A. Duff, Scott A. Duff, Export, PA, 1993. 210 pp., illus. Paper covers. $39.95.
The most comprehensive study available to the collector and historian on the M1 Garand of World War II.

Modern Beretta Firearms, by Gene Gangarosa, Jr., Stoeger Publishing Co., So. Hackensack, NJ, 1994. 288 pp., illus. Paper covers. $16.95.
Traces all models of modern Beretta pistols, rifles, machine guns and combat shotguns.

Modern Gun Values, The Gun Digest Book of, 10th Edition, by the Editors of Gun Digest, DBI Books, a division of Krause Publications, Iola, WI, 1996. 560 pp. illus. Paper covers. $21.95.
Greatly updated and expanded edition describing and valuing over 7,000 firearms manufactured from 1900 to 1996. The standard for valuing modern firearms.

Modern Guns Identification & Value Guide, Eleventh Edition, by Russell and Steve Quertermous, Collector Books, Paducah, KY, 1996. 504 pp., illus. Paper covers. $12.95.
A popular guidebook featuring 2500 models of rifle, handgun and shotgun from 1900 to the present with detailed descriptions and prices.

THE HANDGUNNER'S LIBRARY

Modern Gun Identification & Value Guide, Twelfth Edition, by Russell and Steve Quertermous, Collector Books, Paducah, KY, 1998. 504 pp., illus. Paper covers. $12.95.
Features current values for over 2,500 models of rifles, shotguns and handguns, with over 1,800 illustrations.

More Single Shot Rifles, by James C. Grant, The Gun Room Press, Highland Park, NJ, 1976. 324 pp., illus. $29.95.
Details the guns made by Frank Wesson, Milt Farrow, Holden, Borchardt, Stevens, Remington, Winchester, Ballard and Peabody-Martini.

Mortimer, the Gunmakers, 1753-1923, by H. Lee Munson, Andrew Mowbray Inc., Lincoln, RI, 1992. 320 pp., illus. $65.00.
Seen through a single, dominant, English gunmaking dynasty this fascinating study provides a window into the classical era of firearms artistry.

The Mosin-Nagant Rifle, by Terence W. Lapin, North Cape Publications, Tustin, CA, 1998. 30 pp., illustrated. Paper covers. $19.95.
The first ever complete book on the Mosin-Nagant rifle written in English. Covers every variation.

Mossberg: More Gun for the Money, by V. and C. Havlin, Investment Rarities, Inc., Minneapolis, MN, 1995. 304 pp., illus. Paper covers. $24.95.
The history of O. F. Mossberg and Sons, Inc.

The Muzzle-Loading Cap Lock Rifle, by Ned H. Roberts, reprinted by Wolfe Publishing Co., Prescott, AZ, 1991. 432 pp., illus. $30.00.
Originally published in 1940, this fascinating study of the muzzle-loading cap lock rifle covers rifles on the frontier to hunting rifles, including the famous Hawken.

The Navy Luger, by Joachim Gortz and John Walter, Handgun Press, Glenview, IL, 1988. 128 pp., illus. $24.95.
The 9mm Pistole 1904 and the Imperial German Navy. A concise illustrated history.

The New World of Russian Small Arms and Ammunition, by Charlie Cutshaw. Paladin Press, Boulder, CO, 1998. 160 pp., illustrated. $39.95.
Detailed descriptions, specifications and first-class illustrations of the AN-94, PSS silent pistol, Bizon SMG, Saifa-12 tactical shotgun, the GP-25 grenade launcher and more cutting edge Russian weapons.

The Number 5 Jungle Carbine, by Alan M. Petrillo, Excalibur Publications, Latham, NY, 1994. 32 pp., illus. Paper covers. $7.95.
A comprehensive treatment of the rifle that collectors have come to call the "Jungle Carbine"—the Lee-Enfield Number 5, Mark 1.

Observations on Colt's Second Contract, November 2, 1847, by G. Maxwell Longfield and David T. Basnett, Museum Restoration Service, Bloomfield, Ontario, Canada, 1997. 36 pp., illus. Paper covers. $6.95.
A much-expanded version of Campbell's *The '03 Springfields,* representing forty years of in-depth research into "all things '03."

Official Guide to Gunmarks, 3rd Edition, by Robert H. Balderson, House of Collectibles, New York, NY, 1996. 367 pp., illus. Paper covers. $15.00.
Identifies manufacturers' marks that appear on American and foreign pistols, rifles and shotguns.

Official Price Guide to Antique and Modern Firearms, by Robert H. Balderson, House of Collectibles, New York, NY, 1996. 300 pp., illus. Paper covers. $17.00.
More than 30,000 updated prices for firearms manufactured from the 1600's to the present.

Official Price Guide to Civil War Collectibles, by Richard Friz, House of Collectibles, New York, NY, 1995. 375 pp., illus. Paper covers. $21.50.
Price listings and current market values for thousands of Civil War items.

Official Price Guide to Gun Collecting, by R.L. Wilson, Ballantine/House of Collectibles, New York, NY, 1998. 450 pp., illus. Paper covers. $20.00.
Covers more than 30,000 prices from Colt revolvers to Winchester rifles and shotguns to German Lugers and British sporting rifles and game guns.

Official Price Guide to Military Collectibles, 6th Edition, by Richard J. Austin, Random House, Inc., New York, NY, 1998. 200 pp., illus. Paper cover. $20.00.
Covers weapons and other collectibles from wars of the distant and recent past. More than 4,000 prices are listed. Illustrated with 400 black & white photos plus a full-color insert.

Old Gunsights: A Collector's Guide, 1850 to 2000, by Nicholas Stroebel, Krause Publications, Iola, WI, 1998. 320 pp., illus. Paper covers. $29.95.
An in-depth and comprehensive examination of old gunsights and the rifles on which they were used to get accurate feel for prices in this expanding market.

The P-08 Parabellum Luger Automatic Pistol, edited by J. David McFarland, Desert Publications, Cornville, AZ, 1982. 20 pp., illus. Paper covers. $11.95.
Covers every facet of the Luger, plus a listing of all known Luger models.

Packing Iron, by Richard C. Rattenbury, Zon International Publishing, Millwood, NY, 1993. 216 pp., illus. $45.00.
The best book yet produced on pistol holsters and rifle scabbards. Over 300 variations of holster and scabbards are illustrated in large, clear plates.

Patents for Inventions, Class 119 (Small Arms), 1855-1930, British Patent Office, Armory Publications, Oceanside, CA, 1993. 7 volume set, $350.00.
Contains 7980 abridged patent descriptions and their sectioned line drawings, plus a 37-page alphabetical index of the patentees.

Pattern Dates for British Ordnance Small Arms, 1718-1783, by DeWitt Bailey, Thomas Publications, Gettysburg, PA, 1997. 116 pp., illus. Paper covers. $20.00.
The weapons discussed in this work are those carried by troops sent to North America between 1737 and 1783, or shipped to them as replacement arms while in America.

Pistols of the World, 3rd Edition, by Ian Hogg and John Weeks, DBI Books, a division of Krause Publications, Iola, WI, 1992. 320 pp., illus. Paper covers. $24.95.
A totally revised edition of one of the leading studies of small arms.

The Pitman Notes on U.S. Martial Small Arms and Ammunition, 1776-1933, Volume 2, Revolvers and Automatic Pistols, by Brig. Gen. John Pitman, Thomas Publications, Gettysburg, PA, 1990. 192 pp., illus. $29.95.
A most important primary source of information on United States military small arms and ammunition.

The Plains Rifle, by Charles Hanson, Gun Room Press, Highland Park, NJ, 1989. 169 pp., illus. $35.00.
All rifles that were made with the plainsman in mind, including pistols.

Powder and Ball Small Arms, by Martin Pegler, Windrow & Green, London, 1998. 128 pp., illus. $39.95.
Part of the new "Live Firing Classic Weapons" series featuring full color photos of experienced shooters dressed in authentic costumes handling, loading and firing historic weapons.

The Powder Flask Book, by Ray Riling, R&R Books, Livonia, NY, 1993. 514 pp., illus. $70.00.
The complete book on flasks of the 19th century. Exactly scaled pictures of 1,600 flasks are illustrated.

Proud Promise: French Autoloading Rifles, 1898-1979, by Jean Huon, Collector Grade Publications, Inc. Coburg, Ont., Canada, 1995. 216 pp., illus. $39.95.
The author has finally set the record straight about the importance of French contributions to modern arms design.

E. C. Prudhomme's Gun Engraving Review, by E. C. Prudhomme, R&R Books, Livonia, NY, 1994. 164 pp., illus. $60.00.
As a source for engravers and collectors, this book is an indispensable guide to styles and techniques of the world's foremost engravers.

Reloading Tools, Sights and Telescopes for Single Shot Rifles, by Gerald O. Kelver, Brighton, CO, 1982. 163 pp., illus. Paper covers. $15.00.
A listing of most of the famous makers of reloading tools, sights and telescopes with a brief description of the products they manufactured.

The Remington-Lee Rifle, by Eugene F. Myszkowski, Excalibur Publications, Latham, NY, 1995. 100 pp., illus. Paper covers. $22.50.
Features detailed descriptions, including serial number ranges, of each model from the first Lee Magazine Rifle produced for the U.S. Navy to the last Remington-Lee Small Bores shipped to the Cuban Rural Guard.

Revolvers of the British Services 1854-1954, by W.H.J. Chamberlain and A.W.F. Taylerson, Museum Restoration Service, Ottawa, Canada, 1989. 80 pp., illus. $27.50.
Covers the types issued among many of the United Kingdom's naval, land or air services.

Rhode Island Arms Makers & Gunsmiths, by William O. Archibald, Andrew Mowbray, Inc., Lincoln, RI, 1990. 108 pp., illus. $16.50.
A serious and informative study of an important area of American arms making.

Rifles of the World, by Jean-Noel Mouret, Book Sales, Edison, NJ, 1998. 144 pp., illus. $17.99.
This highly illustrated book recounts the fascinating story of the rifle and its development. Military, sporting and hunting.

Rifles of the World, 2nd Edition, by John Walter, DBI Books, a division of Krause Publications, Iola, WI, 512 pp., illus. Paper covers. $24.95.

Rifles of the World, by Oliver Achard, Chartwell Books, Inc., Edison, NJ, 141 pp., illus. $18.95.
A unique insight into the world of long guns, not just rifles, but also shotguns, carbines and all the usual multi-barreled guns that once were so popular with European hunters, especially in Germany and Austria.

The Rock Island '03, by C.S. Ferris, C.S. Ferris, Arvada, CO, 1993. 58 pp., illus. Paper covers. $12.50.
A monograph of interest to the collector or historian concentrating on the U.S. M1903 rifle made by the less publicized of our two producing facilities.

Round Ball to Rimfire, Vol. 1, by Dean Thomas, Thomas Publications, Gettysburg, PA, 1997. 144 pp., illus. $40.00.
The first of a two-volume set of the most complete history and guide for all small arms ammunition used in the Civil War. The information includes data from research and development to the arsenals that created it.

Ruger and his Guns, by R.L. Wilson, Simon & Schuster, New York, NY, 1996. 358 pp., illus. $65.00.
A history of the man, the company and their firearms.

Russell M. Catron and His Pistols, by Warren H. Buxton, Ucross Books, Los Alamos, NM, 1998. 210 pp., illustrated. Paper covers. $35.00.
An unknown American firearms inventor and manufacturer of the mid twentieth century. Military commerical ammunition.

The SAFN-49 and The FAL, by Joe Poyer and Dr. Richard Feirman, North Cape Publications, Tustin, CA, 1998. 160 pp., illus. Paper covers. $14.95.
The first complete overview of the SAFN-49 battle rifle, from its pre-World War 2 beginnings to its military service in countries as diverse as the Belgian Congo and Argentina. The FAL was "light" version of the SAFN-49 and it became the Free World's most adopted battle rifle.

Sam Colt's Own Record 1847, by John Parsons, Wolfe Publishing Co., Prescott, AZ, 1992. 167 pp., illus. $24.50.
Chronologically presented, the correspondence published here completes the account of the manufacture, in 1847, of the Walker Model Colt revolver.

J.P. Sauer & Sohn, Suhl, by Jim Cate & Nico Van Gun, CBC Book Co., Chattanooga, TN, 1998. 406 pp., illus. $65.00.
A historical study of Sauer automatic pistols. Over 500 photos showing the different variations of pistols, grips, magazines and holsters.

THE HANDGUNNER'S LIBRARY

Scottish Firearms, by Claude Blair and Robert Woosnam-Savage, Museum Restoration Service, Bloomfield, Ont., Canada, 1995. 52 pp., illus. Paper covers. $4.95.
This revision of the first book devoted entirely to Scottish firearms is supplemented by a register of surviving Scottish long guns.

The Scottish Pistol, by Martin Kelvin. Fairleigh Dickinson University Press, Dist. By Associated University Presses, Cranbury, NJ, 1997. 256 pp., illus. $49.50.
The Scottish pistol, its history, manufacture and design.

Scouts, Peacemakers and New Frontiers in .22 Caliber, by Don Wilkerson, Cherokee Publications, Kansas City, MO, 1995. 224 pp., illus. $40.00.
Covers the 48 variations and numerous subvariants of the later rimfire Single Actions.

Sharps Firearms, by Frank Seller, Frank M. Seller, Denver, CO, 1982. 358 pp., illus. $50.00.
Traces the development of Sharps firearms with full range of guns made including all martial variations.

Simeon North: First Official Pistol Maker of the United States, by S. North and R. North, The Gun Room Press, Highland Park, NJ, 1972. 207 pp., illus. $15.95.
Reprint of the rare first edition.

The SKS Carbine, by Steve Kehaya and Joe Poyer, North Cape Publications, Tustin, CA, 1997. 150 pp., illus. Paper covers. $16.95.
The first comprehensive examination of a major historical firearm used through the Vietnam conflict to the diamond fields of Angola.

The SKS Type 45 Carbines, by Duncan Long, Desert Publications, El Dorado, AZ, 1992. 110 pp., illus. Paper covers.
Covers the history and practical aspects of operating, maintaining and modifying this abundantly available rifle.

Small Arms of the East India Company 1600-1856, by D. F. Harding, Volume 1 & 2, Foresight Books, London, England, $185.00.
Over 100 patterns of East India Company muskets, fusils, rifles, carbines, pistols, blunderbusses, wallpieces and bayonets identified for the first time in print.

Smith & Wesson 1857-1945, by Robert J. Neal and Roy G. Jinks, R&R Books, Livonia, NY, 1996. 434 pp., illus. $50.00.
The bible for all existing and aspiring Smith & Wesson collectors.

Sniper Variations of the German K98k Rifle, by Richard D. Law, Collector Grade Publications, Ontario, Canada, 1997. 240 pp., illus. $47.50.
Volume 2 of "Backbone of the Wehrmacht" the author's in-depth study of the German K98k rifle. This volume concentrates on the telescopic-sighted rifle of choice for most German snipers during World War 2.

Southern Derringers of the Mississippi Valley, by Turner Kirkland, Pioneer Press, Tenn. 1971. 80 pp. illus., paper covers. $10.00.
A guide for the collector, and a much-needed study.

Soviet Russian Postwar Military Pistols and Cartridges, by Fred A. Datig, Handgun Press, Glenview, IL, 1988. 152 pp., illus. $29.95.
Thoroughly researched, this definitive sourcebook covers the development and adoption of the Makarov, Stechkin and the new PSM pistols. Also included in this source book is coverage on Russian clandestine weapons and pistol cartridges.

Soviet Russian Tokarev "TT" Pistols and Cartridges 1929-1953, by Fred Datig, Graphic Publishers, Santa Ana, CA, 1993. 168 pp., illus. $39.95.
Details of rare arms and their accessories are shown in hundreds of photos. It also contains a complete bibliography and index.

Soviet Small-Arms and Ammunition, by David Bolotin, Handgun Press, Glenview, IL, 1996. 264 pp., illus. $49.95.
An authoritative and complete book on Soviet small arms.

Sporting Collectibles, by Jim and Vivian Karsnitz, Schiffer Publishing Ltd., West Chester, PA, 1992. 160 pp., illus. Paper covers. $29.95.
The fascinating world of hunting related collectibles presented in an informative text.

The Springfield 1903 Rifles, by Lt. Col. William S. Brophy, USAR, Ret., Stackpole Books Inc., Harrisburg, PA, 1985. 608 pp., illus. $75.00.
The illustrated, documented story of the design, development, and production of all the models, appendages, and accessories.

Springfield Armory Shoulder Weapons 1795-1968, by Robert W.D. Ball, Antique Trader Books, Dubuque, IA, 1998. 264 pp., illus. $34.95.
This book documents the 255 basic models of rifles, including test and trial rifles, produced by the Springfield Armory. It features the entire history of rifles and carbines manufactured at the Armory, the development of each weapon with specific operating characteristics and procedures.

Springfield Model 1903 Service Rifle Production and Lateration, 1905-1910, by C.S. Ferris and John Beard, Arvada, CO, 1995. 66 pp., illus. Paper covers. $12.50.
A highly recommended work for any serious student of the Springfield Model 1903 rifle.

Springfield Shoulder Arms 1795-1865, by Claud E. Fuller, S. & S. Firearms, Glendale, NY, 1986. 76 pp., illus. Paper covers. $17.95.
Exact reprint of the scarce 1930 edition of one of the most definitive works on Springfield flintlock and percussion muskets ever published.

Standard Catalog of Smith and Wesson, by Jim Supica and Richard Nahas, Krause Publications, Iola, WI, 1996. 240 pp., illus. $29.95.
Clearly details hundreds of products by the legendary manufacturer. How to identify, evaluate the condition and assess the value of 752 Smith & Wesson models and variations.

Steel Canvas: The Art of American Arms, by R.L. Wilson, Random House, NY, 1995. 384 pp., illus. $65.00.
Presented here for the first time is the breathtaking panorama of America's extraordinary engravers and embellishers of arms, from the 1700s to modern times.

Stevens Pistols & Pocket Rifles, by K.L. Cope, Museum Restoration Service, Alexandria Bay, NY, 1992. 114 pp., illus. $24.50.
This is the story of the guns and the man who designed them and the company which he founded to make them.

A Study of Colt Conversions and Other Percussion Revolvers, by R. Bruce McDowell, Krause Publications, Iola, WI, 1997. 464 pp., illus. $39.95.
The ultimate reference detailing Colt revolvers that have been converted from percussion to cartridge.

The Sumptuous Flaske, by Herbert G. Houze, Andrew Mowbray, Inc., Lincoln, RI, 1989. 158 pp., illus. Soft covers. $35.00.
Catalog of a recent show at the Buffalo Bill Historical Center bringing together some of the finest European and American powder flasks of the 16th to 19th centuries.

Textbook of Automatic Pistols, by R.K. Wilson, Wolfe Publishing Co., Prescott, AZ, 1990. 349 pp., illus. $54.00.
Reprint of the 1943 classic being a treatise on the history, development and functioning of modern military self-loading pistols.

Thompson: The American Legend, by Tracie L. Hill, Collector Grade Publications, Ontario, Canada, 1996. 584 pp., illus. $85.00.
The story of the first American submachine gun. All models are featured and discussed.

Toys That Shoot and Other Neat Stuff, by James Dundas, Schiffer Books, Atglen, PA, 1999. 112 pp. illustrated. Paper covers $24.95.
Shooting toys from the twentieth century, especially 1920's to 1960's, in over 420 color photographs of BB guns, cap shooters, marble shooters, squirt guns and more. Complete with a price guide.

Trade Guns of the Hudson's Bay Company, 1670-1870, by S. James Gooding, Museum Restoration Service, Bloomfield, Ontario, Canada, 1998. 35 pp., illus. Paper covers. $6.95.
The various styles and patterns of muzzle loading guns brought by the Hudson Bay Co. to North America to trade with the Indians.

The Trapdoor Springfield, by M.D. Waite and B.D. Ernst, The Gun Room Press, Highland Park, NJ, 1983. 250 pp., illus. $39.95.
The first comprehensive book on the famous standard military rifle of the 1873-92 period.

U.S. Breech-Loading Rifles and Carbines, Cal. 45, by Gen. John Pitman, Thomas Publications, Gettysburg, PA, 1992. 192 pp., illus. $29.95.
The third volume in the Pitman Notes on U.S. Martial Small Arms and Ammunition, 1776-1933. This book centers on the "Trapdoor Springfield" models.

U.S. Handguns of World War 2: The Secondary Pistols and Revolvers, by Charles W. Pate, Andrew Mowbray, Inc., Lincoln, RI, 1998. 515 pp., illus. $39.00.
This indispensable new book covers all of the American military handguns of World War 2 except for the M1911A1 Colt automatic.

United States Martial Flintlocks, by Robert M. Reilly, Mowbray Publishing Co., Lincoln, RI, 1997. 264 pp., illus. $40.00.
A comprehensive history of American flintlock longarms and handguns (mostly military) c. 1775 to c. 1840.

U.S. Martial Single Shot Pistols, by Daniel D. Hartzler and James B. Whisker, Old Bedford Village Pess, Bedford, PA, 1998. 128 pp., illus. $45.00.
A photographic chronicle of military and semi-martial pistols supplied to the U.S. Government and the several States.

U.S. Military Arms Dates of Manufacture from 1795, by George Madis, David Madis, Dallas, TX, 1989. 64 pp. Soft covers. $5.00.
Lists all U.S. military arms of collector interest alphabetically, covering about 250 models.

U.S. Military Small Arms 1816-1865, by Robert M. Reilly, The Gun Room Press, Highland Park, NJ, 1983. 270 pp., illus. $39.95.
Covers every known type of primary and secondary martial firearms used by Federal forces.

U.S. M1 Carbines: Wartime Production, by Craig Riesch, North Cape Publications, Tustin, CA, 1994. 72 pp., illus. Paper covers. $15.95.
Presents only verifiable and accurate information. Each part of the M1 Carbine is discussed fully in its own section; including markings and finishes.

U.S. Naval Handguns, 1808-1911, by Fredrick R. Winter, Andrew Mowbray Publishers, Lincoln, RI, 1990. 128 pp., illus. $26.00.
The story of U.S. Naval Handguns spans an entire century—included are sections on each of the important naval handguns within the period.

Walther Models PP and PPK, 1929-1945, by James L. Rankin, assisted by Gary Green, James L. Rankin, Coral Gables, FL, 1974. 142 pp., illus. $35.00.
Complete coverage on the subject as to finish, proofmarks and Nazi Party inscriptions.

Walther P-38 Pistol, by Maj. George Nonte, Desert Publications, Cornville, AZ, 1982. 100 pp., illus. Paper covers. $11.95.
Complete volume on one of the most famous handguns to come out of WWII. All models covered.

Walther Volume II, Engraved, Presentation and Standard Models, by James L. Rankin, J.L. Rankin, Coral Gables, FL, 1977. 112 pp., illus. $35.00.
The new Walther book on embellished versions and standard models. Has 88 photographs, including many color plates.

Walther, Volume III, 1908-1980, by James L. Rankin, Coral Gables, FL, 1981. 226 pp., illus. $35.00.
Covers all models of Walther handguns from 1908 to date, includes holsters, grips and magazines.

The Whitney Firearms, by Claud Fuller, Standard Publications, Huntington, WV, 1946. 334 pp., many plates and drawings, $50.00.
An authoritative history of all Whitney arms and their maker. Highly recommended. An exclusive with Ray Riling Arms Books Co.

THE HANDGUNNER'S LIBRARY

REFERENCE

Winchester: An American Legend, by R.L. Wilson, Random House, New York, NY, 1991. 403 pp., illus. $65.00.
The official history of Winchester firearms from 1849 to the present.

Winchester Bolt Action Military & Sporting Rifles 1877 to 1937, by Herbert G. Houze, Andrew Mowbray Publishing, Lincoln, RI, 1998. 295 pp., illus. $45.00.
Winchester was the first American arms maker to commercially manufacture a bolt action repeating rifle, and this book tells the exciting story of these Winchester bolt actions.

The Winchester Book, by George Madis, David Madis Gun Book Distributor, Dallas, TX, 1986. 650 pp., illus. $49.50.
A new, revised 25th anniversary edition of this classic book on Winchester firearms. Complete serial ranges have been added.

Winchester Dates of Manufacture 1849-1984, by George Madis, Art & Reference House, Brownsboro, TX, 1984. 59 pp. $5.95.
A most useful work, compiled from records of the Winchester factory.

Winchester Engraving, by R.L. Wilson, Beinfeld Books, Springs, CA, 1989. 500 pp., illus. $125.00.
A classic reference work of value to all arms collectors.

The Winchester Handbook, by George Madis, Art & Reference House, Lancaster, TX, 1982. 287 pp., illus. $19.95.
The complete line of Winchester guns, with dates of manufacture, serial numbers, etc.

Winchester Lever Action Repeating Firearms, Vol. 1, The Models of 1866, 1873 and 1876, by Arthur Pirkle, North Cape Publications, Tustin, CA, 1995. 112 pp., illus. Paper covers, $19.95.
Complete, part-by-part description, including dimensions, finishes, markings and variations throughout the production run of these fine, collectible guns.

Winchester Lever Action Repeating Rifles, Vol. 2, The Models of 1886 and 1892, by Arthur Pirkle, North Cape Publications, Tustin, CA, 1996. 150 pp. illus. Paper covers, $19.95.
Describes each model on a part-by-part basis by serial number range complete with finishes, markings and changes.

Winchester Lever Action Repeating Rifles, Volume 3, The Model of 1894, by Arthur Pirkle, North Cape Publications, Tustin, CA, 1998. 150 pp., illus. Paper covers, $16.95.
The first book ever to provide a detailed description of the Model 1894 rifle and carbine.

The Winchester Model 94: The First 100 Years, by Robert C. Renneberg, Krause Publications, Iola, WI, 1991. 208 pp., illus. $34.95.
Covers the design and evolution from the early years up to the many different editions that exist today.

Winchester Shotguns and Shotshells, by Ronald W. Stadt, Krause Publications, Iola, WI, 1995. 256 pp., illus. $34.95.
The definitive book on collectible Winchester shotguns and shotshells manufactured through 1961.

The Winchester Single-Shot, by John Campbell, Andrew Mowbray, Inc., Lincoln RI, 1995. 272 pp., illus. $55.00.
Covers every important aspect of this highly-collectible firearm.

Winchester Slide-Action Rifles, Volume 1: Model 1890 & Model 1906, by Ned Schwing, Krause Publications, Iola, WI, 1992. 352 pp., illus. $39.95.
First book length treatment of models 1890 & 1906 with over 50 charts and tables showing significant new information about caliber style and rarity.

Winchester Slide-Action Rifles, Volume 2: Model 61 & Model 62, by Ned Schwing, Krause Publications, Iola, WI, 1993. 256 pp., illus. $34.95.
A complete historic look into the Model 61 and the Model 62. These favorite slide-action guns receive a thorough presentation which takes you to the factory to explore receivers, barrels, markings, stocks, stampings and engraving in complete detail.

Winchester's 30-30, Model 94, by Sam Fadala, Stackpole Books, Inc., Harrisburg, PA, 1986. 223 pp., illus. $24.95.
The story of the rifle America loves.

GENERAL

Advanced Muzzleloader's Guide, by Toby Bridges, Stoeger Publishing Co., So. Hackensack, NJ, 1985. 256 pp., illus. Paper covers, $14.95.
The complete guide to muzzle-loading rifles, pistols and shotguns—flintlock and percussion.

Aids to Musketry for Officers & NCOs, by Capt. B.J. Friend, Excalibur Publications, Latham, NY, 1996. 40 pp., illus. Paper covers, $7.95.
A facsimile edition of a pre-WWI British manual filled with useful information for training the common soldier.

Air Gun Digest, 3rd Edition, by J.I. Galan, DBI Books, a division of Krause Publications, Iola, WI, 1995. 258 pp., illus. Paper covers, $19.95.
Everything from A to Z on air gun history, trends and technology.

American Gunsmiths, by Frank M. Sellers, The Gun Room Press, Highland Park, NJ, 1983. 349 pp. $39.95.
A comprehensive listing of the American gun maker, patentee, gunsmith and entrepreneur.

American and Imported Arms, Ammunition and Shooting Accessories, Catalog No. 18 of the Shooter's Bible, Stoeger, Inc., reprinted by Fayette Arsenal, Fayetteville, NC, 1988. 142 pp., illus. Paper covers, $10.95.
A facsimile reprint of the 1932 Stoeger's Shooter's Bible.

America's Great Gunmakers, by Wayne van Zwoll, Stoeger Publishing Co., So. Hackensack, NJ, 1992. 288 pp., illus. Paper covers, $16.95.
This book traces in great detail the evolution of guns and ammunition in America and the men who formed the companies that produced them.

Armed and Female, by Paxton Quigley, E.P. Dutton, New York, NY, 1989. 237 pp., illus. $16.95.
The first complete book on one of the hottest subjects in the media today, the arming of the American woman.

Arming the Glorious Cause: Weapons of the Second War for Independence, by James B. Whisker, Daniel D. Hartzler and Larry W. Yantz, R&R Books, Livonia, NY, 1998. 175 pp., illustrated. $45.00.
A photographic study of Confederate weapons.

Arms and Armour in Antiquity and the Middle Ages, by Charles Boutell, Stackpole Books, Mechanicsburg, PA, 1996. 352 pp., illus. $22.95.
Detailed descriptions of arms and armor, the development of tactics and the outcome of specific battles.

Arms & Armor in the Art Institute of Chicago, by Walter J. Karcheski, Jr., Bulfinch Press, Boston, MA, 1995. 128 pp., illus. $35.00.
Now, for the first time, the Art Institute of Chicago's arms and armor collection is presented in the visual delight of 103 color illustrations.

Arms for the Nation: Springfield Longarms, edited by David C. Clark, Scott A. Duff, Export, PA, 1994. 73 pp., illus. Paper covers, $9.95.
A brief history of the Springfield Armory and the arms made there.

Arsenal of Freedom, The Springfield Armory, 1890-1948: A Year-by-Year Account Drawn from Official Records, compiled and edited by Lt. Col. William S. Brophy, USAR Ret., Andrew Mowbray, Inc., Lincoln, RI, 1991. 400 pp., illus. Soft covers, $29.95.
A "must buy" for all students of American military weapons, equipment and accoutrements.

Assault Weapons, 4th Edition, The Gun Digest Book of, edited by Jack Lewis, DBI Books, a division of Krause Publications, Iola, WI. 256 pp. illus. Paper covers, $19.95.
An in-depth look at the history and uses of these arms.

The Belgian Rattlesnake: The Lewis Automatic Machine Gun, by William M. Easterly, Collector Grade Publications, Inc., Cobourg, Ont. Canada, 1998. 542 pp., illus. $79.95.
A social and technical biography of the Lewis automatic machine gun and its inventors.

The Big Bang: A History of Explosives, by G.I. Brown, Sutton Publishing, Herndon, VA, 1998. 240 pp., illustrated. $35.00.
The first scientific history of explosives from gunpowder to the nuclear bomb.

The Big Guns: Civil War Siege, Seacoast, and Naval Cannon, by Edwin Olmstead, Wayne E. Stark and Spencer C. Tucker, Museum Restoration Service, Bloomfield, Ontario, Canada, 1997. 360 pp. illus. $80.00.
This book is designed to identify and record the heavy guns available to both sides during the Civil War.

Blackpowder Loading Manual, 3rd Edition, by Sam Fadala, DBI Books, a division of Krause Publications, Iola, WI, 1995. 368 pp., illus. Paper covers, $20.95.
Revised and expanded edition of this landmark blackpowder loading book. Covers hundreds of loads for most of the popular blackpowder rifles, handguns and shotguns.

The Blackpowder Notebook, by Sam Fadala, Wolfe Publishing Co., Prescott, AZ, 1994. 212 pp., illus. $22.50.
For anyone interested in shooting muzzleloaders, this book will help improve scores and obtain accuracy and reliability.

Bolt Action Rifles, 3rd Edition, by Frank de Haas, DBI Books, a division of Krause Publications, Iola, WI, 1995. 528 pp., illus. Paper covers, $24.95.
A revised edition of the most definitive work on all major bolt-action rifle designs.

The Book of the Crossbow, by Sir Ralph Payne-Gallwey, Dover Publications, Mineola, NY, 1996. 416 pp., illus. Paper covers, $14.95.
Unabridged republication of the scarce 1907 London edition of the book on one of the most devastating hand weapons of the Middle Ages.

Bows and Arrows of the Native Americans, by Jim Hamm, Lyons & Burford Publishers, New York, NY, 1991. 156 pp., illus. $19.95.
A complete step-by-step guide to wooden bows, sinew-backed bows, composite bows, strings, arrows and quivers.

Bowhunter's Digest, 3rd Edition, by Chuck Adams, DBI Books, a division of Krause Publications, Iola, WI, 1990. 288 pp., illus. Soft covers, $17.95.
All-new edition covers all the necessary equipment and how to use it, plus the fine points on how to improve your skill.

British Small Arms of World War 2, by Ian D. Skennerton, I.D.S.A. Books, Piqua, OH, 1988. 110 pp., 37 illus. $25.00.

British Sniper, by Ian Skennerton, I.D.S.A. Books, Piqua, OH, 1983. 26 pp., over 375 illus. $40.00.

"Carbine," the Story of David Marshall Williams, by Ross E. Beard, Jr. Phillips Publications, Williamstown, NJ, 1999. 225 pp., illus. $29.95.
The story of the firearms genius, David Marshall "Carbine" Williams. From prison to the pinnacles of fame, the tale of this North Carolinian is inspiring. The author details many of Williams firearms inventions and developments.

Cartridges of the World, 8th Edition, by Frank Barnes, edited by M.L. McPherson, DBI Books, a division of Krause Publications, Iola, WI, 1997. 480 pp., illus. Paper covers, $24.95.
Completely revised edition of the general purpose reference work for which collectors, police, scientists and laymen reach first for answers to cartridge identification questions.

THE HANDGUNNER'S LIBRARY

Combat Handgunnery, 4th Edition, The Gun Digest Book of, by Chuck Taylor, DBI Books, a division of Krause Publications, Iola, WI, 1997. 256 pp., illus. Paper covers. $18.95.
This edition looks at real world combat handgunnery from three different perspectives—military, police and civilian.

The Complete Blackpowder Handbook, 3rd Edition, by Sam Fadala, DBI Books, a division of Krause Publications, Iola, WI, 1997. 400 pp., illus. Paper covers. $21.95.
Expanded and completely rewritten edition of the definitive book on the subject of blackpowder.

The Complete Guide to Game Care and Cookery, 3rd Edition, by Sam Fadala, DBI Books, a division of Krause Publications, Iola, WI, 1994. 320 pp., illus. Paper covers. $18.95.
Over 500 photos illustrating the care of wild game in the field and at home with a separate recipe section providing over 400 tested recipes.

Complete Guide to Guns & Shooting, by John Malloy, DBI Books, a division of Krause Publications, Iola, WI, 1995. 256 pp., illus. Paper covers. $18.95.
What every shooter and gun owner should know about firearms, ammunition, gun safety, collecting and much more.

Cowboy Action Shooting, by Charly Gullett, Wolfe Publishing Co., Prescott, AZ, 1995. 400 pp., illus. Paper covers. $24.50.
The fast growing of the shooting sports is comprehensively covered in this text—the guns, loads, tactics and the fun and flavor of this Old West era competition.

Crossbows, edited by Roger Combs, DBI Books, a division of Krause Publications, Iola, WI, 1986. 192 pp., illus. Paper covers. $15.95.
Complete, up-to-date coverage of the hottest bow going—and the most controversial.

Dead On, by Tony Noblitt and Warren Gabrilska, Paladin Press, Boulder, CO, 1998. 176 pp., illustrated. Paper covers. $20.00
The long-range marksman's guide to extreme accuracy.

Death from Above: The German FG42 Paratrooper Rifle, by Thomas B. Dugelby and R. Blake Stevens, Collector Grade Publications, Toronto, Canada, 1990. 147 pp., illus. $39.95.
The first comprehensive study of all seven models of the FG42.

The Emma Gees, by H.W. McBride, Lancer Militaria, Mt. Ida, AR, 1998. 220 pp., illustrated. Paper cover. $19.95
Originally published in 1918, this was McBride's first book about his service with the machine gun section in World War One.

Encyclopedia of Modern Firearms, Vol. 1, compiled and publ. by Bob Brownell, Montezuma, IA, 1959. 1057 pp. plus index, illus. $60.00. Dist. By Bob Brownell, Montezuma, IA 50171.
Massive accumulation of basic information of nearly all modern arms pertaining to "parts and assembly." Replete with arms photographs, exploded drawings, manufacturers' lists of parts, etc.

Exploded Handgun Drawings, The Gun Digest Book of, edited by Harold A. Murtz, DBI Books, a division of Krause Publications, Iola, WI, 1992. 512 pp., illus. Paper covers. $20.95.
Exploded or isometric drawings for 494 of the most popular handguns.

Exploded Long Gun Drawings, The Gun Digest Book of, edited by Harold A. Murtz, DBI Books, a division of Krause Publications, Iola, WI, 512 pp., illus. Paper covers. $20.95.
Containing almost 500 rifle and shotgun exploded drawings.

Firearms Engraving as Decorative Art, by Dr. Fredric A. Harris, Barbara R. Harris, Seattle, WA, 1989. 172 pp., illus. $115.00.
The origin of American firearms engraving motifs in the decorative art of the Middle East. Illustrated with magnificent color photographs.

Fireworks: A Gunsight Anthology, by Jeff Cooper, Paladin Press, Boulder, CO, 1998. 192 pp., illus. Paper cover. $25.00
A collection of wild, hilarious, shocking and always meaningful tales from the remarkable life of an American firearms legend.

Firing Back, by Clayton E. Cramer, Krause Publications, Iola, WI, 1995. 208 pp., Paper covers. $9.95.
Proposes answers and arguments to counter the popular anti-gun sentiments.

Frank Pachmayr: The Story of America's Master Gunsmith and his Guns, by John Lachuk, Safari Press, Huntington Beach, CA, 1996. 254 pp., illus. First edition, limited, signed and slipcased. $85.00; Second printing trade edition. $50.00.
The colorful and historically significant biography of Frank A. Pachmayr, America's own gunsmith emeritus.

The Frontier Rifleman, by H.B. LaCrosse Jr., Pioneer Press, Union City, TN, 1989. 183 pp., illus. Soft covers. $14.95.
The Frontier rifleman's clothing and equipment during the era of the American Revolution, 1760-1800.

The Gatling Gun: 19th Century Machine Gun to 21st Century Vulcan, by Joseph Berk, Paladin Press, Boulder, CO, 1991. 136 pp., illus. $29.95.
Here is the fascinating on-going story of a truly timeless weapon, from its beginnings during the Civil War to its current role as a state-of-the-art modern combat system.

German Artillery of World War Two, by Ian V. Hogg, Stackpole Books, Mechanicsburg, PA, 1997. 304 pp., illus. $44.95.
Complete details of German artillery use in WWII.

Good Guns Again, by Stephen Bodio, Wilderness Adventures Press, Bozeman, MT, 1994. 183 pp., illus. $29.00.
A celebration of fine sporting arms.

Grand Old Lady of No Man's Land: The Vickers Machine Gun, by Dolf L. Goldsmith, Collector Grade Publications, Cobourg, Canada, 1994. 600 pp., illus. $79.95.
Goldsmith brings his years of experience as a U.S. Army armourer, machine gun collector and shooter to bear on the Vickers, in a book sure to become a classic in its field.

Great Shooters of the World, by Sam Fadala, Stoeger Publishing Co., So. Hackensack, NJ, 1991. 288 pp., illus. Paper covers. $18.95.
This book offers gun enthusiasts an overview of the men and women who have forged the history of firearms over the past 150 years.

The Grenade Recognition Manual, Volume 1, U.S. Grenades & Accessories, by Darryl W. Lynn, Service Publications, Ottawa, Canada, 1998. 112 pp., illus. Paper covers. $29.95.
This new book examines the hand grenades of the United States beginning with the hand grenades of the U.S. Civil War and continues through to the present.

Gun Digest Treasury, 7th Edition, edited by Harold A. Murtz, DBI Books, a division of Krause Publications, Iola, WI, 1994. 320 pp., illus. Paper covers. $17.95.
A collection of some of the most interesting articles which have appeared in Gun Digest over its first 45 years.

Gun Digest 2000, 54th Edition, edited by Ken Warner, DBI Books a division of Krause Publications, Iola, WI, 1999. 544 pp., illustrated. Paper covers. $24.95.
This all new 54th edition continues the editorial excellence, quality, content and comprehensive cataloguing that firearms enthusiasts have come to know and expect. The most read gun book in the world for the last half century.

Gun Engraving, by C. Austyn, Safari Press Publication, Huntington Beach, CA, 1998. 128 pp., plus 24 pages of color photos. $50.00.
A well-illustrated book on fine English and European gun engravers. Includes a fantastic pictorial section that lists types of engravings and prices.

Gun Notes, Volume 2, by Elmer Keith, Safari Press, Huntington Beach, CA, 1997. 292 pp., illus. Limited 1st edition, numbered and signed by Keith's son. Slipcased. $75.00. Second edition. $35.00.
Covers articles from Keith's monthly column in "Guns & Ammo" magazine during the period from 1971 through Keith's passing in 1982.

Gunshot Injuries: How They Are Inflicted, Their Complications and Treatment, by Col. Louis A. La Garde, 2nd revised edition, Lancer Militaria, Mt. Ida, AR, 1991. 480 pp., illus. $34.95.
A classic work which was the standard textbook on the subject at the time of WWI.

Gun Talk, edited by Dave Moreton, Winchester Press, Piscataway, NJ, 1973. 256 pp., illus. $9.95.
A treasury of original writing by the top gun writers and editors in America. Practical advice about every aspect of the shooting sports.

The Gun That Made the Twenties Roar, by Wm. J. Helmer, rev. and enlarged by George C. Nonte, Jr., The Gun Room Press, Highland Park, NJ, 1977. Over 300 pp., illus. $24.95.
Historical account of John T. Thompson and his invention, the infamous "Tommy Gun."

Gun Trader's Guide, 22nd Edition, published by Stoeger Publishing Co., Wayne, NJ, 1999. 592 pp., illus. Paper covers. $23.95.
Complete specifications and current prices for used guns. Prices of over 5,000 handguns, rifles and shotguns both foreign and domestic.

Gun Writers of Yesteryear, compiled by James Foral, Wolfe Publishing Co., Prescott, AZ, 1993. 449 pp. $35.00.
Here, from the pre-American rifleman days of 1898-1920, are collected some 80 articles by 34 writers from eight magazines.

The Gunfighter, Man or Myth? by Joseph G. Rosa, Oklahoma Press, Norman, OK, 1969. 229 pp., illus. (including weapons). Paper covers. $14.95.
A well-documented work on gunfights and gunfighters of the West and elsewhere. Great treat for all gunfighter buffs.

Gunfitting: The Quest for Perfection, by Michael Yardley, Safari Press, Huntington Beach, CA, 1995. 128 pp., illus. $24.95.
The author, a very experienced shooting instructor, examines gun stocks and gunfitting in depth.

Guns Illustrated 2000, 32nd Edition, edited by Harold A. Murtz, DBI Books a division of Krause Publications, Iola, WI, 1999. 352 pp., illustrated. Paper covers. $22.95.
Highly informative, technical articles on a wide range of shooting topics by some of the top writers in the industry. A catalog section lists more than 3,000 firearms currently manufactured in or imported to the U.S.

Guns in Combat, edited by Chris Bishop, Book Sales Inc., Edison, NJ, 1998. 192 pp., illustrated. $19.95.
Here the most used and important small arms - pistols, rifles, machine guns, and submachine guns - are each illustrated by a large, full-color cutaway, annotated artwork showing the gun's working parts to full effect. Along with a detailed and accurate text.

Guns of the Wild West, by George Markham, Sterling Publishing Co., New York, NY, 1993. 160 pp., illus. Paper covers. $19.95.
Firearms of the American Frontier, 1849-1917.

Guns, Who Should Have Them, edited by David B. Kopel, Prometheus Books, Amherst, NY, 1995. 475 pp., illustrated. $26.95.
Topics include the increasing rates of gun ownership and use; arms and women; background checks and waiting periods; the 2nd amendment "Assault Weapons", and children and guns.

Guns & Shooting: A Selected Bibliography, by Ray Riling, Ray Riling Arms Books Co., Phila., PA, 1982. 434 pp., illus. Limited, numbered edition. $75.
A limited edition of this superb bibliographical work, the only modern listing of books devoted to guns and shooting.

Guns, Bullets, and Gunfighters, by Jim Cirillo, Paladin Press, Boulder, CO, 1996. 119 pp., illus. Paper covers. $15.00.
Lessons and tales from a modern-day gunfighter.

THE HANDGUNNER'S LIBRARY

Guns, Loads, and Hunting Tips, by Bob Hagel, Wolfe Publishing Co., Prescott, AZ, 1986, 509 pp., illus. $19.95.
A large hardcover book packed with shooting, hunting and handloading wisdom.

Handgun Digest, 3rd Edition, edited by Chris Christian, DBI Books, a division of Krause Publications, Iola, WI, 1995, 256 pp., illus. Paper covers. $18.95.
Full coverage of all aspects of handguns and handgunning from a highly readable and knowledgeable author.

HK Assault Rifle Systems, by Duncan Long, Paladin Press, Boulder, CO, 1995, 110 pp., illus. Paper covers. $27.95.
The little known history behind this fascinating family of weapons tracing its beginnings from the ashes of World War Two to the present time.

I Remember Skeeter, compiled by Sally Jim Skelton, Wolfe Publishing Co., Prescott, AZ, 1998, 401 pp., illus. Paper covers. $19.95.
A collection of some of the beloved storyteller's famous works interspersed with anecdotes and tales from the people who knew best.

Jim Dougherty's Guide to Bowhunting Deer, by Jim Dougherty, DBI Books, a division of Krause Publications, Iola, WI, 1992, 256 pp., illus. Paper covers. $17.95.
Dougherty sets down some important guidelines for bowhunting and bowhunting equipment.

Kill or Get Killed, by Col. Rex Applegate, Paladin Press, Boulder, CO, 1996, 400 pp., illus. $29.95.
The best and longest-selling book on close combat in history.

The Long-Range War: Sniping in Vietnam, by Peter R. Senich, Paladin Press, Boulder, CO, 1994, 280 pp., illus. $39.95.
The most complete report on Vietnam-era sniping ever documented.

Machine Guns of World War I, by Robert Bruce, Windrow & Greene, London, 1997, 128 pp., illustrated, $39.95.
Seven classic automatic weapons of W.W.I are illustrated in some 250 color photographs. Detailed sequences show them in close-up during field stripping and handling.

Manual for H&R Reising Submachine Gun and Semi-Auto Rifle, edited by George P. Dillman, Desert Publications, El Dorado, AZ, 1994, 81 pp., illus. Paper covers. $12.95.

The Manufacture of Gunflints, by Sydney B.J. Skertchly, facsimile reprint with new introduction by Seymour de Lotbiniere, Museum Restoration Service, Ontario, Canada, 1984, 90 pp., illus. $24.50.
Limited edition reprinting of the very scarce London edition of 1879.

Master Tips, by J. Winokur, Potshot Press, Pacific Palisades, CA, 1985, 96 pp., illus. Paper covers. $11.95.
Basics of practical shooting.

The Military and Police Sniper, by Mike R. Lau, Precision Shooting, Inc., Manchester, CT, 1998, 352 pp., illustrated. Paper covers. $39.95.
Advanced precision shooting for combat and law enforcement.

Military Rifle & Machine Gun Cartridges, by Jean Huon, Paladin Press, Boulder, CO, 1990, 392 pp., illus. $34.95.
Describes the primary types of military cartridges and their principal loadings, as well as their characteristics, origin and use.

Military Small Arms of the 20th Century, 6th Edition, by Ian V. Hogg, DBI Books, a division of Krause Publications, Iola, WI, 1991, 352 pp., illus. Paper covers. $21.95.
Fully revised and updated edition of the standard reference in its field.

Modern Custom Guns, Walnut, Steel, and Uncommon Artistry, by Tom Turpin, Krause Publications, Iola, WI, 1997, 206 pp., illus. $49.95.
From exquisite engraving to breathtaking exotic woods, the mystique of today's custom guns is expertly detailed in word and awe-inspiring color photos of rifles, shotguns and handguns.

Modern Guns Identification & Values, 13th Edition, by Russell & Steve Quertermous, Collector Books, Paducah, KY, 1999. 516 pp., illus. Paper covers. $12.95.
A standard reference for over 20 years. Over 1,800 illustrations of over 2,500 models with their current values.

Modern Law Enforcement Weapons & Tactics, 2nd Edition, by Tom Ferguson, DBI Books, a division of Krause Publications, Iola, WI, 1991. 256 pp., illus. Paper covers. $18.95.
An in-depth look at the weapons and equipment used by law enforcement agencies of today.

Modern Sporting Guns, by Christopher Austyn, Safari Press, Huntington Beach, CA, 1994, 128 pp., illus. $40.00.
A discussion of the "best" English guns; round action, over-and-under, boxlocks, hammer guns, bolt action and double rifles as well as accessories.

The More Complete Cannoneer, by M.C. Switlik, Museum & Collectors Specialties Co., Monroe, MI, 1990. 199 pp., illus. $19.95.
Compiled agreeably to the regulations for the U.S. War Department, 1861, and containing current observations on the use of antique cannons.

The MP-40 Machine Gun, Desert Publications, El Dorado, AZ, 1995. 32 pp., illus. Paper covers. $11.95.

Naval Percussion Locks and Primers, by Lt. J.A. Dahlgren, Museum Restoration Service, Bloomfield, Canada, 1996. 140 pp., illus. $35.00
First published as an Ordnance Memoranda in 1853, this is the finest existing study of percussion locks and primers origin and development.

L.D. Nimschke Firearms Engraver, by R.L. Wilson, R&R Books, Livonia, NY, 1992. 108 pp., illus. $100.00.
The personal work record of one of the 19th century America's foremost engravers. Augmented by a comprehensive text, photographs of deluxe-engraved firearms, and detailed indexes.

1999 Standard Catalog of Firearms, the Collector's Price & Reference Guide, 9th Edition, by Ned Schwing, Krause Publications, Iola, WI, 1999. 1,248 pp., illus. Paper covers. $29.95.
40,000 updated gun prices with more than 4,600 photos. Easy to use master index listing every firearm model.

The Official Soviet AKM Manual, translated by Maj. James F. Gebhardt (Ret.), Paladin Press, Boulder, CO, 1999. 120 pp., illustrated. Paper covers. $16.00.
This official military manual, available in English for the first time, was originally published by the Soviet Ministry of Defence. Covers the history, function, maintenance, assembly and disassembly, etc. of the 7.62mm AKM assault rifle.

The One-Round War: U.S.M.C. Scout-Snipers in Vietnam, by Peter Senich, Paladin Press, Boulder, CO, 1996, 384 pp., illus. $59.95.
Sniping in Vietnam focusing specifically on the Marine Corps program.

OSS Weapons, by Dr. John W. Brunner, Phillips Publications, Williamstown, NJ, 1996. 224 pp., illus. $44.95.
The most definitive book ever written on the weapons and equipment used by the supersecret warriors of the Office of Strategic Services.

Pin Shooting: A Complete Guide, by Mitchell A. Ota, Wolfe Publishing Co., Prescott, AZ, 1992. 145 pp., illus. Paper covers. $14.95.
Traces the sport from its humble origins to today's thoroughly enjoyable social event, including the mammoth eight-day Second Chance Pin Shoot in Michigan.

Powder and Ball Small Arms, by Martin Pegler, Windrow & Greene Publishing, London, 1998, 128 pp., illustrated with 200 color photos, $39.95.
Part of the new "Live Firing Classic Weapons" series. Full-color photos of experienced shooters dressed in authentic costumes handling, loading and firing historic weapons.

E.C. Prudhomme, Master Gun Engraver, A Retrospective Exhibition: 1946-1973, intro. by John T. Amber, The R. W. Norton Art Gallery, Shreveport, LA, 1973, 32 pp., illus. Paper covers. $9.95.
Examples of master gun engravings by Jack Prudhomme.

A Rifleman Went to War, by H. W. McBride, Lancer Militaria, Mt. Ida, AR, 1987. 398 pp., illus. $24.95.
The classic account of practical marksmanship on the battlefields of World War I.

Sharpshooting for Sport and War, by W. W. Greener, Wolfe Publishing Co., Prescott, AZ, 1995, 192 pp., illus. $30.00.
This classic reprint explores the *first* expanding bullet; service rifles; shooting positions; trajectories; recoil; external ballistics; and other valuable information.

The Shooter's Bible 2000, No. 91, edited by William S. Jarrett, Stoeger Publishing Co., Wayne, NJ, 1999. 576 pp., illustrated. Paper covers. $23.95.
Over 3,000 firearms currently offered by major American and foreign gunmakers. Represented are handguns, rifles, shotguns and black powder arms with complete specifications and retail prices.

Shooting, by J.H. FitzGerald, Wolfe Publishing Co., Prescott, AZ, 1993, 421 pp., illus. $29.00.
A classic book and reference for anyone interested in pistol and revolver shooting.

Shooting Sixguns of the Old West, by Mike Venturino, MLV Enterprises, Livingston, MT, 1997. 221 pp., illus. Paper covers. $26.50.
A comprehensive look at the guns of the early West; Colts, Smith & Wesson and Remingtons, plus blackpowder and reloading specs.

Sniper: The World of Combat Sniping, by Adrian Gilbert, St Martin's Press, NY, 1995, 290 pp., illus. $24.95.
The skills, the weapons and the experiences.

Sniper Training, FM 23-10, Reprint of the U.S. Army field manual of August, 1994, Paladin Press, Boulder, CO, 1995, 352pp., illus. Paper covers. $25.00
The most up-to-date U.S. military sniping information and doctrine.

Sniping in France, by Major H. Hesketh-Prichard, Lancer Militaria, Mt. Ida, AR, 1993. 224 pp., illus. $24.95.
The author was a well-known British adventurer and big game hunter. He was called upon in the early days of "The Great War" to develop a program to offset an initial German advantage in sniping. How the British forces came to overcome this advantage.

Special Warfare: Special Weapons, by Kevin Dockery, Emperor's Press, Chicago, IL, 1997. 192 pp., illus. Paper covers. $29.95.
The arms and equipment of the UDT and SEALS from 1943 to the present.

Sporting Collectibles, by Dr. Stephen R. Irwin, Stoeger Publishing Co, Wayne, NJ, 1997, 256 pp., illus. Paper covers. $19.95.
A must book for serious collectors and admirers of sporting collectibles.

The Sporting Craftsmen: A Complete Guide to Contemporary Makers of Custom-Built Sporting Equipment, by Art Carter, Countrysport Press, Traverse City, MI, 1994, 240 pp., illus. $49.50.
Profiles leading makers of centerfire rifles; muzzleloading rifles; bamboo fly rods; fly reels; flies; waterfowl calls; decoys; handmade knives; and traditional longbows and recurves.

Sporting Rifle Takedown & Reassembly Guide, 2nd Edition, by J.B. Wood, DBI Books, a division of Krause Publications, Iola, WI, 1997. 480 pp., illus. Paper covers. $19.95.
An updated edition of the reference guide for anyone who wants to properly care for their sporting rifle. (Available September 1997)

The Street Smart Gun Book, by John Farnam, Police Bookshelf, Concord, NH, 1986. 45 pp., illus. Paper covers. $11.95.
Weapon selection, defensive shooting techniques, and gunfight-winning tactics from one of the world's leading authorities.

Stress Fire, Vol. 1: Stress Fighting for Police, by Massad Ayoob, Police Bookshelf, Concord, NH, 1984. 149 pp., illus. Paper covers. $9.95.
Gunfighting for police, advanced tactics and techniques.

THE HANDGUNNER'S LIBRARY

Survival Guns, by Mel Tappan, Desert Publications, El Dorado, AZ, 1993. 456 pp., illus. Paper covers. $21.95.

Discusses in a frank and forthright manner which handguns, rifles and shotguns to buy for personal defense and securing food, and the ones to avoid.

The Tactical Advantage, by Gabriel Suarez, Paladin Press, Boulder, CO, 1998. 216 pp., illustrated. Paper covers. $20.00.

Learn combat tactics that have been tested in the world's toughest schools.

Tactical Marksman, by Dave M. Lauch, Paladin Press, Boulder, CO, 1996. 165 pp., illus. Paper covers. $35.00.

A complete training manual for police and practical shooters.

Thompson Guns 1921-1945, Anubis Press, Houston, TX, 1980. 215 pp., illus. Paper covers. $15.95.

Facsimile reprinting of five complete manuals on the Thompson submachine gun.

Trailriders Guide to Cowboy Action Shooting, by James W. Barnard, Pioneer Press, Union City, TN, 1998. 134 pp., plus 91 photos, drawings and charts. Paper covers. $24.95.

Covers the complete spectrum of this shooting discipline, from how to dress to authentic leather goods, which guns are legal, calibers, loads and ballistics.

The Ultimate Sniper, by Major John L. Plaster, Paladin Press, Boulder, CO, 1994. 464 pp., illus. Paper covers. $39.95.

An advanced training manual for military and police snipers.

U.S. Marine Corp Rifle and Pistol Marksmanship, 1935, reprinting of a government publication, Lancer Militaria, Mt. Ida, AR, 1991. 99 pp., illus. Paper covers. $11.95.

The old corps method of precision shooting.

U.S. Marine Corps Scout/Sniper Training Manual, Lancer Militaria, Mt. Ida, AR, 1989. Soft covers. $14.95.

Reprint of the original sniper training manual used by the Marksmanship Training Unit of the Marine Corps Development and Education Command in Quantico, Virginia.

U.S. Marine Corps Scout-Sniper, World War II and Korea, by Peter R. Senich, Paladin Press, Boulder, CO, 1994. 236 pp., illus. $39.95.

The most thorough and accurate account ever printed on the training, equipment and combat experiences of the U.S. Marine Corps Scout-Snipers.

U.S. Marine Corps Sniping, Lancer Militaria, Mt. Ida, AR, 1989. Irregular pagination. Soft covers. $14.95.

A reprint of the official Marine Corps FMFM1-3B.

Unrepentant Sinner, by Charles Askins, Tejano Publications, San Antonio, TX, 1985. 322 pp., illus. Soft covers. $19.95.

The autobiography of Colonel Charles Askins.

Weapons of the Waffen-SS, by Bruce Quarrie, Sterling Publishing Co., Inc., 1991. 168 pp., illus. $24.95.

An in-depth look at the weapons that made Hitler's Waffen-SS the fearsome fighting machine it was.

Weatherby: The Man, The Gun, The Legend, by Grits and Tom Gresham, Cane River Publishing Co., Natchitoches, LA, 1992. 290 pp., illus. $24.95.

A fascinating look at the life of the man who changed the course of firearms development in America.

The Winchester Era, by David Madis, Art & Reference House, Brownsville, TX, 1984. 100 pp., illus. $14.95.

Story of the Winchester company, management, employees, etc.

Winchester Repeating Arms Company by Herbert Houze, Krause Publications, Iola, WI. 512 pp., illus. $50.00.

The World's Sniping Rifles, by Ian V. Hogg, Paladin Press, Boulder, CO, 1998. 144 pp., illustrated. Paper covers. $22.95.

A detailed manual with descriptions and illustrations of more than 50 high-precision rifles from 14 countries and a complete analysis of sights and systems.

You Can't Miss, by John Shaw and Michael Bane, John Shaw, Memphis, TN, 1983. 152 pp., illus. Paper covers. $12.95.

The secrets of a successful combat shooter; how to better defensive shooting skills.

Black Powder Hobby Gunsmithing, by Sam Fadala and Dale Storey, DBI Books, a division of Krause Publications, Iola, WI, 1994. 256 pp., illus. Paper covers. $18.95.

A how-to guide for gunsmithing blackpowder pistols, rifles and shotguns from two men at the top of their respective fields.

Checkering and Carving of Gun Stocks, by Monte Kennedy, Stackpole Books, Harrisburg, PA, 1962. 175 pp., illus. $39.95.

Revised, enlarged cloth-bound edition of a much sought-after, dependable work.

The Complete Metal Finishing Book, by Harold Hoffman, H&P Publishers, San Angelo, TX, 1992. 364 pp., illus. Paper covers. $29.95.

Instructions for the different metal finishing operations that the normal craftsman or shop will use. Primarily firearm related.

Custom Gunstock Carving, by Philip Eck, Stackpole Books, Mechanicsburg, PA, 1995. 232 pp., illus. $34.95.

Featuring a gallery of more than 100 full-size patterns for buttstocks, grips, accents and borders that carvers can use for their own projects.

Exploded Handgun Drawings, The Gun Digest Book of, edited by Harold A. Murtz, DBI Books, a division of Krause Publications, Iola, WI. 1992. 512 pp., illus. Paper covers. $20.95.

Exploded or isometric drawings for 494 of the most popular handguns.

Exploded Long Gun Drawings, The Gun Digest Book of, edited by Harold A. Murtz, DBI Books, a division of Krause Publications, Iola, WI. 512 pp., illus. Paper covers. $20.95.

Containing almost 500 rifle and shotgun exploded drawings. An invaluable aid to both professionals and hobbyists.

The Finishing of Gun Stocks, by Harold Hoffman, H&P Publishers, San Angelo, TX, 1994. 98 pp., illus. Paper covers. $17.95.

Covers different types of finishing methods and finishes.

Firearms Assembly/Disassembly, Part I: Automatic Pistols, Revised Edition, The Gun Digest Book of, by J.B. Wood, DBI Books, a division of Krause Publications, Iola, WI, 1990. 480 pp., illus. Paper covers. $19.95.

Covers 58 popular autoloading pistols plus nearly 200 variants of those models integrated into the text and completely cross-referenced in the index.

Firearms Assembly/Disassembly Part II: Revolvers, Revised Edition, The Gun Digest Book of, by J.B. Wood, DBI Books, a division of Krause Publications, Iola, WI, 1990. 480 pp., illus. Paper covers. $19.95.

Covers 49 popular revolvers plus 130 variants. The most comprehensive and professional presentation available to either hobbyist or gunsmith.

Firearms Assembly/Disassembly Part III: Rimfire Rifles, Revised Edition, The Gun Digest Book of, by J. B. Wood, DBI Books, a division of Krause Publications, Iola, WI., 1994. 480 pp., illus. Paper covers. $19.95.

Greatly expanded edition covering 65 popular rimfire rifles plus over 100 variants all completely cross-referenced in the index.

Firearms Assembly/Disassembly Part IV: Centerfire Rifles, Revised Edition, The Gun Digest Book of, by J.B. Wood, DBI Books, a division of Krause Publications, Iola, WI, 1991. 480 pp., illus. Paper covers. $19.95.

Covers 54 popular centerfire rifles plus 300 variants. The most comprehensive and professional presentation available to either hobbyist or gunsmith.

Firearms Assembly/Disassembly, Part V: Shotguns, Revised Edition, The Gun Digest Book of, by J.B. Wood, DBI Books, a division of Krause Publications, Iola, WI, 1992. 480 pp., illus. Paper covers. $19.95.

Covers 46 popular shotguns plus over 250 variants with step-by-step instructions on how to dismantle and reassemble each. The most comprehensive and professional presentation available to either hobbyist or gunsmith.

Firearms Assembly/Disassembly Part VI: Law Enforcement Weapons, The Gun Digest Book of, by J.B. Wood, DBI Books, a division of Krause Publications, Iola, WI, 1981. 288 pp., illus. Paper covers. $16.95.

Step-by-step instructions on how to completely dismantle and reassemble the most commonly used firearms found in law enforcement arsenals.

Firearms Assembly 3: The NRA Guide to Rifle and Shotguns, NRA Books, Wash., DC, 1980. 264 pp., illus. Paper covers. $13.95.

Text and illustrations explaining the takedown of 125 rifles and shotguns, domestic and foreign.

Firearms Assembly 4: The NRA Guide to Pistols and Revolvers, NRA Books, Wash., DC, 1980. 253 pp., illus. Paper covers. $13.95.

Text and illustrations explaining the takedown of 124 pistol and revolver models, domestic and foreign.

Firearms Bluing and Browning, By R.H. Angier, Stackpole Books, Harrisburg, PA, 151 pp., illus. $19.95.

A world master gunsmith reveals his secrets of building, repairing and renewing a gun, quite literally, lock, stock and barrel. A useful, concise text on chemical coloring methods for the gunsmith and mechanic.

Firearms Disassembly—With Exploded Views, by John A. Karns & John E. Traister, Stoeger Publishing Co., S. Hackensack, NJ, 1995. 320 pp. illus. Paper covers. $19.95.

Provides the do's and don'ts of firearms disassembly. Enables owners and gunsmiths to disassemble firearms in a professional manner.

Guns and Gunmaking Tools of Southern Appalachia, by John Rice Irwin, Schiffer Publishing Ltd., 1983. 118 pp., illus. Paper covers. $9.95.

The story of the Kentucky rifle.

Gunsmithing Tips and Projects, a collection of the best articles from the *Hand-loader* and *Rifle* magazines, by various authors, Wolfe Publishing Co., Prescott, AZ, 1992. 443 pp., illus. Paper covers. $25.00.

Includes such subjects as shop, stocks, actions, tuning, triggers, barrels, customizing, etc.

GUNSMITHING

Advanced Rebarreling of the Sporting Rifle, by Willis H. Fowler, Jr., Willis H. Fowler, Jr., Anchorage, AK, 1994. 127 pp., illus. Paper covers. $32.50.

A manual outlining a superior method of fitting barrels and doing chamber work on the sporting rifle.

The Art of Engraving, by James B. Meek, F. Brownell & Son, Montezuma, IA, 1973. 196 pp., illus. $33.95.

A complete, authoritative, imaginative and detailed study in training for gun engraving. The first book of its kind—and a great one.

Artistry in Arms, The R. W. Norton Gallery, Shreveport, LA, 1970. 42 pp., illus. Paper covers. $9.95.

The art of gunsmithing and engraving.

Barrels & Actions, by Harold Hoffman, H&P Publishers, San Angelo, TX, 1990. 309 pp., illus. Sprial bound. $27.95.

A manual on barrel making.

THE HANDGUNNER'S LIBRARY

HANDGUNS

Gunsmith Kinks, by F.R. (Bob) Brownell, F. Brownell & Son, Montezuma, IA, 1st ed., 1969, 496 pp., well illus. $18.95.
A widely useful accumulation of shop kinks, short cuts, techniques and pertinent comments by practicing gunsmiths from all over the world.

Gunsmith Kinks 2, by Bob Brownell, F. Brownell & Son, Publishers, Montezuma, IA, 1983, 496 pp., illus. $18.95.
A collection of gunsmithing knowledge, shop kinks, new and old techniques, shortcuts and general know-how straight from those who do them best—the gunsmiths.

Gunsmith Kinks 3, edited by Frank Brownell, Brownells Inc., Montezuma, IA, 1993, 504 pp., illus. $19.95.
Hundreds of valuable ideas are given in this volume.

Gunsmithing, by Roy F. Dunlap, Stackpole Books, Harrisburg, PA, 1990, 742 pp., illus. $34.95.
A manual of firearm design, construction, alteration and remodeling. For amateur and professional gunsmiths and users of modern firearms.

Gunsmithing at Home: Lock, Stock and Barrel, by John Traister, Stoeger Publishing Co., Wayne, NJ, 1997, 320 pp., illus. Paper covers. $19.95.
A Complete step-by-step fully illustrated guide to the art of gunsmithing.

Gunsmithing: Pistols & Revolvers, by Patrick Sweeney, DBI Books, a division of Krause Publications, Iola, WI, 1998, 352 pp., illus. Paper covers. $24.95.
Do-it-Yourself projects, diagnosis and repair for pistols and revolvers.

The Gunsmith's Manual, by J.P. Stelle and Wm. B. Harrison, The Gun Room Press, Highland Park, NJ, 1982, 376 pp., illus. $19.95.
For the gunsmith in all branches of the trade.

Handbook of Hard-to Find Guns Parts Drawings, by LeeRoy Wisner, Brownells, Inc., Montezuma, IA, 1997. Unpaginated. Deluxe edition, $54.95.
Over 2901 dimensioned drawings covering 147 guns from 36 manufacturers. The most valuable tool you'll ever buy for your shop.

Home Gunsmithing the Colt Single Action Revolvers, by Loren W. Smith, Ray Riling Arms Books, Co., Phila., PA, 1995, 119 pp., illus. $24.95.
Affords the Colt Single Action owner detailed, pertinent information on the operating and servicing of this famous and historic handgun.

How to Convert Military Rifles, Williams Gun Sight Co., Davision, MI, new and enlarged seventh edition, 1997. 76 pp., illus. Paper covers. $13.95.
This latest edition updated the changes that have occured over the past thirty years. Tips, instructions and illustrations on how to convert popular military rifles as the Enfield, Mauser 96 nad SKS just to name a few are presented.

Mr. Single Shot's Gunsmithing-Idea-Book, by Frank de Haas, Mark de Haas, Orange City, IA, 1996, 168 pp., illus. Paper covers. $21.50.
Offers easy to follow, step-by-step instructions for a wide variety of gunsmithing procedures all reinforced by plenty of photos.

The NRA Gunsmithing Guide—Updated, by Ken Raynor and Brad Fenton, National Rifle Association, Wash., DC, 1984. 336 pp., illus. Paper covers. $19.95.
Material includes chapters and articles on all facets of the gunsmithing art.

Pistolsmithing, The Gun Digest Book of, by Jack Mitchell, DBI Books, a division of Krause Publications, Iola, WI, 1980. 256 pp., illus. Paper covers. $16.95.
An expert's guide to the operation of each of the handgun actions with all the major functions of pistolsmithing explained.

Pistolsmithing, by George C. Nonte, Jr., Stackpole Books, Harrisburg, PA, 1974, 560 pp., illus. $29.95.
A single source reference to handgun maintenance, repair, and modification at home, unequaled in value.

Practical Gunsmithing, by the editors of American Gunsmith, DBI Books, a division of Krause Publications, Iola, WI, 1996. 256 pp., illus. Paper covers. $19.95.
A book intended primarily for home gunsmithing, but one that will be extremely helpful to professionals as well.

Professional Stockmaking, by D. Wesbrook, Wolfe Publishing Co., Prescott AZ, 1995. 308 pp., illus. $54.00.
A step-by-step how-to with complete photographic support for every detail of the art of working wood into riflestocks.

Riflesmithing, The Gun Digest Book of, by Jack Mitchell, DBI Books, a division of Krause Publications, Iola, WI, 1982. 256 pp., illus. Paper covers. $16.95.
The art and science of rifle gunsmithing. Covers tools, techniques, designs, finishing wood and metal, custom alterations.

Shotgun Gunsmithing, The Gun Digest Book of, by Ralph Walker, DBI Books, a division of Krause Publications, Iola, WI, 1983. 256 pp., illus. Paper covers. $16.95.
The principles and practices of repairing, individualizing and accurizing modern shotguns by one of the world's premier shotgun gunsmiths.

Sporting Rifle Take Down & reassembly Guide, 2nd Edition, by J.B. Wood, Krause Publications, Iola, WI, 1997, 480 pp., illus. Paper covers. $19.95.
Hunters and shooting enthusiasts must have this reference featuring 52 of the most popular and widely used sporting centerfire and rimfire rifles.

The Story of Pope's Barrels, by Ray M. Smith, R&R Books, Livonia, NY, 1993. 203 pp., illus. $39.00.
A reissue of a 1960 book whose author knew Pope personally. It will be of special interest to Schuetzen rifle fans, since Pope's greatest days were at the height of the Schuetzen-era before WWI.

Survival Gunsmithing, by J.B. Wood, Desert Publications, Cornville, AZ, 1986. 92 pp., illus. Paper covers. $11.95.
A guide to repair and maintenance of the most popular rifles, shotguns and handguns.

The Tactical 1911, by Dave Lauck, Paladin Press, Boulder, CO, 1998. 137 pp., illus. Paper covers. $20.00.
Here is the only book you will ever need to teach you how to select, modify, employ and maintain your Colt.

The Trade Rifle Sketchbook, by Charles E. Hanson, The Fur Press, Chadron, NE, 1979, 48 pp., illus. Paper covers. $9.95.
Includes full-scale plans for 10 rifles made for Indian and mountain men; from 1790 to 1860, plus plans for building three pistols.

Advanced Master Handgunning, by Charles Stephens, Paladin Press, Boulder, CO, 1994. 72 pp., illus. Paper covers. $10.00.
Secrets and surefire techniques for winning handgun competitions.

The Ayoob Files: The Book, by Massad Ayoob, Police Bookshelf, Concord, NH, 1995, 223 pp., illus. Paper covers. $14.95.
The best of Massad Ayoob's acclaimed series in American Handgunner magazine.

Big Bore Sixguns, by John Taffin, Krause Publications, Iola, WI, 1997, 336 pp., illus. $39.95.
The author takes aim on the entire range of big bores from .357 Magnums to .500 Maximums, single actions and cap-and-ball sixguns to custom touches for big bores.

Black Powder Hobby Gunsmithing, by Sam Fadala and Dale Storey, DBI Books, a division of Krause Publications, Iola, WI, 1994. 256 pp., illus. Paper covers. $18.95.
A how-to guide for gunsmithing blackpowder pistols, rifles and shotguns from two men at the top of their respective fields.

Browning Hi-Power Pistols, Desert Publications, Cornville, AZ, 1982, 20 pp., illus. Paper covers. $9.95.
Covers all facets of the various military and civilian models of the Browning Hi-Power pistol.

The Colt .45 Auto Pistol, compiled from U.S. War Dept. Technical Manuals, and reprinted by Desert Publications, Cornville, AZ, 1978. 80 pp., illus. Paper covers. $9.95.
Covers every facet of this famous pistol from mechanical training, manual of arms, disassembly, repair and replacement of parts.

Combat Handgunnery, 4th Edition, by Chuck Taylor, DBI Books, a division of Krause Publications, Iola, WI, 1997. 256 pp., illus. Paper covers. $18.95.
This all-new edition looks at real world combat handgunnery from three different perspectives—military, police and civilian. Available. October, 1996.

Combat Raceguns, by J.M. Ramos, Paladin Press, Boulder, CO, 1994. 168 pp., illus. Paper covers. $26.00.
Learn how to put together precision combat raceguns with the best compensators, frames, controls, sights and custom accessories.

Competitive Pistol Shooting, by Dr. Laslo Antal, A&C Black, London, England, 2nd edition, 1995. 176 pp., illus. Paper covers. $24.95.
Covers the basic principles followed in each case by a well illustrated and detailed discussion of the rules, technique, and training as well as the choice and maintenance of weapons.

The Complete Book of Combat Handgunning, by Chuck Taylor, Desert Publications, Cornville, AZ, 1982. 168 pp., illus. Paper covers. $20.00.
Covers virtually every aspect of combat handgunning.

Complete Guide to Compact Handguns, by Gene Gangarosa, Jr., Stoeger Publishing Co., Wayne, NJ, 1997. 228 pp., illus. Paper covers. $22.95.
Includes hundreds of compact firearms, along with text results conducted by the author.

Complete Guide to Service Handguns, by Gene Gangarosa, Jr., Stoeger Publishing Co., Wayne, NJ, 1998. 320 pp., illus. Paper covers. $22.95.
The author explores the revolvers and pistols that are used around the globe by military, law enforcement and civilians.

The Custom Government Model Pistol, by Layne Simpson, Wolfe Publishing Co., Prescott, AZ, 1994. 639 pp., illus. Paper covers. $24.50.
The book about one of the world's greatest firearms and the things pistolsmiths do to make it even greater.

The CZ-75 Family: The Ultimate Combat Handgun, by J.M. Ramos, Paladin Press, Boulder, CO, 1990. 100 pp., illus. Soft covers. $21.00.
An in-depth discussion of the early-and-late model CZ-75s, as well as the many newest additions to the Czech pistol family.

Encyclopedia of Pistols & Revolvers, by A.E. Hartink, Knickerbocker Press, New York, NY, 1997. 272 pp., illus. $19.95.
A comprehensive encyclopedia specially written for collectors and owners of pistols and revolvers.

Experiments of a Handgunner, by Walter Roper, Wolfe Publishing Co., Prescott, AZ, 1989. 202 pp., illus. $37.00.
A limited edition reprint. A listing of experiments with functioning parts of handguns, with targets, stocks, rests, handloading, etc.

Exploded Handgun Drawings, DBI Books, a division of Krause Publications, Iola, WI, 1992. 512 pp., illus. Paper covers. $20.95.
Exploded or isometric drawings for 494 of the most popular handguns.

The Farnam Method of Defensive Handgunning, by John S. Farnam, DTI, Inc., Seattle, WA, 1994. 191 pp., illus. Paper covers. $13.95.
A book intended to not only educate the new shooter, but also to serve as a guide and textbook for his and his instructor's training courses.

Fast and Fancy Revolver Shooting, by Ed. McGivern, Anniversary Edition, Winchester Press, Piscataway, NJ, 1984. 484 pp., illus. $18.95.
A fascinating volume, packed with handgun lore and solid information by the acknowledged dean of revolver shooters.

THE HANDGUNNER'S LIBRARY

Firearms Assembly/Disassembly, Part I: Automatic Pistols, Revised Edition, The Gun Digest Book of, by J.B. Wood, DBI Books, a division of Krause Publications, Iola, WI, 1990. 480 pp., illus. Soft covers. $19.95.
Covers 58 popular autoloading pistols plus nearly 200 variants of those models integrated into the text and completely cross-referenced in the index.

Firearms Assembly/Disassembly Part II: Revolvers, Revised Edition, The Gun Digest Book of, by J.B. Wood, DBI Books, a division of Krause Publications, Iola, WI, 1990. 480 pp., illus. Soft covers. $19.95.
Covers 49 popular revolvers plus 130 variants. The most comprehensive and professional presentation available to either hobbyist or gunsmith.

.45 ACP Super Guns, by J.M. Ramos, Paladin Press, Boulder, CO, 1991. 144 pp., illus. Paper covers. $24.00.
Modified .45 automatic pistols for competition, hunting and personal defense.

The .45, The Gun Digest Book of, by Dean A. Grennell, DBI Books, a division of Krause Publications, Iola, WI, 1989. 256 pp., illus. Paper covers. $17.95.
Definitive work on one of America's favorite calibers.

Glock: The New Wave in Combat Handguns, by Peter Alan Kasler, Paladin Press, Boulder, CO, 1993. 304 pp., illus. $25.00.
Kasler debunks the myths that surround what is the most innovative handgun to be introduced in some time.

Glock's Handguns, by Duncan Long, Desert Publications, El Dorado, AR, 1996. 180 pp., illus. Paper covers. $18.95.
An outstanding volume on one of the world's newest and most successful firearms of the century.

Hand Cannons: The World's Most Powerful Handguns, by Duncan Long, Paladin Press, Boulder, CO, 1995. 208 pp., illus. Paper covers. $20.00.
Long describes and evaluates each powerful gun according to their features.

Handguns 2000, 12th Edition, edited by Harold A. Murtz, DBI Books a division of Krause Publications, Iola, WI, 1999. 352 pp., illustrated. Paper covers. $22.95.
Top writers in the handgun industry give you a complete report on new handgun developments, testfire reports on the newest introductions and previews on what's ahead.

Handgun Digest, 3rd Edition, edited by Chris Christian, DBI Books, a division of Krause Publications, Iola, WI, 1995. 256 pp., illus. Paper covers. $18.95.
Full coverage of all aspects of handguns and handgunning from a highly readable and knowledgeable author.

Handgun Reloading, The Gun Digest Book of, by Dean A. Grennell and Wiley M. Clapp, DBI Books, a division of Krause Publications, Iola, WI, 1987. 256 pp., illus. Paper covers. $16.95.
Detailed discussions of all aspects of reloading for handguns, from basic to complex. New loading data.

Heckler & Koch's Handguns, by Duncan Long, Desert Publications, El Dorado, AR, 1996. 142 pp., illus. Paper covers. $18.95.
Traces the history and the evolution of H&K's pistols from the company's beginning at the sight of WWII to the present.

Hidden in Plain Sight, by Trey Bloodworth & Mike Raley, Professional Press, Chapel Hill, NC, 1995. Paper covers. $13.00.
A practical guide to concealed handgun carry.

High Standard Automatic Pistols 1932-1950, by Charles E. Petty, The Gunroom Press, Highland Park, NJ, 1989. 124 pp., illus. $19.95.
A definitive source of information for the collector of High Standard arms.

The Hi-Standard Pistol Guide, by Burr Leyson, Duckett's Sporting Books, Tempe AZ, 1995. 128 pp., illus. Paper covers. $22.00.
Complete information on selection, care and repair, ammunition, parts, and accessories.

How to Become a Master Handgunner: The Mechanics of X-Count Shooting, by Charles Stephens, Paladin Press, Boulder, CO, 1993. 64 pp., illus. Paper covers. $12.00.
Offers a simple formula for success to the handgunner who strives to master the technique of shooting accurately.

Hunting for Handgunners, by Larry Kelly and J.D. Jones, DBI Books, a division of Krause Publications, Iola, WI, 1990. 256 pp., illus. Paper covers. $16.95.
Covers the entire spectrum of hunting with handguns in an amusing, easy-flowing manner that combines entertainment with solid information.

Illustrated Encyclopedia of Handguns, by A.B. Zhuk, Stackpole Books, Mechanicsburg, PA, 1994. 256 pp., illus. Cloth cover, $49.95; paper cover, $29.95.
Identifies more than 2,000 military and commercial pistols and revolvers with details of more than 100 popular handgun cartridges.

Instinct Combat Shooting, by Chuck Klein, Chuck Klein, The Goose Creek, IN, 1989. 49 pp., illus. Paper covers. $12.00.
Defensive handgunning for police.

Know Your Czechoslovakian Pistols, by R.J. Berger, Blacksmith Corp., Chino Valley, AZ, 1989. 96 pp., illus. Soft covers. $9.95.
A comprehensive reference which presents the fascinating story of Czech pistols.

Know Your 45 Auto Pistols—Models 1911 & A1, by E.J. Hoffschmidt, Blacksmith Corp., Southport, CT, 1974. 58 pp., illus. Paper covers. $9.95.
A concise history of the gun with a wide variety of types and copies.

Know Your Walther P38 Pistols, by E.J. Hoffschmidt, Blacksmith Corp., Southport, CT, 1974. 77 pp., illus. Paper covers. $9.95.
Covers the Walther models Armee, M.P., H.P., P.38—history and variations.

Know Your Walther PP & PPK Pistols, by E.J. Hoffschmidt, Blacksmith Corp., Southport, CT, 1975. 87 pp., illus. Paper covers. $9.95.
A concise history of the guns with a guide to the variety and types.

The Gordon Macquarrie Treasury, with introduction and commentary by Zack Taylor, Willow Creek Press, Minocqua, WI, 1998. $29.50.
This new treasury draws 20 of the very best of Macquarrie's best stories that appeared in his trilogy plus 19 newly discovered stories never before published in book form.

The Mauser Self-Loading Pistol, by Belford & Dunlap, Borden Publ. Co., Alhambra, CA. Over 200 pp., 300 illus., large format. $24.95.
The long-awaited book on the "Broom Handles," covering their inception in 1894 to the end of production. Complete and in detail: pocket pistols, Chinese and Spanish copies, etc.

Modern American Pistols and Revolvers, by A.C. Gould, Wolfe Publishing Co., Prescott, AZ, 1988. 222 pp., illus. $37.00.
A limited edition reprint. An account of the development of those arms as well as the manner of shooting them.

The Modern Technique of the Pistol, by Gregory Boyce Morrison, Gunsite Press, Paulden, AZ, 1991. 153 pp., illus. $45.00.
The theory of effective defensive use of modern handguns.

9mm Handguns, 2nd Edition, The Gun Digest Book of, edited by Steve Comus, DBI Books, a division of Krause Publications, Iola, WI, 1993. 256 pp., illus. Paper covers. $18.95.
Covers the 9mmP cartridge and the guns that have been made for it in greater depth than any other work available.

9mm Parabellum: The History & Developement of the World's 9mm Pistols & Ammunition, by Klaus-Peter König and Martin Hugo, Schiffer Publishing Ltd., Atglen, PA, 1993. 304 pp., illus. $39.95.
Detailed history of 9mm weapons from Belgium, Italy, Germany, Israel, France, USA, Czechoslovakia, Hungary, Poland, Brazil, Finland and Spain.

The Official 9mm Markarov Pistol Manual, translated into English by Major James Gebhardt, U.S. Army (Ret.), Desert Publications, El Dorado, AR, 1996. 84 pp., illus. Paper covers. $12.95.
The information found in this book will be of enormous benefit and interest to the owner or a prospective owner of one of these pistols.

The 100 Greatest Combat Pistols, by Timothy J. Mullin, Paladin Press, Boulder, CO, 1994. 409 pp., illus. Paper covers. $40.00.
Hands-on tests and evaluations of handguns from around the world.

P-38 Automatic Pistol, by Gene Gangarosa, Jr., Stoeger Publishing Co., S. Hackensack, NJ, 1993. 272 pp., illus. Paper covers. $16.95
This book traces the origins and development of the P-38, including the momentous political forces of the World War II era that caused its near demise and, later, its rebirth.

Pistol & Revolver Guide, 3rd Ed., by George C. Nonte, Stoeger Publ. Co., So. Hackensack, NJ, 1975. 224 pp., illus. Paper covers. $11.95.
The standard reference work on military and sporting handguns.

Pistol Guide, by George C. Nonte, Jr., Stoeger Publishing Co., So. Hackensack, NJ, 1991. 280 pp., illus. Paper covers. $13.95.
Covers handling and marksmanship, care and maintenance, pistol ammunition, how to buy a used gun, military pistols, air pistols and repairs.

Pistols of the World, 3rd Edition, by Ian Hogg and John Weeks, DBI Books, a division of Krause Publications, Iola, WI, 1992. 352 pp., illus. Paper covers. $20.95.
A totally revised edition of one of the leading studies of small arms.

Pistolsmithing, The Gun Digest Book of, by Jack Mitchell, DBI Books, a division of Krause Publications, Iola, WI, 1980. 288 pp., illus. Paper covers. $16.95.
An expert's guide to the operation of each of the handgun actions with all the major functions of pistolsmithing explained.

Practical Shooting: Beyond Fundamentals, by Brian Enos, Zediker Publishing, Clifton, CO, 1997. 201 pp., illus. $27.95.
This prize-winning master covers technique of combat shooting in all its aspects.

Report of Board on Tests of Revolvers and Automatic Pistols, From the Annual Report of the Chief of Ordnance, 1907. Reprinted by J.C. Tillinghast, Marlow, NH, 1969. 34 pp., 7 plates, paper covers. $9.95.
A comparison of handguns, including Luger, Savage, Colt, Webley-Fosbery and other makes.

Revolver Guide, by George C. Nonte, Jr., Stoeger Publishing Co., So. Hackensack, NJ, 1991. 288 pp., illus. Paper covers. $10.95.
A detailed and practical encyclopedia of the revolver, the most common handgun to be found.

Ruger Automatic Pistols and Single Action Revolvers, by Hugo A. Lueders, edited by Don Findley, Blacksmith Corp., Chino Valley, AZ, 1993. 79 pp., illus. Paper covers. $14.95.
The definitive work on Ruger automatic pistols and single action revolvers.

The Ruger "P" Family of Handguns, by Duncan Long, Desert Publications, El Dorado, AR, 1993. 128 pp., illus. Paper covers. $14.95.
A full-fledged documentary on a remarkable series of Sturm Ruger handguns.

The Ruger .22 Automatic Pistol, Standard/Mark I/Mark II Series, by Duncan Long, Paladin Press, Boulder, CO, 1989. 168 pp., illus. Paper covers. $12.00.
The definitive book about the pistol that has served more than 1 million owners so well.

The Semiautomatic Pistols in Police Service and Self Defense, by Massad Ayoob, Police Bookshelf, Concord, NH, 1990. 25 pp., illus. Soft covers. $9.95.
First quantitative, documented look at actual police experience with 9mm and 45 police service automatics.

The Sharpshooter—How to Stand and Shoot Handgun Metallic Silhouettes, by Charles Stephens, Yucca Tree Press, Las Cruces, NM, 1993. 86 pp., illus. Paper covers. $10.00.
A narration of some of the author's early experiences in silhouette shooting, plus how-to information.

THE HANDGUNNER'S LIBRARY

REFERENCE

Shoot to Win, by John Shaw, Blacksmith Corp., Southport, CT, 1985, 160 pp., illus. Paper covers. $15.50. The lessons taught here are of interest and value to all handgun shooters.

Shooting, by J.H. FitzGerald, Wolfe Publishing Co., Prescott, AZ, 1993, 421 pp., illus. $29.00. Exhaustive coverage of handguns and their use for target shooting, defense, trick shooting, and in police work by a noted firearms expert.

Shooting Colt Single Actions, by Mike Venturino, Livingston, MT, 1995. A definitive work on the famous Colt SAA and the ammunition it shoots.

Sig/Sauer Handguns, by Duncan Long, Desert Publications, El Dorado, AZ, 1995, 150 pp., illus. Paper covers. $16.95. The history of Sig/Sauer handguns, including Sig, Sig-Hammerli and Sig/Sauer variants.

Sixgun Cartridges and Loads, by Elmer Keith, reprint edition by The Gun Room Press, Highland Park, NJ, 1984, 151 pp., illus. $24.95. A manual covering the selection, use and loading of the most suitable and popular revolver cartridges.

Sixguns, by Elmer Keith, Wolfe Publishing Company, Prescott, AZ, 1992, 336 pp. Paper covers. $29.95. The history, selection, repair, care, loading, and use of this historic frontiersman's friend—the one-hand firearm.

Smith & Wesson's Automatics, by Larry Combs, Desert Publications, El Dorado, AZ, 1994, 143 pp., illus. Paper covers. $19.95. A must for every S&W auto owner or prospective owner.

Standard Catalog of Smith and Wesson by Jim Supica and Richard Nahas, Krause Publications, Inc. Iola, WI, 1996, 240 pp., illus. $29.95. Clearly details hundreds of products by the legendary manufacturer. How to identify, evaluate the conditions and assesses the value of 752 Smith & Wesson models and variations.

Street Stoppers: The Latest Handgun Stopping Power Street Results, by Evan P. Marshall & Edwin J. Sandow, Paladin Press, Boulder, CO, 1997, 392 pp., illus. Paper covers, $39.95. Compilation of the results of real-life shooting incidents involving every major handgun caliber.

The Tactical Pistol, by Gabriel Suarez with a foreword by Jeff Cooper, Paladin Press, Boulder, CO, 1996, 216 pp., illus. Paper covers. $25.00. Advanced gunfighting concepts and techniques.

The Thompson/Center Contender Pistol, by Charles Tephens, Paladin, Press, Boulder, CO, 1997, 58 pp., illus. Paper covers. $12.00. How to tune and time, load and shoot accurately with the Contender pistol.

The .380 Enfield No. 2 Revolver, by Mark Stamps and Ian Skennerton, I.D.S.A. Books, Piqua, OH, 1993, 124 pp., 80 illus. Paper covers. $19.95.

The Truth About Handguns, by Duane Thomas, Paladin Press, Boulder, CO, 1997, 136 pp., illus. Paper covers. $14.00.

U.S. Handguns of World War 2, The Secondary Pistols and Revolvers, by Charles W. Pate, Mowbray Publishers, Lincoln, RI, 1997, 368 pp., illus. $39.00. This indispensable new book covers all of the American military handguns of W.W.2 except for the M1911A1.

World's Deadliest Rimfire Battleguns, by J.M. Ramos, Paladin Press, Boulder, CO, 1990, 184 pp., illus. Paper covers. $14.00. Exploding the myths, hype, and misinformation about handguns. This heavily illustrated book shows international rimfire assault weapon innovations from World War II to the present.

HUNTING

NORTH AMERICA

Advanced Black Powder Hunting, by Toby Bridges, Stoeger Publishing Co., Wayne, NJ, 1998, 288 pp., illus. Paper covers. $21.95. The first modern day publication to be filled from cover to cover with guns, loads, projectiles, accessories and the techniques to get the most from today's front loading guns.

Advanced Strategies for Trophy Whitetails, by David Morris, Safari Press, Inc., Huntington Beach, CA, 1998, 399 pp., illustrated. $29.95. An in-depth look into the critical where-to and when-to strategies, covering exactly where in North America the great trophies are found and how to pick the best time to hunt.

Advanced Wild Turkey Hunting & World Records, by Dave Harbour, Winchester Press, Piscataway, NJ, 1983, 264 pp., illus. $19.95. The definitive book, written by an authority who has studied turkeys and turkey calling for over 40 years.

After the Hunt With Lovett Williams, by Lovett Williams, Krause Publications, Iola, WI, 1996, 256 pp., illus. Paper covers. $15.95. The author carefully instructs you on how to prepare your trophy turkey for a trip to the taxidermist. Plus help on planning a grand slam hunt.

Aggressive Whitetail Hunting, by Greg Miller, Krause Publications, Iola, WI, 1995, 208 pp., illus. Paper covers. $14.95. Learn how to hunt trophy bucks in public forests, private farmlands and exclusive hunting grounds from one of America's foremost hunters.

Alaskan Adventures, Volume 2, by Russell Annabel, Safari Press, Inc., Huntington Beach, CA, 1997, 351 pp., illus. $50.00. More of this famous writer's previously unpublished magazine articles in book form.

All About Bears, by Duncan Gilchrist, Stoneydale Press Publishing Co., Stevensville, MT, 1989, 176 pp., illus. $19.95. Covers all kinds of bears—black, grizzly, Alaskan brown, polar and leans on a lifetime of hunting and guiding experiences to explore proper hunting techniques.

All-American Deer Hunter's Guide, edited by Jim Zumbo and Robert Elman, Winchester Press, Piscataway, NJ, 1983, 320 pp., illus. $29.95. The most comprehensive, thorough book yet published on American deer hunting.

American Duck Shooting, by George Bird Grinnell, Stackpole Books, Harrisburg, PA, 1991, 640 pp., illus. Paper covers. $19.95. First published in 1901 at the height of the author's career. Describes 50 species of waterfowl, and discusses hunting methods common at the turn of the century.

American Hunting and Fishing Books, 1800-1970, Volume 1, by Morris Heller, Nimrod and Piscator Press, Mesilla, NM, 1997, 220 pp., illus. A limited, numbered edition. $125.00. An up-to-date, profusely illustrated, annotated bibliography on American hunting and fishing books and booklets.

The Art of Super-Accurate Hunting with Scoped Rifles, by Don Judd, Wolfe Publishing Co., Prescott, AZ, 1996, 99 pp., illus. Paper covers. $14.95. The philosophy of super-accurate hunting and the rewards of making your shot a trophy.

Autumn Passages, Compiled by the editors of Ducks Unlimited Magazine, Willow Creek Press, Minocqua, WI, 1997, 320 pp. $27.50. An exceptional collection of duck hunting stories.

Awesome Antlers of North America, by Odie Sudbeck, HTW Publications, Seneca, KS, 1993, 150 pp., illus. $35.00. 500 world-class bucks in color and black and white. This book starts up where the Boone & Crockett recordbook leaves off.

Bare November Days, by George Bird Evans et al, Countrysport Press, Traverse City, MI, 1992, 136 pp., illus. $39.50. A new, original anthology, a tribute to ruffed grouse, king of upland birds.

Bear Attacks, by K. Etling, Safari Press, Long Beach, CA, 1998, 574 pp., illus. In 2 volumes. $80.00. Classic tales of dangerous North American bears.

The Bear Hunter's Century, by Paul Schullery, Stackpole Books, Harrisburg, PA, 1989, 240 pp., illus. $19.95. Thrilling tales of the bygone days of wilderness hunting.

The Best of Babcock, by Havilah Babcock, selected and with an introduction by Hugh Grey, The Gunnerman Press, Auburn Hills, MI, 1985, 262 pp., illus. $19.95. A treasury of memorable pieces, 21 of which have never before appeared in book form.

The Best of Nash Buckingham, by Nash Buckingham, selected, edited and annotated by George Bird Evans, Winchester Press, Piscataway, NJ, 1973, 320 pp., illus. $35.00. Thirty pieces that represent the very cream of Nash's output on his whole range of outdoor interests—upland shooting, duck hunting, even fishing.

The Best of Sheep Hunting, by John Batten, Amwell Press, Clinton, NJ, 1992, 616 pp., illus. $47.50. This "Memorial Edition" is a collection of 40 articles and appendices covering sheep hunting in the North American area of Canada, Alaska, the West and Midwest as well as Africa and Europe.

Better on a Rising Tide, by Tom Kelly, Lyons & Burford Publishers, New York, NY, 1995, 184 pp. $22.95. Tales of wild turkeys, turkey hunting and Southern folk.

Big Bucks the Benoit Way, by Bryce Towsley, Krause Publications Iola, WI, 1998, 208 pp., illus. $24.95. Secrets from America's first family of whitetail hunting.

Big December Canvasbacks, by Worth Mathewson, Sand Lake Press, Amity, OR, 1997, 171 pp., illus. By David Hagenbaumer. Limited, signed and numbered edition. $29.95. Duck hunting stories.

Big Woods, by William Faulkner, wilderness adventures, Gallatin Gateway, MT, 1998, 208 pp., illus. Slipcased, $60.00. A collection of Faulkner's best hunting stories that belongs in the library of every sportsman.

Birdhunter, by Richard S. Grozik, Safari Press, Huntington Beach, CA, 1998, 180 pp., illus. Limited, numbered and signed edition. Slipcased, $60.00. An entertaining salute to the closeness between man and his dog, man and his gun, and man and the great outdoors.

Bird Dog Days, Wingshooting Ways, by Archibald Rutledge, edited by Jim Casada, Wilderness Adventure Press, Gallatin Gateway, MT, 1998, 200 pp., illus. $35.00. One of the most popular and enduring outdoor writers of this century, the poet laureate of South Carolina.

Birds on the Horizon, by Stuart Williams, Countrysport Press, Traverse City, MI, 1993, 288 pp., illus. $49.50. Wingshooting adventures around the world.

Blacktail Trophy Tactics, by Boyd Iverson, Stoneydale Press, Stevensville, MI, 1992, 166 pp., illus. Paper covers. $14.95. A comprehensive analysis of blacktail deer habits, describing a deer's and man's use of scents, still hunting, tree techniques, etc.

Bowhunter's Digest, 3rd Edition, by Chuck Adams, DBI Books, a division of Krause Publications, Iola, WI, 1990, 288 pp., illus. Soft covers. $17.95. All-new edition covers all the necessary equipment and how to use it, plus the fine points on how to improve your skill.

THE HANDGUNNER'S LIBRARY

Bowhunter's Handbook, Expert Strategies and Techniques, by M.R. James with Fred Asbell, Dave Holt, Dwight Schuh & Dave Samuel, DBI Books, a division of Krause Publications, Iola, WI, 1997. 256 pp., illus. Paper covers. $19.95.
Tips from the top on taking your bowhunting skills to the next level.

The Buffalo Harvest, by Frank Mayer as told to Charles Roth, Pioneer Press, Union City, TN, 1995. 96 pp., illus. Paper covers. $7.50.
The story of a hide hunter during his buffalo hunting days on the plains.

Bugling for Elk, by Dwight Schuh, Stoneydale Press Publishing Co., Stevensville, MT, 1983. 162 pp., illus. $18.95.
A complete guide to early season elk hunting.

Call of the Quail: A Tribute to the Gentleman Game Bird, by Michael McIntosh, et al., Countrysport Press, Traverse City, MI, 1990. 175 pp., illus. $39.50.
A new anthology on quail hunting.

Calling All Elk, by Jim Zumbo, Cody, WY, 1989. 169 pp., illus. Paper covers. $14.95.
The only book on the subject of elk hunting that covers every aspect of elk vocalization.

Campfires and Game Trails: Hunting North American Big Game, by Craig Boddington, Winchester Press, Piscataway, NJ, 1985. 295 pp., illus. $23.95.
How to hunt North America's big game species.

Come October, by Gene Hill et al, Countrysport Press, Inc., Traverse City, MI, 1991. 176 pp., illus. $39.50.
A new and all-original anthology on the woodcock and woodcock hunting.

The Complete Guide to Bird Dog Training, by John R. Falk, Lyons & Burford, New York, NY, 1994. 288 pp., illus. $22.95.
The latest on live-game field training techniques using released quail and recall pens. A new chapter on the services available for entering field trials and other bird dog competitions.

The Complete Guide to Bowhunting Deer, by Chuck Adams, DBI Books, a division of Krause Publications, Iola, WI, 1984. 256 pp., illus. Paper covers. $16.95.
Plenty on equipment, bows, sights, quivers, arrows, clothes, lures and scents, stands and blinds, etc.

The Complete Guide to Game Care & Cookery, 3rd Edition, by Sam Fadala, DBI Books, a division of Krause Publications, Iola, WI, 1994. 320 pp., illus. Paper covers. $18.95.
Over 500 photos illustrating the care of wild game in the field and at home with a separate recipe section providing over 400 tested recipes.

Coveys and Singles: The Handbook of Quail Hunting, by Robert Gooch, A.S. Barnes, San Diego, CA, 1981. 196 pp., illus. $11.95.
The story of the quail in North America.

Coyote Hunting, by Phil Simonski, Stoneydale Press, Stevensville, MT, 1994. 126 pp., illus. Paper covers. $12.95.
Probably the most thorough "How-to-do-it" book on coyote hunting ever written.

Dabblers & Divers: A Duck Hunter's Book, compiled by the editors of Ducks Unlimited Magazine, Willow Creek Press, Minocqua, WI, 1997. 160 pp., illus. $39.95.
In-depth information from the editor of "Deer & Deer Hunting" magazine.

Dancers in the Sunset Sky, by Robert F. Jones, The Lyons Press, New York, NY, 1997. 192 pp., illus. $22.95.
The musings of a bird hunter.

Deer & Deer Hunting, by Al Hofacker, Krause Publications, Iola, WI, 1993. 208 pp., illus. $34.95.
Coffee-table volume packed full of how-to-information that will guide hunts for years to come.

Deer and Deer Hunting: The Serious Hunter's Guide, by Dr. Robert Wegner, Stackpole Books, Harrisburg, PA, 1984. 384 pp., illus. Paper covers. $18.95.
In-depth information from the editor of "Deer & Deer Hunting" magazine.
Major bibliography of English language books on deer and deer hunting from 1838-1984.

Deer and Deer Hunting Book 2, by Dr. Robert Wegner, Stackpole Books, Harrisburg, PA, 1987. 400 pp., illus. Paper covers. $18.95.
Strategies and tactics for the advanced hunter.

Deer and Deer Hunting, Book 3, by Dr. Robert Wegner, Stackpole Books, Harrisburg, PA, 1990. 368 pp., illus. $29.95.
This comprehensive volume covers natural history, deer hunting lore, profiles of deer hunters, and discussion of important issues facing deer hunters today.

Deer Hunter's Guide to Guns, Ammunition, and Equipment, by Edward A. Matunas, an Outdoor Life Book, distributed by Stackpole Books, Harrisburg, PA, 1983. 352 pp., illus. $24.95.
Where to hunt for North American deer. An authoritative guide that will help every deer hunter get maximum enjoyment and satisfaction from his sport.

The Deer Hunters: The Tactics, Lore, Legacy and Allure of American Deer Hunting, Edited by Patrick Durkin, Krause Publications, Iola, WI, 1997. 208 pp., illus. $29.95.
More than twenty years of research from America's top whitetail hunters, researchers, and photographers have gone in to the making of this book.

Deer Hunting, by R. Smith, Stackpole Books, Harrisburg, PA, 1978. 224 pp., illus. Paper covers. $14.95.
A professional guide leads the hunt for North America's most popular big game animal.

Deer Hunting Coast to Coast, by C. Boddington and R. Robb, Safari Press, Long Beach, CA, 1989. 248 pp., illus. $24.95.
Join the authors as they hunt whitetail deer in eastern woodlot, southern swamps, midwestern prairies, and western river bottom; mule deer in badland, deserts, and high alpine basins; blacktails in oak grasslands and coastal jungles.

Doves and Dove Shooting, by Byron W. Dalrymple, New Win Publishing, Inc., Hampton, NJ, 1992. 256 pp., illus. $17.95.
The author reveals in this classic book his penchant for observing, hunting, and photographing this elegantly fashioned bird.

Dove Hunting, by Charley Dickey, Galahad Books, NY, 1976. 112 pp., illus. $10.00.
This indispensable guide for hunters deals with equipment, techniques, types of dove shooting, hunting dogs, etc.

Dreaming the Lion, by Thomas McIntyre, Countrysport Press, Traverse City, MI, 1994. 309 pp., illus. $35.00.
Reflections on hunting, fishing, and a search for the wild. Twenty-three stories by *Sports Afield* editor, Tom McIntyre.

Drummer in the Woods, by Burton L. Spiller, Stackpole Books, Harrisburg, PA, 1990. 240 pp., illus. Soft covers. $16.95.
Twenty-one wonderful stories on grouse shooting by "the Poet Laureate of Grouse."

Duck Decoys and How to Rig Them, by Ralf Coykendall, revised by Ralf Coykendall, Jr., Nick Lyons Books, New York, NY, 1990. 137 pp., illus. Paper covers. $14.95.
Sage and practical advice on the art of decoying ducks and geese.

The Duck Hunter's Handbook, by Bob Hinman, revised, expanded, updated edition, Winchester Press, Piscataway, NJ, 1985. 288 pp., illus. $15.95.
The duck hunting book that has it all.

Eastern Upland Shooting, by Dr. Charles C. Norris, Countrysport Press, Traverse City, MI, 1990. 424 pp., illus. $29.50.
A new printing of this 1946 classic with a new, original Foreword by the author's friend and hunting companion, renowned author George Bird Evans.

Elk and Elk Hunting, by Hart Wixom, Stackpole Books, Harrisburg, PA, 1986. 288 pp., illus. $34.95.
Your practical guide to fundamentals and fine points of elk hunting.

Elk Hunting in the Northern Rockies, by Ed. Wolff, Stoneydale Press, Stevensville, MT, 1984. 162 pp., illus. $18.95.
Helpful information about hunting the premier elk country of the northern Rocky Mountain states—Wyoming, Montana and Idaho.

Elk Hunting with the Experts, by Bob Robb, Stoneydale Press, Stevensville, MT, 1992. 176 pp., illus. Paper covers. $15.95.
A complete guide to elk hunting in North America by America's top elk hunting expert.

Elk Rifles, Cartridges and Hunting Tactics, by Wayne van Zwoll, Larsen's Outdoor Publishing, Lakeland, FL, 1992. 414 pp., illus. $24.95.
The definitive work on which rifles and cartridges are proper for hunting elk plus the tactics for hunting them.

Encyclopedia of Deer, by G. Kenneth Whitehead, Safari Press, Huntington, CA, 1993. 704 pp., illus. $130.00.
This massive tome will be the reference work on deer for well into the next century.

Fair Chase, by Jim Rikhoff, Amwell Press, Clinton, NJ, 1984. 323 pp., illus. $25.00.
A collection of hunting experiences from the Arctic to Africa, Mongolia to Montana, taken from over 25 years of writing.

A Fall of Woodcock, by Tom Huggler, Countrysport Press, Selman, AL, 1997. 256 pp., illus. $39.00.
A book devoted to the woodcock and to those who await his return to their favorite coverts each autumn.

Firelight, by Burton L. Spiller, Gunnerman Press, Auburn Hills, MI, 1990. 196 pp., illus. $19.95.
Enjoyable tales of the outdoors and stalwart companions.

The Formidable Game, by John H. Batten, Amwell Press, Clinton, NJ, 1983. 264 pp., illus. $40.00.
Big game hunting in India, Africa and North America by a world famous hunter.

Fresh Looks at Deer Hunting, by Byron W. Dalrymple, New Win Publishing, Inc., Hampton, NJ, 1993. 288 pp., illus. $24.95.
Tips and techniques used throughout the pages of this latest work by Mr. Dalrymple whose name is synonymous with hunting proficiency.

From the Peace to the Fraser, by Prentis N. Gray, Boone and Crockett Club, Missoula, MT, 1995. 400 pp., illus. $49.95.
Newly discovered North American hunting and exploration journals from 1900 to 1930.

Fur Trapping in North America, by Steven Geary, Winchester Press, Piscataway, NJ, 1985. 160 pp., illus. Paper covers. $19.95.
A comprehensive guide to techniques and equipment, together with fascinating facts about fur bearers.

A Gallery of Waterfowl and Upland Birds, by Gene Hill, with illustrations by David Maass, Petersen Prints, Los Angeles, CA, 1978. 132 pp., illus. $44.95.
Gene Hill at his best. Liberally illustrated with 51 full-color reproductions of David Maass' finest paintings.

Game in the Desert Revisited, by Jack O'Connor, Amwell Press, Clinton, NJ, 1984. 306 pp., illus. $27.50.
Reprint of a Derrydale Press classic on hunting in the Southwest

THE HANDGUNNER'S LIBRARY

Getting the Most Out of Modern Waterfowling, by John O. Cartier, St. Martin's Press, NY, 1974, 396 pp., illus. $22.50.
The most comprehensive, up-to-date book on waterfowling imaginable.

Getting a Stand, by Miles Gilbert, Pioneer Press, Union City, TN, 1993, 204 pp., illus. Paper covers, $10.95.
An anthology of 18 short personal experiences by buffalo hunters of the late 1800s, specifically from 1870-1882.

Gordon MacQuarrie Trilogy: Stories of the Old Duck Hunters, by Gordon MacQuarrie, Willow Creek Press, Minocqua, WI, 1994, $49.00.
A slip-cased three volume set of masterpieces by one of America's finest outdoor writers.

The Grand Passage: A Chronicle of North American Waterfowling, by Gene Hill, et al., Countrysport Press, Traverse City, MI, 1990, 175 pp., illus. $39.50.
A new original anthology by renowned sporting authors on our world of waterfowling.

Grouse and Woodcock, A Gunner's Guide, by Don Johnson, Krause Publications, Iola, WI, 1995, 256 pp., illus. Paper covers, $14.95.
A cross-continental hunting guide.

Grouse of North America, by Tom Huggler, NorthWord Press, Inc, Minocqua, WI, 1990, 160 pp., illus. $29.95.
A cross-continental hunting guide.

Grouse Hunter's Guide, by Dennis Walrod, Stackpole Books, Harrisburg, PA, 1985, 192 pp., illus. $18.95.
Find out what you need in guns, ammo, equipment, dogs and terrain.

Gunning for Sea Ducks, by George Howard Gillelan, Tidewater Publishers, Centreville, MD, 1988, 144 pp., illus. $14.95.
A book that introduces you to a practically untouched arena of waterfowling.

Heartland Trophy Whitetails, by Odie Sudbeck, HTW Publications, Seneca, KS, 1992, 130 pp., illus. $35.00.
A completely revised and expanded edition which includes over 500 photos of Boone & Crockett class whitetail, major mulies and unusual racks.

The Heck with Moose Hunting, by Jim Zumbo, Wapiti Valley Publishing Co., Cody, WY, 1996, 199 pp., illus. $17.95.
Jim's hunts around the continent including encounters with moose, caribou, sheep, antelope and mountain goats.

High Pressure Elk Hunting, by Mike Lapinski, Stoneydale Press Publishing Co., Stevensville, MT, 1996, 192 pp., illus. $19.95.
The secrets of hunting educated elk revealed.

Hill Country, by Gene Hill, Countrysport Press, Traverse City, MI, 1996, 180 pp., illus. $25.00.
Stories about hunting, fishing, dogs and guns.

Home from the Hill, by Fred Webb, Safari Press, Huntington Beach, CA, 1997, 283 pp., Limited edition, signed and numbered. In a slipcase. $50.00.
The story of a big-game guide in the Canadian wilderness.

Horns in the High Country, by Andy Russell, Alfred A. Knopf, NY, 1973, 259 pp., illus. Paper covers, $12.95.
A many-sided view of wild sheep and their natural world.

How to Hunt, by Dave Bowring, Winchester Press, Piscataway, NJ, 1982, 208 pp., illus. Paper covers, $10.95; cloth, $15.00.
An outdoor book that will appeal to every person who spends time in the field—or who wishes he could.

A Hunter's Road, by Jim Fergus, Henry Holt & Co., NY, 1992, 290 pp., $22.50.
A journey with gun and dog across the American uplands.

Hunt Alaska Now: Self-Guiding for Trophy Moose & Caribou, by Dennis W. Confer, Wily Ventures, Anchorage, AK, 1997, 309 pp., illus. Paper covers, $26.95.
How to plan affordable, successfull, safe hunts you can do yourself.

Hunt High for Rocky Mountain Goats, Bighorn Sheep, Chamois & Tahr, by Duncan Gilchrist, Stoneydale Press, Stevensville, MT, 1992, 192 pp., illus. Paper covers, $19.95.
The source book for hunting mountain goats.

The Hunters and the Hunted, by George Laycock, Outdoor Life Books, New York, NY, 1990, 280 pp., illus. $34.95.
The pursuit of game in America from Indian times to the present.

A Hunter's Fireside Book, by Gene Hill, Winchester Press, Piscataway, NJ, 1972, 192 pp., illus. $16.95.

The Hunter's World, by Charles F. Waterman, Winchester Press, Piscataway, NJ, 1983, 250 pp., illus. $29.95.
A classic.

The Hunter's Shooting Guide, by Jack O'Connor, Outdoor Life Books, New York, NY, 1982, 176 pp., illus. Paper covers, $5.95.
A classic covering rifles, cartridges, shooting techniques for shotguns/rifles/handguns.

Hunting Adventure of Me and Joe, by Walt Prothero, Safari Press, Huntington Beach, CA, 1995, 220 pp., illus. $22.50.
A collection of the author's best and favorite stories.

Hunting America's Game Animals and Birds, by Robert Elman and George Peper, Winchester Press, Piscataway, NJ, 1975, 368 pp., illus. $16.95.
A how-to, where-to, when-to guide—by 40 top experts—covering the continent's big, small, upland game and waterfowl.

Hunting Ducks and Geese, by Steven Smith, Stackpole Books, Harrisburg, PA, 1984, 160 pp., illus. $19.95.
Hard facts, good bets, and serious advice from a duck hunter you can trust.

Hunting for Handgunners, by Larry Kelly and J.D. Jones, DBI Books, a division of Krause Publications, Iola, WI, 1990, 256 pp., illus. Soft covers, $16.95.
A definitive work on an increasingly popular sport.

Hunting in Many Lands, edited by Theodore Roosevelt and George Bird Grinnell, et al., Boone & Crockett Club, Dumphries, VA, 1990, 447 pp., illus. $40.00.
A limited edition reprinting of the original Boone & Crockett Club 1895 printing.

Hunting Mature Bucks, by Larry L. Weishuhn, Krause Publications, Iola, WI, 1995, 256 pp., illus. Paper covers, $14.95.
One of North America's top white-tailed deer authorities shares his expertise on hunting those big, smart and elusive bucks.

Hunting Open-Country Mule Deer, by Dwight Schuh, Sage Press, Nampa, ID, 1989, 180 pp., illus. $18.95.
A guide taking the hunter through every step of the hunting/marketing process.

Hunting Predators for Hides and Profits, by Wilf E. Pyle, Stoeger Publishing Co., So. Hackensack, NJ, 1985, 224 pp., illus. Paper covers, $11.95.
The author takes the hunter through every step of the hunting/marketing process.

Hunting the American Wild Turkey, by Dave Harbour, Stackpole Books, Harrisburg, PA, 1975, 256 pp., illus. $24.95.
The techniques and tactics of hunting North America's largest, and most popular, woodland game bird.

Hunting the Rockies, Home of the Giants, by Kirk Darner, Marceline, MO, 1996, 291 pp., illus. $25.00.
Understand how and where to hunt Western game in the Rockies.

Hunting the Sun, by Ted Nelson Lundrigan, Countrysport Press, Selma, AL, 1997, 240 pp., illus. $30.00.
One of the best books on grouse and woodcock ever published.

Hunting Trips in North America, by F.C. Selous, Wolfe Publishing Co, Prescott, AZ, 1988, 395 pp., illus. $52.00.
A limited edition reprint. Coverage of caribou, moose and other big game hunting in virgin wilds.

Hunting Trophy Deer, by John Wootters, The Lyons Press, New York, NY, 1997, 272 pp., illus. $24.95.
A revised edition of the definitive manual for identifying, scouting, and successfully hunting a deer of a lifetime.

Hunting Trophy Whitetails, by David Morris, Stoneydale Press, Stevensville, MT, 1993, 483 pp., illus. $29.95.
This is one of the best whitetail books published in the last two decades.

Hunting Upland Birds, by Charles F. Waterman, Countrysport Press, Selma, AL, 1997, 220 pp., illus. $30.00.
Originally published a quarter of a century ago, this classic has been newly updated with the latest information for today's wingshooter.

Hunting Western Deer, by Jim and Wes Brown, Stoneydale Press, Stevensville, MT, 1994, 174 pp., illus. Paper covers, $14.95.
A pair of expert Oregon hunters provide insight into hunting mule deer and blacktail deer in the western states.

Hunting Wild Turkeys in the West, by John Higley, Stoneydale Press, Stevensville, MT, 1992, 154 pp., illus. Paper covers, $12.95.
Covers the basics of calling, locating and hunting turkeys in the western states.

Hunting with the Twenty-two, by Charles Singer Landis, R&R Books, Livonia, NY, 1994, 429 pp., illus. $45.00.
A miscellany of articles touching on the hunting and shooting of small game.

I Don't Want to Shoot an Elephant, by Havilah Babcock, The Gunnerman Press, Auburn Hills, MI, 1985, 184 pp., illus. $19.95.
Eighteen delightful stories that will enthrall the upland gunner for many pleasureable hours.

In Search of the Buffalo, by Charles G. Anderson, Pioneer Press, Union City, TN, 1996, 144 pp., illus. Paper covers, $13.95.
The primary study of the life of J. Wright Mooar, one of the few hunters fortunate enough to kill a white buffalo.

In Search of the Wild Turkey, by Bob Gooch, Greatlakes Living Press, Ltd., Waukegan, IL, 1978, 182 pp., illus. $9.95.
A state-by-state guide to wild turkey hot spots, with tips on gear and methods for bagging your bird.

Indian Hunts and Indian Hunters of the Old West, by Dr. Frank C. Hibben, Safari Press, Long Beach, CA, 1989, 228 pp., illus. $24.95.
Tales of some of the most famous American Indian hunters of the Old West as told to the author by an old Navajo hunter.

Jack O'Connor's Gun Book, by Jack O'Connor, Wolfe Publishing Company, Prescott, AZ, 1992, 208 pp. Hardcover. $26.00.
Jack O'Connor imparts a cross-section of his knowledge on guns and hunting. Brings back some of his writings that have here-to-fore been lost.

Jaybirds Go to Hell on Friday, by Havilah Babcock, The Gunnerman Press, Auburn Hills, MI, 1985, 149 pp., illus. $19.95.

Jim Dougherty's Guide to Bowhunting Deer, by Jim Dougherty, DBI Books, a division of Krause Publications, Iola, WI, 1992, 256 pp., illus. Paper covers, $17.95.
Dougherty sets down some important guidelines for bowhunting and bowhunting equipment.

Last Casts and Stolen Hunts, edited by Jim Casada and Chuck Wechsler, Countrysport Press, Traverse City, MI, 1994, 270 pp., illus. $29.95.
Sixteen jewels that reestablish the lost art of good old-fashioned yarn telling.

A Listening Walk...and Other Stories, by Jim Corbett, Jack O'Connor, Archibald Rutledge and others, NJ, 1965, 208 pp., illus. $15.95.
Vintage Hill. Over 60 stories.

THE HANDGUNNER'S LIBRARY

Longbows in the Far North, by E. Donnall Thomas, Jr. Stackpole Books, Mechanicsburg, PA, 1994. 200 pp., illus. $18.95.
An archer's adventures in Alaska and Siberia.

The Longwalkers: 25 Years of Tracking the Northern Cougar, by Jerry A. Lewis, Wolfe Publishing Co., Prescott, AZ, 1996. 140 pp., illus. Paper covers. $24.95.
Trek the snow-covered mountain forests of Idaho, Montana, British Columbia, and Alberta with the author as he follows cougars/mountain lions on foot, guided by his keen hounds.

Mammoth Monarchs of North America, by Odie Sudbeck, HTW Publications, Seneca, KA, 1995. 288 pp., illus. $35.00.
This book reveals eye-opening big buck secrets.

Matching the Gun to the Game, by Clair Rees, Winchester Press, Piscataway, NJ, 1982. 272 pp., illus. $17.95.
Covers selection and use of handguns, blackpowder firearms for hunting, matching rifle type to the hunter, calibers for multiple use, tailoring factory loads to the game.

Measuring and Scoring North American Big Game Trophies, by Wm. H. Nesbitt and Philip L. Wright, The Boone and Crockett Club, Alexandria, VA, 1986. 176 pp., illus. $15.00.
The Boone and Crockett Club official scoring system, with tips for trophy evaluation.

Meditation on Hunting, by Jose Ortega y Gasset, Wilderness Adventures Press, Bozeman, MT, 1996. 140 pp., illus. In a slipcase. $60.00.
The classic work on the philosophy of hunting.

Mixed Bag, by Jim Rikhoff, National Rifle Association of America, Wash., DC, 1981. 284 pp., illus. Paper covers. $9.95.
Reminiscences of a master raconteur.

Modern Pheasant Hunting, by Steve Grooms, Stackpole Books, Harrisburg, PA, 1982. 224 pp., illus. Paper covers. $10.95.
New look at pheasants and hunters from an experienced hunter who respects this splendid gamebird.

Modern Waterfowl Guns and Gunning, by Don Zutz, Stoeger Publishing Co., So. Hackensack, NJ, 1985. 224 pp., illus. Paper covers. $11.95.
Up-to-date information on the fast-changing world of waterfowl guns and loads.

Montana—Land of Giant Rams, by Duncan Gilchrist, Stoneydale Press Publishing Co., Stevensville, MT, 1990. 208 pp., illus. $19.95.
Latest information on Montana bighorn sheep and why so many Montana bighorn rams are growing to trophy size.

Montana—Land of Giant Rams, Volume 2, by Duncan Gilchrist, Outdoor Expeditions and Books, Corvallis, MT, 1992. 208 pp., illus. $34.95.
The reader will find stories of how many of the top-scoring trophies were taken.

More and Better Pheasant Hunting, by Steve Smith, Winchester Press, Piscataway, NJ, 1986. 192 pp., illus. $15.95.
Complete, fully illustrated, expert coverage of the bird itself, the dogs, the hunt, the guns, and the best places to hunt.

More Grouse Feathers, by Burton L. Spiller, Crown Publ., NY, 1972. 238 pp., illus. $25.00.
Facsimile of the original Derrydale Press issue of 1938. Guns and dogs, the habits and shooting of grouse, woodcock, ducks, etc. Illus. by Lynn Bogue Hunt.

More Tracks: 78 Years of Mountains, People & Happiness, by Howard Copenhaver, Stoneydale Press, Stevensville, MT, 1992. 150 pp., illus. $18.95.
A collection of stories by one of the back country's best storytellers about the people who shared with Howard his great adventure in the high places and wild Montana country.

Moss, Mallards and Mules, by Robert Brister, Countrysport Books, Selma, AL, 1998. 216 pp., illustrated by David Maass. $30.00.
Twenty-seven short stories on hunting and fishing on the Gulf Coast.

Mostly Huntin', by Bill Jordan, Everett Publishing Co., Bossier City, LA, 1987. 254 pp., illus. $21.95.
Jordan's hunting adventures in North America, Africa, Australia, South America and Mexico.

Mostly Tailfeathers, by Gene Hill, Winchester Press, Piscataway, NJ, 1975. 192 pp., illus. $15.95.
An interesting, general book about bird hunting.

"Mr. Buck": The Autobiography of Nash Buckingham, by Nash Buckingham, Countrysport Press, Traverse City, MI, 1990. 288 pp., illus. $39.50.
A lifetime of shooting, hunting, dogs, guns, and Nash's reflections on the sporting life, along with previously unknown pictures and stories written especially for this book.

Mule Deer: Hunting Today's Trophies, by Tom Carpenter and Jim Van Norman, Krause Publications, Iola, WI, 1998. 256 pp., illustrated. Paper covers. $19.95.
A tribute to both the deer and the people who hunt them. Includes info on where to look for big deer, prime mule deer habitat and effective weapons for the hunt.

Murry Burnham's Hunting Secrets, by Murry Burnham with Russell Tinsley, Winchester Press, Piscataway, NJ, 1984. 244 pp., illus. $17.95.
One of the great hunters of our time gives the reasons for his success in the field.

My Health is Better in November, by Havilah Babcock, University of S. Carolina Press, Columbia, SC, 1985. 284 pp., illus. $19.95.
Adventures in the field set in the plantation country and backwater streams of SC.

North American Big Game Animals, by Byron W. Dalrymple and Erwin Bauer, Outdoor Life Books/Stackpole Books, Harrisburg, PA, 1985. 258 pp., illus. $29.95.
Complete illustrated natural histories. Habitat, movements, breeding, birth and development, signs, and hunting.

North American Elk: Ecology and Management, edited by Jack Ward Thomas and Dale E. Toweill, Stackpole Books, Harrisburg, PA, 1982. 576 pp., illus. $39.95.
The definitive, exhaustive, classic work on the North American elk.

The North American Waterfowler, by Paul S. Bernsen, Superior Publ. Co., Seattle, WA, 1972. 206 pp. Paper covers. $9.95.
The complete inside and outside story of duck and goose shooting. Big and colorful, illustrations by Les Kouba.

Of Bears and Man, by Mike Cramond, University of Oklahoma Press, Norman, OK, 1986. 433 pp., illus. $29.95.
The author's lifetime association with bears of North America. Interviews with survivors of bear attacks.

The Old Man and the Boy, by Robert Ruark, Henry Holt & Co., New York, NY, 303 pp., illus. $24.95.
A timeless classic, telling the story of a remarkable friendship between a young boy and his grandfather as they hunt and fish together.

The Old Man's Boy Grows Older, by Robert Ruark, Henry Holt & Co., Inc., New York, NY, 1993. 300 pp., illus. $24.95.
The heartwarming sequel to the best-selling *The Old Man and the Boy.*

Old Wildfowling Tales, Volume 2, edited by Worth Mathewson, Sand Lake Press, Amity, OR, 1996. 240 pp. $21.95.
A collection of duck and geese hunting stories based around accounts from the past.

Once Upon a Time, by Nash Buckingham, Beaver Dam Press, Brentwood, TN, 1995. 170 pp., illus. $29.50.
Fifty or so stories by two good sports.

161 Waterfowling Secrets, edited by Matt Young, Willow Creek Press, Minocqua, WI, 1997. 78 pp., illus. Paper covers. $10.95.
Time-honored, field-tested waterfowling tips and advice.

The Only Good Bear is a Dead Bear, by Jeanette Hortick Prodgers, Falcon Press, Helena, MT, 1986. 204 pp. Paper covers. $12.50.
A collection of the West's best bear stories.

Outdoor Pastimes of an American Hunter, by Theodore Roosevelt, Stackpole Books, Mechanicsburg, PA, 1994. 480 pp., illus. Paper covers. $18.95.
Stories of hunting big game in the West and notes about animals pursued and observed.

Outdoor Yarns & Outright Lies, by Gene Hill and Steve Smith, Stackpole Books, Harrisburg, PA, 1984. 168 pp., illus. $18.95.
Fifty or so stories by two good sports.

The Outlaw Gunner, by Harry M. Walsh, Tidewater Publishers, Cambridge, MD, 1973. 178 pp., illus. $22.95.
A colorful story of market gunning in both its legal and illegal phases.

Passing of a Good Time, by Gene Hill, Countrysport Press, Traverse City, MI, 1996. 200 pp., illus. $25.00.
Filled with insights and observations of guns, dogs and fly rods that make Gene Hill a master essayist.

Pear Flat Philosophies, by Larry Weishuhn, Safari Press, Huntington Beach, CA, 1995. 234 pp., illus. $24.95.
The author describes his more lighthearted adventures and funny anecdotes while out hunting.

Pheasant Days, by Chris Dorsey, Voyageur Press, Stillwater, MN, 1992. 233 pp., illus. $24.95.
The definitive resource on ringnecks. Includes everything from basic hunting techniques to the life cycle of the bird.

Pheasant Hunter's Harvest, by Steve Grooms, Lyons & Burford Publishers, New York, NY, 1990. 180 pp. $22.95.
A celebration of pheasant, pheasant dogs and pheasant hunting. Practical advice from a passionate hunter.

Pheasant Tales, by Gene Hill et al, Countrysport Press, Traverse City, MI, 1996. 202 pp., illus. $39.00.
Charley Waterman, Michael McIntosh and Phil Bourjaily join the author to tell some of the stories that illustrate why the pheasant is America's favorite game bird.

Pheasants of the Mind, by Datus Proper, Wilderness Adventures Press, Bozeman, MT, 1994. 154 pp., illus. $25.00.
No single title sums up the life of the solitary pheasant hunter like this masterful work.

Pinnell and Talifson: Last of the Great Brown Bear Men, by Marvin H. Clark, Jr., Great Northwest Publishing and Distributing Co., Spokane, WA, 19880. 224 pp., Illus. $39.95.
The story of these famous Alaskan guides and some of the record bears taken by both of them.

Predator Calling with Gerry Blair, by Gerry Blair, Krause Publications, Iola, WI, 1996. 208 pp., illus. Paper covers. $14.95.
Time-tested secrets lure predators closer to your camera or gun.

Proven Whitetail Tactics, by Greg Miller, Krause Publications, Iola, WI, 1997. 224 pp., illus. Paper covers. $19.95.
Proven tactics for scouting, calling and still-hunting whitetail.

Quail Hunting in America, by Tom Huggler, Stackpole Books, Harrisburg, PA, 1987. 288 pp., illus. $19.95.
Tactics for finding and taking bobwhite, valleys, Gambel's, Mountain, scaled-blue, and Mearn's quail by season and habitat.

Quest for Dall Rams, by Duncan Gilchrist, Outdoor Expeditions and Books, Corvallis, MT, 1997. 224 pp., illus. Limited numbered edition. $34.95.
The most complete book of Dall sheep ever written. Covers information on Alaska and provinces with Dall sheep and explains hunting techniques, equipment, etc.

Quest for Giant Bighorns, by Duncan Gilchrist, Outdoor Expeditions and Books, Corvallis, MT, 1994. 224 pp., illus. Paper covers. $19.95.
How some of the most successful sheep hunters hunt and how some of the best bighorns were taken.

REFERENCE

THE HANDGUNNER'S LIBRARY

Radical Elk Hunting Strategies, by Mike Lapinski, Stoneydale Press Publishing Co., Stevensville, MT, 1988, 161 pp., illus. $18.95. Secrets of calling elk in close.

Records of North American Big Game 1932, by Prentis N. Grey, Boone and Crockett Club, Dumfries, VA, 1988, 178 pp., illus. $79.95. A reprint of the book that started the Club's record keeping for native North American big game.

Records of North American Caribou and Moose, Craig Boddington et al, The Boone & Crockett Club, Missoula, MT, 1997, 250 pp., illus. $24.95. More than 1,800 caribou listings, and more than 1,500 moose listings, organized by the state or Canadian province where they were taken.

Records of North American Elk and Mule Deer, 2nd Edition, edited by Jack and Susan Reneau, Boone & Crockett Club, Missoula, MT, 1996, 360 pp., illus. Paper cover, $18.95; hardcover, $24.95. Updated and expanded edition featuring more than 150 trophy, field and historical photos of the finest elk and mule deer trophies ever recorded.

Records of North American Sheep, Rocky Mountain Goats and Pronghorn edited by Jack and Susan Reneau, Boone & Crockett Club, Missoula, MT, 1996, 400 pp., illus. Paper cover, $18.95; hardcover, $24.95. The first B&C Club records book featuring all 3941 accepted wild sheep, Rocky Mountain goats and pronghorn trophies.

The Rifles, the Cartridges, and the Game, by Clay Harvey, Stackpole Books, Harrisburg, PA, 1991, 254 pp., illus. $32.95. A complete collection of previously unpublished magazine articles in book form by this gifted outdoor writer.

Ringneck! Pheasants & Pheasant Hunting, by Ted Janes, Crown Publ., NY, 1975, 120 pp., illus. $15.95. A thorough study of one of our more popular game birds.

Ruffed Grouse, edited by Sally Atwater and Judith Schnell, Stackpole Books, Harrisburg, PA, 1989, 370 pp., illus. $59.95. Everything you ever wanted to know about the ruffed grouse. More than 25 wildlife professionals provided in-depth information on every aspect of this popular game bird's life. Lavishly illustrated with over 300 full-color photos.

The Russell Annabel Adventure Series, by Russell Anabel, Safari Press, Huntington Beach, CA: Vol. 1, Alaskan Adventure, The Early Years, $35.00, Vol. 2, Adventure is My Business, 1951-1955, $35.00, Vol. 3, Adventure is in My Blood, 1957-1964, $35.00, Vol. 4, High Road to Adventure, 1964-1970, $35.00, Vol. 5, The Way We Were, 1970-1979, $35.00.

The Season, by Tom Kelly, Lyons & Burford, New York, NY, 1997, 160 pp., illus. $22.95. The delight and challenges of a turkey hunter's Spring season.

Secret Strategies from North America's Top Whitetail Hunters, compiled by Nick Sisley, Krause Publications, Iola, WI, 1995, 256 pp., illus. Paper covers, $14.95. Bow and gun hunters share their success stories.

Sheep Hunting in Alaska—The Dall Sheep Hunter's Guide, by Tony Russ, Outdoor Expeditions and Books, Corvallis, MT, 1994, 160 pp., illus. Paper covers, $19.95. A how-to guide for the Dall sheep hunter.

Shorebirds: The Birds, The Hunters, The Decoys, by John M. Levinson & Somers G. Headley, Tidewater Publishers, Centreville, MD, 1991, 160 pp., illus. $49.95. A thorough study of shorebirds and the decoys used to hunt them. Photographs of more than 200 of the decoys created by prominent carvers are shown.

Shots at Big Game, by Craig Boddington, Stackpole Books, Harrisburg, PA, 1989, 198 pp., illus. $24.95. How to shoot a rifle accurately under hunting conditions.

Some Bears Kill: True-Life Tales of Terror, by Larry Kanuit, Safari Press, Huntington Beach, CA, 1997, 313 pp., illus. $24.95. A collection of 38 stories as told by the victims, and in the case of fatality, recounted by the author from institutional records, episodes involve all three species of North American bears.

Southern Deer & Deer Hunting, by Larry Weishuhn and Bill Bynum, Krause Publications, Iola, WI, 1995, 256 pp., illus. Paper covers, $14.95. Mount a trophy southern whitetail on your wall with this firsthand account of stalking big bucks below the Mason-Dixon line.

Spring Gobbler Fever, by Michael Hanback, Krause Publications, Iola, WI, 1996, 256 pp., illus. Paper covers. $15.95. Your complete guide to spring turkey hunting.

Spirit of the Wilderness, Compiled by Theodore J. Holsten, Jr., Susan C. Reneau and Jack Reneau, the Boone & Crockett Club, Missoula, MT, 1997 300 pp., illus. $29.95. Stalking wild sheep, tracking a trophy cougar, hiking the back country of British Columbia, fishing for striped bass and coming face-to-face with a grizzly bear are some of the adventures found in this book.

Stand Hunting for Whitetails, by Richard P. Smith, Krause Publications, Iola, WI, 1996, 256 pp., illus. Paper covers. $14.95. The author explains the tricks and strategies for successful stand hunting.

Successful Goose Hunting, by Charles L. Cadieux, Stone Wall Press, Inc, Washington, DC, 1986, 223 pp., illus. $24.95. Here is a complete book on modern goose hunting by a lifetime waterfowler and professional wildlifer.

The Sultan of Spring: A Hunter's Odyssey Through the World of the Wild Turkey, by Bob Saile, The Lyons Press, New York, NY, 1998, 176 pp., illus. $22.95. A literary salute to the magic and mysticism of spring turkey hunting.

Taking Big Bucks, by Ed Wolff, Stoneydale Press, Stevensville, MT, 1987, 169 pp., illus. $18.95. Solving the whitetail riddle.

Taking Chances in the High Country, compiled and with an introduction by Jim Rikhoff, The Amwell Press, Clinton, NJ, 1995, 411 pp., illus. In a slipcase. $85.00. An anthology by some thirty stories by different authors on hunting sheep in the high country.

Taking More Birds, by Dan Carlisle and Dolph Adams, Lyons & Burford Publishers, New York, NY, 1993, 160 pp., illus. Paper covers, $15.95. A practical handbook for success at Sporting Clays and wing shooting.

Tales of Alaska's Big Bears, by Jim Rearden, Wolfe Publishing Co, Prescott, AZ, 1989, 125 pp., illus. Soft covers, $12.95. A collection of bear yarns covering nearly three-quarters of a century.

Tales of Quails 'n Such, by Havilah Babcock, University of S. Carolina Press, Columbia, SC, 1985, 237 pp., illus. $19.95. A group of hunting stories, told in informal style, on field experiences in the South in quest of small game.

Tears and Laughter, by Gene Hill, Countrysport Press, Traverse City, MI, 1996, 176 pp., illus. $25.00. In twenty-six stories, Gene Hill explores the ancient and honored bond between man and dog.

Tenth Legion, by Tom Kelly, the Lyons Press, New York, NY, 1998, 128 pp., illus. $18.95. The classic work on that frustrating, yet wonderful sport of turkey hunting.

They Left Their Tracks, by Howard Copenhaver, Stoneydale Press Publishing Co, Stevensville, MT, 1990, 190 pp., illus. $18.95. Recollections of 60 years as an outfitter in the Bob Marshall Wilderness.

Timberdoodle, by Frank Woolner, Nick Lyons Books, N. Y., NY, 1987, 168 pp., illus. $18.95. The classic guide to woodcock and woodcock hunting.

Timberdoodle Tales, by T. Waters, Safari Press, Inc, Huntington Beach, CA, 1997, 220 pp., illus. $30.00. A fresh appreciation of this captivating bird and the ethics of its hunt.

Timberdoodle Tales: Adventures of a Minnesota Woodcock Hunter, Safari Press, Huntington Beach, CA, 1997, 220 pp., illus. $35.00.

To Heck with Moose Hunting, by Jim Zumbo, Wapiti Publishing Co., Cody, WY, 1996, 199 pp., illus. $17.95. Jim's hunts around the continent and even an African adventure.

Trail and Campfire, edited by George Bird Grinnel and Theodore Roosevelt, The Boone and Crockett Club, Dumfries, VA, 1989, 357 pp., illus. $39.50. Reprint of the Boone and Crockett Club's 3rd book published in 1897.

Trailing a Bear, by Robert S. Munger, The Munger Foundation, Albion, MI, 1997, 352 pp., illus. Paper covers, $19.95. An exciting and humorous account of hunting with legendary archer Fred Bear.

The Trickiest Thing in Feathers, by Corey Ford; compiled and edited by Laurie Morrow and illustrated by Christopher Smith, Wilderness Adventures, Gallatin Gateway, MT, 1998, 208 pp., illus. $29.95. Here is a collection of Corey Ford's best wing-shooting stories, many of them previously unpublished.

Trophy Mule Deer: Finding & Evaluating Your Trophy, by Lance Stapleton, Outdoor Experiences Unlimited, Salem, OR, 1993, 290 pp., illus. Paper covers. The most comprehensive reference book on mule deer.

The Turkey Hunter's Book, by John M. McDaniel, Amwell Press, Clinton, NJ, 1980, 147 pp., illus. Paper covers, $11.95. One of the most original turkey hunting books to be published in many years.

Turkey Hunter's Digest, Revised Edition, by Dwain Bland, DBI Books, a division of Krause Publications, Iola, WI, 1994, 256 pp., illus. Paper covers, $17.95. A no-nonsense approach to hunting all five sub-species of the North American wild turkey that make up the Royal Grand Slam.

Turkey Hunting with Gerry Blair, by Gerry Blair, Krause Publications, Iola, WI, 1993, 280 pp., illus $19.95. Novice and veteran turkey hunters alike will enjoy this complete examination of the varied wild turkey subspecies, their environments, equipment needed to pursue them and the tactics to outwit them.

The Upland Equation: A Modern Bird-Hunter's Code, by Charles Fergus, Lyons & Burford Publishers, New York, NY, 1996, 86 pp., illus. $18.00. A book that deserves space in every sportsman's library. Observations based on firsthand experience.

The Upland Gunner's Book, edited by George Bird Evans, The Amwell Press, Clinton, NJ, 1985, 263 pp., illus. In slipcase. $27.50. An anthology of the finest stories ever written on the sport of upland game hunting.

Upland Tales, by Worth Mathewson (Ed.), Sand Lake Press, Amity, OR, 1996, 271 pp., illus. $21.95. A collection of articles on grouse, snipe and quail.

Varmint and Small Game Rifles and Cartridges, by various authors, Wolfe Publishing Co., Prescott, AZ, 1993, 228 pp., illus. Paper covers, $26.00. This is a collection of reprints of articles originally appearing in Wolfe's Rifle and Handloader magazines from 1966 through 1990.

Waterfowling Horizons: Shooting Ducks and Geese in the 21st Century, by Chris and Jason Smith, Wilderness Adventures, Gallatin Gateway, MT, 1998, 320 pp., illus. $49.95. A compendium of the very latest in everything for the duck and goose hunter today.

Waterfowling These Past 50 Years, Especially Brant, by David Hagerbaumer, Sand Lake Press, Amity, OR, 1998, 182 pp., illustrated. $35.00. The author's autobiography from the time he mustered out of the Marines in 1946 to the present day. Dave has done 209 pencil drawings, plus a color frontispiece for the book.

THE HANDGUNNER'S LIBRARY

Wegner's Bibliography on Dear and Deer Hunting, by Robert Wegner, St. Hubert's Press, Deforest, WI, 1993. 333 pp., 16 full-page illustrations. $45.00.
A comprehensive annotated compilation of books in English pertaining to deer and their hunting 1413-1991.

Western Hunting Guide, by Mike Lapinski, Stoneydale Press Publishing Co., Stevensville, MT, 1989. 168 pp., illus. $18.95.
A complete where-to-go and how-to-do-it guide to Western hunting.

Whispering Wings of Autumn, by Gene Hill and Steve Smith, Wilderness Adventures Press, Bozeman, MT, 1994. 150 pp., illus. $29.00.
Hill and Smith, masters of hunting literature, treat the reader to the best stories of grouse and woodcock hunting.

Whitetail: Behavior Through the Seasons, by Charles J. Alsheimer, Krause Publications, Iola, WI, 1996. 208 pp., illus. $34.95.
In-depth coverage of whitetail behavior presented through striking portraits of the whitetail in every season.

Whitetail: The Ultimate Challenge, by Charles J. Alsheimer, Krause Publications, Iola, WI, 1995. 228 pp., illus. Paper covers. $14.95.
Learn deer hunting's most intriguing secrets—fooling deer using decoys, scents and calls—from America's premier authority.

Wildfowlers Season, by Chris Dorsey, Lyons & Burford Publishers, New York, NY, 1998. 224 pp., illus. $37.95.
Modern methods for a classic sport.

The Wild Turkey Book, edited and with special commentary by J. Wayne Fears. Amwell Press, Clinton, NJ, 1982. 303 pp., illus. $22.50.
An anthology of the finest stories on wild turkey ever assembled under one cover.

The Wilderness Hunter, by Theodore Roosevelt, Wolfe Publishing Co., Prescott, AZ, 1994. 200 pp., illus. $25.00.
Reprint of a classic by one of America's most famous big game hunters.

Wildfowling Tales 1888-1913, Volume One, edited by Worth Mathewson, Sand Lake Press, Amity, OR, 1998. 186 pp., illustrated by David Hagerbaumer. $22.50.
A collection of some of the best accounts from our literary heritage.

Windward Crossings: A Treasury of Original Waterfowling Tales, edited and with a foreword by Chuck Petrie et al, Willow Creek Press, Minocqua, WI, 1998. $35.00.
An illustrated, modern anthology of previously unpublished waterfowl hunting (fiction and creative non-fiction) stories by America's finest outdoor journalists.

Wings of Thunder: New Grouse Hunting Revisited, by Steven Mulak, Countrysport Books, Selma, AL, 1998. 168 pp. illustrated. $30.00.
The author examines every aspect of New England grouse hunting as it is today - the bird and its habits, the hunter and his dog, guns and loads, shooting and hunting techniques, practice on clay targets, clothing and equipment.

Wings for the Heart, by Jerry A. Lewis, West River Press, Corvallis, MT, 1991. 324 pp., illus. Paper covers. $14.95.
A delightful book on hunting Montana's upland birds and waterfowl.

Wisconsin Hunting, by Brian Lovett, Krause Publications, Iola, WI, 1997. 208 pp., illus. Paper covers. $16.95.
A comprehensive guide to Wisconsin's public hunting lands.

The Woodchuck Hunter, by Paul C. Estey, R&R Books, Livonia, NY, 1994. 135 pp., illus. $25.00.
This book contains information on woodchuck equipment, the rifle, telescopic sights and includes interesting stories.

Woodcock Shooting, by Steve Smith, Stackpole Books, Inc., Harrisburg, PA, 1988. 142 pp., illus. $16.95.
A definitive book on woodcock hunting and the characteristics of a good woodcock dog.

World Record Whitetail: The Hanson Buck Story, by Milo Hanson with Ian McMurchy, Krause Publications, Iola, WI, 1995. 144 pp., illus. Paper covers. $9.95.
How do you top a deer hunting record that stood for 80 years? Milo Hanson shares in his firsthand account of bagging the largest whitetail ever scored in the history of B&C measurements.

World Record Whitetails, by Gordon Whittington, Safari Press Books, Inc., Huntington Beach, CA, 1998. 246 pp., illustrated. $39.95.
The first and only complete chronicle of all the bucks that have ever held the title "World Record Whitetail." Covers the greatest trophies ever recorded in their categories, typical, non-typical, gun, bow, and muzzleloader.

The Working Retrievers, by Tom Quinn, The Lyons Press, New York, NY, 1998. 257 pp., illus. $40.00.
The author covers every aspect of the training of dogs for hunting and field trials - from the beginning to the most advanced levels - for Labradors, Chesapeakes, Goldens and others.

AFRICA/ASIA/ELSEWHERE

African Adventures, by J.F. Burger, Safari Press, Huntington Beach, CA, 1993. 222 pp., illus. $35.00.
The reader shares adventures on the trail of the lion, the elephant and buffalo.

The African Adventures: A Return to the Silent Places, by Peter Hathaway Capstick. St. Martin's Press, New York, NY, 1992. 220 pp., illus. $22.95.
This book brings to life four turn-of-the-century adventurers and the savage frontier they braved. Frederick Selous, Constatine "Iodine" Ionides, Johnny Boyes and Jim Sutherland.

African Camp-fire Nights, by J.E. Burger, Safari Press, Huntington Beach, CA, 1993. 192 pp., illus. $32.50.
In this book the author writes of the men who made hunting their life's profession.

African Game Trails, by Theodore Roosevelt, Peter Capstick, Series Editor, St. Martin's Press, New York, NY 1988. 583 pp., illustrated. $24.95.
The famed safari of the noted sportsman, conservationist, and President.

African Hunter, by James Mellon, Safari Press, Huntington Beach, CA, 1996. 522 pp., illus. Clothbound, $125.00; paper covers, $75.00.
Regarded as the most comprehensive title ever published on African hunting.

African Hunting and Adventure, by William Charles Baldwin, Books of Zimbabwe, Bulawayo, 1981. 451 pp., illus. $75.00.
Facsimile reprint of the scarce 1863 London edition. African hunting and adventure from Natal to the Zambezi.

African Jungle Memories, by J.F. Burger, Safari Press, Huntington Beach, CA, 1993. 192 pp., illus. $32.50.
A book of reminiscences in which the reader is taken on many exciting adventures on the trail of the buffalo, lion, elephant and leopard.

African Rifles & Cartridges, by John Taylor, The Gun Room Press, Highland Park, NJ, 1977. 431 pp., illus. $35.00.
Experiences and opinions of a professional ivory hunter in Africa describing his knowledge of numerous arms and cartridges for big game. A reprint.

African Safaris, by Major G.H. Anderson, Safari Press, Long Beach, CA, 1997. 173 pp., illus. $35.00.
A reprinting of one of the rarest books on African hunting, with a foreword by Tony Sanchez.

African Twilight, by Robert F. Jones, Wilderness Adventure Press, Bozeman, MT, 1994. 208 pp., illus. $36.00.
Details the hunt, danger and changing face of Africa over a span of three decades.

After Big Game in Central Africa, by Edouard Foa, St. Martin's Press, New York, NY, 1989. 400 pp., illus. $16.95.
Reprint of the scarce 1899 edition. This sportsman covered 7200 miles, mostly on foot—from Zambezi delta on the east coast to the mouth of the Congo on the west.

A Man Called Lion: The Life and Times of John Howar "Pondoro" Taylor, by P.H. Capstick, Safari Press, Huntington Beach, CA, 1994. 240 pp., illus. $24.95.
With the help of Brian Marsh, an old Taylor acquaintance, Peter Capstick has accumulated over ten years of research into the life of this mysterious man.

Argali: High-Mountain Hunting, by Ricardo Medem, Safari Press, Huntington Beach, CA, 1995. 304 pp., illus. Limited, signed edition. $150.00.
Medem describes hunting seven different countries in the pursuit of sheep and other mountain game.

Baron in Africa, by W. Alvensleben, Safari Press, Inc., Huntington Beach, CA, 1997. 100 pp., illus. $60.00.
A must-read adventure story one of the most interesting characters to have come out of Africa after WWII.

The Best of Big Game, by Terry Wieland, John Culler and Sons, Camden, SC, 1996. 200 pp., illus. $49.95.
Twenty detailed accounts of the best hunters from around the world.

Big Game and Big Game Rifles, by John Taylor, Safari Press, Inc., Huntington Beach, CA, 1993. 215 pp., illus. $24.95.
A classic reprint and one of the most interesting characters to have come out of Africa after WWII.

The Big Five, by Tony Dyer, Trophy Room Books, Angoura, CA, 1996. 224 pp., illus. Limited, numbered edition signed by both the artist and author. $100.00.
A classic for African game than any other hunter.

Big Game Hunting and Collecting in East Africa 1903-1926, by Kalman Kittenberger, St. Martin's Press, New York, NY, 1989. 496 pp., illus. $16.95.
One of the most heart stopping, charming and funny accounts of adventure in the Kenya Colony ever penned.

Big Game Hunting Around the World, by Bert Klineburger and Vernon W. Hurst, Exposition Press, Jericho, NY, 1969. 376 pp., illus. $30.00.
The first book that takes you on a safari all over the world.

Big Game Hunting in Asia, Africa, and Elsewhere, by Jacques Vettier, Trophy Room Books, Agoura, CA, 1993. 400 pp., illus. Limited, numbered edition. $150.00.
A new edition of this classic study of the big five by two of the men who know them best.

Big Game Hunting in North-Eastern Rhodesia, by Owen Letcher, St. Martin's Press, New York, NY, 1986. 272 pp., illus. $15.95.
A classic reprint and one of the very few books to concentrate on this fascinating area, a region that today is still very much safari country.

Big Game Shooting in Cooch Behar, the Duars and Assam, by The Maharajah of Cooch Behar, Wolfe Publishing Co., Prescott, AZ, 1993. 461 pp., illus. $49.50.
A reprinting of the book that has become legendary. This is the Maharajah's personal diary of killing 365 tigers.

The Book of the Lion, by Sir Alfred E. Pease, St. Martin's Press, New York, NY, 1986. 305 pp., illus. $15.95.
Reprint of the finest book ever published on the subject. The author describes all aspects of lion history and lion hunting, drawing heavily on his own experiences in British East Africa.

Bwana Cotton, by Cotton Gordon, Trophy Room Books, Agoura, CA, 1996. 300 pp., illus. Limited, numbered and signed edition. $85.00.
Rambling, witty, wonderful reminiscences of an African hunter.

Chull A Guide to Hunting the African Leopard, by Lou Hallamore and Bruce Woods, Trophy Room Books, Agoura, CA, 1994. 239 pp., illus. $75.00.
Tales of exciting leopard encounters by one of today's most respected pros.

THE HANDGUNNER'S LIBRARY

A Country Boy in Africa, by George Hoffman, Trophy Room Books, Agoura, CA, 1998. 267 pp., illustrated with over 100 photos. Limited, numbered edition signed by the author. $85.00.
In addition to the author's long and successful hunting career, he is known for developing a most effective big game cartridge, the .416 Hoffman.

Death in a Lonely Land, by Peter Capstick, St. Martin's Press, New York, NY, 1990. 284 pp., illus. $22.95.
Twenty-three stories of hunting as only the master can tell them.

Death in the Dark Continent, by Peter Capstick, St. Martin's Press, New York, NY, 1983. 238 pp., illus. $22.95.
A book that brings to life the suspense, fear and exhilaration of stalking ferocious killers under primitive, savage conditions, with the ever present threat of death.

Death in the Long Grass, by Peter Hathaway Capstick, St. Martin's Press, New York, NY, 1977. 297 pp., illus. $22.95.

Death in the Silent Places, by Peter Capstick, St. Martin's Press, New York, NY, 1981. 243 pp., illus. $22.95.
The author recalls the extraordinary careers of legendary hunters such as Corbett, Karamojo Bell, Stigand and others.

Duck Hunting in Australia, by Dick Eussen, Australia Outdoor Publishers Pty Ltd., Victoria, Australia, 1994. 106 pp., illus. Paper covers, $17.95.
Covers the many aspects of duck hunting from hides to hunting methods.

East Africa and its Big Game, by Captain Sir John C. Willoughby, Wolfe Publishing Co., Prescott, AZ, 1990. 312 pp., illus. $52.00.
A deluxe limited edition reprint of the very scarce 1889 edition of a narrative of a sporting trip from Zanzibar to the borders of the Masai.

East of the Sun and West of the Moon, by Theodore and Kermit Roosevelt, Wolfe Publishing Co., Prescott, AZ, 1988. 284 pp., illus. $25.00.
A limited edition reprint. A classic on Marco Polo sheep hunting. A life experience unique to hunters of big game.

Elephant Hunting in East Equatorial Africa, by A. Neumann, St. Martin's Press, New York, NY, 1994. 455 pp., illus. $26.95.
This is a reprint of one of the rarest elephant hunting titles ever.

Elephants of Africa, by Dr. Anthony Hall-Martin, New Holland Publishers, London, England, 1987. 120 pp., illus. $75.00.
A superbly illustrated overview of the African elephant with reproductions of paintings by the internationally acclaimed wildlife artist Paul Bosman.

Encounters with Lions, by Jan Hemsing, Trophy Room books, Agoura, CA, 1995. 302 pp., illus. $75.00.
Some stories fierce, fatal, frightening and even humorous of when man and lion meet.

First Wheel, by Bunny Allen, Amwell Press, Clinton, NJ, 1984. Limited, signed and numbered edition in the NSFL "African Hunting Heritage Series." 292 pp., illus. $100.00.
Autobiography of one of the breed of "hard safari men" whose lives are full of changes and charges.

Fourteen Years in the African Bush, by A. Marsh, Safari Press Publication, Huntington Beach, CA, 1998. 312 pp., illus. Limited, signed, numbered, slipcased. $70.00.
An account of a Kenyan game warden. A graphic and well-written story.

"For the Honour of a Hunter....", by A.M.D. (Tony) Seth-Smith, Trophy Room Books, Agoura, CA, 1996. 320 pp., illus. Limited, numbered and signed edition. $85.00.
Only a handful of men can boast of having a fifty-year professional hunting career throughout Africa as John Northcote has had.

From Sailor to Professional Hunter: The Autobiography of John Northcote, Trophy Room Books, Agoura, CA, 1997. 400 pp., illus. Limited, signed and numbered. $125.00.

The Formidable Game, by John Batten, The Amwell Press, Clinton, NJ, 1994. 336 pp., illus. $40.00.
Batten and his wife cover the globe in search of the world's dangerous game. Includes a section on the development of the big bore rifle for formidable game.

Glory Days of Baja, by Larry Stanton, John Culler and Sons, Camden, SC, 1996. 184 pp., illus. $21.95.
This book represents twenty-five years of hunting in Mexico's Baja.

The Great Arc of the Wild Sheep, by J.L. Clark, Safari Press, Huntington Beach, CA, 1994. 247 pp., illus. $24.95.
Perhaps the most complete work done on all the species and subspecies of the wild sheep of the world.

Great Hunters: Their Trophy Rooms & Collections, Volume 2, compiled and published by Safari Press, Inc., Huntington Beach, CA, 1998. 224 pp., illustrated in color. $60.00.
Volume two of the world's finest, best produced series of books on trophy rooms and game collections. 46 sportsmen sharing sights you'll never forget on this guided tour.

Great Hunters: Their Trophy Rooms and Collections, Volume 1, compiled and published by Safari Press, Inc., Huntington Beach, CA, 1997. 172 pp., illustrated in color. $60.00.
A rare glimpse into the trophy rooms of top international hunters. A few of these trophy rooms are museums.

Horn of the Hunter, by Robert Ruark, Safari Press, Long Beach, CA, 1987. 315 pp., illus. $35.00.
Ruark's most sought-after title on African hunting, here in reprint.

Horned Death, by John F. Burger, Safari Press, Huntington Beach, CA, 1992. 343 pp., illus. $35.00.
The classic work on hunting the African buffalo.

Hunter, by J.A. Hunter, Safari Press Publications, Huntington Beach, CA, 1999. 263 pp., illus. $24.95.
Hunter's best known book on African big-game hunting. Internationally recognized as being one of the all-time African hunting classics.

A Hunter's Africa, by Gordon Cundill, Trophy Room Books, Agoura, CA, 1998. 298 pp., over 125 photographic illustrations, Limited numbered edition signed by the author. $125.00.
A good look by the author at the African safari experience - elephant, lion, spiral-horned antelope, firearms, people and events, as well as the clients that make it worthwhile.

Hunter's Tracks, by J.A. Hunter, Safari Press Publications, Huntington Beach, CA, 1999. 240 pp., illustrated. $24.95.
One of the most well-written stories of East African hunting, big game, and eccentric characters.

Hunters of Man, by Capt. J. Brandt, Safari Press, Huntington Beach, CA, 1997. 242 pp., illus. Paper covers, $18.95.
True stories of man-eaters, man killers and rogues in Southeast Asia.

Hunting Adventures Worldwide, by Jack Atcheson, Jack Atcheson & Sons, Butte, MT, 1995. 256 pp., illus. $29.95.
The author chronicles the richest adventures of a lifetime spent in quest of big game across the world – including Africa, North America and Asia.

Hunting in Ethiopia, An Anthology, by Tony Sanchez-Arino, Safari Press, Huntington Beach, CA, 1996. 350 pp., illus. Limited, signed and numbered edition. $135.00.
The finest selection of hunting stories ever compiled on hunting in this great game country.

Hunting in Many Lands, by Theodore Roosevelt and George Bird Grinnel, The Boone and Crockett Club, Dumfries, VA, 1987. 447 pp., illus. $40.00.
Limited edition reprint of this 1895 classic work on hunting in Africa, India, Mongolia, etc.

Hunting in the Sudan, An Anthology, compiled by Tony Sanchez-Arino, Safari Press, Huntington Beach, CA, 1992. 350 pp., illus. Limited, signed and numbered edition in a slipcase. $125.00.
The finest selection of hunting stories ever compiled on hunting in this great game country.

Hunting the Dangerous Game of Africa, by John Kingsley-Heath, Sycamore Island Books, Boulder, CO, 1998. 477 pp., illustrated. $95.00.
Written by one of the most respected, successful, and ethical P.H.'s to trek the sunlit plains of Botswana, Kenya, Uganda, Tanganyika, Somaliland, Eritrea, Ethiopia, and Mozambique. Filled with some of the most gripping and terrifying tales ever to come out of Africa.

Hunting the Elephant in Africa, by Captain C.H. Stigand, St. Martin's Press, New York, NY, 1986. 379 pp., illus. $30.00.
A reprint of the scarce 1913 edition; vintage Africana at its best.

Hunting, Settling and Remembering, by Philip H. Percival, Trophy Room Books, Agoura, CA, 1997. 230 pp., illus. Limited, numbered and signed edition. $85.00.
If Philip Percival is to come alive again, it will be through this, the first edition of his easy, intricate and magical book illustrated with some of the best historical big game hunting photos ever taken.

Jaguar Hunting in the Mato Grosso and Bolivia, by T. Almedia, Safari Press, Long Beach, CA, 1989. 256 pp., illus. $35.00.
Not since Sacha Siemel has there been a book on jaguar hunting like this one.

Jim Corbett, Master of the Jungle, by Tim Werling, Safari Press, Huntington Beach, CA, 1998. 215 pp., illus. $30.00.
A biography of India's most famous hunter of man-eating tigers and leopards.

King of the Wa-Kikuyu, by John Boyes, St. Martin Press, New York, NY, 1993. 240 pp., illus. $19.95.
In the 19th and 20th centuries, Africa drew to it a large number of great hunters, explorers, adventurers and rogues. Many have become legendary, but John Boyes (1874-1951) was the most legendary of them all.

Lake Ngami, by Charles Anderson, New Holland Press, London, England, 1987. 576 pp., illus. $35.00.
Originally published in 1856. Describes two expeditions into what is now Botswana, depicting every detail of landscape and wildlife.

Last Horizons: Hunting, Fishing and Shooting on Five Continents, by Peter Capstick, St. Martin's Press, New York, NY, 1989. 288 pp., illus. $19.95.
The first in a two volume collection of hunting, fishing and shooting tales from the selected pages of The American Hunter, Guns & Ammo and Outdoor Life.

Last of the Few: Forty-Two Years of African Hunting, by Tony Sanchez-Arino, Safari Press, Huntington Beach, CA, 1996. 250 pp., illus. $85.00.
The story of the author's career with all the highlights that come from pursuing the unusual and dangerous animals that are native to Africa.

Last of the Ivory Hunters, by John Taylor, Safari Press, Long Beach, CA, 1990. 354 pp., illus. $29.95.
Reprint of the classic book "Pondoro" by one of the most famous elephant hunters of all time.

Legends of the Field: More Early Hunters in Africa, by W.R. Foran, Trophy Room Press, Agoura, CA, 1997. 319 pp., illus. Limited edition. $100.00.
This book contains the biographies of some very famous hunters: William Cotton Oswell, F.C. Selous, Sir Samuel Baker, Arthur Neumann, Jim Sutherland, W.D.M. Bell and others.

The Lost Classics, by Robert Ruark, Safari Press, Huntington Beach, CA, 1996. 260 pp., illus. $35.00.
The magazine stories that Ruark wrote in the 1950s and 1960s finally in print in book form.

THE HANDGUNNER'S LIBRARY

The Magic of Big Games, by Terry Wieland, Countrysport Books, Selma, AL, 1998. 200 pp., illus. $39.00.
Original essays on hunting big game around the world.

Mahohboh, by Ron Thomson, African Safari Press, Hartbeespoort, South Africa, 1997. 312 pp., illustrated. Limited edition, signed and numbered. $70.00.
Elephants and elephant hunting in South Central Africa.

The Man-Eaters of Tsavo, by Lt. Colonel J.H. Patterson, Peter Capstick, series editor, St. Martin's Press, New York, NY, 1986. 5th printing, 346 pp., illus. $22.95.
The classic man-eating story of the lions that halted construction of a railway line and reportedly killed one hundred people, told by the man who risked his life to successfully shoot them.

Memoirs of an African Hunter, by Terry Irwin, Safari Press Publications, Huntington Beach, CA, 1998. 421 pp., illustrated. Limited numbered, signed and slipcased. $125.00.
A narrative of a professional hunter's experiences in Africa.

Men for all Seasons: The Hunters and Pioneers, by Tony Dyers, Trophy Room Books, Agoura, CA, 1996. 440 pp., illus. Limited, numbered and signed edition. $125.00.
The men, women and warriors who created the great Safari Industry of East Africa.

Months of the Sun; Forty Years of Elephant Hunting in the Zambezi Valley, by Ian Nyschens, Safari Press, Huntington Beach, CA, 1998. 420 pp., illus. Limited signed and numbered edition. Slipcased. $85.00.
The author has shot equally as many elephants as Walter Bell, and under much more difficult circumstances. His book will rank, or surpass, the best elephant-ivory hunting books published this century.

Mundjamba: The Life Story of an African Hunter, by Hugo Seia, Trophy Room Books, Agoura, CA, 1996. 400 pp., illus. Limited, numbered and signed by the author. $125.00.
An autobiography of one of the most respected and appreciated professional African hunters.

My Last Kambaku, by Leo Kroger, Safari Press, Huntington Beach, CA, 1997. 272 pp., illus. Limited edition signed and numbered and slipcased. $60.00.
One of the most engaging hunting memoirs ever published.

The Nature of the Game, by Ben Hoskyns, Quiller Press, Ltd., London, England, 1994. 160 pp., illus. $37.50.
The first complete guide to British, European and North American game.

One Happy Hunter, by George Barrington, Safari Press, Huntington Beach, CA, 1994. 240 pp., illus. $40.00.
A candid, straightforward look at safari hunting.

One Long Safari, by Peter Hay, Trophy Room Books, Agoura, CA, 1998. 350 pp., with over 200 photographic illustrations and 7 maps. Limited numbered edition signed by the author. $100.00.
Contains hunts for leopards, sitatunga, hippo, rhino, snakes and, of course, the general African big game bag.

The Path of a Hunter, by Gilles Tre-Hardy, Trophy Room Books, Agoura, CA, 1997. 318 pp., illus. Limited Edition, signed and numbered. $85.00.
A most unusual hunting autobiography with much about elephant hunting in Africa.

Peter Capstick's Africa: A Return to the Long Grass, by Peter Hathaway Capstick, St. Martin's Press, N. Y., NY, 1987. 213 pp., illus. $29.95.
A first-person adventure in which the author returns to the long grass for his own dangerous and very personal excursion.

The Recollections of an Elephant Hunter 1864-1875, by William Finaughty, Books of Zimbabwe, Bulawayo, Zimbabwe, 1980. 244 pp., illus. $85.00.
Reprint of the scarce 1916 privately published edition. The early game hunting exploits of William Finaughty in Matabeleland and Nashonaland.

Safari: A Chronicle of Adventure, by Bartle Bull, Viking/Penguin, London, England, 1989. 383 pp., illus. $40.00.
The thrilling history of the African safari, highlighting some of Africa's best-known personalities.

Safari Rifles: Double, Magazine Rifles and Cartridges for African Hunting, by Craig Boddington, Safari Press, Huntington Beach, CA, 1990. 416 pp., illus. $24.95.
A wealth of knowledge on the safari rifle. Historical and present double-rifle makers, ballistics for the large bores, and much, much more.

Safari: The Last Adventure, by Peter Capstick, St. Martin's Press, New York, NY, 1984. 291 pp., illus. $19.95.
A modern comprehensive guide to the African Safari.

Sands of Silence, by Peter H. Capstick, Saint Martin's Press, New York, NY, 1991. 224 pp., illus. $35.00.
Join the author on safari in Namibia for his latest big-game hunting adventures.

Shoot Straight and Stay Alive: A Lifetime of Hunting Experiences, by Fred Bartlett, Trophy Room Books, Argoura, CA, 1994. 262 pp., illus. $85.00.
A book written by a man who has left his mark on the maps of Africa's great gamelands.

Skyline Pursuits, by John Batten, The Amwell Press, Clinton, NJ, 1994. 372 pp., illus. $40.00.
A chronicle of Batten's own hunting adventures in the high country on four continents since 1928, traces a sheep hunting career that has accounted for both North American and International Grand Slams.

Solo Safari, by T. Cacek, Safari Press, Huntington Beach, CA, 1995. 270 pp., illus. $30.00.
Here is the story of Terry Cacek who hunted elephant, buffalo, leopard and plains game in Zimbabwe and Botswana on his own.

South Pacific Trophy Hunter, by Murray Thomas, Safari Press, Long Beach, CA, 1988. 181 pp., illus. $37.50.
A record of a hunter's search for a trophy of each of the 15 major game species in the South Pacific region.

Spiral-Horn Dreams, by Terry Wieland, Trophy Room Books, Agoura, CA, 1996. 362 pp., illus. Limited, numbered and signed by the author. $85.00.
Everyone who goes to hunt in Africa is looking for something; this is for those who go to hunt the spiral-horned antelope—the bongo, nyala, mountain nyala, greater and lesser kudu, etc.

Sport on the Pamirs and Turkestan Steppes, by Major C.S. Cumberland, Moncrieff & Smith, Victoria, Autralia, 1992. 278 pp., illus. $45.00.
The first in a series of facsimile reprints of great trophy hunting books by Moncrieff & Smith.

Tales of the African Frontier, by J.A. Hunter, Safari Press Publications, Huntington Beach, CA, 1999. 308 pp., illus. $24.95.
The early days of East Africa is the subject of this powerful John Hunter book.

Theodore Roosevelt Outdoorsman, by R.L. Wilson, Trophy Room Books, Agoura, CA, 1994. 326 pp., illus. $85.00.
This book presents Theodore Roosevelt as a rancher, Rough Rider, Governor, President, naturalist and international big game hunter.

Those Were the Days, by Rudolf Sand, Safari Press, Huntington Beach, CA, 1993. 300 pp., illus. $100.00.
Travel with Rudolf Sand to the pinnacles of the world in his pursuit of wild sheep and goats.

Through the Brazilian Wilderness, by Theodore Roosevelt, Stackpole Books, Mechanicsburg, PA, 1994. 448 pp., illus. Paper covers. $16.95.
Adventure and drama in the South American jungle.

Trophy Hunter in Africa, by Elgin Gates, Safari Press, Huntington Beach, CA, 1994. 315 pp., illus. $29.95.
This is the story of one man's adventure in Africa's wildlife paradise.

Uganda Safaris, by Brian Herne, Winchester Press, Piscataway, NJ, 1979. 236 pp., illus. $12.95.
The chronicle of a professional hunter's adventures in Africa.

Under the Shadow of Man Eaters, by Jerry Jaleel, The Jim Corbett Foundation, Edmonton, Alberta, Canada, 1997. 152 pp., illus. A limited, numbered and signed edition. Paper covers. $35.00.
The life and legend of Jim Corbett of Kumaon.

Use Enough Gun, by Robert Ruark, Safari Press, Huntington Beach, CA, 1997. 333 pp., illus. $35.00.
Robert Ruark on big game hunting.

Warrior: The Legend of Col. Richard Meinertzhagen, by Peter H. Capstick, St. Martins Press, New York, NY, 1998. 320 pp., illus. $23.95.
A stirring and vivid biography of the famous British colonial officer Richard Meinertzhagen, whose exploits earned him fame and notoriety as one of the most daring and ruthless men to serve during the glory days of the British Empire.

Where Lions Roar: Ten More Years of African Hunting, by Craig Boddington, Safari Press, Huntington Beach, CA, 1997. 250 pp., illus. Limited edition, signed and numbered. In a slipcase. $60.00.
The story of Boddington's hunts in the Dark Continent during the last ten years.

White Hunter, by J.A. Hunter, Safari Press Publications, Huntington Beach, CA, 1999. 282 pp., illustrated. $24.95.
This book is a seldom-seen account of John Hunter's adventures in pre-WW2 Africa.

A White Hunters Life, by Angus MacLagan, an African Heritage Book, published by Amwell Press, Clinton, NJ, 1983. 283 pp., illus. Limited, signed, and numbered deluxe edition, in slipcase. $100.00.
True to life, a sometimes harsh yet intriguing story.

Wild Sports of Southern Africa, by William Cornwallis Harris, New Holland Press, London, England, 1987. 376 pp., illus. $35.00.
Originally published in 1863, describes the author's travels in Southern Africa.

With a Gun in Good Country, by Ian Manning, Trophy Room Books, Agoura, CA, 1996. Limited, numbered and signed by the author. $85.00.
A book written about that splendid period before the poaching onslaught which almost closed Zambia and continues to the granting of her independence. It then goes on to recount Manning's experiences in Botswana, Congo, and briefly in South Africa.

DIRECTORY OF THE HANDGUNNING TRADE

HANDGUNS 2001

PRODUCT & SERVICE DIRECTORY

AMMUNITION, COMMERCIAL

American Ammunition
Arizona Ammunition, Inc.
Atlantic Rose, Inc.
Bergman & Williams
Big Bear Arms & Sporting Goods, Inc.
Black Hills Ammunition, Inc.
Blammo Ammo
Blount, Inc., Sporting Equipment Div.
Brown Dog Ent.
Buffalo Bullet Co., Inc.
BulletMakers Workshop, The
Bull-X, Inc.
California Magnum
CBC
Colorado Sutlers Arsenal
Cor-Bon Bullet & Ammo Co.
Cumberland States Arsenal
Daisy Mfg. Co.
Dead Eye's Sport Center
Delta Frangible Ammunition, LLC
Denver Bullets, Inc.
Dynamit Nobel-RWS, Inc.
Eldorado Cartridge Corp.
Eley Ltd.
Elite Ammunition
Estate Cartridge, Inc.
Federal Cartridge Co.
4W Ammunition
Hunters Supply
GOEX, Inc.
Goldcoast Reloaders, Inc.
Hansen & Co.
Hansen Cartridge Co.
Hart & Son, Inc., Robert W.
Hirtenberger Aktiengesellschaft
Hornady Mfg. Co.
ICI-America
IMI
Israel Military Industries Ltd.
Jones, J.D.
Keng's Firearms Specialty, Inc.
Kent Cartridge Mfg. Co. Ltd.
Lapua Ltd.
M&D Munitions Ltd.
MagSafe Ammo Co.
Markell, Inc.
Mathews & Son, Inc., George E.
Men—Metallwerk Elisenhuette, GmbH
Mullins Ammunition
NECO
New England Ammunition Co.
Oklahoma Ammunition Co.
Old Western Scrounger, Inc.
Omark Industries
Pacific Cartridge, Inc.
PMC/Eldorado Cartridge Corp.
Pony Express Reloaders
Precision Delta Corp.
Pro Load Ammunition, Inc.
Remington Arms Co., Inc.
Rucker Dist. Inc.
RWS
Spence, George W.
SSK Industries
Talon Mfg. Co., Inc.
Taylor & Robbins
Thompson Bullet Lube Co.
3-D Ammunition & Bullets
3-Ten Corp.
USAC
Valor Corp.
Victory USA
Vihtavuori Oy/Kaltron-Pettibone
Voere-KGH m.b.H.
Widener's Reloading & Shooting Supply, Inc.
Winchester Div., Olin Corp.
Zero Ammunition Co., Inc.

AMMUNITION, CUSTOM

Accuracy Unlimited (Littleton, CO)
AFSCO Ammunition
American Derringer Corp.
Arizona Ammunition, Inc.
Arms Corporation of the Philippines
Atlantic Rose, Inc.
Black Hills Ammunition, Inc.
Bruno Shooters Supply
Brynin, Milton
Buckskin Bullet Co.
BulletMakers Workshop, The
CBC
Country Armourer, The
Custom Tackle and Ammo
Dead Eye's Sport Center
Delta Frangible Ammunition, LLC
DKT, Inc.
Elite Ammunition
Estate Cartridge, Inc.
4W Ammunition
Freedom Arms, Inc.
GDL Enterprises
Glaser Safety Slug, Inc.
GOEX, Inc.
"Gramps" Antique Cartridges
Granite Custom Bullets
Gun Accessories
Heidenstrom Bullets
Hirtenberger Aktiengesellschaft
Hoelscher, Virgil
Horizons Unlimited
Hornady Mfg. Co.
Hunters Supply
IMI
Israel Military Industries Ltd.
Kaswer Custom, Inc.
Keeler, R.H.
Kent Cartridge Mfg. Co. Ltd.
KJM Fabritek, Inc.
Lindsley Arms Cartridge Co.
MagSafe Ammo Co.
MAST Technology
McMurdo, Lynn
Men-Metallwerk Elisenhuette, GmbH
Milstor Corp.
Mullins Ammunition
Naval Ordnance Works
NECO
Northern Precision Custom Swaged Bullets
Old Western Scrounger, Inc.
Oklahoma Ammunition Company
Precision Delta Corp.
Precision Munitions, Inc.
Precision Reloading, Inc.
Professional Hunter Supplies
Sanders Custom Gun Service
Sandia Die & Cartridge Co.
SOS Products Co.
Specialty Gunsmithing
Spence, George W.
Spencer's Custom Guns
Star Custom Bullets
State Arms Gun Co.
Stewart's Gunsmithing
Talon Mfg. Co., Inc.
3-D Ammunition & Bullets
3-Ten Corp.
Unmussig Bullets, D.L.
Vulpes Ventures, Inc.
Warren Muzzleloading Co., Inc.
Weaver Arms Corp. Gun Shop
Worthy Products, Inc.
Yukon Arms Classic Ammunition

AMMUNITION, FOREIGN

AFSCO Ammunition
Armscorp USA, Inc.
Atlantic Rose, Inc.
BulletMakers Workshop, The
CBC
Dead Eye's Sport Center
Diana
DKT, Inc.
Dynamit Nobel-RWS, Inc.
First, Inc., Jack
Fisher Enterprises, Inc.
Fisher, R. Kermit
FN Herstal
Forgett Jr., Valmore J.
GOEX, Inc.
Hansen & Co.
Hansen Cartridge Co.
Heidenstrom Bullets
Hirtenberger Aktiengesellschaft
Hornady Mfg. Co.
IMI
IMI Services USA, Inc.
Israel Military Industries Ltd.
JägerSport, Ltd.
K.B.I., Inc.
Keng's Firearms Specialty, Inc.
Magnum Research, Inc.
MagSafe Ammo Co.
MagTech Recreational Products, Inc.
Maionchi-L.M.I.
MAST Technology
Merkuria Ltd.
Mullins Ammunition
Oklahoma Ammunition Co.
Old Western Scrounger, Inc.
Petro-Explo, Inc.
Precision Delta Corp.
R.E.T. Enterprises
RWS
Sentinel Arms
Southern Ammunition Co., Inc.
Spence, George W.
Stratco, Inc.
SwaroSports, Inc.
T.F.C. S.p.A.
Vihtavuori Oy/Kaltron-Pettibone
Yukon Arms Classic Ammunition

AMMUNITION COMPONENTS—BULLETS, POWDER

PRIMERS, CASES

Acadian Ballistic Specialties
Accuracy Unlimited (Littleton, CO)
Accurate Arms Co., Inc.
Accurate Bullet Co.
Action Bullets, Inc.
Alaska Bullet Works, Inc.
Alliant Techsystems
Allred Bullet Co.
American Products Inc.
Arco Powder
Atlantic Rose, Inc.
Baer's Hollows
Ballard Built
Barnes Bullets, Inc.
Beartooth Bullets
Beeline Custom Bullets Limited
Bell Reloading, Inc.
Belt MTN Arms
Berger Bullets, Ltd.
Bergman & Williams
Berry's Mfg., Inc.
Bertram Bullet Co.
Big Bore Bullets of Alaska
Big Bore Express
Bitterroot Bullet Co.
Black Belt Bullets
Black Hills Shooters Supply
Black Powder Products
Blount, Inc., Sporting Equipment Div.
Briese Bullet Co., Inc.
Brown Co., E. Arthur
Brown Dog Ent.
Brownells, Inc.
BRP, Inc.
Bruno Shooters Supply
Buck Stix

PRODUCT & SERVICE DIRECTORY

AMMUNITION COMPONENTS—BULLETS, POWDER (continued)

Buckeye Custom Bullets
Buckskin Bullet Co.
Buffalo Arms Co.
Buffalo Rock Shooters Supply
Bullet, Inc.
Bullseye Bullets
Bull-X, Inc.
Butler Enterprises
Canyon Cartridge Corp.
Carnahan Bullets
Cast Performance Bullet Company
CCI
Champion's Choice, Inc.
Cheddite France, S.A.
CheVron Bullets
C.J. Ballistics, Inc.
Colorado Sutlers Arsenal
Competitor Corp., Inc.
Cook Engineering Service
Copperhead Bullets, Inc.
Cor-Bon Bullet & Ammo Co.
Cumberland States Arsenal
Cummings Bullets
Curtis Cast Bullets
Custom Bullets by Hoffman
Cutsinger Bench Rest Bullets
D&J Bullet Co. & Custom Gun Shop, Inc.
Dixie Gun Works, Inc.
DKT., Inc.
Dohring Bullets
Double A Ltd.
Eichelberger Bullets, Wm.
Eldorado Cartridge Corp.
Elkhorn Bullets
Epps, Ellwood
Federal Cartridge Co.
Forkin, Ben
4W Ammunition
Fowler, Bob
Fowler Bullets
Foy Custom Bullets
Freedom Arms, Inc.
Fusilier Bullets
G&C Bullet Co., Inc.

Gander Mountain, Inc.
Gehmann, Walter
GOEX, Inc.
Golden Bear Bullets
Gotz Bullets
"Gramps" Antique Cartridges
Granite Custom Bullets
Grayback Wildcats
Green Mountain Rifle Barrel Co., Inc.
Grier's Hard Cast Bullets
Group Tight Bullets
Gun City
Hammets VLD Bullets
Hardin Specialty Dist.
Harris Enterprises
Harrison Bullets
Hart & Son, Inc., Robert W.
Hawk, Inc.
Haydon Shooters' Supply, Russ
Heidenstrom Bullets
Hi-Performance Ammunition Company
Hirtenberger Aktiengesellschaft
Hobson Precision Mfg. Co.
Hodgdon Powder Co.
Hornady Mfg. Co.
HT Bullets
Huntington Die Specialties
Hunters Supply
IMI Services USA, Inc.
IMR Powder Co.
J-4, Inc.
J&D Components
J&L Superior Bullets
Jensen Bullets
Jensen's Firearms Academy
Jericho Tool & Die Co., Inc.
Jester Bullets
JLK Bullets
JRP Custom Bullets
Ka Pu Kapili
Kaswer Custom, Inc.
Keith's Bullets
Ken's Kustom Kartridge
Keng's Firearms Specialty, Inc.

Kent Cartridge Mfg. Co. Ltd.
KJM Fabritek, Inc.
KLA Enterprises
Kodiak Custom Bullets
Lapua Ltd.
Legend Products Corp.
Liberty Shooting Supplies
Lightning Performance Innovations, Inc.
Lindsley Arms Cartridge Co.
Lomont Precision Bullets
M&D Munitions Ltd.
Magnus Bullets
Maine Custom Bullets
Maionchi-L.M.I.
Marchmon Bullets
Markesbery Muzzle Loaders, Inc.
Marple & Associates, Dick
MAST Technology
Mathews & Son, Inc., George E.
McMurdo, Lynn
Meister Bullets
Men—Metallwerk Elisenhuette, GmbH
Merkuria Ltd.
Mitchell Bullets, R.F.
Mi-TE Bullets
Modern Muzzleloading, Inc.
MoLoc Bullets
Montana Armory, Inc.
Montana Precision Swaging
Mountain State Muzzleloading Supplies, Inc.
Mt. Baldy Bullet Co.
Mulhern, Rick
Mushroom Express Bullet Co.
Nagel's Bullets
National Bullet Co.
Navy Arms Co.
Necromancer Industries, Inc.
Norma
North American Shooting Systems
North Devon Firearms Services

Northern Precision Custom Swaged Bullets
Nosler, Inc.
Oklahoma Ammunition Co.
Old Wagon Bullets
Old Western Scrounger, Inc.
Omark Industries
Ordnance Works, The
Oregon Trail Bullet Company
Pacific Cartridge, Inc.
Page Custom Bullets
Patrick Bullets
Pease Accuracy, Bob
Petro-Explo, Inc.
Phillippi Custom Bullets, Justin
Pinetree Bullets
PMC/Eldorado Cartridge Corp.
Pomeroy, Robert
Precision Components
Precision Delta Corp.
Precision Munitions, Inc.
Price Bullets, Patrick W.
PRL Bullets
Professional Hunter Supplies
Rainier Ballistics Corp.
Ranger Products
Red Cedar Precision Mfg.
Redwood Bullet Works
Remington Arms Co., Inc.
Rhino
Rifle Works & Armory
R.I.S. Co., Inc.
R.M. Precision, Inc.
Robinson H.V. Bullets
Rolston, Inc., Fred W.
Rubright Bullets
SAECO
Scharch Mfg., Inc.
Schmidtman Custom Ammunition
Schneider Bullets
Schroeder Bullets
Scot Powder
Seebeck Assoc., R.E.

Shappy Bullets
Sierra Bullets
Silhouette, The
SOS Products Co.
Specialty Gunsmithing
Speer Products
Spencer's Custom Guns
Stanley Bullets
Star Ammunition, Inc.
Star Custom Bullets
Stark's Bullet Mfg.
Starke Bullet Company
Stewart's Gunsmithing
Talon Mfg. Co., Inc.
TCSR
T.F.C. S.p.A.
Thompson Precision
3-D Ammunition & Bullets
TMI Products
Traditions, Inc.
Trophy Bonded Bullets, Inc.
True Flight Bullet Co.
Tucson Mold, Inc.
Unmussig Bullets, D.L.
USAC
Vann Custom Bullets
Vihtavuori Oy/Kaltron-Pettibone
Vincent's Shop
Viper Bullet and Brass Works
Warren Muzzleloading Co., Inc.
Watson Trophy Match Bullets
Western Nevada West Coast Bullets
Widener's Reloading & Shooting Supply
Williams Bullet Co., J.R.
Winchester Div., Olin Corp.
Winkle Bullets
Worthy Products, Inc.
Wyant Bullets
Wyoming Custom Bullets
Yukon Arms Classic Ammunition
Zero Ammunition Co., Inc.

ANTIQUE ARMS DEALERS

Ackerman & Co.
Ad Hominem
Antique American Firearms
Antique Arms Co.
Aplan Antiques & Art, James O.
Armoury, Inc., The
Bear Mountain Gun & Tool
Bob's Tactical Indoor Shooting

Range & Gun Shop
British Antiques
Buckskin Machine Works
Buffalo Arms Co.
Cape Outfitters
Carlson, Douglas R.
Chadick's Ltd.
Chambers Flintlocks Ltd., Jim
Champlin Firearms, Inc.
Chuck's Gun Shop

Classic Guns, Inc.
Clements' Custom Leathercraft, Chas
Cole's Gun Works
Colonial Arms, Inc.
D&D Gunsmiths, Ltd.
Dixie Gun Works, Inc.
Dixon Muzzleloading Shop, Inc.
Duffy, Charles E.
Dyson & Son Ltd., Peter
Ed's Gun House

Enguix Import-Export
Fagan & Co., William
Fish Mfg. Gunsmith Sptg. Co., Marshall F.
Flayderman & Co., N.
Forgett Jr., Valmore J.
Frielich Police Equipment
Fulmer's Antique Firearms, Chet
Getz Barrel Co.

Glass, Herb
Goergen's Gun Shop, Inc.
Golden Age Arms Co.
Gun Room, The
Gun Room Press, The
Guncraft Sports, Inc.
Gun Works, The
Guns Antique & Modern DBA/Charles E. Duffy
Hallowell & Co.
HandiCrafts Unltd.

PRODUCT & SERVICE DIRECTORY

ANTIQUE ARMS DEALERS (continued)

Hansen & Co.
Hunkeler, A.
Johns Master Engraver, Bill
Kelley's
Ledbetter Airguns, Riley
LeFever Arms Co., Inc.
Lever Arms Service Ltd.
Lock's Philadelphia Gun Exchange
Log Cabin Sport Shop
Mandall Shooting Supplies, Inc.
Martin's Gun Shop
Montana Outfitters
Museum of Historical Arms, Inc.
Muzzleloaders Etcetera, Inc.
New England Arms Co.
Pony Express Sport Shop, Inc.
Retting, Inc., Martin B.
R.G.-G., Inc.
Scott Fine Guns, Inc., Thad
Shootin' Shack, Inc.
Steves House of Guns
Stott's Creek Armory, Inc.
Strawbridge, Victor W.
Vic's Gun Refinishing
Vintage Arms, Inc.
Westley Richards & Co.
Wiest, M.C.
Winchester Sutler, Inc., The
Wood, Frank
Yearout, Lewis E.

APPRAISERS—GUNS, ETC.

Antique Arms Co.
Armoury, Inc., The
Arundel Arms & Ammunition, Inc., A.
Barsotti, Bruce
Beitzinger, George
Blue Book Publications, Inc.
Bob's Tactical Indoor Shooting Range & Gun Shop
British Antiques
Bustani, Leo
Butterfield & Butterfield
Camilli, Lou
Cannon's, Andy Cannons
Cape Outfitters
Chadick's Ltd.
Champlin Firearms, Inc.
Christie's East
Clark Firearms Engraving
Classic Guns, Inc.
Clements' Custom Leathercraft, Chas
Cole's Gun Works
Colonial Arms, Inc.
Colonial Repair
Corry, John
Custom Tackle and Ammo
D&D Gunsmiths, Ltd.
DGR Custom Rifles
Dixon Muzzleloading Shop, Inc.
Duane's Gun Repair
Ed's Gun House
Epps, Ellwood
Eversull Co., Inc., K.
Fagan & Co., William
Ferris Firearms
Fish Mfg. Gunsmith Sptg. Co., Marshall F.
Flayderman & Co., Inc., N.
Forgett, Valmore J., Jr.
Forty Five Ranch Enterprises
Francotte & Cie S.A., Auguste
Frontier Arms Co., Inc.
Getz Barrel Co.
Gillmann, Edwin
Golden Age Arms Co.
Gonzalez Guns, Ramon B.
Griffin & Howe, Inc.
Gun City
Gun Hunter Trading Co.
Gun Room Press, The
Gun Shop, The
Guncraft Sports, Inc.
Guns
Hallowell & Co.
Hammans, Charles E.
HandiCrafts Unltd.
Hank's Gun Shop
Hansen & Co.
Hughes, Steven Dodd
Irwin, Campbell H.
Island Pond Gun Shop
Jackalope Gun Shop
Jaeger, Inc., Paul/Dunn's
Jensen's Custom Ammunition
Kelley's
LaRocca Gun Works, Inc.
Ledbetter Airguns, Riley
LeFever Arms Co., Inc.
L.L. Bean, Inc.
Lock's Philadelphia Gun Exchange
Mac's .45 Shop
Madis, George
Mandall Shooting Supplies, Inc.
Martin's Gun Shop
McCann's Muzzle-Gun Works
Montana Outfitters
Museum of Historical Arms, Inc.
Muzzleloaders Etcetera, Inc.
Navy Arms Co.
New England Arms Co.
Nitex, Inc.
Orvis Co., The
Pasadena Gun Center
Pentheny de Pentheny
Perazzi USA, Inc.
Peterson Gun Shop, Inc., A.W.
Pettinger Books, Gerald
Pony Express Sport Shop, Inc.
R.E.T. Enterprises
Retting, Inc., Martin B.
Richards, John
Safari Outfitters Ltd.
Scott Fine Guns, Inc., Thad
Shootin' Shack, Inc.
Steger, James R.
Stratco, Inc.
Strawbridge, Victor W.
Swampfire Shop, The
Thurston Sports, Inc.
Vic's Gun Refinishing
Wayne Firearms for Collectors and Investors, James
Wells Custom Gunsmith, R.A.
Whildin & Sons Ltd., E.H.
Wiest, M.C.
Williams Shootin' Iron Service
Winchester Sutler, Inc., The
Wood, Frank
Yearout, Lewis E.
Yee, Mike

AUCTIONEERS—GUNS, ETC.

Butterfield & Butterfield
Christie's East
Kelley's
"Little John's" Antique Arms
Sotheby's

BOOKS (Publishers and Dealers)

Action Direct, Inc.
American Handgunner Magazine
Armory Publications, Inc.
Arms & Armour Press
Barnes Bullets, Inc.
Blackhawk West
Blacksmith Corp.
Blacktail Mountain Books
Blue Book Publications, Inc.
Blue Ridge Machinery & Tools, Inc.
Brown Co., E. Arthur
Brownell Checkering Tools, W.E.
Brownell's, Inc.
Bullet'n Press
Calibre Press, Inc.
Cape Outfitters
Colonial Repair
Colorado Sutlers Arsenal
Corbin Mfg. & Supply, Inc.
Cumberland States Arsenal
DBI Books
Flores Publications, Inc., J.
Forgett Jr., Valmore J.
Golden Age Arms Co.
Gun City
Gun Hunter Books
Gun Hunter Trading Co.
Gun List
Gun Parts Corp., The
Gun Room Press, The
Gun Works, The
Guncraft Books
Guncraft Sports, Inc.
Gunnerman Books
GUNS Magazine
H&P Publishing
Handgun Press
Harris Publications
Hawk Laboratories, Inc.
Heritage/VSP Gun Books
Hodgdon Powder Co., Inc.
Home Shop Machinist, The
Hornady Mfg. Co.
Hungry Horse Books
I.D.S.A. Books
Info-Arm
Ironside International Publishers, Inc.
Koval Knives
Krause Publications, Inc.
Lane Publishing
Lapua Ltd.
Lethal Force Institute
Liberty Shooting Supplies
Lyman Products Corp.
Madis Books
Martin Bookseller, J.
McKee Publications
MI-TE Bullets
Montana Armory, Inc.
Mountain South
New Win Publishing, Inc.
NgraveR Co., The
OK Weber, Inc.
Outdoorsman's Bookstore, The
Paintball Games International Magazine (Aceville Publications)
Paintball Sports Magazine
Pejsa Ballistics
Petersen Publishing Co.
Pettinger Books, Gerald
Police Bookshelf
PWL Gunleather
R.G.-G., Inc.
Riling Arms Books Co., Ray
Rocky Mountain Wildlife Products
Rutgers Book Center
S&S Firearms
Safari Press, Inc.
Saunders Gun & Machine Shop
Semmer, Charles
Shootin' Accessories, Ltd.
Sierra Bullets
SPG, Inc.
Stackpole Books
Stewart Game Calls, Inc., Johnny
Stoeger Publishing Co.
"Su-Press-On," Inc.
Thomas, Charles C.
Track of the Wolf, Inc.
Trafalgar Square
Trotman, Ken
Vintage Industries, Inc.
VSP Publishers
WAMCO—New Mexico
Wiest, M.C.
Wilderness Sound Products Ltd.
Williams Gun Sight Co.
Winchester Press
Wolfe Publishing Co.
Wolf's Western Traders

PRODUCT & SERVICE DIRECTORY

BULLET AND CASE LUBRICANTS

Blackhawk West
Brown Co., E. Arthur
Camp-Cap Products
Chem-Pak, Inc.
C-H Tool & Die Corp.
Cooper-Woodward
CVA
Elkhorn Bullets
E-Z-Way Systems
Forster Products
4-D Custom Die Co.
Guardsman Products
HEBB Resources
Hollywood Engineering
Hornady Mfg. Co.
Le Clear Industries
Lee Precision, Inc.
Lestrom Laboratories,
Lithi Bee Bullet Lube
M&N Bullet Lube
Michaels of Oregon Co.
MI-TE Bullets
NECO
Paco's
RCBS
Reardon Products
Rooster Laboratories
Shay's Gunsmithing
Small Custom Mould &
  Bullet Co.
Tamarack Products, Inc.
Uncle Mike's
Warren Muzzleloading
  Co., Inc.
Widener's Reloading &
  Shooting
  Supply, Inc.
Young Country Arms

BULLET SWAGE DIES AND TOOLS

Brynin, Milton
Bullet Swaging Supply,
  Inc.
Camdex, Inc.
Corbin Mfg. & Supply,
  Inc.
Cumberland Arms
Eagan, Donald V.
Heidenstrom Bullets
Holland's
Hollywood Engineering
Necromancer Industries,
  Inc.
Niemi Engineering, W.B.
North Devon Firearms
  Services
Rorschach Precision
  Products
Sport Flite
  Manufacturing Co.

CARTRIDGES FOR COLLECTORS

Ad Hominem
Buck Stix—SOS
  Products Co.
Cameron's
Campbell, Dick
Cartridge Transfer
  Group
Cole's Gun Works
Colonial Repair
Country Armourer, The
de Coux, Pete
DGR Custom Rifles
Duane's Gun Repair
Ed's Gun House
Enguix Import-Export
Epps, Ellwood
First, Inc., Jack
Fitz Pistol Grip Co.
Forty Five Ranch
  Enterprises
Goergen's Gun Shop,
  Inc.
"Gramps" Antique
  Cartridges
Gun City
Gun Parts Corp., The
Gun Room Press, The
Mandall Shooting
  Supplies, Inc.
MAST Technology
Michael's Antiques
Montana Outfitters
Mountain Bear Rifle
  Works, Inc.
Pasadena Gun Center
San Francisco Gun
  Exchange
Samco Global Arms, Inc.
Scott Fine Guns, Inc.,
  Thad
SOS Products Co.
Stone Enterprises, Ltd.
Ward & Van Valkenburg
Yearout, Lewis E.

CASES, CABINETS, RACKS AND SAFES—GUN

Abel Safe & File, Inc.
Alco Carrying Cases
All Rite Products, Inc.
Allen Co., Bob
Allen Co., Inc.
Alumna Sport by Dee
  Zee
American Display Co.
American Security
  Products Co.
Americase
Ansen Enterprises
Arizona Custom Case
Arkfeld Mfg. & Dist. Co.,
  Inc.
Art Jewel Enterprises
  Ltd.
Bagmaster Mfg., Inc.
Barramundi Corp.
BEC, Inc.
Berry's Mfg., Inc.
Big Sky Racks, Inc.
Big Spring Enterprises
  "Bore Stores"
Bill's Custom Cases
Bison Studios
Black Sheep Brand
Boyt
Brauer Bros. Mfg. Co.
Brown, H.R.
Browning Arms Co.
Bucheimer, J.M.
Bushmaster Hunting &
  Fishing
Cannon Safe, Inc.
Chipmunk
Cobalt Mfg., Inc.
CONKKO
Connecticut Shotgun
  Mfg. Co.
D&L Industries
Dara-Nes, Inc.
Deepeeka Exports Pvt.
  Ltd.
D.J. Marketing
Doskocil Mfg. Co., Inc.
DTM International, Inc.
Elk River, Inc.
English, Inc., A.G.
Enhanced
  Presentations, Inc.
Eutaw Co., Inc., The
Eversull Co., Inc., K.
Fort Knox Security
  Products
Frontier Safe Co.
Galati Internationl
GALCO International
  Ltd.
Granite Custom Bullets
Gun Locker
Gun-Ho Sports Cases
Gusdorf Corp.
Hafner Creations, Inc.
Hall Plastics, Inc., John
Harrison-Hurtz
  Enterprises, Inc.
Hastings Barrels
Homak
Hoppe's Div.
Huey Gun Cases
Hugger Hooks Co.
Hunter Co., Inc.
Impact Case Co.
Johansson
Vapentillbehor, Bert
Johnston Bros.
Jumbo Sports Products
Kalispel Case Line
Kane Products, Inc.
KK Air International
Knock on Wood
  Antiques
Kolpin Mfg., Inc.
Lakewood Products,
  LLC
Liberty Safe
Marsh, Mike
Maximum Security Corp.
McWelco Products
Morton Booth Co.
MPC
MTM Molded Products
  Co., Inc.
Nalpak
National Security Safe
  Co., Inc.
Necessary Concepts,
  Inc.
Nesci Enterprises, Inc.
Oregon Arms, Inc.
Outa-Site Gun Carriers
Outdoor Connection,
  Inc., The
Pachmayr Ltd.
Palmer Security
  Products
Penguin Industries, Inc.
Pflumm Mfg. Co.
Poburka, Philip
Powell & Son
  (Gunmakers) Ltd.,
  William
Protecto Plastics
Prototech Industries, Inc.
Quality Arms, Inc.
Rogue Rifle Co., Inc.
Schulz Industries
Silhouette Leathers
Southern Security
Sportsman's
  Communicators
Sun Welding Safe Co.
Surecase Co., The
Sweet Home, Inc.
Tinks & Ben Lee Hunting
  Products
Waller & Son, Inc., W.
WAMCO, Inc.
Wilson Case, Inc.
Woodstream
Zanotti Armor, Inc.
Ziegel Engineering

CHRONOGRAPHS AND PRESSURE TOOLS

Brown Co., E. Arthur
Canons Delcour
Competition Electronics,
  Inc.
Custom Chronograph,
  Inc.
D&H Precision Tooling
Hege Jagd-u.
  Sporthandels, GmbH
Hornady Mfg. Co.
Kent Cartridge Mfg. Co.
  Ltd.
Oehler Research, Inc.
P.A.C.T., Inc.
Shooting Chrony, Inc.
SKAN A.R.
Stratco, Inc.
Tepeco

CLEANING AND REFINISHING SUPPLIES

AC Dyna-tite Corp.
Acculube II, Inc.
Accupro Gun Care
American Gas &
  Chemical Co., Ltd.
Answer Products Co.
Armite Laboratories
Atlantic Mills, Inc.
Atsko/Sno-Seal, Inc.
Barnes Bullets, Inc.
Birchwood Casey
Blackhawk East
Blount, Inc., Sporting
  Equipment Div.
Blue and Gray Products,
  Inc.
Break-Free, Inc.
Bridgers Best
Brown Co., E. Arthur
Camp-Cap Products
Cape Outfitters
Chem-Pak, Inc.
CONKKO
Crane & Crane Ltd.

PRODUCT & SERVICE DIRECTORY

CLEANING AND REFINISHING SUPPLIES (continued)

Creedmoor Sports, Inc.
CRR, Inc./Marble's Inc.
Custom Products
D&H Prods. Co., Inc.
Dara-Nes, Inc.
Decker Shooting Products
Deepeeka Exports Pvt. Ltd.
Dewey Mfg. Co., Inc., J.
Du-Lite Corp.
Dutchman's Firearms, Inc., The
Dykstra, Doug
E&L Mfg., Inc.
Eezox, Inc.
Ekol Leather Care
Faith Associates, Inc.
Flitz International Ltd.
Fluoramics, Inc.
Frontier Products Co.
G96 Products Co., Inc.
Goddard, Allen
Golden Age Arms Co.
Gozon Corp., U.S.A.
Great Lakes Airguns
Guardsman Products
Half Moon Rifle Shop
Heatbath Corp.
Hoppe's Div.
Hornady Mfg. Co.
Hydrosorbent Products
Iosso Products
Johnston Bros.
Kellogg's Professional Products
Kent Cartridge Mfg. Co. Ltd.
Kesselring Gun Shop
Kleen-Bore, Inc.
Laurel Mountain Forge
Lee Supplies, Mark
LEM Gun Specialties, Inc.
Lewis Lead Remover, The
List Precision Engineering
LPS Laboratories, Inc.
Marble Arms
Micro Sight Co.
Minute Man High Tech Industries
Mountain View Sports, Inc.
MTM Molded Products Co., Inc.
Muscle Products Corp.
Nesci Enterprises, Inc.
Northern Precision Custom Swaged Bullets
Now Products, Inc.
Old World Oil Products
Omark Industries
Original Mink Oil, Inc.
Outers Laboratories, Div. of Blount
Ox-Yoke Originals, Inc.
P&M Sales and Service
Pachmayr Ltd.
PanaVise Products, Inc.
Parker Gun Finishes
Pendleton Royal
Penguin Industries, Inc.
Precision Reloading, Inc.
Prolix® Lubricants
Pro-Shot Products, Inc.
R&S Industries Corp.
Radiator Specialty Co.
Rickard, Inc., Pete
RIG Products Co.
Rod Guide Co.
Rooster Laboratories
Rusteprufe Laboratories
Rusty Duck Premium Gun Care Products
Saunders Gun & Machine Shop
Shiloh Creek
Shooter's Choice
Shootin' Accessories, Ltd.
Silencio/Safety Direct
Sno-Seal, Inc.
Spencer's Custom Guns
Stoney Point Products, Inc.
Svon Corp.
Tag Distributors
TDP Industries, Inc.
Tetra Gun Lubricants
Texas Platers Supply Co.
T.F.C. S.p.A.
Thompson Bullet Lube Co.
Thompson/Center Arms
Track of the Wolf, Inc.
United States Products Co.
Van Gorden & Son, Inc., C.S.
Venco Industries, Inc.
VibraShine, Inc.
Warren Muzzleloading Co., Inc.
WD-40 Co.
Wick, David E.
Willow Bend
Young Country Arms
Z-Coat Industrial Coatings, Inc.

COMPUTER SOFTWARE—BALLISTICS

ADC, Inc.
Action Target, Inc.
AmBr Software Group Ltd.
Arms, Programming Solutions
Arms Software
Ballistic Engineering & Software, Inc.
Ballistic Program Co., Inc., The
Barnes Bullets, Inc.
Beartooth Bullets
Blackwell, W.
Canons Delcour
Corbin Mfg. & Supply, Inc.
Country Armourer, The
Data Tech Software Systems
Exe, Inc.
FlashTek, Inc.
Hodgdon Powder Co., Inc.
Hutton Rifle Ranch
Jensen Bullets
J.I.T. Ltd.
JWH: Software
Kent Cartridge Mfg. Co. Ltd.
Load From A Disk
Maionchi-L.M.I.
Oehler Research, Inc.
P.A.C.T., Inc.
PC Bullet/ADC, Inc.
Pejsa Ballistics
Powley Computer
RCBS
Sierra Bullets
Tioga Engineering Co., Inc.
Vancini, Carl
W. Square Enterprises

CUSTOM METALSMITHS

Ahlman Guns
Aldis Gunsmithing & Shooting Supply
Amrine's Gun Shop
Answer Products Co.
Arnold Arms Co., Inc.
Arundel Arms & Ammunition, Inc., A.
Baer Custom, Inc., Les
Bansner's Gunsmithing Specialties
Baron Technology
Barsotti, Bruce
Bear Mountain Gun & Tool
Behlert Precision, Inc.
Beitzinger, George
Bell, Sid
Benchmark Guns
Bengtson Arms Co., L.
Biesen, Al
Billeb, Stephen L.
Billingsley & Brownell
Brace, Larry D.
Briganti, A.J.
Brown Precision, Inc.
Buckhorn Gun Works
Bullberry Barrel Works, Ltd.
Campbell, Dick
Carter's Gun Shop
Champlin Firearms, Inc.
Checkmate Refinishing
Chicasaw Gun Works
Christman Jr., David
Classic Guns, Inc.
Cochran, Oliver
Colonial Repair
Colorado Gunsmithing Academy
Craftguard
Crandall Tool & Machine Co.
Cullity Restoration, Daniel
Custom Gun Products
Custom Gunsmiths
Custom Shop, The
D&D Gunsmiths, Ltd.
D&H Precision Tooling
DAMASCUS-U.S.A.
Delorge, Ed
DGS, Inc.
Dietz Gun Shop & Range, Inc.
Duane's Gun Repair
Duncan's Gunworks, Inc.
Eversull Co., Inc., K.
Eyster Heritage Gunsmiths, Inc., Ken
Ferris Firearms
Forster, Larry L.
Forthofer's Gunsmithing & Knifemaking
Francesca, Inc.
Frank Custom Classic Arms, Ron
Fullmer, Geo. M.
Gilkes, Anthony W.
Gordie's Gun Shop
Grace, Charles E.
Graybill's Gun Shop
Green, Roger M.
Gun Shop, The
Guns
Hamilton, Alex B.
Hartmann & Weiss GmbH
Harwood, Jack O.
Hecht, Hubert J.
Heilmann, Stephen
Heritage Wildlife Carvings
Highline Machine Co.
Hiptmayer, Armurier
Hiptmayer, Klaus
Hoag, James W.
Hoelscher, Virgil
Holland's
Hollis Gun Shop
Hyper-Single, Inc.
Island Pond Gun Shop
Ivanoff, Thomas G.
J&S Heat Treat
Jaeger, Inc., Paul/Dunn's
Jamison's Forge Works
Jeffredo Gunsight
Johnston, James
KDF, Inc.
Ken's Gun Specialties
Kilham & Co.
Klein Custom Guns, Don
Kleinendorst, K.W.
Kopp, Terry K.
Lampert, Ron
Lawson Co., Harry
List Precision Engineering
Mac's .45 Shop
Makinson, Nicholas
McCament, Jay
McCann's Machine & Gun Shop
McFarland, Stan
Morrow, Bud
Mullis Guncraft
Nelson, Stephen
Nettestad Gun Works
New England Custom Gun Service
Nicholson Custom
Nitex, Inc.
Noreen, Peter H.
North Fork Custom Gunsmithing
Nu-Line Guns, Inc.
Olson, Vic
Ozark Gun Works
P&S Gun Service
Pagel Gun Works, Inc.
Parker Gun Finishes
Pasadena Gun Center
Penrod Precision
Precision Metal Finishing
Precise Metalsmithing Enterprises
Precision Metal Finishing, John Westrom
Precision Specialties
Rice, Keith
Rifles Inc.
Robar Co.'s, Inc., The
Rocky Mountain Arms, Inc.
Score High Gunsmithing
Simmons Gun Repair, Inc.
Sipes Gun Shop
Skeoch, Brian R.
Smith, Art
Snapp's Gunshop
Spencer's Custom Guns
Sportsmen's Exchange & Western Gun Traders, Inc.

PRODUCT & SERVICE DIRECTORY

CUSTOM METALSMITHS (continued)

Starnes Gunmaker, Ken
Steffens, Ron
Steger, James R.
Stiles Custom Guns
Storey, Dale A.
Strawbridge, Victor W.
Ten-Ring Precision, Inc.
Thompson, Randall

Tom's Gun Repair
Tooley Custom Rifles
Van Horn, Gil
Van Patten, J.W.
Von Minden Gunsmithing Services
Waldron, Herman

Weber & Markin Custom Gunsmiths
Wells, Fred F.
Westrom, John
Wells Custom Gunsmith, R.A.
Welsh, Bud
Werth, T.W.

Wessinger Custom Guns & Engraving
Williamson Precision Gunsmithing
Wise Guns, Dale
Wood, Frank
Williams Gun Sight Co.

Williams Shootin' Iron Service
Zufall, Joseph F.

ENGRAVERS, ENGRAVING TOOLS

Ackerman & Co.
Adair Custom Shop, Bill
Adams, John J. & Son Engravers
Ahlman Guns
Alfano, Sam
Allard, Gary
Allen Firearm Engraving
Altamont Co.
American Pioneer Video
Anthony and George Ltd.
Baron Technology
Barraclough, John K.
Bates Engraving, Billy
Bell, Sid
Blair Engraving, J.R.
Bleile, C. Roger
Boessler, Erich
Bone Engraving, Ralph
Bratcher, Dan
Brgoch, Frank
Brooker, Dennis
Brownell Checkering Tools, W.E.
Burgess, Byron
CAM Enterprises
Churchill, Winston
Clark Firearms Engraving
Collings, Ronald
Creek Side Metal & Woodcrafters
Cullity Restoration, Daniel

Cupp, Custom Engraver, Alana
Custom Gun Engraving
DAMASCUS-U.S.A.
Davidson, Jere
Dayton Traister
Delorge, Ed
Desquesnes, Gerald
Dixon Muzzleloading Shop, Inc.
Dolbare, Elizabeth
Drain, Mark
Dubber, Michael W.
Engraving Artistry
Evans Engraving, Robert
Eversull Co., Inc., K.
Eyster Heritage Gunsmiths, Inc., Ken
Fanzoj GmbH
Firearms Engraver's Guild of America
Flannery Engraving Co., Jeff W.
Forty Five Ranch Enterprises
Fountain Products
Francotte & Cie S.A., Auguste
Frank Knives
French, Artistic Engraving, J.R.
Gene's Custom Guns
George, Tim
Gilmm, Jerome C.
Golden Age Arms Co.
Gournet, Geoffroy

Grant, Howard V.
Griffin & Howe, Inc.
GRS Corp., Glendo
Gun Room, The
Guns
Gurney, F.R.
Gwinnell, Bryson J.
Hale/Engraver, Peter
Half Moon Rifle Shop
Hands Engraving, Barry
Harris Gunworks
Harris Hand Engraving, Paul A.
Harwood, Jack O.
Hawken Shop, The
Hendricks, Frank E.
Heritage Wildlife Carvings
Hiptmayer, Armurier
Hiptmayer, Heidemarie
Horst, Alan K.
Ingle, Engraver, Ralph W.
Jaeger, Inc., Paul/Dunn's
Jantz Supply
Johns Master Engraver, Bill
Kamyk Engraving Co., Steve
Kane, Edward
Kehr, Roger
Kelly, Lance
Klingler Woodcarving
Koevenig's Engraving Service

Kudlas, John M.
LeFever Arms Co., Inc.
Leibowitz, Leonard
Lindsay, Steve
Little Trees Ramble
Lutz Engraving, Ron
Master Engravers, Inc.
McCombs, Leo
McDonald, Dennis
McKenzie, Lynton
Mele, Frank
Metals Hand Engraver
Mittermeier, Inc., Frank
Montgomery Community College
Moschetti, Mitchell R.
Mountain States Engraving
Nelson, Gary K.
New England Custom Gun Service
New Orleans Jewelers Supply Co.
NgraveR Co., The
Oker's Engraving
P&S Gun Service
Pedersen, C.R.
Pedersen, Rex C.
Pilgrim Pewter, Inc.
Pilkington, Scott
Piquette, Paul R.
Potts, Wayne E.
Rabeno, Martin
Reed, Dave
Reno, Wayne
Riggs, Jim
Roberts, J.J.

Rohner, Hans
Rohner, John
Rosser, Bob
Rundell's Gun Shop
Runge, Robert P.
Sampson, Roger
Schiffman, Mike
Sherwood, George
Singletary, Kent
Smith, Mark A.
Smith, Ron
Smokey Valley Rifles
Theis, Terry
Thiewes, George W.
Thirion Gun Engraving, Denise
Thompson/Center Arms
Valade Engraving, Robert
Vest, John
Viramontez, Ray
Vorhes, David
Wagoner, Vernon G.
Wallace, Terry
Warenski, Julie
Warren, Kenneth W.
Weber & Markin Custom Gunsmiths
Welch, Sam
Wells, Rachel
Wessinger Custom Guns & Engraving
Wood, Mel
Yee, Mike

GUN PARTS, U.S. AND FOREIGN

Accuracy Gun Shop
Actions by "T"
Ahlman Guns
Amherst Arms
Aro-Tek, Ltd.
Auto-Ordnance Corp.
Badger Shooters Supply, Inc.
Bear Mountain Gun & Tool
Billings Gunsmiths, Inc.
Bob's Gun Shop
Bowen Classic Arms Corp.
Briese Bullet Co., Inc.
British Antiques
Buffer Technologies
Bushmaster Firearms
Bustani, Leo
Cape Outfitters
Caspian Arms Ltd.

Chicasaw Gun Works
Clark Custom Guns, Inc.
Cochran, Oliver
Cole's Gun Works
Colonial Repair
Cylinder & Slide, Inc.
Dayton Traister
Delta Arms Ltd.
DGR Custom Rifles
Dibble, Derek A.
Duane's Gun Repair
Duffy, Charles E.
Dyson & Son Ltd., Peter
EGW Evolution Gun Works
Elliott Inc., G.W.
EMF Co., Inc.
Enguix Import-Export
Flemning Firearms

Forrest, Inc., TomGalati
Glimm, Jerome C.
Goodwin, Fred
Greider Precision
Groenewold, John
Gun Parts Corp., The
Gun Shop, The
Guns Antique & Modern DBA/Charles E. Duffy
Gunsmithing, Inc.
Gun-Tec
Hastings Barrels
Hawken Shop, The
High Performance International
Irwin, Campbell H.
I.S.S.
Jaeger, Inc.; Paul/Dunn's
Jamison's Forge Works

Johnson's Gunsmithing, Inc., Neal G
J.R. Distributing (Wolf competition guns)
K&T Co.
Kimber of America, Inc.
K.K. Arms Co.
Krico Jagd-und Sportwaffen GmbH
Laughridge, William R.
List Precision Engineering
Lodewick, Walter H.
Long, George F.
Lothar Walther Precision Tool, Inc.
Mac's .45 Shop
Mandall Shooting Supplies, Inc.
Markell, Inc.
Martin's Gun Shop

Martz, John V.
McCormick Corp., Chip
MCS, Inc.
Merkuria Ltd.
Mid-America Recreation, Inc.
Mo's Competitor Supplies
Morrow, Bud
NCP Products, Inc.
North Star West
Nu-Line Guns, Inc.
Olympic Arms
Pachmayr Ltd.
Parts & Surplus
Pennsylvania Gun Parts
Perazone, Brian
Performance Specialists
Peterson Gun Shop, Inc., A.W.
P.S.M.G. Gun Co.

PRODUCT & SERVICE DIRECTORY

GUN PARTS, U.S. AND FOREIGN (continued)

Quality Firearms of Idaho, Inc.
Quality Parts Co.
Randco UK
Ravell Ltd.
Retting, Inc., Martin B.
R.G.-G., Inc.
Ruger
S&S Firearms
Sabatti S.R.L.
Sarco, Inc.
Scherer

Shockley, Harold H.
Shootin' Shack, Inc.
Silver Ridge Gun Shop
Simmons Gun Repair, Inc.
Sipes Gun Shop
Smires, C.L.
Smith & Wesson
Southern Ammunition Co., Inc.
Southern Armory, The

Sportsmen's Exchange & Western Gun Traders, Inc.
Springfield, Inc.
Springfield Sporters, Inc.
Starr Trading Co., Jedediah
Steyr Mannlicher AG & CO KG
Sturm, Ruger & Co., Inc.
"Su-Press-On," Inc.
Swampfire Shop, The

Tank's Rifle Shop
Tarnhelm Supply Co., Inc.
Triple-K Mfg. Co., Inc.
Twin Pine Armory
USA Sporting Inc.
Vintage Arms, Inc.
Volquartsen Custom Ltd.
Walker Arms Co., Inc.
Waller & Son, Inc. W.
Weaver Arms Corp. Gun Shop

Wescombe, Bill
Westfield Engineering
Whitestone Lumber Corp.
Williams Mfg. of Oregon
Winchester Sutler, Inc., The
Wise Guns, Dale
Wolff Co., W.C.

GUNS, AIR

Airrow
Beeman Precision Airguns
Benjamin/Sheridan Co.
Brass Eagle, Inc.
Brocock Ltd.
BSA Guns Ltd.
Crosman Airguns
Crosman Products of Canada Ltd.
Daisy Mfg. Co.
Diana
Dynamit Nobel-RWS, Inc.

FAS
Frankonia Jagd
FWB
Gamo USA, Inc.
Gaucher Armes, S.A.
Great Lakes Airguns
Hebard Guns, Gil
Hofmann & Co.
Interarms
Labanu, Inc.
List Precision Engineering
Mac-1 Distributors
Marksman Products

Maryland Paintball Supply
Merkuria Ltd.
Pardini Armi Srl
Penguin Industries, Inc.
Precision Airgun Sales, Inc.
Precision Sales Int'l., Inc.
Ripley Rifles
Robinson, Don
RWS
S.G.S. Sporting Guns Srl
SKAN A.R.

Smart Parts
Steyr Mannlicher AG & CO KG
Stone Enterprises Ltd.
Swivel Machine Works, Inc.
Theoben Engineering
Tippmann Pneumatics, Inc.
Tristar Sporting Arms, Ltd.
Trooper Walsh
UltraSport Arms, Inc.
Valor Corp.

Vortek Products
Walther GmbH, Carl
Webley and Scott Ltd.
Weihrauch KG, Hermann
Whiscombe
World Class Airguns

GUNS, FOREIGN—IMPORTERS (Manufacturers)

Accuracy International (Anschutz GmbH target rifles)
AcuSport Corporation (Anschutz GmbH)
Air Rifle Specialists (airguns)
American Arms, Inc. (Fausti Cav. Stefano & Figlie snc; Franchi S.p.A.; Grulla Armes; Uberti; Aldo; Zabala Hermanos S.A.; blackpowder arms)
American Frontier Firearms Mfg. Inc. (single-action revolvers)
Amtec 2000, Inc. (Erma Werke GmbH)
Anics Firm, Inc. (Anics)
Arms United Corp. (Gamo)
Armsport, Inc. (Bernardelli S.p.A., Vincenzo)
Aspen Outfitting Co. (Ugartechea S.A., Ignacio)
Auto-Ordnance Corp. (Techno Arms)
Autumn Sales, Inc. (Blaser Jagdwaffen GmbH)
Beauchamp & Son, Inc. (Pedersoli and Co., Davide)

Beeman Precision Airguns (Beeman Precision Airguns, Inc.; FWB; Webley & Scott Ltd.; Weihrauch KG, Hermann)
Beretta U.S.A. Corp. (Beretta S.p.A., Pietro)
Big Bear Arms & Sporting Goods, Inc. (Russian/Big Bear Arms)
Bohemia Arms Co. (BRNO)
British Sporting Arms
Browning Arms Co. (Browning Arms Co.)
Cabela's (Pedersoli and Co., Davide; Uberti, Aldo; blackpowder arms)
Cape Outfitters (Armi Sport; Pedersoli and Co., Davide; San Marco; Societa Armi Bresciane Srl.; blackpowder arms)
Century International Arms, Inc. (FEG)
Champion Shooters' Supply (Anschutz GmbH)
Champion's Choice (Anschutz GmbH; Walther GmbH, Carl; target rifles)
Chapuis USA (Chapuis Armes)

Champlin Firearms, Inc. (Chapuis Armes; M.Thys)
Christopher Firearms Co., Inc., E.
Cimarron Arms (Uberti, Aldo; Armi San Marco; Pedersoli)
CVA (blackpowder arms)
CZ USA
Daisy Mfg. Co. (Daisy Mfg. Co.; Gamo)
Dixie Gun Works, Inc. (Pedersoli and Co., Davide; Uberti, Aldo; blackpowder arms)
Dynamit Nobel-RWS, Inc. (Brenneke KG, Wilhelm; Diana; Gamo; Norma Precision AB; RWS)
E.A.A. Corp. (Astra-Sport, S.A.; Sabatti S.r.l.; Tanfoglio Fratelli S.r.l.; Weihrauch KG, Hermann; Star Bonifacio Echeverria S.A.)
Eagle Imports, Inc. (Bersa S.A.)
EMF Co., Inc. (Dakota; Hartford; Pedersoli and Co., Davide; San Marco; Uberti, Aldo; blackpowder arms)
Euroarms of America, Inc. (blackpowder arms)

Eversull Co., Inc., K.
Fiocchi of America, Inc. (Fiocchi Munizioni S.p.A.)
Forgett Jr., Valmore J. (Navy Arms Co.; Uberti, Aldo)
Franzen International, Inc. (Peters Stahl GmbH)
Gamba, USA (Societa Armi Bresciane Srl.)
Gamo USA, Inc. (Gamo airguns)
Giacomo Sporting, Inc.
Glock, Inc. (Glock GmbH)
Great Lakes Airguns (air pistols & rifles)
Groenewold, John (BSA Guns Ltd.; Webley & Scott Ltd.)
GSI, Inc. (Mauser Werke Oberndorf; Merkel Freres; Steyr-Mannlicher AG)
Gun Shop, The (Ugartechea S.A., Ignacio)
Hammerli USA (Hammerli Ltd.)
Hanus Birdguns, Bill (Ugartechea S.A., Ignacio)
Heckler & Koch, Inc. (Benelli Armi S.p.A.; Heckler & Koch, GmbH)

IAR, Inc. (Uberti, Kimar, Armi San Marco, S.I.A.C.E.)
Import Sports Inc. (Llama Gabilondo Y Cia)
Israel Arms International, Inc. (KSN Industries, Ltd.)
Ithaca Gun Co., LLC (Fabarm S.p.A.)
JägerSport, Ltd. (Voere-KGH m.b.H.)
J.R. Distributing (Wolf competition guns)
K.B.I., Inc. (FEG; Miroku, B.C./Daly, Charles)
Kemen American (Armas Kemen S.A.)
Keng's Firearms Specialty, Inc. (Lapua Ltd.; Ultralux)
Kongsberg America L.L.C. (Kongsberg)
K-Sports Imports, Inc.
Lion Country Supply
London Guns Ltd. (London Guns Ltd.)
Mac-1 Distributors
Magnum Research, Inc.
MagTech Recreational Products, Inc. (MagTech)

PRODUCT & SERVICE DIRECTORY

GUNS, FOREIGN—IMPORTERS (Manufacturers) (continued)

Mandall Shooting Supplies, Inc. (Arizaga; Atamec-Bretton; Cabanas; Crucelegui, Hermanos; Erma Werke GmbH; Firearms Co. Ltd./Alpine; Hammerli Ltd.; Korth; Krico Jagd- und Sportwaffen GmbH; Morini; SIG; Tanner; Zanoletti, Pietro; blackpowder arms)

Marx, Harry (FERLIB)

MCS, Inc. (Pardini)

MEC-Gar U.S.A., Inc. (MEC-Gar S.R.L.)

Moore & Co., Wm.

Larkin (Garbi; Piotti; Rizzini, Battista; Rizzini F.lli)

Nationwide Sports Distributors, Inc. (Arizaga; Daewoo Precision Industries Ltd.)

Navy Arms Co. (Navy Arms Co.

Pedersoli and Co., Davide; Pietta; Uberti, Aldo; blackpowder and cartridge arms)

Nevada Cartridge Co. (Effebi SNC-Dr. Franco Beretta)

Nygord Precision Products (FAS; Morini; Pardini Armi Srl; Steyr- Mannlicher AG; TOZ; Unique/M.A.P.F.)

Pachmayr Ltd.

Para-Ordnance, Inc. (Para- Ordnance Mfg., Inc.)

Powell Agency, William, The (William Powell & Son [Gunmakers] Ltd.)

P.S.M.G. Gun Co. (Astra Sport, S.A.; Interarms; Star Bonifacio Echeverria S.A.; Walther GmbH, Carl)

Sarco, Inc.

Schuetzen Pistol Works (Peters Stahl GmbH)

Sigarms, Inc. (Hammerli Ltd.; Sauer rifles; SIG- Sauer)

Specialty Shooters Supply, Inc. (JSL Ltd.)

Sphinx USA Inc. (Sphinx Engineering SA)

Springfield, Inc.

Stoeger Industries (IGA; Sako Ltd.; Tikka; target pistols)

Stone Enterprises Ltd.

Swarovski Optik North America Ltd.

Taurus Firearms, Inc. (Taurus International Firearms)

Taylor's & Co., Inc. (Armi San Marco; Armi Sport; I.A.B.; Pedersoli and Co., Davide; Pietta; Uberti, Aldo)

Tradewinds, Inc. (blackpowder arms)

Tristar Sporting Arms, Ltd. (Turkish, German, Italian and Spanish made firearms)

Trooper Walsh

Turkish Firearms Corp. (Turkish Firearms)

Uberti USA, Inc. (Uberti, Aldo; blackpowder arms)

USA Sporting Inc. (Armas Kemen S.A.)

Vintage Arms, Inc.

Whitestone Lumber Corp. (Heckler & Koch; Bennelli Armi S.p.A.)

World Class Airguns (Air Arms)

GUNS, FOREIGN—MANUFACTURERS (Importers)

Accuracy International Precision Rifles (Gunsite Custom Shop; Gunsite Training Center)

Air Arms (World Class Airguns)

Anics (Anics Firm, Inc.)

Anschutz GmbH (Accuracy International; AcuSport Corporation; Champion Shooters' Supply; Champion's Choice; Gunsmithing, Inc.

Astra Sport, S.A. (E.A.A. Corp.; P.S.M.G. Gun Co.)

Atamec-Bretton (Mandall Shooting Supplies, Inc.)

BEC Scopes (BEC, Inc.)

Beeman Precision Airguns, Inc. (Beeman Precision Airguns)

Benelli Armi S.p.A. (Heckler & Koch, Inc.; Whitestone Lumber Co.)

Beretta S.p.A., Pietro (Beretta U.S.A. Corp.)

Bersa S.A. (Eagle Imports, Inc.)

Bondini Paolo (blackpowder arms)

Borovnik KG, Ludwig

BRNO (Bohemia Arms Co.)

Brocock Ltd.

Browning Arms Co. (Browning Arms Co.)

BSA Guns Ltd. (Groenewold, John; Precision Sales International, Inc.)

CBC

Daisy Mfg. Co. (Daisy Mfg. Co.)

Diana (Dynamit Nobel-RWS, Inc.)

Erma Werke GmbH (Amtec 2000, Inc.; Mandall Shooting Supplies, Inc.)

F.A.I.R. Techni-Mec s.n.c.

FAS (Nygord Precision Products)

FEG (Century International Arms, Inc.; K.B.I., Inc.)

Firearms Co. Ltd./Alpine (Mandall Shooting Supplies, Inc.)

FN Herstal

FWB (Beeman Precision Airguns)

Gamba S.p.A.-Societa Armi Bresciane Srl.

Gamo (Arms United Corp.; Daisy Mfg. Co.; Dynamit Nobel-RWS, Inc.; Gamo USA, Inc.)

Gaucher Armes S.A.

Glock GmbH (Glock, Inc.)

Hammerli Ltd. (Hammerli USA;

Mandall Shooting Supplies, Inc.; Sigarms, Inc.)

Hartford (EMF Co., Inc.)

Hartmann & Weiss GmbH

Heckler & Koch, GmbH (Heckler & Koch, Inc.)

Hege Jagd-u. Sporthandels, GmbH

Helwan (Interarms)

I.A.B. (Taylor's & Co., Inc.)

IGA (Stoeger Industries)

IMI

Interarms (Interarms; P.S.M.G. Gun Co.)

JSL Ltd. (Specialty Shooters Supply, Inc.)

Kimar (IAR, Inc.)

Kongsberg (Kongsberg America L.L.C.)

Korth (Interarms; Mandall Shooting Supplies, Inc.)

KSN Industries, Ltd. (Israel Arms International, Inc.)

Lapua Ltd. (Keng's Firearms Specialty, Inc.)

Llama Gabilondo Y Cia (Import Sports Inc.)

MagTech (MagTech Recreational Products, Inc.)

Mandall Shooting Supplies, Inc.;

Mauser Werke Oberndorf (GSI, Inc.)

MEC-Gar S.R.L. (MEC- Gar U.S.A., Inc.)

Navy Arms Co. (Forgett Jr., Valmore J.; Navy Arms Co.)

Norinco (Century International Arms, Inc.; Interarms)

Norma Precision AB (Dynamit Nobel-RWS Inc.; The Paul Co., Inc.)

Para-Ordnance Mfg., Inc. (Para- Ordnance, Inc.)

Pardini Armi Srl. (Nygord Precision Products; MCS, Inc.)

Powell & Son Ltd., William (Powell Agency, The, William)

RWS (Dynamit Nobel- RWS, Inc.)

SIG (Mandall Shooting Supplies, Inc.)

SIG-Sauer (Sigarms, Inc.)

Sphinx Engineering SA (Sphinx USA Inc.)

Springfield, Inc. (Springfield, Inc.)

Star Bonifacio Echeverria S.A. (E.A.A. Corp.; Interarms; P.S.M.G. Gun Co.)

Steyr-Mannlicher AG (GSI, Inc.; Nygord Precision Products)

Tanner (Mandall Shooting Supplies, Inc.)

Taurus International Firearms (Taurus Firearms, Inc.)

Taurus S.A., Forjas Techno Arms (Auto- Ordnance Corp.)

T.F.C. S.p.A. (Turkish Firearms Corp.)

Turkish Firearms Corp. (Turkish Firearms Corp.)

Uberti, Aldo (American Arms, Inc.; Cabela's; Cimarron Arms; Dixie Gun Works, Inc.; EMF Co., Inc.; Forgett Jr., Valmore J.; IAR, Inc.; Navy Arms Co.; Taylor's & Co., Inc.; Uberti USA, Inc.)

Ultralux (Keng's Firearms Specialty, Inc.)

Unique/M.A.P.F. (Nygord Precision Products)

Walther GmbH, Carl (Champion's Choice; Interarms; P.S.M.G. Gun Co.)

Webley & Scott Ltd. (Beeman Precision Airguns; Groenewold, John; Hermann Weihrauch KG, Precision Airguns; E.A.A. Corp.)

PRODUCT & SERVICE DIRECTORY

GUNS, U.S.-MADE

A.A. Arms, Inc.
Accu-Tek
Airrow
American Arms, Inc.
American Derringer Corp.
American Frontier Firearms Co.
A.M.T.
Auto-Ordnance Corp.
Baer Custom, Inc., Les
Beretta S.p.A., Pietro
Beretta U.S.A. Corp.
Bond Arms, Inc.
Braverman Corp., R.J.
Brolin Arms
Brown Co., E. Arthur
Brown Products, Inc., Ed
Browning Arms Co.
Calico Light Weapon Systems
Casull Arms Corp.
Century Gun Dist., Inc.
Champlin Firearms, Inc.
Colt's Mfg. Co., Inc.
Competitor Corp., Inc.
Connecticut Valley Classics
Coonan Arms
Cumberland Arms
Cumberland Mountain Arms
CVA
CVC
Davis Industries
Dayton Traister
Dixie Gun Works, Inc.
Downsizer Corp.
Eagle Arms, Inc.
Emerging Technologies, Inc.
FN Herstal
Forgett Jr., Valmore J.
Fort Worth Firearms
Frank Custom Classic Arms, Ron
Freedom Arms, Inc.
Fullmer, Geo. M.
Gonic Arms, Inc.
Gunsite Custom Shop
Gunsite Gunsmithy
H&R 1871, Inc.
Harris Gunworks
Harrington & Richardson
Heritage Firearms
Heritage Manufacturing, Inc.
Hesco-Meprolight
High Standard Mfg. Co., Inc.
Hi-Point Firearms
HJS Arms, Inc.
Holston Ent. Inc.
IAR, Inc.
Imperial Russian Armory
Intratec
Jones, J.D.
J.P. Enterprises, Inc.
JS Worldwide DBA
Kahr Arms
Kel-Tec CNC Industries, Inc.
Kimber of America, Inc.
K.K. Arms Co.
Knight's Mfg. Co.
L.A.R. Mfg., Inc.
Laseraim, Inc.
Lever Arms Service Ltd.
Ljutic Industries, Inc.
Lorcin Engineering Co., Inc.
Mag-Na-Port International, Inc.
Magnum Research, Inc.
MKS Supply, Inc.
M.O.A. Corp.
Montana Armory, Inc.
NCP Products, Inc.
North American Arms, Inc.
North Star West
Nowlin Mfg. Co.
Olympic Arms, Inc.
Oregon Arms, Inc.
Phillips & Rogers, Inc.
Phoenix Arms
Precision Small Arms
Professional Ordnance, Inc.
Raptor Arms Co., Inc.
Recoilless Technologies, Inc.
Remington Arms Co., Inc.
Republic Arms, Inc.
Rocky Mountain Arms, Inc.
Ruger
Scattergun Technologies, Inc.
Seecamp Co., Inc., L.W.
Shepherd & Turpin Dist. Company
Small Arms Specialties
Smith & Wesson
Springfield, Inc.
SSK Industries
STI International
Stoeger Industries
Sturm, Ruger & Co., Inc.
Sundance Industries, Inc.
Sunny Hill Enterprizes, Inc.
Survival Arms, Inc.
Swivel Machine Works, Inc.
Texas Armory
Taurus Firearms, Inc.
Taylor & Robbins
Texas Longhorn Arms, Inc.
Thompson/Center Arms
Time Precision, Inc.
Tristar Sporting Arms, Ltd.
Ultra Light Arms, Inc.
UFA, Inc.
Wells, Fred F.
Wescombe, Bill
Wesson Firearms Co., Inc.
Wesson Firearms, Dan
Wildey, Inc.
Wilkinson Arms
Z-M Weapons

GUNS AND GUN PARTS, REPLICA AND ANTIQUE

Armi San Paolo
Auto-Ordnance Corp.
Bear Mountain Gun & Tool
Beauchamp & Son, Inc.
Billings Gunsmiths, Inc.
Bob's Gun Shop
British Antiques
Buckskin Machine Works
Buffalo Arms Co.
Burgess & Son Gunsmiths, R.W.
Cache La Poudre Rifleworks
Cape Outfitters
Chambers Flintlocks Ltd., Jim
Chicasaw Gun Works
Cochran, Oliver
Cogar's Gunsmithing
Cole's Gun Works
Colonial Arms, Inc.
Colonial Repair
Custom Riflestocks, Inc.
Dangler, Homer L.
Day & Sons, Inc., Leonard
Delhi Gun House
Delta Arms Ltd.
Dilliott Gunsmithing, Inc.
Dixon Muzzleloading Shop, Inc.
Dyson & Son., Ltd. Peter
Ed's Gun House
Flintlocks, Etc.
Forgett, Valmore J., Jr.
Getz Barrel Co.
Golden Age Arms Co.
Goodwin, Fred
Groenewold, John
Gun Parts Corp., The
Gun Works, The
Guns
Gun-Tec
Hastings Barrels
Hunkeler, A.
IAR, Inc.
Kokolus, Michael
Liberty Antique Gunworks
List Precision Engineering
L&R Lock Co.
Lucas, Edw. E.
Mandall Shooting Supplies, Inc.
Martin's Gun Shop
McKee Publications
McKinney, R.P.
Mountain Bear Rifle Works, Inc.
Mountain State Muzzleloading Supplies, Inc.
Munsch Gunsmithing, Tommy
Museum of Historical Arms, Inc.
Navy Arms Co.
Neumann GmbH
North Star West
October Country
Pasadena Gun Center
Pecatonica River Longrifle
PEM's Mfg. Co.
Pony Express Sport Shop, Inc.
Precise Metalsmithing Enterprises
Quality Firearms of Idaho, Inc.
Ranch Products
Randco UK
Ravell Ltd.
Retting, Inc., Martin B.
R.G.-G., Inc.
S&S Firearms
Sarco, Inc.
Shootin' Shack, Inc.
Silver Ridge Gun Shop
Simmons Gun Repair, Inc.
Southern Ammunition Co., Inc.
Starnes Gunmaker, Ken
Stott's Creek Armory, Inc.
Taylor's & Co., Inc.
Tennessee Valley Mfg.
Triple-K Mfg. Co., Inc.
Uberti USA, Inc.
Vintage Industries, Inc.
Vortek Products, Inc.
Walker Arms Co., Inc.
Weisz Parts
Wescombe, Bill
Winchester Sutler, Inc., The

GUNS, SURPLUS—PARTS AND AMMUNITION

Ad Hominem
Alpha 1 Drop Zone
Armscorp USA, Inc.
Arundel Arms & Ammunition, Inc., A.
Ballistica Maximus North
Bohemia Arms Co.
Bondini Paolo
Century International Arms, Inc.
Chuck's Gun Shop
Cole's Gun Works
Combat Military Ordnance Ltd.
Delta Arms Ltd.
Ed's Gun House
First, Inc., Jack
Flaig's
Fleming Firearms
Forgett, Valmore J., Jr.
Forrest, Inc., Tom
Frankonia Jagd
Fulton Armory
Garcia National Gun Traders, Inc.
Goodwin, Fred
Gun City
Gun Parts Corp., The
Hart & Son, Inc., Robert W.
Hege Jagd-u. Sporthandels, GmbH
Hofmann & Co.
Interarms
Jackalope Gun Shop
LaRocca Gun Works, Inc.
Lever Arms Service Ltd.
Lomont Precision Bullets
Mandall Shooting Supplies, Inc.
Navy Arms Co.
Nevada Pistol Academy Inc.
Oil Rod and Gun Shop
Paragon Sales & Services, Inc.
Parts & Surplus
Pasadena Gun Center
Perazone, Brian
Quality Firearms of Idaho, Inc.
Raptor Arms. Inc., Co.
Ravell Ltd.
Retting, Inc., Martin B.
Samco Global Arms, Inc.
San Francisco Gun Exchange
Sanders Custom Gun Service
Sarco, Inc.
Shootin' Shack, Inc.
Silver Ridge Gun Shop

PRODUCT & SERVICE DIRECTORY

GUNS, SURPLUS—PARTS AND AMMUNITION (continued)

Simmons Gun Repair, Inc.

Sportsmen's Exchange & Western Gun Traders, Inc.
Springfield Sporters, Inc.

Starnes Gunmaker, Ken
Tarnhelm Supply Co., Inc.
T.F.C. S.p.A.

Thurston Sports, Inc.
Westfield Engineering
Williams Shootin' Iron Service

Whitestone Lumber Corp.

GUNSMITH SCHOOLS

Bull Mountain Rifle Co.
Colorado Gunsmithing Academy
Colorado School of Trades
Lassen Community College,

Gunsmithing Dept.
Laughridge, William R.
Modern Gun Repair School
Montgomery Community College
Murray State College

North American Correspondence Schools
Nowlin Mfg. Co.
NRI Gunsmith School
Pennsylvania Gunsmith School

Piedmont Community College
Pine Technical College
Professional Gunsmiths of America
Southeastern Community College
Smith & Wesson

Spencer's Custom Guns
Trinidad State Junior College Gunsmithing Dept.
Trinidad State Junior College
Wright's Hardwood Gunstock Blanks
Yavapai College

GUNSMITH SUPPLIES, TOOLS, SERVICES

Ace Custom 45's, Inc.
Actions by "T"
Aldis Gunsmithing & Shooting Supply
Allred Bullet Co.
American Frontier Firearms Co.
Bar-Sto Precision Machine
Baer Custom, Inc., Les
Bauska Barrels
Bear Mountain Gun & Tool
Belt MTN Arms
Bengtson Arms Co., L.
Biesen, Al
Biesen, Roger
Bill's Gun Repair
Blue Ridge Machinery & Tools, Inc.
Bowen Classic Arms Corp.
Break-Free, Inc.
Briganti, A.J.
Briley Mfg., Inc.
Brownells, Inc.
B-Square Co., Inc.
Bull Mountain Rifle Co.
Burgess & Son Gunsmiths, R.W.
Carbide Checkering Tools
Chapman Manufacturing Co.
Chem-Pak, Inc.
Choate Machine & Tool Co., Inc.
Chopie Mfg., Inc.
Chuck's Gun Shop
Colonial Arms, Inc.
Colorado School of Trades
Conetrol Scope Mounts

Craig Custom Ltd.
CRR, Inc./Marble's Inc.
Cumberland Arms
Cumberland Mountain Arms
Custom Checkering Service
Custom Gun Products
D&J Bullet Co. & Custom Gun Shop, Inc.
Dakota Arms, Inc.
Decker Shooting Products
Dem-Bart Checkering Tools, Inc.
Dever Co., Jack
Dewey Mfg. Co., Inc., J.
Dremel Mfg. Co.
Du-Lite Corp.
Danuser Machine Co.
Dutchman's Firearms, Inc., The
Dyson & Son, Ltd., Peter
Echols & Co., D'Arcy
EGW Evolution Gun Works
Faith Associates, Inc.
FERLIB
Fisher, Jerry A.
Forgreens Tool Mfg., Inc.
Forkin, Ben
Forster, Kathy
Frazier Brothers Enterprises
Gentry Custom Gunmaker, David
Gilkes, Anthony W.
Grace Metal Products, Inc.
Greider Precision
Gr.-Tan Rifles
Gunline Tools
Gun-Tec

Half Moon Rifle Shop
Halstead, Rick
Hammon Custom Guns Ltd.
Hastings Barrels
Henriksen Tool Co., Inc.
High Performance International
Hoelscher, Virgil
Holland's
Huey Gun Cases
Ivanoff, Thomas G.
J&R Engineering
J&S Heat Treat
Jacobson, Teddy
Jantz Supply
JGS Precision Tool Mfg.
Kasenit Co., Inc.
KenPatable Ent., Inc.
Kimball, Gary
Kleinendorst, K.W.
Kmount
Kopp Professional Gunsmithing, Terry K.
Korzinek Riflesmith, J.
Kwik Mount Corp.
LaBounty Precision Reboring
Lawson Co., Harry
Lea Mfg. Co.
Lee's Red Ramps
Lee Supplies, Mark
List Precision Engineering
London Guns Ltd.
Mahovsky's Metalife
Marble Arms
Marsh, Mike
McKillen & Heyer, Inc.
Meier Works
Menck, Thomas W.
Metalife Industries
Metaloy Inc.
Michael's Antiques

MMC
Morrow, Bud
Mo's Competitor Supplies
Mowrey's Guns & Gunsmithing
N&J Sales
New England Custom Gun Service
Nowlin Custom Mfg.
Nu-Line Guns, Inc.
Ole Frontier Gunsmith Shop
Parker Gun Finishes
PEM's Mfg. Co.
Perazone, Brian
P.M. Enterprises, Inc.
Power Custom, Inc.
Practical Tools, Inc.
Precision Metal Finishing
Precision Specialties
Professional Gunsmiths of America
Prolix® Lubricants
Ransom International Corp.
Reardon Products
Rice, Keith
Robar Co.'s, Inc., The
Romain's Custom Guns, Inc.
Roto Carve
Royal Arms Gunstocks
Rusteprufe Laboratories
Scott, McDougall & Associates
Shooter's Choice
Simmons Gun Repair, Inc.
Smith Abrasives, Inc.
Spradlin's
Starrett Co., L.S.
Stiles Custom Guns

Sullivan, David S.
Texas Platers Supply
Theis, Terry
Time Precision, Inc.
Tom's Gun Repair
Track of the Wolf, Inc.
Trinidad State Junior College Gunsmithing Dept.
Trulock Tool
Turnbull Restoration, Doug
Van Gorden & Son, Inc., C.S.
Venco Industries, Inc.
Volquartsen Custom Ltd.
Warne Manufacturing Co.
Washita Mountain Whetstone Co.
Weaver Arms Corp. Gun Shop
Weigand Combat Handguns, Inc.
Welsh, Bud
Wessinger Custom Guns & Engraving
Westfield Engineering
Westrom, John
Westwind Rifles, Inc.
White Rock Tool & Die
Wicox All-Pro Tools & Supply
Will-Burt Co.
Williams Gun Sight Co.
Williams Shootin' Iron Service
Willow Bend
Wilson's Gun Shop
Wise Guns, Dale
Wright's Hardwood Gunstock Blanks
Yavapai College

HANDGUN ACCESSORIES

A.A. Arms, Inc.
Ace Custom 45's, Inc.
Action Direct, Inc.
ADCO Sales, Inc.
Adventurer's Outpost
African Import Co.
Aimpoint U.S.A.

Aimtech Mount Systems
Ajax Custom Grips, Inc.
Alpha Gunsmith Division
American Derringer Corp.
American Frontier Firearms Co.

Arms Corporation of the Philippines
Aro-Tek, Ltd.
Astra Sport, S.A.
Baer Custom, Inc., Les
Bar-Sto Precision Machine

BEC, Inc.
Behlert Precision, Inc.
Blue and Gray Products, Inc.
Bond Custom Firearms
Bowen Classic Arms Corp.

Broken Gun Ranch
Brown Products, Inc., Ed
Brownells, Inc.
Bucheimer, J.M.
Bushmaster Firearms
Bushmaster Hunting & Fishing

PRODUCT & SERVICE DIRECTORY

HANDGUN ACCESSORIES (continued)

Butler Creek Corp.
C3 Systems
Centaur Systems, Inc.
Central Specialties Ltd.
Clark Custom Guns, Inc.
Conetrol Scope Mounts
Craig Custom Ltd.
CRR, Inc./Marble's Inc.
D&L Industries
Dade Screw Machine Products
Dayson Arms Ltd.
Delhi Gun House
D.J. Marketing
Doskocil Mfg. Co., Inc
E&L Mfg., Inc.
E.A.A. Corp.
Eagle International
European American Armory Corp.
Faith Associates, Inc.
Feminine Protection, Inc.
Fisher Custom Firearms
Flashette Co.
Fleming Firearms
Flores Publications, Inc., J.
Frielich Police Equipment
FWB
Gage Manufacturing
Galati International
GALCO International Ltd.
G.G. & G.
Glock, Inc.
Greider Precision
Gremmel Enterprises
Gun Parts Corp., The
Gun-Alert
Gun-Ho Sports Cases
Hebard Guns, Gil
Heinie Specialty Products
Henigson & Associates
Hill Speed Leather, Ernie
H.K.S. Products
Hoppe's Div.
Hunter Co., Inc.
Impact Case Co.
Jarvis, Inc.
JB Custom
Jeffredo Gunsight
Jones, J.D.
J.P. Enterprises, Inc.
Jumbo Sports Products
KeeCo Impressions
KK Air International
Keller Co., The
King's Gun Works
K.K. Arms Co.
L&S Technologies, Inc.
Lee's Red Ramps Lem Sports, Inc.
Loch Leven Industries
Lohman Mfg. Co., Inc.
Mac's .45 Shop
Mag-Na-Port International, Inc.
Magnolia Sports, Inc.
Marble Arms
Markell, Inc.
Maxi-Mount
MCA Sports
McCormick Corp., Chip
MEC-Gar S.R.L.
Merkuria Ltd.
Mid-America Guns and Ammo
Middlebrooks Custom Shop
Millett Sights
MTM Molded Products Co., Inc.
MCA Sports
Noble Co., Jim
No-Sho Mfg. Co.
Omega Sales
Ox-Yoke Originals, Inc.
PAST Sporting Goods, Inc.
Pearce Grip, Inc.
Penguin Industries, Inc.
Phoenix Arms
Power Custom, Inc.
Practical Tools, Inc.
Protector Mfg. Co., Inc., The
Quality Parts Co.
Ram-Line Blount, Inc.
Ranch Products
Ransom International Corp.
Recoilless Technologies, Inc.
Redfield, Inc.
Robar Co.'s, Inc., The
Round Edge, Inc.
RPM
Simmons Gun Repair, Inc.
Slings 'N Things, Inc.
Southwind Sanctions
SSK Industries
STI International
TacStar Industries, Inc.
TacTell, Inc.
Tanfoglio Fratelli S.r.l.
T.F.C. S.p.A.
Thompson/Center Arms
Trigger Lock Division
Trijicon, Inc.
Triple-K Mfg. Co., Inc.
Tyler Manufacturing & Distributing
Valor Corp.
Volquartsen Custom Ltd.
Waller & Son, Inc., W.
Weigand Combat Handguns, Inc.
Wessinger Custom Guns & Engraving
Western Design
Wichita Arms, Inc.
Wilson Gun Shop

HANDGUN GRIPS

A.A. Arms, Inc.
Ahrends, Kim
Ajax Custom Grips, Inc.
Altamont Co.
American Derringer Corp.
American Frontier Firearms Co.
American Gripcraft
Arms Corporation of the Philippines
Art Jewel Enterprises Ltd.
Baelder, Harry
Baer Custom, Inc., Les
Barami Corp.
Bear Hug Grips, Inc.
Big Bear Arms & Sporting Goods, Inc.
Boone's Custom Ivory Grips, Inc.
Boyds' Gunstock Industries, Inc.
Brooks Tactical Systems
Brown Products, Inc., Ed
CAM Enterprises
Cole-Grip
Colonial Repair
Custom Firearms
Dayson Arms Ltd.
E.A.A. Corp.
EMF Co., Inc.
Essex Arms
European American Armory Corp.
Eyears Insurance
Fisher Custom Firearms
Fitz Pistol Grip Co.
Forrest, Inc., Tom
FWB
Harrison-Hurtz Enterprises, Inc.
Herrett's Stocks, Inc.
Hogue Grips
Huebner, Corey O.
KeeCo Impressions
Knight's Mfg. Co.
Korth
Lee's Red Ramps
Lett Custom Grips
Linebaugh Custom Sixgun & Rifle Works
Mac's .45 Shop
Masen Co., Inc., John
Michaels of Oregon Co.
Mid-America Guns and Ammo
Millett Sights
N.C. Ordnance Co.
Newell, Robert H.
Nickels, Paul R.
Pacific Rifle Co.
Pardini Armi Srl
Phoenix Arms
Pilgrim Pewter, Inc.
Radical Concepts
Recoilless Technologies, Inc.
Rosenberg & Sons, Jack A.
Roy's Custom Grips
Sile Distributors, Inc.
Smith & Wesson
Speedfeed, Inc.
Spegel, Craig
Stoeger Industries
Taurus Firearms, Inc.
Tyler Manufacturing & Distributing
Uncle Mike's
Vintage Industries, Inc.
Volquartsen Custom Ltd.
Western Gunstock Mfg. Co.

HEARING PROTECTORS

Aero Peltor
Ajax Custom Grips, Inc.
Autauga Arms, Inc.
Brown Co., E. Arthur
Brown Products, Inc., Ed
Browning Arms Co.
Clark Co., Inc., David
E-A-R, Inc.
Electronic Shooters Protection, Inc.
Faith Associates, Inc.
Flents Products Co., Inc.
Gentex Corp.
Hoppe's Div.
Kesselring Gun Shop
North Specialty Products
Paterson Gunsmithing
Peltor, Inc.
Penguin Industries, Inc.
R.E.T. Enterprises
Rucker Dist. Inc.
Silencio/Safety Direct
Willson Safety Prods. Div.

HOLSTERS AND LEATHER GOODS

A&B Industries, Inc.
Action Direct, Inc.
Action Products, Inc.
Aker Leather Products
Alessi Holsters, Inc.
American Sales & Kirkpatrick
Arratoonian, Andy
Bagmaster Mfg., Inc.
Baker's Leather Goods, Roy
Bandcor Industries
Bang-Bang Boutique
Barami Corp.
Bear Hug Grips, Inc.
Beretta S.p.A., Pietro
Bianchi International, Inc.
Bill's Custom Cases
Blocker Holsters, Inc., Ted
Brauer Bros. Mfg. Co.
Brown, H.R.
Browning Arms Co.
Bucheimer, J.M.
Bull-X, Inc.
Bushwacker Backpack & Supply Co.
Carvajal Belts & Holsters
Cathey Enterprises, Inc.
Chace Leather Products
Churchill Glove Co., James
Cimarron Arms
Clements' Custom Leathercraft, Chas
Cobra Sport
Colonial Repair
Counter Assault
Creedmoor Sports, Inc.
Davis Leather Co., G. Wm.
Delhi Gun House
DeSantis Holster & Leather Goods, Inc.
Dixie Gun Works, Inc.
D-Max, Inc.
Easy Pull Outlaw Products
Ekol Leather Care
El Dorado Leather (c/o Dill)
El Paso Saddlery Co.
EMF Co., Inc.
Eutaw Co., Inc., The
F&A Inc.
Faust, Inc., T.G.
Feminine Protection, Inc.
Ferdinand, Inc.

PRODUCT & SERVICE DIRECTORY

HOLSTERS AND LEATHER GOODS (continued)

Flores Publications, Inc., J.
Fobus International Ltd.
Forgett Jr., Valmore J.
Frankonia Jagd
Gage Manufacturing
GALCO International Ltd.
GML Products, Inc.
Gould & Goodrich
Gun Leather Limited
Gunfitters, The
Gun Works, The
Gusty Winds Corp.
Hafner Creations, Inc.
HandiCrafts Unltd.
Hank's Gun Shop
Hebard Guns, Gil
Heinie Specialty Products
Hellweg Ltd.
Henigson & Associates, Steve
Hill Speed Leather, Ernie
Hofmann & Co.
Holster Shop, The
Horseshoe Leather Products
Hoyt Holster Co., Inc.
Hume, Don
Hunter Co., Inc.
John's Custom Leather
Jumbo Sports Products
Kane Products, Inc.
Keller Co., The
Kirkpatrick Leather Co.
Kolpin Mfg., Inc.
Korth
Kramer Handgun Leather, Inc.
L.A.R. Mfg., Inc.
Law Concealment Systems, Inc.
Lawrence Leather Co.
Leather Arsenal
Lone Star Gunleather
Magnolia Sports, Inc.
Markell, Inc.
Michaels of Oregon Co.
Minute Man High Tech Industries
Mixson Corp.
Noble Co., Jim
No-Sho Mfg. Co.
Null Holsters Ltd., K.L.
October Country
Ojala Holsters, Arvo
Oklahoma Leather Products, Inc.
Old West Reproductions, Inc.
Pathfinder Sports Leather
PWL Gunleather
Recoilless Technologies, Inc.
Renegade
Ringler Custom Leather Co.
Rybka Custom Leather Equipment, Thad
Safariland Ltd., Inc.
Safety Speed Holster, Inc.
Schulz Industries
Second Chance Body Armor
Shoemaker & Sons, Inc., Tex
ShurKatch Corporation
Silhouette Leathers
Smith Saddlery, Jesse W.
Southwind Sanctions
Sparks, Milt
Stalker, Inc.
Star Trading Co.
Strong Holster Co.
Stuart, V. Pat
Tabler Marketing
Texas Longhorn Arms, Inc.
Top-Line USA Inc.
Torel, Inc.
Triple-K Mfg. Co., Inc.
Tristar Sporting Arms, Ltd.
Tyler
Tyler Manufacturing & Distributing
Uncle Mike's
Valor Corp.
Venus Industries
Viking Leathercraft, Inc.
Watt's Custom Leather
Westley Richards & Co.
Whinnery, Walt
Wild Bill's Originals
Wilson Gun Shop

LABELS, BOXES, CARTRIDGE HOLDERS

Ballistic Products, Inc.
Berry's Mfg., Inc.
Brown Co., E. Arthur
Cabinet Mountain Outfitters Scents & Lures
Cape Outfitters
Crane & Crane Ltd.
Del Rey Products
DeSantis Holster & Leather Goods, Inc.
Fitz Pistol Grip Co.
Flambeau Products
J&J Products Co.
Koipin Mfg., Inc.
Liberty Shooting Supplies
Midway Arms, Inc.
MTM Molded Products
Pendleton Royal

LOAD TESTING AND PRODUCT TESTING (Chronographing, Ballistic Studies)

Ballistic Research
Bartlett, Don
Briese Bullet Co., Inc.
Buck Stix—SOS Products Co.
Clearview Products
Clerke Co., J.A.
D&H Precision Tooling
Defense Training International, Inc.
DGR Custom Rifles
Duane's Gun Repair
Hensler, Steve
Henigson & Associates, Steve
Hoelscher, Jerry
Hoeschler, Virgil
Jackalope Gun Shop
Jensen Bullets
Lomont Precision Bullets
Maionchi-L.M.I.
MAST Technology
McMurdo, Lynn
Middlebrooks Custom Shop
Multiplex International
Oil Rod and Gun Shop
Rupert's Gun Shop
SOS Products Co.
Spencer's Custom Guns
Vancini, Carl
Vulpes Ventures, Inc.
Wells Custom Gunsmith, R.A.
White Laboratory, Inc., H.P.
X-Spand Target Systems

MUZZLE-LOADING GUNS, BARRELS AND EQUIPMENT

Accuracy Unlimited (Littleton, CO)
Adkins, Luther
Aimtech Mount Systems
Allen Manufacturing
Anderson Manufacturing Co., Inc.
Armi San Paolo
Armoury, Inc., The
Bauska Barrels
Beauchamp & Son, Inc.
Beaver Lodge
Bentley, John
Big Bore Bullets
Birdsong & Associates, W.E.
Blackhawk West
Black Powder Products
Blue and Gray Products, Inc.
Bridgers Best
Buckskin Bullet Co.
Buckskin Machine Works
Burgess & Son Gunsmiths, R.W.
Butter Creek Corp.
Cache La Poudre Rifleworks
California Sights
Cash Manufacturing Co., Inc.
CenterMark
Chambers Flintlocks, Ltd., Jim
Chopie Mfg., Inc.
Cimarron Arms
Cogar's Gunsmithing
Colonial Repair
Colt Blackpowder Arms Co.
Conetrol Scope Mounts
Cousin Bob's Mountain Products
Cumberland Arms
Cumberland Mountain Arms
Cumberland Knife & Gun Works
Curly Maple Stock Blanks
CVA
Dangler, Homer L.
Day & Sons, Inc., Leonard
Dayton Traister
deHaas Barrels
Delhi Gun House
Dixie Gun Works, Inc.
Dyson & Son Ltd., Peter
EMF Co., Inc.
Euroarms of America, Inc.
Eutaw Co., Inc., The
Fautheree, Andy
Feken, Dennis
Fellowes, Ted
Fire'n Five
Flintlocks, Etc.
Forgett Jr., Valmore J.
Fort Hill Gunstocks
Fowler, Bob
Frankonia Jagd
Frontier
Gain Twist Barrel Co.
Getz Barrel Co.
Golden Age Arms Co.
Gonic Arms, Inc.
Green Mountain Rifle Barrel Co., Inc.
Gun Works, The
Hastings Barrels
Hawken Shop, The
Hege Jagd-u. Sporthandels, GmbH
Hodgdon Powder Co., Inc.
Hoppe's Div.
Hornady Mfg. Co.
House of Muskets, Inc., The
Hunkeler, A.
Impact Case Co.
Jamison's Forge Works
Jones Co., Dale
K&M Industries, Inc.
Kennedy Firearms
Knight Rifles
Knight's Mfg. Co.
Kwik-Site Co.
L&R Lock Co.
L&S Technologies, Inc.
Legend Products Corp.
Lestrom Laboratories, Inc.
Log Cabin Sport Shop
Lone Star Rifle Company
Lothar Walther Precision Tool, Inc.
Lyons Gunworks, Larry
Lyman
Marlin Firearms Co.
Mathews & Son, Inc., George E.
McCann's Muzzle-Gun Works
Michaels of Oregon Co.
MMP
Modern MuzzleLoading, Inc.
Montana Precision Swaging
Mountain State Muzzleloading Supplies, Inc.
Mowrey Gun Works
MSC Industrial Supply Co.

PRODUCT & SERVICE DIRECTORY

MUZZLE-LOADING GUNS, BARRELS AND EQUIPMENT (continued)

Mt. Alto Outdoor Products
Mushroom Express Bullet Co.
Muzzleloaders Etcetera, Inc.
Naval Ordnance Works
North Star West
October Country
Oklahoma Leather Products, Inc.
Olson, Myron
Orion Rifle Barrel Co.
Ox-Yoke Originals, Inc.
Pacific Rifle Co.
Parker Gun Finishes
Pecatonica River Longrifle
Pedersoli and Co., Davide
Penguin Industries, Inc.
Pioneer Arms Co.
Prairie River Arms
R.E. Davis
Rusty Duck Premium Gun Care Products
R.V.I.
S&B Industries
S&S Firearms
Selsi Co., Inc.
Shiloh Creek
Shooter's Choice
Sile Distributors
Simmons Gun Repair, Inc.
Sklany's Machine Shop
Slings 'N Things, Inc.
Smokey Valley Rifles
South Bend Replicas, Inc.
Southern Bloomer Mfg. Co.
Starr Trading Co., Jedediah
Stone Mountain Arms
Taylor's & Co., Inc.
Tennessee Valley Mfg.
Thompson Bullet Lube Co.
Thompson/Center Arms
Thunder Mountain Arms
Tiger-Hunt
Track of the Wolf, Inc.
Traditions, Inc.
Treso, Inc.
UFA, Inc.
Uberti, Aldo
Uncle Mike's
Upper Missouri Trading Co.
Venco Industries, Inc.
Voere-KGH m.b.H.
Walters, John
Warren Muzzleloading Co., Inc.
Wescombe, Bill
White Owl Enterprises
White Muzzleloading Systems
White Shooting Systems, Inc.
Williams Gun Sight Co.
Woodworker's Supply
Wright's Hardwood Gunstock Blanks
Young Country Arms

PISTOLSMITHS

Acadian Ballistic Specialties
Accuracy Gun Shop
Accuracy Unlimited (Glendale, AZ)
Actions by "T"
Adair Custom Shop, Bill
Ahlman Guns
Ahrends, Kim
Aldis Gunsmithing & Shooting Supply
Alpha Precision, Inc.
Alpine's Precision Gunsmithing & Indoor Shooting Range
Armament Gunsmithing Co., Inc.
Arundel Arms & Ammunition, Inc., A.
Baer Custom, Inc., Les
Bain & Davis, Inc.
Baity's Custom Gunworks
Banks, Ed
Bear Arms
Behlert Precision, Inc.
Bellm Contenders
Belt MTN Arms
Bengtson Arms Co., L.
Bowen Classic Arms Corp.
Broken Gun Ranch
Campbell, Dick
Cannon's, Andy Cannon
Caraville Manufacturing
Carter's Gun Shop
Chicasaw Gun Works
Clark Custom Guns, Inc.
Cochran, Oliver
Colonial Repair
Colorado School of Trades
Corkys Gun Clinic
Craig Custom Ltd.
Curtis Custom Shop
Custom Firearms
Custom Gunsmiths
D&D Gunsmiths, Ltd.
D&L Sports
Davis Service Center, Bill
Dayton Traister
Dilliott Gunsmithing, Inc.
EGW Evolution Gun Works
Ellicott Arms, Inc./Woods Pistolsmithing
Ferris Firearms
Fisher Custom Firearms
Forkin, Ben
Francesca, Inc.
Frielich Police Equipment
Garthwaite, Pistolsmith, Inc., Jim
G.G. & G.
Gonzalez Guns, Ramon B.
Greider Precision
Gun Room Press, The
Guncraft Sports, Inc.
Gunsite Custom Shop
Gunsite Gunsmithy
Gunsite Training Center
Hamilton, Alex B.
Hamilton, Keith
Hammond Custom Guns Ltd.
Hank's Gun Shop
Hanson's Gun Center, Dick
Harwood, Jack O.
Harris Gunworks
Hawken Shop, The
Hebard Guns, Gil
Heinie Specialty Products
High Bridge Arms, Inc.
Highline Machine Co.
Hoag, James W.
Irwin, Campbell H.
Island Pond Gun Shop
Ivanoff, Thomas G.
J&S Heat Treat
Jacobson, Teddy
Jarvis, Inc.
Jensen's Custom Ammunition
Johnston, James
Jones, J.D.
Jungkind, Reeves C.
K-D, Inc.
Kaswer Custom, Inc.
Ken's Gun Specialties
Kilham & Co.
Kimball, Gary
Kopp, Terry K.
La Clinique du .45
LaFrance Specialties
LaRocca Gun Works, Inc.
Lathrop's, Inc.
Lawson, John G.
Lee's Red Ramps
Leckie Professional Gunsmithing
Liberty Antique Gunworks
Linebaugh Custom Sixguns & Rifle Works
List Precision Engineering
Long, George F.
Mac's .45 Shop
Mag-Na-Port International, Inc.
Mahony, Philip Bruce
Mandall Shooting Supplies, Inc.
Marent, Rudolf
Marvel, Alan
Maxi-Mount
McCann's Machine & Gun Shop
MCS, Inc.
Middlebrooks Custom Shop
Miller Custom
Mitchell's Accuracy Shop
MJK Gunsmithing, Inc.
Mo's Competitor Supplies
Mountain Bear Rifle Works, Inc.
Mowrey's Guns & Gunsmithing
Mullis Guncraft
Nastoff's 45 Shop, Inc., Steve
NCP Products, Inc.
Novak's Inc.
Nowlin Custom Mfg.
Nygord Precision Products
Oglesby & Oglesby Gunmakers, Inc.
Paris, Frank J.
Pace Marketing, Inc.
Pasadena Gun Center
Peacemaker Specialists
PEM's Mfg. Co.
Performance Specialists
Pierce Pistols
Plaxco, J. Michael
Precision Specialties
Randco UK
Ries, Chuck
Rim Pac Sports, Inc.
Robar Co.'s, Inc., The
RPM
Score High Gunsmithing
Scott, McDougall & Associates
Seecamp Co., Inc., L.W.
Shooter Shop, The
Shooters Supply
Shootin' Shack, Inc.
Sight Shop, The
Singletary, Kent
Sipes Gun Shop
Spokhandguns, Inc.
Springfield, Inc.
SSK Industries
Starnes Gunmaker, Ken
Steger, James R.
Swenson's 45 Shop, A.D.
Swift River Gunworks
Ten-Ring Precision, Inc.
Thompson, Randall
300 Gunsmith Service, Inc.
Thurston Sports, Inc.
Tom's Gun Repair
Vic's Gun Refinishing
Volquartsen Custom Ltd.
Walker Arms Co., Inc.
Walters Industries
Wardell Precision Handguns Ltd.
Weigand Combat Handguns, Inc.
Wessinger Custom Guns & Engraving
Williams Gun Sight Co.
Williamson Precision Gunsmithing
Wilson Gun Shop
Wichita Arms, Inc.

REBORING AND RERIFLING

A.M.T.
Arundel Arms & Ammunition, Inc., A.
BlackStar AccuMax Barrels
BlackStar Barrel Accurizing
Chicasaw Gun Works
Cochran, Oliver
Ed's Gun House
Flaig's
Gun Works, The
IAI
H&S Liner Service
Ivanoff, Thomas G.
Jackalope Gun Shop
K-D, Inc.
Kopp, Terry K.
LaBounty Precision Reboring
Matco, Inc.
NCP Products, Inc.
Pence Precision Barrels
Pro-Port Ltd.
Ranch Products
Redman's Rifling & Reboring
Rice, Keith
Ridgetop Sporting Goods
Shaw, Inc., E.R.
Siegrist Gun Shop
Simmons Gun Repair, Inc.
Stratco, Inc.

PRODUCT & SERVICE DIRECTORY

REBORING AND RERIFLING (continued)

300 Gunsmith Service, Inc.
Time Precision, Inc.
Tom's Gun Repair
Van Patten, J.W.
West, Robert G.
White Rock Tool & Die
Zufall, Joseph F.

RELOADING TOOLS AND ACCESSORIES

Action Bullets, Inc.
Advance Car Mover Co., Rowell Div.
Alaska Bullet Works, Inc.
American Products Inc.
Ames Metal Products
Ammo Load, Inc.
Anderson Manufacturing Co., Inc.
Armite Laboratories
Arms Corporation of the Philippines
Atlantic Rose, Inc.
Atsko/Sno-Seal, Inc.
Bald Eagle Precision Machine Co.
Ballistic Products, Inc.
Ballisti-Cast, Inc.
Belltown, Ltd.
Ben's Machines
Berger Bullets, Ltd.
Berry's Mfg., Inc.
Birchwood Casey
Blount, Inc., Sporting Equipment Div.
Blue Ridge Machinery & Tools, Inc.
Bonanza
Break-Free, Inc.
Brobst, Jim
Brown Co., E. Arthur
Bruno Shooters Supply
Brynin, Milton
B-Square Co., Inc.
Buck Stix—SOS Products Co.
Bull Mountain Rifle Co.
Bullet Swaging Supply, Inc.
Bullseye Bullets
C&D Special Products
Camdex, Inc.
Camp-Cap Products
Canyon Cartridge Corp.
Carbide Die & Mfg. Co., Inc.
Case Sorting System
CFVentures
C-H Tool & Die Corp.
Chem-Pak, Inc.
CheVron Case Master
Claybuster Wads & Harvester Bullets
Cleanzoil Corp.
Clearview Products
Clymer Manufacturing Co., Inc.
Coats, Mrs. Lester
Colorado Shooter's Supply
CONKKO
Cook Engineering Service
Cooper-Woodward
Crouse's Country Cover
Cumberland Arms

Custom Products, Neil A. Jones
CVA
Davis, Don
Davis Products, Mike
D.C.C. Enterprises
Denver Bullets, Inc.
Denver Instrument Co.
Dever Co., Jack
Dewey Mfg. Co., Inc., J. Dillon Precision Products, Inc.
Dropkick
Dutchman's Firearms, Inc.
E&L Mfg., Inc.
Eagan, Donald V.
Eezox, Inc.
Eichelberger Bullets, Wm.
Elkhorn Bullets
Engineered Accessories
Enguix Import-Export
Estate Cartridge, Inc.
E-Z-Way Systems
F&A Inc.
Federal Cartridge Co.
Federated-Fry
Feken, Dennis
Ferguson, Bill
First, Inc., Jack
Fisher Custom Firearms
Fitz Pistol Grip Co.
Flambeau Products Corp.
Flitz International Ltd.
Forgett Jr., Valmore J.
Forgreens Tool Mfg., Inc.
Forster Products
4-D Custom Die Co.
4W Ammunition
Fremont Tool Works
Fry Metals
Fusilier Bullets
G&C Bullet Co., Inc.
GAR
Gehmann, Walter
Goddard, Allen
Gozon Corp., U.S.A.
Graf & Sons
"Gramps" Antique Cartridges
Graphics Direct
Graves Co.
Green, Arthur S.
Green, Mr. & Mrs. Steve
Greenwood Precision
Gun Works, The
Hanned Line, The
Hanned Precision
Harrell's Precision
Harris Enterprises
Harrison Bullets
Haselbauer Products, Jerry

Haydon Shooters' Supply, Russ
Heidenstrom Bullets
Hensley & Gibbs
Hirtenberger Aktiengesellschaft
Hobson Precision Mfg.
Hoch Custom Bullet Moulds
Hodgdon Powder Co., Inc.
Hoehn Sales, Inc.
Hoelscher, Virgil
Holland's Gunsmithing
Hondo Industries
Hornady Mfg. Co.
Howell Machine
Hunters Supply
Huntington Die Specialties
Image Ind. Inc.
IMI Services USA, Inc.
Imperial
Imperial Magnum Corp.
INTEC International, Inc.
Iosso Products
Javelina Lube Products
JGS Precision Tool Mfg.
J&L Superior Bullets
JLK Bullets
Jonad Corp.
Jones Custom Products, Neil A.
Jones Moulds, Paul
K&M Services
Kapro Mfg. Co., Inc.
King & Co.
Kleen-Bore, Inc.
Korzinek Riflesmith, J.
Lane Bullets, Inc.
Lapua Ltd.
LBT
Le Clear Industries
Lee Precision, Inc.
Legend Products Corp.
Liberty Metals
Liberty Shooting Supplies
Lightning Performance Innovations, Inc.
Litchi Bee Bullet Lube
Littleton, J.F.
Lortone, Inc.
Loweth Firearms, Richard H.R.
Luch Metal Merchants, Barbara
Lyman Instant Targets, Inc.
Lyman Products Corp.
M&D Munitions Ltd.
MA Systems
Magma Engineering Co.

ManMik, Inc.
Marquart Precision Co.
MAST Technology
Match Prep—Doyle Gracey
Mayville Engineering Co.
McKillen & Heyer, Inc.
MCRW Associates Shooting Supplies
MCS, Inc.
MEC, Inc.
Midway Arms, Inc.
Miller Engineering
MI-TE Bullets
MMP
Mo's Competitor Supplies
Montana Armory, Inc.
Montana State Muzzleloading Supplies, Inc.
Mt. Baldy Bullet Co.
MTM Molded Products Co., Inc.
Multi-Scale Charge Ltd.
MWG Company
Necromancer Industries, Inc.
NEI Handtools, Inc.
Niemi Engineering, W.B.
North Devon Firearms Services
Northern Precision Custom Swaged Bullets
October Country
Old West Bullet Moulds
Omark Industries
Original Box, Inc.
Paco's
Pattern Control
Pease Accuracy, Bob
Pedersoli and Co., Davide
Peerless Alloy, Inc.
Pend Oreille Sport Shop
Pinetree Bullets
Plum City Ballistic Range
Pomeroy, Robert
Ponsness/Warren
Prairie River Arms
Precision Castings & Equipment, Inc.
Precision Reloading, Inc.
Prime Reloading
Professional Hunter Supplies
Prolix® Lubricants
Pro-Shot Products, Inc.
Protector Mfg. Co., Inc., The
Quinetics Corp.
R&D Engineering & Manufacturing

Rapine Bullet Mould Mfg. Co.
Raytech
RCBS
R.D.P. Tool Co., Inc.
Redding Reloading Equipment
R.E.I.
Reloading Specialties, Inc.
Rice, Keith
Riebe Co., W.J.
RIG Products
R.I.S. Co., Inc.
Roberts Products
Rochester Lead Works, Inc.
Rolston, Inc., Fred. W.
Rooster Laboratories
Rorschach Precision Products
Rosenthal, Brad and Sallie
SAECO
Sandia Die & Cartridge Co.
Saunders Gun & Machine Shop
Saville Iron Co.
Scharch Mfg. Inc.
Scot Powder Co. of Ohio, Inc.
Scott, Dwight
Seebeck Assoc., R.E.
Sharp Shooter Supply
Sharps Arms Co. Inc., C.
Shiloh Creek
Shiloh Rifle Mfg.
Shooter's Choice
ShurKatch Corporation
Sierra Specialty Prod.
Silhouette, The
Silver Eagle Machining
Simmons, Jerry
Sinclair International, Inc.
Skip's Machine
S.L.A.P. Industries
Small Custom Mould & Bullet Co.
Sno-Seal
SOS Products Co.
Spence, George W.
Spencer's Custom Guns
SPG, Inc.
Sport Flite Manufacturing Co.
Sportsman Supply Co.
Stalwart Corp.
Star Custom Bullets
Star Machine Works
Starr Trading Co., Jedediah
Stillwell, Robert

PRODUCT & SERVICE DIRECTORY

RELOADING TOOLS AND ACCESSORIES (continued)

Stoney Point Products, Inc.
Stratco, Inc.
Taracorp Industries
TCCI
TCSR
TDP Industries, Inc.
Tetra Gun Lubricants
Thompson Bullet Lube Co.
Thompson/Center Arms
Timber Heirloom Products
Time Precision, Inc.
TMI Products
TR Metals Corp.
Trammco, Inc.
Tru-Square Metal Prods., Inc.
TTM
Varner's Service
Vega Tool Co.
Venco Industries, Inc.
VibraShine, Inc.
Vibra-Tek Co.
Vintavuori Oy/Kaltron-Pettibone
Vitt/Boos
Von Minden Gunsmithing Services
Walters, John
Webster Scale Mfg. Co.
WD-40 Co.
Welsh, Bud
Wells Custom Gunsmith, R.A.
Werner, Carl
Westfield Engineering
White Rock Tool & Die
Whitetail Design & Engineering Ltd.
Widener's Reloading & Shooting Supply
William's Gun Shop, Ben
Wilson, Inc., L.E.
Wise Guns, Dale
Wolf's Western Traders
Woodleigh
WTA Manufacturing, Bill Wood
Yesteryear Armory & Supply
Young Country Arms

RESTS—BENCH, PORTABLE—AND ACCESSORIES

Accuright
Adventure 16, Inc.
Armor Metal Products
Bald Eagle Precision Machine Co.
Bartlett Engineering
Borden's Accuracy
Browning Arms Co.
B-Square Co., Inc.
Bull Mountain Rifle Co.
Canons Delcour
Chem-Pak, Inc.
Clift Mfg., L.R.
Clift Welding Supply
Cravener's Gun Shop
Decker Shooting Products
Desert Mountain Mfg.
Erickson's Mfg., Inc., C.W.
F&A Inc.
Greenwood Precision
Harris Engineering, Inc.
Hidalgo, Tony
Hoehn Sales, Inc.
Hoelscher, Virgil
Hoppe's Div.
Kolpin Mfg., Inc.
Kramer Designs
Midway Arms, Inc.
Millett Sights
MJM Manufacturing
Outdoor Connection, Inc., The
PAST Sporting Goods, Inc.
Penguin Industries, Inc.
Portus, Robert
Protektor Model
Ransom International Corp
Saville Iron Co.
ShurKatch Corporation
Stoney Point Products, Inc.
Thompson Target Technology
T.H.U. Enterprises, Inc.
Tonoloway Tack Drivers
Varner's Service
Wichita Arms, Inc.
Zanotti Armor, Inc.

SCOPES, MOUNTS, ACCESSORIES, OPTICAL EQUIPMENT

ADCO Sales, Inc.
Aimpoint U.S.A.
Aimtech Mount Systems
Anderson Manufacturing Co., Inc.
Apel GmbH, Ernst
Baer Custom, Inc., Les
Barrett Firearms Mfg., Inc.
Bausch & Lomb Sports Optics Div.
Blount, Inc., Sporting Equipment Div.
Brown Co., E. Arthur
Brownells, Inc.
Brunton U.S.A.
Burris
Bushnell Sports Optics Worldwide
Butler Creek Corp.
Celestron International
Center Lock Scope Rings
Combat Military Ordnance Ltd.
Compass Industries, Inc.
Concept Development Corp.
Conetrol Scope Mounts
CRDC Laser Systems Group
Custom Quality Products, Inc.
Doctor Optic Technologies, Inc.
Emerging Technologies, Inc.
Excalibur Enterprises
Fotar Optics
Fujinon, Inc.
Great Lakes Airguns
Hammerli USA
Ironsighter Co.
Jeffredo Gunsight
Kahles, A Swarovski Company
KDF, Inc.
Knight's Mfg. Co.
Kowa Optimed, Inc.
Kris Mounts
KVH Industries, Inc.
Kwik Mount Corp.
Kwik-Site Co.
L&S Technologies, Inc.
L.A.R. Mfg., Inc.
Laser Devices, Inc.
Laseraim
LaserMax, Inc.
Leica USA, Inc.
Leupold & Stevens, Inc.
Lightforce U.S.A. Inc.
Lyte Optronics
Mac's .45 Shop
Mag-Na-Port International, Inc.
Masen Co., Inc., John
Maxi-Mount
MCS, Inc.
Merit Corp.
Michaels of Oregon Co.
Military Armament Corp.
Millett Sights
Mirador Optical Corp.
Mitchell Optics Inc.
Nightforce
Nikon, Inc.
Norincoptics
Olympic Optical Co.
Optical Services Co.
Outdoor Connection, Inc., The
Parsons Optical Mfg. Co.
PECAR Herbert Schwarz, GmbH
Pentax Corp.
Precision Sport Optics
Quarton USA, Ltd. Co.
Ram-Line Blount, Inc.
Ranch Products
Randolph Engineering, Inc.
Ranging, Inc.
Redfield, Inc.
Rocky Mountain High Sports Glasses
RPM
S&K Mfg. Co.
Saunders Gun & Machine Shop
Schmidt & Bender, Inc.
Scope Control Inc.
ScopLevel
Score High Gunsmithing
Seattle Binocular & Scope Repair Co.
Segway Industries
Selsi Co., Inc.
Sightron, Inc.
Simmons Enterprises, Ernie
Simmons Outdoor Corp.
Springfield, Inc.
Stoeger Industries
SwaroSports, Inc.
Swarovski Optik North America Ltd.
Swift Instruments, Inc.
TacStar Industires, Inc.
Tasco Sales, Inc.
Tele-Optics
Thompson/Center Arms
Trijicon, Inc.
Ultra Dot Distribution
Uncle Mike's
Unertl Optical Co., Inc., John
United Binocular Co.
United States Optics Tech., Inc.
Voere-KGH m.b.H.
Warne Manufacturing Co.
Warren Muzzleloading Co., Inc.
WASP Shooting Systems
Weaver Products
Weaver Scope Repair Service
Weigand Combat Handguns, Inc.
Westfield Engineering
White Muzzleloading Systems
White Shooting Systems, Inc.
White Rock Tool & Die
Wideview Scope Mount Corp.
Williams Gun Sight Co.
York M-1 Conversions
Zanotti Armor, Inc.
Zeiss Optical, Carl

SHOOTING/TRAINING SCHOOLS

Accuracy Gun Shop
Alpine Precision Gunsmithing & Indoor Shooting Range
American Small Arms Academy
Auto Arms
Barsotti, Bruce
Bob's Tactical Indoor Shooting Range & Gun Shop
Cannon's, Andy Cannon
Chapman Academy of Practical Shooting
Chelsea Gun Club of New York City, Inc.
CQB Training
Daisy Mfg. Co.
Defense Training International, Inc.
Dowtin Gunworks
Executive Protection Institute
Feminine Protection, Inc.
Ferris Firearms
Firearm Training Center, The
Firearms Academy of Seattle
G.H. Enterprises Ltd.
Front Sight Firearms Training Institute
Gunsite Training Center
Guncraft Sports, Inc.
Henigson & Associates, Steve
International Shootists, Inc.
Jensen's Custom Ammunition
Jensen's Firearms Academy
L.L. Bean, Inc.
McMurdo, Lynn
Mendez, John A.

PRODUCT & SERVICE DIRECTORY

SHOOTING/TRAINING SCHOOLS (continued)

Montgomery Community College
NCP Products, Inc.
Nevada Pistol Academy, Inc.
North American Shooting Systems

North Mountain Pine Training Center
Performance Specialists
Quigley's Personal Protection
SAFE
Shooter's World
Smith & Wesson
Specialty Gunsmithing
Starlight Training Center, Inc.
Steger, James R.

Shooting Gallery, The
Strategies, Paxton
300 Gunsmith Service, Inc.
Thunder Ranch
Western Missouri Shooters Alliance

Tactical Defense Institute
Yankee Gunsmith
Yavapai Firearms Academy Ltd.

SIGHTS, METALLIC

Alpec Team, Inc.
Anschutz GmbH
Baer Custom, Inc., Les
BEC, Inc.
Bo-Mar Tool & Mfg. Co.
Bowen Classic Arms Corp.
Brown Co., E. Arthur
Brown Products, Inc., Ed
Center Lock Scope Rings
C-More Systems

CRR, Inc./Marble's Inc.
Eagle International
Engineered Accessories
Forgett Jr., Valmore J.
Gun Works, The
Heinie Specialty Products
Hesco-Meprolight
Innovative Weaponry, Inc.
J.P. Enterprises, Inc.

Kris Mounts
Lee's Red Ramps
List Precision Engineering
London Guns Ltd.
L.P.A. Snc
Lyman Products Corp.
Mac's .45 Shop
Marble Arms
MCS, Inc.
MEC-Gar S.R.L.
Meier Works

Meprolight
Merit Corp.
Millett Sights
MMC
Novak's Inc.
Oakshore Electronic Sights, Inc.
P.M. Enterprises, Inc.
Quarton USA, Ltd. Co.
RPM
STI International
Talley, Dave

T.F.C. S.p.A.
Thompson/Center Arms
Trijicon, Inc.
Wichita Arms, Inc.
Wild West Guns, Inc.
Williams Gun Sight Co.
Wilson Gun Shop

TARGETS, BULLET AND CLAYBIRD TRAPS

Action Target, Inc.
American Target
American Whitetail Target Systems
A-Tech Corp.
Autauga Arms, Inc.
Beomat of America Inc.
Birchwood Casey
Blount, Inc., Sporting Equipment Div.
Blue and Gray Products, Inc.
Brown Manufacturing
Bull-X, Inc.
Camp-Cap Products
Caswell International Corp.

Champion Target Co.
Cunningham Co., Eaton
Dapkus Co., Inc., J.G.
Datumtech Corp.
Dayson Arms Ltd.
D.C.C. Enterprises
Detroit-Armor Corp.
Diamond Mfg. Co.
Estate Cartridge, Inc.
Federal Champion Target Co.
Freeman Animal Targets
G.H. Enterprises Ltd.
Gun Parts Corp., The
Hiti-Schuch, Atelier Wilma
H-S Precision, Inc.

Hunterjohn
Innovision Enterprises
JWH: Software
Kennebec Journal
Kleen-Bore, Inc.
Lakefield Arms Ltd.
Litter Sales Co.
Lyman Instant Targets, Inc.
Lyman Products Corp.
M&D Munitions Ltd.
Mendez, John A.
MSR Targets
National Target Co.
N.B.B., Inc.
North American Shooting Systems

Nu-Teck
Outers Laboratories, Div. of Blount
Ox-Yoke Originals, Inc.
Passive Bullet Traps, Inc.
PlumFire Press, Inc.
Remington Arms Co., Inc.
Rockwood Corp., Speedwell Div.
Rocky Mountain Target Co.
Savage Arms (Canada), Inc.
Savage Range Systems, Inc.

Schaefer Shooting Sports
Seligman Shooting Products
Shooters Supply
Shoot-N-C Targets
Thompson Target Technology
Trius Products, Inc.
World of Targets
X-Spand Target Systems
Z's Metal Targets & Frames
Zriny's Metal Targets

TAXIDERMY

African Import Co.
Jonas Appraisers—Taxidermy

Animals, Jack
Kulis Freeze Dry Taxidermy

Montgomery Community College
Parker, Mark D.

World Trek, Inc.

TRIGGERS, RELATED EQUIPMENT

A.M.T.
B&D Trading Co., Inc.
Baer Custom, Inc., Les
Behlert Precision, Inc.
Bond Custom Firearms
Boyds' Gunstock Industries, Inc.
Bull Mountain Rifle Co.
Canjar Co., M.H.
Cycle Dynamics, Inc.

Dayton Traister Electronic Trigger Systems, Inc.
Eversull Co., Inc., K.
FWB
Galati International
Gentry Custom Gunmaker, David
Hastings Barrels
Hawken Shop, The

Hoelscher, Virgil
Holland's
IAI
Impact Case Co.
Jacobson, Teddy
Jaeger, Inc.,
Paul/Dunn's
Jewell Triggers, Inc.
J.P. Enterprises, Inc.
KK Air International

L&R Lock Co.
List Precision Engineering
Mahony, Philip Bruce
Masen Co., Inc., John
Master Lock Co.
NCP Products, Inc.
OK Weber, Inc.
PEM's Mfg. Co.
Penrod Precision

Perazone, Brian
S&B Industries
Shilen, Inc.
Simmons Gun Repair, Inc.
STI International
Timney Mfg., Inc.

MANUFACTURER'S DIRECTORY

A

A Zone Bullets, 2039 Walter Rd., Billings, MT 59105 / 800-252-3111; FAX: 406-248-1961

A&B Industries,Inc (See Top-Line USA Inc)

A&M Waterfowl,Inc., P.O. Box 102, Ripley, TN 38063 / 901-635-4003; FAX: 901-635-2320

A&W Repair, 2930 Schneider Dr., Arnold, MO 63010 / 314-287-3725

A-Square Co.,Inc., One Industrial Park, Bedford, KY 40006-9667 / 502-255-7456; FAX: 502-255-7657

A-Tech Corp., P.O. Box 1281, Cottage Grove, OR 97424

A.A. Arms, Inc., 4811 Persimmont Ct, Monroe, NC 28110 / 704-289-5356 or 800-935-1119; FAX: 704-289-5859

A.B.S. III, 9238 St. Morritz Dr., Fern Creek, KY 40291

A.G. Russell Knives,Inc., 1705 Hwy. 71B North, Springdale, AR 72764 / 501-751-7341

A.R.M.S., Inc., 230 W. Center St., West Bridgewater, MA 02379-1620 / 508-584-7816; FAX: 508-588-8045

A.W. Peterson Gun Shop, Inc., 4255 W. Old U.S. 441, Mt. Dora, FL 32757-3299 / 352-383-4258; FAX: 352-735-1001

ABO (USA) Inc, 615 SW 2nd Avenue, Miami, FL 33130 / 305-859-2010 FAX: 305-859-2099

AC Dyna-tite Corp., 155 Kelly St., P.O. Box 0984, Elk Grove Village, IL 60007 / 847-593-5566; FAX: 847-593-1304

Acadian Ballistic Specialties, P.O. Box 787, folsom, LA 70437 / 504-796-0078 gunsmith@neasolt.com

Accu-Tek, 4510 Carter Ct, Chino, CA 91710

Accupro Gun Care, 15512-109 Ave., Surrey, BC U3R 7E8 CANADA / 604-583-7807

Accura-Site (See All's, The Jim Tembelis Co., Inc.)

Accuracy Innovations, Inc., P.O. Box 376, New Paris, PA 15554 / 814-839-4517; FAX: 814-839-2601

Accuracy Int'l. North America, Inc., PO Box 5267, Oak Ridge, TN 37831 / 423-482-0330; FAX: 423-482-0336

Accuracy International, 9115 Trooper Trail, P.O. Box 2019, Bozeman, MT 59715 / 406-587-7922; FAX: 406-585-9434

Accuracy Internationl Precision Rifles (See U.S. Importer-Gunsite Custom Shop; Gunsite Training Center)

Accuracy Unlimited, 16036 N. 49 Ave., Glendale, AZ 85306 / 602-978-9089; FAX: 602-978-9089

Accuracy Unlimited, 7479 S. DePew St., Littleton, CO 80123

Accurate Arms Co., Inc., 5891 Hwy. 230 West, McEwen, TN 37101 / 800-416-3006 FAX: 931-729-4211

Accuright, RR 2 Box 397, Sebeka, MN 56477 / 218-472-3383

Ace Custom 45's, Inc., 1880 1/2 Upper Turtle Creek Rd., Kerrville, TX 78028 / 830-257-4290; FAX: 830-257-5724

Ace Sportswear, Inc., 700 Quality Rd., Fayetteville, NC 28306 / 919-323-1223; FAX: 919-323-5392

Ackerman & Co., Box 133 US Highway Rt. 7, Pownal, VT 05261 / 802-823-9874 muskets@togsther.net

Ackerman, Bill (See Optical Services Co)

Acra-Bond Laminates, 134 Zimmerman Rd., Kalispell, MT 59901 / 406-257-9003; FAX: 406-257-9003

Action Bullets & Alloy Inc, RR 1, P.O. Box 189, Quinter, KS 67752 / 913-754-3609; FAX: 913-754-3629

Action Direct, Inc., P.O. Box 830760, Miami, FL 33283 / 305-559-4652; FAX: 305-559-4652 action-direct.com

Action Products, Inc., 22 N. Mulberry St., Hagerstown, MD 21740 / 301-797-1414; FAX: 301-733-2073

Action Target, Inc., P.O. Box 636, Provo, UT 84603 / 801-377-8033; FAX: 801-377-8096

Actions by "T" Teddy Jacobson, 16315 Redwood Forest Ct., Sugar Land, TX 77478 / 281-277-4008

AcuSport Corporation, 1 Hunter Place, Bellefontaine, OH 43311-3001 / 513-593-7010 FAX: 513-592-5625

Ad Hominem, 3130 Gun Club Lane, RR, Orillia, ON L3V 6H3 CANADA / 705-689-5303; FAX: 705-689-5303

Adair Custom Shop, Bill, 2886 Westridge, Carrollton, TX 75006

Adams & Son Engravers, John J, 87 Acorn Rd, Dennis, MA 02638 / 508-385-7971

Adams Jr., John J., 87 Acorn Rd., Dennis, MA 02638 / 508-385-7971

ADCO Sales, Inc., 4 Draper St. #A, Woburn, MA 01801 / 781-935-1799; FAX: 781-935-1011

Adkins, Luther, 1292 E. McKay Rd., Shelbyville, IN 46176-8706 / 317-392-3795

Advance Car Mover Co., Rowell Div., P.O. Box 1, 240 N. Depot St., Juneau, WI 53039 / 414-386-4464; FAX: 414-386-4416

Adventure 16, Inc., 4620 Alvarado Canyon Rd., San Diego, CA 92120 / 619-283-6314

Adventure Game Calls, R.D. 1, Leonard Rd., Spencer, NY 14883 / 607-589-4611

Adventurer's Outpost, P.O. Box 547, Cottonwood, AZ 86326-0547 / 800-762-7471; FAX: 602-634-8781

Aero Peltor, 90 Mechanic St, Southbridge, MA 01550 / 508-764-5500; FAX: 508-764-0188

African Import Co., 22 Goodwin Rd, Plymouth, MA 02360 / 508-746-8552 FAX: 508-746-0404

AFSCO Ammunition, 731 W. Third St., P.O. Box L, Owen, WI 54460 / 715-229-2516

Ahlman Guns, 9525 W. 230th St., Morristown, MN 55052 / 507-685-4243; FAX: 507-685-4280

Ahrends, Kim (See Custom Firearms, Inc), Box 203, Clarion, IA 50525 / 515-532-3449; FAX: 515-532-3926

Aimpoint c/o Springfield, Inc., 420 W. Main St, Geneseo, IL 61254 / 309-944-1702

Aimtech Mount Systems, P.O. Box 223, Thomasville, GA 31799-1638 / 912-226-4313; FAX: 912-227-0222 aimtech@surfsouth.com www.aimtech-mounts.com

Air Arms, Hailsham Industrial Park, Diplocks Way, Hailsham, E. Sussex, BN27 3JF ENGLAND / 011-0323-845853

Air Rifle Specialists, P.O. Box 138, 130 Holden Rd., Pine City, NY 14871-0138 / 607-734-7340; FAX: 607-733-3261

Air Venture Airguns, 9752 E. Flower St., Bellflower, CA 90706 / 310-867-6355

Airgun Repair Centre, 3227 Garden Meadows, Lawrenceburg, IN 47025 / 812-637-1463; FAX: 812-637-1463

Airrow, 11 Monitor Hill Rd, Newtown, CT 06470 / 203-270-6343

Aitor-Cuchilleria Del Norte S.A., Izelaieta, 17, 48260, Ermua, S SPAIN / 43-17-08-50

Ajax Custom Grips, Inc., 9130 Viscount Row, Dallas, TX 75247 / 214-630-8893; FAX: 214-630-4942

Aker International, Inc., 2248 Main St., Suite 6, Chula Vista, CA 91911 / 619-423-5182; FAX: 619-423-1363

Al Lind Custom Guns, 7821 76th Ave. SW, Tacoma, WA 98498 / 206-584-6361

Alana Cupp Custom Engraver, P.O. Box 207, Annabella, UT 84711 / 801-896-4834

Alaska Bullet Works, Inc., 9978 Crazy Horse Drive, Juneau, AK 99801 / 907-789-3834; FAX: 907-789-3433

Alco Carrying Cases, 601 W. 26th St., New York, NY 10001 / 212-675-5820; FAX: 212-691-5935

Aldis Gunsmithing & Shooting Supply, 525 S. Montezuma St., Prescott, AZ 86303 / 602-445-6723; FAX: 602-445-6763

Alessi Holsters, Inc., 2465 Niagara Falls Blvd., Amherst, NY 14228-3527 / 716-691-5615

Alex, Inc., Box 3034, Bozeman, MT 59772 / 406-282-7396; FAX: 406-282-7396

Alfano, Sam, 36180 Henry Gaines Rd., Pearl River, LA 70452 / 504-863-3364; FAX: 504-863-7715

All American Lead Shot Corp., P.O. Box 224566, Dallas, TX 75062

All Rite Products, Inc., 5752 N. Silverstone Circle, Mountain Green, UT 84050 / 801-876-3330; FAX: 801-876-2216

All's, The Jim J. Tembelis Co., Inc., 216 Loper Ct, Neenah, WI 54956 / 920-725-5251; FAX: 920-725-5251

Allard, Gary/Creek Side Metal & Woodcrafters, Fishers Hill, VA 22626 / 703-465-3903

Allen Co., Bob, 214 SW Jackson, P.O. Box 477, Des Moines, IA 50315 / 515-283-2191 or 800-685-7020; FAX: 515-283-0779

Allen Co., Inc., 525 Burbank St., Broomfield, CO 80020 / 303-469-1857 or 800-876-8600; FAX: 303-466-7437

Allen Firearm Engraving, 339 Grove Ave., Prescott, AZ 86301 / 520-778-1237

Allen Mfg., 6449 Hodgson Rd., Circle Pines, MN 55014 / 612-429-8231

Allen Sportswear, Bob (See Allen Co., Bob)

Alley Supply Co., P.O. Box 848, Gardnerville, NV 89410 / 702-782-3800

Alliant Techsystems Smokeless Powder Group, 200 Valley Rd., Suite 305, Mt. Arlington, NJ 07856 / 800-276-9337; FAX: 201-770-2528

Allred Bullet Co., 932 Evergreen Drive, Logan, UT 84321 / 435-752-6983; FAX: 435-752-6983

Alpec Team, Inc., 201 Ricken Backer Cir., Livermore, CA 94550 / 510-606-8245; FAX: 510-606-4279

Alpha 1 Drop Zone, 2121 N. Tyler, Wichita, KS 67212 / 316-729-0800

Alpha Gunsmith Division, 1629 Via Monserate, Fallbrook, CA 92028 / 619-723-9279 or 619-728-2663

Alpha LaFranck Enterprises, P.O. Box 81072, Lincoln, NE 68501 / 402-466-3193

Alpha Precision, Inc., 2765-B Preston Rd. NE, Good Hope, GA 30641 / 770-267-6163

Alpine Indoor Shooting Range, 2401 Government Way, Coeur d'Alene, ID 83814 / 208-676-8824 FAX: 208-676-8824

Altamont Co., 901 N. Church St., P.O. Box 309, Thomasboro, IL 61878 / 217-643-3125 or 800-626-5774; FAX: 217-643-7973

Alumna Sport by Dee Zee, 1572 NE 58th Ave., P.O. Box 3090, Des Moines, IA 50316 / 800-798-9899

Amadeo Rossi S.A., Rua: Amadeo Rossi, 143, Sao Leopoldo, RS 93030-220 BRAZIL / 051-592-5566

AmBr Software Group Ltd., P.O. Box 301, Reistertown, MD 21136-0301 / 800-888-1917; FAX: 410-526-7212

American Ammunition, 3545 NW 71st St., Miami, FL 33147 / 305-835-7400; FAX: 305-694-0037

American Arms Inc., 2604 NE Industrial Dr, N. Kansas City, MO 64116 / 816-474-3161; FAX: 816-474-1225

American Bullet, 1512 W Chester Pike #298, West Chester, PA 19382-7754 / 610-399-6584

American Custom Gunmakers Guild, PO Box 812, Burlington, IA 52601 / 318-752-6114; FAX: 319-752-6114 acgg@acgg.org acgg.org

American Derringer Corp., 127 N. Lacy Dr., Waco, TX 76705 / 800-642-7817 or 817-799-9111; FAX: 817-799-7935

American Display Co., 55 Cromwell St., Providence, RI 02907 / 401-331-2464; FAX: 401-421-1264

American Frontier Firearms Mfg., Inc, PO Box 744, Aguanga, CA 92536 / 909-763-0014; FAX: 909-763-0014

American Gas & Chemical Co., Ltd, 220 Pegasus Ave, Northvale, NJ 07647 / 201-767-7300

American Gripcraft, 3230 S Dodge 2, Tucson, AZ 85713 / 602-790-1222

American Gunsmithing Institute, 1325 Imola Ave #504, Napa, CA 94559 / 707-253-0462; FAX: 707-253-7149

American Handgunner Magazine, 591 Camino de la Reina, Ste 200, San Diego, CA 92108 / 619-297-5350; FAX: 619-297-5353

American Pioneer Video, PO Box 50049, Bowling Green, KY 42102-2649 / 800-743-4675

American Products, Inc., 14729 Spring Valley Road, Morrison, IL 61270 / 815-772-3336; FAX: 815-772-8046

American Safe Arms, Inc., 1240 Riverview Dr., Garland, UT 84312 / 801-257-7472; FAX: 801-785-8156

American Sales & Kirkpatrick Mfg. Co., P.O. Box 677, Laredo, TX 78042 / 210-723-6893; FAX: 210-725-0672

American Sales & Mfg. Co., PO Box 677, Laredo, TX 78042 / 956-723-6893; FAX: 956-725-0672 holsters@kirkpatrickleather.com http://kirkpatrickleather.com

American Security Products Co., 11925 Pacific Ave., Fontana, CA 92337 / 909-685-9680 or 800-421-6142; FAX: 909-685-9685

American Small Arms Academy, P.O. Box 12111, Prescott, AZ 86304 / 602-778-5623

American Target, 1328 S. Jason St., Denver, CO 80223 / 303-733-0433; FAX: 303-777-0311

American Target Knives, 1030 Brownwood NW, Grand Rapids, MI 49504 / 616-453-1998

American Western Arms, Inc., 1450 S.W. 10th St., Suite 3B, Delray Beach, FL 33444 / 877-292-4867; FAX: 561-330-0881

American Whitetail Target Systems, P.O. Box 41, 106 S. Church St., Tennyson, IN 47637 / 812-567-4527

Americase, P.O. Box 271, 1610 E. Main, Waxahachie, TX 75165 / 800-880-3629; FAX: 214-937-8373

Ames Metal Products, 4323 S. Western Blvd., Chicago, IL 60609 / 773-523-3230; or 800-255-6937 FAX: 773-523-3854

Amherst Arms, P.O. Box 1457, Englewood, FL 34295 / 941-475-2020; FAX: 941-473-1212

Ammo Load, Inc., 1560 E. Edinger, Suite G, Santa Ana, CA 92705 / 714-558-8858; FAX: 714-569-0319

Amrine's Gun Shop, 937 La Luna, Ojai, CA 93023 / 805-646-2376

Amsec, 11925 Pacific Ave., Fontana, CA 92337

Amtec 2000, Inc., 84 Industrial Rowe, Gardner, MA 01440 / 508-632-9608; FAX: 508-632-2300

Anderson Manufacturing Co., Inc. 22602 53rd Ave. SE, Bothell, WA 98021 / 206-481-1858; FAX: 206-481-7839

Andres & Dworsky, Bergstrasse 18, A-3822 Karlstein, Thaya, AUSTRIA / 0 28 44-285

Angel Arms, Inc., 1825 Addison Way, Haywood, CA 94545 / 510-783-7122

Angelo & Little Custom Gun Stock Blanks, P.O. Box 240046, Dell, MT 59724-0046

Anics Firm Inc3 Commerce Park Square, 23200 Chagrin Blvd., Suite 240, Beechwood, OH 44122 / 800-556-1582; FAX: 216-292-2588

Anschutz GmbH, Postfach 1128, D-89001 Ulm, Donau, GERMANY / 731-40120

Answer Products Co., 1519 Westbury Drive, Davison, MI 48423 / 810-653-2911

Anthony and George Ltd., Rt. 1, P.O. Box 45, Evington, VA 24550 / 804-821-8117

Antique American Firearms, P.O. Box 71035, Dept. GD, Des Moines, IA 50325 / 515-224-6552

Arco Powder, HC-Rt. 1 P.O. Box 102, County Rd. 357, Mayo, FL 32066 / 904-294-3882; FAX:

Antique Arms Co., 1110 Cleveland Ave., Monett, MO 65708 / 417-235-6501

Apel GmbH, Ernst, Am Kirschberg 3, D-97218, Gerbrunn, GERMANY / 0 (931) 707192

Aplan Antiques & Art, James O., HC 80, Box 793-25, Piedmont, SD 57769 / 605-347-5016

Arizona Ammunition, Inc., 21421 No. 14th Ave., Suite E, Phoenix, AZ 85027 / 623-516-9004; FAX: 623-516-9012 azammo.com

Arkansas Mallard Duck Calls, Rt. Box 182, England, AR 72046 / 501-842-3597

ArmaLite, Inc., P.O. Box 299, Geneseo, IL 61254 / 309-944-6939; FAX: 309-944-6949

Armament Gunsmithing Co., Inc., 525 Rt. 22, Hillside, NJ 07205 / 908-686-0960 FAX: 718-738-5019

Armas Kemen S. A. (See U.S. Importers)

Armas Urki Garbi, 12-14 20,600, Eibar (Guipuzcoa), / 43-11 38 73

Armfield Custom Bullets, 4775 Caroline Drive, San Diego, CA 92115 / 619-582-7188; FAX: 619-287-3238

Armi Perazzi S.p.A., Via Fontanelle 1/3, 1-25080, Botticino Matrina, / 030-2692591; FAX: 030 2692594+

Armi San Marco (See U.S. Importers-Taylor's & Co I

Armi San Paolo, 172-A, I-25062, via Europa, ITALY / 030-2751725

Armi Sport (See U.S. Importers-Cape Outfitters)

Armite Laboratories, 1845 Randolph St., Los Angeles, CA 90001 / 213-587-7768; FAX: 213-587-5075

Armoloy Co., of Ft. Worth, 204 E. Daggett St., Fort Worth, TX 76104 / 817-332-5604; FAX:

Armor (See Buck Stop Lure Co., Inc.)

Armor Metal Products, P.O. Box 4609, Helena, MT 59604 / 406-442-5560; FAX: 406-442-5650

Armoury Publications, 17171 Bothall Way NE, #276, Seattle, WA 98155 / 208-664-9906 armorypub.com

Arms & Armour Press, Wellington House, 125 Strand, London, WC2R 0BB ENGLAND / 0171-420-5555;

Arms Corporation of the Philippines, Bo. Parang Marikina, Metro Manila, PHILIPPINES / 632-941-6243 or 632-941-6244; FAX: 632-941-0682

Arms Craft Gunsmithing, 1106 Linda Dr., Arroyo Grande, CA 93420 / 805-481-2830

Arms Ingenuity Co., P.O. Box 1, 51 Canal St., Weatogue, CT 06089 / 203-658-5624

Arms Software, P.O. Box 1526, Lake Oswego, OR 97035 / 800-366-5559 or 503-697-3337

Arms, Programming Solutions (See Arms Software)

Armsport, Inc., 3950 NW 49th St., Miami, FL 33142 / 305-635-7850; FAX: 305-633-2877

Arnold Arms Co., Inc., P.O. Box 1011, Arlington, WA 98223 / 800-371-1011 or 360-435-1011; FAX: 360-435-7304

Aro-Tek Ltd., 206 Frontage Rd. North, Suite C, Pacific, WA 98047 / 206-351-2984; FAX: 206-833-4483

Arratoonian, Andy (See Horseshoe Leather Products)

Arrieta S.L., Morkaiko 5, 20870, Elgoibar, SPAIN / 34-43-743150; FAX: 34-43-743154+

Art Jewel Enterprises Ltd., Eagle Business Ctr., 460 Randy Rd., Carol Stream, IL 60188 / 708-260-0400

Art's Gun & Sport Shop, Inc., 6008 Hwy. Y, Hillsboro, MO 63050

Artistry in Wood, 134 Zimmerman Rd., Kalispell, MT 59901 / 406-257-9003

Arundel Arms & Ammunition, Inc., A., 24A Defense St., Annapolis, MD 21401 / 410-224-8683

Arvo Ojala Holsters, P.O. Box 98, N. Hollywood, CA 91603 / 818-222-9700; FAX: 818-222-0401

Ashby Turkey Calls, P.O. Box 1466, Ava, MO 65608-1466 / 417-967-3787

Ashley Outdoors, Inc., 2401 Ludelle St, Fort Worth, TX 76105 / 888-744-4880; FAX: 800-734-7939

Aspen Outfitting Co., Jon Hollinger, 9 Dean St, Aspen, CO 81611 / 970-925-3406

Astra Sport, S.A., Apartado 3, 48300 Guernica, Espagne, SPAIN / 34-4-6250100; FAX: 34-4-6255186+

Atamec-Bretton, 19 rue Victor Grignard, F-42026, St.-Etienne (Cedex 1, / 77-93-54-69; FAX: 33-77-93-57-98+

Atlanta Cutlery Corp., 2143 Gees Mill Rd., Box 839 CIS, Conyers, GA 30207 / 800-883-0300; FAX:

Atlantic Mills, Inc., 1295 Towbin Ave., Lakewood, NJ 08701-5934 / 800-242-7374

Atlantic Rose, Inc., P.O. Box 10717, Bradenton, FL 34282-0717

Atsko/Sno-Seal, Inc., 2664 Russell St., Orangeburg, SC 29115 / 803-531-1820; FAX: 803-531-2139

Auguste Francotte & Cie S.A., rue du Trois Juin 109, 4400 Herstal-Liege, BELGIUM / 32-4-248-13-18;

Austin & Halleck, 1099 Welt, Weston, MO 64098 / 816-386-2176; FAX: 816-386-2177

Austin Sheridan USA, Inc., P.O. Box 577, 36 Haddam Quarter Rd., Durham, CT 06422 / 860-349-1772; FAX: 860-349-1771 swalzer@palm.net

Autauga Arms, Inc., Pratt Plaza Mall No. 13, Prattville, AL 36067 / 800-262-9563; FAX: 334-361-2961

Auto Arms, 738 Clearview, San Antonio, TX 78228 / 512-434-5450

Auto-Ordnance Corp., PO Box 220, Blauvelt, NY 10913 / 914-353-7770

Automatic Equipment Sales, 627 E. Railroad Ave., Salesburg, MD 21801

Autumn Sales, Inc. (Blaser), 1320 Lake St., Fort Worth, TX 76102 / 817-335-1634; FAX: 817-338-0119

Avnda Otaola Norica, 16 Apartado 68, 20600, Eibar, SPAIN

AWC Systems Technology, P.O. Box 41938, Phoenix, AZ 85080-1938 / 602-780-1050 FAX: 602-780-2967

AYA (See U.S. Importer-New England Custom Gun Service)

B & P America, 12321 Brittany Cir, Dallas, TX 75230 / 972-726-9069

B&D Trading Co., Inc., 3935 Fair Hill Rd., Fair Oaks, CA 95628 / 800-334-3790 or 916-967-9366; FAX: 916-967-4873

B-Square Company, Inc., P.O. Box 11281, 2708 St. Louis Ave., Ft. Worth, TX 76110 / 817-923-0964 or 800-433-2909 FAX: 817-926-7012

B-West Imports, Inc., 2425 N. Huachuca Dr., Tucson, AZ 85745-1201 / 602-628-1990; FAX: 602-628-3602

B.B. Walker Co., PO Box 1167, 414 E Dixie Dr, Asheboro, NC 27203 / 910-625-1380; FAX: 910-625-8125

B.C. Outdoors, Larry McGhee, PO Box 61497, Boulder City, NV 89006 / 702-294-0025

B.M.F. Activator, Inc., 12145 Mill Creek Run, Plantersville, TX 77363 / 936-894-2397 or 800-527-2881 FAX: 936-894-2397

Badger Shooters Supply, Inc., P.O. Box 397, Owen, WI 54460 / 800-424-9069; FAX: 715-229-2332

Baekgaard Ltd., 1855 Janke Dr., Northbrook, IL 60062 / 708-498-3040; FAX: 708-493-3106

Baelder, Harry, Alte Goennebeker Strasse 5, 24635, Rickling, GERMANY / 04328-722732; FAX: 04328-722733

Baer Custom, Inc., Les, 29601 34th Ave., Hillsdale, IL 61257 / 309-658-2716; FAX: 309-658-2610

Baer's Hollows, P.O. Box 284, Eads, CO 81036 / 719-438-5718

Bagmaster Mfg., Inc., 2731 Sutton Ave., St. Louis, MO 63143 / 314-781-8002; FAX: 314-781-3363

Bain & Davis, Inc., 307 E. Valley Blvd., San Gabriel, CA 91776-3522 / 818-573-4241 or 213-283-7449 cain-davis@aol.com

Baker, Stan, 10000 Lake City Way, Seattle, WA 98125 / 206-522-4575

Baker's Leather Goods, Roy, PO Box 893, Magnolia, AR 71753 / 501-234-0344

Balance Co., 340-39 Ave., S.E., Box 505, Calgary, AB T2G 1X6 CANADA

Bald Eagle Precision Machine Co., 101-A Allison St., Lock Haven, PA 17745 / 570-748-6772; FAX: 570-748-4443

Balickie, Joe, 408 Trelawney Lane, Apex, NC 27502 / 919-362-5185

Ballard Industries, 10271 Lockwood Dr., Suite B, Cupertino, CA 95014 / 408-996-0957; FAX: 408-257-6828

Ballard Rifle & Cartridge Co., LLC, 113 W Yellowstone Ave, Cody, WY 82414 / 307-587-4914; FAX: 307-527-6097

Ballisti-Cast, Inc., 6347 49th St. NW, Plaza, ND 58771 / 701-497-3333; FAX: 701-497-3335

Ballistic Engineering & Software, Inc., 185 N. Park Blvd., Suite 330, Lake Orion, MI 48362 /

Ballistic Product, Inc., 20015 75th Ave. North, Corcoran, MN 55340-9456 / 612-494-9237; FAX: 612-494-9236 info@ballisticproducts.com www.ballisticproducts.com

Ballistic Research, 1108 W. May Ave., McHenry, IL 60050 / 815-385-0037

Bandcor Industries, Div. of Man-Sew Corp., 6108 Sherwin Dr., Port Richey, FL 34668 / 813-848-0432

Bang-Bang Boutique (See Holster Shop, The)

Banks, Ed, 2762 Hwy. 41 N., Ft. Valley, GA 31030 / 912-987-4665

Bansner's Gunsmithing Specialties, 261 East Main St. Box VH, Adamstown, PA 19501 / 800-368-2379; FAX: 717-484-0523

Bar-Sto Precision Machine, 73377 Sullivan Rd., P.O. Box 1838, Twentynine Palms, CA 92277 / 760-367-2747; FAX: 760-367-2407

Barbour, Inc., 55 Meadowbrook Dr., Milford, NH 03055 / 603-673-1313; FAX: 603-673-6510

Barnes, 110 Borner St S, Prescott, WI 54021-1149 / 608-987-8416

Barnes Bullets, Inc., P.O. Box 215, American Fork, UT 84003 / 801-756-4222 or 800-574-9200; FAX: 801-756-2465 email@barnesbullets.com barnesbullets.com

Baron Technology, 62 Spring Hill Rd., Trumbull, CT 06611 / 203-452-0515; FAX: 203-452-0663

Barraclough, John K., 55 Merit Park Dr., Gardena, CA 90247 / 310-324-2574

Barramundi Corp., P.O. Drawer 4259, Homosassa Springs, FL 32687 / 904-628-0200

Barrett Firearms Manufacturer, Inc., P.O. Box 1077, Murfreesboro, TN 37133 / 615-896-2938; FAX: 615-896-7313

Barry Lee Hands Engraving, 26192 E. Shore Route, Bigfork, MT 59911 / 406-837-0035

Barta's Gunsmithing, 10231 US Hwy. 10, Cato, WI 54206 / 920-732-4472

Barteaux Machete, 1916 SE 50th Ave., Portland, OR 97215-3238 / 503-233-5880

Bartlett Engineering, 40 South 200 East, Smithfield, UT 84335-1645 / 801-563-5910

Basics Information Systems, Inc., 1141 Georgia Ave., Suite 515, Wheaton, MD 20902 / 301-949-1070; FAX: 301-949-5326

Bates Engraving, Billy, 2302 Winthrop Dr, Decatur, AL 35603 / 256-355-3690

Bauer, Eddie, 15010 NE 36th St., Redmond, WA 98052

Baumgartner Bullets, 3011 S. Alane St., W. Valley City, UT 84120

MANUFACTURER'S DIRECTORY

Bauska Barrels, 105 9th Ave. W., Kalispell, MT 59901 / 406-752-7706

Bear Archery, RR 4, 4600 Southwest 41st Blvd., Gainesville, FL 32601 / 904-376-2327

Bear Arms, 121 Rhodes St., Jackson, SC 29831 / 803-471-9859

Bear Hug Grip, Inc., P.O. Box 16649, Colorado Springs, CO 80935-6649 / 800-232-7710

Bear Mountain Gun & Tool, 120 N. Plymouth, New Plymouth, ID 83655 / 208-278-5221; FAX: 208-278-5221

Beartooth Bullets, P.O. Box 491, Dept. HLD, Dover, ID 83825-0491 / 208-448-1865 beartooth@trasport.com

Beaver Lodge (See Fellowes, Ted)

Beaver Park Product, Inc., 840 J St., Penrose, CO 81240 / 719-372-6744

BEC, Inc, 1227 W. Valley Blvd., Suite 204, Alhambra, CA 91803 / 626-281-5751; FAX: 626-293-7073

Beeline Custom Bullets Limited, P.O. Box 85, Yarmouth, NS B5A 4B1 CANADA / 902-648-3494; FAX: 902-648-0253

Beeman Precision Airguns, 5454 Argosy Dr., Huntington Beach, CA 92649 / 714-890-4800; FAX: 714-890-4808

Behlert Precision, Inc., P.O. Box 288, 7067 Easton Rd., Pipersville, PA 18947 / 215-766-8681 or 215-766-7301; FAX: 215-766-8681

Beitzinger, George, 116-20 Atlantic Ave, Richmond Hill, NY 11419 / 718-847-7661

Belding's Custom Gun Shop, 10691 Sayers Rd., Munith, MI 49259 / 517-596-2388

Bell & Carlson, Inc., Dodge City Industrial Park, 101 Allen Rd., Dodge City, KS 67801 / 800-634-8586 or 316-225-6688; FAX: 316-225-9095

Bell Reloading, Inc., 1725 Harlin Lane Rd., Villa Rica, GA 30180

Bell's Gun & Sport Shop, 3309-19 Mannheim Rd, Franklin Park, IL 60131

Bell's Legendary Country Wear, 22 Circle Dr., Bellmore, NY 11710 / 516-679-1158

Bellm Contenders, P.O. Box 459, Cleveland, UT 84518 / 801-653-2530

Belltown Ltd., 11 Camps Rd., Kent, CT 06757 / 860-354-5750 FAX: 860-354-6764

Ben William's Gun Shop, 1151 S. Cedar Ridge, Duncanville, TX 75137 / 214-780-1807

Benchmark Guns, 12593 S. Ave. 5 East, Yuma, AZ 85365

Benchmark Knives (See Gerber Legendary Blades)

Benelli Armi S.p.A., Via della Stazione, 61029, Urbino, ITALY / 39-722-307-1; FAX: 39-722-327427+

Benelli USA Corp, 17603 Indian Head Hwy, Accokeek, MD 20607 / 301-283-6981; FAX: 301-283-6988 benelliusa.com

Bengtson Arms Co., L., 6345-B E. Akron St., Mesa, AZ 85205 / 602-981-6375

Benjamin/Sheridan Co., Crossman, Rts. 5 and 20, E. Bloomfield, NY 14443 / 716-657-6161; FAX: 716-657-5405

Bentley, John, 128-D Watson Dr., Turtle Creek, PA 15145

Beomat of America, Inc., 300 Railway Ave., Campbell, CA 95008 / 408-379-4829

Beretta S.p.A., Pietro, Via Beretta, 18-25063, Gardone V.T., ITALY / 39-30-8341-1 FAX: 39-30-8341-421

Beretta U.S.A. Corp., 17601 Beretta Drive, Accokeek, MD 20607 / 301-283-2191; FAX: 301-283-0316

Berger Bullets Ltd., 5342 W. Camelback Rd., Suite 200, Glendale, AZ 85301 / 602-842-4001; FAX: 602-934-9083

Bernardelli S.p.A., Vincenzo, 125 Via Matteotti, PO Box 74, Brescia, ITALY / 39-30-8912851-2-3; FAX: 39-30-8910249

Berry's Mfg., Inc., 401 North 3050 East St., St. George, UT 84770 / 435-634-1682; FAX: 435-634-1683 sales@berrysmfg.com / www.berrysmfg.com

Bersa S.A., Gonzales Castillo 312, 1704, Ramos Mejia, ARGENTINA / 541-656-2377; FAX: 541-656-2093+

Bert Johanssons Vapentillbehor, S-430 20 Veddige, SWEDEN

Bertuzzi (See U.S. Importer-New England Arms Co)

Better Concepts Co., 663 New Castle Rd., Butler, PA 16001 / 412-285-9000

Beverly, Mary, 3201 Horseshoe Trail, Tallahassee, FL 32312

Bianchi International, Inc., 100 Calle Cortez, Temecula, CA 92590 / 909-676-5621; FAX: 909-676-6777

Biesen, Al, 5021 Rosewood, Spokane, WA 99208 / 509-328-9340

Biesen, Roger, 5021 W. Rosewood, Spokane, WA 99208 / 509-328-9340

Big Bear Arms & Sporting Goods, Inc., 1112 Milam Way, Carrollton, TX 75006 / 972-416-8051 or 800-400-BEAR; FAX: 972-416-0771

Big Bore Bullets of Alaska, P.O. Box 872785, Wasilla, AK 99687 / 907-373-2673; FAX: 907-373-2673 doug@mtaonline.net ww.awloo.com/bbb/index.

Big Bore Express, 7154 W. State St., Boise, ID 83703 / 800-376-4010; FAX: 208-376-4020

Big Sky Racks, Inc., P.O. Box 729, Bozeman, MT 59771-0729 / 406-586-9393; FAX: 406-585-7378

Big Spring Enterprises "Bore Stores", P.O. Box 1115, Big Spring Rd., Yellville, AR 72687 / 870-449-5297; FAX: 870-449-4446

Bilal, Mustafa, 908 NW 50th St., Seattle, WA 98107-3634 / 206-782-4164

Bilinski, Bryan. See: FIELDSPORT LTD

Bill Austin's Calls, Box 284, Kaycee, WY 82639 / 307-738-2552

Bill Adair Custom Shop, 2886 Westridge, Carrollton, TX 75006 / 972-418-0950

Bill Hanus Birdguns LLC, P.O. Box 533, Newport, OR 97365 / 541-265-7433; FAX: 541-265-7400

Bill Johns Master Engraver, 7927 Ranch Roach 965, Fredericksburg, TX 78624-9545 / 830-997-6795

Bill Wiseman and Co., P.O. Box 3427, Bryan, TX 77805 / 409-690-3456; FAX: 409-690-0156

Bill's Custom Cases, P.O. Box 2, Dunsmuir, CA 96025 / 530-235-0177; FAX: 530-235-4959

Bill's Gun Repair, 1007 Burlington St., Mendota, IL 61342 / 815-539-5786

Billeb, Stephen L., 1101 N. 7th St., Burlington, IA 52601 / 319-753-2110

Billings Gunsmiths Inc., 1841 Grand Ave., Billings, MT 59102 / 406-256-8390

Billingsley & Brownell, P.O. Box 25, Dayton, WY 82836 / 307-655-9344

Billy Bates Engraving, 2302 Winthrop Dr., Decatur, AL 35603 / 205-355-3690

Birchwood Casey, 7900 Fuller Rd., Eden Prairie, MN 55344 / 800-328-6156 or 612-937-7933; FAX: 612-937-7979

Birdsong & Assoc., W. E., 1435 Monterey Rd, Florence, MS 39073-9748 / 601-366-8270

Bismuth Cartridge Co., 3500 Maple Ave., Suite 1650, Dallas, TX 75219 / 214-521-5880; FAX: 214-521-9035

Bison Studios, 1409 South Commerce St., Las Vegas, NV 89102 / 702-388-2891; FAX: 702-383-9967

Bitterroot Bullet Co., PO Box 412, Lewiston, ID 83501-0412 / 208-743-5635 FAX: 208-743-5635

BKL Technologies, PO Box 5237, Brownsville, TX 78523

Black Belt Bullets (See Big Bore Express)

Black Hills Ammunition, Inc., P.O. Box 3090, Rapid City, SD 57709-3090 / 605-348-5150; FAX: 605-348-9827

Black Hills Shooters Supply, P.O. Box 4220, Rapid City, SD 57709 / 800-289-2506

Black Powder Products, 67 Township Rd. 1411, Chesapeake, OH 45619 / 614-867-8047

Black Sheep Brand, 3220 W. Gentry Parkway, Tyler, TX 75702 / 903-592-3853; FAX: 903-592-0527

Blackhawk East, Box 2274, Loves Park, IL 61131

Blacksmith Corp., PO Box 280, North Hampton, OH 45349 / 800-531-2665; FAX: 937-969-8399 bc-books@glasscity.net

BlackStar AccuMax Barrels, 11501 Brittmoore Park Drive, Houston, TX 77041 / 281-721-6040; FAX: 281-721-6041

BlackStar Barrel Accurizing (See BlackStar AccuMax Barrels)

Blacktail Mountain Books, 42 First Ave. W., Kalispell, MT 59901 / 406-257-5573

Blair Engraving, J. R., PO Box 64, Glenrock, WY 82637 / 307-436-8115

Blammo Ammo, P.O. Box 1677, Seneca, SC 29679 / 803-882-1768

Blaser Jagdwaffen GmbH, D-88316, Isny Im Allgau, GERMANY

Bleile, C. Roger, 5040 Ralph Ave., Cincinnati, OH 45238 / 513-251-0249

Blount, Inc., Sporting Equipment Div., 2299 Snake River Ave., P.O. Box 856, Lewiston, ID 83501 /

800-627-3640 or 208-746-2351; FAX: 208-799-3904

Blue and Gray Products Inc (See Ox-Yoke Originals, Inc..)

Blue Book Publications, Inc., One Appletree Square, 8009 34th Ave. S. Suite 175, Minneapolis, MN 55425 / 800-877-4867 or 612-854-5229; FAX: 612-853-1486

Blue Mountain Bullets, HCR 77, P.O. Box 231, John Day, OR 97845 / 541-820-4594

Blue Ridge Machinery & Tools, Inc., P.O. Box 536-GD, Hurricane, WV 25526 / 800-872-6500; FAX: 304-562-5311

BMC Supply, Inc., 26051 - 179th Ave. S.E., Kent, WA 98042

Bo-Mar Tool & Mfg. Co., Rt. 8, Box 405, Longview, TX 75604 / 903-759-4784; FAX: 903-759-9141

Bob Allen Co.214 SW Jackson, P.O. Box 477, Des Moines, IA 50315 / 800-685-7020 FAX: 515-283-0779

Bob Rogers Gunsmithing, P.O. Box 305, 344 S. Walnut St., Franklin Grove, IL 61031 / 815-456-2685; FAX: 815-288-7142

Bob Schrimsher's Custom Knifemaker's Supply, P.O. Box 308, Emory, TX 75440 / 903-473-3330; FAX: 903-473-2235

Bob's Gun Shop, P.O. Box 200, Royal, AR 71968 / 501-767-1970; FAX: 501-767-1970

Bob's Tactical Indoor Shooting Range & Gun Shop, 90 Lafayette Rd., Salisbury, MA 01952 / 508-465-5561

Boessler, Erich, Am Vogeltal 3, 97702, Munnerstadt, GERMANY

Bohemia Arms Co., 17101 Los Modelos St., Fountain Valley, CA 92708 / 619-442-7005; FAX: 619-442-7005

Boker USA, Inc., 1550 Balsam Street, Lakewood, CO 80215 / 303-462-0662; FAX: 303-462-0668 bokerusa@worldnet.att.net bokerusa.com

Boltin, John M., P.O. Box 644, Estill, SC 29918 / 803-625-2185

Bonanza (See Forster Products), 310 E Lanark Ave, Lanark, IL 61046 / 815-493-6360; FAX: 815-493-2371

Bond Arms, Inc., P.O. Box 1296, Granbury, TX 76048 / 817-573-4445; FAX: 817-573-5636

Bond Custom Firearms, 8954 N. Lewis Ln., Bloomington, IN 47408 / 812-332-4519

Bondini Paolo, Via Sorrento 345, San Carlo di Cesena, ITALY / 0547-663-240; FAX: 0547-663-780

Bone Engraving, Ralph, 718 N Atlanta, Owasso, OK 74055 / 918-272-9745

Boone Trading Co., Inc., P.O. Box BB, Brinnan, WA 98320

Boone's Custom Ivory Grips, Inc., 562 Coyote Rd., Brinnon, WA 98320 / 206-796-4330

Boonie Packer Products, P.O. Box 12204, Salem, OR 97309 / 800-477-3244 or 503-581-3244; FAX: 503-581-3191

Borden Ridges Rimrock Stocks, RR 1 Box 250 BC, Springville, PA 18844 / 570-965-2505 FAX: 570-965-2328

Borden Rifles Inc., RD 1, Box 250BC, Springville, PA 18844 / 717-965-2505; FAX: 717-965-2328

Border Barrels Ltd., Riccarton Farm, Newcastleton, SCOTLAND UK

Borovnik KG, Ludwig, 9170 Ferlach, Bahnhofstrasse 7, AUSTRIA / 042 27 24 42; FAX: 042 26 43 49

Bosis (See U.S. Importer-New England Arms Co.)

Boss Manufacturing Co., 221 W. First St., Kewanee, IL 61443 / 309-852-2131 or 800-447-4581; FAX: 309-852-0848

Bostick Wildlife Calls, Inc., P.O. Box 728, Estill, SC 29918 / 803-625-2210 or 803-625-4512

Bowen Classic Arms Corp., P.O. Box 67, Louisville, TN 37777 / 865-984-3583 bowsarms.com

Bowen Knife Co., Inc., P.O. Box 590, Blackshear, GA 31516 / 912-449-4794

Bowerly, Kent, 710 Golden Pheasant Dr, Redmond, OR 97756 / 541-595-6028

Boyds Gunstock Industries, Inc., 25376 403RD AVE, MITCHELL, SD 57301 / 605-996-5011; FAX: 605-996-9878

Brace, Larry D., 771 Blackfoot Ave., Eugene, OR 97404 / 541-688-1278; FAX: 541-607-5833

Bradley Gunsight Co., P.O. Box 340, Plymouth, VT 05056 / 860-589-0531; FAX: 860-582-6294

Brass Eagle, Inc., 7050A Bramalea Rd., Unit 19, Mississauga, ON L4Z 1C7 CANADA / 416-848-4844

MANUFACTURER'S DIRECTORY

Bratcher, Dan, 311 Belle Air Pl., Carthage, MO 64836 / 417-358-1518

Brauer Bros. Mfg. Co., 2020 Delmar Blvd., St. Louis, MO 63103 / 314-231-2864; FAX: 314-249-4952

Break-Free, Inc., P.O. Box 25020, Santa Ana, CA 92799 / 714-953-1900; FAX: 714-953-0402

Brenneke KG, Wilhelm, Ilmenauweg 2, 30851 Langenhagen, GERMANY / 0511-97262-0; FAX: 0511-97262-62

Brian Perazone-Gunsmith, Cold Spring Rd., Roxbury, NY 12474 / 607-326-4088; FAX: 607-326-3140

Bridgeman Products, Harry Jaffin, 153 B Cross Slope Court, Englishtown, NJ 07726 / 732-972-1004; FAX: 732-972-1004

Bridgers Best, P.O. Box 1410, Berthoud, CO 80513

Briese Bullet Co., Inc., RR1, Box 108, Tappen, ND 58487 / 701-327-4578; FAX: 701-327-4579

Brigade Quartermasters, 1025 Cobb International Blvd., Dept. VH, Kennesaw, GA 30144-4300 / 404-428-1248 or 800-241-3125; FAX:

Briganti, A.J., 512 Rt. 32, Highland Mills, NY 10930 / 404-426-7726

Briley Mfg. Inc., 1230 Lumpkin, Houston, TX 77043 / 800-331-5718 or 713-932-6995; FAX: 713-932-1043

British Antiques, P.O. Box 35369, Tucson, AZ 85740 / 520-575-9063 britishantiques@hotmail.com

British Sporting Arms, RR1, Box 130, Millbrook, NY 12545 / 914-677-8303

BRNO (See U.S. Importers-Bohemia Arms Co.)

Broad Creek Rifle Works, Ltd., 120 Horsey Ave., Laurel, DE 19956 / 302-875-5446; FAX: 302-875-1449

Brockman's Custom Gunsmithing, P.O. Box 357, Gooding, ID 83330 / 208-934-5050

Brocock Ltd. 43 River Street, Digbeth, Birmingham, B5 5SA ENGLAND / 011-021-773-1200

Broken Gun Ranch, 10739 126 Rd., Spearville, KS 67876 / 316-385-2587; FAX: 316-385-2597

Brolin Arms, 2755 Thompson Creek Rd., Pomona, CA 91767 / 909-392-7822; FAX: 909-392-7824

Brooker, Dennis, Rt. 1, Box 12A, Derby, IA 50068 / 515-533-2103

Brooks Tactical Systems, 279-C Shorewood Ct., Fox Island, WA 98333 / 253-549-2866 FAX: 253-549-2703 brooks@brookstactical.com www.brookstactical.com

Brown Products, Inc., Ed, 43885 Muldrow Trail, Perry, MO 63462 / 573-565-3261; FAX: 573-565-2791

Brown Dog Ent., 2200 Calle Camelia, 1000 Oaks, CA 91360 / 805-497-2318; FAX: 805-497-1618

Brown Manufacturing, P.O. Box 9219, Akron, OH 44305 / 800-837-GUNS

Brown Precision, Inc. 7786 Molinos Ave., Los Molinos, CA 96055 FAX: 916-384-1638

Brown, H. R. (See Silhouette Leathers)

Brown Co., E. Arthur, 3404 Pawnee Dr, Alexandria, MN 56308 / 320-762-8847

Brownells, Inc., 200 S. Front St., Montezuma, IA 50171 / 515-623-5401; FAX: 515-623-3896

Browning Arms Co., One Browning Place, Morgan, UT 84050 / 801-876-2711; FAX: 801-876-3331

Browning Arms Co. (Parts & Service), 3005 Arnold Tenbrook Rd., Arnold, MO 63010 / 314-287-6800; FAX: 314-287-9751

BRP, Inc. High Performance Cast Bullets, 1210 Alexander Rd., Colorado Springs, CO 80909 / 719-633-0658

Brunton U.S.A., 620 E. Monroe Ave., Riverton, WY 82501 / 307-856-6559; FAX: 307-856-1840

Bryan & Assoc., R D Sauls, PO Box 5772, Anderson, SC 29623-5772 / 864-261-6810

Brynin, Milton, P.O. Box 383, Yonkers, NY 10710 / 914-779-4333

BSA Guns Ltd., Armoury Rd. Small Heath, Birmingham, ENGLAND / 011-021-772-8543; FAX: 011-021-773-084

BSA Optics, 3911 SW 47th Ave #914, Ft Lauderdale, FL 33314 / 954-581-2144 FAX: 954-581-3165

Buchheimer, J.M. (See Jumbo Sports Products)

Buchheimer, J. (See JUMBO SPORTS PRODUCTS)

Buck Knives, Inc., 1900 Weld Blvd., P.O. Box 1267, El Cajon, CA 92020 / 619-449-1100 or 800-326-2825; FAX: 619-562-5774 8

Buck Stix—SOS Products Co., Box 3, Neenah, WI 54496

Buck Stop Lure Co., Inc., 3600 Grow Rd. NW, P.O. Box 636, Stanton, MI 48888 / 517-762-5091; FAX: 517-762-5124

Buckeye Custom Bullets, 6490 Stewart Rd., Elida, OH 45807 / 419-641-4463

Buckhorn Gun Works, 8109 Woodland Dr., Black Hawk, SD 57718 / 605-787-6472

Buckskin Bullet Co., P.O. Box 1893, Cedar City, UT 84721 / 435-586-3286

Buckskin Machine Works, A. Hunkeler, 3235 S. 358th St., Auburn, WA 98001 / 206-927-5412

Budin, Dave, Main St., Margaretville, NY 12455 / 914-586-4103; FAX: 914-586-4105

Buenger Enterprises/Goldenrod Dehumidifier, 3600 S. Harbor Blvd., Oxnard, CA 93035 / 800-451-6797 or 805-985-5828; FAX: 805-985-1534

Buffalo Bullet Co., Inc., 12637 Los Nietos Rd., Unit A, / 208-263-6953; FAX: 208-265-2096 Santa Fe Springs, CA 90670 FAX: 562-944-5054

Buffalo Rock Shooters Supply, R.R. 1, Ottawa, IL 61350 / 815-433-2471

Buffer Technologies, P.O. Box 104930, Jefferson City, MO 65110 / 573-634-8529; FAX: 573-634-8522

Bull Mountain Rifle Co., 6327 Golden West Terrace, Billings, MT 59106 / 406-656-0778

Bull-X, Inc. 520 N. Main, Farmer City, IL 61842 / 309-928-2574 or 800-248-3845; FAX: 309-928-2130

Bullberry Barrel Works, Ltd., 2430 W. Bullberry Ln., #67-5, Hurricane, UT 84737 / 435-635-9866; FAX: 435-635-0348

Bullet Metals, P.O. Box 1238, Sierra Vista, AZ 85636 / 520-458-5321; FAX: 520-458-1421 alloymetalsmith@theriver.com

Bullet Swaging Supply Inc., P.O. Box 1056, 303 McMillan Rd., West Monroe, LA 71291 / 318-387-3266; FAX: 318-387-7779

Bullet, Inc., 3745 Hiram Alworth Rd., Dallas, GA 30132 /

Bullseye Bullets, 8100 E Broadway Ave #A, Tampa, FL 33619-2223 / 813-630-9186

Burgess, Byron, PO Box 6853, Los Osos, CA 93412 / 805-528-1005

Burkhart Gunsmithing, Don, P.O. Box 852, Rawlins, WY 82301 / 307-324-6007

Burnham Bros., P.O. Box 1148, Menard, TX 78659 / 915-396-4572; FAX: 915-396-4574

Burris Co., Inc., P.O. Box 1747, 331 E. 8th St., Greeley, CO 80631 / 970-356-1670; FAX: 970-356-8702

Bushman Hunters & Safaris, P.O. Box 293088, Lewisville, TX 75029 / 214-317-0768

Bushmaster Firearms (See Quality Parts Co/Bushmaster Firearms)

Bushmaster Hunting & Fishing, 451 Alliance Ave., Toronto, ON M6N 2J1 Canada / 416-763-4040; FAX: 416-763-0623

Bushnell Sports Optics Worldwide, 9200 Cody, Overland Park, KS 66214 / 913-752-3400 or 800-423-3537; FAX: 913-752-3550

Bushwacker Backpack & Supply Co (See Counter Assault)

Bustani, Leo, P.O. Box 8125, W. Palm Beach, FL 33410 / 305-622-2710

Buster's Custom Knives, P.O. Box 214, Richfield, UT 84701 / 801-896-5319

Butler Creek Corp, 290 Arden Dr., Belgrade, MT 59714 / 800-423-8327 or 406-388-1356; FAX: 406-388-7204

Butler Enterprises, 834 Oberting Rd., Lawrenceburg, IN 47025 / 812-537-3584

Butterfield & Butterfield, 220 San Bruno Ave., San Francisco, CA 94103 / 415-861-7500

Buzztail Brass (See Grayback Wildcats)

Byron Burgess, P.O. Box 6853, Los Osos, CA 93412 / 805-528-1005

C

C&D Special Products (See Claybuster Wads & Harvester Bullets)

C&H Research, 115 Sunnyside Dr., Box 351, Lewis, KS 67552 / 316-324-5445 www.09.net(chr)

C-More Systems, P.O. Box 1750, 7553 Gary Rd., Manassas, VA 20108 / 703-361-2663; FAX: 703-361-5881

C. Palmer Manufacturing Co., Inc., P.O. Box 220, West Newton, PA 15089 / 412-872-8200; FAX: 412-872-8302

C. Sharps Arms Co., Inc., 100 Centennial, Box 885, Big Timber, MT 59011 / 406-932-4353; FAX:

C.S. Van Gorden & Son, Inc., 1815 Main St., Bloomer, WI 54724 / 715-568-2612

C.W. Erickson's Mfg. Inc., 530 Garrison Ave NE, PO Box 522, Buffalo, MN 55313 / 612-682-3665; FAX: 612-682-4328

Cabanas (See U.S. Importer-Mandall Shooting Supplies, Inc.)

Cabela's, 812-13th Ave., Sidney, NE 69160 / 308-254-6644 or 800-237-4444; FAX: 308-254-6745

Cabinet Mtn. Outfitters Scents & Lures, P.O. Box 766, Plains, MT 59859 / 406-826-3970

Cache La Poudre Rifleworks, 140 N. College, Ft. Collins, CO 80524 / 303-482-6913

Cali'co Hardwoods, Inc., 3580 Westwind Blvd., Santa Rosa, CA 95403 / 707-546-4045; FAX:

Calibre Press, Inc., 666 Dundee Rd., Suite 1607, Northbrook, IL 60062 / 800-323-0037; FAX:

Calico Light Weapon Systems, 1489 Greg St., Sparks, NV 89431

California Sights (See Fautheree, Andy)

Cambos Outdoorsman, 532 E. Idaho Ave., Ontario, OR 97914 / 541-889-3138 FAX: 541-889-2633

Camdex, Inc., 2330 Alger, Troy, MI 48083 / 810-528-2300; FAX: 810-528-0989

Cameron's, 16690 W. 11th Ave., Golden, CO 80401 / 303-279-7365; FAX: 303-628-5413

Camilli, Lou, 600 Sandtree Dr., Suite 212, Lake Park, FL 33403

Camillus Cutlery Co., 54 Main St., Camillus, NY 13031 / 315-672-8111; FAX: 315-672-8832

Camp-Cap Products, P.O. Box 3805, Chesterfield, MO 63006 / 314-532-4340; FAX: 314-532-4340

Campbell, Dick, 20000 Silver Ranch Rd., Conifer, CO 80433 / 303-697-0150; FAX: 303-697-0150

Cannon, Andy. (See CANNON'S)

Cannon Safe, Inc., 9358 Stephens St., Pico Rivera, CA 90660 / 310-692-0636 or 800-242-1055; FAX: 310-692-7252

Cannon's, Andy Cannon, Box 1026, 320 Main St., Polson, MT 59860 / 406-887-2048

Canons Delcour, Rue J.B. Cools, B-4040, Herstal, BELGIUM / +32(0)42.40.61.40; FAX: +32(0)42.40.22.88

Canyon Cartridge Corp., P.O. Box 152, Albertson, NY 11507 FAX: 516-294-8946

Cape Outfitters, 599 County Rd. 206, Cape Girardeau, MO 63701 / 573-335-4103; FAX: 573-335-1555

Caraville Manufacturing, P.O. Box 4545, Thousand Oaks, CA 91359 / 805-499-1234

Carbide Checkering Tools (See J&R Engineering)

Carbide Die & Mfg. Co., Inc., 15615 E. Arrow Hwy., Irwindale, CA 91706 / 626-337-2518

Carhartt, Inc., P.O. Box 600, 3 Parklane Blvd., Dearborn, MI 48121 / 800-358-3825 or 313-271-8460; FAX: 313-271-3455

Carl Walther GmbH, B.P. 4325, D-89033, Ulm, GERMANY

Carl Walther USA, PO Box 208, Ten Prince St, Alexandria, VA 22313 / 703-548-1400; FAX: 703-549-7826

Carl Zeiss Inc, 13017 N Kingston Ave, Chester, VA 23836-2743 / 804-861-0033 or 800-388-2984; FAX: 804-733-4024

Carlson, Douglas R, Antique American Firearms, PO Box 71035, Dept GD, Des Moines, IA 50325 / 515-224-6552

Carnahan Bullets, 17645 110th Ave. SE, Renton, WA 98055

Carolina Precision Rifles, 1200 Old Jackson Hwy., Jackson, SC 29831 / 803-827-2069

Carrell's Precision Firearms, 643 Clark Ave., Billings, MT 59101-1614 / 406-962-3593

Carry-Lite, Inc., 5203 W. Clinton Ave., Milwaukee, WI 53223 / 414-355-3520; FAX: 414-355-4775

Carter's Gun Shop, 225 G St., Penrose, CO 81240 /

Cartridge Transfer Group, Pete de Coux, 235 Oak St., Butler, PA 16001 / 412-282-3426

Cascade Bullet Co., Inc., 2355 South 6th St., Klamath Falls, OR 97601 / 503-884-9316

Cascade Shooters, 2155 N.W. 12th St., Redwood, OR 97756

Case & Sons Cutlery Co., W R, Owens Way, Bradford, PA 16701 / 814-368-4123 or 800-523-6350; FAX: 814-768-5369

Case Sorting System, 12695 Cobblestone Creek Rd., Poway, CA 92064 / 619-486-9340

Cash Mfg. Co., Inc., P.O. Box 130, 201 S. Klein Dr., Waunakee, WI 53597-0130 / 608-849-5664; FAX: 608-849-5664

Caspian Arms, Ltd., 14 North Main St., Hardwick, VT 05843 / 802-472-6454; FAX: 802-472-6709

Cast Performance Bullet Company, 113 Riggs Rd, Shoshoni, WY 82649 / 307-856-4347

Casull Arms Corp., P.O. Box 1629, Afton, WY 83110 / 307-886-0200

Caswell Detroit Armor Companies, 1221 Marshall St. NE, Minneapolis, MN 55413-1055 / 612-379-2000; FAX: 612-379-2367

Catco-Ambush, Inc., P.O.Box 300, Corte Madera, CA 94926

Cathey Enterprises, Inc., P. O. Box 2202, Brownwood, TX 76804 / 915-643-2553; FAX: 915-643-3653

Cation, 2341 Alger St., Troy, MI 48083 / 810-689-0658; FAX: 810-689-7558

Caywood, Shane J., P.O. Box 321, Minocqua, WI 54548 / 715-277-3866

CBC, Avenida Humberto de Campos 3220, 09400-000, Ribeirao Pires, SP, BRAZIL / 55-11-742-7500; FAX: 55-11-459-7385

CBC-BRAZIL, 3 Cuckoo Lane, Honley, Yorkshire HD7 2BR, ENGLAND / 44-1484-661062; FAX: 44-1484-663709

CCG Enterprises, 5217 E. Belknap St., Halton City, TX 76117 / 800-819-7464

CCI Div. of Blount, Inc., Sporting Equipment Div.2299 Sn, P.O. Box 856, Lewiston, ID 83501 / 800-627-3640 or 208-746-2351; FAX: 208-746-2915

CCL Security Products, 199 Whiting St, New Britain, CT 06051 / 800-733-8588

Cedar Hill Game Calls Inc., 238 Vic Allen Rd, Downsville, LA 71234 / 318-982-5632; FAX: 318-368-2245

Celestron International, P.O. Box 3578, 2835 Columbia St., Torrance, CA 90503 / 310-328-9560; FAX: 310-212-5835

Centaur Systems, Inc., 1602 Foothill Rd., Kalispell, MT 59901 / 406-755-8609; FAX: 406-755-8609

Center Lock Scope Rings, 9901 France Ct., Lakeville, MN 55044 / 612-461-2114

Central Specialties Ltd. (See Trigger Lock Division/Central Specialties Ltd.)

Century Gun Dist. Inc., 1467 Jason Rd., Greenfield, IN 46140 / 317-462-4524

Century International Arms, Inc., 1161 Holland Dr, Boca Raton, FL 33487

CFVentures, 509 Harvey Dr., Bloomington, IN 47403-1715

CH Tool & Die Co (See 4-D Custom Die Co), 711 N Sandusky St, PO Box 889, Mt Vernon, OH 43050-0889 / 740-397-7214; FAX: 740-397-6600

Chace Leather Products, 507 Alden St., Fall River, MA 02722 / 508-678-7556; FAX: 508-675-9666

Chadick's Ltd., P.O. Box 100, Terrell, TX 75160 / 214-563-7577

Chambers Flintlocks Ltd., Jim, 116 Sams Branch Rd., Candler, NC 28715 / 828-667-8361 FAX: 828-665-0852

Champion Shooters' Supply, P.O. Box 303, New Albany, OH 43054 / 614-855-1603; FAX: 614-855-1209

Champion Target Co. 232 Industrial Parkway, Richmond, IN 47374 / 800-441-4971

Champion's Choice, Inc., 201 International Blvd., LaVergne, TN 37086 / 615-793-4066; FAX: 615-793-4070

Champlin Firearms, Inc., P.O. Box 3191, Woodring Airport, Enid, OK 73701 / 580-237-7388; FAX: 580-242-6922

Chapman Academy of Practical Shooting, 4350 Academy Rd., Hallsville, MO 65255 / 573-696-5544 or 573-696-2266

Chapman, Jack. (See OLD WEST BULLET MOULDS J ken Chapman)

Chapman Manufacturing Co., 471 New Haven Rd., P.O. Box 250, Durham, CT 06422 / 860-349-9228; FAX: 860-349-0084

Chapuis Armes, 21 La Gravoux, BP15, 42380, St. Bonnet-le-Chatea, FRANCE / (33)77.50.06.96+

Chapuis USA, 416 Business Park, Bedford, KY 40006

Charter 2000, 273 Canal St, Shelton, CT 06484 / 203-922-1652

Checkmate Refinishing, 370 Champion Dr., Brooksville, FL 34601 / 352-799-5774 FAX: 352-799-2986

Cheddite France S.A., 99 Route de Lyon, F-26501, Bourg-les-Valence, FRANCE / 33-75-56-4545; FAX: 33-75-56-3587

Chelsea Gun Club of New York City Inc., 237 Ovington Ave., Apt. D53, Brooklyn, NY 11209 / 718-836-9422 or 718-833-2704

Chem-Pak Inc., PO Box 2058, Winchester, VA 22604-1258 / 800-336-9828 or 703-667-1341 FAX: 703-722-3993

Cherry Creek State Park Shooting Center, 12500 E. Belleview Ave., Englewood, CO 80111 / 303-693-1765

Chet Fulmer's Antique Firearms, P.O. Box 792, Rt. 2 Buffalo Lake, Detroit Lakes, MN 56501 / 218-847-7712

CheVron Bullets, RR1, Ottawa, IL 61350 / 815-433-2471

Cheyenne Pioneer Products, PO Box 28425, Kansas City, MO 64188 / 816-413-9196 FAX: 816-455-2859 cheyennepp@aol.com www.cartridgeboxes.com

Chicago Cutlery Co., 1536 Beech St., Terre Haute, IN 47804 / 800-457-2665

Chicasaw Gun Works, 4 Mi. Mkr., Pluto Rd. Box 868, Shady Spring, WV 25918-0868 / 304-763-2848 FAX: 304-763-3725

Chipmunk (See Oregon Arms, Inc.)

Choate Machine & Tool Co., Inc., P.O. Box 218, 116 Lovers Ln., Bald Knob, AR 72010 / 501-724-6193 or 800-972-6390; FAX: 501-724-5873

Chopie Mfg.,Inc., 700 Copeland Ave., LaCrosse, WI 54603 / 608-784-0926

Christensen Arms, 385 N. 3050 E., St. George, UT 84790 / 435-624-9535; FAX: 435-674-9293

Christie's East, 219 E. 67th St., New York, NY 10021 / 212-606-0400

Chu Tani Ind., Inc., P.O. Box 2064, Cody, WY 82414-2064

Chuck's Gun Shop, P.O. Box 597, Waldo, FL 32694 / 904-468-2264

Churchill (See U.S. Importer-Ellett Bros)

Churchill, Winston, Twenty Mile Stream Rd., RFD P.O. Box 29B, Proctorsville, VT 05153 / 802-226-7772

Churchill Glove Co., James, PO Box 298, Centralia, WA 98531 / 360-736-2816 FAX: 360-330-0151

CIDCO, 21480 Pacific Blvd., Sterling, VA 22170 / 703-444-5353

Ciener Inc., Jonathan Arthur, 8700 Commerce St., Cape Canaveral, FL 32920 / 407-868-2200; FAX: 407-868-2201

Cimarron F.A. Co., P.O. Box 906, Fredericksburg, TX 78624-0906 / 210-997-9090; FAX: 210-997-0802

Cincinnati Swaging, 2605 Marlington Ave., Cincinnati, OH 45208

Clark Custom Guns, Inc., 336 Shootout Lane, Princeton, LA 71067 / 318-949-9884; FAX: 318-949-9829

Clark Firearms Engraving, P.O. Box 80746, San Marino, CA 91118 / 818-287-1652

Clarkfield Enterprises, Inc., 1032 10th Ave., Clarkfield, MN 56223 / 612-669-7140

Claro Walnut Gunstock Co., 1235 Stanley Ave., Chico, CA 95928 / 530-342-5188; FAX: 530-342-5199

Classic Arms Company, Rt 1 Box 120F, Burnet, TX 78611 / 512-756-4001

Classic Arms Corp., P.O. Box 106, Dunsmuir, CA 96025-0106 / 530-235-2000

Classic Guns, Inc., Frank S. Wood, 3230 Medlock Bridge Rd., Suite 110, Norcross, GA 30092 / 404-242-7944

Classic Old West Styles, 1060 Doniphan Park Circle C, El Paso, TX 79936 / 915-587-0684

Claybuster Wads & Harvester Bullets, 309 Sequoya Dr., Hopkinsville, KY 42240 / 800-922-6287 or 800-284-1746; FAX: 502-885-8088 50

Clean Shot Technologies, 21218 St. Andrews Blvd. Ste 504, Boca Raton, FL 33433 / 888-866-2532

Clear Creek Outdoors, Pat LaBoone, 2550 Hwy 23, Wrenshall, MN 55797 / 218-384-3670

Clearview Mfg. Co., Inc., 413 S. Oakley St., Fordyce, AR 71742 / 501-352-8557; FAX: 501-352-7120

Clearview Products, 3021 N. Portland, Oklahoma City, OK 73107

Cleland's Outdoor World, Inc, 10306 Airport Hwy, Swanton, OH 43558 / 419-865-4713; FAX: 419-865-5865

Clements' Custom Leathercraft, Chas, 1741 Dallas St., Aurora, CO 80010-2018 / 303-364-0403; FAX: 303-739-9824

Clenzoil Corp., P.O. Box 80226, Sta. C, Canton, OH 44708-0226 / 330-833-9758; FAX: 330-833-4724

Clift Mfg., L. R., 3821 hammonton Rd, Marysville, CA 95901 / 916-755-3390; FAX: 916-755-3393

Clift Welding Supply & Cases, 1332-A Colusa Hwy., Yuba City, CA 95993 / 916-755-3390 FAX: 916-755-3393

Cloward's Gun Shop, 4023 Aurora Ave. N, Seattle, WA 98103 / 206-632-2072

Clymer Manufacturing Co. Inc., 1645 W. Hamlin Rd., Rochester Hills, MI 48309-3312 / 248-853-5555; FAX: 248-853-1530

Cobalt Mfg., Inc., 4020 Mcewen Rd Ste 180, Dallas, TX 75244-5090 / 817-382-8986 FAX: 817-383-4281

Cobra Sport S.r.l., Via Caduti Nei Lager No. 1, 56020 San Romano, Montopoli v/Arno (Pi) ITALY / 0039-571-450490; FAX: 0039-571-450492

Coffin, Charles H., 3719 Scarlet Ave., Odessa, TX 79762 / 915-366-4729 FAX: 915-366-4729

Coffin, Jim. (See Working Guns)

Coffin, Jim. (See WORKING GUNS)

Cogar's Gunsmithing, P.O. Box 755, Houghton Lake, MI 48629 / 517-422-4591

Coghlan's Ltd., 121 Irene St., Winnipeg, MB R3T 4C7 CANADA / 204-284-9550; FAX: 204-475-4127

Cold Steel Inc., 2128-D Knoll Dr., Ventura, CA 93003 / 800-255-4716 or 800-624-2363 FAX:

Cole's Gun Works, Old Bank Building, Rt. 4 Box 250, Moyock, NC 27958 / 919-435-2345

Cole-Grip, 16135 Cohasset St., Van Nuys, CA 91406 / 818-782-4424

Coleman Co., Inc., 250 N. St. Francis, Wichita, KS 67201

Coleman's Custom Repair, 4035 N. 20th Rd., Arlington, VA 22207 / 703-528-4486

Collectors Firearms Etc, P.O. Box 62, Minnesota City, MN 55959 / 507-689-2925

Collings, Ronald, 1006 Cielta Linda, Vista, CA 92083

Colonial Arms, Inc., P.O. Box 636, Selma, AL 36702-0636 / 334-872-9455; FAX: 334-872-9540 colonialarms@mindspring.com www.colonialarms.com

Colonial Knife Co., Inc., P.O. Box 3327, Providence, RI 02909 / 401-421-1600; FAX: 401-421-2047

Colonial Repair, 47 NAVARRE ST, ROSLINDALE, MA 02131-4725 / 617-469-4951

Colorado Gunsmithing Academy, 27533 Highway 287 South, Lamar, CO 81052 / 719-336-4099 or 800-754-2046; FAX: 719-336-9642

Colorado School of Trades, 1575 Hoyt St., Lakewood, CO 80215 / 800-234-4594; FAX: 303-233-4723

Colorado Sutlers Arsenal (See Cumberland States Arsenal)

Colt Blackpowder Arms Co., 110 8th Street, Brooklyn, NY 11215 / 212-925-2159; FAX: 212-966-4986

Colt's Mfg. Co., Inc., P.O. Box 1868, Hartford, CT 06144-1868 / 800-962-COLT or 860-236-6311; FAX: 860-244-1449

Compass Industries, Inc., 104 East 25th St., New York, NY 10010 / 212-473-2614 or 800-221-9904; FAX: 212-353-0826

Component Concepts, Inc., 530 S Springbrook Dr, Newberg, OR 97132-7056 / 503-554-8095 FAX: 503-554-9370

Compasseco, Ltd., 151 Atkinson Hill Ave., Bardtown, KY 40004 / 502-349-0910

Competition Electronics, Inc., 3469 Precision Dr., Rockford, IL 61109 / 815-874-8001; FAX: 815-874-8181

Competitor Corp. Inc., Appleton Business Center, 30 Tricnit Road Unit 16, New Ipswich, NH 03071 / 603-878-3891; FAX: 603-878-3950

CONKKO, P.O. Box 40, Broomall, PA 19008 / 215-356-0711

Concept Development Corp., 14715 N. 78th Way, Suite 300, Scottsdale, AZ 85260 / 800-472-4405; FAX: 602-948-7560

Conetrol Scope Mounts, 10225 Hwy., 123 S., Seguin, TX 78155 / 210-379-3030 or 800-CONETROL; FAX: 210-379-3030

Connecticut Shotgun Mfg. Co., P.O. Box 1692, 35 Woodland St., New Britain, CT 06051 / 860-225-6581; FAX: 860-832-8707

Connecticut Valley Classics (See CVC)

Conrad, C. A., 3964 Ebert St., Winston-Salem, NC 27127 / 919-788-5469

MANUFACTURER'S DIRECTORY

Cook Engineering Service, 891 Highbury Rd., Vict., 3133 AUSTRALIA

Coonan Arms (JS Worldwide DBA), 1745 Hwy. 36 E., Maplewood, MN 55109 / 612-777-3156; FAX: 612-777-3683

Cooper Arms, P.O. Box 114, Stevensville, MT 59870 / 406-777-5534; FAX: 406-777-5228

Cooper-Woodward, 3800 Pelican Rd., Helena, MT 59602 / 406-458-3800

Cor-Bon Bullet & Ammo Co., 1311 Industry Rd., Sturgis, SD 57785; FAX: 800-923-2666

Corbin Mfg. & Supply, Inc., 600 Industrial Circle, P.O. Box 2659, White City, OR 97503 / 541-826-5211; FAX: 541-826-8669

Corkys Gun Clinic, 4401 Hot Springs Dr., Greeley, CO 80634-9226 / 970-330-0516

Corry, John, 861 Princeton Ct., Neshanic Station, NJ 08853 / 908-369-8019

Cosmi Americo & Figlio s.n.c., Via Flaminia 307, Ancona, ITALY / 071-888208; FAX: 39-071-887006+

Coulston Products, Inc., P.O. Box 30, 201 Ferry St., Suite 212, Easton, PA 18044-0030 / 215-253-0167 or 800-445-9927; FAX: 215-252-1511

Counter Assault, Box 4721, Missoula, MT 59806 / 406-728-6241 FAX: 406-728-8800

Cousin Bob's Mountain Products, 7119 Ohio River Blvd., Ben Avon, PA 15202 / 412-766-5114 FAX: 412-766-5114

Cox, Ed. C., RD 2, Box 192, Prosperity, PA 15329 /

CP Bullets, 1310 Industrial Hwy #5-6, South Hampton, PA 18966 / 215-953-7264; FAX: 215-953-7275

CQB Training, P.O. Box 1739, Manchester, MO 63011

Craftguard, 3624 Logan Ave., Waterloo, IA 50703 / 319-232-2959 FAX: 319-234-0804

Craig, Spegel, P.O. Box 3108, Bay City, OR 97107 / 503-377-2697

Craig Custom Ltd., Research & Development, 629 E. 10th, Hutchinson, KS 67501 / 316-669-0601

Crandall Tool & Machine Co., 19163 21 Mile Rd., Tustin, MI 49688 / 616-829-4430

Creative Concepts USA, Inc., P.O. Box 1705, Dickson, TN 37056 / 615-446-8346 or 800-874-6965; FAX: 615-446-0646

Creedmoor Sports, Inc., P.O. Box 1040, Oceanside, CA 92051 / 619-757-5529

Creek Side Metal & Woodcrafters, Fishers Hill VA 22626 / 703-465-3903

Creekside Gun Shop Inc., Main St., Holcomb, NY 14469 / 716-657-6338 FAX: 716-657-7900

Creighton Audette, 19 Highland Circle, Springfield, VT 05156 / 802-885-2331

Crimson Trace Lasers, 1433 N.W. Quimby, Portland, OR 97209 / 503-295-2406; FAX: 503-295-2225

CritR Call (See Rocky Mountain Wildlife Products)

Crosman Airguns, Rts. 5 and 20, E. Bloomfield, NY 14443 / 716-657-6161 FAX: 716-657-5405

Crosman Blades (See Coleman Co., Inc.)

Crosman Products of Canada Ltd., 1173 N. Service Rd. West, Oakville, ON L6M 2V9 CANADA / 905-827-1822

Crossfire, L.L.C., 2169 Greenville Rd., La Grange, GA 30241 / 706-882-8070 FAX: 706-882-9050

Crosse's Country Cover, P.O. Box 160, Storrs, CT 06268 / 860-423-8736

CRR, Inc./Marble's Inc., 420 Industrial Park, P.O. Box 111, Gladstone, MI 49837 / 906-428-3710; FAX: 906-428-3711

Crucelegui, Hermanos (See U.S. Importer-Mandall Shooting Supplies Inc.)

Cryo-Accurizing, 2250 N. 1500 West, Ogden, UT 84404 / 801-395-2796 or 888-279-6266

Cubic Shot Shell Co., Inc., 98 Fatima Dr., Campbell, OH 44405 / 330-755-0349

Cullity Restoration, 209 Old County Rd., East Sandwich, MA 02537 / 508-888-1147

Cumberland Arms, 514 Shafer Road, Manchester, TN 37355 / 800-797-8414

Cumberland Mountain Arms, P.O. Box 710, Winchester, TN 37398 / 615-967-8414; FAX: 615-967-9199

Cumberland States Arsenal, 1124 Palmyra Road, Clarksville, TN 37040

Cummings Bullets, 1417 Esperanza Way, Escondido, CA 92027

Cupp, Alana, Custom Engraver, PO Box 207, Annabella, UT 84711 / 801-896-4834

Curly Maple Stock Blanks (See Tiger-Hunt)

Curtis Cast Bullets, 527 W. Babcock St., Bozeman, MT 59715 / 406-587-8117; FAX: 406-587-8117

Curtis Custom Shop, RR1, Box 193A, Wallingford, KY 41093 / 703-659-4265

Curtis Gun Shop (See Curtis Cast Bullets)

Custom Bullets by Hoffman, 2604 Peconic Ave., Seaford, NY 11783

Custom Calls, 607 N. 5th St., Burlington, IA 52601 / 319-752-4465

Custom Checkering Service, Kathy Forster, 2124 SE Yamhill St., Portland, OR 97214 / 503-236-5874

Custom Chronograph, Inc., 5305 Reese Hill Rd., Sumas, WA 98295 / 360-988-7801

Custom Firearms (See Ahrends, Kim)

Custom Gun Products, 5021 W. Rosewood, Spokane, WA 99208 / 509-328-9340

Custom Gun Stocks, 3062 Turners Bend Rd, McMinnville, TN 37110 / 615-668-3912

Custom Products (See Jones Custom Products)

Custom Quality Products, Inc., 345 W. Girard Ave., P.O. Box 71129, Madison Heights, MI 48071 /

Custom Riflestocks, Inc., Michael M. Kokolus, 7005 Herber Rd., New Tripoli, PA 18066 / 610-298-3013

Custom Tackle and Ammo, P.O. Box 1886, Farmington, NM 87499 / 505-632-3539

Cutco Cutlery, P.O. Box 810, Olean, NY 14760 / 716-372-3111

CVA, 5988 Peachtree Corners East, Norcross, GA 30071 / 800-251-9412; FAX: 404-242-8546

CVC, 5988 Peachtree Crns East, Norcross, GA 30071

Cylinder & Slide, Inc., William R. Laughridge, 245 E. 4th St., Fremont, NE 68025 / 402-721-4277; FAX: 402-721-0263

CZ USA, PO Box 171073, Kansas City, KS 66117 / 913-321-1811; FAX: 913-321-4901

D

D&D Gunsmiths, Ltd., 363 E. Elmwood, Troy, MI 48083 / 810-583-1512; FAX: 810-583-1524

D&G Precision Duplicators (See Greene Precision Duplicators)

D&H Precision Tooling, 7522 Barnard Mill Rd., Ringwood, IL 60072 / 815-653-4011

D&H Prods. Co., Inc., 465 Denny Rd., Valencia, PA 16059 / 412-898-2840 or 800-776-0281; FAX: 412-898-2013

D&J Bullet Co. & Custom Gun Shop, Inc., 426 Ferry St., Russell, KY 41169 / 606-836-2663; FAX:

D&L Industries (See D.J. Marketing)

D&L Sports, P.O. Box 651, Gillette, WY 82717 /

D&R Distributing, 308 S.E. Valley St., Myrtle Creek, OR 97457 / 503-863-6850

D-Boone Ent., Inc., 5900 Colwyn Dr., Harrisburg, PA 17109

D.C.C. Enterprises, 259 Wynburn Ave., Athens, GA 30601

D.D. Custom Stocks, R.H. "Dick" Devereaux, 5240 Mule Deer Dr., Colorado Springs, CO 80919 / 719-548-8468

D.J. Marketing, 10602 Horton Ave., Downey, CA 90241 / 310-806-0891; FAX: 310-806-6231

Da-Mar Gunsmith's Inc., 102 1st St., Solvay, NY 13209 /

Dade Screw Machine Products, 2319 NW 7th Ave., Miami, FL 33127 / 305-573-5050

Daewoo Precision Industries Ltd., 34-3 Yeoeuido-Dong, Yeongdeungpo-GU 15th Fl., Seoul, KOREA

Daisy Mfg. Co., P.O. Box 220, Rogers, AR 72757 / 501-621-4210; FAX: 501-636-0573

Dakota (See U.S. Importer-EMF Co., Inc.)

Dakota Arms, Inc., HC 55, Box 326, Sturgis, SD 57785 / 605-347-4686; FAX: 605-347-4459

Dakota Corp., 77 Wales St., P.O. Box 543, Rutland, VT 05701 / 802-775-6062 or 800-451-4167; FAX: 802-773-3919

DAMASCUS-U.S.A., 149 Deans Farm Rd., Tyner, NC 27980 / 252-221-2010; FAX: 252-221-2009

DAN WESSON FIREARMS, 119 Kemper Lane, Norwich, NY 13815 / 607-336-1174; FAX: 607-336-2730

Dan's Whetstone Co., Inc., 130 Timbs Place, Hot Springs, AR 71913 / 501-767-1616; FAX: 501-767-9598

Danforth, Mikael. (See VEKTOR USA, Mikael Danforth)

Dangler, Homer L., Box 254, Addison, MI 49220 / 517-547-6745

Danner Shoe Mfg. Co., 12722 NE Airport Way, Portland, OR 97230 / 503-251-1100 or 800-345-0430; FAX: 503-251-1119

Danuser Machine Co., 550 E. Third St., P.O. Box 368, Fulton, MO 65251 / 573-642-2246; FAX: 573-642-2240

Dara-Nes, Inc. (See Nesci Enterprises, Inc.)

Darlington Gun Works, Inc., P.O. Box 698, 516 S. 52 Bypass, Darlington, SC 29532 / 803-393-3931

Darwin Hensley Gunmaker, P.O. Box 329, Brightwood, OR 97011 / 503-622-5411

Data Tech Software Systems, 19312 East Eldorado Drive, Aurora, CO 80013

Datumtech Corp., 2275 Wehrle Dr., Buffalo, NY 14221

Dave Norin Schrank's Smoke & Gun, 2010 Washington St., Waukegan, IL 60085 / 708-662-4034

Dave's Gun Shop, 555 Wood Street, Powell, WY 82435

Davide Pedersoli and Co., Via Artigiani 57, Gardone VT. Brescia 25063, ITALY / 030-8912402; FAX: 030-8911019

David Clark Co., Inc., PO Box 15054, Worcester, MA 01615-0054 / 508-756-6216; FAX: 508-753-5827

David Condon, Inc., 109 E. Washington St., Middleburg, VA 22117 / 703-687-5642

David Miller Co., 3131 E Greenlee Rd, Tucson, AZ 85716 / 520-326-3117

David R. Chicoine, 19 Key St., Eastport, ME 04631 / 207-853-4116 gnpress@nemaine.com

David W. Schwartz Custom Guns, 2505 Waller St., Eau Claire, WI 54703 / 715-832-1735

Davidson, Jere, Rt. 1, Box 132, Rustburg, VA 24588 / 804-821-3637

Davis Industries, 15150 Sierra Bonita Ln., Chino, CA 91710 / 909-597-4726; FAX: 909-393-9771

Davis Products, Mike, 643 Loop Dr., Moses Lake, WA 98837 / 509-765-6178 or 509-766-7281

Davis, Don, 1619 Heights, Katy, TX 77493 /

Daystate Ltd., Birch House Lanee, Cotes Heath Staffs, ST15.022, ENGLAND / 01782-791755; FAX: 01782-791617

Dayton Traister, 4778 N. Monkey Hill Rd., P.O. Box 593, Oak Harbor, WA 98277 / 360-679-4657; FAX: 360-675-1114

DBI Books Division of Krause Publications 700 E State St, Iola, WI 54990-0001 / 630-759-1229

de Coux, Pete (See Cartridge Transfer Group)

Dead Eye's Sport Center, RD 1, 76 Baer Rd, Shickshinny, PA 18655 / 570-256-7432

Decker Shooting Products, 1729 Laguna Ave., Schofield, WI 54476 / 715-359-5873

Deepeeka Exports Pvt. Ltd., D-78, Saket, Meerut-250-006, INDIA / 011-91-121-512889 or 011-91-121-545363; FAX: 011-91-121-542988

Deer Me Products Co., Box 34, 1208 Park St., Anoka, MN 55303 / 612-421-8971; FAX: 612-422-0526

Defense Training International, Inc., 749 S. Lemay, Ste. A3-337, Ft. Collins, CO 80524 / 303-482-2520; FAX: 303-482-0548

Degen Inc. (See Aristocrat Knives)

deHaas Barrels, RR 3, Box 77, Ridgeway, MO 64481 / 816-872-6308

Del Rey Products, P.O. Box 5134, Playa Del Rey, CA 90296-5134 / 213-823-0494

Del-Sports, Inc., Box 685, Main St., Margaretville, NY 12455 / 914-586-4103; FAX: 914-586-4105

Delhi Gun House, 1374 Kashmere Gate, Delhi, 0110 006 INDIA / 011-2917344

Delorge, Ed, 6734 W. Main, Houma, LA 70360 / 504-223-0206

Delta Arms Ltd., P.O. Box 1000, Delta, VT 84624-1000

Delta Enterprises, 284 Hagemann Drive, Livermore, CA 94550

Delta Frangible Ammunition LLC, P.O. Box 2350, Stafford, VA 22555-2350 / 540-720-5778 or 800-339-1933; FAX: 540-720-5667

Dem-Bart Checkering Tools, Inc., 6807 Bickford Ave., Old Hwy. 2, Snohomish, WA 98290 / 360-568-7356; FAX: 360-568-7356

Denver Instrument Co., 6542 Fig St., Arvada, CO 80004 / 800-321-1135 or 303-431-7225; FAX: 303-423-4831

DeSantis Holster & Leather Goods, Inc., P.O. Box 2039, 149 Denton Ave., New Hyde Park, NY 11040-0701 / 516-354-8000; FAX: 516-354-7501

Desert Mountain Mfg., P.O. Box 130184, Coram, MT 59913 / 800-477-0762 or 406-387-5361; FAX: 406-387-5361

MANUFACTURER'S DIRECTORY

Detroit-Armor Corp., 720 Industrial Dr. No. 112, Cary, IL 60013 / 708-639-7666; FAX: 708-639-7694

Dever Co, Jack, 8590 NW 90, Oklahoma City, OK 73132 / 405-721-6393

Devereaux, R.H. "Dick" (See D.D. Custom Stocks, R.H. "Dick Devereaux)

Dewey Mfg. Co., Inc. J., P.O. Box 2014, Southbury, CT 06488 / 203-264-3064; FAX: 203-262-6907 deweyrods@worldnet.att.net www.dgsrifle.com

DGR Custom Rifles, 4191 37th Ave SE, Tappen, ND 58487 / 701-327-8135

DGS, Inc., Dale A. Storey, 1117 E. 12th, Casper, WY 82601 / 307-237-2414 FAX: 307-237-2414 dalest@trib.com www.dgsrifle.com

DHB Products, P.O. Box 3092, Alexandria, VA 22302 / 703-836-2648

Diamond Machining Technology, Inc. (See DMT)

Diamond Mfg. Co., P.O. Box 174, Wyoming, PA 18644 / 800-233-9601

Diana (See U.S. Importer - Dynamit Nobel-RWS, Inc., 81 Ruckman Rd., Closter, NJ 07624 / 201-767-7971; (FAX: 201-767-1589)

Dibble, Derek A., 555 John Downey Dr., New Britain, CT 06051 / 203-224-2630

Dick Marple & Associates, 21 Dartmouth St, Hooksett, NH 03106 / 603-627-1837; FAX: 603-627-1837

Dietz Gun Shop & Range, Inc., 421 Range Rd., New Braunfels, TX 78132 / 210-885-4662

Dilliott Gunsmithing, Inc., 657 Scarlett Rd., Dandridge, TN 37725 / 865-397-9204 gunsmithd@aol.com dilliottgunsmithing.com

Dillon, Ed, 1035 War Eagle Dr. N., Colorado Springs, CO 80919 / 719-598-4929; FAX: 719-598-4929

Dillon Precision Products, Inc., 8009 East Dillon's Way, Scottsdale, AZ 85260 / 602-948-8009 or 800-762-3845; FAX: 602-998-2786

Dina Arms Corporation, P.O. Box 46, Royersford, PA 19468 / 610-287-0266; FAX: 610-287-0266

Division Lead Co., 7742 W. 61st Pl., Summit, IL 60502

Dixie Gun Works, Inc., Hwy. 51 South, Union City, TN 38261 / order 800-238-6785;

Dixon Muzzleloading Shop, Inc., 9952 Kunkels Mill Rd., Kempton, PA 19529 / 610-756-6271

DKT, Inc., 14623 Vera Drive, Union, MI 49130-9744 / 800-741-7083 orders; FAX: 616-641-2015

DLO Mfg., 10807 SE Foster Ave., Arcadia, FL 33821-7304

DMT--Diamond Machining Technology Inc., 85 Hayes Memorial Dr., Marlborough, MA 01752 FAX: 508-485-3924

Doctor Optic Technologies, Inc., 4685 Boulder Highway, Suite A, Las Vegas, NV 89121 / 800-290-3634 or 702-898-7161; FAX: 702-898-3737

Dohring Bullets, 100 W. 8 Mile Rd., Ferndale, MI 48220

Dolbare, Elizabeth, P.O. Box 222, Sunburst, MT 59482-0222

Domino, PO Box 108, 20019 Settimo Milanese, Milano, ITALY / 1-39-2-33512040; FAX: 1-39-2-33511587

Donnelly, C. P., 405 Kubli Rd., Grants Pass, OR 97527 / 541-846-6604

Doskocil Mfg. Co., Inc., P.O. Box 1246, 4209 Barnett, Arlington, TX 76017 / 817-467-5116; FAX: 817-472-9810

Double A Ltd., P.O. Box 11306, Minneapolis, MN 55411 / 612-522-0306

Douglas Barrels Inc., 5504 Big Tyler Rd., Charleston, WV 25313-1398 / 304-776-1341; FAX: 304-776-8560

Downsizer Corp., P.O. Box 710316, Santee, CA 92072-0316 / 619-448-5510; FAX: 619-448-5780 www.downsizer.com

Dr. O's Products Ltd., P.O. Box 111, Niverville, NY 12130 / 518-784-3333; FAX: 518-784-2800

Drain, Mark, SE 3211 Kamilche Point Rd., Shelton, WA 98584 / 206-426-5452

Dremel Mfg. Co., 4915-21st St., Racine, WI 53406

Dressel Jr., Paul G., 209 N. 92nd Ave., Yakima, WA 98908 / 509-966-9233; FAX: 509-966-3365

Dri-Slide, Inc., 411 N. Darling, Fremont, MI 49412 / 616-924-3950

Dropkick, 1460 Washington Blvd., Williamsport, PA 17701 / 717-326-6561; FAX: 717-326-4950

DTM International, Inc., 40 Joslyn Rd., P.O. Box 5, Lake Orion, MI 48362 / 313-693-6670

Du-Lite Corp., 171 River Rd., Middletown, CT 06457 / 203-347-2505; FAX: 203-347-9404

Duane A. Hobbie Gunsmithing, 2412 Pattie Ave, Wichita, KS 67216 / 316-264-8266

Duane's Gun Repair (See DGR Custom Rifles)

Dubber, Michael W., P.O. Box 312, Evansville, IN 47702 / 812-424-9000; FAX: 812-424-6551

Duck Call Specialists, P.O. Box 124, Jerseyville, IL 62052 / 618-498-9855

Duffy, Charles E (See Guns Antique & Modern DBA), Williams Lane, PO Box 2, West Hurley, NY 12491 / 914-679-2997

Dumoulin, Ernest, Rue Florent Boclinville 8-10, 13-4041, Votten, BELGIUM / 41 27 78 92

Duncan's Gun Works, Inc., 1619 Grand Ave., San Marcos, CA 92069 / 619-727-0515

Dunham Boots, 1 Keuka business Park #300, Penn Yan, NY 14527-8995 / 800-254-2316

Duofold, P.O. Box RD 3 Rt. 309, Valley Square Mall, Tamaqua, PA 18252 / 717-386-2666; FAX: 717-386-3652

Dybala Gun Shop, P.O. Box 1024, FM 3156, Bay City, TX 77414 / 409-245-0866

Dykstra, Doug, 411 N. Darling, Fremont, MI 49412 / 616-924-3950

Dynalite Products, Inc., 215 S. Washington St., Greenfield, OH 45123 / 513-981-2124

Dynamit Nobel-RWS, Inc., 81 Ruckman Rd., Closter, NJ 07624 / 201-767-7971; FAX: 201-767-1589

E

E&L Mfg., Inc., 4177 Riddle By Pass Rd., Riddle, OR 97469 / 541-874-2137; FAX: 541-874-3107

E-A-R, Inc., Div. of Cabot Safety Corp., 5457 W. 79th St., Indianapolis, IN 46268 / 800-327-3431; FAX: 800-488-8007

E-Z-Way Systems, P.O. Box 4310, Newark, OH 43058-4310 / 614-345-6645 or 800-848-2072; FAX: 614-345-6600

E. Arthur Brown Co., 3404 Pawnee Dr., Alexandria, MN 56308 / 320-762-8847

E.A.A. Corp., P.O. Box 1299, Sharpes, FL 32959 / 407-639-4842 or 800-536-4442; FAX: 407-639-7006

Eagan, Donald V., P.O. Box 196, Benton, PA 17814 / 717-925-6134

Eagle Arms, Inc. (See ArmaLite, Inc.)

Eagle Grips, Eagle Business Center, 460 Randy Rd., Carol Stream, IL 60188 / 800-323-6144 or 708-260-0400; FAX: 708-260-0486

Edenpine, Inc. c/o Six Enterprises, Inc., 320 D Turtle Creek Ct., San Jose, CA 95125 / 408-999-0201; FAX: 408-999-0216

Eagle Imports, Inc., 1750 Brielle Ave., Unit B1, Wanamassa, NJ 07712 / 908-493-0333

EAW (See U.S. Importer-New England Custom Gun Service)

Echols & Co., D'Arcy, 164 W. 580 S., Providence, UT 84332 / 801-753-2367

Eckelman Gunsmithing, 3125 133rd St. SW, Fort Ripley, MN 56449 / 218-829-3176

Eclectic Technologies, Inc., 45 Grandview Dr., Suite A, Farmington, CT 06034

Ed- Brown Products, Inc., 43825 Muldrow Trail, Perry, MO 63462 / 573-565-3261; FAX: 573-565-2791

Eddie Salter Calls, Inc., Hwy. 31 South-Brewton Industrial, Park, Brewton, AL 36426 / 205-867-2584; FAX: 206-867-9005

EdgeCraft Corp., S. Weiner, 825 Southwood Road, Avondale, PA 19311 / 610-268-0500 or 800-342-3255; FAX: 610-268-3545 www.chefschoice.com

Edmisten Co., P.O. Box 1293, Boone, NC 28607

Edmund Scientific Co., 101 E. Gloucester Pike, Barrington, NJ 08033 / 609-543-6250

Ednar, Inc., 2-4-8 Kayabacho, Nihonbashi Chuo-ku, Tokyo, JAPAN / 81(Japan)-3-3667-1651; FAX: 81-3-3661-8113

Eezox, Inc., P.O. Box 772, Waterford, CT 06385-0772 / 800-462-3331; FAX: 860-447-3484

Effebi SNC-Dr. Franco Beretta, via Rossa, 4, 25062, IT-ALY / 030-2751955; FAX: 030-2180414

Efficient Machinery Co, 12878 NE 15th Pl, Bellevue, WA 98005

Eggleston, Jere D., 400 Saluda Ave., Columbia, SC 29205 / 803-799-3402

EGW Evolution Gun Works, 4050 B-8 Skyron Dr., Doylestown, PA 18901 / 215-348-9892; FAX: 215-348-1056

Eichelberger Bullets, Wm, 158 Crossfield Rd., King Of Prussia, PA 19406

Ekol Leather Care, P.O. Box 2652, West Lafayette, IN 47906 / 317-463-2250; FAX: 317-463-7004

El Dorado Leather (c/o Dill), P.O. Box 566, Benson, AZ 85602 / 520-586-4791; FAX: 520-586-4791

El Paso Saddlery Co., P.O. Box 27194, El Paso, TX 79926 / 915-544-2233; FAX: 915-544-2535

Eldorado Cartridge Corp (See PMC/Eldorado Cartridge Corp.)

Electro Prismatic Collimators, Inc., 1441 Manatt St., Lincoln, NE 68521

Electronic Shooters Protection, Inc., 11997 West 85th Place, Arvada, CO 80005 / 800-797-7791; FAX: 303-456-7179

Electronic Trigger Systems, Inc., P.O. Box 13, 230 Main St. S., Hector, MN 55342 / 320-848-2760; FAX: 320-848-2760

Eley Ltd., P.O. Box 705, Witton, Birmingham, B6 7UT ENGLAND / 021-356-8899; FAX: 021-331-4173

Elite Ammunition, P.O. Box 3251, Oakbrook, IL 60522 / 708-366-9006

Elk River, Inc., 1225 Paonia St., Colorado Springs, CO 80915 / 719-574-4407

Elkhorn Bullets, P.O. Box 5293, Central Point, OR 97502 / 541-826-7440

Ellett Bros., 267 Columbia Ave., P.O. Box 128, Chapin, SC 29036 / 803-345-3751 or 800-845-3711; FAX: 803-345-1820

Ellicott Arms, Inc./Woods Pistolsmithing, 3840 Dahlgren Ct., Ellicott City, MD 21042 / 410-465-7979

Elliott Inc., G. W., 514 Burnside Ave, East Hartford, CT 06108 / 203-289-5741; FAX: 203-289-3137

Elsen Inc., Pete, 1523 S 113th St, West Allis, WI 53214 / 414-541-5420

Emerging Technologies, Inc. (See Laseraim Technologies, Inc.)

Emap USA, 6420 Wilshire Blvd., Los Angeles, CA 90048 / 213-782-2000; FAX: 213-782-2867

EMF Co., Inc., 1900 E. Warner Ave., Suite 1-D, Santa Ana, CA 92705 / 714-261-6611; FAX: 714-756-0133

Empire Cutlery Corp., 12 Kruger Ct., Clifton, NJ 07013 / 201-472-5155; FAX: 201-779-0759

English, Inc., A.G., 708 S. 12th St., Broken Arrow, OK 74012 / 918-251-3399

Engraving Artistry, 36 Alto Rd., RFD 2, Burlington, CT 06013 / 203-673-6837

Enguix Import-Export, Alpujarras 58, Alzira, Valencia, SPAIN / (96) 241 43 95; FAX: (96) (241 43 95

Enhanced Presentations, Inc., 5929 Market St., Wilmington, NC 28405 / 910-799-1622; FAX: 910-799-5004

Enlow, Charles, 895 Box, Beaver, OK 73932 / 405-625-4487

Entre'prise Arms, Inc., 15861 Business Center Dr., Irwindale, CA 91706

EPC, 1441 Manatt St., Lincoln, NE 68521 / 402-476-3946

Epps, Ellwood (See "Gramps" Antique, Box 341, Washago, ON L0K 2B0 CANADA / 705-689-5348

Erhardt, Dennis, 3280 Green Meadow Dr., Helena, MT 59601 / 406-442-4533

Erma Werke GmbH, Johan Ziegler St., 13/15/FeldigISt., D-8060 Dachau, GERMANY

Eskridge Rifles, Steven Eskridge, 218 N. Emerson, Mart, TX 76664 / 817-876-3544

Eskridge, Steven. (See ESKRIDGE RIFLES)

Essex Arms, P.O. Box 363, Island Pond, VT 05846 / 802-723-6203 FAX: 802-723-6203

Essex Metals, 1000 Brighton St., Union, NJ 07083 / 800-282-8369

Estate Cartridge, Inc., 12161 FM 830, Willis, TX 77378 / 409-856-7277; FAX: 409-856-5486

Euber Bullets, No. Orwell Rd., Orwell, VT 05760 / 802-948-2621

Euro-Imports, 905 West Main St Ste E, El Cajon, CA 92020 / 619-442-7005; FAX: 619-442-7005

Euroarms of America, Inc., P.O. Box 3277, Winchester, VA 22604 / 540-662-1863; FAX: 540-662-4464

European American Armory Corp (See E.A.A. Corp)

Evans, Andrew, 2325 NW Squire St., Albany, OR 97321 / 541-928-3190; FAX: 541-928-4128

Evans Engraving, Robert, 332 Vine St, Oregon City, OR 97045 / 503-656-5693

Evans Gunsmithing (See Evans, Andrew)

Eversull Co., Inc., K., 1 Tracemont, Boyce, LA 71409 / 318-793-8728; FAX: 318-793-5483

Excalibur Electro Optics Inc, P.O. Box 400, Fogelsville, PA 18051-0400 / 610-391-9105; FAX: 610-391-9220

Excel Industries Inc., 4510 Carter Ct., Chino, CA 91710 / 909-627-2404; FAX: 909-627-7817

MANUFACTURER'S DIRECTORY

Executive Protection Institute, PO Box 802, Berryville, VA 22611 / 540-955-1128

Eyster Heritage Gunsmiths, Inc., Ken, 6441 Bishop Rd., Centerburg, OH 43011 / 614-625-6131

Eze-Lap Diamond Prods., P.O. Box 2229, 15164 West State St., Westminster, CA 92683 / 714-847-1555; FAX: 714-897-0280

F

F&A Inc. (See ShurKatch Corporation)

F.A.I.R. Techni-Mec s.n.c. di Isidoro Rizzini & C., Via Gitti, 41 Zona Industrial, 25060 Marcheno (Bres, IT-ALY / 030/861162-8610344; FAX: 030/8610179

Fabarm S.p.A., Via Averolda 31, 25039 Travagliato, Brescia, ITALY / 030-6863629; FAX: 030-6863684

Fagan & Co,Inc, 22952 15 Mile Rd., Clinton Township, MI 48035 / 810-465-4637; FAX: 810-792-6996

Fair Game International, P.O. Box 77234-34053, Houston, TX 77234 / 713-941-6269

Faith Associates, Inc., PO Box 549, Flat Rock, NC 28731-0549 / 828-692-1916; FAX: 828-697-6827

Fanzoj GmbH, Griessgasse 1, 9170 Ferlach, 9170 AUS-TRIA / (43) 04227-2283; FAX: (43) 04227-2867

Far North Outfitters, Box 1252, Bethel, AK 99559

Farm Form Decoys, Inc., 1602 Biovu, P.O. Box 748, Galveston, TX 77553 / 409-744-0762 or 409-765-6361; FAX: 409-765-8513

Farmer-Dressel, Sharon, 209 N. 92nd Ave., Yakima, WA 98908 / 509-966-9233; FAX: 509-966-3365

Farr Studio, Inc, 1231 Robinhood Rd., Greeneville, TN 37743 / 615-638-8825

Farrar Tool Co., Inc., 12150 Bloomfield Ave., Suite E, Santa Fe Springs, CA 90670 / 310-863-5123

Faulhaber Wildlocker, Dipl.-Ing. Norbert Wittasek, Seil-ergasse 2, A-1010 Wien, AUSTRIA /

Faulk's Game Call Co., Inc., 616 18th St., Lake Charles, LA 70601 / 318-436-9726 FAX: 318-494-7205

Faust Inc., T. G., 544 minor St., Reading, PA 19602 /

Fausti Cav. Stefano & Figlie snc, Via Martini Dell In-dipendenza, 70, Marcheno, 25060 ITALY

Feather, Flex Decoys, 1655 Swan Lake Rd., Bossier City, LA 71111 / 318-746-8596; FAX: 318-742-4815

Featherce, Andy, P.O. Box 4607, Pagosa Springs, CO 81157 / 970-731-5003; FAX: 970-731-5009

Federal Arms Corp. of America, 7928 University Ave., Fridley, MN 55432 / 612-780-8780; FAX:

Federal Cartridge Co., 900 Ehlen Dr., Anoka, MN 55303 / 612-323-2300; FAX: 612-323-2506

Federal Champion Target Co., 232 Industrial Parkway, Richmond, IN 47374 / 800-441-4971; FAX:

Federated-Fry (See Fry Metals)

FEG, Budapest, Soroksariut 158, H-1095, HUNGARY

Feken, Dennis, Rt. 2, Box 124, Perry, OK 73077 / 405-336-5611

Felk, Inc, 2121 Castlebridge Rd., Midlothian, VA 23113 / 804-794-3744

Fellowes, Ted, Beaver Lodge, 9245 16th Ave. SW, Se-attle, WA 98106 / 206-763-1698

Feminine Protection, Inc, 949 W. Kearney Ste. 100, Mesquite, TX 75149 / 972-289-8997 FAX: 972-289-4410

Ferguson, Bill, P.O. Box 1238, Sierra Vista, AZ 85636 /

FERLIB, Via Costa 46, 25063, Gardone V.T., ITALY / 30-89-12-586; FAX: 30-89-12-586

Ferris Firearms, 7110 F.M. 1863, Buiverde, TX 78163 / 210-980-4424

Fibron Products, Inc., P.O. Box 430, Buffalo, NY 14209-0430 / 716-886-2378; FAX: 716-886-2394

Fieldsport Ltd, Bryan Bilinski, 3313 W South Airport Rd, Traverse Vity, MI 49684 / 616-933-0767

Fiocchi Munizioni S.p.A. (See U.S. Importer-Fiocchi of America, Inc.)

Fiocchi of America Inc., 5030 Fremont Rd., Ozark, MO 65721 / 417-725-4118 or 800-721-2666 FAX: 417-725-1039

Firearms Co Ltd/Alpine (See U.S. Importer-Mandall Shooting Supplies, Inc.)

Firearms Engraver's Guild of America, 332 Vine St., Or-egon City, OR 97045 / 503-656-5693

Firearms International, 5709 Hartsdale, Houston, TX 77036 / 713-460-2447

First Inc., Jack, 1201 Turbine Dr., Rapid City, SD 57701 / 605-343-9544; FAX: 605-343-9420

Fish Mfg. Gunsmith Sptg., Co., Marshall F, Rd. Box 2439, Rt. 22 N, Westport, NY 12993 / 518-962-4897 FAX: 518-962-4897

Fisher, Jerry A., 553 Crane Mt. Rd., Big Fork, MT 59911 / 406-837-2722

Fisher Custom Firearms, 2199 S. Kittredge Way, Auro-ra, CO 80013 / 303-755-3710

Fisher Enterprises, Inc., 1071 4th Ave. S., Suite 303, Edmonds, WA 98020-4143 / 206-771-5382

Fisher, R. Kermit (See Fisher Enterprises, Inc), 1071 4th Ave S Ste 303, Edmonds, WA 98020-4143 / 206-771-5382

Fitz Pistol Grip Co., P.O. Box 744, LEWISTON, CA 96052-0744 / 916-778-0240

Flambeau Products Corp., 15981 Valplast Rd., Middle-field, OH 44062 / 216-632-1631; FAX: 216-632-1581

Flannery Engraving Co., Jeff W., 11034 Riddles Run Rd, Union, KY 41091 / 606-384-3127

Flashette Co., 4725 S. Kolin Ave., Chicago, IL 60632 FAX: 773-927-3083

Flayderman & Co., Inc., P.O. Box 2446, Ft Lauderdale, FL 33303 / 954-761-8855

Fleming Firearms, 7720 E 126th St. N, Collinsville, OK 74021-7016 / 918-665-3624

Flents Products Co., Inc., P.O. Box 2109, Norwalk, CT 06852 / 203-866-2581; FAX: 203-854-9322

Flintlocks Etc., 160 Rositter Rd, Richmond, MA 01254 / 413-698-3822

Flintlocks, Etc., 160 Rossiter Rd., P.O. Box 181, Rich-mond, MA 01254 / 413-698-3822; FAX:

Flitz International Ltd., 821 Mohr Ave., Waterford, WI 53185 / 414-534-5898; FAX: 414-534-2991

Flores Publications Inc., J (See Action Direct Inc), PO Box 830760, Miami, FL 33283 / 305-559-4652; FAX: 305-559-4652

Fluoramics, Inc., 18 Industrial Ave., Mahwah, NJ 07430 / 800-922-0075; FAX: 201-825-7035

Flynn's Custom Guns, P.O. Box 7461, Alexandria, LA 71306 / 318-455-7130

FN Herstal, Voie de Liege 33, Herstal, 4040 Belgium / (3241.40.82.83; FAX: (32)41.40.86.79

Fobus International Ltd., P.O. Box 64, Kfar Hess, 40692 ISRAEL / 972-9-7964170; FAX: 972-9-7964169

Folks, Donald E., 205 W. Lincoln St., Pontiac, IL 61764 / 815-844-7901

Foothills Video Productions, Inc., P.O. Box 651, Spar-tanburg, SC 29304 / 803-573-7023 or 800-782-5358

Foredom Electric Co., Rt. 6, 16 Stony Hill Rd., Bethel, CT 06801 / 203-792-8622

Forgett Jr., Valmore J., 689 Bergen Blvd., Ridgefield, NJ 07657 / 201-945-2500; FAX: 201-945-6859

Forgreens Tool Mfg., Inc., P.O. Box 990, 723 Austin St., Robert Lee, TX 76945 / 915-453-2800; FAX: 915-453-2460

Forkin, Ben (See Belt MTN Arms)

Forkin Arms, 205 10th Ave SW, White Sulphur Spring, MT 59645 / 406-547-2344; FAX: 406-547-2456

Forrest Inc., Tom, PO Box 326, Lakeside, CA 92040 / 619-561-5800; FAX: 619-561-0227

Forrest Tool Co., P.O. Box 768, 44380 Gordon Lane, Mendocino, CA 95460 / 707-937-2141; FAX: 717-937-1817

Forster, Kathy (See Custom Checkering Service, Kathy Forster)

Forster, Larry L., P.O. Box 212, 220 First St. NE, Gwin-ner, ND 58040-0212 / 701-678-2475

Forster Products, 310 E Lanark Ave, Lanark, IL 61046 / 815-493-6360; FAX: 815-493-2371

Fort Hill Gunstocks, 12807 Fort Hill Rd., Hillsboro, OH 45133 / 513-466-2763

Fort Knox Security Products, 1051 N. Industrial Park Rd., Orem, UT 84057 / 801-224-7233 or 800-821-5216; FAX: 801-226-5493

Fort Worth Firearms, 2006-B, Martin Luther King Fwy., Ft. Worth, TX 76104-6303 / 817-536-0718; FAX: 817-535-0290

Forthofer's Gunsmithing & Knifemaking, 5535 U.S. Hwy 93S, Whitefish, MT 59937-8411 / 406-862-2674

Fortune Products, Inc., HC04, Box 303, Marble Falls, TX 78654 / 210-693-6111; FAX: 210-693-6394

Forty Five Ranch Enterprises, Box 1080, Miami, OK 74355-1080 / 918-542-5875

Fountain Products, 492 Prospect Ave., West Spring-field, MA 01089 / 413-781-4651; FAX: 413-733-8217

4-D Custom Die Co., 711 N. Sandusky St., P.O. Box 889, Mt. Vernon, OH 43050-0889 / 740-397-7214; FAX: 740-397-6600

Fowler Bullets, 806 Dogwood Dr., Gastonia, NC 28054 / 704-867-3259

Fowler, Bob (See Black Powder Products)

Fox River Mills, Inc., P.O. Box 298, 227 Poplar St., Os-age, IA 50461 / 515-732-3798; FAX: 515-732-5128

Foy Custom Bullets, 104 Wells Ave, Daleville, AL 36322

Francesca, Inc., 3115 Old Ranch Rd., San Antonio, TX 78217 / 512-826-2584; FAX: 512-826-8211

Franchi S.p.A., Via del Serpente 12, 25131, Brescia, IT-ALY / 030-3581833; FAX: 030-3581554

Francotte & Cie S.A. Auguste, rue de Trois Juin 109, 4400 Herstal-Liege, BELGIUM / 32-4-248-13-18; FAX: 32-4-248-11-79

Frank Custom Classic Arms, Ron, 7131 Richland Rd, Ft Worth, TX 76118 / 817-284-9300; FAX:

Frank E. Hendricks Master Engravers, Inc., HC03, Box 434, Dripping Springs, TX 78620 / 512-858-7828

Frank Knives, 13868 NW Keleka Pl., Seal Rock, OR 97376 / 541-563-3041; FAX: 541-563-3041

Frank Mittermeier, Inc., P.O. Box 2G, 3577 E. Tremont Ave., Bronx, NY 10465 / 718-828-3843

Frankonia Jagd Hofmann & Co., D-97064 Wurzburg, Wurzburg, GERMANY / 09302-200; FAX: 09302-20200

Franzen International,Inc (U.S. Importer for Peters Stahl GmbH)

Fred F. Wells/Wells Sport Store, 110 N Summit St, Prescott, AZ 86301 / 520-445-3655

Freedom Arms, Inc., P.O. Box 150, Freedom, WY 83120 / 307-883-2468 or 800-833-4432; FAX: 307-883-2005

Freeman Animal Targets, 5519 East County Road, 100 South, Plainsfield, IN 46168 / 317-272-2663; FAX:

Fremont Tool Works, 1214 Prairie, Ford, KS 67842 / 316-369-2327

French, Artistic Engraving, J. R., 1712 Creek Ridge Ct, Irving, TX 75060 / 214-254-2654

Frielich Police Equipment, 211 East 21st St., New York, NY 10010 / 212-254-3045

Front Sight Firearms Training Institute, P.O. Box 2619, Aptos, CA 95001 / 800-987-7719; FAX: 408-684-2137

Frontier, 2910 San Bernardo, Laredo, TX 78040 / 956-723-5409; FAX: 956-723-1774

Frontier Arms Co., Inc., 401 W. Rio Santa Cruz, Green Valley, AZ 85614-3932

Frontier Products Co., 2401 Walker Rd., Roswell, NM 88201-8950 / 614-262-9357

Frost Cutlery Co., P.O. Box 22636, Chattanooga, TN 37422 / 615-894-6079; FAX: 615-894-9576

Fry Metals, 4100 6th Ave., Altoona, PA 16602 / 814-946-1611

Fujinon, Inc., 10 High Point Dr., Wayne, NJ 07470 / 201-633-5600; FAX: 201-633-5216

Fullmer, Geo. M., 2499 Mavis St., Oakland, CA 94601 / 510-533-4193

Fulmer's Antique Firearms, Chet, PO Box 792, Rt 2 Buf-falo Lake, Detroit Lakes, MN 56501 / 218-847-7712

Fulton Armory, 8725 Bollman Place No. 1, Savage, MD 20763 / 301-490-9485; FAX: 301-490-9547

Furr Arms, 91 N. 970 W., Orem, UT 84057 / 801-226-3877; FAX: 801-226-3877

Fusilier Bullets, 10010 N. 6000 W., Highland, UT 84003 / 801-756-6813

FWB, Neckarstrasse 43, 78727, Oberndorf a. N., GER-MANY / 07423-814-0; FAX: 07423-814-89

G

G&H Decoys,Inc., P.O. Box 1208, Hwy. 75 North, Hen-ryetta, OK 74437 / 918-652-3314; FAX: 918-652-3400

G.C.C.T., 4455 Torrance Blvd., Ste. 453, Torrance, CA 90503-4398

G. G. & G., 3602 E. 42nd Stravenue, Tucson, AZ 85713 / 520-748-7167; FAX: 520-748-7583

G.H. Enterprises Ltd., Bag 10, Okotoks, AB T0L 1T0 CANADA / 403-938-6070

MANUFACTURER'S DIRECTORY

G.U. Inc (See U.S. Importer for New SKB Arms Co)

G.W. Elliott, Inc., 514 Burnside Ave., East Hartford, CT 06108 / 203-289-5741; FAX: 203-289-3137

G96 Products Co., Inc., 85 5th Ave, Bldg #6, Paterson, NJ 07544 / 973-684-4050 FAX: 973-684-4050

Gage Manufacturing, 663 W. 7th St., A, San Pedro, CA 90731 / 310-832-3546

Gaillard Barrels, P.O. Box 21, Pathlow, SK S0K 3B0 CANADA / 306-752-3769; FAX: 306-752-5969

Gain Twist Barrel Co. Rifle Works and Armory, 707 12th Street, Cody, WY 82414 / 307-587-4919; FAX: 307-527-6097

Galati International, PO Box 10, Wesco, MO 65586 / 314-257-4837; FAX: 314-257-2268

Galaxy Imports Ltd.,Inc., P.O. Box 3361, Victoria, TX 77903 / 361-573-4867; FAX: 361-576-9622 galaxy@tisd.net

GALCO International Ltd., 2019 W. Quail Ave., Phoenix, AZ 85027 / 602-258-8295 or 800-874-2526; FAX: 602-582-6854

Galena Industries AMT, 3551 Mayer Ave., Sturgis, SD 57785 / 605-423-4105

Gamba S.p.A. Societa Armi Bresciane Srl, Renato, Via Artigiani 93, ITALY / 30-8911640; FAX: 30-8911648

Gamba, USA, P.O. Box 60452, Colorado Springs, CO 80960 / 719-578-1145; FAX: 719-444-0731

Game Haven Gunstocks, 13750 Shire Rd., Wolverine, MI 49799 / 616-525-8257

Game Winner, Inc., 2625 Cumberland Parkway, Suite 220, Atlanta, GA 30339 / 770-434-9210; FAX: 770-434-9215

Gamebore Division, Polywad Inc, PO Box 7916, Macon, GA 31209 / 912-477-0669

Gamo (See U.S. Importers-Arms United Corp, Daisy Mfg. Co.)

Gamo USA, Inc., 3911 SW 47th Ave., Suite 914, Ft. Lauderdale, FL 33314 / 954-581-5822; FAX: 954-581-3165

Gander Mountain, Inc., 12400 Fox River Rd., Wilmont, WI 53192 / 414-862-6848

GAR, 590 McBride Avenue, West Paterson, NJ 07424 / 973-754-1114; FAX: 973-754-1114

Garbi, Armas Urki, 12-14 20.600 Eibar, Guipuzcoa, SPAIN

Garcia National Gun Traders, Inc., 225 SW 22nd Ave., Miami, FL 33135 / 305-642-2355

Garrett Cartridges Inc., P.O. Box 178, Chehalis, WA 98532 / 360-736-0702

Garthwaite Pistolsmith, Inc., Jim, Rt 2 Box 310, Watsontown, PA 17777 / 570-538-1566; FAX: 570-538-2965

GDL Enterprises, 409 Le Gardeur, Slidell, LA 70460 / 504-649-0693

Gehmann, Walter (See Huntington Die Specialties)

Genco, P.O. Box 5704, Asheville, NC 28803

Gene's Custom Guns, 2710 N Steves Blvd. #22, Flagstaff, AZ 86004 / 520-526-3313; FAX: 520-527-0840 gary@reedercustomguns.com www.reedercustomguns.com

Genecco Gun Works, K, 10512 Lower Sacramento Rd., Stockton, CA 95210 / 209-951-0706 FAX: 209-931-3872

Gentex Corp., 5 Tinkham Ave., Derry, NH 03038 / 603-434-0311; FAX: 603-434-3002 sales@derry.gentexcorp.com www.derry.gentexcorp.com

Gentner Bullets, 109 Woodlawn Ave., Upper Darby, PA 19082 / 610-352-9396

Gentry Custom Gunmaker, David, 314 N Hoffman, Belgrade, MT 59714 / 406-388-GUNS

George & Roy's, PO Box 2125, Sisters, OR 97759-2125 / 503-228-5424 or 800-553-3022; FAX: 503-225-9409

George, Tim, Rt. 1, P.O. Box 45, Evington, VA 24550 / 804-821-8117

George E. Mathews & Son, Inc., 10224 S. Paramount Blvd., Downey, CA 90241 / 562-862-6719; FAX: 562-862-6719

George Ibberson (Sheffield) Ltd., 25-31 Allen St., Sheffield, S3 7AW ENGLAND / 0114-2766123; FAX: 0114-2738465

Gerald Pettinger Books, see Pettinger Books, G, Rt. 2, Box 125, Russell, IA 50238 / 515-535-2239

Gerber Legendary Blades, 14200 SW 72nd Ave., Portland, OR 97223 / 503-639-6161 or 800-950-6161; FAX: 503-684-7008

Gervais, Mike, 3804 S. Cruise Dr., Salt Lake City, UT 84109 / 801-277-7729

Getz Barrel Co., P.O. Box 88, Beavertown, PA 17813 / 717-658-7263

Giacomo Sporting USA, 6234 Stokes Lee Center Rd., Lee Center, NY 13363

Gibbs Rifle Co., Inc., 211 Lawn St, Martinsburg, WV 25401 / 304-262-1651; FAX: 304-262-1658

Gil Hebard Guns, 125-129 Public Square, Knoxville, IL 61448 / 309-289-2700 FAX: 309-289-2233

Gilbert Equipment Co., Inc., 960 Downtowner Rd., Mobile, AL 36609 / 205-344-3322

Gilkes, Anthony W., 26574 HILLMAN HWY, MEADOWVIEW, VA 24361-3142 / 303-657-1873; FAX: 303-657-1885

Gillmann, Edwin, 33 Valley View Dr., Hanover, PA 17331 / 717-632-1662

Gilman-Mayfield, Inc., 3279 E. Shields, Fresno, CA 93703 / 209-221-9415; FAX: 209-221-9419

Gilmore Sports Concepts, 5949 S. Garnett, Tulsa, OK 74146 / 918-250-3810; FAX: 918-250-3845 gilmore@webzone.net www.gilmoresports.com

Giron, Robert E., 1328 Pocono St., Pittsburgh, PA 15218 / 412-731-6041

Glacier Glove, 4890 Aircenter Circle, Suite 210, Reno, NV 89502 / 702-825-8225; FAX: 702-825-6544

Glaser Safety Slug, Inc., P.O. Box 8223, Foster City, CA 94404 / 800-221-3489; FAX: 510-785-6685 safetyslug.com

Glass, Herb, P.O. Box 25, Bullville, NY 10915 / 914-361-3021

Glimm, Jerome C., 19 S. Maryland, Conrad, MT 59425 / 406-278-3574

Glock GmbH, P.O. Box 50, A-2232, Deutsch Wagram, AUSTRIA

Glock, Inc., PO Box 369, Smyrna, GA 30081 / 770-432-1202; FAX: 770-433-8719

Glynn Scobey Duck & Goose Calls, Rt. 3, Box 37, Newbern, TN 38059 / 901-643-6241

GML Products, Inc., 394 Laredo Dr., Birmingham, AL 35226 / 205-979-4867

Gner's Hard Cast Bullets, 1107 11th St., LaGrande, OR 97850 / 503-963-8796

Goens, Dale W., P.O. Box 224, Cedar Crest, NM 87008 / 505-281-5419

Goergen's Gunsmithing, R.D. 1, Box 1097, Spring Grove, PA 17362 / 717-225-3350

Goodwin, Fred, Silver Ridge Gun Shop, Sherman Mills, ME 04776 / 207-365-4451

Gordie's Gun Shop, 1401 Fulton St., Streator, IL 61364 / 815-672-7202

Gordon Wm. Davis Leather Co., P.O. Box 2270, Walnut, CA 91788 / 909-598-5620

Gotz Bullets, 7313 Rogers St., Rockford, IL 61111

Gould & Goodrich, 709 E. McNeil, Lillington, NC 27546 / 910-893-2071; FAX: 910-893-4742

Gournet, Geoffroy, 820 Paxinosa Ave., Easton, PA 18042 / 610-559-0710

Gozon Corp. U.S.A., P.O. Box 6278, Folson, CA 95763 / 916-983-2026; FAX: 916-983-9500

Grace, Charles E., 1305 Arizona Ave., Trinidad, CO 81082 / 719-846-9435

Grace Metal Products, P.O. Box 67, Elk Rapids, MI 49629 / 616-264-8133

Graf & Sons, 4050 S Clark St, Mexico, MO 65265 / 573-581-2266 FAX: 573-581-2875

"Gramps" Antique Cartridges, Box 341, Washago, ON L0K 2B0 CANADA / 705-689-5348

Granite Mountain Arms, Inc, 3145 W Hidden Acres Trail, Prescott, AZ 86305 / 520-541-9758; FAX: 520-445-6826

Grant, Howard V., Hiawatha 15, Woodruff, WI 54568 / 715-356-7146

Graphics Direct, P.O. Box 372421, Reseda, CA 91337-2421 / 818-344-9002

Graves Co., 1800 Andrews Ave., Pompano Beach, FL 33069 / 800-327-9103; FAX: 305-960-0301

Grayback Wildcats, 5306 Bryant Ave., Klamath Falls, OR 97603 / 541-884-1072

Graybill's Gun Shop, 1035 Ironville Pike, Columbia, PA 17512 / 717-684-2739

GrE-Tan Rifles, 29742 W.C.R. 50, Kersey, CO 80644 / 970-353-6176; FAX: 970-356-9133

Great American Gunstock Co., 3420 Industrial Drive, Yuba City, CA 95993 / 530-671-4570; FAX: 530-671-3906

Great Lakes Airguns, 6175 S. Park Ave, New York, NY 14075 / 716-648-6666; FAX: 716-648-5279

Green, Arthur S., 485 S. Robertson Blvd., Beverly Hills, CA 90211 / 310-274-1283

Green, Roger M., P.O. Box 984, 435 E. Birch, Glenrock, WY 82637 / 307-436-9804

Green Genie, Box 114, Cusseta, GA 31805

Green Head Game Call Co., RR 1, Box 33, Lacon, IL 61540 / 309-246-2155

Green Mountain Rifle Barrel Co., Inc., P.O. Box 2670, 153 West Main St., Conway, NH 03818 / 603-447-1095; FAX: 603-447-1099

Greenwood Precision, P.O. Box 468, Nixa, MO 65714-0468 / 417-725-2330

Greg Gunsmithing Repair, 3732 26th Ave. North, Robbinsdale, MN 55422 / 612-529-8103

Greg's Superior Products, P.O. Box 46219, Seattle, WA 98146

Greider Precision, 431 Santa Marina Ct., Escondido, CA 92029 / 619-480-8892; FAX: 619-480-9800

Gremmel Enterprises, 2111 Carriage Drive, Eugene, OR 97408-7537 / 541-302-3000

Grier's Hard Cast Bullets, 1107 11th St., LaGrande, OR 97850 / 503-963-8796

Griffin & Howe, Inc., 36 W. 44th St., Suite 1011, New York, NY 10036 / 212-921-0980

Griffin & Howe, Inc., 33 Claremont Rd., Bernardsville, NJ 07924 / 908-766-2287

Grifon, Inc., 58 Guinam St., Waltham, MS 02154

Groenewold, John, P.O. Box 830, Mundelein, IL 60060 / 847-566-2365

GRS Corp., Glendo, P.O. Box 1153, 900 Overlander St., Emporia, KS 66801 / 316-343-1084 or 800-835-3519

Gruaisi, Robert. (See WILCOX INDUSTRIES CORP)

Grulla Armes, Apartado 453, Avda Otaloa 12, Eiber, SPAIN

Gruning Precision Inc, 7101 Jurupa Ave., No. 12, Riverside, CA 92504 / 909-689-6692 FAX: 909-689-7791

GSI, Inc., 7661 Commerce Ln., Trussville, AL 35173 / 205-655-8299

GTB, 482 Comerwood Court, San Francisco, CA 94080 / 650-583-1550

Gun Accessories (See Glaser Safety Slug, Inc.), PO Box 8223, Foster City, CA 94404 / 800-221-3489; FAX: 510-785-5685

Gun City, 212 W. Main Ave., Bismarck, ND 58501 / 701-223-2304

Gun Hunter Books (See Gun Hunter Trading Co), 5075 Heisig St, Beaumont, TX 77705 / 409-835-3006

Gun Hunter Trading Co., 5075 Heisig St., Beaumont, TX 77705 / 409-835-3006

Gun Leather Limited, 116 Lipscomb, Ft. Worth, TX 76104 / 817-334-0225; FAX: 800-247-0609

Gun List (See Krause Publications), 700 E State St, Iola, WI 54945 / 715-445-2214; FAX: 715-445-4087

Gun Locker Div. of Airmold W.R. Grace & Co.-Conn., Becker Farms Ind. Park, P.O. Box 610, Roanoke Rapids, NC 27870 / 800-344-5716; FAX: 919-536-2201

Gun South, Inc. (See GSI, Inc.)

Gun Vault, 7339 E Acoma Dr., Ste. 7, Scottsdale, AZ 85260 / 602-951-6855

Gun-Alert, 1010 N. Maclay Ave., San Fernando, CA 91340 / 818-365-0864; FAX: 818-365-1308

Gun-Ho Sports Cases, 110 E. 10th St., St. Paul, MN 55101 / 612-224-9491

MANUFACTURER'S DIRECTORY

Guncraft Books (See Guncraft Sports Inc), 10737 Dutchtown Rd, Knoxville, TN 37932 / 423-966-4545; FAX: 423-966-4500

Guncraft Sports Inc., 10737 Dutchtown Rd., Knoxville, TN 37932 / 423-966-4545; FAX: 423-966-4500

Gunfitters, P.O. 426, Cambridge, WI 53523-0426 / 608-764-8128 gunfitters@aol.com www.gunfitters.com

Gunline Tools, 2950 Saturn St., "O", Brea, CA 92821 / 714-993-5100; FAX: 714-572-4128

Gunnerman Books, P.O. Box 217, Owosso, MI 48867 / 517-729-7018; FAX: 517-725-9391

Guns, 81 E. Streetsboro St., Hudson, OH 44236 / 330-650-4563

Guns Antique & Modern DBA/Charles E. Duffy, Williams Lane, West Hurley, NY 12491 / 914-679-2997

Guns Div. of D.C. Engineering, Inc., 8633 Southfield Fwy., Detroit, MI 48228 / 313-271-7111 or 800-886-7623; FAX: 313-271-7112

GUNS Magazine, 591 Camino de la Reina, Suite 200, San Diego, CA 92108 / 619-297-8350 FAX: 619-297-5353

Gunsite Custom Shop, P.O. Box 451, Paulden, AZ 86334 / 520-636-4104; FAX: 520-636-1236

Gunsite Gunsmithy (See Gunsite Custom Shop)

Gunsite Training Center, P.O. Box 700, Paulden, AZ 86334 / 520-636-4565; FAX: 520-636-1236

Gunsmithing, Inc., 57 Unquowa Rd., Fairfield, CT 06430 / 203-254-0436; FAX: 203-254-1535

Gunsmithing Ltd., 57 Unquowa Rd., Fairfield, CT 06430 / 203-254-0436; FAX: 203-254-1535

Gurney, F. R., Box 13, Sooke, BC V0S 1N0 CANADA / 604-642-5282; FAX: 604-642-7859

Gwinnell, Bryson J., P.O. Box 248C, Maple Hill Rd., Rochester, VT 05767 / 802-767-3664

H

H&B Forge Co., Rt. 2, Geisinger Rd., Shiloh, OH 44878 / 419-895-1856

H&P Publishing, 7174 Hoffman Rd., San Angelo, TX 76905 / 915-655-5953

H&R 1871, Inc., 60 Industrial Rowe, Gardner, MA 01440 / 978-632-9393; FAX: 978-632-2300

H&S Liner Service, 515 E. 8th, Odessa, TX 79761 / 915-332-1021

H-S Precision, Inc., 1301 Turbine Dr., Rapid City, SD 57701 / 605-341-3006; FAX: 605-342-8964

H. Krieghoff Gun Co., Boschstrasse 22, D-89079, Ulm, GERMANY / 731-401820; FAX: 731-4018270

H.K.S. Products, 7841 Founion Dr., Florence, KY 41042 / 606-342-7841 or 800-354-9814; FAX: 606-342-5865

H.P. White Laboratory, Inc., 3114 Scarboro Rd., Street, MD 21154 / 410-838-6550; FAX: 410-838-2802

Hafner World Wide, Inc., P.O. Box 1987, Lake City, FL 32055 / 904-755-6481; FAX: 904-755-6595

Hagn Rifles & Actions, Martin, PO Box 444, Cranbrook, BC V1C 4H9 CANADA / 604-489-4861

Hakko Co., Ltd., 1-13-12, Narimasu, Itabashiku Tokyo, JAPAN / 03-5997-7870/2; FAX: 81-3-5997-7840

Hale, Engraver, Peter, 800 E Canyon Rd., Spanish Fork, UT 84660 / 801-798-8215

Half Moon Rifle Shop, 490 Halfmoon Rd., Columbia Falls, MT 59912 / 406-892-4409

Hall Manufacturing, 142 CR 406, Clanton, AL 35045 / 205-755-4094

Hall Plastics, Inc., John, P.O. Box 1526, Alvin, TX 77512 / 713-489-8709

Hallberg Gunsmith, Fritz, 532 E. Idaho Ave, Ontario, OR 97914 / 541-889-3135; FAX: 541-889-2633

Hallowell & Co., P.O. Box 1445, Livingston, MT 59047 / 406-222-4770 FAX: 406-222-4792 morris@hallowellco.com blaine.hallowellco.com

Hally Caller, 443 Wells Rd., Doylestown, PA 18901 / 215-345-6354

Halstead, Rick, 313 TURF ST, CARL JUNCTION, MO 64834-9658 / 918-540-0933

Hamilton, Jim, Rte. 5, Box 278, Guthrie, OK 73044 / 405-282-3634

Hamilton, Alex B (See Ten-Ring Precision, Inc)

Hammans, Charles E., P.O. Box 788, 2022 McCracken, Stuttgart, AR 72106 / 870-673-1388

Hammerli Ltd, Seonerstrasse 37, CH-5600, SWITZERLAND / 064-50 11 44; FAX: 064-51 38 27

Hammerli USA, 19296 Oak Grove Circle, Groveland, CA 95321 FAX: 209-962-5311

Hammets VLD Bullets, P.O. Box 479, Rayville, LA 71269 / 318-728-2019

Hammond Custom Guns Ltd., 619 S. Pandora, Gilbert, AZ 85234 / 602-892-3437

Hammonds Rifles, RD 4, Box 504, Red Lion, PA 17356 / 717-244-7879

HandCrafts Unltd (See Clements' Custom Leathercraft, Chas.), 1741 Dallas St., Aurora, CO 80010-2018 / 303-364-0403; FAX: 303-739-9824

Handgun Press, P.O. Box 406, Glenview, IL 60025 / 847-657-6500; FAX: 847-724-8831 jschroed@inter-access.com

Hands Engraving, Barry Lee, 26192 E Shore Route, Bigfork, MT 59911 / 406-837-0035

Hank's Gun Shop, Box 370, 50 West 100 South, Monroe, UT 84754 / 801-527-4456

Hanned Precision (See Hanned Line, The)

Hansen & Co. (See Hansen Cartridge Co.), Old Post Rd., Southport, CT 06490 / 203-259-6222; FAX: 203-254-3832

Hanson's Gun Center, Dick, 233 Everett Dr, Colorado Springs, CO 80911

Hanus Birdguns Bill, PO Box 533, Newport, OR 97365 / 541-265-7433; FAX: 541-265-7400

Hanusin, John, 3306 Commercial, Northbrook, IL 60062 / 708-564-2706

Hardin Specialty Dist., P.O. Box 338, Radcliff, KY 40159-0338 / 502-351-6649

Harford (See U.S. Importer-EMF Co., Inc.)

Harper's Custom Stocks, 928 Lombrano St., San Antonio, TX 78207 / 210-732-5780

Harrell's Precision, 5756 Hickory Dr., Salem, VA 24133 / 703-380-2683

Harrington & Richardson (See H&R 1871, Inc.)

Harris Engineering Inc, Dept GD54, Barlow, KY 42024 / 502-334-3633 FAX: 502-334-3000

Harris Enterprises, P.O. Box 105, Bly, OR 97622 / 503-353-2625

Harris Gunworks, 20813 N. 19th Ave., PO Box 9249, Phoenix, AZ 85027 / 602-582-9627; FAX: 602-582-5178

Harris Hand Engraving, Paul A., 113 Rusty Ln, Boerne, TX 78006-5746 / 512-391-5121

Harris Publications, 1115 Broadway, New York, NY 10010 / 212-807-7100 FAX: 212-627-4678

Harrison Bullets, 6437 E. Hobart St., Mesa, AZ 85205

Harry Lawson Co., 3328 N. Richey Blvd., Tucson, AZ 85716 / 520-326-1117

Hart & Son, Inc., Robert W., 401 Montgomery St, Nescopeck, PA 18635 / 717-752-3655; FAX: 717-752-1088

Hart Rifle Barrels,Inc., P.O. Box 182, 1690 Apulia Rd., Lafayette, NY 13084 / 315-677-9841; FAX: 315-677-9610 hartb@hartbarrels.com

Hartford (See U.S. Importer-EMF Co, Inc.)

Hartmann & Weiss GmbH, Rahlstedter Bahnhofstr. 47, 22143, Hamburg, GERMANY / (40) 677 55 85; FAX: (40) 677 55 92

Harvey, Frank, 218 Nightfall, Terrace, NV 89015 / 702-558-6998

Harwood, Jack O., 1191 S. Pendlebury Lane, Blackfoot, ID 83221 / 208-785-5368

Hastings Barrels, 320 Court St., Clay Center, KS 67432 / 913-632-3169; FAX: 913-632-6554

Hatfield Gun, 224 N. 4th St., St. Joseph, MO 64501

Hawk Laboratories, Inc. (See Hawk, Inc.), 849 Hawks Bridge Rd., Salem, NJ 08079 / 609-299-2800

Hawk, Inc., 849 Hawks Bridge Rd., Salem, NJ 08079 / 609-299-2700; FAX: 609-299-2800

Hawken Shop, The (See Dayton Traister)

Haydel's Game Calls, Inc., 5018 Hazel Jones Rd., Bossier City, LA 71111 / 800-HAYDELS; FAX: 318-746-3711

Haydon Shooters Supply, Russ, 15018 Goodrich Dr NW, Gig Harbor, WA 98329-9738 / 253-857-7557; FAX: 253-857-7884

Heatbath Corp., P.O. Box 2978, Springfield, MA 01101 / 413-543-3381

Hebard Guns, Gil, 125-129 Public Square, Knoxville, IL 61448

HEBB Resources, P.O. Box 999, Mead, WA 99021-0999 / 509-466-1292

Hecht, Hubert J., Waffen-Hecht, PO Box 2635, Fair Oaks, CA 95628 / 916-966-1020

Heckler & Koch GmbH, P.O. Box 1329, 78722 Oberndorf, Neckar, GERMANY / 49-7423179-0; FAX: 49-7423179-246

Heckler & Koch, Inc., 21480 Pacific Blvd., Sterling, VA 20166-8900 / 703-450-1900; FAX: 703-450-8160

Hege Jagd-u. Sporthandels GmbH, P.O. Box 101461, W-7770, Ueberlingen a. Boden, GERMANY

Heidenstrom Bullets, Urdngt 1, 3937 Heroya, NORWAY,

Heilmann, Stephen, P.O. Box 657, Grass Valley, CA 95945 / 530-272-8758

Heinie Specialty Products, 301 Oak St., Quincy, IL 62301-2500 / 217-228-9500; FAX: 217-228-9502 rheinie@heinie.com www.heinie.com

Hellweg Ltd., 40356 Oak Park Way, Suite W, Oakhurst, CA 93644 / 209-683-3030; FAX: 209-683-3422

Helwan (See U.S. Importer-Interarms)

Hendricks, Frank E, Inc., Master Engravers, HC 03, Box 434, Dripping Springs, TX 78620 / 512-858-7828

Henigson & Associates, Steve, PO Box 2726, Culver City, CA 90231 / 310-305-8288; FAX:

Henriksen Tool Co., Inc., 8515 Wagner Creek Rd., Talent, OR 97540 / 541-535-2309 FAX: 541-535-2309

Henry Repeating Arms Co., 110 8th St., Brooklyn, NY 11215 / 718-499-5600

Hensley, Gunmaker, Darwin, PO Box 329, Brightwood, OR 97011 / 503-622-5411

Heppler, Keith. (See KEITH'S CUSTOM GUN-STOCKS)

Heppler's Machining, 2240 Calle Del Mundo, Santa Clara, CA 95054 / 408-748-9166; FAX: 408-988-7711

Heppner, Keith M, Keith's Custom Gunstocks, 540 Banyan Cir, Walnut Creek, CA 94598 / 510-934-3509; FAX: 510-934-3143

Hercules, Inc. (See Alliant Techsystems, Smokeless Powder Group)

Heritage Firearms (See Heritage Mfg., Inc.)

Heritage Manufacturing, Inc., 4600 NW 135th St., Opa Locka, FL 33054 or 305-685-5966; FAX: 305-687-6721

Heritage Wildlife Carvings, 2145 Wagner Hollow Rd., Fort Plain, NY 13339 / 518-993-3983

Heritage/VSP Gun Books, P.O. Box 887, McCall, ID 83638 / 208-634-4104; FAX: 208-634-3101

Herrett's Stocks, Inc., P.O. Box 741, Twin Falls, ID 83303 / 208-733-1498

Hertel & Reuss, Werk fr Optik und Feinmechanik GmbH, Quellhofstrasse 67, 34 127, GERMANY / 0561-83006; FAX: 0561-893308

Herter's Manufacturing, Inc., 111 E. Burnett St., P.O. Box 518, Beaver Dam, WI 53916 / 414-887-1765; FAX: 414-887-8444

Hesco-Meprolight, 2139 Greenville Rd., LaGrange, GA 30241 / 706-884-7967; FAX: 706-882-4683

Heydenberk, Warren R., 1059 W. Sawmill Rd., Quakertown, PA 18951 / 215-538-2682

Hi-Grade Imports, 8655 Monterey Rd., Gilroy, CA 95021 / 408-842-9301; FAX: 408-842-2374

Hi-Performance Ammunition Company, 484 State Route 366, Apollo, PA 15613 / 412-327-8100

Hi-Point Firearms, 5990 Philadelphia Dr., Dayton, OH 45415 / 513-275-4991; FAX: 513-522-8330

Hickman, Jaclyn, Box 1900, Glenrock, WY 82637

Hidalgo, Tony, 12701 SW 9th Pl., Davie, FL 33325 / 954-476-7645

High Bridge Arms, Inc, 3185 Mission St., San Francisco, CA 94110 / 415-282-8358

High North Products, Inc., P.O. Box 2, Antigo, WI 54409 / 715-627-2331 FAX: 715-623-5451

High Performance International, 5734 W. Florist Ave., Milwaukee, WI 53218 / 414-466-9040

High Standard Mfg. Co., Inc. 10606 Hempstead Hwy., Suite 116, Houston, TX 77092 / 713-462-4200, 800-467-2228

High Tech Specialties, Inc., P.O. Box 387R, Adamstown, PA 19501 / 215-484-0405 or 800-231-9385

Highline Machine Co., Randall Thompson, 654 Lela Place, Grand Junction, CO 81504 / 970-434-4971

Hill, Loring F., 304 Cedar Rd., Elkins Park, PA 19027

Hill Speed Leather, Ernie, 4507 N 195th Ave, Litchfield Park, AZ 85340 / 602-853-9222; FAX:

Hines Co., S C, PO Box 423, Tijeras, NM 87059 / 505-281-3783

Hinman Outfitters, Bob, 107 N Sanderson Ave, Bartonville, IL 61607-1839 / 309-691-8132

HIP-GRIP Barami Corp., 6689 Orchard Lake Rd. No. 148, West Bloomfield, MI 48322 / 248-738-0462; FAX: 248-738-2542

MANUFACTURER'S DIRECTORY

Hiptmayer, Armurier, RR 112 750, P.O. Box 136, Eastman, PQ J0E 1P0 CANADA / 514-297-2492

Hiptmayer, Heidemarie, RR 112 750, P.O. Box 136, Eastman, PQ J0E 1P0 CANADA / 514-297-2492

Hiptmayer, Klaus, RR 112 750, P.O. Box 136, Eastman, PQ J0E 1P0 CANADA / 514-297-2492

Hirtenberger Aktiengesellschaft, Leobersdorferstrasse 31, A-2552, Hirtenberg. / 43(0)2256 81184; FAX: 43(0)2256 81807

HiTek International, 484 El Camino Real, Redwood City, CA 94063 / 415-363-1404 or 800-54-NIGHT FAX: 415-363-1408

Hiti-Schuch, Atelier Wilma, A-8863 Preditz, Pirming, Y1 AUSTRIA / 0355418278

HJS Arms,Inc., P.O. Box 3711, Brownsville, TX 78523-3711 / 800-453-2767; FAX: 210-542-2767

Hoag, James W., 8523 Canoga Ave., Suite C, Canoga Park, CA 91304 / 818-998-1510

Hobson Precision Mfg. Co., 210 Big Oak Ln, Brent, AL 35034 / 205-926-4662 FAX: 205-926-3193 cahobbob@dbtech.net

Hoch Custom Bullet Moulds (See Colorado Shooter's

Hodgdon Powder Co. 6231 Robinson, Shawnee Mission, KS 66202 / 913-362-9455; FAX: 913-362-1307

Hodgman, Inc., 1750 Orchard Rd., Montgomery, IL 60538 / 708-897-7555; FAX: 708-897-7558

Hodgson, Richard, 9081 Tahoe Lane, Boulder, CO 80301

Hoehn Sales, Inc., 2045 Kohn Road, Wright City, MO 63390 / 636-745-8144; FAX: 636-745-7868 hoehnsal@usmo.com benchrestcentral.com

Hoelscher, Virgil, 8230 Hillrose St, Sunland, CA 91040-2404 / 310-631-8545

Hoenig & Rodman, 6521 Morton Dr., Boise, ID 83704 / 208-375-1116

Hofer Jagdwaffen, P., Buchsenmachermeister, Kirchgasse 24, A-9170 Ferlach, AUSTRIA

Hoffman New Ideas, 821 Northmoor Rd., Lake Forest, IL 60045 / 312-234-4075

Hogue Grips, P.O. Box 1138, Paso Robles, CA 93447 / 800-438-4747 or 805-239-1440; FAX: 805-239-2553

Holland & Holland Ltd., 33 Bruton St., London, ENGLAND / 44-171-499-4411; FAX: 44-171-408-7962

Holland's Gunsmithing, P.O. Box 69, Powers, OR 97466 / 541-439-5155; FAX: 541-439-5155

Hollinger, Jon. (See ASPEN OUTFITTING CO)

Hollis Gun Shop, 917 Rex St., Carlsbad, NM 88220 / 505-885-3782

Hollywood Engineering, 10642 Arminta St., Sun Valley, CA 91352 / 818-842-8376

Homak, 5151 W. 73rd St., Chicago, IL 60638-6613 / 312-523-3100; FAX: 312-523-9455

Home Shop Machinist The Village Press Publications, P.O. Box 1810, Traverse City, MI 49685 / 800-447-7367; FAX: 616-946-3289

Hondo Ind., 510 S. 52nd St., I04, Tempe, AZ 85281

Hoover, Harvey, 5750 Pearl Dr., Paradise, CA 95969-4829

Hoppe's Div. Penguin Industries, Inc., Airport Industrial Mall, Coatesville, PA 19320 / 610-384-6000

Horizons Unlimited, P.O. Box 426, Warm Springs, GA 31830 / 706-655-3603; FAX: 706-655-3603

Hornady Mfg. Co., P.O. Box 1848, Grand Island, NE 68802 / 800-338-3220 or 308-382-1390; FAX: 308-382-5761

Horseshoe Leather Products, Andy Arratoonian, The Cottage Sharow, Ripon, ENGLAND / 44-1765-605858

Houtz & Barwick, P.O. Box 435, W. Church St., Elizabeth City, NC 27909 / 800-775-0337 or 919-335-4191; FAX: 919-335-1152

Howa Machinery, Ltd., Sukaguchi, Shinkawa-cho Nishikasugai-gun, Aichi 452, JAPAN

Hoyt Holster Co., Inc., P.O. Box 69, Coupeville, WA 98239-0069 / 360-678-6640; FAX: 360-678-6549

HT Bullets, 204 Belleville Rd., New Bedford, MA 02745 / 508-999-3338

Hubert J. Hecht Waffen-Hecht, P.O. Box 2635, Fair Oaks, CA 95628 / 916-966-1020

Hubertus Schneidwarenfabrik, P.O. Box 180 106, D-42626, Solingen, GERMANY / 01149-212-59-19-94; FAX: 01149-212-59-19-92

Huebner, Corey O., P.O. Box 2074, Missoula, MT 59806-2074 / 406-721-7168

Huey Gun Cases, P.O. Box 22456, Kansas City, MO 64113 / 816-444-1637; FAX: 816-444-1637

Hugger Hooks Co., 3900 Easley Way, Golden, CO 80403 / 303-279-0600

Hughes, Steven Dodd, P.O. Box 545, Livingston, MT 59047 / 406-222-9377; FAX: 406-222-9377

Hume, Don, P.O. Box 351, Miami, OK 74355 / 800-331-2686 FAX: 918-542-4340

Hungry Horse Books, 4605 Hwy. 93 South, Whitefish, MT 59937 / 406-862-7997

Hunkeler, A (See Buckskin Machine Works, A. Hunkeler) 3235 S 358th St., Auburn, WA 98001 / 206-927-5412

Hunter Co., Inc., 3300 W. 71st Ave., Westminster, CO 80030 / 303-427-4626; FAX: 303-428-3980

Hunter's Specialties Inc., 6000 Huntington Ct. NE, Cedar Rapids, IA 52402-1268 / 319-395-0321; FAX: 319-395-0326

Hunterjohn, P.O. Box 771457, St. Louis, MO 63177 / 314-531-7250

Hunters Supply, Inc., PO Box 313, Tioga, TX 76271 / 940-437-2458; FAX: 940-437-2228 hunterssupply@hotmail.com hunterssupply.net

Hunting Classics Ltd., P.O. Box 2089, Gastonia, NC 28053 / 704-867-1307; FAX: 704-867-0491

Huntington Die Specialties, 601 Oro Dam Blvd., Oroville, CA 95965 / 530-534-1210; FAX: 530-534-1212

Hutton Rifle Ranch, P.O. Box 45236, Boise, ID 83711 / 208-345-8781

Hydrosorbent Products, P.O. Box 437, Ashley Falls, MA 01222 / 413-229-2967; or 800-229-8743 FAX: 413-229-8743 orders@dehumidify.com www.dehumidify.com

Hyper-Single, Inc., 520 E. Beaver, Jenks, OK 74037 / 918-299-2391

I

I.A.B. (See U.S. Importer-Taylor's & Co. Inc.)

I.D.S.A. Books, 1324 Stratford Drive, Piqua, OH 45356 / 937-773-4203; FAX: 937-778-1922

I.N.C. Inc (See Kick Eez)

I.S.S., P.O. Box 185234, Ft. Worth, TX 76181 / 817-595-2090

I.S.W., 106 E. Cairo Dr., Tempe, AZ 85282

IAR Inc., 33171 Camino Capistrano, San Juan Capistrano, CA 92675 / 949-443-3642; FAX: 949-443-3647

IGA (See U.S. Importer-Stoeger Industries)

Ignacio Ugartechea S.A., Chonta 26, Eibar, 20600 SPAIN / 43-121257; FAX: 43-121669

Illinois Lead Shop, 7742 W. 61st Place, Summit, IL 60501

Image Ind. Inc., 382 Balm Court, Wood Dale, IL 60191 / 630-766-2402; FAX: 630-766-7373

IMI, P.O. Box 1044, Ramat Hasharon, 47100 ISRAEL / 972-3-5485617; FAX: 972-3-5406908

IMI Services USA, Inc., 2 Wisconsin Circle, Suite 420, Chevy Chase, MD 20815 / 301-215-4800; FAX: 301-657-1446

Impact Case Co., P.O. Box 9912, Spokane, WA 99209-0912 / 800-262-3322 or 509-467-3303; FAX: 509-326-5436 kkair.com

Imperial (See E-Z-Way Systems), PO Box 4310, Newark, OH 43058-4310 / 614-345-6645; FAX: 614-345-6600

Imperial Magnum Corp., P.O. Box 249, Oroville, WA 98844 / 604-495-3131; FAX: 604-495-2816

Imperial Miniature Armory, 10547 S. Post Oak, Houston, TX 77035 / 713-729-8428 FAX: 713-729-2274

Imperial Schrade Corp., 7 Schrade Ct., Box 7000, Ellenville, NY 12428 / 914-647-7601; FAX: 914-647-8701

Import Sports Inc., 1750 Brielle Ave., Unit B1, Wanamassa, NJ 07712 / 908-493-0302; FAX: 908-493-0301

IMR Powder Co., 1080 Military Turnpike, Suite 2, Plattsburgh, NY 12901 / 518-563-2253; FAX: 518-563-6916

Info-Arm, P.O. Box 1262, Champlain, NY 12919 / 514-955-0355; FAX: 514-955-0357

Ingle, Ralph W., Engraver, 112 Manchester Ct., Centerville, GA 31028 / 912-953-5824

Innovative Weaponry Inc., 2513 E. Loop 820 N., Fort Worth, TX 76118 / 817-284-0099; or 800-334-3573

Innovision Enterprises, 728 Skinner Dr., Kalamazoo, MI 49001 / 616-382-1681 FAX: 616-382-1830

INTEC International, Inc., P.O. Box 5708, Scottsdale, AZ 85261 / 602-483-1708

Inter Ordnance of America LP, 3305 Westwood Industrial Dr, Monroe, NC 28110-5204 / 704-821-8337; FAX: 704-821-8523

Intercontinental Distributors, Ltd., PO Box 815, Beulah, ND 58523

Intrac Arms International, 5005 Chapman Hwy., Knoxville, TN 37920

Intratec, 12405 SW 130th St., Miami, FL 33186-6224 / 305-232-1821; FAX: 305-253-7207

Ion Industries, Inc, 3508 E Allerton Ave, Cudahy, WI 53110 / 414-486-2007; FAX: 414-486-2017

Iosso Products, 1485 Lively Blvd., Elk Grove Village, IL 60007 / 847-437-8400; FAX: 847-437-8478

Iron Bench, 12619 Bailey Rd., Redding, CA 96003 / 916-241-4623

Ironside International Publishers, Inc., P.O. Box 55, 800 Slaters Lane, Alexandria, VA 22313 / 703-684-6111; FAX: 703-683-5486

Ironsighter Co., P.O. Box 85070, Westland, MI 48185 / 734-326-8731; FAX: 734-326-3378

Irwin, Campbell H., 140 Hartland Blvd., East Hartland, CT 06027 / 203-653-3901

Island Pond Gun Shop, Cross St., Island Pond, VT 05846 / 802-723-4546

Israel Arms International, Inc., 5709 Hartsdale, Houston, TX 77036 / 713-789-0745; FAX: 713-789-7513

Israel Military Industries Ltd. (See IMI), PO Box 1044, Ramat Hasharon, ISRAEL / 972-3-5485617; FAX: 972-3-5406908

Ithaca Classic Doubles, Stephen Lamboy, PO Box 665, Mendon, NY 14506 / 706-569-6760; FAX: 706-561-9248

Ithaca Gun Co. LLC, 891 Route 34-B, King Ferry, NY 13081 / 888-9ITHACA; FAX: 315-364-5134

Ivanoff, Thomas G (See Tom's Gun Repair)

J

J J Roberts Firearm Engraver, 7808 Lake Dr, Manassas, VA 20111 / 703-330-0448 FAX: 703-264-8600

J Martin Inc, PO Drawer AP, Beckley, WV 25802 / 304-255-4073; FAX: 304-255-4077

J&D Components, 75 East 350 North, Orem, UT 84057-4719 / 801-225-7007

J&J Products, Inc., 9240 Whitmore, El Monte, CA 91731 / 818-571-5228; FAX: 800-927-8361

J&J Sales, 1501 21st Ave. S., Great Falls, MT 59405 / 406-453-7549

J&L Superior Bullets (See Huntington Die Specialties)

J&R Engineering, P.O. Box 77, 200 Lyons Hill Rd., Athol, MA 01331 / 508-249-9241

J&R Enterprises, 4550 Scotts Valley Rd., Lakeport, CA 95453

J&S Heat Treat, 803 S. 16th St., Blue Springs, MO 64015 / 816-229-2149; FAX: 816-229-1135

J-4, Inc., 1700 Via Burton, Anaheim, CA 92806 / 714-254-8315; FAX: 714-956-4421

J-Gar Co., 183 Turnpike Rd., Dept. 3, Petersham, MA 01366-9604

J. Dewey Mfg. Co., Inc., P.O. Box 2014, Southbury, CT 06488 / 203-264-3064; FAX: 203-262-6907

J.A. Blades, Inc. (See Christopher Firearms Co.)

J.A. Henckels Zwillingswerk Inc., 9 Skyline Dr., Hawthorne, NY 10532 / 914-592-7370

J.G. Dapkus Co., Inc., Commerce Circle, P.O. Box 293, Durham, CT 06422

J.I.T. Ltd., P.O. Box 230, Freedom, WY 83120 / 708-494-0937

J.J. Roberts/Engraver, 7808 Lake Dr., Manassas, VA 22111 / 703-330-0448

J.M. Bucheimer Jumbo Sports Products, 721 N. 20th St. Louis, MO 63103 / 314-241-1020

J.P. Enterprises Inc., P.O. Box 26324, Shoreview, MN 55126 / 612-486-9064; FAX: 612-482-0970

J.P. Gunstocks, Inc., 4508 San Miguel Ave., North Las Vegas, NV 89030 / 702-645-0718

J.R. Blair Engraving, P.O. Box 64, Glenrock, WY 82637 / 307-436-8115

J.R. Williams Bullet Co., 2008 Tucker Rd., Perry, GA 31069 / 912-987-0274

J.W. Morrison Custom Rifles, 4015 W. Sharon, Phoenix, AZ 85029 / 602-978-3754

J/B Adventures & Safaris Inc., 2275 E. Arapahoe Rd., Ste. 109, Littleton, CO 80122-1521 / 303-771-0977

MANUFACTURER'S DIRECTORY

Jack Dever Co., 8590 NW 90, Oklahoma City, OK 73132 / 405-721-6393

Jack A. Rosenberg & Sons, 12229 Cox Ln., Dallas, TX 75234 / 214-241-6302

Jack First, Inc., 1201 Turbine Dr., Rapid City, SD 57701 / 605-343-9544; FAX: 605-343-9420

Jackalope Gun Shop, 1048 S. 5th St., Douglas, WY 82663 / 307-358-3441

Jaffin, Harry, (See BRIDGEMAN PRODUCTS)

Jagdwaffen, P. Hofer, Buchsenmachermeister, Kirchgasse 24 A-9170, Ferlach, AUSTRIA / 04227-3683

James Churchill Glove Co., P.O. Box 298, Centralia, WA 98531

James Calhoon Mfg., Rt. 304, Havre, MT 59501 / 406-395-4079

James Wayne Firearms for Collectors and Investors, 2608 N. Laurent, Victoria, TX 77901 / 512-578-1258; FAX: 512-578-3559

Jamison's Forge Works, 4527 Rd. 6.5 NE, Moses Lake, WA 98837 / 509-762-2659

Jantz Supply, P.O. Box 584-GD, Davis, OK 73030-0584 / 580-369-2316; FAX: 580-369-3082

Jarrett Rifles, Inc., 383 Brown Rd., Jackson, SC 29831 / 803-471-3616

Jarvis, Inc., 1123 Cherry Orchard Lane, Hamilton, MT 59840 / 406-961-4392

JAS, Inc., P.O. Box 0, Rosemount, MN 55068 / 612-890-7631

Javelina Lube Products, P.O. Box 337, San Bernardino, CA 92402 / 714-882-5847; FAX: 714-434-6937

JB Custom, P.O. Box 6912, Leawood, KS 66206 / 913-381-2329

Jeff W. Flannery Engraving Co., 11034 Riddles Run Rd., Union, KY 41091 / 606-384-3127

Jeffredo Gunsight, P.O. Box 669, San Marcos, CA 92079 / 619-728-2695

Jena Eur, PO Box 319, Dunmore, PA 18512

Jenco Sales, Inc., P.O. Box 1000, Manchaca, TX 78652 / 800-531-5301 FAX: 800-266-2373

Jenkins Recoil Pads, Inc., 5438 E. Frontage Ln., Olney, IL 62450 / 618-395-3416

Jensen Bullets, 86 North, 400 West, Blackfoot, ID 83221 / 208-785-5590

Jensen's Custom Ammunition, 5146 E. Pima, Tucson, AZ 85712 / 602-325-3346 FAX: 602-322-5704

Jensen's Firearms Academy, 1280 W. Prince, Tucson, AZ 85705 / 602-293-8516

Jericho Tool & Die Co., Inc., RD 3 Box 70, Route 7, Bainbridge, NY 13733-9496 / 607-563-8222; FAX: 607-563-8560

Jerry Phillips Optics, P.O. Box L632, Langhorne, PA 19047 / 215-757-5037 FAX: 215-757-7097

Jesse W. Smith Saddlery, 16909 E. Jackson Road, Elk, WA 99009-9600 / 509-325-0622

Jester Bullets, Rt. 1 Box 27, Orienta, OK 73737

Jewell Triggers, Inc., 3620 Hwy. 123, San Marcos, TX 78666 / 512-353-2999

JGS Precision Tool Mfg., 100 Main Sumner, Coos Bay, OR 97420 / 541-267-4331 FAX: 541-267-5996

Jim Chambers Flintlocks Ltd., Rt. 1, Box 513-A, Candler, NC 28715 / 704-667-8361

Jim Garthwaite Pistolsmith, Inc., Rt. 2 Box 310, Watsontown, PA 17777 / 717-538-1566

Jim Noble Co., 1305 Columbia St., Vancouver, WA 98660 / 360-695-1309; FAX: 360-695-6835 jnoblbeco@aol.com

Jim Norman Custom Gunstocks, 14281 Cane Rd. Valley Center, CA 92082 / 619-749-6252

Jim's Gun Shop (See Spradlin's)

Jim's Precision, Jim Ketchum, 1725 Moclips Dr., Petaluma, CA 94952 / 707-762-3014

JLK Bullets, 414 Turner Rd., Dover, AR 72837 / 501-331-4194

Johanssons Vapentillbehor, Bert, S-430 20, Veddige, SWEDEN

John Hall Plastics, Inc., Inc., P.O. Box 1526, Alvin, TX 77512 / 713-489-8709

John J. Adams & Son Engravers, PO Box 66, Vershire, VT 05079 / 802-685-0019

John Masen Co. Inc., 1305 Jelmak, Grand Prairie, TX 75050 / 817-430-8732; FAX: 817-430-1715

John Norrell Arms, 2608 Grist Mill Rd, Little Rock, AR 72207 / 501-225-7864

John Partridge Sales Ltd., Trent Meadows Rugeley, Staffordshire, WS15 2HS ENGLAND

John Rigby & Co., 1317 Spring St., Paso Robles, CA 93446 / 805-227-4236; FAX: 805-227-4723

John Unertl Optical Co., Inc., 308-310 Clay Ave., Mars, PA 16046-0818 / 724-625-3810

John's Custom Leather, 523 S. Liberty St., Blairsville, PA 15717 / 412-459-6802

Johnny Stewart Game Calls, Inc., P.O. Box 7954, 5100 Fort Ave., Waco, TX 76714 / 817-772-3261; FAX: 817-772-3670

Johnson Wood Products, 34968 Crystal Road, Strawberry Point, IA 52076 / 319-933-4930

Johnson's Gunsmithing, Inc., Neal, 208 W Buchanan St, Ste B, Colorado Springs, CO 80907 / 800-284-8671; FAX: 719-632-3493

Johnston Bros. (See C&T Corp. TA Johnson Brothers)

Johnston, James (See North Fork Custom Gunsmithing, James Johnston)

Jonad Corp., 2091 Lakeland Ave., Lakewood, OH 44107 / 216-226-3161

Jonathan Arthur Ciener, Inc., 8700 Commerce St., Cape Canaveral, FL 32920 / 407-868-2200; FAX: 407-868-2201

Jones Co., Dale, 680 Hoffman Draw, Kila, MT 59920 / 406-755-4684

Jones Custom Products, Neil A., 17217 Brookhouser Rd., Saegertown, PA 16433 / 814-763-2769; FAX: 814-763-4228

Jones Moulds, Paul, 4901 Telegraph Rd, Los Angeles, CA 90022 / 213-262-1510

Jones, J.D./SSK Industries, 590 Woodvue Ln., Wintersville, OH 43953 / 740-264-0176; FAX: 740-264-2257

JP Sales, Box 307, Anderson, TX 77830

JRP Custom Bullets, RR2 2233 Carlton Rd., Whitehall, NY 12887 / 518-282-0084 or 802-438-5548

JS Worldwide DBA (See Coonan Arms)

JSL Ltd (See U.S. Importer-Specialty Shooters Supply, Inc.)

Juenke, Vern, 25 Bitterbush Rd., Reno, NV 89523 / 702-345-0225

Jumbo Sports Products, J. M. Bucheimer, 721 N. 20th St., St. Louis, MO 63103 / 314-241-1020

Jungkind, Reeves Co., 5001 Buckskin Pass, Austin, TX 78745-2841 / 512-442-1094

Jurras, L. E., P.O. Box 680, Washington, IN 47501 / 812-254-7698

Justin Phillippi Custom Bullets, P.O. Box 773, Ligonier, PA 15658 / 412-238-9671

K

K&M Industries, Inc., Box 66, 510 S. Main, Troy, ID 83871 / 208-835-2281; FAX: 208-835-5211

K&M Services, 5430 Salmon Run Rd., Dover, PA 17315 / 717-292-3175; FAX: 717-292-3175

K-D, Inc., Box 459, 585 N. Hwy. 155, Cleveland, UT 84518 / 801-653-2530

K-Sports Imports Inc., 2755 Thompson Creek Rd., Pomona, CA 91767 / 909-392-2354

K. Eversull Co., Inc., 1 Tracemont, Boyce, LA 71409 / 318-793-8728

K.B.I. Inc., PO Box 6625, Harrisburg, PA 17112 / 717-540-8518; FAX: 717-540-8567

K.K. Arms Co., Star Route Box 671, Kerrville, TX 78028 / 210-257-4718 FAX: 210-257-4891

K.L. Null Holsters Ltd., 161 School St. NW, Hill City Station, Resaca, GA 30735 / 706-625-5643; FAX: 706-625-9392

Ka Pu Kapili, P.O. Box 745, Honokaa, HI 96727 / 808-776-1644; FAX: 808-776-1731

KA-BAR Knives, 1116 E. State St., Olean, NY 14760 / 800-282-0130; FAX: 716-373-6245

Kahles A Swarovski Company, 1 Wholesale Way, Cranston, RI 02920-5540 / 401-946-2220; FAX: 401-946-2587

Kahr Arms, P.O. Box 220, 630 Route 303, Blauvelt, NY 10913 / 914-353-5996; FAX: 914-353-7833

Kalispel Case Line, P.O. Box 267, Cusick, WA 99119 / 509-445-1121

Kamik Outdoor Footwear, 554 Montee de Liesse, Montreal, PQ H4T 1P1 CANADA / 514-341-3950; FAX: 514-341-1861

Kamyk Engraving Co., Steve, 9 Grandview Dr, Westfield, MA 01085-1810 / 413-568-0457

Kane Products, Inc., 5572 Brecksville Rd., Cleveland, OH 44131 / 216-524-9962

Kane, Edward, P.O. Box 385, Ukiah, CA 95482 / 707-462-2937

Kapro Mfg. Co. Inc. (See R.E.I.)

Kasenit Co., Inc., 13 Park Ave., Highland Mills, NY 10930 / 914-928-9595; FAX: 914-928-7292

Kasmarsik Bullets, 4016 7th Ave. SW, Puyallup, WA 98373

Kasmer Custom, Inc., 13 Surrey Drive, Brookfield, CT 06804 / 203-775-0564; FAX: 203-775-6872

KDF, Inc., 2485 Hwy. 46 N., Seguin, TX 78155 / 210-379-8141; FAX: 210-379-5420

KeeCo Impressions, Inc., 346 Wood Ave., North Brunswick, NJ 08902 / 800-468-0546

Keeler, R. H., 817 "N" St., Port Angeles, WA 98362 / 206-457-4702

Kehr, Roger, 2131 Agate Ct. SE, Lacy, WA 98503 / 360-456-0831

Keith's Bullets, 942 Twisted Oak, Algonquin, IL 60102 / 708-658-3520

Keith's Custom Gunstocks (See Heppler, Keith M)

Keith's Custom Gunstocks, Keith M Heppler, 540 Banyan Circle, Walnut Creek, CA 94598 / 925-934-3509; FAX: 925-934-3143

Kel-Tec CNC Industries, Inc., P.O. Box 3427, Cocoa, FL 32924 / 407-631-0068; FAX: 407-631-1169

Kelbly, Inc., 7222 Dalton Fox Lake Rd., North Lawrence, OH 44666 / 216-683-4674; FAX: 216-683-7349

Kelley's, P.O. Box 125, Woburn, MA 01801 / 617-935-3389

Kellogg's Professional Products, 325 Pearl St., Sandusky, OH 44870 / 419-625-6551; FAX: 419-625-6167

Kelly, Lance, 1723 Willow Oak Dr., Edgewater, FL 32132 / 904-423-4933

Kemen America, 2550 Hwy. 23, Wrenshall, MN 55797 / 218-424-3595

Ken Eyster Heritage Gunsmiths, Inc., 6441 Bishop Rd., Centerburg, OH 43011 / 614-625-6131

Ken Starnes Gunmaker, 15940 SW Holly Hill Rd., Hillsboro, OR 97123-9033 / 503-628-0705; FAX: 503-628-6005

Ken's Gun Specialties, Rt. 1, Box 147, Lakeview, AR 72642 / 501-431-5606

Ken's Kustom Kartridges, 331 Jacobs Rd., Hubbard, OH 44425 / 216-534-4595

Ken's Rifle Blanks, Ken McCullough, Rt. 2, P.O. Box 85B, Weston, OR 97886 / 503-566-3879

Keng's Firearms Specialty, Inc./US Tactical Systems, 875 Wharton Dr., P.O. Box 44405, Atlanta, GA 30336-1405 / 404-691-7611; FAX: 404-505-8445

Kennebec Journal, 274 Western Ave., Augusta, ME 04330 / 207-622-6288

Kennedy Firearms, 10 N. Market St., Muncy, PA 17756 / 717-546-6695

Kenneth W. Warren Engraver, P.O. Box 2842, Wenatchee, WA 98807 / 509-663-6123 FAX: 509-665-6123

KenPatable Ent., Inc., P.O. Box 19422, Louisville, KY 40259 / 502-239-5447

Kent Cartridge America, Inc, PO Box 849, 1000 Zigor Rd., Kearneysville, WV 25430

Kent Cartridge Mfg. Co. Ltd., Unit 16 Branbridges Industrial Esta. Tonbridge, Kent, ENGLAND / 622-872255; FAX: 622-872645

Keowee Game Calls, 608 Hwy. 25 North, Travelers Rest, SC 29690 / 864-834-7204; FAX: 864-834-7831

Kershaw Knives, 25300 SW Parkway Ave., Wilsonville, OR 97070 / 503-682-1966 or 800-325-2891; FAX: 503-682-7168

Kesselring Gun Shop, 400 Hwy. 99 North, Burlington, WA 98233 / 206-724-3113; FAX: 206-724-7003

Ketchum, Jim (See Jim's Precision)

Kickeez Inc., 301 Industrial Dr., Carl Junction, MO 64834-8806 / 419-649-2100; FAX: 417-649-2200 kickey@ipa.net

Kilham & Co., Main St., P.O. Box 37, Lyme, NH 03768 / 603-795-4112

Kim Ahrends Custom Firearms, Inc., Box 203, Clarion, IA 50525 / 515-532-3449; FAX: 515-532-3926

Kimar (See U.S. Importer-IAR,Inc)

Kimball, Gary, 1526 N. Circle Dr., Colorado Springs, CO 80909 / 719-634-1274

Kimber of America, Inc., 1 Lawton St., Yonkers, NY 10705 / 800-880-2418; FAX: 914-964-9340

King & Co., P.O. Box 1242, Bloomington, IL 61702 / 309-473-2161

King's Gun Works, 1837 W. Glenoaks Blvd., Glendale, CA 91201 / 818-956-6010; FAX: 818-548-8606

Kingyon, Paul L. (See Custom Calls)

Kirkpatrick Leather Co., PO Box 677, Laredo, TX 78040 / 956-723-6631; FAX: 956-725-0672

MANUFACTURER'S DIRECTORY

KK Air International (See Impact Case Co.)

KLA Enterprises, P.O. Box 2028, Eaton Park, FL 33840 / 941-682-2829 FAX: 941-682-2829

Kleen-Bore, Inc., 16 Industrial Pkwy., Easthampton, MA 01027 / 413-527-0300; FAX: 413-527-2522 info@kleen-bore.com www.kleen-bore.com

Klein Custom Guns, Don, 433 Murray Park Dr, Ripon, WI 54971 / 920-748-2931

Kleinendorst, K. W., RR 1, Box 1500, Hop Bottom, PA 18824 / 717-289-4687

Klingler Woodcarving, P.O. Box 141, Thistle Hill, Cabot, VT 05647 / 802-426-3811

Kmount, P.O. Box 19422, Louisville, KY 40259 / 502-239-5447

Kneiper, James, P.O. Box 1516, Basalt, CO 81621-1516 / 303-963-9880

Knife Importers, Inc., P.O. Box 1000, Manchaca, TX 78652 / 512-282-6860

Knight & Hale Game Calls, Box 468, Industrial Park, Cadiz, KY 42211 / 502-924-1755; FAX: 502-924-1763

Knight Rifles, 21852 hwy j46, P.O. Box 130, Centerville, IA 52544 / 515-856-2626; FAX: 515-856-2628

Knight Rifles (See Modern Muzzle Loading, Inc.)

Knight's Mfg. Co., 7750 9th St. SW, Vero Beach, FL 32968 / 561-562-5697; FAX: 561-569-2955

Knippel, Richard, 500 Gayle Ave Apt 213, Modesto, CA 95350-4241 / 209-869-1469

Knock on Wood Antiques, 355 Post Rd., Darien, CT 06820 / 203-655-9031

Knoell, David, 9737 McCardle Way, Santee, CA 92071

Koevenig's Engraving Service, Box 55 Rabbit Gulch, Hill City, SD 57745 / 605-574-2239

KOGOT, 410 College, Trinidad, CO 81082 / 719-846-9406 FAX: 719-846-9406

Kokolus, Michael M. (See Custom Riflestocks, Inc., Michael M. Kokolus)

Kolar, 1925 Roosevelt Ave, Racine, WI 53406 / 414-554-0800; FAX: 414-554-9093

Kolpin Mfg., Inc., P.O. Box 107, 205 Depot St., Fox Lake, WI 53933 / 414-928-3118; FAX: 414-928-3687

Korth, Robert-Bosch-Str. 4, P.O. Box 1320, 23909 Ratzeburg, GERMANY / 451-4991497; FAX: 451-4993230

Korzinek Riflesmith, J, RD 2 Box 73D, Canton, PA 17724 / 717-673-8512

Koval Knives, 5819 Zarley St., Suite A, New Albany, OH 43054 / 614-855-0777; FAX: 614-855-0945

Kowa Optimed, Inc., 20001 S. Vermont Ave., Torrance, CA 90502 / 310-327-1913; FAX: 310-327-4177

Kramer Designs, P.O. Box 129, Clancy, MT 59634 / 406-933-8658; FAX: 406-933-8658

Kramer Handgun Leather, P.O. Box 112154, Tacoma, WA 98411 / 206-564-6652; FAX: 206-564-1214

Krause Publications, Inc., 700 E. State St., Iola, WI 54990 / 715-445-2214; FAX: 715-445-4087

Krico-Jagd-und Sportwaffen GmbH. Nürmbergerstrasse 6, D-90602, Pyrbaum, GERMANY / 09180-2780; FAX: 09180-2661

Krieger Barrels, Inc., N114 W18697 Clinton Dr., Germantown, WI 53022 / 414-255-9593; FAX: 414-255-9586

Krieghoff Gun Co., H., Boschstrasse 22, D-89079 Elm, GERMANY or 731-4018270

Krieghoff International,Inc., 7528 Easton Rd., Ottsville, PA 18942 / 610-847-5173; FAX: 610-847-8691

Kris Mounts, 108 Lehigh St., Johnstown, PA 15905 / 814-539-9751

KSN Industries Ltd (See U.S. Importer-Israel Arms International, Inc.,)

Kudlas, John M., 622 14th St. SE, Rochester, MN 55904 / 507-288-5579

Kulis Freeze Dry Taxidermy, 725 Broadway Ave., Bedford, OH 44146 / 216-232-8352; FAX: 216-232-7305 jkulis@kastaway.com

KVH Industries, Inc., 110 Enterprise Center, Middletown, RI 02842 / 401-847-3327; FAX: 401-849-0045

Kwik Mount Corp., P.O. Box 19422, Louisville, KY 40259 / 502-239-5447

Kwik-Site Co., 5555 Treadwell, Wayne, MI 48184 / 734-326-1500; FAX: 734-326-4120

L

L&R Lock Co., 1137 Pocalla Rd., Sumter, SC 29150 / 803-775-6127 FAX: 803-775-5171

L&S Technologies Inc (See Aimtech Mount Systems)

L. Bengtson Arms Co., 6345-B E. Akron St., Mesa, AZ 85205 / 602-981-6375

L.A.R. Mfg., Inc., 4133 W. Farm Rd., West Jordan, UT 84088 / 801-280-3505; FAX: 801-280-1972

L.E. Wilson, Inc., Box 324, 404 Pioneer Ave., Cashmere, WA 98815 / 509-782-1328; FAX: 509-782-7200

L.L. Bean, Inc., Freeport, ME 04032 / 207-865-4761; FAX: 207-552-2802

L.P.A. Snc, Via Alfieri 26, Gardone V.T., Brescia, ITALY / 30-891-14-81; FAX: 30-891-09-51

L.R. Clift Mfg., 3821 Hammonton Rd., Marysville, CA 95901 / 916-755-3390; FAX: 916-755-3393

L.S. Starrett Co., 121 Crescent St., Athol, MA 01331 / 617-249-3551

L.W. Seecamp Co., Inc., P.O. Box 255, New Haven, CT 06502 / 203-877-3429

La Clinique du .45, 1432 Rougemont, Chambly, PQ J3L 2L8 CANADA / 514-658-1144

Labanu, Inc., 2201-F Fifth Ave., Ronkonkoma, NY 11779 / 516-467-6197; FAX: 516-981-4112

LaBoone, Pat. (See CLEAR CREEK OUTDOORS)

LaBounty Precision Reboring, Inc., 7968 Silver Lake Rd, PO Box 186, Maple Falls, WA 98266 / 360-599-2047 FAX: 360-599-3018

LaCrosse Footwear, Inc., P.O. Box 1328, La Crosse, WI 54602 / 608-782-3020 or 800-323-2668; FAX: 800-658-9444

LaFrance Specialties, P.O. Box 87933, San Diego, CA 92138-7933 / 619-293-3373; FAX: 619-293-7087

Lage Uniwad, P.O. Box 2302, Davenport, IA 52809 / 319-388-LAGE; FAX: 319-388-LAGE

Lair, Sam, 520 E. Beaver, Jenks, OK 74037 / 918-299-2391

Lake Center, P.O. Box 38, St. Charles, MO 63302 / 314-946-7500

Lakefield Arms Ltd (See Savage Arms Inc)

Lakewood Products LLC, 275 June St., Berlin, WI 54923 / 800-872-8458; FAX: 920-361-7719

Lamboy, Stephen. (See ITHACA CLASSIC DOUBLES)

Lampert, Ron, Rt. 1, Box 177, Guthrie, MN 56461 / 218-854-7345

Lamson & Goodnow Mfg. Co., 45 Conway St., Shelburne Falls, MA 03170 / 413-625-6564; or 800-872-6564 FAX: 413-625-9816 www.lamsonsharp.com

Lanber Armas, S.A., Zubiaurre 5, Zaldibar, 48250 SPAIN / 34-4-6827702; FAX: 34-4-6827999

Langenberg Hat Co., P.O. Box 1860, Washington, MO 63090 / 800-428-1860; FAX: 314-239-3151

Lanphert, Paul, P.O. Box 1985, Wenatchee, WA 98807 / 408-373-0701; FAX: 408-373-0903

Lansky Levine, Arthur. (See LANSKY SHARPENERS)

Lansky Sharpeners, Arthur Lansky Levine, PO Box 50830, Las Vegas, NV 89016 / 702-361-7511; FAX: 702-896-9511

Lapua Ltd., P.O. Box 5, Lapua, FINLAND / 6-310111; FAX: 6-4388991

LaRocca Gun Works, 51 Union Place, Worcester, MA 01608 / 508-754-2887; FAX: 508-754-2887

Larry Lyons Gunworks, 110 Hamilton St., Dowagiac, MI 49047 / 616-782-9478

Laser Devices, Inc., 2 Harris Ct. A-4, Monterey, CA 93940 / 408-373-0701; FAX: 408-373-0903

Laseraim Technologies, Inc., P.O. Box 3548, Little Rock, AR 72203 / 501-375-2227

LaserMax, Inc., 3495 Winton Place, Bldg, B, Rochester, NY 14623-2807 / 800-527-3703 FAX: 716-272-5427

Lassen Community College, Gunsmithing Dept., P.O. Box 3000, Hwy. 139, Susanville, CA 96130 / 916-251-8800; FAX: 916-251-8838

Lathrop's, Inc., Inc., 5146 E. Pima, Tucson, AZ 85712 / 520-881-0266 or 800-875-4867; FAX: 520-322-5704

Laughridge, William R (See Cylinder & Slide Inc)

Laurel Mountain Forge, P.O. Box 52, Crown Point, IN 48065 / 219-548-2950; FAX: 219-548-2950

Laurona Armas Eibar, S.A.L., Avenida de Otaola 25, P.O. Box 260, Eibar 20600, SPAIN / 34-43-700600; FAX: 34-43-700616

Lawrence Brand Shot (See Precision Reloading, Inc.)

Lawrence Leather Co., P.O. Box 1479, Lillington, NC 27546 / 910-893-2071; FAX: 910-893-4742

Lawson Co., Harry, 3328 N Richey Blvd., Tucson, AZ 85716 / 520-326-1117 FAX: 520-326-1117

Lawson, John. (See THE SIGHT SHOP)

Lazzeroni Arms Co., PO Box 26696, Tucson, AZ 85726 / 888-492-7247; FAX: 520-624-4250

LBT, HCR 62, Box 145, Moyie Springs, ID 83845 / 208-267-3588

Le Clear Industries (See E-Z-Way Systems), PO Box 4310, Newark, OH 43058-4310 / 614-345-6645; FAX: 614-345-6600

Lea Mfg. Co., 237 E. Aurora St., Waterbury, CT 06720 / 203-753-5116

Leapers, Inc., 7675 Five Mile Rd., Northville, MI 48167 / 248-486-1231; FAX: 248-486-1430

Leatherman Tool Group, Inc., 12106 NE Ainsworth Cir., P.O. Box 20595, Portland, OR 97294 / 503-253-7826; FAX: 503-253-7830

Lebeau-Courally, Rue St. Gilles, 386 4000, Liege, BELGIUM / 042-52-48-43; FAX: 32-042-52-20-08

Leckie Professional Gunsmithing, 546 Quarry Rd., Ottsville, PA 18942 / 215-847-8594

Lectro Science, Inc., 6410 W. Ridge Rd., Erie, PA 16506 / 814-833-6487; FAX: 814-833-0447

Ledbetter Airguns, Riley, 1804 E Sprague St, Winston Salem, NC 27107-3521 / 919-784-0676

Lee Co., T. K., 1282 Branchwater Ln, Birmingham, AL 35216 / 205-913-5222

Lee Precision, Inc., 4275 Hwy. U, Hartford, WI 53027 / 414-673-3075; FAX: 414-673-9273 leeprecision.com

Lee Supplies, Mark, 9901 France Ct., Lakeville, MN 55044 / 612-461-2114

Lee's Red Ramps, 4 Kristine Ln., Silver City, NM 88061 / 505-538-8529

LeFever Arms Co., Inc., 6234 Stokes, Lee Center Rd., Lee Center, NY 13363 / 315-337-6722; FAX: 315-337-1543

Legacy Sports International, 10 Prince St., Alexandria, VA 22314 / 703-548-4837

Legend Products Corp., 21218 Saint Andrews Blvd., Boca Raton, FL 33433-2435

Leibowitz, Leonard, 1205 Murrayhill Ave., Pittsburgh, PA 15217 / 412-361-5455

Leica USA, Inc., 156 Ludlow Ave., Northvale, NJ 07647 / 201-767-7500; FAX: 201-767-8666

LEM Gun Specialties Inc. The Lewis Lead Remover, P.O. Box 2855, Peachtree City, GA 30269-2024

Leonard Day, 6 Linseed Rd Box 1, West Hatfield, MA 01088-7505 / 413-337-8369

Les Baer Custom,Inc., 29601 34th Ave., Hillsdale, IL 61257 / 309-658-2716; FAX: 309-658-2610

Lestrom Laboratories, Inc., P.O. Box 628, Mexico, NY 13114-0628 / 315-343-3076; FAX: 315-592-3370

Lethal Force Institute (See Police Bookshelf), PO Box 122, Concord, NH 03301 / 603-224-6814; FAX: 603-226-3554

Lett Custom Grips, 672 Currier Rd., Hopkinton, NH 03229-2652 / 800-421-5388 FAX: 603-226-4580

Leupold & Stevens, Inc., 14400 NW Greenbrier Pky., Beaverton, OR 97006 / 503-646-9171; FAX: 503-526-1455

Lever Arms Service Ltd., 2131 Burrard St., Vancouver, BC V6J 3H7 CANADA / 604-736-2711; FAX: 604-738-3503

Lew Horton Dist. Co., Inc., 15 Walkup Dr., Westboro, MA 01581 / 508-366-7400; FAX: 508-366-5332

Liberty Metals, 2233 East 16th St., Los Angeles, CA 90021 / 213-581-9171; FAX: 213-581-9351

Liberty Safe, 1060 N. Spring Creek Pl., Springville, UT 84663 / 800-247-5625; FAX: 801-489-6409

Liberty Shooting Supplies, P.O. Box 357, Hillsboro, OR 97123 / 503-640-5518; FAX: 503-640-5518

Liberty Trouser Co., 3500 6 Ave S., Birmingham, AL 35222-2406 / 205-251-9143

Lightfield Ammunition Corp. (See Slug Group, Inc.), PO Box 376, New Paris, PA 15554 / 814-839-4517; FAX: 814-839-2601

Lightforce U.S.A. Inc., 19226 66th Ave. So., L-103, Kent, WA 98032 / 206-656-1577; FAX: 206-656-1578

Lightning Performance Innovations, Inc., RD1 Box 555, Mohawk, NY 13407 / 800-242-5873; FAX: 315-866-1578

Lilja Precision Rifle Barrels, P.O. Box 372, Plains, MT 59859 / 406-826-3084; FAX: 406-826-3083 lilja@riflebarrels.com www.riflebarrels.com

Lincoln, Dean, Box 1886, Farmington, NM 87401

Lind Custom Guns, Al, 7821 76th Ave SW, Tacoma, WA 98498 / 253-584-6361 lindcustguns@worldnot.att.net

Lindsay, Steve, RR 2 Cedar Hills, Kearney, NE 68847 / 308-236-7885

Linder Solingen Knives, 4401 Sentry Dr., Tucker, GA 30084 / 770-939-6915; FAX: 770-939-6738

MANUFACTURER'S DIRECTORY

Lindsley Arms Cartridge Co., P.O. Box 757, 20 College Hill Rd., Henniker, NH 03242 / 603-428-3127

Linebaugh Custom Sixguns, Route 2, Box 100, Maryville, MO 64468 / 660-562-3031 sixgunner.com

Lion Country Supply, P.O. Box 480, Port Matilda, PA 16870

List Precision Engineering, Unit 1 Ingley Works, 13 River Road, Barking, ENGLAND / 011-081-594-1686

Lithi Bee Bullet Lube, 1728 Carr Rd., Muskegon, MI 49442 / 616-788-4479

"Little John's" Antique Arms, 1740 W. Laveta, Orange, CA 92668

Little Trees Ramble (See Scott Pilkington, Little

Litter Sales Co., 20815 W. Chicago, Detroit, MI 48228 / 313-273-6888; FAX: 313-273-1099

Littleton, J. F., 275 Pinedale Ave., Oroville, CA 95966 / 916-533-6084

Ljutic Industries, Inc., 732 N. 16th Ave., Suite 22, Yakima, WA 98907 / 509-248-0476; FAX: 509-576-8233

Llama Gabilondo Y Cia, Apartado 290, E-01080, Victoria, spain, SPAIN

Loch Leven Industries, P.O. Box 2751, Santa Rosa, CA 95405 / 707-573-8735; FAX: 707-573-0369

Lock's Philadelphia Gun Exchange, 6700 Rowland Ave., Philadelphia, PA 19149/215-332-6225; FAX: 215-332-4800

Lodewick, Walter H., 2816 NE Halsey St., Portland, OR 97232 / 503-284-2554

Log Cabin Sport Shop, 8010 Lafayette Rd., Lodi, OH 44254 / 330-948-1082; FAX: 330-948-4307

Logan, Harry M., Box 745, Honokaa, HI 96727 / 808-776-1644

Lohman Mfg. Co., Inc., 4500 Doniphan Dr., P.O. Box 220, Neosho, MO 64850 / 417-451-4438; FAX: 417-451-2576

Lomont Precision Bullets, RR 1, Box 34, Salmon, ID 83467 / 208-756-6819; FAX: 208-756-6824

London Guns Ltd., Box3750, Santa Barbara, CA 93130 / 805-683-4141; FAX: 805-683-1712

Lone Star Gunleather, 1301 Brushy Bend Dr., Round Rock, TX 78681 / 512-255-1805

Lone Star Rifle Company, 11231 Rose Road, Conroe, TX 77303 / 409-856-3363

Long, George F., 1500 Rogue River Hwy., Ste. F, Grants Pass, OR 97527 / 541-476-7552

Lortone Inc., 2856 NW Market St., Seattle, WA 98107

Lothar Walther Precision Tool Inc., 3425 Hutchinson Rd., Cumming, GA 30040 / 770-889-9998; FAX: www.lotharwalther.com

Loweth, Richard H.R., 29 Hedgegrow Lane, Kirby Muxloe, Leics, LE9 2BN ENGLAND / (0) 116 238 6295

LPS Laboratories, Inc., 4647 Hugh Howell Rd., P.O. Box 3050, Tucker, GA 30084 / 404-934-7800

Lucas, Edward E., 32 Garfield Ave., East Brunswick, NJ 08816 / 201-251-5526

Lucas, Mike, 1631 Jessamine Rd., Lexington, SC 29073

Lupton, Keith. (See PAWLING MOUNTAIN CLUB)

Lutz Engraving, Ron E., E1998 Smokey Valley Rd., Scandinavia, WI 54977 / 715-467-2674

Lyman Instant Targets, Inc. (See Lyman Products, Corp.)

Lyman Products Corp., 475 Smith Street, Middletown, CT 06457-1541 / 860-632-2020 or 800-632-1699; FAX: 860-632-1699

Lyman Products Corporation, 475 Smith Street, Middletown, CT 06457-1529 / 800-22-LYMAN or 860-632-2020; FAX: 860-632-1699

Lyte Optronics (See TracStar Industries Inc)

M

M.Thys (See U.S. Importer-Champlin Firearms Inc)

M.H. Canjar Co., 500 E. 45th Ave., Denver, CO 80216 / 303-295-2638; FAX: 303-295-2638

M.O.A. Corp., 2451 Old Camden Pike, Eaton, OH 45320 / 937-456-3669

MA Systems, P.O. Box 1143, Chouteau, OK 74337 / 918-479-6378

Mac-1 Airgun Distributors, 13974 Van Ness Ave., Gardena, CA 90249 / 310-327-3581; FAX: 310-327-0238 mac1@airgun.com

Macbean, Stan, 754 North 1200 West, Orem, UT 84057 / 801-224-6446

Madis, George, P.O. Box 545, Brownsboro, TX 75756 / 903-852-6480

Madis Books, 2453 West Five Mile Pkwy., Dallas, TX 75233 / 214-330-7168

MAG Instrument, Inc., 1635 S. Sacramento Ave., Ontario, CA 91761 / 909-947-1006; FAX: 909-947-3116

Mag-Na-Port International, Inc., 41302 Executive Dr., Harrison Twp., MI 48045-1306 / 810-469-6727; FAX: 810-469-0425

Mag-Pack Corp., P.O. Box 846, Chesterland, OH 44026

Magma Engineering Co., P.O. Box 161, 20955 E. Ocotillo Rd., Queen Creek, AZ 85242 / 602-987-9008; FAX: 602-987-0148

Magnolia Sports,Inc., 211 W. Main, Magnolia, AR 71753 / 501-234-8410 or 800-530-7816; FAX: 501-234-8117

Magnum Power Products, Inc., P.O. Box 17768, Fountain Hills, AZ 85268

Magnum Research, Inc., 7110 University Ave. NE, Minneapolis, MN 55432 / 800-772-6168 or 612-574-1868; FAX: 612-574-0109 magnumresearch.com

Magnus Bullets, P.O. Box 239, Toney, AL 35773 / 256-420-8359; FAX: 256-420-8360

MagSafe Ammo Co., 4700 S US Highway 17/92, Casselberry, FL 32707-3814 / 407-834-9966; FAX: 407-834-8185

Magtech Ammunition Co. Inc., 837 Boston Rd #12, Madison, CT 06443 / 203-245-8983; FAX: 203-245-2883 rfinemtek@aol.com

Mahony, Philip Bruce, 67 White Hollow Rd., Lime Rock, CT 06039-2418 / 203-435-9341

Mahovsky's Metalife, R.D. 1, Box 149a Eureka Road, Grand Valley, PA 16420 / 814-436-7747

Maine Custom Bullets, RFD 1, Box 1755, Brooks, ME 04921

Maionchi-L.M.I., Via Di Coselli-Zona, Industriale Di Guamo 55060, Lucca, ITALY / 011 39-583 94291

Makinson, Nicholas, RR 3, Komoka, ON N0L 1R0 CANADA / 519-471-5462

Malcolm Enterprises, 1023 E. Prien Lake Rd., Lake Charles, LA 70601

Mallardtone Game Calls, 2901 16th St., Moline, IL 61265 / 309-762-8089

Mandall Shooting Supplies Inc., 3616 N. Scottsdale Rd., Scottsdale, AZ 85252 / 480-945-2553; FAX: 480-949-0734

Marathon Rubber Prods. Co., Inc., 1009 3rd St., Wausau, WI 54403-4765 / 715-845-6255

Marble Arms (See CRR, Inc./Marble's Inc.)

Marchmon Bullets, 8191 Woodland Shore Dr., Brighton, MI 48116

Marent, Rudolf, 9711 Tiltree St., Houston, TX 77075 / 713-946-7028

Mark Lee Supplies, 9901 France Ct., Lakeville, MN 55044 / 612-461-2114

Markell,Inc., 422 Larkfield Center 235, Santa Rosa, CA 95403 / 707-573-0792; FAX: 707-573-9867

Markesbery Muzzle Loaders, Inc., 7785 Foundation Dr., Ste. 6, Florence, KY 41042 / 606-342-2380

Marksman Products, 5482 Argosy Dr., Huntington Beach, CA 92649 / 714-898-7535 or 800-822-8005; FAX: 714-891-0782

Marlin Firearms Co., 100 Kenna Dr., North Haven, CT 06473 / 203-239-5621; FAX: 203-234-7991

MarMik, Inc., 2116 S. Woodland Ave., Michigan City, IN 46360 / 219-872-7231; FAX: 219-872-7231

Marocchi F.lli S.p.A., Via Galileo Galilei 8, I-25068 Zanano, ITALY

Marquart Precision Co., (See Morrison Precision)

Marsh, Johnny, 1007 Drummond Dr., Nashville, TN 37211 / 615-833-3259

Marsh, Mike, Croft Cottage, Main St., Derbyshire, DE4 2BY ENGLAND / 01629 650 669

Marshall Enterprises, 792 Canyon Rd., Redwood City, CA 94062

Marshall F. Fish Mfg. Gunsmith Sptg. Co., Rd. Box 2439, Rt. 22 North, Westport, NY 12993 / 518-962-4897 FAX: 518-962-4897

Martin B. Retting Inc., 11029 Washington, Culver City, CA 90232 / 213-837-2412

Martin Hagn Rifles & Actions, P.O. Box 444, Cranbrook, BC V1C 4H9 CANADA / 604-489-4861

Martin's Gun Shop, 937 S. Sheridan Blvd., Lakewood, CO 80226 / 303-922-2184

Martz, John V., 8060 Lakeview Lane, Lincoln, CA 95648 FAX: 916-645-3815

Marvel, Alan, 3922 Madonna Rd., Jarretsville, MD 21084 / 301-557-6545

Marx, Harry (See U.S. Importer for FERLIB)

Maryland Paintball Supply, 8507 Harford Rd., Parkville, MD 21234 / 410-882-5607

MAST Technology, 4350 S. Arville, Suite 3, Las Vegas, NV 89103 / 702-362-5043; FAX: 702-362-9554

Master Engravers, Inc. (See Hendricks, Frank E)

Master Lock Co., 2600 N. 32nd St., Milwaukee, WI 53245 / 414-444-2800

Match Prep-Doyle Gracey, P.O. Box 155, Tehachapi, CA 93581 / 661-822-5383; FAX: 661-823-8680

Matco, Inc., 1003-2nd St., N. Manchester, IN 46962 / 219-982-8282

Mathews & Son, Inc., George E., 10224 S Paramount Blvd., Downey, CA 90241 / 562-862-6719; FAX: 562-862-6719

Matthews Cutlery, 4401 Sentry Dr., Tucker, GA 30084 / 770-939-6915

Mauser Werke Oberndorf Waffensysteme GmbH, Postfach 1349, 78722, Oberndorf/N, GERMANY

Maverick Arms, Inc., 7 Grasso Ave., P.O. Box 497, North Haven, CT 06473 / 203-230-5300; FAX: 203-230-5420

Maxi-Mount, P.O. Box 291, Willoughby Hills, OH 44094-0291 / 216-944-9456; FAX: 216-944-9456

Maximum Security Corp., 32841 Calle Perfecto, San Juan Capistrano, CA 92675 / 714-493-3684; FAX: 714-496-7733

Mayville Engineering Co. (See MEC, Inc.)

Mazur Restoration, Pete, 13083 Drummer Way, Grass Valley, CA 95949 / 530-268-2412

McBros Rifle Co., P.O. Box 86549, Phoenix, AZ 85080 / 602-582-3713; FAX: 602-581-3825

McCament, Jay, 1730-134th St. Ct. S., Tacoma, WA 98444 / 253-531-8832

McCann Industries, P.O. Box 641, Spanaway, WA 98387 / 253-537-6919; FAX: 253-537-6919 mccann.machine@worldnet.att.net www.mccannindustries.com

McCann's Machine & Gun Shop, P.O. Box 641, Spanaway, WA 98387 / 253-537-6919; FAX: 253-537-6993 mccann.machine@worldnet.att.net

McCann's Muzzle-Gun Works, 14 Walton Dr., New Hope, PA 18938 / 215-862-2728

McCluskey Precision Rifles, 10502 14th Ave. NW, Seattle, WA 98177 / 206-781-2776

McCombs, Leo, 1862 White Cemetery Rd., Patriot, OH 45658 / 614-256-1714

McCormick Corp., Chip, 1825 Fortview Rd Ste 115, Austin, TX 78704 / 800-328-CHIP; FAX: 512-462-0009

McCullough, Ken. (See KEN'S RIFLE BLANKS)

McDonald, Dennis, 8359 Brady St., Peosta, IA 52068 / 319-556-7940

McFarland, Stan, 2221 Idella Ct., Grand Junction, CO 81505 / 970-243-4704

McGhee, Larry, (See B.C. OUTDOORS)

McGowen Rifle Barrels, 5961 Spruce Lane, St. Anne, IL 60964 / 815-937-9816; FAX: 815-937-4024

McGuire, Bill, 1600 N. Eastmont Ave., East Wenatchee, WA 98802 / 509-884-6021

Mchalik, Gary (See ROSSI FIREARMS, BRAZTECH)

McKenzie, Lynton, 6940 N. Alvernon Way, Tucson, AZ 85718 / 520-299-5090

McKillen & Heyer, Inc., 35535 Euclid Ave., Suite 11, Willoughby, OH 44094 / 216-942-2044

McKinney, R.P. (See Schuetzen Gun Co.)

McMillan Fiberglass Stocks, Inc, 21421 N. 14th Ave., Suite B, Phoenix, AZ 85027 / 602-582-9635; FAX: 602-581-3825

McMillan Optical Gunsight Co., 28638 N. 42nd St., Cave Creek, AZ 85331 / 602-585-7868; FAX: 602-585-7872

McMillan Rifle Barrels, P.O. Box 3427, Bryan, TX 77805 / 409-690-3456; FAX: 409-690-0156

McMurdo, Lynn (See Specialty Gunsmithing), PO Box 404, Afton, WY 83110 / 307-886-5535

MCRW Associates Shooting Supplies, R.R. 1, Box 1425, Sweet Valley, PA 18656 / 717-864-3967; FAX: 717-864-2669

MCS, Inc., 34 Delmar Dr., Brookfield, CT 06804 / 203-775-1013; FAX: 203-775-9462

McWelco Products, 6730 Santa Fe Ave., Hesperia, CA 92345 / 619-244-8876; FAX: 619-244-9398

MDS, P.O. Box 1441, Brandon, FL 33509-1441 / 813-653-1180; FAX: 813-684-5953

MANUFACTURER'S DIRECTORY

Meadow Industries, 24 Club Lane, Palmyra, VA 22963 / 804-589-7672; FAX: 804-589-7672

Measurement Group Inc., Box 27777, Raleigh, NC 27611

Measures, Leon. (See SHOOT WHERE YOU LOOK)

MEC, Inc., 715 South St., Mayville, WI 53050 / 414-387-4500; FAX: 414-387-5802 reloaders@mayvl.com www.mayvl.com

MEC-Gar S.r.l., Via Madonnina 64, Gardone V.T. Brescia, ITALY / 39-30-8912687; FAX: 39-30-8910065

MEC-Gar U.S.A., Inc., Box 112, 500B Monroe Turnpike, Monroe, CT 06468 / 203-635-8662; FAX: 203-635-8662

Mech-Tech Systems, Inc., 1602 Foothill Rd., Kalispell, MT 59901 / 406-755-8055

Meister Bullets (See Gander Mountain)

Mele, Frank, 201 S. Wellow Ave., Cookeville, TN 38501 / 615-526-4860

Melton Shirt Co., Inc., 56 Harvester Ave., Batavia, NY 14020 / 716-343-8750; FAX: 716-343-6887

Men-Metalwerk Elisenhuette GmbH, D-56372 GERMANY / 2604-7819

Menck, Gunsmith Inc., T.W., 5703 S 77th St, Ralston, NE 68127

Mendez, John A., P.O. Box 620984, Orlando, FL 32862 / 407-344-2791

Meprolight (See Hesco-Meprolight)

Mercer Custom Stocks, R. M., 216 S Whitewater Ave, Jefferson, WI 53549 / 920-674-3839

Merit Corp., Box 9044, Schenectady, NY 12309 / 518-346-1420

Merkel Freres, Strasse 7 October, 10, Suhl, GERMANY

Merkuria Ltd., Argentinska 38, 17005, Praha 7 CZECH. REPUBLIC / 422-875117; FAX: 422-809152

Metal Merchants, PO Box 186, Walled Lake, MI 48390-0186

Metalife Industries (See Mahovsky's Metalife)

Metaloy, Inc., Rt. 5, Box 595, Berryville, AR 72616 / 501-545-3611

Metals Hand Engraver/European Hand Engraving, Ste. 216, 12 South First St., San Jose, CA 95113 / 408-293-6559

MI-TE Bullets, 1396 Ave. K, Ellsworth, KS 67439 / 785-472-4575; FAX: 785-472-5579

Michael's Antiques, Box 591, Waldoboro, ME 04572

Michaels Of Oregon, 1710 Red Soils Ct., Oregon City, OR 97045

Micro Sight Co., 242 Harbor Blvd., Belmont, CA 94002 / 415-591-0769; FAX: 415-591-7531

Microfusion Alfa S.A., Paseo San Andres N8, P.O. Box 271, Eibar, 20600 SPAIN / 34-43-11-89-16; FAX: 34-43-11-40-38

Mid-America Guns and Ammo, 1205 W. Jefferson, Suite E, Effingham, IL 62401 / 800-820-5177

Mid-America Recreation, Inc., 1328 5th Ave., Moline, IL 61265 / 309-764-5089; FAX: 309-764-2722

Middlebrooks Custom Shop, 7366 Colonial Trail East, Surry, VA 23883 / 757-357-0881; FAX: 757-365-0442

Midway Arms, Inc., 5875 W. Van Horn Tavern Rd., Columbia, MO 65203 / 800-243-3220 or 573-445-6363; FAX: 573-446-1018

Midwest Gun Sport, 1108 Herbert Dr., Zebulon, NC 27597 / 919-269-5570

Midwest Sport Distributors, Box 129, Fayette, MO 65248

Mike Davis Products, 643 Loop Dr., Moses Lake, WA 98817 / 509-765-6178 or 509-766-7281

Milberry House Publishing, PO Box 575, Corydon, IN 47112 / 888-738-1567; FAX: 888-738-1567

Military Armament Corp., P.O. Box 120, Mt. Zion Rd., Lingleville, TX 76461 / 817-965-3253

Millennium Designed Muzzleloaders, PO Box 536, Routes 11 & 25, Limington, ME 04049 / 207-637-2316

Miller Arms, Inc., P.O. Box 260 Purl St., St. Onge, SD 57779 / 605-642-5160; FAX: 605-642-5160

Miller Custom, 210 E. Julia, Clinton, IL 61727 / 217-935-9362

Miller Single Trigger Mfg. Co., Rt. 209, Box 1275, Millersburg, PA 17061 / 717-692-3704

Millett Sights, 7275 Murdy Circle, Adm. Office, Huntington Beach, CA 92647 / 714-842-5575 or 800-645-5388; FAX: 714-843-5707

Mills Jr., Hugh B., 3615 Canterbury Rd., New Bern, NC 28560 / 919-637-4631

Milstor Corp., 80-975 Indio Blvd., Indio, CA 92201 / 760-775-9998; FAX: 760-775-5229 milstor@webtv.net

---

Miltex, Inc., 700 S Lee St., Alexandria, VA 22314-4332 / 888-642-9123; FAX: 301-645-1430

Minute Man High Tech Industries, 10611 Canyon Rd. E., Suite 151, Puyallup, WA 98373 / 800-233-2734

Mirador Optical Corp., P.O. Box 11614, Marina Del Rey, CA 90295-7614 / 310-821-5587; FAX: 310-305-0386

Miroku, B C/Daly, Charles (See U.S. Importer-Bell's)

Mitchell, Jack, c/o Geoff Gaebe, Addieville East Farm, 200 Pheasant Dr, Mapleville, RI 02839 /

Mitchell Bullets, R.F., 430 Walnut St, Westernport, MD 21562

Mitchell Optics, Inc., 2072 CR 1100 N, Sidney, IL 61877 / 217-688-2219 or 217-621-3018; FAX: 217-688-2505

Mitchell's Accuracy Shop, 68 Greenridge Dr., Stafford, VA 22554 / 703-659-0165

Mittermeier, Inc., Frank, PO Box 2G, 3577 E Tremont Ave, Bronx, NY 10465 / 718-828-3843

Mixson Corp., 7635 W. 28th Ave., Hialeah, FL 33016 / 305-821-5190 or 800-327-0078; FAX: 305-558-9318

MJK Gunsmithing, Inc., 417 N. Huber Ct., E. Wenatchee, WA 98802 / 509-884-7683

MJM Mfg., 3283 Rocky Water Ln., Suite B, San Jose, CA 95148 / 408-270-4207

MKS Supply, Inc. (See Hi-Point Firearms)

MMC, 2513 East Loop 820 North, Ft. Worth, TX 76118 / 817-595-0404; FAX: 817-595-3074

MMP, Rt. 6, Box 384, Harrison, AR 72601 / 501-741-5019; FAX: 501-741-3104

Mo's Competitor Supplies (See MCS Inc)

Modern Gun Repair School, P.O. Box 92577, Southlake, TX 76092 / 800-493-4114; FAX: 800-556-5112

Modern Muzzleloading, Inc, PO Box 130, Centerville, IA 52544 / 515-856-2626

Moeller, Steve, 1213 4th St., Fulton, IL 61252 / 815-589-2300

Molin Industries, Tru-Nord Division, P.O. Box 365, 204 North 9th St., Brainerd, MN 56401 / 218-829-2870

Monell Custom Guns, 228 Red Mills Rd., Pine Bush, NY 12566 / 914-744-3021

Moneymaker Guncraft Corp., 1420 Military Ave., Omaha, NE 68131 / 402-556-0226

Montana Armory, Inc (See C. Sharps Arms Co. Inc.), 100 Centennial, Box 885, Big Timber, MT 59011 / 406-932-4353

Montana Outfitters, Lewis E. Yearout, 308 Riverview Dr. E., Great Falls, MT 59404 / 406-761-0859

Montana Precision Swaging, P.O. Box 4746, Butte, MT 59702 / 406-782-7502

Montana Vintage Arms, 2354 Bear Canyon Rd., Bozeman, MT 59715

Montgomery Community College, P.O. Box 787-GD, Troy, NC 27371 / 910-576-6222 or 800-839-6222; FAX: 910-576-2176

Morini (See U.S. Importers-Mandall Shooting Supplies, Inc..)

Morrison Custom Rifles, J. W., 4015 W Sharon, Phoenix, AZ 85029 / 602-978-3754

Morrison Precision, 6719 Calle Mango, Hereford, AZ 85615 / 520-378-6207 / morprec@c2i2.com (e-mail)

Morrow, Bud, 11 Hillside Lane, Sheridan, WY 82801-9729 / 307-674-8360

Morton Booth Co., P.O. Box 123, Joplin, MO 64802 / 417-673-1962; FAX: 417-673-3642

Moss Double Tone, Inc., P.O. Box 1112, 2101 S. Kentucky, Sedalia, MO 65301 / 816-827-0827

Mountain Hollow Game Calls, Box 121, Cascade, MD 21719 / 301-241-3282

Mountain Plains, Inc., 244 Glass Hollow Rd., Alton, VA 22920 / 800-687-3000

Mountain Rifles, Inc., P.O. Box 2789, Palmer, AK 99645 / 907-373-4194; FAX: 907-373-4195

Mountain South, P.O. Box 381, Barnwell, SC 29812 / FAX: 803-259-3227

Mountain State Muzzleloading Supplies, Inc., Box 154-1, Rt. 2, Williamstown, WV 26187 / 304-375-7842; FAX: 304-375-3737

Mountain View Sports, Inc., Box 188, Troy, NH 03465 / 603-357-9690; FAX: 603-357-9691

Mowrey Gun Works, P.O. Box 246, Waldron, IN 46182 / 317-525-6181; FAX: 317-525-9595

Mowrey's Guns & Gunsmithing, 119 Fredericks St., Canajoharie, NY 13317 / 518-673-3483

MPC, P.O. Box 450, McMinnville, TN 37110-0450 / 615-473-5513; FAX: 615-473-5516

MPI Stocks, PO Box 83266, Portland, OR 97283 / 503-226-1215; FAX: 503-226-2661

MSC Industrial Supply Co., 151 Sunnyside Blvd., Plainview, NY 11803-9915 / 516-349-0330

MSR Targets, P.O. Box 1042, West Covina, CA 91793 / 818-331-7840

Mt. Alto Outdoor Products, Rt. 735, Howardsville, VA 24562

Mt. Baldy Bullet Co., 12981 Old Hill City Rd., Keystone, SD 57751-6623 / 605-666-4725

MTM Molded Products Co., Inc., 3370 Obco Ct., Dayton, OH 45414 / 937-890-7461; FAX: 937-890-1747

Mulhern, Rick, Rt. 5, Box 152, Rayville, LA 71269 / 318-728-2688

Mullins Ammunition, Rt. 2, Box 304K, Clintwood, VA 24228 / 540-926-6772; FAX: 540-926-6092

Mullis Guncraft, 3523 Lawyers Road E., Monroe, NC 28110 / 704-283-6683

Multi-Scale Charge Ltd., 3269 Niagara Falls Blvd., N. Tonawanda, NY 14120 / 905-566-1255; FAX: 905-276-6295

Multiplex International, 26 S. Main St., Concord, NH 03301 / FAX: 603-796-2223

Multipropulseurs, La Bertrandiere, 42580, FRANCE / 77 74 01 30; FAX: 77 93 19 34

Mundy, Thomas A., 69 Robbins Road, Somerville, NJ 08876 / 201-722-2199

Murmur Corp., 2823 N. Westmoreland Ave., Dallas, TX 75222 / 214-630-5400

Murray State College, 1 Murray Campus St., Tishomingo, OK 73460 / 508-371-2371

Muscle Products Corp., 112 Fennell Dr., Butler, PA 16001 / 800-227-7049 or 412-283-0567; FAX: 412-283-8310

Museum of Historical Arms, Inc., 2750 Coral Way, Suite 204, Miami, FL 33145 / 305-444-9199

Mushroom Express Bullet Co., 601 W. 6th St., Greenfield, IN 46140-1728 / 317-462-6332

Muzzleloaders Etcetera, Inc., 9901 Lyndale Ave. S., Bloomington, MN 55420 / 612-884-1161 muzzleloaders-etcetera.com

Muzzleloading Technologies, Inc, 25 E. Hwy. 40, Suite 330-12, Roosevelt, UT 84066 / 801-722-5996; FAX: 801-722-5909

MWG Co., P.O. Box 971202, Miami, FL 33197 / 800-428-9394 or 305-253-8393; FAX: 305-232-1247

N

N&J Sales, Lime Kiln Rd., Northford, CT 06472 / 203-484-0247

N.B.B., Inc., 24 Elliot Rd., Sterling, MA 01564 / 508-422-7538 or 800-942-9444

N.C. Ordnance Co., P.O. Box 3254, Wilson, NC 27895 / 919-237-2440; FAX: 919-243-9845

Nagel's Custom Bullets, 100 Scott St., Baytown, TX 77520-2849

Nalpak, 1937-C Friendship Drive, El Cajon, CA 92020 / 619-258-1200

Nastoff's 45 Shop, Inc., Steve, 12288 Mahoning Ave, PO Box 446, North Jackson, OH 44451 / 330-538-2977

National Bullet Co., 1585 E. 361 St., Eastlake, OH 44095 / 216-951-1854; FAX: 216-951-7761

National Target Co., 4690 Wyaconda Rd., Rockville, MD 20852 / 800-827-7060 or 301-770-7060; FAX: 301-770-7892

Naval Ordnance Works, Rt. 2, Box 919, Sheperdstown, WV 25443 / 304-876-0098

Navy Arms Co., 689 Bergen Blvd., Ridgefield, NJ 07657 / 201-945-2500; FAX: 201-945-6859

NCP Products, Inc., 3500 12th St. N.W., Canton, OH 44708 / 330-456-5130; FAX: 330-456-5234

Neal Johnson's Gunsmithing, Inc., 208 W. Buchanan St., Suite B, Colorado Springs, CO 80907 / 800-284-8671; FAX: 719-632-3493

Necessary Concepts, Inc., P.O. Box 571, Deer Park, NY 11729 / 516-667-8509; FAX: 516-667-8588

Necromancer Industries, Inc., 14 Communications Way, West Newton, PA 15089 / 412-872-8722

NEI Handtools, Inc., 51583 Columbia River Hwy., Scappoose, OR 97056 / 503-543-6776; FAX: 503-543-6799

Neil A. Jones Custom Products, 17217 Brookhouser Road, Saegertown, PA 16433 / 814-763-2769; FAX: 814-763-4228

MANUFACTURER'S DIRECTORY

Nelson, Gary K., 975 Terrace Dr., Oakdale, CA 95361 / 209-847-4590

Nelson, Stephen, 7365 NW Spring Creek Dr., Corvallis, OR 97330 / 541-745-5232

Nelson/Weather-Rite, Inc., 14760 Santa Fe Trail Dr., Lenexa, KS 66215 / 913-492-3200; FAX:

Nesci Enterprises Inc., P.O. Box 119, Summit St., East Hampton, CT 06424 / 203-267-2588

Nesika Bay Precision, 22239 Big Valley Rd., Poulsbo, WA 98370 / 206-697-3830

Nettestad Gun Works, RR 1, Box 160, Pelican Rapids, MN 56572 / 218-863-4301

Neumann GmbH, Am Galgenberg 6, 90575, GERMA-NY / 09101/8256; FAX: 09101/6356

Nevada Pistol Academy, Inc., 4610 Blue Diamond Rd., Las Vegas, NV 89139 / 702-897-1100

New England Ammunition Co., 1771 Post Rd. East, Suite 223, Westport, CT 06880 / 203-254-8048

New England Arms Co., Box 278, Lawrence Lane, Kittery Point, ME 03905 / 207-439-0593; FAX:

New England Custom Gun Service, 438 Willow Brook Rd., Plainfield, NH 03781 / 603-469-3450; FAX: 603-469-3471 www.newenglandarms.com info@newenglandarms.com

New England Firearms, 60 Industrial Rowe, Gardner, MA 01440 / 508-632-9393; FAX: 508-632-2300

New Orleans Jewelers Supply Co., 206 Charters St., New Orleans, LA 70130 / 504-523-3839; FAX: 504-523-3836

New SKB Arms Co., C.P.O. Box 1401, Tokyo, JAPAN / 81-3-3943-9550; FAX: 81-3-3943-0695

New Win Publishing, Inc., 186 Center St., Clinton, NJ 08809 / 908-735-9701; FAX: 908-735-9703

Newark Electronics, 4801 N. Ravenswood Ave., Chicago, IL 60640

Newell, Robert H., 55 Coyote, Los Alamos, NM 87544 / 505-662-7135

Newman Gunshop, 119 Miller Rd., Agency, IA 52530 / 515-937-5775

Nicholson Custom, 17285 Thornlay Road, Hughesville, MO 65334 / 816-826-8746

Nickels, Paul R., 4789 Summerhill Rd., Las Vegas, NV 89121 / 702-435-5318

Nicklas, Ted, 5504 Hegel Rd., Goodrich, MI 48438 / 810-797-4493

Niemi Engineering, W. B., Box 126 Center Rd., Greensboro, VT 05841 / 802-533-7180; FAX:

Nightforce (See Lightforce USA Inc)

Nikolai leather, 15451 Electronic In, Huntington Beach, CA 92649 / 714-373-2721 FAX: 714-373-2723

Nikon, Inc., 1300 Walt Whitman Rd., Melville, NY 11747 / 516-547-8623; FAX: 516-547-0309

Nitex, Inc., P.O. Box 1706, Uvalde, TX 78801 / 888-543-8843

No-Sho Mfg. Co., 10727 Glenfield Ct., Houston, TX 77096 / 713-723-5332

Noreen, Peter H., 5075 Buena Vista Dr., Belgrade, MT 59714 / 406-586-7383

Norica, Avnda Otaola, 16 Apartado 68, Eibar, SPAIN

Norinco, 7A Yun Tan N, Beijing, CHINA

Norincoptics (See BEC, Inc.)

Norma Precision AB (See U.S. Importers-Dynamit Nobel-RWS, Inc.)

Normark Corp., 10395 Yellow Circle Dr., Minnetonka, MN 55343-9101 / 612-933-7060 FAX:

North American Arms, Inc., 2150 South 950 East, Provo, UT 84606-6285 / 800-821-5783 or 801-374-9990; FAX: 801-374-9998

North American Correspondence Schools The Gun Pro, Oak & Pawney St., Scranton, PA 18515 / 717-342-7701

North American Shooting Systems, P.O. Box 306, Osoyoos, BC V0H 1V0 CANADA / 604-495-3131; FAX: 604-495-2816

North Devon Firearms Services, 3 North St., Braunton, EX33 1AJ ENGLAND / 01271 813624; FAX: 01271 813624

North Fork Custom Gunsmithing, James Johnston, 428 Del Rio Rd., Roseburg, OR 97470 / 503-673-4467

North Mountain Pine Training Center (See Executive Protection Institute)

North Pass, 425 South Bowen St., Ste. 6, Longmount, CO 80501 / 303-682-4315; FAX: 303-678-7109

North Specialty Products, 2664-B Saturn St., Brea, CA 92621 / 714-524-1665

North Star West, P.O. Box 488, Glencoe, CA 95232 / 209-293-7010

North Wind Decoy Co., 1005 N. Tower Rd., Fergus Falls, MN 56537 / 218-736-4378; FAX:

Northern Precision Custom Swaged Bullets, 329 S. James St., Carthage, NY 13619 / 315-493-1711

Northlake Outdoor Footwear, P.O. Box 10, Franklin, TN 37065-0010 / 615-794-1556; FAX: 615-790-8005

Northside Gun Shop, 2725 NW 109th, Oklahoma City, OK 73120 / 405-840-2353

Northwest Arms, 26884 Pearl Rd., Parma, ID 83660 / 208-722-6771; FAX: 208-722-1062

Nosler, Inc., P.O. Box 671, Bend, OR 97709 / 800-285-3701 or 541-382-3921; FAX:

Novak's, Inc., 1206 1/2 30th St., P.O. Box 4045, Parkersburg, WV 26101 / 304-485-9295; FAX: 304-428-6722

Now Products, Inc., PO Box 27608, Tempe, AZ 85285 / 800-662-6063; FAX: 480-966-0890

Nowlin Mfg. Co., 20622 S 4092 Rd., Claremore, OK 74017 / 918-342-0689; FAX: 918-342-0624

NRI Gunsmith School, 4401 Connecticut Ave. NW, Washington, DC 20008

Nu-Line Guns,Inc., 1053 Caulks Hill Rd., Harvester, MO 63304 / 314-441-4500 or 314-447-4501; FAX: 314-447-5018

Null Holsters Ltd. K.L., 161 School St NW, Resaca, GA 30735 / 706-625-5643; FAX: 706-625-9392

Numrich Arms Corp., 203 Broadway, W. Hurley, NY 12491

NW Sinker and Tackle, 380 Valley Dr., Myrtle Creek, OR 97457-9717

Nygord Precision Products, P.O. Box 12578, Prescott, AZ 86304 / 520-717-2315; FAX: 520-717-2198

O

O.F. Mossberg & Sons,Inc., 7 Grasso Ave., North Haven, CT 06473 / 203-230-5300; FAX: 203-230-5420

Oakland Custom Arms,Inc., 4690 W. Walton Blvd., Waterford, MI 48329 / 810-674-8261

Oakman Turkey Calls, RD 1, Box 825, Harrisonville, PA 17228 / 717-485-4620

Obermeyer Rifled Barrels, 23122 60th St., Bristol, WI 53104 / 262-843-3537; FAX: 262-843-2129

October Country Muzzleloading, P.O. Box 969, Dept. GD, Hayden, ID 83835 / 208-772-2068; FAX: 208-772-9230 octobercountry.com

Oehler Research,Inc., P.O. Box 9135, Austin, TX 78766 / 512-327-6900 or 800-531-5125; FAX: 512-327-6903

Oil Rod and Gun Shop, 69 Oak St., East Douglas, MA 01516 / 508-476-3687

Ojala Holsters, Arvo, PO Box 98, N Hollywood, CA 91603 / 503-669-1404

OK Weber,Inc., P.O. Box 7485, Eugene, OR 97401 / 541-747-0458; FAX: 541-747-5927

Oker's Engraving, 365 Bell Rd., P.O. Box 126, Shawnee, CO 80475 / 303-838-6042

Oklahoma Ammunition Co., 3701A S. Harvard Ave., No. 367, Tulsa, OK 74135-2265 / 918-396-3187; FAX: 918-396-4270

Oklahoma Leather Products,Inc., 500 26th NW, Miami, OK 74354 / 918-542-6651; FAX: 918-542-6653

Old Wagon Bullets, 32 Old Wagon Rd., Wilton, CT 06897

Old West Bullet Moulds, J Ken Chapman, P.O. Box 519, Flora Vista, NM 87415 / 505-334-6970

Old West Reproductions,Inc. R.M. Bachman, 446 Florence S. Loop, Florence, MT 59833 / 406-273-2615; FAX: 406-273-2615

Old Western Scrounger,Inc., 12924 Hwy. A-12, Montague, CA 96064 / 916-459-5445; FAX: 916-459-3944

Old World Gunsmithing, 2901 SE 122nd St., Portland, OR 97236 / 503-760-7681

Old World Oil Products, 3827 Queen Ave. N., Minneapolis, MN 55412 / 612-522-5037

Ole Frontier Gunsmith Shop, 2617 Hwy. 29 S., Cantonment, FL 32533 / 904-477-8074

Olson, Myron, 989 W. Kemp, Watertown, SD 57201 / 605-886-9787

Olson, Vic, 5002 Countryside Dr., Imperial, MO 63052 / 314-296-8086

Olympic Arms Inc., 620-626 Old Pacific Hwy. SE, Olympia, WA 98513 / 360-491-3447; FAX: 360-491-3447

Olympic Optical Co., P.O. Box 752377, Memphis, TN 38175-2377 / 901-794-3890 or 800-238-7120; FAX: 901-794-0676 80

Omark Industries,Div. of Blount,Inc., 2299 Snake River Ave., P.O. Box 856, Lewiston, ID 83501 / 208-746-2351

Omega Sales, P.O. Box 1066, Mt. Clemens, MI 48043 / 810-469-7323; FAX: 810-469-0425

One Of A Kind, 15610 Purple Sage, San Antonio, TX 78255 / 512-695-3364

Op-Tec, P.O. Box L632, Langhorn, PA 19047 / 215-757-5037

Optical Services Co., P.O. Box 1174, Santa Teresa, NM 88008-1174 / 505-589-3833

Orchard Park Enterprise, P.O. Box 563, Orchard Park, NY 14227 / 616-656-0356

Oregon Arms, Inc. (See Rogue Rifle Co., Inc.)

Oregon Trail Bullet Company, P.O. Box 529, Dept. P, Baker City, OR 97814 / 800-811-0548; FAX:

Original Box, nc., 700 Linden Ave., York, PA 17404 / 717-854-2897; FAX: 717-845-4276

Original Mink Oil,Inc., 10652 NE Holman, Portland, OR 97220 / 503-255-2814 or 800-547-5895; FAX: 503-255-2487

Orion Rifle Barrel Co., RR2, 137 Cobler Village, Kalispell, MT 59901 / 406-257-5649

Otis Technology, Inc, RR 1 Box 84, Boonville, NY 13309 / 315-942-3320

Ottmar, Maurice, Box 657, 113 E. Fir, Coulee City, WA 99115 / 509-632-5717

Outa-Site Gun Carriers, 219 Market St., Laredo, TX 78040 / 210-722-4678 or 800-880-9715; FAX:

Outdoor Edge Cutlery Corp., 2888 Bluff St., Suite 130, Boulder, CO 80301 / 303-652-8212; FAX:

Outdoor Enthusiast, 3784 W. Woodland, Springfield, MO 65807 / 417-883-9841

Outdoor Sports Headquarters,Inc., 967 Watertower Ln., West Carrollton, OH 45449 / 513-865-5855; FAX: 513-865-5962

Outers Laboratories Div. of Blount, Inc.Sporting E, Route 2, P.O. Box 39, Onalaska, WI 54650 / 608-781-5800; FAX: 608-781-0368

Ox-Yoke Originals, Inc., 34 Main St., Milo, ME 04463 / 800-231-8313 or 207-943-7351; FAX:

Ozark Gun Works, 11830 Cemetery Rd., Rogers, AR 72756 / 501-631-6944; FAX: 501-631-6944 ogw@hotmail.com http://members.tripod.com-ozarkw1

P

P&M Sales and Service, 5724 Gainsborough Pl., Oak Forest, IL 60452 / 708-687-7149

P.A.C.T., Inc., P.O. Box 531525, Grand Prairie, TX 75053 / 214-641-0049

P.M. Enterprises,Inc. 146 Curtis Hill Rd., Chehalis, WA 98532 / 360-748-3743; FAX: 360-748-1802

P.S.M.G. Gun Co., 10 Park Ave., Arlington, MA 02174 / 617-646-8845; FAX: 617-646-2133

Pac-Nor Barreling, 99299 Overlook Rd., P.O. Box 6188, Brookings, OR 97415 / 503-469-7330; FAX: 503-469-7331

Pace Marketing, Inc., P.O. Box 2039, Stuart, FL 34995 / 561-871-9682; FAX: 561-871-6552

Pachmayr Div. Lyman Products, 1875 S. Mountain Ave., Monrovia, CA 91016 / 626-357-7771

Pacific Cartridge, Inc., 2425 Salashan Loop Road, Ferndale, WA 98248 / 360-366-4444; FAX: 360-366-4445

Pacific Research Laboratories, Inc. (See Rimrock R

Pacific Rifle Co., PO Box 1473, Lake Oswego, OR 97035 / 503-538-7437

Paco's (See Small Custom Mould & Bullet Co)

Page Custom Bullets, P.O. Box 25, Port Moresby, NEW GUINEA

Pagel Gun Works, Inc., 1407 4th St. NW, Grand Rapids, MN 55744 / 218-326-3003

Pager Pal, 200 W Pleasantview, Hurst, TX 76054 / 800-561-1603 FAX: 817-285-8769 www.pagerpal.com

Paintball Games International Magazine (Aceville Publications, Castle House) 97 High St., Essex, ENGLAND / 011-44-206-564840

Palmer Security Products, 2930 N. Campbell Ave., Chicago, IL 60618 / 800-788-7725; FAX: 773-267-8080

Palsa Outdoor Products, P.O. Box 81336, Lincoln, NE 68501 / 402-488-5288; FAX: 402-488-2321

Para-Ordnance Mfg., Inc., 980 Tapscott Rd., Scarborough, ON M1X 1E7 CANADA / 416-297-7855; FAX: 416-297-1289

Para-Ordnance, Inc., 1919 NE 45th St., Ste 215, Ft. Lauderdale, FL 33308

Paragon Sales & Services, Inc., 2501 Theodore St, Crest Hill, IL 60435-1613 / 815-725-9212; FAX: 815-725-8974

Pardini Armi Srl, Via Italica 154, 55043, Lido Di Camaiore Lu, ITALY / 584-90121; FAX: 584-90122

Paris, Frank J., 17417 Pershing St., Livonia, MI 48152-3822

Parker & Sons Shooting Supply, 9337 Smoky Row Rd, Straw Plains, TN 97871-1257

Parker Gun Finishes, 9337 Smokey Row Rd., Strawberry Plains, TN 37871 / 423-933-3286

Parker Reproductions, 124 River Rd., Middlesex, NJ 08846 / 908-469-0100 FAX: 908-469-9692

Parsons Optical Mfg. Co., P.O. Box 192, Ross, OH 45061 / 513-867-0820; FAX: 513-867-8380

Partridge Sales Ltd., John, Trent Meadows, Rugeley, ENGLAND

Parts & Surplus, P.O. Box 22074, Memphis, TN 38122 / 901-683-4007

Pasadena Gun Center, 206 E. Shaw, Pasadena, TX 77506 / 713-472-0417; FAX: 713-472-1322

Passive Bullet Traps, Inc. (See Savage Range Systems, Inc..)

PAST Sporting Goods,Inc., P.O. Box 1035, Columbia, MO 65205 / 314-445-9200; FAX: 314-446-6606

Paterson Gunsmithing, 438 Main St., Paterson, NJ 07502 / 201-345-4100

Pathfinder Sports Leather, 2920 E. Chambers St., Phoenix, AZ 85040 / 602-276-0016

Patrick Bullets, P.O. Box 172, Warwick, QSLD, 4370 AUSTRALIA

Patrick W. Price Bullets, 16520 Worthley Drive, San Lorenzo, CA 94580 / 510-278-1547

Pattern Control, 114 N. Third St., P.O. Box 462105, Garland, TX 75046 / 214-494-3551; FAX: 214-272-8447

Paul A. Harris Hand Engraving, 113 Rusty Lane, Boerne, TX 78006-5746 / 512-391-5121

Paul D. Hillmer Custom Gunstocks, 7251 Hudson Heights, Hudson, IA 50643 / 319-988-3941

Paul Jones Moulds, 4901 Telegraph Rd., Los Angeles, CA 90022 / 213-262-1510

Paulsen Gunstocks, Rt. 71, Box 11, Chinook, MT 59523 / 406-357-3403

Pawling Mountain Club, Keith Lupton, PO Box 573, Pawling, NY 12564 / 914-855-3825

Paxton Quigley's Personal Protection Strategies, 9903 Santa Monica Blvd., 300, Beverly Hills, CA 90212 / 310-281-1762 www.defend-net.com/paxton

Payne Photography, Robert, Robert, P.O. Box 141471, Austin, TX 78714 / 512-272-4554

PC Co., 5942 Secor Rd., Toledo, OH 43623 / 419-472-6222

Peacemaker Specialists, P.O. Box 157, Whitmore, CA 96096 / 916-472-3438

Pearce Grip, Inc., P.O. Box 187, Bothell, WA 98011-0187 / 206-485-5488; FAX: 206-488-9497

Pease Accuracy, Bob, P.O. Box 310787, New Braunfels, TX 78131 / 210-625-1342

Pedersen, Rex C., 2717 S. Pere Marquette Hwy., Ludington, MI 49431 / 616-843-2061

Peebles Alloy, Inc., 1445 Osage St., Denver, CO 80204-2439 / 303-825-6394 or 800-253-1278

Peet Shoe Dryer, Inc., 130 S. 5th St., P.O. Box 618, St. Maries, ID 83861 / 208-245-2095 or 800-222-PEET; FAX: 208-245-5441

Peifer Rifle Co., P.O. Box 192, Nokomis, IL 62075-0192 / 217-563-7050; FAX: 217-563-7060

Pejsa Ballistics, 2120 Kenwood Pkwy., Minneapolis, MN 55405 / 612-374-3337; FAX: 612-374-5383

Pelaire Products, 5346 Bonky Ct., W. Palm Beach, FL 33415 / 561-439-0691; FAX: 561-967-0052

Pell, John T. (See KOGOT)

Peltor, Inc. (See Aero Peltor)

PEM's Mfg. Co., 5063 Waterloo Rd., Atwater, OH 44201 / 216-947-3721

Pence Precision Barrels, 7567 E. 900 S., S. Whitley, IN 46787 / 219-839-4745

Pendleton Royal, c/o Swingler Buckland Ltd., 4/7 Highgate St, Birmingham, ENGLAND/ 44 121 440 3060 or 44 121 446 5898; FAX: 44 121 446 4165

Pendleton Woolen Mills, P.O. Box 3030, 220 N.W. Broadway, Portland, OR 97208 / 503-226-4801

Penn Bullets, P.O. Box 756, Indianola, PA 15051

Penn's Woods Products, Inc., 19 W. Pittsburgh St., Delmont, PA 15626 / 412-468-8311; FAX: 412-468-8975

Pennsylvania Gun Parts Inc, PO Box 665, 300 Third St, East Berlin, PA 17316-0665 / 717-259-8010; FAX: 717-259-0057

Pennsylvania Gunsmith School, 812 Ohio River Blvd., Avalon, Pittsburgh, PA 15202 / 412-766-1812 FAX: 412-766-0855 pgs@pagunsmith.com www.pagunsmith.com

Penrod Precision, 312 College Ave., P.O. Box 307, N. Manchester, IN 46962 / 219-982-8385

Pentax Corp., 35 Inverness Dr. E., Englewood, CO 80112 / 303-799-8000; FAX: 303-790-1131

Penthouse de Pentheny, 108 Petaluma Ave #202, Sebastopol, CA 95472-4220 / 707-573-1390; FAX: 707-573-1390

Perazone-Gunsmith, Brian, Cold Spring Rd, Roxbury, NY 12474 / 607-326-4088; FAX: 607-326-3140

Perazzi USA, Inc., 1207 S. Shamrock Ave., Monrovia, CA 91016 / 626-303-0068; FAX: 626-303-2081

Performance Specialists, 308 Eanes School Rd., Austin, TX 78746 / 512-327-0119

Perugini Visini & Co. S.r.l., Via Camprelle, 126, 25080 Nuvolera, ITALY / 30-6897535; FAX: 30-6897821

Pete Elsen, Inc., 1529 S. 113th St., West Allis, WI 53214

Pete Mazur Restoration, 13083 Drummer Way, Grass Valley, CA 95949 / 916-268-2412

Pete Rickard, Inc., 115 Roy Walsh Rd, Cobleskill, NY 12043 / 518-234-2731: FAX: 518-234-2454 rickard@telenet.net peterickard.com

Peter Dyson & Son Ltd., 3 Cuckoo Lane, Honley Huddersfield, Yorkshire, HD7 2BR ENGLAND / 44-1484-661062; FAX: 44-1484-663709

Peter Hale/Engraver, 800 E. Canyon Rd., Spanish Fork, UT 84660 / 801-798-8215

Peters Stahl GmbH, Stettiner Strasse 42, D-33106, Paderborn, / 05251-750025; FAX: 05251-75611

Petersen Publishing Co., (See Emap USA)

Peterson Gun Shop, Inc., A.W., 4255 W. Old U.S. 441, Mt. Dora, FL 32757-3299 / 352-383-4258; FAX: 352-735-1001

Petro-Explo Inc., 7650 U.S. Hwy., 287, Suite 100, Arlington, TX 76017 / 817-478-8888

Pettinger Books, Gerald, Rt. 2, Box 125, Russell, IA 50238 / 515-535-2239

Pflumm Mfg. Co., 10662 Widmer Rd., Lenexa, KS 66215 / 800-888-4867; FAX: 913-451-7857

PFRB Co., P.O. Box 1242, Bloomington, IL 61702 / 309-473-3964; FAX: 309-473-2161

Philip S. Olt Co., P.O. Box 550, 12662 Fifth St., Pekin, IL 61554 / 309-348-3633; FAX: 309-348-3300

Phillippi Custom Bullets, Justin, P.O. Box 773, Ligonier, PA 15658 / 724-238-2962; FAX: 724-238-9671

Phillips & Rogers, Inc., 100 Hilbig #C, Conroe, TX 77301 / 409-435-0011

Phoenix Arms, 1420 S. Archibald Ave., Ontario, CA 91761 / 909-947-4843; FAX: 909-947-6798

Photronic Systems Engineering Company, 6731 Via De La Reina, Bonsall, CA 92003 / 619-758-8000

Piedmont Community College, P.O. Box 1197, Roxboro, NC 27573 / 336-599-1181 FAX: 336-597-3817 www.piedmont.cc.nc.us

Pierce Pistols, 55 Sorrelwood Lane, Sharpsburg, GA 30277-9523 / 404-253-8192

Pietta (See U.S. Importers-Navy Arms Co, Taylor's & Co..)

Pilgrim Pewter,Inc. (See Bell Originals Inc. Sid)

Pilkington, Scott (See Little Trees Ramble)

Pine Technical College, 1100 4th St., Pine City, MN 55063 / 800-521-7463; FAX: 612-629-6766

Pinetree Bullets, 133 Skeena St., Kitimat, BC V8C 1Z1 CANADA / 604-632-3768; FAX: 604-632-3768

Pioneer Arms Co., 355 Lawrence Rd., Broomall, PA 19008 / 215-356-5203

Piotti (See U.S. Importer-Moore & Co, Wm. Larkin)

Piquette, Paul R., 80 Bradford Dr., Feeding Hills, MA 01030 / 413-786-8118; or 413-789-4582

Plaxco, J. Michael, Rt. 1, P.O. Box 203, Roland, AR 72135 / 501-868-9787

Plaza Cutlery, Inc., 3333 Bristol, 161 South Coast Plaza, Costa Mesa, CA 92626 / 714-549-3932

Plum City Ballistic Range, N2162 80th St., Plum City, WI 54761 / 715-647-2539

PlumFire Press, Inc., 30-A Grove Ave., Patchogue, NY 11772-4112 / 800-695-7246; FAX: 516-758-4071

PMC/Eldorado Cartridge Corp., P.O. Box 62508, 12801 U.S. Hwy. 95 S., Boulder City, NV 89005 / 702-294-0025; FAX: 702-294-0121

Poburka, Philip (See Bison Studios)

Pohl, Henry A. (See Great American Gun Co.

Pointing Dog Journal, Village Press Publications, P.O. Box 968, Dept. PGD, Traverse City, MI 49685 / 800-272-3246; FAX: 616-946-3289

Police Bookshelf, P.O. Box 122, Concord, NH 03301 / 603-224-6814; FAX: 603-226-3554

Polywad, Inc., P.O. Box 7916, Macon, GA 31209 / 912-477-0669 polywadmpb@aol.com www.polywad.com

Pomeroy, Robert, RR1, Box 50, E. Corinth, ME 04427 / 207-285-7721

Ponsness/Warren, P.O. Box 8, Rathdrum, ID 83858 / 208-687-2231; FAX: 208-687-2233

Pony Express Reloaders, 608 E. Co. Rd. D, Suite 3, St. Paul, MN 55117 / 612-483-9406; FAX: 612-483-9884

Pony Express Sport Shop, 16606 Schoenborn St., North Hills, CA 91343 / 818-895-1231

Potts, Wayne E., 912 Poplar St, Denver, CO 80220 / 303-355-5462

Powder Horn Antiques, P.O. Box 4196, Ft. Lauderdale, FL 33338 / 305-565-6060

Powell & Son (Gunmakers) Ltd., William, 35-37 Carrs Lane, Birmingham, B4 7SX ENGLAND / 121-643-0689; FAX: 121-631-3504

Powell Agency, William, 22 Circle Dr., Bellmore, NY 11710 / 516-679-1158

Power Custom, Inc., 29739 Hwy. J, Gravois Mills, MO 65037 / 513-372-5684; FAX: 573-372-5799 pwpowers@laurie.net www.powercustom.com

Power Plus Enterprises, Inc., PO Box 38, Warm Springs, GA 31830 / 706-655-2132

Powley Computer (See Hutton Rifle Ranch)

Practical Tools, Inc., 7067 Easton Rd., P.O. Box 133, Pipersville, PA 18947 / 215-766-7301; FAX: 215-766-8681

Prairie Gun Works, 1-761 Marion St., Winnipeg, MB R2J 0K6 Canada / 204-231-2976; FAX: 204-231-8566

Prairie River Arms, 1220 N. Sixth St., Princeton, IL 61356 / 815-875-1616 or 800-445-1541; FAX: 815-875-1402

Pranger, Ed G., 1414 7th St., Anacortes, WA 98221 / 206-293-3488

Pre-Winchester 92-90-62 Parts Co., P.O. Box 8125, W. Palm Beach, FL 33407

Precise Metalsmithing Enterprises, 146 Curtis Hill Rd., Chehalis, WA 98532 / 206-748-3743; FAX: 206-748-8102

Precision Airgun Sales, Inc., 5247 Warrensville Ctr Rd, Maple Hts., OH 44137 / 216-587-5005 FAX: 216-587-5005

Precision Cartridge, 176 Eastside Rd., Deer Lodge, MT 59722 / 800-397-3901 or 406-846-3900

Precision Cast Bullets, 101 Mud Creek Lane, Ronan, MT 59864 / 406-676-5135

Precision Castings & Equipment, P.O. Box 326, Jasper, IN 47547-0135 / 812-634-9167

Precision Components, 3177 Sunrise Lake, Milford, PA 18337 / 570-686-4414

Precision Components and Guns, Rt. 55, P.O. Box 337, Pawling, NY 12564 / 914-855-3040

Precision Delta Corp., P.O. Box 128, Ruleville, MS 38771 / 601-756-2810; FAX: 601-756-2590

Precision Gun Works, 104 Sierra Rd Dept. GD, Kerrville, TX 78028 / 830-367-4587

Precision Munitions, Inc., P.O. Box 326, Jasper, IN 47547

Precision Reloading, Inc., P.O. Box 122, Stafford Springs, CT 06076 / 860-684-5680 FAX: 860-684-6788

Precision Sales International, Inc., P.O. Box 1776, Westfield, MA 01086 / 413-562-5055; FAX: 413-562-5056

MANUFACTURER'S DIRECTORY

Precision Shooting,Inc., 222 McKee St., Manchester, CT 06040 / 860-645-8776; FAX: 860-643-8215

Precision Small Arms, 9777 Wilshire Blvd., Suite 1005, Beverly Hills, CA 90212 / 310-859-4867; FAX: 310-859-2868

Precision Small Arms Inc., 9272 Jeronimo Rd, Ste 121, Irvine, CA 92618 / 800-554-5515; FAX: 949-768-4808 www.tcbebe.com

Precision Specialties, 131 Hendom Dr., Feeding Hills, MA 01030 / 413-786-3365; FAX: 413-786-3365

Precision Sport Optics, 15571 Producer Lane, Unit G, Huntington Beach, CA 92649/714-891-1309; FAX: 714-892-6920

Premier Reticles, 920 Breckinridge Lane, Winchester, VA 22601-6707/ 540-722-0601; FAX: 540-722-3522

Prescott Projectile Co., 1808 Meadowbrook Road, Prescott, AZ 86303

Presik's Gunstocks, 4245 Keith Ln., Chico, CA 95926/ 916-891-8236

Price Bullets, Patrick W., 16520 Worthley Dr., San Lorenzo, CA 94580 / 510-278-1547

Prime Reloading, 30 Chiswick End, Meldreth, ROYS-TON UK / 0763-260636

Primos, Inc., P.O. Box 12785, Jackson, MS 39236-2785 / 601-366-1288; FAX: 601-362-3274

PRL Bullets, c/o Blackburn Enterprises, 114 Stuart Rd., Ste. 110, Cleveland, TN 37312 / 423-559-0340

Pro Load Ammunition, Inc., 5180 E. Seltice Way, Post Falls, ID 83854 / 208-773-9444; FAX:

Pro-Mark Div. of Wells Lamont, 6640 W. Touhy, Chicago, IL 60648 / 312-647-8200

Pro-Port Ltd., 41302 Executive Dr., Harrison Twp., MI 48045-1306 / 810-469-6727 FAX: 810-469-0425

Pro-Shot Products, Inc., P.O. Box 763, Taylorville, IL 62568 / 217-824-9133; FAX: 217-824-8861

Professional Gunsmiths of America,Inc., Route 1, Box 224f, Lexington, MO 64067 / 816-259-2636

Professional Hunter Supplies (See Star Custom Bullets), PO Box 608, 468 Main St, Ferndale, CA 95536 / 707-786-9140; FAX: 707-786-9117

Professional Ordnance, Inc., 1215 E. Airport Dr., Box 182, Ontario, CA 91761 / 909-923-5559; FAX:

Prolixr Lubricants, P.O. Box 1348, Victorville, CA 92393 / 800-248-5823 or 760-243-3129; FAX: 760-241-0148

Proofmark Corp., P.O. Box 610, Burgess, VA 22432 / 804-453-4337; FAX: 804-453-4337 proofmark@nv-net.net

Protektor Model, 1-11 Bridge St., Galeton, PA 16922 / 814-435-2442

Prototech Industries, Inc., Rt. 1, Box 81, Delia, KS 66418 / 913-771-3571; FAX: 913-771-2531

ProWare, Inc., 15847 NE Hancock St., Portland, OR 97230 / 503-239-0159

PWL Gunleather, P.O. Box 450432, Atlanta, GA 31145 / 770-822-1640; FAX: 770-822-1704 covert@pwlusa.com www.pwlusa.com

Pyramid, Inc., 3292 S. Highway 97, Redmond, OR 97756 / 503-548-1041; FAX: 503-923-1004

Q

Quack Decoy & Sporting Clays, 4 Ann & Hope Way, P.O. Box 98, Cumberland, RI 02864 / 401-723-8202; FAX: 401-722-5910

Quaker Boy, Inc., 5455 Webster Rd., Orchard Parks, NY 14127 / 716-662-3979; FAX: 716-662-9426

Quality Arms, Inc., Box 19477, Dept. GD, Houston, TX 77224 / 281-870-8377; FAX: 281-870-8524 arrieta2@excite.com www.gunshop.com

Quality Firearms of Idaho, Inc., 659 Harmon Way, Middleton, ID 83644-3065 / 208-466-1631

Quality Parts Co./Bushmaster Firearms, 999 Roosevelt Trail Bldg. 3, Windham, ME 04062 / 207-892-2005; FAX: 207-892-8068

Quarton USA, Ltd. Co., 7042 Alamo Downs Pkwy., Suite 370, San Antonio, TX 78238-4518 / 800-520-8435 or 210-520-8430; FAX:

Que Industries, Inc., P.O. Box 2471, Everett, WA 98203 / 800-769-6930 or 206-347-9843; FAX: 206-514-3266

Queen Cutlery Co., P.O. Box 500, Franklinville, NY 14737 / 800-222-5233; FAX: 216-876-2618

R

R&C Knives & Such, 2136 CANDY CANE WALK, Manteca, CA 95336-9501 / 209-239-3722; FAX: 209-825-6947

R&D Gun Repair, Kenny Howell, RR1 Box 283, Beloit, WI 53511

R&J Gun Shop, 337 S Humbolt St, Canyon City, OR 97820 / 541-575-2130 rjgunshop@highdesert-net.com

R&S Industries Corp., 8255 Brentwood Industrial Dr., St. Louis, MO 63144 / 314-781-5400 polishing-cloth.com

R. Murphy Co., Inc., 13 Groton-Harvard Rd., P.O. Box 376, Ayer, MA 01432 / 617-772-3481

R.A. Wells Custom Gunsmith, 3452 1st Ave., Racine, WI 53402 / 414-639-5223

R.E. Seebeck Assoc., P.O. Box 59752, Dallas, TX 75229

R.E.I., P.O. Box 88, Tallevast, FL 34270 /

R.E.T. Enterprises, 2608 S. Chestnut, Broken Arrow, OK 74012 / 918-251-GUNS; FAX: 918-251-0587

R.F. Mitchell Bullets, 430 Walnut St., Westernport, MD 21562

R.I.S. Co., Inc., 718 Timberlake Circle, Richardson, TX 75080 / 214-235-0933

R.M. Precision, Inc., P.O. Box 210, LaVerkin, UT 84745 / 801-635-4656; FAX: 801-635-4430

R.T. Eastman Products, P.O. Box 1531, Jackson, WY 83001 / 307-733-3217 or 800-624-4311

Rabeno, Martin, 92 Spook Hole Rd., Ellenville, NY 12428 / 914-647-4567; FAX: 914-647-2129

Radack Photography, Lauren, 21140 Jib Court L-12, Aventura, FL 33180 / 305-931-3110

Radiator Specialty Co., 1900 Wilkinson Blvd., P.O. Box 34689, Charlotte, NC 28234 / 800-438-6947; FAX: 800-421-9525

Radical Concepts, P.O. Box 1473, Lake Grove, OR 97035 / 503-538-7437

Rainier Ballistics Corp., 4500 15th St. East, Tacoma, WA 98424 / 800-638-8722 or 206-922-7589; FAX: 206-922-7854

Ralph Bone Engraving, 718 N. Atlanta, Owasso, OK 74055 / 918-272-9745

Ramon B. Gonzalez Guns, P.O. Box 370, 93 St. Joseph's Hill Road, Monticello, NY 12701 / 914-794-4515

Rampart International, 2781 W. MacArthur Blvd., B-283, Santa Ana, CA 92704 / 800-976-7240 or 714-557-6405

Ranch Products, P.O. Box 145, Malinta, OH 43535 / 313-277-3118; FAX: 313-565-8536

Randall-Made Knives, P.O. Box 1988, Orlando, FL 32802 / 407-855-8075

Randco UK, 286 Gipsy Rd., Welling, DA16 1JJ EN-GLAND / 44 81 303 4118

Randolph Engineering, Inc., 26 Thomas Patten Dr., Randolph, MA 02368 / 800-541-1405; FAX: 800-875-4200

Randy Duane Custom Stocks, 110 W. North Ave., Winchester, VA 22601 /703-667-9461; FAX: 703-722-3993

Range Brass Products Company, P.O. Box 218, Rockport, TX 78381

Ranger Products, 2623 Grand Blvd., Suite 209, Holiday, FL 34609 / 813-942-4652 or 800-407-7007; FAX: 813-942-6221

Ranger Shooting Glasses, 26 Thomas Patten Dr., Randolph, MA 02368 / 800-541-1405; FAX: 617-986-0337

Ranging, Inc., Routes 5 & 20, East Bloomfield, NY 14443 / 716-657-6161; FAX: 716-657-5405

Ransom International Corp., 1027 Spire Dr, Prescott, AZ 86302 / 520-778-7899; FAX: 520-778-7993 ransom@primenet.com www.ransom-intl.com

Rapine Bullet Mould Mfg. Co., 9503 Landis Lane, East Greenville, PA 18041 / 215-679-5413; FAX: 215-679-9795

Raptor Arms Co., Inc., 273 Canal St, #179, Shelton, CT 06484 / 203-924-7618; FAX: 203-924-7624

Ravell Ltd., 289 Diputacion St., 08009, Barcelona, SPAIN / 34(3) 4874486; FAX: 34(3) 4881394

Ray Riling Arms Books Co., 6844 Gorsten St., P.O. Box 18925, Philadelphia, PA 19119 / 215-438-2456; FAX: 215-438-5395

Ray's Gunsmith Shop, 3199 Elm Ave., Grand Junction, CO 81504 / 970-434-6162; FAX: 970-434-6162

Raytech Div. of Lyman Products Corp., 475 Smith Street, Middletown, CT 06457-1541 / 860-632-2020; FAX: 860-632-1699

RCBS Div. of Blount, 605 Oro Dam Blvd., Oroville, CA 95965 / 800-533-5000 or 916-533-5191; FAX: 916-533-1647 www.rcbs.com

Reagent Chemical & Research, Inc. (See Calico Hardwoods, Inc.)

Reardon Products, P.O. Box 126, Morrison, IL 61270 / 815-772-3155

Red Diamond Dist. Co., 1304 Snowdon Dr., Knoxville, TN 37912

Redding Reloading Equipment, 1089 Starr Rd., Cortland, NY 13045 / 607-753-3331; FAX: 607-756-8445

Redfield Media Resource Center, 4607 N.E. Cedar Creek Rd., Woodland, WA 98674 / 360-225-5000 FAX: 360-225-7616

Redfield, Inc., 5800 E Jewell Ave, Denver, CO 80224 / 303-757-6411; FAX: 303-756-2338

Redfield/Blount, PO Box 39, Onalaska, WI 54650 / 800-635-7656

Redman's Rifling & Reboring, 189 Nichols Rd., Omak, WA 98841 / 509-826-5512

Redwood Bullet Works, 3559 Bay Rd., Redwood City, CA 94063 / 415-367-6741

Reed, Dave, Rt. 1, Box 374, Minnesota City, MN 55959 / 507-689-2944

Reiswig, Wallace E. (See Claro Walnut Gunstock Co.)

Reloaders Equipment Co., 4680 High St., Ecorse, ML 48229

Reloading Specialties, Inc., Box 1130, Pine Island, MN 55463 / 507-356-8500; FAX: 507-356-8800

Remington Arms Co., Inc., 870 Remington Drive, P.O. Box 700, Madison, NC 27025-0700/800-243-9700; FAX: 910-548-8700

Remington Double Shotguns, 7885 Cyd Dr., Denver, CO 80221 / 303-429-6947

Renato Gamba S.p.A.-Societa Armi Bresciane Srl, Via Artigiani 93, 25063 Gardone, Val Trompia (BS), IT-ALY / 30-8911640; FAX: 30-8911648

Renegade, P.O. Box 31546, Phoenix, AZ 85046 / 602-482-6777; FAX: 602-482-1952

Renfrew Guns & Supplies, R.R. 4, Renfrew, ON K7V 3Z7 CANADA / 613-432-7080

Reno, Wayne, 2808 Stagestop Rd, Jefferson, CO 80456 / 719-836-3452

Republic Arms, Inc., 15167 Sierra Bonita Lane, Chino, CA 91710 / 909-597-3873; FAX: 909-597-2612

Retting, Inc., Martin B, 11029 Washington, Culver City, CA 90232 / 213-837-2412

RG-G, Inc., PO Box 935, Trinidad, CO 81082 / 719-845-1436

Rhino, P.O. Box 787, Locust, NC 28097 / 704-753-2198

Rhodeside, Inc., 1704 Commerce Dr., Piqua, OH 45356 / 513-773-5781

Rice, Keith (See White Rock Tool & Die)

Richard H.R. Loveth (Firearms), 29 Hedgegrow Lane, Kirby Muxloe, Leics. LE9 2BN, ENGLAND

Richards Micro-Fit Stocks, 8331 N. San Fernando Ave., Sun Valley, CA 91352 / 818-767-6097; FAX: 818-767-7121

Rickard, Pete, RD 1, Box 292, Cobleskill, NY 12043 / 800-282-5663; FAX: 518-234-2454

Ridgeline, Inc., Bruce Sheldon, PO Box 930, Dewey, AZ 86327-0930/ 800-632-5900; FAX: 520-632-5900

Ridgetop Sporting Goods, P.O. Box 306, 42907 Hilligoss Ln. East, Eatonville, WA 98328 / 360-832-6422; FAX: 360-832-6422

Ries, Chuck, 415 Ridgecrest Dr., Grants Pass, OR 97527 / 503-476-5623

Rifles, Inc., 873 W. 5400 N., Cedar City, UT 84720 / 801-586-5996; FAX: 801-586-5996

Rigby & Co., John, 66 Great Suffolk St, London, EN-GLAND / 0171-620-0690; FAX: 0171-928-9205

Riggs, Jim, 206 Azalea, Boerne, TX 78006 / 210-249-8567

Riley Ledbetter Airguns, 1804 E. Sprague St., Winston Salem, NC 27107-3521 / 919-784-0676

Riling Arms Books Co., Ray, 6844 Gorsten St, PO Box 18925, Philadelphia, PA 19119 / 215-438-2456; FAX: 215-438-5395

Rim Pac Sports, Inc., 1034 N. Soldano Ave., Azusa, CA 91702-2135

Ringler Custom Leather Co., 31 Shining Mtn. Rd., Powell, WY 82435 / 307-645-3255

Ripley Rifles, 42 Fletcher Street, Ripley, Derbyshire, DE5 3LP ENGLAND / 011-0773-748353

River Road Sporting Clays, Bruce Barsotti, P.O. Box 3016, Gonzales, CA 93926 / 408-675-2473

Rizzini F.lli (See U.S. Importers-Moore & C England)

Rizzini SNC, Via 2 Giugno, 7/7Bis-25060, Marcheno (Brescia), ITALY

RLCM Enterprises, 110 Hill Crest Drive, Burleson, TX 76028

RMS Custom Gunsmithing, 4120 N. Bitterwell, Prescott Valley, AZ 86314 / 520-772-7626

Robert Evans Engraving, 332 Vine St., Oregon City, OR 97045 / 503-656-5693

Robert Valade Engraving, 931 3rd Ave., Seaside, OR 97138 / 503-738-7672

Roberts Products, 25328 SE Iss. Beaver Lk. Rd., Issaquah, WA 98029 / 206-392-8172

Robinett, R. G., P.O. Box 72, Madrid, IA 50156 / 515-795-2906

Robinson, Don, Pennsylvaia Hse, 36 Fairfax Crescent, W Yorkshire, ENGLAND / 0422-364458

Robinson Firearms Mfg. Ltd., 1699 Blondeaux Crescent, Kelowna, BC V1Y 4J8 CANADA / 604-868-9596

Robinson H.V. Bullets, 3145 Church St., Zachary, LA 70791 / 504-654-4029

Rochester Lead Works, 76 Anderson Ave., Rochester, NY 14607 / 716-442-8500; FAX: 716-442-4712

Rock River Arms, 101 Noble St., Cleveland, IL 61241

Rockwood Corp., Speedwell Division, 136 Lincoln Blvd., Middlesex, NJ 08846 / 800-243-8274; FAX: 980-560-7475

Rodgers & Sons Ltd., Joseph (See George Ibberson (Sheffield) Ltd.)

Rocky Mountain Arms, Inc., 1813 Sunset Pl, Unit D, Longmont, CO 80501 / 800-375-0846; FAX: 303-678-8766

Rocky Mountain High Sports Glasses, 8121 N. Central Park Ave., Skokie, IL 60076 / 847-679-1012 or 800-323-1418; FAX: 847-679-0184

Rocky Mountain Rifle Works Ltd., 1707 14th St., Boulder, CO 80302 / 303-443-9189

Rocky Mountain Target Co., 3 Aloe Way, Leesburg, FL 34788 / 352-365-9598

Rocky Mountain Wildlife Products, P.O. Box 999, La Porte, CO 80535 / 970-484-2768; FAX: 970-484-0807

Rocky Shoes & Boots, 294 Harper St., Nelsonville, OH 45764 / 800-848-9452 or 614-753-1951; FAX: 614-753-4024

Rogue Rifle Co., Inc., P.O. Box 20, Prospect, OR 97536 / 541-560-4040; FAX: 541-560-4041

Rogue River Rifleworks, 1317 Spring St., Paso Robles, CA 93446 / 805-227-4706; FAX: FAX:805-227-4723

Rohner, Hans, 1148 Twin Sisters Ranch Rd., Nederland, CO 80466-9600

Rohner, John, 186 Virginia Ave., Asheville, NC 28806 / 303-444-3841

Romain's Custom Guns, Inc., RD 1, Whetstone Rd., Brockport, PA 15823 / 814-265-1948

Ron Frank Custom Classic Arms, 7131 Richland Rd., Ft. Worth, TX 76118 / 817-284-9300; FAX: 817-284-9300

Ron Lutz Engraving, E. 1998 Smokey Valley Rd., Scandinavia, WI 54977 / 715-467-2674

Rooster Laboratories, P.O. Box 412514, Kansas City, MO 64141 / 816-474-1622; FAX: 816-474-1307

Rorschach Precision Products, P.O. Box 151613, Irving, TX 75015 / 214-790-3487

Rosenberg & Son, Jack A., 12229 Cox Ln, Dallas, TX 75234 / 214-241-6302

Rosenthal, Brad and Sallie, 19303 Ossenfort Ct., St. Louis, MO 63038 / 314-273-5159; FAX: 314-273-5149

Ross, Don, 12813 West 83 Terrace, Lenexa, KS 66215 / 913-492-6982

Rosser, Bob, 1824 29th Ave., Suite 214, Birmingham, AL 35209 / 205-870-4422; FAX: 205-870-4421

Rossi Firearms, Braztech, Gary Mchalik, 16175 NW 49th Ave, Miami, FL 33014-6314 / 305-474-0401

Roto Carve, 2754 Garden Ave., Janesville, IA 50647

Rottweil Compe, 1330 Glassell, Orange, CA 92667

Round Edge, Inc., P.O. Box 723, Lansdale, PA 19446 / 215-361-0859

Roy Baker's Leather Goods, P.O. Box 893, Magnolia, AR 71753 / 501-234-0344

Roy's Custom Grips, Rt. 3, Box 174-E, Lynchburg, VA 24504 / 804-993-3470

Royal Arms Gunstocks, 919 8th Ave. NW, Great Falls, MT 59404 / 406-453-1149 FAX: 406-453-1194 royalarms@lmt.net lmt.net/~royalarms

RPM, 15481 N. Twin Lakes Dr., Tucson, AZ 85739 / 520-825-1233; FAX: 520-825-3333

Rubright Bullets, 1008 S. Quince Rd., Walnutport, PA 18088 / 215-767-1339

Rucker Dist. Inc., P.O. Box 479, Terrell, TX 75160 / 214-563-2094

Ruger (See Sturm, Ruger & Co., Inc.)

Rumanya Inc., 11513 Piney Lodge Rd, Gaithersburg, MD 20878-2443 / 281-345-2077; FAX: 281-345-2005

Rundell's Gun Shop, 6198 Frances Rd., Clio, MI 48420 / 313-687-0559

Runge, Robert P., 94 Grove St., Ilion, NY 13357 / 315-894-3036

Rupert's Gun Shop, 2202 Dick Rd., Suite B, Fenwick, MI 48834 / 517-248-3252

Russ Haydon Shooters' Supply, 15018 Goodrich Dr. NW., Gig Harbor, WA 98329 / 253-857-7557; FAX: 253-857-7884

Russ Trading Post, William A. Russ, 23 William St., Addison, NY 14801-1326 / 607-359-3896

Russ, William. (See RUSS TRADING POST)

Rusteprufe Laboratories, 1319 Jefferson Ave., Sparta, WI 54656 / 608-269-4144

Rusty Duck Premium Gun Care Products, 7785 Foundation Dr., Suite 6, Florence, KY 41042 / 606-342-5553; FAX: 606-342-5556

Rutgers Book Center, 127 Raritan Ave., Highland Park, NJ 08904 / 732-545-4344 FAX: 732-545-6686

Rutten (See U.S. Importer-Labanu Inc)

RWS (See US Importer-Dynamit Nobel-RWS, Inc.), 81 Ruckman Rd, Closter, NJ 07624 / 201-767-7971; FAX: 201-767-1589

Ryan, Chad L., RR 3, Box 72, Cresco, IA 52136 / 319-547-4384

S

S&B Industries, 11238 McKinley Rd., Montrose, MI 48457 / 810-639-5491

S&K Mfg. Co., P.O. Box 247, Pittsfield, PA 16340 / 814-563-7808; FAX: 814-563-4067

S&S Firearms, 74-11 Myrtle Ave., Glendale, NY 11385 / 718-497-1100; FAX: 718-497-1105

S.A.R.L. G. Granger, 66 cours Fauriel, 42100, Saint Etienne, FRANCE / 04 77 25 14 73; FAX: 04 77 38 66 99

S.C.R.C., P.O. Box 660, Katy, TX 77492-0660 FAX: 713-578-2124

S.D. Meacham, 1070 Angel Ridge, Peck, ID 83545

S.G.S. Sporting Guns Srl., Via Della Resistenza, 37 20090, Buccinasco, ITALY / 2-45702464; FAX: 2-45702464

S.I.A.C.E. (See U.S. Importer-IAR Inc)

S.L.A.P. Industries, P.O. Box 1121, Parklands, 02121 SOUTH AFRICA / 27-11-788-0030; FAX: 27-11-788-0030

Sabatti S.r.l., via Alessandro Volta 90, 25063 Gardone V.T., Brescia, ITALY / 030-8912207-831312; FAX: 030-8912059

SAECO (See Redding Reloading Equipment)

Saf-T-Lok, 5713 Corporate Way, Suite 100, W. Palm Beach, FL 33407

Safari Outfitters Ltd., 71 Ethan Allan Hwy., Ridgefield, CT 06877 / 203-544-9505

Safari Press, Inc., 15621 Chemical Lane B, Huntington Beach, CA 92649 / 714-894-9080; FAX: 714-894-4949

Safariland Ltd., Inc., 3120 E. Mission Blvd., P.O. Box 51478, Ontario, CA 91761 / 909-923-7300; FAX: 909-923-7400

SAFE, P.O. Box 864, Post Falls, ID 83854 / 208-773-3624 FAX: 208-773-6819 stay-safe@safe-llc.com www.safe-llc.com

Safety Speed Holster, Inc., 910 S. Vail Ave., Montebello, CA 90640 / 323-723-4140; FAX: 323-726-6973

Sako Ltd (See U.S. Importer-Stoeger Industries)

Samco Global Arms, Inc., 6995 NW 43rd St., Miami, FL 33166 / 305-593-9782 FAX: 305-593-1014

Sampson, Roger, 2316 Mahogany St., Mora, MN 55051 / 612-679-4868

San Francisco Gun Exchange, 124 Second St., San Francisco, CA 94105 / 415-982-6097

San Marco (See U.S. Importers-Cape Outfitters-EMF)

Sanders Custom Gun Service, 2358 Tyler Lane, Louisville, KY 40205 / 502-454-3338; FAX: 502-451-8857

Sanders Gun and Machine Shop, 145 Delhi Road, Manchester, IA 52057

Sandia Die & Cartridge Co., 37 Atancacio Rd. NE, Auquerque, NM 87123 / 505-298-5729

Sarco, Inc., 323 Union St., Stirling, NJ 07980 / 908-647-3800; FAX: 908-647-9413

Sauer (See U.S. Importers-Paul Co., The, Sigarms Inc.,)

Sauls, R. (See BRYAN & ASSOC)

Saunders Gun & Machine Shop, R.R. 2, Delhi Road, Manchester, IA 52057

Savage Arms (Canada), Inc., 248 Water St., P.O. Box 1240, Lakefield, ON K0L 2H0 CANADA / 705-652-8000; FAX: 705-652-8431

Savage Arms, Inc., 100 Springdale Rd., Westfield, MA 01085 / 413-568-7001; FAX: 413-562-7764

Savage Range Systems, Inc., 100 Springdale RD., Westfield, MA 01085 / 413-568-7001; FAX: 413-562-1152

Saville Iron Co. (See Greenwood Precision)

Savino, Barbara J., P.O. Box 51, West Burke, VT 05871-0051

Scanco Environmental Systems, 5000 Highlands Parkway, Suite 180, Atlanta, GA 30082 / 770-431-0025; FAX: 770-431-0028

Scansport, Inc., P.O. Box 700, Enfield, NH 03748 / 603-632-7654

Scattergun Technologies, Inc., 620 8th Ave. South, Nashville, TN 37203 / 615-254-1441; FAX: 615-254-1449

Sceery Game Calls, P.O. Box 6520, Sante Fe, NM 87502 / 505-471-9110; FAX: 505-471-3476

Schaefer Shooting Sports, P.O. Box 1515, Melville, NY 11747-0515 / 516-643-5466 FAX: 516-643-2426 rschaefe@optonline.net www.schaefershooting.com

Scharch Mfg., Inc., 10325 CR 120, Salida, CO 81201 / 719-539-7242 or 800-836-4683; FAX: 719-539-3021

Scherer, Box 250, Ewing, VA 24240 / 615-733-2615; FAX: 615-733-2073

Schiffman, Curt, 3017 Kevin Cr., Idaho Falls, ID 83402 / 208-524-4684

Schiffman, Mike, 8233 S. Crystal Springs, McCammon, ID 83250 / 208-254-9114

Schiffman, Norman, 3017 Kevin Cr., Idaho Falls, ID 83402 / 208-524-4684

Schmidt & Bender, Inc., 438 Willow Brook Rd., Meriden, NH 03770 / 800-468-3450 or 800-468-3450; FAX: 603-469-3471

Schmidtke Group, 17050 W. Salentine Dr., New Berlin, WI 53151-7349

Schmidtman Custom Ammunition, 6 Gilbert Court, Cotati, CA 94931

Schneider Bullets, 3655 West 214th St., Fairview Park, OH 44126

Schneider Rifle Barrels, Inc, Gary, 12202 N 62nd Pl, Scottsdale, AZ 85254 / 602-948-2525

Schroeder Bullets, 1421 Thermal Ave., San Diego, CA 92154 / 619-423-3523; FAX: 619-423-8124

Schuetzen Pistol Works, 620-626 Old Pacific Hwy. SE, Olympia, WA 98513 / 360-459-3471; FAX: 360-491-3447

Schulz Industries, 16247 Minnesota Ave., Paramount, CA 90723 / 213-439-5903

Schumakers Gun Shop, 512 Prouty Corner Lp. A, Colville, WA 99114 / 509-684-4848

Scope Control, Inc., 5775 Co. Rd. 23 SE, Alexandria, MN 56308 / 612-762-7295

ScopLevel, 151 Lindbergh Ave., Suite C, Livermore, CA 94550 / 925-449-5052; FAX: 925-373-0861

Score High Gunsmithing, 9812-A, Cochiti SE, Albuquerque, NM 087123 / 800-326-5632 or 505-292-5532; FAX: 505-292-2592

Scot Powder, Rt.1 Box 167, McEwen, TN 37101 / 800-416-3006; FAX: 615-729-4211

Scot Powder Co. of Ohio, Inc., Box GD96, Only, TN 37140 / 615-729-4207 or 800-416-3006; FAX: 615-729-4217

Scott, Dwight, 23089 Englehardt St., Clair Shores, MI 48080 / 313-779-4735

Scott Fine Guns Inc., Thad, PO Box 412, Indianola, MS 38751 / 601-887-5929

Scott McDougall & Associates, 7950 Redwood Dr., Suite 13, Cotati, CA 94931 / 707-546-2264; FAX: 707-795-1911 www.colt380.com

Searcy Enterprises, PO Box 584, Boron, CA 93596 / 760-762-6771 FAX: 760-762-0191

MANUFACTURER'S DIRECTORY

Second Chance Body Armor, P.O. Box 578, Central Lake, MI 49622 / 616-544-5721; FAX: 616-544-9824

Seebeck Assoc., R.E., P. O. Box 59752, Dallas, TX 75229

Seecamp Co. Inc., L.W., PO Box 255, New Haven, CT 06502 / 203-877-3429

Segway Industries, P.O. Box 783, Suffern, NY 10901-0783 / 914-357-5510

Seligman Shooting Products, Box 133, Seligman, AZ 86337 / 602-422-3607

Sellier & Bellot, USA Inc, PO Box 27006, Shawnee Mission, KS 66225 / 913-685-0916; FAX: 913-685-0917

Selsi Co. Inc., P.O. Box 10, Midland Park, NJ 07432-0010 / 201-935-0388; FAX: 201-935-5851

Semmer, Charles (See Remington Double Shotguns)

Sentinel Arms, P.O. Box 57, Detroit, MI 48231 / 313-331-1951; FAX: 313-331-1456

Service Armament, 689 Bergen Blvd., Ridgefield, NJ 07657

Servus Footwear Co., 1136 2nd St., Rock Island, IL 61204 / 309-786-7741; FAX: 309-786-9808

Shappy Bullets, 76 Milldale Ave., Plantsville, CT 06479 / 203-621-3704

Sharp Shooter Supply, 4970 Lehman Road, Delphos, OH 45833 / 419-695-3179

Sharps Arms Co., Inc., C., 100 Centennial, Box 885, Big Timber, MT 59011 / 406-932-4353

Shaw, Inc., E. R. (See Small Arms Mfg. Co.)

Shay's Gunsmithing, 931 Marvin Ave., Lebanon, PA 17042

Sheffield Knifemakers Supply, Inc., P.O. Box 741107, Orange City, FL 32774-1107 / 904-775-6453; FAX: 904-774-5754

Sheldon, Bruce. (See RIDGELINE, INC)

Shepherd Enterprises, Inc., Box 189, Waterloo, NE 68069 / 402-779-2424; FAX: 402-779-4010 sshepherd@shepherdscopes.com www.shepherdscopes.com

Sherwood, George, 46 N. River Dr., Roseburg, OR 97470 / 541-672-3159

Shilen, Inc., 205 Metro Park Blvd., Ennis, TX 75119 / 972-875-5318; FAX: 972-875-5402

Shiloh Creek, Box 357, Cottleville, MO 63338 / 314-925-1842; FAX: 314-925-1842

Shiloh Rifle Mfg., 201 Centennial Dr., Big Timber, MT 59011 / 406-932-4454; FAX: 406-932-5627

Shockley, Harold H., 204 E. Farmington Rd., Hanna City, IL 61536 / 309-565-4524

Shoemaker & Sons Inc., Tex, 714 W Cienega Ave, San Dimas, CA 91773 / 909-592-2071; FAX: 909-592-2378

Shoot Where You Look, Leon Measures, Dept GD, 408 Fair, Livingston, TX 77351

Shoot-N-C Targets (See Birchwood Casey)

Shooter's Choice, 16770 Hilltop Park Place, Chagrin Falls, OH 44023 / 216-543-8808; FAX:

Shooter's Edge Inc., P.O.Box 769, Trinidad, CO 81082

Shooter's World, 3828 N. 28th Ave., Phoenix, AZ 85017 / 602-266-0170

Shooters Supply, 1120 Tieton Dr., Yakima, WA 98902 / 509-452-1181

Shootin' Accessories, Ltd., P.O. Box 6810, Auburn, CA 95604 / 916-889-2220

Shootin' Shack, Inc., 1065 Silver Beach Rd., Riviera Beach, FL 33403 / 561-842-0990

Shooting Chrony, Inc., 3269 Niagara Falls Blvd., N. Tonawanda, NY 14120 / 905-276-6292; FAX: 416-276-6295

Shooting Specialties (See Titus, Daniel)

Shooting Star, 1715 FM 1626 Ste 105, Manchaca, TX 78652 / 512-462-0009

Shotgun Sports, PO Box 6810, Auburn, CA 95604 / 530-889-2220; FAX: 530-889-9106

Shotguns Unlimited, 2307 Fon Du Lac Rd., Richmond, VA 23229 / 804-752-7115

ShurKatch Corporation, PO Box 850, Richfield Springs, NY 13439 / 315-858-1470; FAX: 315-858-2969

Siegrist Gun Shop, 8752 Turtle Road, Whittemore, MI 48770

Sierra Bullets, 1400 W. Henry St., Sedalia, MO 65301 / 816-827-6300; FAX: 816-827-6300

Sierra Specialty Prod. Co., 1344 Oakhurst Ave., Los Altos, CA 94024 FAX: 415-965-1536

SIG, CH-8212 Neuhausen, SWITZERLAND

SIG-Sauer (See U.S. Importer-Sigarms Inc.)

Sigarms, Inc., Corporate Park, Exeter, NH 03833 / 603-772-2302; FAX: 603-772-9082

Sighton, Inc., 1672B Hwy. 96, Franklinton, NC 27525 / 919-528-8783; FAX: 919-528-0995

Signet Metal Corp., 551 Stewart Ave., Brooklyn, NY 11222 / 718-384-5400; FAX: 718-388-7488

Sile Distributors, Inc., 7 Centre Market Pl., New York, NY 10013 / 212-925-4111; FAX: 212-925-3149

Silencio/Safety Direct, 56 Coney Island Dr., Sparks, NV 89431 / 800-648-1812 or 702-354-4451; FAX: 702-359-1074

Silent Hunter, 1100 Newton Ave., W. Collingswood, NJ 08107 / 609-854-3276

Silhouette Leathers, P.O. Box 1161, Gunnison, CO 81230 / 303-641-6639

Silver Eagle Machining, 18007 N. 69th Ave., Glendale, AZ 85308

Silver Ridge Gun Shop (See Goodwin, Fred)

Simmons, Jerry, 715 Middlebury St., Goshen, IN 46526

Simmons Gun Repair, Inc., 700 S. Rogers Rd., Olathe, KS 66062 / 913-782-3131; FAX: 913-782-4189

Simmons Outdoor Corp., PO Box 217, Heflin, AL 36264 / 219-533-8546

Sinclair International, Inc., 2330 Wayne Haven St., Fort Wayne, IN 46803 / 219-493-1858; FAX:

Singletary, Kent, 2915 W. Ross, Phoenix, AZ 85027 / 602-582-4900

Sipes Gun Shop, 7415 Asher Ave., Little Rock, AR 72204 / 501-771-6133

Siskiyou Gun Works (See Donnelly, C. P.)

Six Enterprises, 320-D Turtle Creek Ct., San Jose, CA 95125 / 408-999-0201; FAX: 408-999-0216

SKAN A.R., 4 St. Catherines Road, Long Melford, Suffolk, O10 9JU ENGLAND / 011-0787-312942

SKB Shotguns, 4325 S. 120th St., Omaha, NE 68137 / 800-752-2767; FAX: 402-330-8029

Skeoch, Brian R., P.O. Box 279, Glenrock, WY 82637 / 307-436-9655 FAX: 307-436-9034

Skip's Machine, 364 29 Road, Grand Junction, CO 81501 / 303-245-5417

Sklany's Machine Shop, 566 Birch Grove Dr., Kalispell, MT 59901 / 406-755-4257

Slezak, Jerome F., 1290 Marlowe, Lakewood (Cleveland), OH 44107 / 216-221-1668

Slug Group, Inc., P.O. Box 376, New Paris, PA 15554 / 814-839-4517; FAX: 814-839-2601

Slug Site, Ozark Wilds, 21300 Hwy. 5, Versailles, MO 65084 / 573-378-6430 john.ebeling.com

Small Arms Mfg. Co., 5312 Thoms Run Rd., Bridgeville, PA 15017 / 412-221-4343; FAX: 412-221-4303

Small Arms Specialists, 443 Firchburg Rd. Mason, NH 03048 / 603-878-0427 FAX: 603-878-3905 miniguns@empire.net miniguns.com

Smart Parts, 1203 Spring St., Latrobe, PA 15650 / 412-539-2660; FAX: 412-539-2298

Smires, C. L., 5222 Windmill Lane, Columbia, MD 21044-1328

Smith & Wesson, 2100 Roosevelt Ave., Springfield, MA 01104 / 413-781-8300; FAX: 413-731-8980

Smith, Art, 230 Main St., Hector, MN 55342 / 320-848-2760; FAX: 320-848-2760

Smith, Mark A., P.O. Box 182, Sinclair, WY 82334 / 307-324-7929

Smith, Michael, 620 Nye Circle, Chattanooga, TN 37405 / 615-267-8341

Smith, Ron, 5869 Straley, Ft. Worth, TX 76114 / 817-732-6768

Smith, Sharmon, 4545 Speas Rd., Fruitland, ID 83619 / 208-452-6329

Smith Abrasives, Inc., 1700 Sleepy Valley Rd., P.O. Box 5095, Hot Springs, AR 71902-5095 / 501-321-2244; FAX: 501-321-9232

Smith Saddlery, Jesse W., 16909 E Jackson Rd, Elk, WA 99009-9600 / 509-325-0622

Smokey Valley Rifles (See Lutz Engraving, Ron E)

Snapp's Gunshop, 6911 E. Washington Rd., Clare, MI 48617 / 517-386-9226

Sno-Seal, Inc. (See Atsko/Sno-Seal)

Societa Armi Bresciane Srl (See U.S. Importer-Cape Outfitters)

SOS Products Co. (See Buck Stix-SOS Products Co.)

Sotheby's, 1334 York Ave. at 72nd St., New York, NY 10021 / 212-606-7260

Sound Technology, Box 391, Pelham, AL 35124 / 205-664-5860 or 907-486-2825

South Bend Replicas, Inc., 61650 Oak Rd., South Bend, IN 46614 / 219-289-4500

Southeastern Community College, 1015 S. Gear Ave., West Burlington, IA 52655 / 319-752-2731

Southern Ammunition Co., Inc., 4232 Meadow St., Loris, SC 29569-3124 / 803-756-3262; FAX: 803-756-3583

Southern Bloomer Mfg. Co., P.O. Box 1621, Bristol, TN 37620 / 615-878-6660; FAX: 615-878-8761

Southern Security, 1700 Oak Hills Dr., Kingston, TN 37763 / 423-376-6297; FAX: 800-251-9992

Southwind Sanctions, P.O. Box 445, Aledo, TX 76008 / 817-441-8917

Sparks, Milt, 605 E. 44th St. No. 2, Boise, ID 83714-4800

Spartan-Realtree Products, Inc., 1390 Box Circle, Columbus, GA 31907 / 706-569-9101; FAX: 706-569-0042

Specialty Gunsmithing, Lynn McMurdo, P.O. Box 404, Afton, WY 83110 / 307-886-5535

Specialty Shooters Supply, Inc., 3325 Griffin Rd., Suite 9mm, Fort Lauderdale, FL 33317

Speedfeed, Inc., PO Box 1146, Rocklin, CA 95677 / 916-630-7720; FAX: 916-630-7719

Speer Products Div. of Blount Inc. Sporting Equipm, P.O. Box 856, Lewiston, ID 83501 / 208-746-2351; FAX: 208-746-2915

Spegel, Craig, PO Box 387, Nehalem, OR 97131 / 503-368-5663

Speiser, Fred D., 2229 Dearborn, Missoula, MT 59801 / 406-549-8133

Spencer Reblue Service, 1820 Tupelo Trail, Holt, MI 48842 / 517-694-7474

Spencer's Custom Guns, 4107 Jacobs Creek Dr, Scottsville, VA 24590 / 804-293-6836 FAX: 804-293-6836

SPG LLC, P.O. Box 1625, Cody, WY 82414 / 307-587-7621; FAX: 307-587-7695

Sphinx Engineering SA, Ch. des Grandex-Vies 2, CH-2900, Porrentruy, SWITZERLAND FAX: 41 66 66 30 90

Spokhandguns, Inc., 1206 Fig St., Benton City, WA 99320 / 509-588-5255

Sport Flite Manufacturing Co., P.O. Box 1082, Bloomfield Hills, MI 48303 / 248-647-3747

Sporting Arms Mfg., Inc., 801 Hall Ave., Littlefield, TX 79339 / 806-385-5665; FAX: 806-385-3394

Sporting Clays Of America, 9257 Buckeye Rd, Sugar Grove, OH 43155-9632 / 740-746-8334; FAX: 740-746-8605

Sports Innovations Inc., P.O. Box 5181, 8505 Jacksboro Hwy., Wichita Falls, TX 76307 / 817-723-6015

Sportsman Safe Mfg. Co., 6309-6311 Paramount Blvd., Long Beach, CA 90805 / 800-266-7150 or 310-984-5445

Sportsman Supply Co., 714 E. Eastwood, P.O. Box 650, Marshall, MO 65340 / 816-886-9393

Sportsman's Communicators, 588 Radcliffe Ave., Pacific Palisades, CA 90272 / 800-538-3752

Sportsmatch U.K. Ltd., 16 Summer St., Leighton Buzzard, Bedfordshire, LU7 8HT ENGLAND / 01525-381638; FAX: 01525-851236

Sportsmen's Exchange & Western Gun Traders, Inc., 560 S. C St., Oxnard, CA 93030 / 805-483-1917

Spradlin's, 457 Shannon Rd, Texas Creek, CO 81223 / 719-275-7105 FAX: 719-275-3852 spradlins@prodigt.net jimspradlin.com

Springfield Sporters, Inc., RD 1, Penn Run, PA 15765 / 412-254-2626; FAX: 412-254-9173

Springfield, Inc., 420 W. Main St., Geneseo, IL 61254 / 309-944-5631; FAX: 309-944-3676

Spyderco, Inc., 4565 N. Hwy. 93, P.O. Box 800, Golden, CO 80403 / 303-279-8383 or 800-525-7770; FAX: 303-278-2229

SSK Industries, 590 Woodvue Lane, Wintersville, OH 43953 / 740-264-0176; FAX: 740-264-2257

Stackpole Books, 5067 Ritter Rd., Mechanicsburg, PA 17055-6921 / 717-796-0411; FAX: 717-796-0412

Stalker, Inc., P.O. Box 21, Fishermans Wharf Rd., Malakoff, TX 75148 / 903-489-1010

Stalwart Corporation, 76 Imperial, Unit A, Evanston, WY 82930 / 307-789-7687; FAX: 307-789-7688

Stan De Treville & Co., 4129 Normal St., San Diego, CA 92103 / 619-298-3393

Stanley Bullets, 2085 Heatheridge Ln., Reno, NV 89509

Stanley Scruggs' Game Calls, Rt. 1, Hwy. 661, Cullen, VA 23934 / 804-542-4241 or 800-323-4828

Star Ammunition, Inc., 5520 Rock Hampton Ct., Indianapolis, IN 46268 / 800-221-5927; FAX: 317-782-5847

Star Bonifacio Echeverria S.A., Torrekva 3, Eibar, 20600 SPAIN / 43-107340; FAX: 43-101524

Star Custom Bullets, P.O. Box 608, 468 Main St., Ferndale, CA 95536 / 707-786-9140; FAX: 707-786-9117

Star Machine Works, PO Box 1872, Pioneer, CA 95666 / 209-295-5000

Stark's Bullet Mfg., 2580 Monroe St., Eugene, OR 97405

Starke Bullet Company, P.O. Box 400, 605 6th St. NW, Cooperstown, ND 58425 / 888-797-3431

Starkey Labs, 6700 Washington Ave. S., Eden Prairie, MN 55344

Starkey's Gun Shop, 9430 McCombs, El Paso, TX 79924 / 915-751-3030

Starlight Training Center, Inc., Rt. 1, P.O. Box 88, Bronaugh, MO 64728 / 417-843-3555

Starline, 1300 W. Henry St., Sedalia, MO 65301 / 660-827-6640 FAX: 660-827-6650 bjhayden@starlinebra.com http://www.starlinebrass.com

Starr Trading Co., Jedediah, P.O. Box 2007, Farmington Hills, MI 48333 / 810-683-4343; FAX: 810-683-3282

Starrett Co., L.S., 121 Crescent St, Athol, MA 01331 / 978-249-3551 FAX: 978-249-8495

State Arms Gun Co., 815 S. Division St., Waunakee, WI 53597 / 608-849-5800

Steelman's Gun Shop, 10465 Beers Rd., Swartz Creek, MI 48473 / 810-735-4884

Steffens, Ron, 18396 Mariposa Creek Rd., Willits, CA 95490 / 707-485-0873

Stegall, James B., 26 Forest Rd., Wallkill, NY 12589

Steger, James R., 1131 Dorsey Pl., Plainfield, NJ 07062

Steve Henigson & Associates, P.O. Box 2726, Culver City, CA 90231 / 310-305-8288; FAX: 310-305-1905

Steve Kamyk Engraver, 9 Grandview Dr., Westfield, MA 01085-1810 / 413-568-0457

Steve Nastoff's 45 Shop, Inc., 12288 Mahoning Ave., P.O. Box 446, North Jackson, OH 44451 / 330-538-2977

Steves House of Guns, Rt. 1, Minnesota City, MN 55959 / 507-689-2573

Stewart Game Calls, Inc., Johnny, PO Box 7954, 5100 Fort Ave, Waco, TX 76714 / 817-772-3261; FAX: 817-772-3670

Stewart's Gunsmithing, P.O. Box 5854, Pietersburg North 0750, Transvaal, SOUTH AFRICA / 01521-89401

Steyr Mannlicher AG & CO KG, Mannlicherstrasse 1, A-4400, Steyr, AUSTRIA / 0043-7252-78621; FAX: 0043-7252-68621

STI International, 114 Halmar Cove, Georgetown, TX 78628 / 800-959-8201; FAX: 512-819-0465

Stiles Custom Guns, 76 Cherry Run Rd., Box 1605, Homer City, PA 15748 / 712-479-9945

Stillwell, Robert, 421 Judith Ann Dr., Schertz, TX 78154

Stoeger Industries, 5 Mansard Ct., Wayne, NJ 07470 / 201-872-9500 or 800-631-0722; FAX: 201-872-2230

Stoeger Publishing Co. (See Stoeger Industries)

Stone Enterprises Ltd., Rt. 609, P.O. Box 335, Wicomico Church, VA 22579 / 804-580-5114; FAX: 804-580-8421

Stone Mountain Arms, 5988 Peachtree Corners E., Norcross, GA 30071 / 800-251-9412

Stoney Point Products, Inc., PO Box 234, 1822 N Minnesota St, New Ulm, MN 56073-0234 / 507-354-3360; FAX: 507-354-7236 stoney@newulmtel.net www.stoneypoint.com

Storage Tech, 1254 Morris Ave., N. Huntingdon, PA 15642 / 800-437-9393

Storey, Dale A. (See DGS Inc.)

Storm, Gary, P.O. Box 5211, Richardson, TX 75083 / 214-385-0862

Stott's Creek Armory, Inc., 2526 S. 475W. Morgantown, IN 46160 / 317-878-5489; FAX: 317-878-9489 www.sccalendar.com

Stratco, Inc., P.O. Box 2270, Kalispell, MT 59901 / 406-755-1221; FAX: 406-755-1226

Strawbridge, Victor W., 6 Pineview Dr., Dover, NH 03820 / 603-742-0013

Strayer, Sandy, (See STRAYER-VOIGT, INC)

Strayer-Voigt, Inc, Sandy Strayer, 3435 Ray Orr Blvd, Grand Prairie, TX 75050 / 972-513-0575

Streamlight, Inc., 1030 W. Germantown Pike, Norristown, PA 19403 / 215-631-0600; FAX: 610-631-0712

Strong Rifle Barrels, Inc., W. C., PO Box 611, Eagle River, WI 54521 / 715-479-4766

Strutz Rifle Barrels, Inc., W., 39 Grove St., Gloucester, MA 01930 / 508-281-3300; FAX: 508-281-6321

Stuart, V. Pat, Rt.1, Box 447-S, Greenville, VA 24440 / 804-556-3845

Sturgeon Valley Sporters, K. Ide, P.O. Box 283, Vanderbilt, MI 49795 / 517-983-4338

Sturm Ruger & Co. Inc., 200 Ruger Rd., Prescott, AZ 86301 / 520-541-8820; FAX: 520-541-8850

Sullivan, David S. (See Westwind Rifles Inc.)

Summit Specialties, Inc., P.O. Box 786, Decatur, AL 35602 / 205-353-0634; FAX: 205-353-9818

Sun Welding Safe Co., 290 Easy St. No.3, Simi Valley, CA 93065 / 805-584-6678 or 800-729-SAFE FAX: 805-584-6169

Sunny Hill Enterprises, Inc., W1790 Cty. HHH, Malone, WI 53049 / 920-795-4722 FAX: 920-795-4822

"Su-Press-On",Inc., P.O. Box 09161, Detroit, MI 48209 / 313-842-4222

Sure-Shot Game Calls, Inc., P.O. Box 816, 6835 Capitol, Groves, TX 77619 / 409-962-1636; FAX: 409-962-5465

Survival Arms, Inc., 273 Canal St., Shelton, CT 06484-3173 / 203-924-6533; FAX: 203-924-2581

Svon Corp., 280 Eliot St., Ashland, MA 01721 / 508-881-8852

Swann, D. J., 5 Orsova Close, Eltham North Vic., 3095 AUSTRALIA / 03-431-0323

Swanndri New Zealand, 152 Elm Ave., Burlingame, CA 94010 / 415-347-6158

SwaroSports, Inc. (See JagerSport Ltd, One Wholesale Way, Cranston, RI 02920 / 800-962-4867; FAX: 401-946-2587

Swarovski Optik North America Ltd., 2 Slater Rd., Cranston, RI 02920 / 401-946-2220 or 800-426-3089 FAX: 401-946-2587

Sweet Home, Inc., P.O. Box 900, Orrville, OH 44667-0900

Swenson's 45 Shop, A. D., 3839 Ladera Vista Rd, Fallbrook, CA 92028-9431

Swift Bullet Co., P.O. Box 27, 201 Main St., Quinter, KS 67752 / 913-754-3959; FAX: 913-754-2359

Swift Instruments, Inc., 952 Dorchester Ave., Boston, MA 02125 / 617-436-2960; FAX: 617-436-3232

Swift River Gunworks, 450 State St., Belchertown, MA 01007 / 413-323-4052

Szweda, Robert (See RMS Custom Gunsmithing)

T

T&S Industries, Inc., 1027 Skyview Dr., W. Carrollton, OH 45449 / 513-859-8414

T.F.C. S.p.A., Via G. Marconi 118, B, Villa Carcina 25069, ITALY / 030-881271; FAX: 030-881826

T.G. Faust, Inc., 544 Minor St., Reading, PA 19602 / 610-375-8549; FAX: 610-375-4488

T.H.U. Enterprises, Inc., P.O. Box 418, Lederach, PA 19450 / 215-256-1665; FAX: 215-256-9718

T.K. Lee Co., 1282 Branchwater Ln., Birmingham, AL 35216 / 205-913-5222

T.W. Menck Gunsmith Inc., 5703 S. 77th St., Ralston, NE 68127

Tabler Marketing, 2554 Lincoln Blvd., Suite 555, Marina Del Rey, CA 90291 / 818-755-4565; FAX: 818-755-0972

Taconic Firearms Ltd., Perry Lane, PO Box 553, Cambridge, NY 12816 / 518-677-2704; FAX: 518-677-5974

TacStar, PO Box 547, Cottonwood, AZ 86326-0547 / 602-639-0072; FAX: 602-634-8781

TacTell, Inc., P.O. Box 5654, Maryville, TN 37802 / 615-982-7855; FAX: 615-558-8294

Tactical Defense Institute, 574 Miami Bluff Ct., Loveland, OH 45140 / 513-677-8229 FAX: 513-677-0447

Talley, Dave, P.O. Box 821, Glenrock, WY 82637 / 307-436-8724 or 307-436-9315

Talmage, William G., 10208 N. County Rd. 425 W., Brazil, IN 47834 / 812-442-0804

Talon Mfg. Co., Inc., 621 W. King St., Martinsburg, WV 25401 / 304-264-9714; FAX: 304-264-9725

Tamarack Products, Inc., P.O. Box 625, Wauconda, IL 60084 / 708-526-9333; FAX: 708-526-9353

Tanfoglio Fratelli S.r.l., via Valtrompia 39, 41, Brescia, ITALY / 30-8910361; FAX: 30-8910183

Tanglefree Industries, 1261 Heavenly Dr., Martinez, CA 94553 / 800-982-4868; FAX: 510-825-3874

Tank's Rifle Shop, P.O. Box 474, Fremont, NE 68026-0474 / 402-727-1317; FAX: 402-721-2573

Tanner (See U.S. Importer-Mandall Shooting Supplies Inc.)

Tar-Hunt Custom Rifles, Inc., RR3, P.O. Box 572, Bloomsburg, PA 17815-9351 / 717-784-6368; FAX: 717-784-6368

Taracorp Industries, Inc., 1200 Sixteenth St., Granite City, IL 62040 / 618-451-4400

Target Shooting, Inc., PO Box 773, Watertown, SD 57201 / 605-882-6955; FAX: 605-882-8840

Tarnhelm Supply Co., Inc. 431 High St., Boscawen, NH 03303 / 603-796-2551; FAX: 603-796-2918

Tasco Sales, Inc., 2889 Commerce Pky., Miramar, FL 33025

Taurus International Firearms, Inc., 16175 NW 49th Ave., Miami, FL 33014 / 305-624-1115; FAX: 305-623-7506

Taurus S.A. Forjas, Avenida Do Forte 511, Porto Alegre, RS BRAZIL 91360 / 55-51-347-4050; FAX: 55-51-347-3065

Taylor & Robbins, P.O. Box 164, Rixford, PA 16745 / 814-966-3233

Taylor's & Co., Inc., 304 Lenoir Dr., Winchester, VA 22603 / 540-722-2017; FAX: 540-722-2018

TCCI, P.O. Box 302, Phoenix, AZ 85001 / 602-237-3823; FAX: 602-237-3858

TCSR, 3998 Hoffman Rd., White Bear Lake, MN 55110-4626 / 800-328-5323; FAX: 612-429-0526

TDP Industries, Inc., 606 Airport Blvd., Doylestown, PA 18901 / 215-345-8687; FAX: 215-345-6057

Techno Arms (See U.S. Importer- Auto-Ordnance Corp.)

Tecnolegno S.p.A., Via A. Locatelli, 6 10, 24019 Zogno, ITALY / 0345-55111; FAX: 0345-55155

Ted Blocker Holsters, Inc., Clackamas Business Park Bldg A, 14787 SE 82nd Dr, Clackamas, OR 97015 / 503-557-7757; FAX: 503-557-3771

Tele-Optics, 630 E. Rockland Rd., PO Box 6313, Libertyville, IL 60048 / 847-362-7757

Ten-Ring Precision, Inc., Alex B. Hamilton, 1449 Blue Crest Lane, San Antonio, TX 78232 / 210-494-3063; FAX: 210-494-3066

TEN-X Products Group, 1905 N Main St, Suite 133, Cleburne, TX 76031-1305 / 972-243-4016 or 800-433-2225; FAX: 972-243-4112

Tennessee Valley Mfg., P.O. Box 1175, Corinth, MS 38834 / 601-286-5014

Tepeco, P.O. Box 342, Friendswood, TX 77546 / 713-482-2702

Terry K. Kopp Professional Gunsmithing, Rt 1 Box 224F, Lexington, MO 64067 / 816-259-2636

Testing Systems, Inc., 220 Pegasus Ave., Northvale, NJ 07647

Teton Arms, Inc., P.O. Box 411, Wilson, WY 83014 / 307-733-3395

Tetra Gun Lubricants (See FTI, Inc.)

Tex Shoemaker & Sons, Inc., 714 W. Cienega Ave., San Dimas, CA 91773 / 909-592-2071; FAX: 909-592-2378

Texas Armory (See Bond Arms, Inc.)

Texas Platers Supply Co., 2453 W. Five Mile Parkway, Dallas, TX 75233 / 214-330-7168

Thad Rybka Custom Leather Equipment, 134 Havilah Hill, Odenville, AL 35120

Thad Scott Fine Guns, Inc., P.O. Box 412, Indianola, MS 38751 / 601-887-5929

The Accuracy Den, 25 Bitterbrush Rd., Reno, NV 89523 / 702-345-0225

The Armoury, Inc., Rt. 202, Box 2340, New Preston, CT 06777 / 860-868-0001; FAX: 860-868-2919

The Ballistic Program Co., Inc., 2417 N. Patterson St., Thomasville, GA 31792 / 912-228-5739 or 800-368-0835

The BulletMakers Workshop, RFD 1 Box 1755, Brooks, ME 04921

The Competitive Pistol Shop, 5233 Palmer Dr., Ft. Worth, TX 76117-2433 / 817-834-8479

The Creative Armourer, P.O. Box 308, Ashby, MA 01431-0308 / 508-827-6797; FAX: 508-827-4845

The Creative Craftsman, Inc., 95 Highway 29 North, P.O. Box 331, Lawrenceville, GA 30246 / 404-963-2112; FAX: 404-513-9488

The Custom Shop, 890 Cochrane Crescent, Peterborough, ON K9H 5N3 CANADA / 705-742-6693

The Dutchman's Firearms, Inc., 4143 Taylor Blvd., Louisville, KY 40215 / 502-366-0555

MANUFACTURER'S DIRECTORY

The Ensign-Bickford Co., 660 Hopmeadow St., Simsbury, CT 06070

The Eutaw Co., Inc., P.O. Box 608, U.S. Hwy. 176 West, Holly Hill, SC 29059 / 803-496-3341

The Firearm Training Center, 9555 Blandville Rd., West Paducah, KY 42086 / 502-554-5886

The Fouling Shot, 6465 Parfet St., Arvada, CO 80004

The Gun Doctor, 435 East Maple, Roselle, IL 60172 / 708-894-0668

The Gun Doctor, P.O. Box 39242, Downey, CA 90242 / 310-862-3158

The Gun Parts Corp., 226 Williams Lane, West Hurley, NY 12491 / 914-679-2417; FAX: 914-679-5849

The Gun Room, 1121 Burlington, Muncie, IN 47302 / 765-282-9073; FAX: 765-282-5270 bshstle-guns@aol.com

The Gun Room Press, 127 Raritan Ave., Highland Park, NJ 08904 / 732-545-4344; FAX: 732-545-4344 sonbullettube.com

The Gun Shop, 5550 S. 900 East, Salt Lake City, UT 84117 / 801-263-3633

The Gun Shop, 62778 Spring Creek Rd., Montrose, CO 81401

The Gun Shop, 716-A South Rogers Road, Olathe, KS 66062

The Gun Works, 247 S. 2nd, Springfield, OR 97477 / 541-741-4118; FAX: 541-988-1097 gun-works@worldnet.att.net www.thegunworks.com

The Gunsight, 1712 North Placentia Ave., Fullerton, CA 92631

The Gunsmith in Elk River, 14021 Victoria Lane, Elk River, MN 55330 / 612-441-7761

The Hanned Line, P.O. Box 2387, Cupertino, CA 95015-2387 smith@hanned.com www.hanned.com

The Holster Shop, 720 N. Flagler Dr., Ft. Lauderdale, FL 33304 / 305-463-7910; FAX: 305-761-1483

The House of Muskets, Inc., P.O. Box 4640, Pagosa Springs, CO 81157 / 970-731-2295

The Keller Co., 4215 McEwen Rd., Dallas, TX 75244 / 214-770-8585

The Lewis Lead Remover (See LEM Gun Specialties Inc.)

The NgraveR Co., 67 Wawecus Hill Rd., Bozrah, CT 06334 / 860-823-1533

The Ordnance Works, 2969 Pidgeon Point Road, Eureka, CA 95501 / 707-443-3252

The Orvis Co., Rt. 7, Manchester, VT 05254 / 802-362-3622; FAX: 802-362-3525

The Outdoor Connection, Inc., 201 Cotton Dr., P.O. Box 7751, Waco, TX 76714-7751 / 800-533-6076 or 817-772-5575; FAX: 817-776-3553

The Protector Mfg. Co., Inc., 443 Ashwood Place, Boca Raton, FL 33431 / 407-394-6011

The Robar Co.'s, Inc., 21438 N. 7th Ave., Suite B, Phoenix, AZ 85027 / 602-581-2648; FAX:

The Outdoorsman's Bookstore, Llangorse, Brecon, LD3 7UE U.K. / 44-1874-658-660; FAX:

The School of Gunsmithing, 6065 Roswell Rd., Atlanta, GA 30328 / 800-223-4542

The Shooting Gallery, 8070 Southern Blvd., Boardman, OH 44512 / 216-726-7788

The Sight Shop, John G. Lawson, 1802 E. Columbia Ave., Tacoma, WA 98404 / 206-474-5465

The Southern Armory, 25 Millstone Road Woodlawn, VA 24381 / 703-236-1343; FAX: 703-236-1453

The Surecase Co., 233 Wilshire Blvd., Ste. 900, Santa Monica, CA 90401 / 800-92ARMLOC

The Swampfire Shop (See Peterson Gun Shop, Inc.)

The Walnut Factory, 235 West Rd. No. 1, Portsmouth, NH 03801 / 603-436-2225; FAX: 603-433-7003

The Wilson Arms Co., 63 Leetes Island Rd., Branford, CT 06405 / 203-488-7297; FAX: 203-488-0135

Theis, Terry, HC 63 Box 213, Harper, TX 78631 /

Theoben Engineering, Stephenson Road, St. Ives Huntingdon, Cambs., PE17 4WJ ENGLAND / 011-0480-461718

Thieves, George W., 14329 W. Parada Dr., Sun City West, AZ 85375

Things Unlimited, 235 N. Kimbau, Casper, WY 82601 / 307-234-5277

Thirion Gun Engraving, Denise, PO Box 408, Graton, CA 95444 / 707-829-1876

Thomas, Charles C., 2600 S. First St., Springfield, IL 62794 / 217-789-8980; FAX: 217-789-9130

Thompson, Norm, 18905 NW Thurman St., Portland, OR 97209

Thompson Bullet Lube Co., P.O. Box 472343, Garland, TX 75047-2343 / 972-271-8063; FAX: 972-840-6743 thomlube@flash.net www.thompsonbullettube.com

Thompson/Center Arms, P.O. Box 5002, Rochester, NH 03867 / 603-332-2394; FAX: 603-332-5133

Thompson Precision, 110 Mary St., P.O. Box 251, Warren, IL 61087 / 815-745-3625

Thompson, Randall. (See HIGHLINE MACHINE CO.)

Thompson Target Technology, 618 Roslyn Ave., SW, Canton, OH 44710 / 216-453-7707; FAX:

3-D Ammunition & Bullets, PO Box 433, Doniphan, NE 68832 / 402-845-2285 or 800-255-6712; FAX:

3-Ten Corp., P.O. Box 269, Feeding Hills, MA 01030 / 413-789-2086; FAX: 413-789-1549

300 Below Services (See Cryo-Accurizing)

Thunden Ranch, HCR 1, Box 53, Mt. Home, TX 78058 / 830-640-3138

Thunder Mountain Arms, P.O. Box 593, Oak Harbor, WA 98277 / 206-679-4657; FAX: 206-675-1114

Thurston Sports, Inc., RD 3 Donovan Rd., Auburn, NY 13021 / 315-253-0966

Tiger-Hunt Gunstocks, Box 379, Beaverdale, PA 15921 / 814-472-5161 tigerhunt4@aol.com www.gun-stockwood.com

Tikka (See U.S. Importer-Stoeger Industries)

Timber Heirloom Products, 618 Roslyn Ave, SW, Canton, OH 44710 / 216-453-7707; FAX: 216-478-4723

Time Precision, Inc., 640 Federal Rd., Brookfield, CT 06804 / 203-775-8343

Tink's Safariland Hunting Corp., P.O. Box 244, 1140 Monticello Rd., Madison, GA 30650 /

Tinks & Ben Lee Hunting Products (See Wellington Outdoors)

Tioga Engineering Co., Inc., P.O. Box 913, 13 Cone St., Wellsboro, PA 16901 / 717-724-3533; FAX:

Tippman Pneumatics, Inc., 3518 Adams Center Rd., Fort Wayne, IN 46806 / 219-749-6022; FAX: 219-749-6619

Tirelli, Snc Di Tirelli Primo E.C., Via Matteotti No. 359, Gardone V.T. Brescia, ITALY / 030-891819; FAX: 030-832240

TM Stockworks, 6355 Maplecrest Rd., Fort Wayne, IN 46835 / 219-485-5389

TMI Products (See Haselbauer Products, Jerry)

Tom Forrest, Inc., P.O. Box 326, Lakeside, CA 92040 / 619-561-5800; FAX: 619-561-0227

Tom's Gun Repair, Thomas G. Ivanoff, 76-6 Rt. Southfork Rd., Cody, WY 82414 / 307-587-6949

Tom's Gunshop, 3601 Central Ave., Hot Springs, AR 71913 / 501-624-3856

Tombstone Smoke'n' Deals, 3218 East Bell Road, Phoenix, AZ 85032 / 602-905-7013; FAX: 602-443-1998

Tonoloway Tack Drives, HCR 81, Box 100, Needmore, PA 17238

Tooley Custom Rifles, 516 Creek Meadow Dr., Gastonia, NC 28054 / 704-864-7525

Top-Line USA, Inc., 7920-28 Hamilton Ave., Cincinnati, OH 45231 / 513-522-2992 or 800-346-6699; FAX: 513-522-0916

Torel, Inc., 1708 N. South St., P.O. Box 592, Yoakum, TX 77995 / 512-293-2341; FAX: 512-293-3413

TOZ (See U.S. Importer-Nygord Precision Products)

Track of the Wolf, Inc., P.O. Box 6, Osseo, MN 55369-0006 / 612-424-2500; FAX: 612-424-9860

TracStar Industries, Inc., 218 Justin Dr., Cottonwood, AZ 86326 / 520-639-0072; FAX: 520-634-8781

Tradewinds, Inc., P.O. Box 1191, 2339-41 Tacoma Ave. S., Tacoma, WA 98401 / 206-272-4887

Traditions Performance Firearms, P.O. Box 776, 1375 Boston Post Rd., Old Saybrook, CT 06475 / 860-388-4656; FAX: 860-388-4657

Trafalgar Square, P.O. Box 257, N. Pomfret, VT 05053

Trail Visions, 5800 N. Ames Terrace, Glendale, WI 53209 / 414-228-1328

Trammco, 839 Gold Run Rd., Boulder, CO 80302

Trax America, Inc., P.O. Box 898, 1150 Eldridge, Forrest City, AR 72335 / 870-633-0410 or 800-232-2327; FAX: 870-633-4788

Treadlock Gun Safe, Inc., 1764 Granby St. NE, Roanoke, VA 24012 / 800-729-8732 or 703-982-6881; FAX: 703-982-1059

Treemaster, P.O. Box 247, Guntersville, AL 35976 / 205-878-3597

Tresco, Inc., P.O. Box 4640, Pagosa Springs, CO 81157 / 303-731-2295

Trevallion Gunstocks, 9 Old Mountain Rd., Cape Neddick, ME 03902 / 207-361-1130

Trico Plastics, 590 S. Vincent Ave., Azusa, CA 91702 / www.ver-lake.com

Trigger Lock Division/Central Specialties Ltd., 1122 Silver Lake Road, Cary, IL 60013 / 847-639-3900;

Trijicon, Inc., 49385 Shafer Ave., P.O. Box 930059, Wixom, MI 48393-0059 / 810-960-7700; FAX: 810-960-7725

Trilux, Inc., P.O. Box 24608, Winston-Salem, NC 27114 / 910-659-9438; FAX: 910-768-7720

Trinidad St. Jr Col Gunsmith Dept, 600 Prospect St., Trinidad, CO 81082 / 719-846-5631; FAX:

Trinity Traps, Inc., P.O. Box 471, 221 S. Miami Ave., Cleves, OH 45002 / 513-941-5682; FAX: 513-941-7970

Trooper Walsh, 2393 N Edgewood St, Arlington, VA 22207

Trophy Bonded Bullets, Inc., 900 S. Loop W., Suite 190, Houston, TX 77054 / 713-645-4499 or 888-308-3006; FAX: 713-741-6393

Triple-K Mfg. Co., Inc., 2222 Commercial St., San Diego, CA 92113 / 619-232-2066; FAX: 619-232-7675

Tristar Sporting Arms, Ltd., 1814-16 Linn St., P.O. Box 7496, N. Kansas City, MO 64116 / 816-421-1400; FAX: 816-421-4182

Trotman, Ken, 135 Ditton Walk, Unit 11, Cambridge, CB5 8PY ENGLAND / 01223-211030; FAX: 01223-212317

Truglo, Inc, P.O. Box 1612, McKinna, TX 75070 / 972-774-0300 FAX: 972-774-0323 www.truglo-sights.com

Trulock Tool, Broad St., Whigham, GA 31797 / 912-762-4678

Tru-Balance Knife Co., P.O. Box 140555, Grand Rapids, MI 49514 / 616-453-3679

TTM, 1550 Solomon Rd., Santa Maria, CA 93455 / 805-934-1281

Tru-Square Metal Prods., Inc., 640 First St., SW, P.O. Box 585, Auburn, WA 98071 / 206-833-2310; FAX: 206-833-2349

True Flight Bullet Co., 5581 Roosevelt St., Whitehall, PA 18052 / 610-262-7630; FAX: 610-262-7806

Tucson Mold, Inc., 930 S. Plumer Ave., Tucson, AZ 85719 / 520-792-1075; FAX: 520-792-1075

Tucker, James C., P.O. Box 1212, Paso Robles, CA 93447-1212

Turkish Firearms Corp., 522 W. Maple St., Allentown, PA 18101 / 610-821-8660; FAX: 610-821-9049

Turnbull Restoration, Doug, 6680 Rt.58 & 20 Dept. SM 2000, PO Box 471, Bloomfield, NY 14469 / 716-657-6338

Tuttle, Dale, 4046 Russell Rd., Muskegon, MI 49445 / 616-766-2250

Tyler Manufacturing & Distributing, 3804 S. Eastern, Oklahoma City, OK 73129 / 405-677-1487 or 800-654-8415

U

U.S. Fire-Arms Mfg. Co. Inc., 55 Van Dyke Ave., Hartford, CT 06106 / 877-227-6901; FAX: 860-724-6809 sales @ usfirearms.com; www.usfirearms.com

U.S. Importer-Wm. Larkin Moore, 8430 E. Raintree Ste. B-7, Scottsdale, AZ 85260

U.S. Repeating Arms Co., Inc., 275 Winchester Ave., Morgan, UT 84050-9333 / 801-876-3440; FAX: 801-876-3737

U.S. Tactical Systems (See Keng's Firearms Specialty)

U.S.A. Magazines, Inc., P.O. Box 39115, Downey, CA 90241 / 800-872-2577

Uberti, Aldo, Casella Postale 43, I-25063 Gardone V.T., ITALY

Uberti USA, Inc., P.O. Box 469, Lakeville, CT 06039 / 860-435-8068; FAX: 860-435-8146

UFA, Inc., 6927 E. Grandview Dr., Scottsdale, AZ 85254 / 800-616-2776

MANUFACTURER'S DIRECTORY

Ugartechea S. A., Ignacio, Chonta 26, Eibar, SPAIN / 43-121257; FAX: 43-121669
Ultimate Accuracy, 121 John Shelton Rd., Jacksonville, AR 72076 / 501-985-2530
Ultra Dot Distribution, 2316 N.E. 8th Rd., Ocala, FL 34470
Ultra Light Arms, Inc., P.O. Box 1270, 214 Price St., Granville, WV 26505 / 304-599-5687; FAX: 304-599-5687
Ultralux (See U.S. Importer-Keng's Firearms Specia
UltraSport Arms, Inc., 1955 Norwood Ct., Racine, WI 53403 / 414-554-3237; FAX: 414-554-9731
Uncle Bud's, HCR 81, Box 100, Needmore, PA 17238 / 717-294-6000; FAX: 717-294-6005
Uncle Mike's (See Michaels of Oregon Co)
Unertl Optical Co. Inc., John, 308 Clay Ave, PO Box 818, Mars, PA 16046-0818 / 412-625-3810
Unique/M.A.P.F., 10 Les Allees, 64700, Hendaye, FRANCE / 33-59 20 71 93
UniTec, 1250 Bedford SW, Canton, OH 44710 / 216-452-4017
United Binocular Co., 9043 S. Western Ave., Chicago, IL 60620
United Cutlery Corp., 1425 United Blvd., Sevierville, TN 37876 / 865-428-2532 or 800-548-0835 FAX: 865-428-2267
United States Optics Technologies, Inc., 5900 Dale St., Buena Park, CA 90621 / 714-994-4901; FAX: 714-994-4904
United States Products Co., 518 Melwood Ave., Pittsburgh, PA 15213 / 412-621-2130; FAX: 412-621-8740
Universal Sports, P.O. Box 532, Vincennes, IN 47591 / 812-882-8680; FAX: 812-882-8680
Unmussig Bullets, D. L., 7862 Brentford Dr., Richmond, VA 23225 / 804-320-1165
Upper Missouri Trading Co., 304 Harold St., Crofton, NE 68730 / 402-388-4844
USAC, 4500-15th St. East, Tacoma, WA 98424 / 206-922-7589
Utica Cutlery Co., 820 Noyes St., Utica, NY 13503 / 315-733-4663; FAX: 315-733-6602

V

V. H. Blackinton & Co., Inc., 221 John L. Dietsch, Attleboro Falls, MA 02763-0300 / 508-699-4436; FAX: 508-695-5349
Valade Engraving, Robert, 931 3rd Ave, Seaside, OR 97138 / 503-738-7672
Valor Corp., 5555 NW 36th Ave., Miami, FL 33142 / 305-633-0127; FAX: 305-634-4536
Valtro USA, Inc., 1281 Andersen Dr., San Rafael, CA 94901 / 415-256-2575; FAX: 415-256-2576
VAM Distribution Co LLC, 1141-B Mechanicsburg Rd., Wooster, OH 44691 www.rex10.com
Van Gorden & Son Inc., C. S., 1815 Main St., Bloomer, WI 54724 / 715-568-2612
Van Horn, Gil, P.O. Box 207, Llano, CA 93544
Van Patten, J. W., P.O. Box 145, Foster Hill, Milford, PA 18337 / 717-296-7069
Van's Gunsmith Service, 224 Route 69-A, Parish, NY 13131 / 315-625-7251
Vancini, Carl (See Bestload, Inc.)
Vann Custom Bullets, 330 Grandview Ave., Novato, CA 94947
Varmint Masters, LLC, Rick Vecqueray, PO Box 6724, Bend, OR 97708 / 541-318-7306; FAX: 541-318-7306 varmintmasters@bendnet.com
Vecqueray, Rick. (See VARMINT MASTERS, LLC)
Vega Tool Co., c/o T.R. Ross, 4865 Tanglewood Ct., Boulder, CO 80301 / 303-530-0174
Vektor USA, Mikael Danforth, 5139 Stanart St. Norfolk, VA 23502 / 888-740-0837; or 757-455-8895; FAX: 757-461-9155
Venco Industries, Inc. (See Shooter's Choice)
Venus Industries, P.O. Box 246, Sialkot-1, PAKISTAN
Vey-Carron, B.P. 72, 54 Boulevard Lyautey, 42002, [FRA]NCE / 33-477791500; FAX: 33-477790702
P.O. Box 1552, Susanville, CA 96130 /
[...] 844 Arroya Rd., Colorado Springs, CO
[...]-8611; FAX: 719-634-6886
Box 577, Taylorsville, MS 39168
[...]8; Milford, PA 18337 /
[...]eview Dr., Dover, NH
[...]228

Victory USA, P.O. Box 1021, Pine Bush, NY 12566 / 914-744-2060; FAX: 914-744-5181
Vihtavuori Oy, FIN-41330 Vihtavuori, FINLAND, / 358-41-3779211; FAX: 358-41-3771643
Vihtavuori Oy/Kaltron-Pettibone, 1241 Ellis St., Bensenville, IL 60106 / 708-350-1116; FAX: 708-350-1606
Viking Video Productions, P.O. Box 251, Roseburg, OR 97470
Vincent's Shop, 210 Antoinette, Fairbanks, AK 99701
Vincenzo Bernardelli S.p.A., 125 Via Matteotti, P.O. Box 74, Gardone V.T., Bresci, 25063 ITALY / 39-30-8912851-2-3; FAX: 39-30-8910249+
Vintage Arms, Inc., 6003 Saddle Horse, Fairfax, VA 22030 / 703-968-0779; FAX: 703-968-0780
Vintage Industries, Inc., 781 Big Tree Dr., Longwood, FL 32750 / 407-831-8949; FAX: 407-831-5346
Viper Bullet and Brass Works, 11 Brock St., Box 582, Norwich, ON N0J 1P0 CANADA
Viramontez, Ray, 601 Springfield Dr., Albany, GA 31707 / 912-432-9683
Virgin Valley Custom Guns, 450 E 800 N #20, Hurricane, UT 84737 / 435-635-8941; FAX: 435-635-8943 vvcguns@infowest.com www.virginvalleyguns.com
Visible Impact Targets, Rts. 5 & 20, E. Bloomfield, NY 14443 / 716-657-6161; FAX: 716-657-5405
Vitt/Boos, 2178 Nichols Ave., Stratford, CT 06614 / 203-375-6859
Voere-KGH m.b.H., P.O. Box 416, A-6333 Kufstein, Tirol, AUSTRIA / 0043-5372-62547; FAX: 0043-5372-65752
Volquartsen Custom Ltd., 24276 240th Street, P.O. Box 397, Carroll, IA 51401 / 712-792-4238; FAX: 712-792-2542
Vom Hoffe (See Old Western Scrounger, Inc., The), 12924 Hwy A-12, Montague, CA 96064 / 916-459-5445; FAX: 916-459-3944
Vorhes, David, 3042 Beecham St., Napa, CA 94558 / 707-226-9116
Vortek Products, Inc., P.O. Box 871181, Canton, MI 48187-6181 / 313-397-5656; FAX: 313-397-5656
VSP Publishers (See Heritage/VSP Gun Books), PO Box 887, McCall, ID 83638 / 208-634-4104; FAX: 208-634-3101
Vulpes Ventures, Inc. Fox Cartridge Division, P.O. Box 1363, Bolingbrook, IL 60440-7363 / 630-759-1229; FAX: 815-439-3945

W

W. Square Enterprises, 9826 Sagedale, Houston, TX 77089 / 713-484-0935; FAX: 281-484-0935
W. Square Enterprises, Load From A Disk, 9826 Sagedale, Houston, TX 77089 / 713-484-0935; FAX: 281-484-0935
W. Waller & Son, Inc., 2221 Stoney Brook Rd., Grantham, NH 03753-7706 / 603-863-4177
W.B. Niemi Engineering, Box 126 Center Road, Greensboro, VT 05841 / 802-533-7180 or 802-533-7141
W.C. Strutz Rifle Barrels, Inc., P.O. Box 611, Eagle River, WI 54521 / 715-479-4766
W.C. Wolff Co., PO Box 458, Newtown Square, PA 19073 / 610-359-9600; FAX: 610-359-9496
W.E. Birdsong & Assoc., 1435 Monterey Rd., Florence, MS 39073-9748 / 601-366-8270
W.E. Brownell Checkering Tools, 9390 Twin Mountain Cir, San Diego, CA 92126 / 619-695-2479; FAX: 619-695-2479
W.J. Riebe Co., 3434 Tucker Rd., Boise, ID 83703
W.R. Case & Sons Cutlery Co., Owens Way, Bradford, PA 16701 / 814-368-4123 or 800-523-6350; FAX: 814-768-5369
Wagoner, Vernon G., 2325 E. Encanto, Mesa, AZ 85213 / 602-835-1307
Wakina by Pic, 24813 Alderbrook Dr., Santa Clarita, CA 91321 / 800-295-8194
Waldron, Herman, Box 475, 80 N. 17th St., Pomeroy, WA 99347 / 509-843-1404
Walker Arms Co., Inc., 499 County Rd. 820, Selma, AL 36701 / 334-872-6231; FAX: 334-872-6262
Walker Mfg., Inc., 8296 S. Channel, Harsen's Island, MI 48028
Wallace, Terry, 385 San Marino, Vallejo, CA 94589 / 707-642-7041
Walls Industries, Inc., P.O. Box 98, 1905 N. Main, Cleburne, TX 76031 / 817-645-4366; FAX: 817-645-7946

Walt's Custom Leather, Walt Whinnery, 1947 Meadow Creek Dr., Louisville, KY 40218 / 502-458-4361
Walters, John, 500 N. Avery Dr., Moore, OK 73160 / 405-799-0376
Walters Industries, 6226 Park Lane, Dallas, TX 75225 / 214-691-6973
Walther GmbH, Carl, B.P. 4325, D-89033 Ulm, GERMANY
WAMCO, Inc., Mingo Loop, P.O. Box 337, Oquossoc, ME 04964-0337 / 207-864-3344
WAMCO--New Mexico, P.O. Box 205, Peralta, NM 87042-0205 / 505-869-0826
Ward & Van Valkenburg, 114 32nd Ave. N., Fargo, ND 58102 / 701-232-2351
Ward Machine, 5620 Lexington Rd., Corpus Christi, TX 78412 / 512-992-1221
Wardell Precision Handguns Ltd., 48851 N. Fig Springs Rd., New River, AZ 85027-8513 / 602-465-7995
Warenski, Julie, 590 E. 500 N., Richfield, UT 84701 / 801-896-5319; FAX: 801-896-5319
Warne Manufacturing Co., 9039 SE Jannsen Rd., Clackamas, OR 97015 / 503-657-5590 or 800-683-5590; FAX: 503-657-5695
Warren & Sweat Mfg. Co., P.O. Box 350440, Grand Island, FL 32784 / 904-669-3166; FAX: 904-669-7272
Warren Muzzleloading Co., Inc., Hwy. 21 North, P.O. Box 100, Ozone, AR 72854 / 501-292-3268
Warren, Kenneth W. (See Mountain States Engraving)
Washita Mountain Whetstone Co., P.O. Box 378, Lake Hamilton, AR 71951 / 501-525-3914
Wasmundt, Jim, P.O. Box 511, Fossil, OR 97830
WASP Shooting Systems, Rt. 1, Box 147, Lakeview, AR 72642 / 501-431-5606
Waterfield Sports, Inc., 13611 Country Lane, Burnsville, MN 55337 / 612-435-8339
Watson Bros., 39 Redcross Way, London Bridge, LONDON U.K. FAX: 44-171-403-336
Watson Trophy Match Bullets, 2404 Wade Hampton Blvd., Greenville, SC 29615 / 864-244-7948 or 941-635-7948
Wayne E. Schwartz Custom Guns, 970 E. Britton Rd., Morrice, MI 48857 / 517-625-4079
Wayne Firearms for Collectors and Investors, James, 2608 N. Laurent, Victoria, TX 77901 / 512-578-1258; FAX: 512-578-3559
Wayne Reno, 2808 Stagestop Rd., Jefferson, CO 80456 / 719-836-3452
Wayne Specialty Services, 260 Waterford Drive, Florissant, MO 63033 / 413-831-7083
WD-40 Co., 1061 Cudahy Pl., San Diego, CA 92110 / 619-275-1400; FAX: 619-275-5823
Weatherby, Inc., 3100 El Camino Real, Atascadero, CA 93422 / 805-466-1767 or 800-227-2016; FAX: 805-466-2527
Weaver Arms Corp. Gun Shop, RR 3, P.O. Box 266, Bloomfield, MO 63825-9528
Weaver Products, P.O. Box 39, Onalaska, WI 54650 / 800-648-9624 or 608-781-5800; FAX: 608-781-0368
Weaver Scope Repair Service, 1121 Larry Mahan Dr., Suite B, El Paso, TX 79925 / 915-593-1005
Webb, Bill, 6504 North Bellefontaine, Kansas City, MO 64119 / 816-453-7431
Weber & Markin Custom Gunsmiths, 4-1691 Powick Rd., Kelowna, BC V1X 4L1 CANADA / 250-762-7575; FAX: 250-861-3655
Weber Jr., Rudolf, P.O. Box 160106, D-5650, GERMANY / 0212-592136
Webley and Scott Ltd., Frankley Industrial Park, Tay Rd., Birmingham, B45 0PA ENGLAND / 011-021-453-1864; FAX: 021-457-7846
Webster Scale Mfg. Co., P.O. Box 188, Sebring, FL 33870 / 813-385-6362
Weems, Cecil, 510 W Hubbard St, Mineral Wells, TX 76067-4847 / 817-325-1462
Weigand Combat Handguns, Inc., 685 South Main Rd., Mountain Top, PA 18707 / 570-868-8358; FAX: 570-868-5218 sales@jackweigand.com www.jackweigand.com
Weihrauch KG, Hermann, Industriestrasse 11, 8744 Mellrichstadt, Mellrichstadt, GERMANY
Weisz Parts, P.O. Box 20038, Columbus, OH 43220-0038 / 614-45-70-500; FAX: 614-846-8585
Welch, Sam, CVSR 2110, Moab, UT 84532 / 801-259-8131
Wellington Outdoors, P.O. Box 244, 1140 Monticello Rd., Madison, GA 30650 / 706-342-4915; FAX: 706-342-7568
Wells, Rachel, 110 N. Summit St., Prescott, AZ 86301 / 520-445-3655

MANUFACTURER'S DIRECTORY

Wells Creek Knife & Gun Works, 32956 State Hwy. 38, Scottsburg, OR 97473 / 541-587-4202; FAX: 541-587-4223

Welsh, Bud, 80 New Road, E. Amherst, NY 14051 / 716-688-6344

Wenger North America/Precise Int'l., 15 Corporate Dr., Orangeburg, NY 10962 / 800-431-2996 FAX: 914-425-4700

Wenig Custom Gunstocks, 103 N. Market St., P.O. Box 249, Lincoln, MO 65338 / 816-547-3334; FAX: 816-547-2881 gunstock@wenig.com www.wenig.com

Werth, T. W., 1203 Woodlawn Rd., Lincoln, IL 62656 / 217-732-1300

Wescombe, Bill (See North Star West)

Wessinger Custom Guns & Engraving, 268 Limestone Rd., Chapin, SC 29036 / 803-345-5677

West, Jack L., 1220 W. Fifth, P.O. Box 427, Arlington, OR 97812

Western Cutlery (See Camillus Cutlery Co.)

Western Design (See Alpha Gunsmith Division)

Western Gunstock Mfg. Co., 550 Valencia School Rd., Aptos, CA 95003 / 408-688-5884

Western Missouri Shooters Alliance, P.O. Box 11144, Kansas City, MO 64119 / 816-597-3950; FAX: 816-229-7350

Western Nevada West Coast Bullets, PO BOX 2270, DAYTON, NV 89403-2270 / 702-246-3941; FAX: 702-246-0836

Westley Richards & Co., 40 Grange Rd., Birmingham, ENGLAND / 010-214722953

Westley Richards Agency USA (See U.S. Importer for Westley Richards & Co.)

Westrom, John (See Precision Metal Finishing)

Westwind Rifles, Inc., David S. Sullivan, P.O. Box 261, 640 Briggs St., Erie, CO 80516 / 303-828-3823

Weyer International, 2740 Nebraska Ave., Toledo, OH 43607 / 419-534-2020; FAX: 419-534-2697

Whildin & Sons Ltd, E.H., RR 2 Box 119, Tamaqua, PA 18252 / 717-668-6743; FAX: 717-668-6745

Whinnery, Walt (See Walt's Custom Leather)

Whiscombe (See U.S. Importer-Pelaire Products)

White Barn Workshop, 431 County Road, Broadlands, IL 61816

White Flyer Targets, 124 River Road, Middlesex, NJ 08846 / 908-469-0100 or 602-972-7528 FAX:

White Owl Enterprises, 2583 Flag Rd., Abilene, KS 67410 / 913-263-2613; FAX: 913-263-2613

White Pine Photographic Services, Hwy. 60, General Delivery, Wilno, ON K0J 2N0 CANADA / 613-756-3452

White Rock Tool & Die, 6400 N. Brighton Ave., Kansas City, MO 64119 / 816-454-0478

Whitestone Lumber Corp., 148-02 14th Ave., Whitestone, NY 11357 / 718-746-4400; FAX: 718-767-1748

Whitetail Design & Engineering Ltd., 9421 E. Mansfield Rd., Clare, MI 48617 / 517-386-3932

Wichita Arms, Inc., 923 E. Gilbert, P.O. Box 11371, Wichita, KS 67211 / 316-265-0661; FAX: 316-265-0760

Wick, David E., 1504 Michigan Ave., Columbus, IN 47201 / 812-376-6960

Widener's Reloading & Shooting Supply, Inc., P.O. Box 3009 CRS, Johnson City, TN 37602 / 615-282-6786; FAX: 615-282-6651

Wideview Scope Mount Corp., 13535 S. Hwy. 16, Rapid City, SD 57701 / 605-341-3220; FAX: 605-341-9142 wvdon@rapidnet.com

Wiebe, Duane, 846 Holly WYA, Placerville, CA 95667-3415

Wiest, M. C., 10737 Dutchtown Rd., Knoxville, TN 37932 / 423-966-4545

Wilcox All-Pro Tools & Supply, 4880 147th St., Montezuma, IA 50171 / 515-623-3104

Wilcox Industries Corp, Robert F Guarasi, 53 Durham St., Portsmouth, NH 03801 / 603-431-1221

Wild Bill's Originals, P.O. Box 13037, Burton, WA 98013 / 206-463-5738; FAX: 206-465-5925

Wild West Guns, 7521 Old Seward Hwy., Unit A, Anchorage, AK 99518 / 800-992-4570 or 907-344-4500; FAX: 907-344-4005

Wilderness Sound Products Ltd., 4015 Main St. A, Springfield, OR 97478 / 503-741-0263 or 800-437-0006; FAX: 503-741-7648

Wildey, Inc., 45 Angevine Rd, Warren, CT 06754-1818 / 203-355-9000; FAX: 203-354-7759

Wildlife Research Center, Inc., 1050 McKinley St., Anoka, MN 55303 / 612-427-3350 or 800-USE-LURE; FAX: 612-427-8354

Wilhelm Brenneke KG, Ilmenauweg 2, 30851, Langenhagen, GERMANY / 0511/97262-0; FAX: 0511/97262-62

Will-Burt Co., 169 S. Main, Orrville, OH 44667

William Fagan & Co., 22952 15 Mile Rd., Clinton Township, MI 48035 / 810-465-4637; FAX: 810-792-6996

William Powell & Son (Gunmakers) Ltd., 35-37 Carrs Lane, Birmingham, B4 7SX ENGLAND /

William Powell Agency, 22 Circle Dr., Bellmore, NY 11710 / 516-679-1158

Williams Gun Sight Co., 7389 Lapeer Rd., Box 329, Davison, MI 48423 / 810-653-2131 or 800-530-9028; FAX: 810-658-2140 williamsgunsight.com

Williams Mfg. of Oregon, 110 East B St., Drain, OR 97435 / 503-836-7461; FAX: 503-836-7245

Williams Shootin' Iron Service, The Lynx-Line, Rt 2 Box 223A, Mountain Grove, MO 65711 / 417-948-0902 FAX: 417-948-0902

Williamson Precision Gunsmithing, 117 W. Pipeline, Hurst, TX 76053 / 817-285-0064; FAX: 817-280-0044

Willow Bend, P.O. Box 203, Chelmsford, MA 01824 / 978-256-8508; FAX: 978-256-8508

Wilson Case, Inc., P.O. Box 1106, Hastings, NE 68902-1106 / 800-322-5493; FAX: 402-463-5276 sales@wilsoncase.com www.wilsoncase.com

Wilson Gun Shop, 2234 County Road 719, Berryville, AR 72616 / 870-545-3618; FAX: 870-545-3310

Wilson Safety Prods. Div., PO Box 622, Reading, PA 19603-0622 / 610-376-6161; FAX: 610-371-7725

Winchester Div. Olin Corp., 427 N. Shamrock, E. Alton, IL 62024 / 618-258-3566; FAX: 618-258-3599

Winchester Press (See New Win Publishing, Inc.), 186 Center St., Clinton, NJ 08809 / 908-735-9701; FAX: 908-735-9703

Winchester Sutler, Inc., The, 270 Shadow Brook Lane, Winchester, VA 22603 / 540-888-3595; FAX: 540-888-4632

Windish, Jim, 2510 Dawn Dr., Alexandria, VA 22306 / 703-765-1994

Windjammer Tournament Wads Inc., 750 W. Hampden Ave., Suite 170, Englewood, CO 80110 / 303-781-6329

Wingshooting Adventures, 0-1845 W. Leonard, Grand Rapids, MI 49544 / 616-677-1980; FAX: 616-677-1986

Winkle Bullets, R.R. 1, Box 316, Heyworth, IL 61745

Winter, Robert M., P.O. Box 484, 42975-287th St., Menno, SD 57045 / 605-387-5322

Wise Custom Guns, 1402 Blanco Rd, San Antonio, TX 78212-2716 / 210-828-3388

Wise Guns, Dale, 333 W Olmos Dr, San Antonio, TX 78212 / 210-828-3388

Wiseman and Co., Bill, PO Box 3427, Bryan, TX 77805 / 409-690-3456; FAX: 409-690-0156

Wisners Inc/Twin Pine Armory, P.O. Box 58, Hwy. 6, Adna, WA 98522 / 360-748-4590; FAX: 360-748-1802

Wolf (See J.R. Distributing)

Wolf's Western Traders, 40 E. Works, No. 3F, Sheridan, WY 82801 / 307-674-5352 patwolf@wave-one.net

Wolfe Publishing Co., 6471 Airpark Dr., Prescott, AZ 86301 / 520-445-7810 or 800-899-7810; FAX: 520-778-5124

Wolverine Footwear Group, 9341 Courtland Dr., NE, Rockford, MI 49351 / 616-866-5500; FAX: 616-866-5658

Wood, Mel, P.O. Box 1255, Sierra Vista, AZ 85636 / 602-455-5541

Wood, Frank (See Classic Guns, Inc.), 3230 Medlock Bridge Rd, Ste 110, Norcross, GA 30092 / 404-242-7944

Woodleigh (See Huntington Die Specialties)

Woods Wise Products, P.O. Box 681552, 2200 Bowman Rd., Franklin, TN 37068 / 800-735-8182; FAX: 615-726-2637

Woodstream, P.O. Box 327, Lititz, PA 17543 / 717-626-2125 FAX: 717-626-1912

Woodworker's Supply, 1108 North Glenn Rd., Casper, WY 82601 / 307-237-5354

Woolrich, Inc., Mill St., Woolrich, PA 17701 / 800-995-1299; FAX: 717-769-6234/6259

Working Guns, Jim Coffin, 1224 NW Fernwood Cir, Corvallis, OR 97330-2909 / 541-928-4391

World Class Airguns, 2736 Morningstar Dr., Indianapolis, IN 46229 / 317-897-5548

World of Targets (See Birchwood Casey)

World Trek, Inc., 7170 Turkey Creek Rd., Pueblo, CO 81007-1046 / 719-546-2121; FAX: 719-543-6886

Worthy Products, Inc., RR 1, P.O. Box 213, Martville, NY 13111 / 315-324-5298

Wosenitz VHP, Inc., Box 741, Dania, FL 33004 / 305-923-3748; FAX: 305-925-2217

Wostenholm (See Ibberson [Sheffield] Ltd., George)

Wright's Hardwood Gunstock Blanks, 8540 SE Kane Rd., Gresham, OR 97080 / 503-666-1705

WTA Manufacturing, P.O. Box 164, Kit Carson, CO 80825 / 800-700-3054; FAX: 719-962-3570

Wyant Bullets, Gen. Del., Swan Lake, MT 59911

Wyant's Outdoor Products, Inc., P.O. Box 9, Broadway, VA 22815

Wyoming Bonded Bullets, Box 91, Sheridan, WY 82801 / 307-674-8091

Wyoming Custom Bullets, 1626 21st St., Cody, WY 82414

Wyoming Knife Corp., 101 Commerce Dr., Ft. Collins, CO 80524 / 303-224-3454

X

X-Spand Target Systems, 26-10th St. SE, Medicine Hat, AB T1A 1P7 CANADA / 403-526-7997; FAX: 403-528-2362

Y

Yankee Gunsmith, 2901 Deer Flat Dr., Copperas Cove, TX 76522 / 817-547-8433

Yavapai College, 1100 E. Sheldon St., Prescott, AZ 86301 / 520-776-2353 FAX: 520-776-2355

Yavapai Firearms Academy Ltd., P.O. Box 27290, Prescott Valley, AZ 86312 / 520-772-8262

Yearout, Lewis E. (See Montana Outfitters), 308 Riverview Dr E., Great Falls, MT 59404 / 406-761-0859

Yee, Mike, 29927 56 Pl. S., Auburn, WA 98001 / 206-839-3991

Yellowstone Wilderness Supply, P.O. Box 129, W. Yellowstone, MT 59758 / 406-646-7613

Yesteryear Armory & Supply, P.O. Box 408, Carthage, TN 37030

York M-1 Conversions, 803 Mill Creek Run, Plantersville, TX 77363 / 800-527-2881 or 713-477-8442

Young Country Arms, William, 1409 Kuehner Dr #13, Simi Valley, CA 93063-4478

Yukon Arms Classic Ammunition, 1916 Brooks, P.O. Box 223, Missoula, MT 59801 / 406-543-9614

Z

Z's Metal Targets & Frames, P.O. Box 78, South Newbury, NH 03255 / 603-938-2826

Z-M Weapons, 203 South St., Bernardston, MA 01337 / 413-648-9501; FAX: 413-648-0219

Zabala Hermanos S.A., P.O. Box 97, Eibar, 20600 SPAIN / 43-768085 or 43-768076; FAX: 34-43-768201

Zander's Sporting Goods, 7525 Hwy 154 West, Baldwin, IL 62217-9706 / 800-851-4373 FAX:

Zanoletti, Pietro, Via Monte Gugielpo, 4, I-25063 Gardone V.T., ITALY

Zanotti Armor, Inc., 123 W. Lone Tree Rd., Cedar Falls, IA 5061...

Zeeryp...
801-4...

Zieger...

Zim...

Zol...

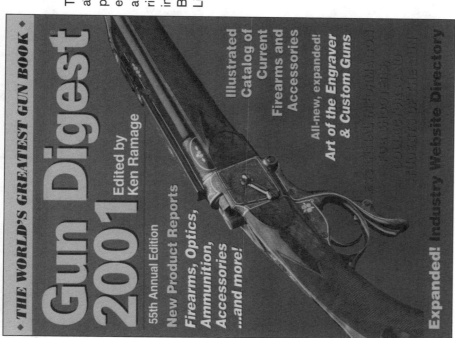

HANDGUNS 2001 READER INTEREST SURVEY

1. **Check all that apply: In which of the following handgunning activities are you currently active?**
   - ☐ Airgunning
   - ☐ Cowboy action shooting
   - ☐ Bullseye shooting
   - ☐ Blackpowder shooting
   - ☐ Action pistol shooting
   - ☐ Silhouette shooting
   - ☐ Informal shooting
   - ☐ Small game hunting
   - ☐ Big game hunting
   - ☐ Handloading
   - ☐ None of these

2. **Choose only one: With which type of handgun do you shoot *most*? (only 1)**
   - ☐ Autoloading pistol ☐ Revolver ☐ Single shot ☐ Not applicable

3. **Choose only one: Which type of ammunition do you use *most*? (only 1)**
   - ☐ Rimfire ☐ Centerfire ☐ Not applicable

4. **Check all that apply: Which of the following handgun-related topics are you interested in reading about?**
   - ☐ Collecting—foreign models
   - ☐ Collecting—U.S. models
   - ☐ Holster/Carry systems
   - ☐ Personal protection
   - ☐ Law enforcement
   - ☐ Political/Legislative news
   - ☐ Handgun history
   - ☐ Military models
   - ☐ New product reports
   - ☐ Vintage/Surplus arms
   - ☐ Used guns
   - ☐ Customized guns
   - ☐ Gun tests
   - ☐ Ammunition
   - ☐ New product reports
   - ☐ Handloading
   - ☐ None of these

5. **Check all that apply: Which of the following publications do you read regularly, that is, at least three out of every four issues?**
   - ☐ American Handgunner
   - ☐ Petersen's Handguns
   - ☐ Shooting Times
   - ☐ Guns & Ammo
   - ☐ Gun Games
   - ☐ Guns
   - ☐ The Sixgunner
   - ☐ Other:__________

6. **Check all that apply: Which of the following did you read in this year's edition of HANDGUNS?**

   FEATURE SECTION:
   - ☐ Trends ☐ Custom & Engraved Guns ☐ Hunting
   - ☐ Gun Tests ☐ Self-Defense/ Concealed Carry
   - ☐ Handloading ☐ Vintage Handguns

   CATALOG SECTION:
   - NEW! ☐ Semi-Custom Handguns ☐ Commercial Handguns

   ACCESSORY SECTION:
   - NEW! ☐ Handgun Grips ☐ Metallic Sights ☐ Laser sights
   - ☐ Metallic Reloading Presses ☐ Brakes & Porting ☐ Sight Mounts
   - ☐ Scopes ☐ Spotting Scopes

   REFERENCE SECTION:
   - ☐ NRA Right to Carry Guide ☐ Arms Periodicals ☐ Directory of the Arms Trade
   - ☐ Arms Associations ☐ Arms Library

7. ADDITIONAL COMMENTS?____________________

Thank you for filling out the HANDGUNS 2001 Reader Interest Survey. Please return your completed survey no later than September 5, 2001. This offer expires on September 5, 2001.

WHICH ONE OF THESE WOULD YOU LIKE FOR TAKING THE TIME TO COMPLETE OUR SURVEY? **

☐ 4 free issues of GUN LIST magazine (a retail value of $22.00). GUN LIST is the leading national newspaper for people who buy and sell quality firearms.

- OR -

☐ 2 free issues of BLADE magazine (a retail value of $9.90). BLADE is the world's #1 knife publication. It is the largest and most comprehensive knife magazine available today.

Name:

Address:

City:

State: Zip Code: Phone: — —

** **PLEASE NOTE: You must complete all of the survey questions and return this by September 5, 2001 to qualify to receive a free gift (4 issues of GUN LIST or 2 issues of BLADE).**

ABAZFA

Cut on dotted line, fold in half, place one piece … in half, place one piece of tape in each corner and mail. Thank you.

Tape Here

BUSINESS REPLY MAIL

FIRST-CLASS MAIL PERMIT NO. 12 IOLA, WI

POSTAGE WILL BE PAID BY ADDRESSEE

KRAUSE PUBLICATIONS
MARKETING RESEARCH DEPT
700 E STATE ST
IOLA WI 54945-9989

Tape Here

Zin! Zin! Zin! a Violin

Zin! Zin! a Violin

By **Lloyd Moss**

Illustrated by **Marjorie Priceman**

Scholastic Inc.
New York Toronto London Auckland Sydney

ISBN 0-590-97554-4

Text copyright © 1995 by Lloyd Moss.
Illustrations copyright © 1995 by Marjorie Priceman.
All rights reserved. Published by Scholastic Inc., 555 Broadway, New York, NY 10012, by arrangement with Simon & Schuster.

12 11 10 9 8 7 6 5 4 3 2 1   6 7 8 9/9 0 1/0

Printed in the U.S.A.   14

First Scholastic printing, October 1996

To Anne, Bradley, Brice, Liana, Nanette—
the music and the poetry in my life
—*L. M.*

For Jonah Squirsky and his descendants
—*M. P.*

With mournful moan and silken tone,
Itself alone comes ONE TROMBONE.
Gliding, sliding, high notes go low;
ONE TROMBONE is playing SOLO.

Next, a TRUMPET comes along,
And sings and stings its swinging song.
It joins TROMBONE, no more alone,
And ONE and TWO-O, they're a DUO.

Fine FRENCH HORN, its valves all oiled,
Bright and brassy, loops all coiled,
Golden yellow; joins its fellows.
TWO, now THREE-O, what a TRIO!

Now, a mellow friend, the CELLO,
Neck extended, bows a "hello";
End pin set upon the floor,
It makes up a QUARTET—that's FOUR.

And soaring high and moving in,

With ZIN! ZIN! ZIN! a VIOLIN,

Stroking strings that come alive;

Now QUINTET. Let's count them: FIVE.

FLUTE, that sends our soul a-shiver;

FLUTE, that slender, silver sliver.

A place among the set it picks

To make a young SEXTET—that's SIX.

With steely keys that softly click,
Its breezy notes so darkly slick,
A sleek, black, woody CLARINET
Is number SEVEN—now SEPTET.

Gleeful, bleating, sobbing, pleading,

Through its throbbing double-reeding;

OBOE, please don't hesitate:

Come, make it an OCTET—that's EIGHT.

That lazy clown, the big BASSOON!
He plays low down, we're laughing soon.
Here, Grumpy, get your place in line,
And give us a NONET—that's NINE.

The HARP descends with angel's wings,
A heaven's blend through magic strings,
And when it joins the others, then
Behold! A CHAMBER GROUP of TEN.

The ORCHESTRA comes in the hall.
They're on the stage; we see them all:
The CELLO, HARP, and CLARINET,
The TRUMPET, whom we've also met,
The OBOE, FLUTE, and big BASSOON,
All eager to get started soon.
TROMBONE, FRENCH HORN, and VIOLIN,
All poised and ready. Now, begin!

The STRINGS all soar, the REEDS implore,
The BRASSES roar with notes galore.
It's music that we all adore.
It's what we go to concerts for.

The minutes fly, the music ends,
And so, good-bye to our new friends.
But when they've bowed and left the floor,
If we clap loud and shout, "Encore!"
They may come out and play once more.

And that would give us great delight
Before we say a late good night.